THE
HOLOG

A GUIDE TO EUROPE'S SITES, MEMORIALS & MUSEUMS

ROSIE WHITEHOUSE

www.bradtguides.com

Bradt Guides Ltd, UK
The Globe Pequot Press Inc, USA

Bradt GUIDES
TRAVEL TAKEN SERIOUSLY

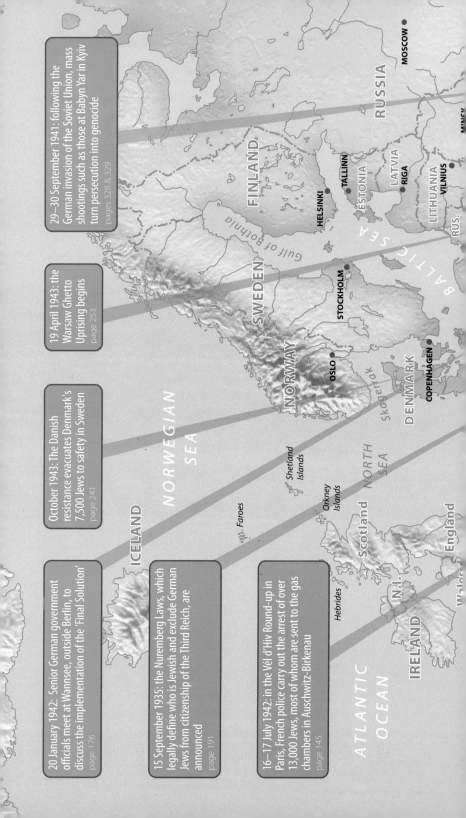

29–30 September 1941: following the German invasion of the Soviet Union, mass shootings such as those at Babyn Yar in Kyiv turn persecution into genocide
pages 328 & 329

19 April 1943: the Warsaw Ghetto Uprising begins
page 253

October 1943: The Danish resistance evacuates Denmark's 7,500 Jews to safety in Sweden
page 241

20 January 1942: Senior German government officials meet at Wannsee, outside Berlin, to discuss the implementation of the 'Final Solution'
page 176

15 September 1935: the Nuremberg Laws, which legally define who is Jewish and exclude German Jews from citizenship of the Third Reich, are announced
page 191

16–17 July 1942: in the Vél d'Hiv Round-up in Paris, French police carry out the arrest of over 13,000 Jews, most of whom are sent to the gas chambers in Auschwitz-Birkenau
page 145

MOSCOW

RUSSIA

MINSK

FINLAND

HELSINKI

TALLINN
ESTONIA
LATVIA
RIGA
LITHUANIA
VILNIUS
RUS.

BALTIC SEA

Gulf of Bothnia

SWEDEN

STOCKHOLM

NORWAY

OSLO

Skagerrak

DENMARK

COPENHAGEN

NORWEGIAN SEA

ICELAND

Faroes

Shetland Islands

Orkney Islands

NORTH SEA

Scotland

Hebrides

N.I.

IRELAND

Wales

England

ATLANTIC OCEAN

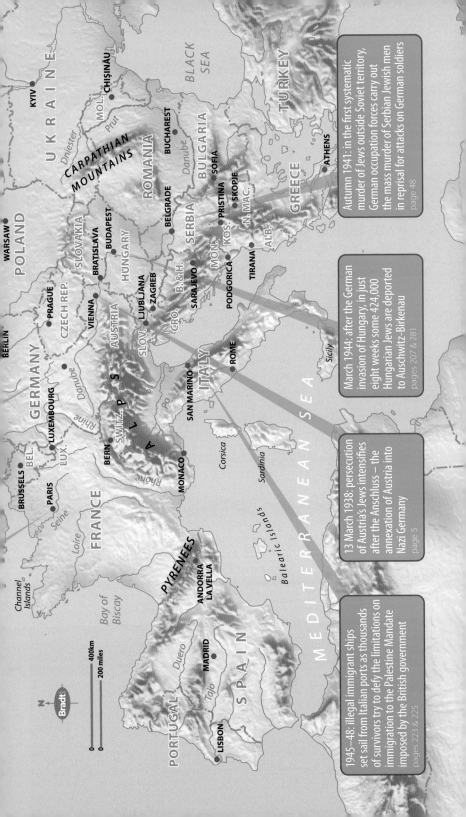

Autumn 1941: in the first systematic murder of Jews outside Soviet territory, German occupation forces carry out the mass murder of Serbian Jewish men in reprisal for attacks on German soldiers
page 48

March 1944: after the German invasion of Hungary, in just eight weeks some 424,000 Hungarian Jews are deported to Auschwitz-Birkenau
pages 207 & 281

13 March 1938: persecution of Austria's Jews intensifies after the Anschluss – the annexation of Austria into Nazi Germany
page 5

1945–48: illegal immigrant ships set sail from Italian ports as thousands of survivors try to defy the limitations on immigration to the Palestine Mandate imposed by the British government
pages 223 & 225

above
(BDB/D)
The 17th-century Portuguese Synagogue in Amsterdam is still a functioning place of worship and also an occasional venue for candlelit concerts PAGE 102

below
(JMP/S)
The Breendonk Memorial Site in northern Belgium commemorates the 3,600 Jews, resistance fighters and political prisoners held there between 1940 and 1944 PAGE 98

A bronze statue of the young diarist Anne Frank stands close to the Anne Frank House museum in Amsterdam PAGE 103   above left (IVU/S)

A memorial to the 102,000 people deported from Westerbork in the Netherlands fills the former Appellplatz at the Camp Westerbork Memorial Centre PAGE 105   above right (MV/S)

The Wall of Names at the Holocaust Memorial in Paris PAGE 144   below left (LM/D)

The Gurs Camp Memorial in southwest France PAGE 161   below right (JK/S)

above
(T/S)

Judenplatz, one of Vienna's most charming squares, is home to the city's Holocaust Memorial PAGE 25

left
(RW)

Tunnels built by forced labour at the former Ebensee concentration camp in Austria PAGE 32

below
(ASc/S)

The Mauthausen Memorial Site complex contains many of the concentration camp's original buildings PAGE 31

A recreation of ghetto living quarters at the Riga Ghetto and Latvian Holocaust Museum PAGE 73 *above (SDV/D)*

A monument at the Klooga Concentration Camp and Holocaust Memorial Site in Estonia PAGE 77 *right (D/D)*

The former ghetto library building in Vilnius was a meeting place of the underground resistance PAGE 67 *below (AP/S)*

top (GB/S)
In 1945, a group of child Holocaust survivors was brought to Windermere in England's Lake District, where today the Lake District Holocaust Project has its headquarters PAGE 116

above left (PP/S)
London's Imperial War Museum houses a permanent exhibition on the Holocaust PAGE 114

above right (RW)
The Odeon, a naval-range finding tower built by forced labour on Alderney in the Channel Islands PAGE 119

below left (AN/D)
A monument to Raoul Wallenberg in Stockholm remembers the Swedish diplomat who saved thousands of Hungarian Jews from deportation PAGES 244 & 245

below right (ASm/S)
Six chairs, seatless and rusted, form Oslo's *Place of Remembrance* memorial, designed by British sculptor Antony Gormley PAGE 240

AUTHOR

Rosie Whitehouse is a travel writer and a journalist specialising in Jewish life after the Holocaust. She writes for *BBC Online, The Observer, The Independent, Tablet* magazine, the *Jewish Chronicle, Haaretz* and others. A graduate of the London School of Economics, she is the author of a number of travel guides, among them Bradt's *Liguria* and an autobiography, *Are We There Yet? Travels with My Frontline Family* (Reportage, 2007); and two books on the Holocaust, *The People on the Beach: Journeys to Freedom after the Holocaust* (Hurst, 2020) and *Two Sisters: Betrayal, Love and Resistance in Wartime France* (Union Square, 2025).

First published October 2024
Bradt Travel Guides Ltd
31a High Street, Chesham, Buckinghamshire, HP5 1BW, England
www.bradtguides.com
Print edition published in the USA by The Globe Pequot Press Inc,
PO Box 480, Guilford, Connecticut 06437-0480

Text copyright © Bradt Travel Guides Ltd, 2024
Maps copyright © Bradt Travel Guides Ltd, 2024; includes map data
© OpenStreetMap contributors. Made with Natural Earth. Free vector
and raster map data @ naturalearthdata.com.
Photographs copyright © Individual photographers, 2024 (see below)
Project Manager: Susannah Lord
Cover research: Pepi Bluck, Perfect Picture

ISBN: 9781804691960

British Library Cataloguing in Publication Data
A catalogue record for this book is available from the British Library

Photographs 4Corners Images: Justin Cliffe (JC/4C); Dreamstime.com: Ark. Neyman
(AN/D), Bert De Boer (BDB/D), Christoph Lischetzki (CL/D), Dimmex (D/D), Luca
Quadrio (LQ/D), Luka Mjeda (LM/D), Pavel Demin (PD/D), Radub85 (R85/D), Rndmst
(R/D), Sean Pavone (SP/D), Sergio Delle Vedove (SDV/D), Slowcentury (S/D), Tatsiana
Hendzel (TH/D); Rosie Whitehouse (RW); Shutterstock.com: agsaz (A/S), Alexey Fedorenko
(AF/S), Anastasia Petrova (AP/S), Andreas Schnaderbeck (ASc/S), Angelika Smile (ASm/S),
Angelina Dimitrova (AD/S), Diego Grandi (DG/S), Garry Basnett (GB/S), Geza Kurka
(GK/S), Ilan Ejzykowicz (IE/S), ItzaVU (IVU/S), JAN KASZUBA (JK/S), Jean-Marc Pierard
(JMP/S), Juliano Galvao Gomes (JGG/S), Konoplytska (K/S), Marc Venema (MV/S),
marekusz (M/S), oksana.perkins (OP/S), Pajor Pawel (PP/S), Philip Willcocks (PW/S),
Robson90 (R90/S), Steven Phraner (SP/S), stoyanh (S/S), trabantos (T/S), uslatar (U/S)
Front cover Stolpersteine ('Stumbling Stones'), an art project by Gunter Demnig: cobblestone-
sized memorials for victims of Nazism, embedded in the pavement in front of their former
homes. Pictured here, *Stolpersteine* in Berlin (JC/4C). See also page 172.
Back cover, clockwise from top left Judenplatz Holocaust Memorial, Vienna, Austria (AD/S), Dossin
Barracks Memorial, Mechelen, Belgium (RW), detail of the Monument of the Ghetto Heroes,
Warsaw, Poland (M/S)
Title page, clockwise from top left Detail of the Emanuel Tree Memorial, Budapest, Hungary
(LQ/D), Auschwitz-Birkenau State Museum (JGG/S), detail of the Memorial to the Murdered Jews
of Europe, Berlin, Germany (AF/S), *The Arrival* Kindertransport memorial, Liverpool Street Station,
London, UK (PW/S)

Maps David McCutcheon FBCart.S. FRGS

Typeset by Ian Spick, Bradt Travel Guides Ltd and Dataworks, India
Production managed by Gutenberg Press Ltd; printed in Malta
Digital conversion by www.dataworks.co.in

Acknowledgements

I am forever grateful to the survivors and their families who shared their stories with me. Nor could I have written this guide without the support and help of my husband, Tim Judah. He has covered politics in southeastern Europe for over 30 years and while reporting on the war in Ukraine took time to visit many of the Holocaust sites and memorials there. I also thank my sons and daughters for their support and guidance.

My thanks also go to the Society of Authors, who supported my research with a generous grant.

In Italy, I must thank historian Professor Marco Cavallarin, who has always offered me a guiding hand in understanding his country's history. I am also grateful to my friend Andreea Arambasa, whom I met in Romania in 1990. The team at the Together Plan in Belarus and the UK were invaluable guides. I am also grateful for the advice of Professor Neil Gregor of Southampton University and an anonymous reviewer for their comments on sections of the text.

I am also lucky to have had a fantastic editor at Bradt, Susannah Lord. Producing a book is a team effort and I thank all of the team at Bradt.

Contents

LIST OF MAPS

HOW TO USE THIS GUIDE

PRICE CODES Throughout this guide we have used price codes, as shown below, to indicate the cost of those places to stay and eat mentioned in the guide. Prices are based on euros or their equivalent in the countries that use a different currency.

Accommodation Based on the price of a double room per night.

€€€€	€250–450
€€€	€150–249
€€	€100–149
€	Less than €100

Eating out Based on the average price of a main course.

€€€€	€26–30
€€€	€21–25
€€	€16–20
€	Less than €15

KOSHER RESTAURANTS Places to eat that serve kosher food are indicated in this guide with a **K**.

ADMISSION FEES The prices given in the guide are for standard adult admission, unless otherwise stated, and are correct at the time of going to press. For up-to-date prices, as well as concessionary and other rates, please consult the website of the relevant site.

MAPS An overview map is provided of each chapter on which cities and key sites are labelled.

Preface

In a roundabout way, you could say that I have been researching this book since I was five years old. In 1966, my family moved into a house on a modern estate near Richmond in Surrey. Our next-door neighbour, Mr Pelczer, often had headaches and had to lie down in a darkened room, and, since the walls were thin, I was sent outside by my mother to play with his son Jeremy, so that we did not disturb him. I was full of questions that my mother could not answer. All she knew was that Mr Pelczer was Jewish and had come to Britain from Austria on the Kindertransport. I was intrigued.

Years later, in 2018, I decided to write a story about Hans Morgenstern, the last Jew of St Pölten. I travelled to the city west of Vienna to meet him. I have spent years driving around Europe recording how the Holocaust is remembered and talking to survivors, but Austria was the last place I expected to find myself part of the story. During our conversation, quite by chance, and to our mutual surprise, I discovered that Morgenstern was Mr Pelczer's cousin. And then, finally, I found out exactly why he had had so many headaches.

Mr Pelczer had indeed lived in Vienna, as my mother had told me, in an apartment on Urban-Loritz Platz. (When I went to look for it, though, it was no longer there. That is how things are in the surreal world of tracing the Holocaust.) Mr Pelczer's mother, Grete, was Morgenstern's aunt. She had been born in Prague and, after the Anschluss, the Pelczer family fled to the Czech capital.

It was from there that Mr Pelczer left for England, as part of a group of Czech children saved by the young humanitarian Sir Nicholas Winton. When the children boarded the train, German soldiers lined the platform. It was the last time Mr Pelczer saw his parents. Grete and Ludwig Pelczer were deported to Theresienstadt, from where they wrote their son a final letter; they were murdered in Majdanek in September 1942.

The move to Richmond also ushered another important group of people into my life. My father soon became very close friends with two Polish doctors at the hospital where he now worked. One was Jewish, the other Catholic. The two doctors were the best of friends and had survived the Katyn Forest massacre together, and were both married to Auschwitz survivors. The wife of the Jewish doctor had lost her first husband and baby in Auschwitz. The wife of the Catholic doctor had been taken to Auschwitz after the Warsaw Uprising of 1944. There the notorious Dr Mengele had carried out medical experiments on her and, as a result, she was unable to have children. My father, a gynaecologist, operated on her to ease the pain of her scar tissue. He operated on many Jewish patients who had been victims of Dr Mengele. The young journalist in me was fascinated by these stories, largely because my father's friends, who were like my aunts and uncles, never stopped talking about the war.

In the 1970s, I accompanied my father on trips to Poland, where he was involved in cultural and scientific diplomacy. People talked in whispers about what had happened to the Jews, and Kazimierz, the Jewish area in Krakow, was deserted – the doors and windows of the empty houses banged in the wind. These trips left me with a lifelong fascination with eastern Europe and led me to study International History at the London School of Economics.

On the student newspaper I met my husband, Tim Judah. On our first date he told me his grandmother had been murdered in Auschwitz. At the time, the present was more consuming than the past. New opportunities for young journalists were opening up in eastern Europe. After the fall of the Berlin Wall, we set off to live in Romania and then Yugoslavia. As the country fell apart in the 1990s, I found myself having to explain the bloody and genocidal world that their father reported on to our five children. Tim has covered the region ever since, and many more wars and conflicts.

In 2013, I wrote the Bradt Guide to Liguria. How that happened is another story, but writing the book changed my life. I stumbled across the story of an illegal immigrant ship overloaded with Holocaust survivors which set out from Liguria to try to smash through the Royal Navy blockade of the Palestine coast. I wondered who the survivors were and how they had made their way to Italy. Answering those questions produced another book, *The People on the Beach: Journeys to Freedom after the Holocaust*. For my research, I travelled from Ukraine to Lithuania and then drove the route the survivors had taken out of Europe. Finally, I went to Israel to ask them why they had decided to leave.

I then became involved in Holocaust education and memorialisation in the UK, where I am the in-house historian for the '45 Aid Society, which represents the child Holocaust survivors and their families who came to Britain between 1945 and 1948. Helping them to chronicle their stories made me realise how little we as a family knew about what had happened to my husband's mother during World War II.

So, I set off on another journey, this time around France. Those travels led to a new book – *Two Sisters: Betrayal, Love and Resistance in Wartime France* – about how my mother-in-law and aunt escaped the Nazis with the help of a young doctor from Val d'Isère in the Alps. For the help he gave our family, he is now recognised as Righteous Among the Nations (page 10) by the Israeli Holocaust memorial, Yad Vashem.

Introduction

I had mixed reactions from people when I told them I was writing this book. Some people were surprised as it is a new and novel idea to look at the Holocaust in this way, which indeed it is. Others welcomed it as a way to tell so many untold stories; but some people thought dark tourism like this seemed a rather odd thing.

So why buy this book and visit some, or hopefully all, of the places in it?

Holocaust tourism has had a bad press recently with reports of people taking inappropriate selfies at sites of mass murder – but put that on one side for a moment. If you are an inquisitive traveller, think how much you learn on the journeys you take, and how they impact on who you are and how you see the world. As a journalist, I have long known that the only way to understand what is happening, or indeed happened somewhere, is to go and have a look for yourself. Archives and books are hugely important but there is nothing like seeing something with your own eyes, asking local people what they think about it and listening to what eyewitnesses have to say. The Holocaust is no different.

It is only when you travel somewhere in search of a specific story – in this case the Holocaust – that you confront truths about contemporary society that cannot be found in history books and memoirs. The traveller who goes in search of the Holocaust will discover much about what Europeans choose to remember, what they prefer to forget and how they have thought about what happened to their Jewish neighbours over the decades. It is a lesson in modern politics. Much of what we know about the Holocaust comes from popular culture, the films we watch, the historical mini-series and the books we read. These have created many misconceptions and they do not tell the stark story of what happened to Europe's Jews.

One of the most typical Holocaust memorials is a freight wagon mounted on a segment of railway track, and the most-visited Holocaust site is the former concentration and extermination camp of Auschwitz-Birkenau. But most of the Jews who were murdered in the Holocaust never stepped foot in Auschwitz, let alone had heard of it.

Education relies heavily on survivor testimony, which, while crucial, can these days also present a selective understanding. Those survivors who remain alive were children in the Holocaust. Their perspective is youthful and often redeeming. Most Jews' experience of the Holocaust was death and not survival.

Looking at the Holocaust in a geographic context, as a guidebook does, highlights how the genocide played out in remarkably different ways across the continent. Although this guide covers some aspects of the murderous policies towards other groups, notably people with physical and learning disabilities and mental health conditions, and Roma and Sinti communities, it unapologetically concentrates on the story of the Jews because they alone were characterised by the Nazis as an implacable global enemy to be fought at every turn and eliminated.

Bradt's ethos has always been about not simply taking but giving back to the communities you visit. In the case of Holocaust tourism this is as important as ever. Jewish museums and memorials empower the Jewish communities that create them, but they also provide cultural spaces where Jews and non-Jews can come together to remember not just the tragedy of the Holocaust but also the richness of Jewish life and the contribution that Jews have made to Europe's society.

This guide covers sites, memorials and museums that deal with the pre-war build-up to the Holocaust, the Holocaust itself and its aftermath. It is hugely selective and would have run into many tomes had we tried to include everything. Treat this book as an introduction and then set out on your own journey to discover more. As you do, don't forget to keep me informed – at X @rosiewhitehouse and @rosieawhitehouse.

IN AN EMERGENCY

In an emergency, dial 112. This pan-European emergency number applies in all European countries – even when it is not the primary number for emergency services locally. It can be dialled from fixed and mobile phones to contact any emergency service: police, ambulance, and the fire brigade.

Part One

GENERAL INFORMATION

1

History

The history of Europe's Jews is a 2,000-year-old story of a flourishing Jewish culture and one in which Jews made an important contribution to European society as a whole. Sadly, it is also a tale punctuated by expulsion, persecution, violence and mass murder. That violence did not make the Holocaust inevitable, but it did provide fertile ground for the Nazis and their collaborators' racist and antisemitic policies.

The genocide that erupted was driven by an ideology that saw Jews as an omnipotent global enemy set on the destruction of Germany. As historian David Cesarani argued in his seminal account *Final Solution: The Fate of the Jews 1933–49* (St Martins, 2016), Hitler was a warrior set on restoring German power, who believed that war would rebuild the German economy and strengthen the German people. Hitler's political ideas were born in the trenches in World War I, and he blamed the Jews for the 1918 defeat; so before Germany would once again embark on war, Jews had to be removed from German society.

Modern-day terms like Holocaust, Shoah and genocide, which did not exist in the 1930s, give a retrospective preordained path to the events that unfurled after the Nazis took power in Germany. Surprisingly, since the 'international Jewish conspiracy' (in which Jews were deemed both communist and capitalist enemies) was one of the Nazi Party's core beliefs and they had a vision of Germany without its Jewish population, the Nazis never had a clear and coherent anti-Jewish policy to render Germany free of Jews. From 1933 to 1945, policy was made on the hoof and determined by developments in the internal nature of the regime, as well as German economic performance, strategic priorities, and military setbacks and successes.

National Socialism embraced an aggressive policy of *Lebensraum*, or 'living space'. It took a narrow definition of German citizenship based on a culturally and ethnically homogenous *Volk* drawn together by strong leadership into a national community, a *Volksgemeinschaft*. Those who did not fit into this ethnic group were to be excluded.

TIMELINE

1933

30 January	Adolf Hitler is appointed Chancellor of Germany.
22 March	Dachau concentration camp opens.
1 April	National boycott in Germany of Jewish shops and businesses.
7 April	Jews are barred from holding civil service, university and state positions.
10 May	Public burning of books written by Jews, political opponents and others not approved of by the state.
14 July	Naturalised Jewish immigrants are stripped of their German citizenship.

1934
19 August   Hitler proclaims himself Führer as well as Reich Chancellor and becomes absolute dictator of Germany with no legal or constitutional limits to his authority. Armed forces must now swear allegiance to him.

1935
21 May   Jews are barred from serving in the German armed forces.
15 September The Nuremberg Laws are declared.

1936
7 March   Germany occupies the Rhineland, a demilitarised area, violating the Treaty of Versailles.
August   The Four-Year Plan sets the economy on a war footing.
25 October   Hitler and Mussolini form the Rome–Berlin Axis.

1938
13 March   Austria is incorporated into the Third Reich.
26 April   Registration of all Jewish property valued at over 5,000 Reichsmarks becomes mandatory.
6 July   The Evian Conference is held in France to address the problem of Jewish refugees.
August   Adolf Eichmann establishes the Office of Jewish Emigration in Vienna to force Jews to leave Austria.
September–November   Italy introduces sweeping antisemitic legislation.
30 September The Munich Conference takes place; Britain, France and Italy agree to German annexation of Czechoslovakia's Sudetenland.
5 October   At the request of the Swiss authorities, Germans mark all passports of Jews living in the Reich with a letter 'J'.
27 October   Some 17,000 Polish Jews living in Germany are expelled.
2 November   Czechoslovakia is partitioned in the First Vienna Award.
7 November   Herschel Grynszpan assassinates German diplomat Ernst vom Rath in Paris.
9–10 November *Kristallnacht* – an anti-Jewish pogrom enacted across the Reich.
12 November   Jews are forced to transfer businesses to Aryan owners.
15 November   Jewish pupils are expelled from German schools.

1939
30 January   Hitler announces in the Reichstag that 'if war erupts, it will mean the *Vernichtung* [annihilation] of European Jews'.
March   Czechoslovakia is dismembered; Slovakia declares independence; Germany occupies Bohemia and Moravia; Transcarpathia is occupied by Hungary.
23 August   The Nazi–Soviet Pact, a non-aggression pact which contained a secret agreement to partition central and eastern Europe, is signed.
1 September   Germany invades Poland. Two days later Britain and France declare war on Germany.

28 October	The first Jewish ghetto in occupied Poland is established in Piotrków.

1940

9 April	Germany attacks Denmark and southern Norway.
10 May	Germany invades the Netherlands, Belgium, Luxembourg and France.
22 June	France surrenders.
July–October	Battle of Britain.

1941

6 April	Germany attacks Yugoslavia and Greece.
22 June	Germany invades the Soviet Union despite the terms of the Nazi–Soviet Pact.
7 December	Japan attacks Pearl Harbor.
11 December	Germany declares war on the USA.

1942

20 January	The Wannsee Conference takes place in Berlin, where senior German government officials meet to discuss the implementation of the 'Final Solution'.
November	Allied victory in North Africa.

1943

February	Germany surrenders at Stalingrad.
19 April	The Warsaw Ghetto Uprising begins.
3 September	Italy capitulates.
October/November	Rescue of Danish Jewry.

1944

19 March	Germany invades Hungary.
6 June	D-Day – Allied invasion of Normandy.

1945

27 January	Auschwitz-Birkenau is liberated by the Red Army.
15 April	The British Army liberates Bergen-Belsen.
29 April	Dachau is liberated by the US Army.
30 April	Hitler commits suicide.
8 May	Germany surrenders, bringing to an end the Third Reich.

INTERWAR YEARS

1933–34 The National Socialists did not rise to power because of their antisemitic policies. Indeed, in 1933 the Nazi leadership had few specific policies regarding the Jews, and it was not clear when Hitler became Chancellor on 30 January 1933 how the new regime would develop and what it would deliver. Initially, the Nazis' main preoccupation was the elimination of political opposition. In March 1933, Dachau concentration camp was established to hold political opponents, not Jews.

Yet from the moment they came to power, the Nazis set out to exclude Jews from German society and public life and to strip them of their rights and property in a series of improvised state-sanctioned persecutions and anti-Jewish legislation.

There was grass-roots violence towards German Jews on the streets; they faced hostility and isolation as their non-Jewish neighbours drew away. Through endless propaganda German Jews were presented instead as 'Jews in Germany', a race apart – what the historian Christopher Browning has called 'an abstract phenomenon to whose fate Germans could be indifferent'.

1935 At the annual Nuremberg rally in September 1935, the Nuremberg Laws heralded a set of new legislation that would legally define who was considered Jewish regardless of whether that individual regarded himself or herself as Jewish or belonged to a Jewish religious community. The Nuremberg Laws excluded German Jews from being citizens of the Third Reich, prohibited them from marrying or having sexual relations with people of 'German or German-related blood' and deprived them of their political rights.

1936–37 During the Winter and Summer Olympic Games the Nazi regime toned down its anti-Jewish rhetoric, but in an alarming development Roma and Sinti were placed in an internment camp on the outskirts of Berlin.

The realignment of the Nazi Party power structure and the Four-Year Plan was designed to put the German economy on a war footing and made 1936 a decisive year. The impoverishment of German Jews, however, limited their ability to start new lives elsewhere, so by 1937 only about a quarter of the German Jewish population had left the country. It had also become increasingly difficult for them to find somewhere to go as states imposed quotas on Jewish immigration. Between April 1933 and 1938, a policy of Aryanisation reduced the number of Jewish-owned businesses by two thirds.

1938

Anschluss Persecution of the Jews intensified after the Anschluss with Austria. The chaotic degradation in which they were made to clean pavements and public toilets was splashed across the front pages of the world's newspapers, but in Germany Hitler's popularity skyrocketed.

Nazi policy, however, was still aimed at getting Jews to emigrate as soon as possible. In Austria, this task was given to Adolf Eichmann. In August 1938, Eichmann opened the Central Office for Jewish Emigration (Zentralstelle für jüdische Auswanderung) in Vienna, and the destiny of Austria's entire Jewish population fell into the hands of the most radical part of the Nazi apparatus, the SS. Eichmann soon showed that this was the area where the security services could reign supreme. Vienna became a laboratory for new ideas through which Jews could be eliminated from the economic life of the country in an 'orderly' manner, which maximised the benefit for the Reich and its preparations for war. The Zentralstelle stripped Jews of their assets prior to emigration and in so doing paid for itself and more.

Kristallnacht The expulsion from Germany on 27 October 1938 of 17,000 Polish Jews was a significant escalation – the first mass deportation of Jews. However, the Poles refused to admit them and 8,000 were left stranded in the frontier village of Zbąszyń. Among them were the parents of 17-year-old Herschel Grynszpan, who at the time was living illegally in Paris. On 7 November, Grynszpan walked into the city's German Embassy and shot the third secretary, Ernst vom Rath, five times in the stomach. The Nazis claimed that Grynszpan was an agent of an international Jewish conspiracy which intended to provoke a war between France and Germany. The assassination sparked a wave of government-backed violence across the Third

Reich, known as Kristallnacht, the Night of the Broken Glass. On this night alone – 9 November 1938 – when synagogues were burned to the ground and Jewish shops attacked, approximately 30,000 Jews were arrested and sent to concentration camps.

The policy, however, remained to force Jews to leave the Third Reich; so the Nazis did not oppose the evacuation of Jewish children on the Kindertransport, which began in the wake of the November pogrom.

1939 On 30 January, Hitler addressed the Reichstag, saying, 'should international financial Jewry in and outside of Europe succeed in plunging the nations once again into a world war, the result will not be the Bolshevisation of the world and thus the victory of Jewry, but the annihilation of the Jewish race in Europe'; although, as historian David Cesarani pointed out, 'Hitler's menacing oration was prophetic but not programmatic'. Anti-Jewish policy remained focused on emigration even after March 1939, when Bohemia and Moravia were occupied and turned into a protectorate.

WORLD WAR II

INVASION OF POLAND When Germany invaded Poland on 1 September 1939, Britain and France declared war on Germany. Hitler blamed the dilemma of a war on two fronts on what he saw as an international Jewish conspiracy. It was a major theme of Nazi propaganda in the autumn of 1939. Jews were now perceived as a real, not a potential, enemy and a fifth column of spies and saboteurs.

Land lost in 1918 was annexed to the Reich, while a colonially administered heartland was created in Poland that would provide a source of labour. As Christopher Browning has shown in *The Origins of the Final Solution: the Evolution of Nazi Jewish Policy 1939–42* (Arrow, 2005), the invasion of Poland was 'an event of decisive importance' which 'swamped Germany with additional Jews on an unprecedented scale'.

Although Lebensraum was a core Nazi policy, how it would be implemented was decided only after the invasion. Germany embarked on a policy of racial imperialism which involved the demographic restructuring of eastern Europe to ensure ethnic German resettlement, which at this point was more important than solving the Jewish question. It was a process in which the Wehrmacht failed to keep control of the occupied territory and the SS, *Einsatzgruppen* (mobile death squads) and Nazi officials took charge. The army put up feeble resistance in the face of atrocities. As Browning has shown, 'The systematic liquidation in 1939–40 of Poles noted for their education, nationalism, or social status made it clear that the Nazis were capable of murdering by the thousands.'

The SS were tasked with creating a Jewish reservation near Lublin, a project known as the Nisko Plan. When that plan failed, a series of ghettos were set up across Poland where Jews were to be concentrated while awaiting expulsion at a future, unspecified, date. The ghettos were never part of a long-term plan. The expulsion of Jews from the Reich continued until 1941, notably in 1940 from Alsace, which was incorporated into the Reich, and the deportation of Jews from southern Germany to the Gurs internment camp.

1940

The Madagascar Plan After the fall of France, plans that had already been floated in the 1930s to resettle Jews in Madagascar (at that time a French colony) were reconsidered in the German Foreign Office. However, since France's colonies

GOOD TO KNOW: HOLOCAUST DENIAL AND DISTORTION

There is nothing new about Holocaust denial; in fact, attempts to deny or distort the truth began during the Holocaust itself. The Nazis used euphemisms like 'Final Solution' when what they meant was the systematic mass murder of Jews. The perpetrators did everything they could to hide their intentions from their victims, and it was only when the Jews realised that the Nazis intended to murder them that a Jewish resistance began. The Germans and their collaborators also tried to eradicate evidence of the Holocaust, forcing prisoners to exhume mass graves and destroy the bodies. After Jewish and Polish underground organisations managed to inform Allied leaders of the unfurling genocide, the Germans attempted to present a misleading picture to keep international critics at bay, as happened in the beautification of the Theresienstadt Ghetto before the 1944 Red Cross visit.

Immediately after the war, the genocide was marginalised. There was reluctance to commemorate the Holocaust in western Europe, while in eastern and central Europe under communism the Jewish experience was treated as no different from that of other victims of the Germans and their allies.

After the fall of the Berlin Wall in 1989, before joining the European Union these countries had to show that they accepted responsibility for what happened there during World War II. All recorded significant progress, but since the late 2000s the erosion of democratic norms, rising antisemitism and nationalism have changed the political atmosphere, just at the moment the last generation of survivors is dying out.

When visiting Holocaust memorials and sites, be aware that you may encounter examples of Holocaust distortion which appear as: minimising national responsibility or collaboration with Nazi Germany; inaccurate representation of history in museums and exhibitions; rehabilitation of figures who played a role in the Holocaust; attempts to limit academic and public discourse; emphasis on the Righteous who saved Jews accompanied by a reluctance to talk about the role of perpetrators.

did not capitulate and the Royal Navy remained in control of the shipping lanes following Germany's failed invasion of Britain, the plan was abandoned. As historians have shown, this failure had an important psychological impact on Nazi thinking and was a key step along the road to genocide.

The T4 programme Significantly, 1940 saw the first implementation of gas chambers and gas vans as tools of mass murder as part of the Nazis' organised euthanasia programme, code-named T4, after the seat of the euthanasia front organisation at Tiergartenstrasse 4 in Berlin. It was designed to systematically murder institutionalised people who were incurably ill, living with physical or cognitive disabilities, or emotionally distraught, as well as those considered elderly. Between January 1940 and August 1941, the T4 programme claimed the lives of more than 70,000 people. Those with disabilities were also the victims of mass murder in the German-occupied east. An estimated 230,000 people with disabilities were murdered by the regime.

1941 The year 1941 was a turning point in history of the Holocaust as it ushered in the era of mass murder.

Invasion of Greece and Yugoslavia In April 1941, Germany invaded Greece and Yugoslavia after a coup in Belgrade toppled the pro-German regime. Hitler blamed Anglo-Saxon warmongers and Jews in Moscow. The Croatian fascist Ustasha, a German ally, unleashed a violent attack on both Jews and Serbs.

Operation Barbarossa On 22 June 1941 Germany invaded the Soviet Union. Most Jews lived in the area to which Jewish settlement had been confined in the Russian Empire, known as the Pale of Settlement. Much of this area had been occupied by the Soviet Union in 1939 or was within its borders. This area soon fell under German control. At this stage the plan was that, after the defeat of the Soviet Union, Europe's Jews would be resettled behind the Urals.

In a significant development the SS were tasked with creating a series of Einsatzgruppen to ensure rear-area security. Military setbacks and the emergence of partisans pushed anti-Jewish measures in a murderous direction. Jews were seen as communist enemies. According to Browning, the army moved from abdication of responsibility to outright participation in this crusade against the 'Jewish-Bolshevik enemy'.

Aided and abetted by local collaborators, they began the mass murder of the Jewish population. Romanian forces allied to Germany also carried out mass murder of Jews. A significant development was the mass killing of children which began in mid-August. August also saw the largest single massacre to date of 44,125 Jews in Kamianets-Podilskyi, now in western Ukraine.

Jews were seen as a drain on food supplies and their rations cut to the minimum. Only Jews useful to the labour force were to be spared. In the late autumn of 1941, the first selections took place when ghettos were created in Lviv and Ivano-Frankivsk.

The invasion of the Soviet Union changed the course of the war, bringing the communists into resistance activity across Europe. The Nazi way of thinking saw Jews at every turn and a dangerous fifth column across the continent.

Serbia German occupation forces facing a communist-led insurgency in Serbia pushed for the deportation of Serbian Jews to Poland. The request was rejected in favour of deporting the Reich Jews first. This led to the mass murder of Serbian Jewish men in reprisal for attacks on German soldiers as in the eyes of the occupying forces Jews equated with communists. It was the first systematic murder of Jews outside Soviet territory.

Deportation of the Reich Jews In the summer of 1941, there were still 250,000 Jews in the Greater Reich and 88,000 in the Protectorate. It was decided in October

TIMING MASS MURDER

During the Holocaust the Germans often deliberately carried out deportations, mass shootings, gassings and the liquidation of ghettos on important Jewish festivals. There are numerous examples of this, but perhaps the best known are the mass shooting at Babyn Yar in Kyiv which took place over Yom Kippur in September 1941 and the mass deportation from the Warsaw Ghetto, which began on Tisha B'av (page 17). Under Nazi persecution, most Jews tried to observe the festivals and holy days as best as they could, but those who refused to work were punished and often executed.

THE PORAJMOS

The Nazis and their allies also carried out a genocide against the Roma and Sinti, known to the Roma as the Porajmos, the 'devouring'.

The Roma, a nomadic people with origins in northern India, have faced centuries of discrimination in Europe. Under a supplementary decree of the Nuremberg Laws issued in November 1935, the Roma were classified as 'enemies of the race-based state'. As was the case with Jewish children, Roma and Sinti children were banned from public schools, while adults found it increasingly difficult to find employment and their freedom of movement was restricted.

Deportations to ghettos and concentration camps began in December 1942. Of the 23,000 Roma and Sinti people imprisoned in Auschwitz-Birkenau, it is estimated that more than 20,000 were murdered. The exact number of Roma victims is not known but historians estimate that as many as half of Europe's Roma population may have been murdered. Though, as historian Christopher Browning has argued in *The Origins of the Final Solution: The Evolution of Nazi Jewish Policy 1939–42* (Arrow, 2005), 'the Nazi regime never committed itself outright to a comprehensive program, analogous to the Final Solution'.

The genocide of the Roma received little attention after World War II and was recognised by the West German government only in 1982.

The Roma genocide was not as well documented as the Holocaust and Romani survivors did not discuss it. In recent years the Roma have begun to memorialise the victims of the Porajmos, but the ongoing discrimination faced by the Roma has also diverted attention from the genocide.

that they would be deported to ghettos in the east. It was a turning point. To make room for them, thousands of Jews already in the overcrowded ghettos of Minsk and Riga were shot, as were many of the Jews deported from the Reich.

Establishing the extermination camps Mass shootings were public, took a toll on the killers and were expensive and time consuming, so in the autumn of 1941 experiments for the use of poisonous gas in mass murder took place in Auschwitz, and the creation of extermination camps at Bełżec, Chełmno and Sobibór began. These experiments came as the German advance across Soviet territory was halted in late October. Expulsion of Jews from Nazi-occupied territory was no longer an assured possibility at the end of a swift defeat of the Soviet Union. In October 1941, a ban on emigration of Jews from Nazi-occupied Europe was implemented. Gas vans were used for mass murder in Belgrade and at Chełmno in December 1941.

War with the USA Hitler was convinced that America's Jews were driving the country to war. After the Japanese attack on Pearl Harbor, on 11 December Hitler declared war on the United States, signalling a turning point in the war for Europe's Jews: there was now a coherent clarity to anti-Jewish policy and Hitler was determined to annihilate the Jews.

1942–45
The Wannsee Conference The year 1942 began with a fateful meeting held in an elegant villa in Wannsee in Berlin, where the logistics of the deportations to

the death camps of millions of Jews was finalised and a timetable for their murder was set.

Extermination camps The first gassing of Jews took place at Auschwitz-Birkenau on 15 February 1942. Extermination camps began operation in Bełżec in March, Sobibór in May and Treblinka in July of the same year. Jews from across occupied Europe were brought to German-occupied Poland to be murdered in the gas chambers.

AFTERMATH

Initially, most survivors hoped they could return home and find family members who had survived, or at least some remnants of the lives they had lived before the Holocaust. Many survivors found that not only were their neighbours not happy to

RIGHTEOUS AMONG THE NATIONS

Yad Vashem is Israel's national Holocaust memorial museum and remembrance authority. On behalf of the State of Israel and the Jewish people, it recognises non-Jews who risked their lives to save Jews during the Holocaust. This is one of its founding duties.

It is a unique attempt by victims to pay tribute to people who stood by their side at a time of persecution when the overwhelming majority of bystanders did nothing.

The criteria for someone to be recognised as Righteous Among the Nations are extremely strict. It must be proved that the victim was indeed in danger of losing their life and that the person who helped them did so for purely altruistic reasons. That help must have been substantial or repeated. Only a Jewish person can put forward a nomination.

Individuals recognised as Righteous Among the Nations are awarded a medal and certificate. Their name is added to the Wall of Honour in the Garden of the Righteous at Yad Vashem. Awards can be given posthumously.

Those who have received the award come from all walks of life, from different countries, economic backgrounds and faiths. Although the Righteous are often used to bolster a country's image of how its population responded to the Holocaust, focus on the Righteous is important as it turns the spotlight away from the victims and asks 'What would you have done to help your neighbours?'.

During the 1961 trial of Adolf Eichmann in Jerusalem, frequent reference was made to the Righteous Among the Nations at the request of David Ben Gurion, Israel's first prime minister, to minimise the negative impact of the trial on Israeli foreign policy. It prompted many Jews to write to Yad Vashem suggesting candidates for an award. In 1963, the Israeli government then set up a special commission to judge applications. Almost 28,000 people have been awarded the title Righteous Among the Nations.

Jews who helped fellow Jews and risked their own lives in the process are not considered for the award. As no such award for Jews exists, it means that the level of Jewish resistance is often underestimated.

For further information, visit w yadvashem.org/righteous.html

see that they had survived, but they had no physical home to return to – someone else was living in their house. There were pogroms in Poland and Slovakia. Again and again, survivors say that they left eastern Europe because they feared for their lives and were not welcome in the towns and villages where their families had previously lived for generations.

The Baltic states, much of pre-war eastern Poland, Transcarpathia and Moldova were absorbed into the Soviet Union and much of eastern Europe became a Soviet zone of influence. Stalinism also drove many Jews to leave as Zionism and the Jewish religion were proscribed under communism.

After liberation, many of the surviving Jews, especially those from eastern Europe, hoped to start a new life far away from Europe, preferably in Palestine. This brought them into conflict with the British Empire, which at this point controlled the Palestine Mandate – the British, who had restricted Jewish immigration in 1939, continued to do so after the war. In 1948, after the declaration of the state of Israel, many survivors then fought in the wars that followed.

In the post-war period, there was little interest in the Jewish wartime experience both in Israel and the wider world. It was only in 1961 during the trial of Adolf Eichmann in Jerusalem that many people heard for the first time about the fate of Europe's Jews.

2

Practical Information

What makes the Holocaust unique as a genocide is that it was a transnational event. Its 6 million victims came from vibrant and diverse European Jewish communities who spoke many different languages, ate an array of different foods and had a variety of approaches to their religious and political beliefs. Traditionally, guidebooks list 'don't miss' highlights that visitors should certainly see, but in the context of the Holocaust that is far from appropriate – it is important to visit sites, both those well and lesser known, across the continent to gain a greater understanding of the breadth of this genocide.

Europe has a wide variety of memorials, sites and museums that commemorate the Holocaust. Some, like Buchenwald and Treblinka, remember victims from across the continent; others give a unique perspective from an individual country's point of view. Many can offer an insight into contemporary politics, notably Budapest's House of Terror Museum and the Jasenovac and Donja Gradina memorials that straddle the Croatia–Bosnia and Herzegovina border. While most tourists flock to see the former concentration and extermination camp at Auschwitz-Birkenau in southern Poland, taking time to visit some of the continent's less-visited sites, like the Škēde Dunes on Latvia's Baltic coast which can be just as moving and informative. Although some sites like the Memorial to the Murdered Jews of Europe near the Brandenburg Gate in Berlin remember the 6 million victims collectively, Holocaust memorialisation is also about remembering 6 million individual people, most of whom died having never heard of Auschwitz-Birkenau.

TOUR OPERATORS

If you prefer to travel in an organised group with a guide, it is possible to join a tour group. Alternatively, many local tourist boards and Jewish organisations offer walking tours and trips to specific sites, but the latter often come with an inflated price tag.

The Cultural Experience
w theculturalexperience.com. Offers Holocaust-themed tours led by an expert in the field.
Educational Tours w eftours.com. Organises a Holocaust tour of central & eastern Europe.
Krakow Travel w krakow-travel.com. Holocaust & Jewish heritage tours.

Leger Holidays w legerbattlefields.co.uk. Holocaust- & resistance-themed tours.
Momentum Tours & Travel w momentumtours.com. Organises a 7-day tour of Jewish Warsaw & Kraków.
World War II Tours w worldwar2tours.com. Offers a 2-week Holocaust Memorial Tour.

SAFETY

Although Holocaust sites and museums are vandalised by right-wing extremists especially at moments of heightened tension in the Middle East, tourists visiting the sites are not themselves targets. While there have been extreme cases such as the 2014 terrorist attack at the Jewish Museum in Brussels, such events are exceptional but, as with visiting any major tourist attraction, it pays to be vigilant. While some museums and memorials have police protection and high levels of security, many do not. Levels of security can also vary considerably at larger sites, notably Auschwitz-Birkenau, where they are intense at the main Auschwitz museum but non-existent at Birkenau.

Many mass graves are situated in remote spots and receive few visitors. As a result, the danger comes not from the nature of the site but simply from its location. If you are a solo traveller, you may feel more secure hiring a taxi and asking the driver to wait.

TRAVELLING WITH A DISABILITY

Access to Holocaust sites, memorials and museums varies across the continent. Some memorials are simply on urban streets, others in fields and forests. Most modern museums are adapted to suit the needs of travellers with a disability; but many of those museums and memorials based in historic buildings can present challenges for travellers with mobility issues, lacking lifts, having uneven walkways and often being in remote locations. It is advisable for visitors who use a wheelchair to take a companion who can assist when visiting sites like Sobibór, Treblinka, and Auschwitz-Birkenau.

Most museums and memorial sites have informative websites, and also offer audio guides and useful apps. The Auschwitz-Birkenau State Museum also produces a braille guide and another in large type for partially sighted visitors, which are both free of charge. It also has a new project that adapts tours of the site for visitors with hearing impairments.

The UK government website (w gov.uk/government/publications/disabled-travellers/disability-and-travel-abroad) has a downloadable guide giving general advice and practical information for travellers with a disability (and their companions) preparing for overseas travel. The website Wheelmap (w wheelmap.org) has an interactive global map showing accessible and partially accessible properties, including museums, hotels and restaurants. The Society for Accessible Travel and Hospitality (w sath.org) also provides some general information. Other useful websites include w disabledaccessibletravel.com and w sagetraveling.com.

TRAVELLING WITH CHILDREN

Most Holocaust museums and memorials put an age limit on visiting, usually 14 years and over. Images in many exhibitions are disturbing and deemed not suitable for younger children. Age limits also apply to prevent children running around and

JEWISH FOOD

Since Jewish dietary laws were created, food has played a symbolic role in religious rituals and celebrations, and the kitchen and the dining table are a central part of Jewish life. European Jewish food covers two worlds: the Ashkenazi and the Sephardi. Ashkenazi cuisine is designed for the cold climate in central and eastern Europe and relies on chicken fat, carp, herring, potatoes and cabbage; while Sephardi cuisine is a taste of the Mediterranean with peppers, tomatoes, freshwater fish, olive oil and rice.

Increasingly popular across Europe today are Middle Eastern restaurants that serve Jewish food originating both from the Middle East and from southeastern Europe, which includes familiar dishes like hummus and falafel. But a journey into the heart of what was Jewish Europe until the 1940s gives visitors a chance to taste some classic Jewish dishes, which have now become part of national cuisines. Among them are pumpkin risotto in Italy, and in Poland *chałka*, a version of the braided Jewish bread *challah*, traditionally eaten on the Sabbath. Bagels have been associated with Ashkenazi Jews since the 17th century but are now eaten across the world.

Many Jewish dishes are eaten at specific Jewish festivals. During Passover, cakes are often made with ground nuts as a substitute for flour and no raising agents are used. At Purim it is traditional to eat triangular biscuits called *hamantaschen*. Small filo pies and pastries filled with cheese are staples on the Sephardi table, while at New Year Ashkenazi Jews traditionally eat *lekach*, a honey cake.

Claudia Roden's *The Book of Jewish Food: an Odyssey from Samarkand and Vilna to the Present Day* (Penguin, 1999) is the perfect companion if you want to explore the world of Jewish food.

making noise that could be considered inappropriate behaviour in this setting. That said, many Holocaust sites are completely unattended and it is up to you to decide if they are suitable to take your children to, although on a practical front, some sites are not suitable for pushchairs.

A good place to start with younger children is to introduce them to Jewish culture. Jewish museums across Europe have events for children, and many towns and cities put up a menorah with candles during the winter festival of Hanukkah.

Books are an excellent way to introduce children to the subject of the Holocaust. The story of Paddington Bear was, after all, based on the Kindertransport experience. Judith Kerr's *When Hitler Stole Pink Rabbit* (HarperCollins, 2017) is a classic in which the author tells the story of how her own family fled Nazi Germany. Michael Rosen's *The Missing: The True Story of My Family in World War II* (Walker Books, 2019) is a powerful account by one of Britain's best-loved children's authors. Michael Morpurgo's *Waiting for Anya* (Egmont, 2007) is an adventure story of Jewish children being smuggled into Spain. However, it is important to think carefully about what you choose to give your child to read as some books, notably John Boyne's *The Boy in the Striped Pyjamas* (Definitions, 2008), can give a distorted view of the history of the Holocaust.

Don't jump in feet first and take teenagers to Auschwitz. When introducing older children to the Holocaust, it helps first to choose sites that they may identify with, such as those linked with children's experiences, like the Maison d'Izieu in France, where Jewish children were hidden during the Holocaust, and Selvino in

Italy or Windermere in the UK, where child Holocaust survivors were cared for after World War II. Or you might take them to see places like Budapest's Dohány Street Synagogue, the synagogues in Kraków, and Berlin's Oranienburger Strasse Synagogue. Introduce the two-millennia story of the Jews in Europe by visiting the old ghetto in Rome. Show them the paintings of Marc Chagall which capture a world that has disappeared in Belarus. Give them a taste of Jewish life – literally – by taking them to a Jewish bakery.

Older primary-school-age children often learn about the Holocaust through the story of Anne Frank and the Kindertransport. There are Kindertransport memorials in Berlin, London, Harwich, Prague and Vienna. Although Anne Frank House museum in Amsterdam sells tickets to all ages it is probably more suited to children over the age of ten.

Whichever site you choose to visit, introduce the history slowly and in an accessible way. Keep initial visits short. Make sure that you have read up and know the history of the site yourself, so you can field any questions.

KEEPING KOSHER

Kosher describes foods that comply with the strict Jewish dietary rules called kashrut. The rules cover what foods can be eaten, and how they are prepared and combined. Not all Jews follow these rules and not all restaurants serving Jewish food are kosher. Kashrut.com (w kashrut.com/travel) has a list of Orthodox synagogues and Chabad centres across Europe. Kosher Traveling (w koshertraveling.co) and Totally Jewish Travel (w totallyjewishtravel.com) are useful websites for finding kosher and Jewish-observant-friendly hotels and kosher restaurants and shops in Europe and beyond.

Restaurants suggested in this guide which serve kosher food are indicated by the symbol **K**.

VISITING THE SITES

When visiting a Holocaust memorial, museum or site, it is important to be respectful and to dress conservatively.

The locations of some museums and memorials were the scene of mass murder and are often the site of mass graves. Always remember you could be standing next to someone who has a familial or other direct connection to the victims.

Some people live near to or actually in former concentration camps. Drancy in France, Mechelen in Belgium and Ebensee am Traunsee in Austria are examples of this. Be mindful not to stare, and respect local people's privacy.

Most sites are happy for you to take photographs and to share them on social media. But think before you post – don't take selfies or family-holiday-style snaps. Pay attention to signs that say photography is not permitted or that flash photography is prohibited.

GOOD TO KNOW

Jewish-run memorials, museums and sites usually close early on Friday and are not open on Saturday or Jewish holidays. At moments of heightened tension in the Middle East, some Holocaust museums and memorials that do not have police protection may close, so check before visiting.

The Jewish calendar follows a lunar cycle and, like other lunisolar calendars, it consists of months of 29 or 30 days which begin and end at approximately the time of the new moon. According to the Jewish calendar, we are now in the sixth millennium. The Hebrew year count starts in year 3761BCE, which the 12th-century Jewish philosopher Maimonides established as the biblical date of creation. Most of 2025 is thus the Jewish year 5786.

In addition to the daily way of life and the spiritual highpoint of the Sabbath (Shabbat) – the Jewish day of rest and worship, lasting from sundown on Friday until sundown on Saturday – there are festivals that add rhythm and colour to Jewish life.

ROSH HASHANAH The Jewish New Year, or Rosh Hashanah, occurs in September/ October. It is the anniversary of the creation of Adam and Eve, the first man and woman according to the Torah (the Jewish Bible), and starts a ten-day period of self-examination and repentance. It is a time for Jews to reflect on their year, including their good and bad deeds.

In the synagogue, the *shofar*, a ram's horn, is blown in a call for repentance. The Tashlich ceremony also takes place during Rosh Hashanah in which sins are symbolically cast out into water by throwing pebbles or breadcrumbs into a river or stream as people ask for God's forgiveness.

Apples are dipped in honey to represent the hope of a sweet new year. Pomegranates are also eaten because of the fruit's appearance in the Torah as the fruit of the land of Israel, and as it is said to have 613 seeds. This is the same number as the number of historic laws governing Jewish life according to tradition.

YOM KIPPUR Also known as the Day of Atonement, this is the holiest day of the Jewish calendar and falls nine days after Rosh Hashanah. There is a 25-hour fast during which nothing must be eaten or drunk. On the eve of Yom Kippur it is traditional for a father to bless his sons and daughters. The service that introduces Yom Kippur is called Kol Nidre after the prayer that is recited. Much of the day is spent in the synagogue in prayer, to repent and seek forgiveness for one's sins over the previous year.

SUCCOT (also Sukkot) Five days after Yom Kippur, the festival of Succot celebrates God's care of the Jewish people in the wilderness after the Exodus and is also the Jewish harvest festival. Succot, which means 'tabernacles', refers to the temporary huts in which the Jews lived in their 40 years in the desert. During Succot a blessing is said over four species of plants mentioned in the Bible. The collective name for these species is a *lulav*, after the palm frond which is the most conspicuous. Meals are taken outside in a flimsy hut called a *succah*.

HANUKKAH Hanukkah, which falls between November and January, celebrates the victory of the Jewish Maccabeans against the Greek rulers who sought to

Avoid touching the former concentration camp sites – they are historic buildings in a fragile state. Walking across delicate structures can damage them.

Jewish people traditionally leave stones on graves and memorials – do not remove them.

impose Hellenistic culture and religion on the Jews. The struggle culminated in the recapture and rededication of the Temple in Jerusalem. The oil burned in the temple had been spoiled, except for one jar. It was enough to last for one day, but by a miracle lasted for eight days. As a result, the festival of Hanukkah lasts for eight days and on each evening a special eight-branched candelabra is lit, starting with one candle on the first night and ending with eight on the last night. It is traditional to eat fried foods, especially potato latkes and doughnuts.

PURIM The deliverance of the Jewish people from the wicked Haman, the royal vizier, in the days of Queen Esther of Persia is celebrated in early spring by reading the story of Purim from a special scroll called the Megilla, eating a festive meal, giving to charity and exchanging gifts of food with family and friends. Children, and sometimes adults, dress up in fancy costumes. The Fast of Esther occurs just before Purim. It commemorates the fast undertaken by the Jewish people when they learned of the decree of annihilation planned against them by Haman. They were saved by Queen Esther and her guardian Mordechai.

PESACH Also known as Passover in English, the festival is held in March or April and celebrates the Jews' escape from slavery in Egypt. It lasts for eight days in the diaspora and begins with the Seder, which consists of a service and a meal. The items on the Seder plate each symbolise a part of the Exodus story, which is retold during the meal using a book called the Haggadah. During Pesach it is not permitted to eat anything which has or may have leaven. Jews eat unleavened bread called matzo. This is symbolic of the fact that when Pharoah ordered the Jews to leave, they did so in such a rush that there was no time for their bread to rise. Only foods that have been specially produced for Passover are permitted, except for fresh fruit and raw vegetables.

SHAVUOT Shavuot, which falls in May or June, celebrates the giving of all the Torah laws, including the Ten Commandments at Mount Sinai after the Exodus. Shavuot means 'weeks' in Hebrew. It is traditional to eat a dairy meal that symbolises the land of milk and honey.

TISHA B'AV The saddest day of the year, falling in July or August, commemorates the destruction of the First Temple in Jerusalem. A major fast is observed which lasts 25 hours, and the Book of Lamentations, which mourns the destruction of Jerusalem, is read in the synagogue.

Other major calamities have happened to the Jewish people on Tisha B'av, among them the start of the First Crusade and the expulsion of the Jews from England, France and Spain. World War I broke out on this day in 1914; and in 1941 the mass deportation from the Warsaw Ghetto began. All of these events are remembered on this day, which has come to be a day of mourning.

If you would like to place a stone, flowers or a candle at a memorial, look out for places where you are permitted to do so.

At most memorial sites you are not allowed to eat or drink, although a water bottle is usually permissible.

In a few short years, the Holocaust brought to an abrupt end the long history of thousands of Jewish communities in central and eastern Europe. One place to start looking for the last testaments of these communities is the cemeteries that were left behind; but perhaps the starkest memorials are the ruined synagogues, notably in Constanța in Romania. Many of the synagogues that remained standing were converted into libraries, museums, cinemas and concert halls.

It is important to understand that, although the rich and vibrant culture of these communities was either erased or moved elsewhere as a result of the Holocaust, Jewish life was not brought to a complete halt; and today there are thriving Jewish communities, large and small, with beautiful active synagogues across the continent.

The following organisations play a key role in preserving and promoting Jewish cultural heritage.

Centropa w centropa.org. This Vienna-based organisation tells the story of Jewish life in central & eastern Europe throughout the 20th century. It has a fantastic collection of testimonies, films & guided walks.

European Association for the Preservation & Promotion of Jewish Culture & Heritage (AEPJ) w jewisheritage.org. The AEPJ serves as a platform to develop cultural initiatives & educational programmes related to European Jewish sites. It runs 2 projects: the 'European Days of Jewish Culture', a cultural festival that takes place across Europe Sep–Dec, is designed to bring an understanding of Jewish culture to non-Jewish European communities; their 'European Routes of Jewish Heritage' programme is aimed at tourists who want to explore Jewish culture (the routes can be seen on an interactive map on the website).

European Jewish Cemeteries Initiative w esjf-cemeteries.org. This German-based non-profit organisation was established in 2015 to protect and preserve Jewish cemeteries in Belarus, Croatia, the Czech Republic, Georgia, Greece, Hungary, Lithuania, Poland, Serbia, Slovakia & Ukraine.

Foundation for Jewish Heritage w historicsynagogueseurope.org. Their website has a useful interactive map that shows the location of synagogues – ruined, converted & those that remain active – across Europe.

JGuideEurope w jguideeurope.org. A cultural guide to Jewish Europe & a useful resource for travellers.

J-Story: Jewish History Tours w j-story.org. Has a useful interactive map.

YIVO Institute for Jewish Research w yivo.org. YIVO was originally set up in Vilnius, Lithuania in 1925. Now based in New York, the organisation preserves, studies and teaches the cultural history of Jewish life throughout eastern Europe, Germany & Russia, as well as promoting studies related to Yiddish. Its website is a useful resource to discover more about Jewish history.

MARCH OF THE LIVING

The International March of the Living (**w** motl.org) is an annual educational programme that brings people from around the world to Poland and Israel to study the history of the Holocaust. Since 1988, the programme has taken more than 300,000 people from 50 countries to the principal Holocaust sites in Poland. The five-day tours are accompanied by survivors. The UK March of the Living website (**w** marchoftheliving.org.uk) has a series of interesting interviews with survivors who have accompanied the trips.

The documentary film *Blind Love: A Holocaust Journey through Poland with Man's Best Friend* (2015) tells of the experience of six blind Israelis who travel with their guide dogs to Poland with March of the Living.

Part Two

THE GUIDE

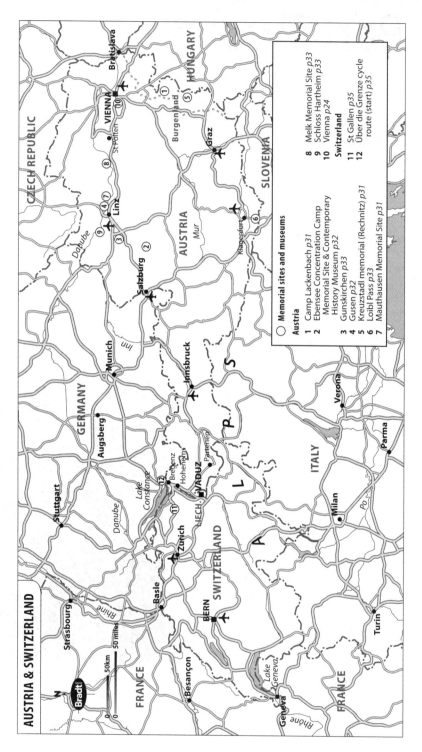

AUSTRIA & SWITZERLAND

Memorial sites and museums

Austria

1 Camp Lackenbach *p31*
2 Ebensee Concentration Camp
   Memorial Site & Contemporary
   History Museum *p32*
3 Gunskirchen *p33*
4 Gusen *p32*
5 Kreuzstadl memorial (Rechnitz) *p31*
6 Loibl Pass *p33*
7 Mauthausen Memorial Site *p31*
8 Melk Memorial Site *p33*
9 Schloss Hartheim *p33*
10 Vienna *p24*

Switzerland

11 St Gallen *p35*
12 Über die Grenze cycle
   route (start) *p35*

3

Austria and Switzerland

Austria is a country packed with history, much of it dark and difficult. While most of the Holocaust and Jewish museums and memorials are to be found in the capital, Vienna, the Mauthausen concentration camp in the west of the country is one of Austria's important Holocaust sites. After the country was annexed by Germany in 1938, many Austrian Jews tried to flee across the border to Switzerland.

Until relatively recently the Swiss national narrative had been one of neutrality and humanitarian assistance. But in the 1990s, historical research exposed the antisemitic asylum policy employed by Switzerland during the 1930s and 40s, which resulted in some 35,000 Jews from Nazi-occupied countries being denied refuge. A 100km cycle path, which begins on the shore of Lake Constance just north of Bregenz in Austria, commemorates the refugee's story as it criss-crosses the border between Austria and Switzerland.

GETTING THERE AND AROUND

Vienna makes a good starting point for exploring central and eastern Europe. It is one of Europe's transport hubs and easy to reach by air, bus, car or train, with an increasing number of night trains (w nightjet.com) from other European capitals and major cities. Switzerland too has excellent air, road and train links, and has an extremely reliable public transport system. The closest airport to St Gallen is Zürich, which is also a train hub with excellent connections to Munich.

To drive on Austrian motorways, you will need to buy a vignette at the border. Car rentals come with a vignette. But you'll need a separate vignette to drive in Switzerland – bear this in mind if you plan to use a car to explore the border area around St Gallen/Lake Constance.

ONLINE RESOURCES

The **Documentation Centre of Austrian Resistance** (w doew.at) has a database of more than 64,000 Jewish victims' names and related information.

AUSTRIA

From the end of the 19th century to the start of World War I, Austria, the beating heart of the Austro-Hungarian Empire, was at the centre of European cultural and intellectual life but it was also home to many of the principal perpetrators of the Holocaust. Adolf Hitler was born in Austria and a larger proportion of Austrians served in the SS than Germans. It is hardly surprising, therefore, that the country has had difficulty coming to terms with its past.

After World War II, most Austrians chose to believe that they were the 'first victim' of the Nazis when the country was annexed to the Reich in the 1938 Anschluss, an event that in fact was welcomed at the time by the majority of Austrians. The 'first victim' myth only began to unravel in the mid 1980s when the Nazi wartime activities of Kurt Waldheim, Austria's president from 1986 to 1992, sparked a national debate on the country's role in the Holocaust. In two highly acclaimed speeches before the Austrian parliament in 1991 and the Israeli Knesset in 1993, Chancellor Franz Vranitzky finally acknowledged the shared responsibility borne by Austrians for Nazi crimes.

Despite the enormous efforts made by recent Austrian governments to commemorate the Holocaust and tackle antisemitism, a 2019 survey by the Conference on Jewish Material Claims Against Germany, also known as the Claims Conference, found more than half of Austrians were unaware that 6 million Jews were murdered in the Holocaust. Research conducted in 2023 on behalf of the Austrian parliament, showed that antisemitism was on the rise with almost 60% of Austrians having witnessed antisemitic language or behaviour in 2022.

A continual point of contention is the stance of the right-wing populist Freedom Party of Austria (Freiheitliche Partei Österreichs; FPÖ), the most popular party in Austria. Although its leaders have repeatedly and publicly disavowed antisemitism, elements within the party still harbour racist and antisemitic views.

Austria now has a Holocaust memorial in Vienna, but it does not have a Holocaust museum.

GETTING AROUND Much of Vienna is accessible on foot. If you need to park your car in the city, download the Easypark app.

The former Mauthausen concentration camp can be reached by public transport, as can Ebensee, Gusen and Melk. For Mauthausen, take a train from Vienna to Linz, which is 22km from the memorial. Then from Linz, take bus 360. If returning by public transport, be aware that the last bus leaves well before the site closes. To explore Burgenland and see the Gunskirchen Memorial Site, it helps to have a car.

HISTORY Jews have lived in Austria since the 3rd century CE and settled in the capital, Vienna, in the 1300s. At that time, Austria was part of territories ruled by the Habsburgs. The community's luck has waxed and waned, the low point was in 1421 when Vienna's entire Jewish population was burned to death, forcibly baptised or expelled. After that there was no Jewish life in Vienna for 150 years. The Jews were expelled again in 1669–70 and only began to return to Vienna in the early 19th century.

In 1782, the Edict of Tolerance – part of a series of reforms by the then Habsburg emperor Joseph II – extended religious freedom to the Jewish community across the Habsburg Empire. Jews played an important part in the leadership of the revolution of 1848, which resulted in the gradual granting of equal rights to Jews and in 1852 permission was granted for the establishment of a Jewish community in Vienna. Austrian Jews put their trust in the German culture the revolution set free. However, the new freedom enjoyed by the press was not all positive, and the antisemitic publications produced soon had a wide readership. Antisemitism continued to be rife particularly in the Austrian capital, where Hitler spent time before World War I. He was influenced by the views of Karl Lueger (1844–1910), Vienna's pre-war mayor, and a rabid antisemite. Lueger's statue, on the Ringstrasse near Stadtpark, is due to be orientated 3.5 degrees to the right in an artistic change of perspective which gives passers-by a sense of insecurity.

By 1938, the Jewish population of Austria was approximately 192,000, 4% of Austria's population, most of whom lived in Vienna, where they made up 10% of the city's inhabitants. In the early 20th century, there was an influx of Jews from Galicia and present-day Slovakia into Vienna and soon they made up 80% of the Jewish community. However, they were less assimilated and were regarded with suspicion by the general population and the established Jewish community; and their poverty stood in stark contrast to the wealth of families like the Rothschilds and Todescos.

Interwar years The new Austria that emerged from the peace treaties following World War I was a deeply unhappy and divided country, its politics fractious and violent. The Treaty of Saint-Germain, which deprived Austria of much of its territory and forbade a union with Germany, angered Austrians as it went against the principles of self-determination laid out in US President Woodrow Wilson's 14 Points. The settlement left 4 million Austrian Germans excluded from the new state. A similar 'stab-in-the-back' myth that the country had been betrayed by Jews and communists developed in Austria as it did in Germany.

The new republic had no defined rights for minorities and left Jews more exposed than they had been under Habsburg rule. In the post-war economic chaos that followed, Jews were accused of stockpiling and price hikes. Hugo Bettauer's 1922 novel *The City without Jews* grew out of the post-war atmosphere. It is a tale of how Jews were hounded out of Vienna but invited back as the city headed towards economic collapse. Bettauer was murdered by a member of the Nazi Party in 1925.

The country's economic instability made many Austrians believe that their future lay in a union with Germany. Hitler, who wanted to unite Austria and Germany, meddled in Austrian politics, supporting the Austrian Nazi Party to destabilise the country. When the party was outlawed, many of its activists fled to Germany, among them those who would become the chief perpetrators of the Holocaust. When Germany and Italy, which borders Austria to the south, became allies, it opened the way for Germany to be invited to 'restore' order, and on 15 March 1938 Hitler made a triumphal entry into Vienna, where he gave a speech from the balcony of the Hofburg Palace, the former royal residence, to a cheering crowd of 200,000 people.

After the **Anschluss**, the annexation of Austria to the Reich, there was panic in the Jewish community as their shops were sacked, their apartments ransacked and their property stolen. Persecution began immediately; famously, Jews were even forced to clean the pavements on their hands and knees. About 120,000 Jewish refugees fled after the Nazis took power in Austria. The second most common destination after the USA was the UK.

Nazi policy was at this point focused on forcing the Jews out of the Reich, and Adolf Eichmann was given the job of ridding Austria of its Jewish population. The Kristallnacht pogroms in November 1938 which occurred across the Reich were especially vicious in Austria, where 42 synagogues were destroyed, and many Jewish businesses vandalised.

World War II Anti-Jewish policy changed after the outbreak of war. Between October 1939 and April 1940, some 1,600 Jewish men were sent to the Nisko concentration camp near Lublin (page 269). Deportations began again in October 1941, when the decision was made to deport the Jews from the Old Reich territories. It was a tipping point that propelled mass murder into genocide. Viennese Jews were deported to Theresienstadt, Auschwitz and ghettos in the east, notably Minsk, Riga and Łódź. The overwhelming majority of those in the Minsk and Riga ghettos were shot. In November 1942, Vienna's Jewish community was officially dissolved.

Aftermath At the end of hostilities, thousands of Jews fleeing continuing antisemitism in Poland and the Soviet Union fled to Austria, which was dotted with displaced persons camps. Many of the survivors left for the Palestine Mandate or the Americas.

In 1945, Austria, like Germany, was divided into four Allied-occupied zones, each with its own military administration. The advent of the Cold War meant that the Allies' interest in prosecuting Nazi war criminals was quickly pushed into the background, and former perpetrators became reintegrated into Austrian society.

VIENNA Vienna, hub of Austria's golden age at the end of the 19th century, was home to the third largest Jewish community in Europe after Warsaw and Budapest. Many of the artists, intellectuals and scientists who contributed to the capital's cultural powerhouse were Jewish, among them some of the most important intellectuals of the era – the composer Gustav Mahler, writers Arthur Schnitzler and Stefan Zweig, and the philosopher Ludwig Wittgenstein to name just a few. The stark reality of what was lost haunts Vienna's splendour.

That said, Vienna today has a small but lively Jewish community, many of its members coming from the former Soviet Union. The Sephardic Jewish community consists of mainly Bukharan Jews from central Asia.

Where to stay and eat Vienna has plenty of chain hotels to choose from, but we'd recommend avoiding the area around Westbahnhof station. An inexpensive option is the **Hotel Babula am Augarten** (Heinestrasse 15; w babulahotel.com; €); if your budget allows, book the suite, which is more stylish than the other rooms. The hotel is next to the site of the former Pazmanitengasse Synagogue which was destroyed in 1938 during Kristallnacht. There is a kosher supermarket, **Shefa Markt**, at Heinestrasse 24.

Vienna is famous for its coffee houses. You may wish to visit the famous **Café Landtmann** (Universitätsring 4; w landtmann.at; ⊕ 07.30–22.00 daily; €€€). In the Leopoldstadt district, where most Jews lived before the Holocaust, in the Augarten, a pretty, peaceful park away from the tourist bustle, is the **Sperling im Augarten restaurant** (Obere Augartenstrasse 1 (main gate); w sperlingwien; ⊕ 09.00–22.00 Tue–Sat, 09.00–18.00 Sun; €€€), which has a nice selection of small platters, as well as main courses. If you are looking for kosher restaurants and shops, **Chabad Haus** (w chabadvienna.com/food) has a useful list.

Be aware that supermarkets and many restaurants close on Sunday.

What to see If you intend to visit all the museums, it is worth investing in a Vienna City Card (w viennacitycard.at). There is a downloadable guide to Jewish Vienna at w wien.info/en/see-do/discover-vienna/jewish-vienna. The JWS Information Point (w jewishinfopoint.at) has information about specialised tours.

The city holds an annual Jewish film festival (w jfw.at) in the spring, and on 9 November, the anniversary of Kristallnacht, light installations are positioned across the city at the sites of synagogues destroyed in the pogrom (for details, see w lichtzeichen.wien).

Judenplatz In the heart of medieval Vienna, Judenplatz is one of the city's most charming squares. This was the site of the Jewish ghetto in the Middle Ages and is the place to put the Holocaust in the context of centuries of Jewish persecution. On the façade of No. 2, the inscription, 'Zum Grossen Jordan' celebrates the pogrom of 1421. The house now contains a public database of 65,000 Austrian Jews murdered by the Nazis. At No. 6, a plaque put up by the Catholic Church begs forgiveness. At the centre of the square stands a statue of the writer and philosopher Ephraim Lessing (1729–81), who was in favour of tolerance towards the Jews. The statue, installed in 1982, is a replica – the original was destroyed by the Nazis in 1938.

Judenplatz is dominated by the **Holocaust Memorial**, which was inaugurated in 2000. Designed by British artist Rachel Whiteread, the monument, an inside-out locked library, is also known as the Nameless Library. The spines of the books face inwards symbolising the untold stories of the victims.

On show in the nearby **Museum Judenplatz** (Judenplatz 8; w jmw.at; ⏁ 10.00–18.00 Sun–Thu, 10.00–17.00 Fri; €15 – both museums), one of two sites belonging to the Jewish Museum of Vienna (see below), are the excavated remains of the medieval synagogue destroyed in 1421. There is also an exhibition of Jewish life in Vienna in the Middle Ages.

Jewish Museum (Jüdisches Museum; Dorotheergasse 11; w jmw.at; ⏁ 10.00–18.00 Sun–Fri; €15 – both museums) Back in the centre, just under 10 minutes' walk from Judenplatz, the main site of the Jewish Museum of Vienna offers an introduction to Jewish life in the city in its informative permanent history exhibition. It also has a good café. Housed in the Palais Eskeles, the museum was founded in 1896, which makes it one of the oldest museums of its kind in the world. Yet, it has been inaccessible for most of its lifetime: it was closed by the Nazis in 1938 and only reopened in 1989. The exhibition on the ground floor traces the rebuilding of Jewish life in the city; the one on the upper floors traces the history of the Jewish community. Among the exhibits is Theodor Herzl's bicycle. Herzl, a journalist and the father of Zionism, set up the headquarters of the Zionist Executive in Vienna. Do not miss the Hanukkah menorah made by two brothers deported to Nisko in Poland. They returned to Vienna in 1940 when the project was discontinued but were then deported again and did not return.

Monument against War and Fascism (Mahnmal Gegen Krieg und Faschismus; Albertinaplatz) It is 5 minutes' walk from the Jewish Museum to the monument, which is located behind the National Opera House. Designed by Austrian sculptor Alfred Hrdlicka in 1988, the memorial is made up of four statues and stands on a bomb site where hundreds of people who had taken shelter in the cellars in March 1945 were killed. The *Gate of Violence* is made of granite quarried by prisoners in the Mauthausen concentration camp. The right column remembers victims of all wars and violence; the left column is dedicated to the victims of the mass murder under National Socialism; the woman giving birth represents the rebirth of Austria. Beyond the gate is the *Kneeling Jew*, a bronze figure of a Jewish man on his hands and knees, cleaning the street with a brush, which many consider degrading and led to calls for a separate Jewish memorial. Behind the bronze Jew is the *Orpheus Enters Hades*, a memorial to the victims of the bombings.

Morzinplatz On the opposite side of the city centre near the Danube Canal, Morzinplatz was once the site of the luxurious Hotel Metropole, which was confiscated from its Jewish owners immediately after the Anschluss. Subsequently, as the Gestapo HQ, it was the most feared address in the city. With a staff of 900, Vienna's Gestapo office was the largest in the Reich; 80% of its agents were former Austrian policemen. Today a post-war apartment block, the Leopold Figl Hof, stands on the spot. The Monument to the Victims of Fascism, which stands in the northwestern corner of Morzinplatz, is topped with a Star of David and a pink triangle, representing the Jewish and homosexual victims of the Nazis.

Not far away, in the **Vienna Wiesenthal Institute for Holocaust Studies** (Das Wiener Wiesenthal Institut für Holocaust-Studien; Rabensteig 3; w vwi.ac.at), there is a small museum (⊕ Sep–Jun 10.00–18.00 Mon–Fri, Jul–Aug 10.00–16.00 Mon–Fri, closed hols; free) dedicated to the Nazi hunter Simon Wiesenthal. Wiesenthal, who wrote the memoir *The Murderers Among Us* (McGraw-Hill, 1967), had been a prisoner in Mauthausen and made it his mission to bring the architects of the Holocaust to justice. On display is his famous magnifying glass.

Just around the corner is the **Stadttempel** (Seitenstettengasse 4; w jewishinfopoint. at; tours at 10.00 Mon–Fri, bookable online; €25), Vienna's main synagogue and the only one of the 93 synagogues and prayer houses in the city in 1938 to survive the Nazis. Its interior was, however, badly damaged during Kristallnacht. Built in 1824–26 in accordance with an edict that ruled only Catholic churches could have façades on public streets, it forms part of an apartment building and is effectively hidden from sight. Its proximity to people's houses saved it from an arson attack in the Nazi period. In the anteroom is a Holocaust memorial, designed by architect Thomas Feiger and inaugurated in 2002. The synagogue was the target of a terrorist attack in 1981.

Aron Menczer was a Zionist activist and Director of Youth Aliyah at the Palestine emigration office at **Marc Aurelstrasse 5**, a short walk from the Stadttempel, which he turned into an oasis for young people and children. He returned to Vienna from escorting a group of children to Mandate Palestine in 1939 despite the pleas of his family who had already settled there. Menczer looked after orphaned children and smuggled them across the border into Yugoslavia. He was deported to Theresienstadt in 1942 and gassed with children in his care at Auschwitz in 1943. On the pavement next to this site is a plaque in his memory.

Sigmund Freud Museum (Berggasse 19; w freud-museum.at; ⊕ 10.00–18.00 Wed–Mon & holidays; €15) To get a feeling for the rich cultural contribution that Jews made to Viennese culture, visit the home of the psychoanalyst Sigmund Freud (1856–1939) north of the city centre. The Freud family lived here from 1891 until they fled to the UK in 1938. The Freud family were among 110,000 Austrian Jews who managed to escape.

From 1939 onwards Jews were ordered into crowded designated buildings as their apartments were confiscated. Freud's apartment was eventually confiscated in 1942. The newly renovated museum commemorates Freud's neighbours and the 76 Jews detained in the building between the autumn of 1939 and spring 1942. Their names are recorded in the stairwell. While some escaped, the majority died in the Theresienstadt Ghetto or were murdered in extermination camps and the Shoah by Bullets (page 316) in Riga and Minsk. Freud's four older sisters were deported to the Theresienstadt Ghetto, where one of them died. The other three were murdered in Treblinka. In London Freud's daughter, the child psychologist Anna Freud, played a key role in the rehabilitation of child Holocaust survivors.

A short walk from the Freud Museum, the elegant Servitengasse was majority Jewish before its residents and shop owners were brutally evicted in 1938; many of them were later murdered. The **Keys of Remembrance** (Schlüssel gegen das Vergessen) memorial, created in 2008, shows 462 keys with name tags set beneath a glass panel lowered in the pavement on the corner of Servitengasse and Grünentorgasse.

Shoah Wall of Names Memorial (Shoah-Namensmauren; Otto-Wagner-Platz; w shoah-namensmauern-wien.at; ⊕ 24hrs daily)

The memorial, a 10-minute walk west of the Freud Museum, was inaugurated in 2021 on the anniversary of Kristallnacht. Inscriptions in English, German and Hebrew at the entrance note the participation in the Holocaust of 'countless Austrians'. Inside, a large 200m elliptical loop of standalone walls are engraved with the names of 65,000 Jewish adults and children from Austria murdered between 1938 and 1945. Outside the memorial, a stone also commemorates the suffering of other groups persecuted, tortured, and killed in Austria by the Nazis and their supporters. The monument is particularly moving at night. It is opposite the Austrian National Bank but more significantly stands next to Vienna University. In 1938, some 2,700 Jewish teachers and students were expelled from the university, which before the Anschluss was a hotbed of antisemitism.

The **headquarters of the Haganah**, the underground Zionist paramilitary organisation run by the Jewish Agency in Mandate Palestine, was located on the second floor of Frankgasse 2. Today, this nondescript building houses various offices, but in 1947, the second floor was a hive of clandestine activity where maps and photographs adorned the walls, phones rang and smoke filled the air as agents chased Hitler's most notorious henchmen. Updated reports on Nazis who evaded capture arrived daily. The Haganah also helped Jews fleeing eastern Europe to travel illegally to the Palestine Mandate, then controlled by Britain, who restricted immigration.

Viktor Frankl Museum Vienna (Viktor Frankl Museum Wien; Mariannengasse 1; w franklzentrum.org; ⊕ 13.00–18.00 Mon, Fri & Sat; €8)

Not far from the Shoah Wall of Names Memorial, this museum remembers Viktor Frankl (1905–97), another great Vienna-born therapist and the founder of logotherapy and existential analysis. Frankl was a Holocaust survivor who spent three years in four camps: Theresienstadt, Auschwitz, Kaufering III and Türkheim. He lost his father in Theresienstadt, his brother and mother at Auschwitz, and his wife in Bergen-Belsen. His sister, Stella, escaped to Australia. After his return from the camps, he wrote *Man's Search for Meaning* (Rider, 2004) in just nine days. The book was published in German in 1946. The English translation, published in 1959, became an international bestseller. The museum is located at the house in which Frankl lived from the end of World War II until his death in 1997.

In the immediate post-war era, thousands of Jews passed through Vienna fleeing from eastern Europe. They converged on the **Rothschild Hospital**, which once stood at 18 Währinger Gürtel, 10 minutes' walk from the Viktor Frankl Museum. In 1946 alone, some 52,000 Jewish refugees passed through its doors.

Westbahnhof (Europaplatz 2/3)

Immediately after Kristallnacht in November 1938, Britain agreed to take in 10,000 Jewish children in a scheme known as the Kindertransport. Visas were given to the children on the condition that they went without their parents. The Westbahnhof railway station was where hundreds of families said goodbye; most of the children never saw their parents again. There is a memorial in the ticket hall called *For the Child* by Flor Kent, where there is also a plaque to the first Austrians sent to Dachau.

Aspangbahnhof Deportation Memorial (Leon-Zelman-Park, Rubin-Bittmann-Promenade 7) Between 1941 and 1942, 47,035 Jewish men, women and children were deported from Aspangbahnhof to camps, ghettos and killing fields of Nazi-occupied eastern Europe. The station – today replaced by the small, scruffy Leon-Zelman-Park – was probably chosen because it was less busy than the Westbahnhof and served regional traffic only. The first transport left in October 1939 for Nisko near Lublin in Poland, where a plan to create a Jewish reservation failed. Transports were restarted in earnest in February 1941. A memorial erected in 2017 comprises two concrete rails leading to a dark, hollow enclosure, from which there is no way back. Nearly all eastern Austrian Roma were deported from Aspangbahnhof, mostly to the Łódź Ghetto in occupied Poland.

Schloss Belvedere (Prinz Eugen-Strasse 27; w belvedere.at; ⊕ 09.00–18.00 daily; €19.00) Tourists flock to the Schloss Belvedere to see the paintings of Gustav Klimt. This Baroque palace houses 24 of the artist's works, including *The Kiss*. Although Klimt himself was not Jewish, many of his patrons were. One of his most famous paintings, *Portrait of Adele Bloch-Bauer I* (also called *The Lady in Gold*), was commissioned by the sitter's husband, Ferdinand Bloch-Bauer, a Jewish banker and sugar producer. Adele died in 1925, and in 1938 Ferdinand fled to Switzerland, leaving his art collection behind. The portrait was stolen by the Nazis in 1941. Ferdinand died in exile in 1945.

In 1998, Austrian journalist Hubertus Czernin, who had previously exposed the Nazi past of former Austrian president Kurt Waldheim, revealed that *The Lady in Gold* was among stolen art works on display in the Belvedere. Ferdinand's niece, Maria Altmann, then demanded the gallery return five works by Klimt that had belonged to her uncle. In 2006, after a hearing in front of the US Supreme Court, an arbitration committee in Vienna agreed that the paintings should be returned to the family. Altmann sold *The Lady in Gold* for a record US$135 million to collector Ronald Lauder. The work now hangs in the Neue Galerie in New York. The film *Woman in Gold* (2015) tells the story.

Not far away, at Prinz-Eugen Strasse 20–22, Adolf Eichmann – who had been dispatched to Vienna to force the Jewish population to emigrate and to strip them of their assets – set up his **Central Office for Jewish Emigration** in the confiscated Rothschild Palace. The palace belonged to Austrian Jews Alphonse and Clarice Rothschild, scions of the Rothschild global banking empire. Eichmann's deputy was a fellow Austrian, Alois Brunner.

Leopoldstadt In 1938, Leopoldstadt was home to many of Vienna's Jews. Today, it remains the centre of the city's 10,000-strong Jewish community, many of whom are Jews from the former Soviet Union who emigrated in the 1970s and 80s, and Hasidic Jews from the United States and Israel. The vast Moorish Leopoldstadt **synagogue** which stood at Tempelgasse 5 was the largest in Vienna. Designed by the architect Ludwig von Förster, who had built the Dohány Street Synagogue (page 209) in Budapest, it had a magnificent façade and could hold 3,750 worshippers. The building was set on fire in an arson attack in October 1938. The four tall white pillars which today mark the site give a sense of the synagogue's enormity and grandeur. The buildings adjacent to the synagogue were left standing and the left annex, which still survives, was home to a children's orphanage from

Jackie Young was brought up in north London. When he was nine, he discovered he was adopted. 'It did not have much of an impact on my life until I was a teenager and my grandmother told me I had been born in Austria,' he says. 'I rushed home to ask my parents if it was true. My father lost his temper and stormed out of the room. I was too nervous to ask more.'

In 1960, when Young was 19 years old, he met his future wife, Lita. To marry in the synagogue, he had to show documents proving he was Jewish. 'My mother kept my adoption papers in a safe deposit box so no-one could see them, but she had to show them to the officials. As the secretary handed them back, I snatched them out of his hand. With utter astonishment I saw that I had been in a concentration camp.'

Young was born Jona Spiegel in Vienna. His mother, Elsa, had left him at the orphanage on Tempelgasse three months before she was deported to Minsk. He was just nine months old when in 1942 he was sent to the Theresienstadt Ghetto, in the modern-day Czech Republic.

Young probably escaped deportation to Auschwitz thanks to the Nazi propaganda film shot in September 1944 that sought to portray Theresienstadt as a model ghetto where Jewish children lived happy lives. Someone who knew Young as a child after he was adopted has told him that he bears a striking resemblance to a small boy in the film.

'People say I am lucky that I don't remember. I reply, "You know what you have lost – but for me the pain is not knowing. I would love to have memories."'

In 1987, Young discovered that his mother was murdered at the Maly Trostenets extermination camp, now in Belarus. Not even the Iron Curtain could stop him from visiting, but it did not bring any kind of closure, he says. 'The excitement turned to unease and resentment. I had a terrible feeling of being totally lost.' Not knowing has become more and more painful to live with as he has grown older.

Young's adoptive mother refused to have any communication with the staff of the charity that had brought him to Britain and funded his care. He now knows that his birth mother had a brother and a married sister. The latter left Austria for Yugoslavia in 1939.

Young brims with frustration. 'Maybe she tried to look for me, who knows?'

Young made a second trip to Maly Trostenets in 2019 for the inauguration of a memorial that bears his mother's name, along with 10,000 others. He also put a stone on the plot identified as his grandmother's grave in Vienna and visited the new wall that commemorates the city's Jews who were deported in the Holocaust.

'It is terrific that finally Austria has put up a vast statement of remorse. It is something they should have done long ago,' he says.

1942 to 1945 and the complex served as a centre for survivors after the war. The ruins of the temple were only removed in the 1950s, when a car park was built on the site. Memorial plaques on the gates of the current building are always accessible.

At Kleine Sperlgasse 2A, a plaque marks the spot where Jews were gathered before deportation. From February to March 1941 and from October 1941 to the end of October 1942, the school at this site served as a transit camp, where tens of thousands of deportees were held. Many people committed suicide here.

Further afield

Burgenland Literally translated as Castle Land, Burgenland is a pretty, hilly piece of country than runs along Austria's border with Hungary. After the collapse of the Austro-Hungarian Empire, the region became a source of contention between the new states of Austria and Hungary. Initially allocated to Hungary, despite its considerable German-speaking population, most of Burgenland was finally allocated to Austria in 1921. It was a dispute that fed pan-German nationalism and had a deep impact on one of the principal Austrian SS perpetrators, Alois Brunner, who was born and brought up in Burgenland. In a frightening precedent, Burgenland was the first place in the Reich from which Jews were expelled in 1938.

HANS MORGENSTERN'S STORY

Situated 60km west of Vienna lies St Pölten, a Baroque Austrian town which before 1938 was home to more than 1,000 Jews. Hans Morgenstern was the last Jew of St Pölten.

When Hitler led his triumphal parade through St Pölten in the days after the Anschluss, Morgenstern's father, a prominent local lawyer, watched from his office window as the crowds cheered. He decided to obtain visas for Palestine and the family settled in Bat Yam south of Tel Aviv in 1939. 'It was just a village in the sand,' Morgenstern told me when we met in 2018. While he adapted to their new home quickly, the adjustment was hard for his father – he could not speak Hebrew, his qualifications were not recognised and, paralysed from polio as a child, he could not walk on crutches in the sandy streets.

In 1947, as war loomed in Palestine, the family returned to St Pölten. Eventually a handful of other Jewish families also returned – but they soon left again. Morgenstern remained, and until his death in 2023 would enjoy a coffee in the same cafés from which 85 years earlier Jews were banned.

He had no children. 'It's the end of the line,' he chuckled. He dedicated his life to recording the stories of St Pölten's Jews, of whom 575 were murdered during the Holocaust. 'There was always a certain loneliness, that there is no Jewish community here anymore. For us Jews it is important to ensure they are not forgotten,' he explained solemnly. 'But the older generation in Austria did not like to commemorate them because they had a guilty conscience.'

The conversation turned to his cousin, who survived and lived in England. 'His name was Otto Pelczer.' I mention that when I was a child our neighbours were called Pelczer. The father was called Otto and the son Jeremy. 'You know him?' says Morgenstern, his pale, faded-blue eyes wide open.

Flummoxed, I had no idea what to ask next. Morgenstern suggested a tour of the town's former synagogue. He was a driving force in its preservation. It is now a museum, the Institute for Jewish History in Austria (w injoest.ac.at).

In the institute's memory book, appropriately called *Displaced Neighbours*, I discovered that Otto Pelczer's mother, Grete, was Hans Morgenstern's aunt. After the Anschluss, the Pelczer family fled to Prague. Otto was one of the 669 children rescued from Czechoslovakia by Sir Nicholas Winton, a young British humanitarian (page 125). His mother and father were then deported to Theresienstadt. They wrote him a final letter from the ghetto before they were murdered in Majdanek in Poland in September 1942.

Camp Lackenbach Lackenbach, located 95km south of Vienna, was the site of Austria's largest concentration camp for Roma and Sinti. About 2,000 of Camp Lackenbach's 4,000 inmates were later murdered in the Łódź Ghetto and the Chełmno extermination camp in occupied Poland; another 400 died in Auschwitz-Birkenau. Smaller *Zigeunerlager* or 'Gypsy camps' were located in Weyer, Salzburg and Vienna. In 1938, 12,000 Roma lived in Austria of whom 9,000–10,000 perished during the Holocaust. The camp buildings were demolished in the 1970s and a housing estate built on the site. A **memorial**, erected in 1984, stands at the junction of Ritzingerstrasse and Bergstrasse.

Rechnitz In the autumn of 1944, the SS used Hungarian Jews to build a defensive wall of anti-tank ditches to slow down the Soviet advance. Six hundred Hungarian Jews were taken to the village of Rechnitz, 47km south of Lackenbach. At a selection, 200 considered unfit for work were shot – some claim by guests attending a party held by local Nazis, at a homestead called Kreuzstadl. The survivors were evacuated on death marches as the war drew to a close. The **Kreuzstadl memorial** (w kreuzstadl.net; ⊕ always accessible) today stands opposite the Billa supermarket.

Mauthausen Austria's most important Holocaust site stands high up on a hill with a stunning view across the Austrian Alps, 4km from Mauthausen station. Many of the original buildings remain and are today part of the Mauthausen Memorial Site, which opened in 1949 and has an excellent museum. Unlike Auschwitz, Mauthausen is not inundated with tourists.

History Based in a purpose-built fortress, Mauthausen concentration camp operated from 1938 to 1945. It also had a system of more than 40 subcamps scattered across the country. After the outbreak of war prisoners were brought to Mauthausen from across Europe, and at the end of the war thousands who had been evacuated from camps closer to the front converged on Mauthausen on death marches. Those who arrived on the death marches were held in a tent camp in the field beyond the barbed wire. The camp had a jail and a gas chamber.

One of the reasons for the establishment of the camp was the nearby granite quarries, where prisoners were forced to work from its inception. It was backbreaking work and the steps to the quarry became known as the 'stairs of death'. From 1943, prisoners were forced to work in the camp's new armaments factories.

The prisoners' barracks were built to hold 300 people, but in the second half of the war they each accommodated up to 2,000. Jews were separated from the other prisoners and housed in Room B of Barracks 5, where conditions were worse than in the rest of the camp.

In total, around 190,000 people were interned in Mauthausen and its subcamps, of whom at least 90,000 were murdered or died as a result of the harsh conditions. On 5 May 1945, the US Army liberated Mauthausen and the nearby Gusen subcamp. Every year thousands of people from across the world take part in a commemorative ceremony.

What to see Before you visit the **Mauthausen Memorial Site** (KZ-Gedenkstätte Mauthausen; Erinnerungsstrasse 1; w mauthausen-memorial.org; ⊕ Mar–Oct 09.00–17.30 daily, Nov–Feb 09.00–15.45 Tue–Sun; free), it is worth browsing the website as it contains extensive information about the camp, including testimonies and a virtual tour with an audio guide (you can also pick up an audio guide at the memorial's visitor centre). If you have time, watch the Spanish film *El Fotógrafo de Mauthausen* (*The Photographer of Mauthausen*; 2018).

You need at least 2 hours to see the whole site, which includes a fascinating museum with full explanations in English. There are copies of the lists of those who arrived here on the death marches, and a detailed part of the exhibition is dedicated to the aftermath of the Holocaust.

Around the complex are numerous national memorials put up in the decades after the war. The memorial to the camp's Jewish victims was unveiled in the 1970s and that to the Roma and Sinti victims in the 1990s. They stand on the site of the SS barracks and administration offices above the granite quarries. From here the gatehouse leads to the section of the camp that held prisoners, where the roll-call area was the focal point.

The subcamps There are interesting memorials at some of Mauthausen's subcamps, which were murderous underground factories producing armaments.

At **Gusen**, 7km west of the Mauthausen Memorial Site, much of the modern village is built on the footprint of the camp destroyed in 1945. Several original buildings survive, but today are used as private residences. While it is difficult to comprehend this, it is far from unusual. There is a small visitors' centre and memorial (Georgestrasse 7, Langenstein; w gusen.org; ⊕ Mar–Oct 09.00–16.45 daily; free). The website has details of an audio-guided tour.

There is far more to see in **Ebensee**, 100km southwest of Mauthausen. Ebensee is a beautiful spot on the banks of a lake and is surrounded by mountains where a network of tunnels was constructed to hold a rocket research facility safe from air raids but which was also used as a petrol refinery. The camp opened in 1943 with the first Jews arriving in June 1944. Prisoners from all over Europe were brought here; 27,278 Jews accounted for a third of the inmates. Conditions in the camp were some of the harshest in the Nazi concentration camp system.

The **Ebensee Contemporary History Museum** (Widerstandsmuseum Verein KZ-Gedenkstätte Ebensee; Kirchengasse 5; w memorial-ebensee.at; museum ⊕ Mar–mid-Jun 10.00–17.00 Tue–Sat, mid-Jun–mid-Sep 09.00–17.00 Tue–Sun, Oct–Feb 09.00–17.00 Tue–Fri; tunnels ⊕ May–mid-Jun & last 2 weeks of Sep 10.00–17.00 Sat–Sun, mid-Jun–mid-Sep 10.00–17.00 Tue–Sun; museum €7, tunnels €6, combined ticket €10) has an excellent exhibition which traces the rise of the Austrian Nazi Party and the local history of the Ebensee camp. The museum is 3 minutes' walk from the station, which is also the easiest place to park. The site of the actual **camp and tunnels** is in Ebensee am Traunsee, a 40-minute walk from the museum. Alternatively take bus 505/555 and walk the last 15 minutes.

The camp itself was demolished in 1949 and is now a suburban housing estate entered through the original camp gateway. It is a peaceful place with kids on bikes and neatly kept gardens. The vast tunnels dug into the foot of the Seeberg Mountain are down a dirt track road to the left of the gateway signposted KZ-Gedenkstollen. It is possible to drive up and park at the site. It is worth visiting even if the tunnels are closed as it is possible to look through the bars into the tunnels and feel the cold air that radiates out of them.

To reach the **cemetery** (⊕ 24hrs daily), drive through the camp gateway and follow the signs. It was built by the Americans after the liberation on the site of the former sickbay. About 900 people are buried here. There are two mass graves. On one is the Lepetit Memorial put up by Hilda Lepetit from Milan whose husband is believed to be buried in the grave. Between 8,500 and 11,000 people died in the Ebensee camp, many of disease and hunger, and in the terrible overcrowding in

Schloss Hartheim (Schlossstrasse 1, Alkoven; w schloss-hartheim.at; ⊕ 09.00–16.00 Mon–Thu, 09.00–15.00 Fri, 10.00–17.00 Sun & public hols; free), 18km west of Linz, was one of six euthanasia centres run by the Nazis as part of the T4 programme (page 7). Here, some 30,000 people with physical and mental disabilities were murdered. A memorial and museum opened in the castle in 2002. The colonnaded courtyard was the site of one of two crematoria. After the war the castle was converted into apartments – the exhibition includes artefacts excavated from the gardens.

When T4 was halted in 1941, after a public outcry, 27 of the staff at Hartheim were deployed at the extermination camps of Chełmno, Sobibór and Treblinka.

An additional 12,000 victims were sent to their deaths at Hartheim, among them Jewish inmates from Mauthausen, sick women from Ravensbrück and political prisoners including priests.

---

the months before the liberation. Today, there is a moving memorial of names. Memorials like this are deeply significant as in the concentration camps people were deprived of their names and identified only by a number.

Melk, Gunskirchen and the **Loibl Pass**, three much smaller subcamps, are also interesting. Famous for its stunning 11th-century abbey, Melk, on the main road and railway line between Linz and Vienna, 83km east of Mauthausen, was also home to an underground forced labour camp. It was operational from 1944 to 1945 and manufactured ball bearings, aeroplane engines and tanks. To visit the **Melk Memorial Site** (KZ-Gedenkstätte Melk; Schießstattweg 2; w melk-memorial. org; ⊕ daily; free), present a valid photo ID at the entrance of the Melk barracks (Freiherr Karl von Birago Pionierkaserne, Prinzlstrasse 22) to get the key.

The **Gunskirchen** camp operated for only three weeks in a forest before being liberated by US forces on 4 May 1945. It was intended to house forced labourers but became the destination for a series of death marches. Typhus and dysentery spread rapidly among the starving prisoners. The smell was something that the liberators never forgot. Captain J D Pletcher recalled that as he entered the camp 'living skeletons crowded to touch the jeep, to kiss our arms – perhaps just to make sure that it was true. The people who couldn't walk crawled out toward our jeep.'

There are two memorials. One is on Route 1 from Wels to Lambach opposite the turning for Saag. On the road leading to Saag, on the left in a tiny glade, there is a small memorial. Birds sing in the trees below which the muddy ground was literally littered with corpses when the Americans arrived.

The tunnel that leads out of Austria into Slovenia at the **Loibl Pass** was partly built by prisoners from Mauthausen. It was a strategically important transport link between the Reich and the Balkans which could be used in winter. The tunnel was completed in 1967. There is a memorial plaque at the north entrance, and some ruins of the camp are visible.

SWITZERLAND

Switzerland was technically neutral in World War II and many international organisations were based here. Reports of the mass murder of European Jews reached Switzerland first and were from there passed on to Allied governments.

Some Swiss agencies also tried to rescue Jews from the Nazis but Swiss banks have also admitted to having wrongfully confiscated accounts of Holocaust victims.

In 2023, the Swiss parliament finally approved plans to build a Holocaust memorial, which will be located in the capital, Bern, but at the time of writing it was not clear when it would be inaugurated or if the memorial, which will have an online database, would reference Swiss complicity. For more information, see w swissmemorial.ch.

HISTORY After the Nazis came to power in January 1933, thousands of German Jews tried to seek refuge in neutral Switzerland. The numbers rose dramatically after Austria was incorporated into the Reich in 1938. Indeed, of the more than 300,000 refugees who passed through Switzerland between 1933 and 1945, some 30,000 were Jewish – but during that time 35,000 Jews were also turned away. The country's existing Jewish aid organisations joined together under one umbrella organisation, the Swiss Aid Society for Jewish Refugees, to consolidate efforts in giving aid to the large numbers of Jewish refugees.

To help control the influx, the Swiss government asked the Reich to mark Jewish passports so that the immigration authorities could distinguish them from other refugees trying to enter the country. In the autumn of 1938, Germany agreed and the passports of all Jews living in the Third Reich were marked with a 'J'.

Since Switzerland was reliant on the German economy, it tried not to offend its northern neighbour. And in October 1939 the Swiss authorities further curtailed the entry of foreigners, especially Jews. After Germany invaded western Europe, the Swiss government, fearful that Germany might invade, interned refugees and prohibited the entry of refugees from France. Despite the stringent regulations, however, many thousands of Jewish refugees managed to enter the country illegally. When Germany invaded Italy in September 1943, immigration rules were loosened and about 20,000 Italians, among them several thousand Jews, were able to cross over the border into Switzerland.

In 1944, as a result of negotiations with Germany, 1,684 Hungarian Jews arrived in Switzerland from Bergen-Belsen as part of the Kasztner Transport. Rudolf Kasztner, a Hungarian Jewish lawyer, negotiated with Adolf Eichmann and organised for a vast ransom to be paid so the Jews could escape Hungary. Although the train contained a cross-section of Jewish society, the richest passengers paid for their own place. The transport was highly controversial and Kasztner was accused of collaboration. He was assassinated in Tel Aviv in 1957. A further 1,200 Jews from Theresienstadt arrived in St Gallen in 1945.

Today, Switzerland's Jewish community numbers 18,500 (a similar size to the Swiss Jewish population on the eve of World War II), making it the tenth largest in Europe.

LAKE CONSTANCE Lake Constance forms the border between Austria, Germany and Switzerland. Thousands of Jews fleeing from the Third Reich tried to reach Switzerland across the Alpine Rhine – as the section of the River Rhine that flows into Lake Constance is known. They are commemorated by an interactive cycle route that begins on the lakeshore. If you don't have your own, bikes can be hired at St Gallen railway station.

Where to stay and eat St Gallen, about 12km south of Lake Constance, makes a good base. The **Hotel Walhalla** (Poststrasse 27; w hotelwalhalla.ch; €€€) is a modern hotel located conveniently opposite the train station. The classic St Gallen

PAUL GRÜNINGER

Paul Grüninger (1891–1972), the police commandant in St Gallen in 1938 when Austria was annexed to the Third Reich, took an enormous risk and disobeyed orders to help Jewish refugees. Between October 1938 and March 1939, he managed to save about 3,600 Jews. He falsified reports about the number of arrivals and the status of the refugees, ignored false papers and impeded efforts to trace refugees who were known to have entered Switzerland illegally.

In the spring of 1939, Grüninger was dismissed from his post, convicted and fined. He received no pension and died in poverty in 1972. Just before his death, he was recognised as Righteous Among the Nations. In 1993, the journalist Stefan Keller wrote a book about Grüninger, *Grüningers Fall* (Rotpunktverlag, 2014), which led to the Swiss federal government finally annulling the former police commandant's conviction in 1995.

Grüninger's heirs received 1.3 million Swiss francs in compensation. The Paul Grüninger Foundation (w paul-grueninger.ch) was established with the money in 1998, and a film of his life, *Akte Grüninger (One Step to Freedom)*, was made in 2013.

bratwurst, a sausage usually made of pork, is sold at stalls in Marktplatz. If you fancy a drink, St Gallen has its own brewery, Schützengarten, whose beers are sold in bars around the city.

What to see The **Über die Grenze** (Crossing the Border) project is a 100km cycle path which begins on the shore of Lake Constance just north of Bregenz in Austria and runs to Partenen. Along the way are 52 markers, sometimes criss-crossing the border into Switzerland and Liechtenstein, linked to refugees' stories and those of the smugglers who helped them. The route is accompanied by an interactive map and audio guide in English (w crossing-the-border.info), which tells the story of the refugees through photographs, documents and personal letters.

The Swiss government intends to create a Holocaust education and information centre in St Gallen in the next few years in co-operation with the **Hohenems Jewish Museum** (Jüdisches Museum Hohenems; Villa Heimann-Rosenthal, Schweizerstrasse 5; w jm-hohenems.at; ⊕ 10.00–17.00 Tue–Sun; €9) across the border in the Austrian town of Hohenems, which has an exhibition on the Alpine Rhine escapes. The centre in St Gallen will be linked to the main memorial in Bern (w swissmemorial.ch).

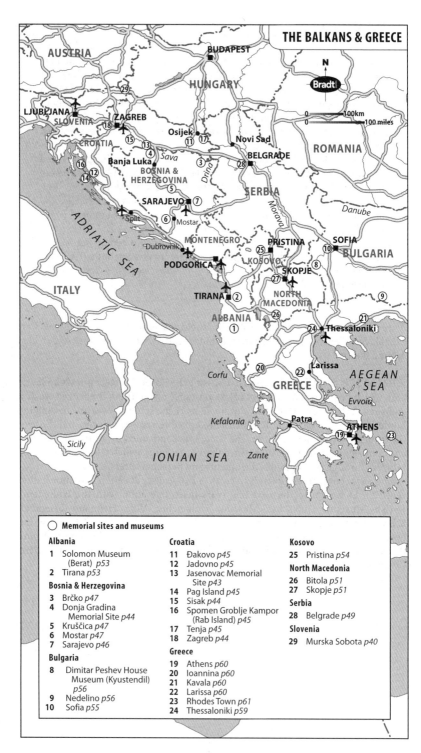

THE BALKANS & GREECE

N

Bradt

0 — 100km
0 — 100 miles

AUSTRIA

BUDAPEST

HUNGARY

LJUBLJANA
SLOVENIA ㉙
ZAGREB ⑱
CROATIA ⑮ ⑬
④
Sava
Banja Luka ③
BOSNIA &
HERZEGOVINA ⑤
⑯
⑭⑫
Osijek ⑪ ⑰
Novi Sad
BELGRADE ㉘
ROMANIA

SERBIA

SARAJEVO ⑦
Split
⑥ Mostar
ADRIATIC SEA
Dubrovnik
MONTENEGRO
PODGORICA
Drina
Morava
Danube
PRISTINA ㉕
KOSOVO
SKOPJE ⑧
㉗
SOFIA ⑩
BULGARIA

ITALY

TIRANA ②
NORTH
MACEDONIA ⑨
ALBANIA ①
㉖
㉔ Thessaloniki ㉑

Corfu ⑳
㉒ Larissa
GREECE
AEGEAN SEA
Evvoia

Kefalonia
Patra
ATHENS ⑲ ㉓

Sicily
IONIAN SEA
Zante

4

The Balkans and Greece

The vast majority of Jews from the Balkans and Greece were murdered in World War II, and yet despite its appalling violence and contemporary significance, the Holocaust in southeastern Europe is a story about which little is known outside the region. Few remember that the Greek port of Thessaloniki was once a majority Jewish city or Albania had more Jews at the end of the war than it did at the beginning.

The German invasion of Yugoslavia in April 1941 was a turning point in history that haunts the politics of modern-day Bosnia and Herzegovina, Croatia, Kosovo, Serbia, Slovenia, North Macedonia and Montenegro, which until the wars of the 1990s were all part of the multi-ethnic Yugoslav state.

Slavko Goldstein in his remarkable account of the Holocaust in Croatia, *1941: The Year that Keeps Returning* (NYRB, 2013), wrote that, when the Germans invaded in 1941, the Jews of the region feared what was probably awaiting them, 'that they would face mistreatment, discrimination, and perhaps expulsion; that their shops and possibly apartments would be confiscated and that they might be sent to concentration camps. But they were all confident that they would not be killed.'

Although there is much to see across the region, there are no Holocaust memorials or museums in Montenegro.

GETTING THERE AND AROUND

The airports best served by flights from the UK are Belgrade, Sofia, Thessaloniki, Tirana and Zagreb. There are regular flights to Zagreb from Ireland, Tel Aviv and Toronto, and direct flights from Tel Aviv to Thessaloniki. Trains and buses connect Zagreb with major European capitals, especially in summer. At present, no trains connect Belgrade to Zagreb, Sarajevo, Sofia, Skopje or Thessaloniki; but check before travelling as some services are being rehabilitated. The quickest way to get around the region is by car or bus.

ONLINE RESOURCES

A useful website that lists memorials in the former Yugoslavia is **Spomenik Database** (**w** spomenikdatabase.org). The **Lost Sephardic World of the Western Balkans** (**w** lostsephardicworld.org) is an online resource run by the Vienna-based organisation Centropa (page 340).

CROATIA
Documenta **w** documenta.hr. A Croatian NGO dealing with history & the truth in the country's 20th-century history.

NORTH MACEDONIA
Monastir-Bitola . Can help tracing roots & organises guided tours of Jewish Bitola (known in Ottoman times as Monastir).

United States Holocaust Memorial Museum w ushmm.org. The Bulgarians, who occupied the region around Bitola during the war, forced the Jews living in the city into a ghetto & collected photographs of every Jewish adult. This was common practice across Nazi-occupied Europe, but the collection from Bitola is one of the few to have survived. It can be viewed on this website.

SERBIA
Mapping the Holocaust: Places of Remembrance in Serbia w holocaust.rs. Has a useful interactive map.
Vojvodina Holocaust Memorials w vhmproject.org. Gives a full list of Holocaust memorials in Vojvodina.

HISTORY

Jews settled in the Balkans in the 4th century BCE. Dubrovnik in Croatia, once the independent Republic of Ragusa, is home to Europe's second oldest synagogue founded in 1352. The remains of one from the Roman period can be seen in Stobi in North Macedonia.

Many Balkan Jews were Ladino-speaking Sephardim, the descendants of those expelled from Spain during the Inquisition of 1492, though Jews in Croatia and Slovenia were mostly Ashkenazi. In Greece, before the arrival of the Sephardim and in other parts of the Balkans, the Greek-speaking Romaniote community predominated.

For centuries the region was divided between the Ottoman and Habsburg empires, the border between them shifting over time. The people who lived in the territory were multi-ethnic and multi-religious. Under the Ottomans, Jewish life flourished and there were no pogroms. The Ottomans welcomed the Jews when they were expelled from Spain because their skills boosted the economy.

By the late 19th century, most of modern-day Slovenia, Croatia and northern Serbia (Vojvodina) had been under Habsburg rule for centuries. In 1878 Bosnia and Herzegovina was seized by what was now called the Austro-Hungarian Empire, only to be formally annexed in 1908.

All of the modern Balkan states were created as they gained independence from the Ottomans and in the dissolution of the Austro-Hungarian Empire. The Greek state emerged in the wake of the Greek War of Independence of 1821. Serbia, then a territory far smaller than today, was an Ottoman principality in the wake of its revolt against the Ottomans in 1804 and was recognised, as was Montenegro, as fully independent in 1878. Bulgaria became a principality under the Ottomans in 1878 and fully independent in 1908. After more than 500 years, the Ottomans were finally expelled from the region during the Balkan Wars of 1912–13. Most of modern Croatia, Slovenia and all of Bosnia and Herzegovina became part of Yugoslavia in 1918, when the Austro-Hungarian Empire vanished, and they united with Serbia and Montenegro. Likewise, Kosovo and North Macedonia, Ottoman until 1912, became first parts of Serbia and then Yugoslavia. Albania declared independence in 1912 and was recognised as independent by the Concert of Europe's ambassadors the following year.

Nationalist politics emerged in the Balkans in the 19th century. On 28 June 1914, Archduke Franz Ferdinand, heir to the Austro-Hungarian throne, was assassinated in Sarajevo by the Bosnian Serb Gavrilo Princip, who hoped to create a Yugoslav state. It was the spark that ignited World War I. The assassination prompted Austria-Hungary to invade Serbia which it held responsible.

INTERWAR YEARS The post-1918 order left many unsatisfied and some extreme nationalists keen to create new, more ethnically pure states. The region was politically unstable and undemocratic regimes soon took control. On the eve of World War II, Jews, Roma and other large ethnic minorities found themselves in an extremely vulnerable position. Nevertheless, in the 1930s, the Balkans provided the escape route for tens of thousands of German and Austrian Jews and remained a place of refuge until the Axis invasion in 1941.

WORLD WAR II In October 1940, Italy invaded Greece from Albania which it had already occupied in 1939. The Greek Army drove the Italian forces back and a stalemate ensued. Hitler ordered the invasion of Yugoslavia and Greece in April 1941 to help the Italians and also to neutralise any threat from the region, where the British had a presence, before his planned invasion of the Soviet Union. On 6 April 1941, Germany and Italy, supported by Hungarian units, attacked Yugoslavia. Germany also attacked Greece. The Yugoslav government fled to London and the leadership of the armed forces surrendered on 18 April. By 28 April, Axis troops had pacified most of the Greek mainland, but Greek resistance on the islands continued until June.

SLOVENIA

Slovenia had a tiny Jewish population of just over 4,500 at the outbreak of World War II, almost 90% of whom, one of the highest proportions anywhere, were killed. Some Slovene Jews managed to save themselves by joining the Yugoslav partisans, who welcomed them. Yet it is a small figure compared with the thousands of Slovene victims of the war and post-war years. In the post-Yugoslav decades, interest and commemorations in Slovenia have focused far more on the murder of more than 11,000 collaborationist Home Guard, the Slovensko domobranstvo, by the communists after the war than the fact they took part in the deportation of the country's Jews.

HISTORY Antisemitism began to intensify in Slovenia as in other parts of the Austro-Hungarian Empire at the end of the 19th century and was promoted by senior members of the Catholic Church.

In 1918–19 in the chaotic transition between Austria-Hungary and the new Kingdom of Serbs, Croats and Slovenes (later officially renamed Yugoslavia), riots broke out against Jews and Hungarians in many places in Prekmurje, the region contested between Slovenes and Yugoslavia on the one side and Hungarians and Hungary on the other.

In the wake of the beginning of the war in Yugoslavia on 6 April 1941, the Germans, Italians and Hungarians divided Slovenia between them. Six villages were also handed over to the quisling Croatian state, the Nezavisna Država Hrvatska (NDH). The Germans introduced racial policies and measures against the Jews. After the fall of Italy's Fascist government in September 1943, Germany occupied the Italian zone, persecuting the few remaining Jews. The Nazis occupied Hungary in the spring of 1944, initiating a mass persecution of Jews in the part of Slovenia the Hungarians had previously annexed.

MURSKA SOBOTA The majority of Slovenia's Jews lived in Prekmurje in the northeast of the country on the border with Hungary, an area that is off the beaten track and receives few visitors. Murska Sobota is the regional capital.

Don't visit Murska Subota without a copy of the novel *Billiards at the Hotel Dobray* (Istros, 2020) by Dušan Šarotar, who was born here. Set in March 1945, just before its liberation by the Soviet Red Army, it is the first novel to address the fate of the Jews in Slovenia.

⌂ Where to stay and eat
Hotel **Belmur** (ul. Slovenska 49; w belmur.si; €) is a modern boutique hotel in a historic building on the main pedestrianised street and has its own parking. Have a drink at the **Hotel Zvezda** (Trg zmage 8; w hotel-zvezda.si), formerly the Dobray, from whose balcony the Murska Republic was declared in 1919.

History
Murska Sobota is a tiny town with a complicated central European story. In 1919, the Murska Republic, also known as the Republic of Prekmurje, declared independence from the short-lived Hungarian Soviet Republic. It was snuffed out barely a week later by Hungarian troops. A few months later the region was incorporated into Yugoslavia. Prekmurje was annexed by Hungary in World War II and then occupied by Germany between 1944 and 1945.

What to see
All the sights in Murska Sobota can be visited on foot. Make your first stop the friendly **tourist office** (ul. Slovenska 41; ⊕ 09.00–16.00 Mon–Fri, 09.00–noon Sat). They will mark out the main sites on a map and can show you a 3D film of the former synagogue. Slovenska, the town's main street, was once home to many Jewish businesses and shops. A minute's walk up the street is the Hotel Zvezda.

Across the road from Hotel Zvezda, the main square has one of the few Soviet war memorials in former Yugoslavia. On ulica Lendavska, a short walk from the hotel, an apartment block on the site of the former synagogue was built using stone from the synagogue which was demolished in the 1950s. It is still known as the **Jewish House**. A small monument outside commemorates the synagogue, where on 26 April 1944 all the town's Jews were ordered to gather, with hand luggage only. They were locked up overnight without food or water, and the next morning transferred to Čakovec in Croatia, and then to the main concentration camp in Nagykanizsa in Hungary before being sent to Auschwitz.

The first **Holocaust memorial** in Slovenia was unveiled on the platform of Murska Sobota railway station on ulica Novaka in 2010. It is a 10-minute walk from the Jewish House. The memorial, a bronze bench with a suitcase next to it, fails to convey the horror of deportation.

Not far from the station, the former **Jewish cemetery** (Judovska pokopališče), is on ulica Panonska, next to the Mol petrol station. The site is always accessible and is marked by a small memorial.

CROATIA

During World War II, the Croatian fascist Ustasha, who came to power on the backs of the invading Nazis and Italians, aligned themselves with Berlin. They orchestrated the murder of most of the country's Jews and Roma and murdered about 300,000 Serbs.

GETTING AROUND The easiest way to get around Croatia is by car – the country has a good motorway system. Buses involve long journeys. You can get to Jasenovac by train from Zagreb. It is 10 minutes' drive from Novska station.

To see the mass graves at Donja Gradina, you will have to cross the border into Bosnia and Herzegovina. Since you will be leaving the EU, you will be asked to show your car papers if you are driving. Cars registered in Croatia, other EU countries and the UK do not need an insurance green card. Queues are shorter at the nearby Kozarska Dubica crossing.

HISTORY When World War II broke out, Croatia was part of the Kingdom of Yugoslavia, but its political elite were dissatisfied with its status and the preceding years had been ones of quarrels between Serb and Croat leaders about the internal organisation of the country. The Ustasha, an extreme right-wing nationalist terrorist group, was formed in 1929. They were allied to the pro-Bulgarian Macedonian who assassinated King Alexander I in Marseille in 1934 and were set on creating a racially pure Croatia. As such, Serbs, almost 17% of the population, were a huge minority in Croatia and were the Ustasha's main target; but so were Jews and Roma. Jews were seen as inherently pro-Yugoslav.

In exile in the interwar years, the Ustasha forged close ties with fascist Italy and Nazi Germany. After the Axis invasion in April 1941, an Ustasha puppet state led by Ante Pavelić, the Independent State of Croatia, the Nezavisna Država Hrvatska (NDH) was created. Italy seized much of the Adriatic coast and the islands, but the

The Balkans and Greece   CROATIA

4

GOOD TO KNOW

Denial or relativisation of the crimes committed by the Ustasha in the NDH is not uncommon in Croatia. The Independent Holocaust Remembrance Alliance gave Croatia a red card in its 2020 report.

In post-war Yugoslavia, the Communists needed to reunify the country. This meant that the Nazis were portrayed as playing a dominant role in the mass murders, as opposed to the Ustasha and other local collaborators, who in turn were defeated by the heroic partisan resistance led by Josip Broz Tito. Memorials commemorated victims of fascism and Yugoslav partisans generally making no reference to ethnicity. 'Brotherhood and Unity' were key foundation stones of the new Yugoslavia and hence it did not serve the interests of Tito's regime to emphasise the sectarian nature of much of the killing during the war.

Civilians in Croatia responded in a variety of ways to the Holocaust. They included those who tried to rescue Jews and showed sympathy for them; but there were those who denounced them, incited violence and demanded a more radical approach to the 'Jewish question'.

History was weaponised and distorted in the late 1980s and during the period of Croatia's war of independence between 1991 and 1995, known in Croatia as the Homeland War. Competing narratives emerged in which Croats saw themselves as the historical victims of the Serbs and vice versa. Both Croats and Serbs rehabilitated politicians and others who had championed and sanctioned genocide during World War II.

Since the late 1980s, historical revisionism has become commonplace. In the years leading to the break-up of Yugoslavia, the issue of how many died in Jasenovac became a real touchstone. Memorials have been erected and streets named after public figures associated with the NDH regime. Many Communist-era monuments have been removed or vandalised but not everywhere. Regional wartime history and sympathies generally determine where they have survived or not.

Croatia joined the EU in 2013.

NDH included all of Bosnia and Herzegovina, parts of what is now Slovenia and parts of Serbia, stretching to Zemun, part of Belgrade. Until the Italian capitulation in 1943, the NDH was divided into two zones of influence by Germany and Italy. On the eve of the Axis invasion of 1941, about 25,000 Jews lived in Croatia.

In NDH territory, Serbs numbered about 2 million, roughly one third of its population. As Marko Attila Hoare notes in his *History of Bosnia* (Saqi, 2007), of 36,000–40,000 Jews in the NDH 'at least 30,000 or over 80%' were to die principally at the hands of the Nazis and Ustashas; but he says that 'smaller numbers were victims of the Chetniks, Muslim SS troops, Italian forces and others.'

The arrest and persecution of Jews began in April 1941, immediately after the Axis invasion and collapse of Yugoslavia. At the same time, a system of 26 concentration and death camps was set up. The Nazis believed that some Slavs, notably Croats and Czechs, could assimilate with the German people and gave their blessing to Pavelić's genocidal plans, but reprimanded the Ustasha on multiple occasions for their extreme violence against the Serbs as it encouraged partisan resistance. The last public activity in which Croatian Jews took part was a football match between the Jewish club Makabi and Ličanin from Zagreb. Makabi won 1:0 in the last minute. The players were among the first to be arrested and all but three killed.

After the Italian capitulation in 1943, Germany occupied Pula and Rijeka (called Fiume in Italian), which were Italian in the interwar years and only became parts of Croatia and Yugoslavia after 1945. The Međimurje region was annexed by Hungary between 1941 and 1945. Between 3,000 and 5,000 Jews from Croatia survived the war, many having joined the partisans. Pavelić died in Spain in 1959.

JASENOVAC Jasenovac, 109km southeast of Zagreb, is the most important Holocaust site in the country. It was one of the largest concentration camps in Europe and the only extermination camp run by a Nazi collaborationist regime. That said, it is off the beaten track and receives just 15,000 visitors a year.

It is evident as you approach the memorial that the conflicts of the 1990s still haunt Jasenovac. The museum complex was on the frontline, and many buildings damaged in the fighting are empty or in ruins. The municipality is made up of ten villages and was 25.9% Serbian in 1991. That figure is now at about 5%.

Where to stay and eat Zepter Hotel (Svetosavska br. 2; w zepterhotel.com; €) in Kozarska Dubica, just on the other side of the border in Bosnia and Herzegovina, is a modern hotel on the banks of the Una River. It is a real oasis if you don't like old-fashioned, heavy, timber countryside places, which are common on both sides of the border here. It has a riverside restaurant and parking. The hotel belongs to the multi-millionaire Filip Zepter, who was born in the town.

History Although Jasenovac was called a concentration and labour camp, in reality it was an extermination camp, and conditions were gruesome. Run by the Ustasha, with no direct Nazi involvement, it was a complex of five camps in operation from August 1941 to April 1945 and was close to the Zagreb–Novska railway line. The neighbouring villages of Uštica, Mlaka and Jablanac were populated by Serbs, who were soon interned in the camp. Many prisoners were murdered on arrival. They were taken by ferry across the Sava River to the Donja Gradina site (page 44), where they were bludgeoned, stabbed and beaten to death. Some 7,000 Jews were also transported from Jasenovac to Auschwitz and Bergen-Belsen.

Exhumations at the site began immediately after the war. Little remains of the original camp as it was cleared and the materials used to build houses. Apart from makeshift memorials by survivors and locals, memorialisation of Jasenovac did not take place until the 1960s.

Since 2016, Jewish and Serbian groups have refused to attend commemorations at the camp arguing that the Croatian government has failed to address historical revisionism. They say that the state has not taken the necessary steps to address the minimisation of the wartime Croatian state's role in the Holocaust.

The number of victims who died at Jasenovac has long been disputed and manipulated for different reasons. Identifying victims was also complicated by the fact that the Ustasha destroyed much of the documentation in the final days of the camp's operation. In Tito's Yugoslavia the number of victims was recorded as being some 700,000 by Vladimir Dedijer, a Serbian politician, historian and biographer of Tito. In 1989, a Croatian demographer put the figure at between 80,000 and 90,000 deaths and many serious sources now coalesce around similar numbers. The Jasenovac Memorial Site's own figure for 'confirmed deaths' is 81,998 of whom 46,685 were Serbs, 16,131 were Roma and 12,982 were Jews, while Croats and Bosniaks comprised the majority of the rest.

As Yugoslavia collapsed in the early 1990s, the numbers of victims of the Ustasha in general and at Jasenovac in particular was a hugely divisive issue. Franjo Tudjman, the president of Croatia when it fought the Serbs from 1991 to 1995, and also a historian, put the death toll at 30,000–40,000. By contrast, Serb historians and politicians put the figure at anything up to 1.1 million. At the Donja Gradina Memorial Site on the Bosnian side of the river, where many of the mass graves are, and which lies in the Republika Srpska, the Serbian-controlled entity within Bosnia, the figure of 500,000 Serbian victims is still used, with an overall total of 700,000 victims.

During the 1991–95 conflict, Jasenovac was occupied by the Serbian-dominated Yugoslav Army and Serbian paramilitaries. Damage had already been inflicted, however, by Croatian forces in 1991 when they had vandalised the site. Part of the contents of the museum, some 7,770 exhibits, were taken to Banja Luka in Bosnia, and Belgrade. They were put on show in 1994 in an exhibition at the Museum of Genocide Victims with the intention of demonstrating what they alleged were Croatian genocidal tendencies.

Repairs at the site began in 1998. Two thirds of the museum's contents were returned after intervention by the United States Holocaust Memorial Museum, but the rest of the collection is still missing. In 2003 restoration work and the demining of the site were completed. The permanent exhibition reopened in 2006.

What to see The camp at Jasenovac was divided into two parts on either side of the Sava River. The Jasenovac Memorial Site is in Croatia, and, while described in this section, the Donja Gradina Memorial Site, where most of the mass killings took place, is across the border in Bosnia and Herzegovina in the Serb-controlled entity of Republika Srpska. After the wars of the 1990s the two sites were separated and there has been no official co-operation between them since.

Jasenovac Memorial Site (Spomen područje Jasenovac; Braće Radić 147; w jusp-jasenovac.hr; ⊕ summer 09.00–17.00 Mon–Fri, 10.00–16.00 Sat–Sun, winter 09.00–16.00 Mon–Fri; free) The Croatian site is dominated by the **Stone Flower** monument that stands in the middle of a field on the site of the former Roma camp. Almost no Roma survived the camp and the treatment they received was particularly inhumane. Their names were not recorded.

Pressures from survivors prompted the commissioning of the Stone Flower in 1963. Designed by Bogdan Bogdanović, it was completed in 1966. On the north face are verses from Ivan Goran Kovačić's poem 'Jama' ('The Pit'). Kovačić's father was a Croat and his mother was Jewish from Transylvania. It was a cruel irony that the 30-year-old author of the most powerful verses condemning the Ustasha, and also a member of the partisans, had his throat slit by Serb nationalist Chetnik forces in 1943. The path that leads to the monument is made from railway sleepers taken from the tracks which once brought wagons crammed with victims to the camp.

The **museum** focuses on victims' stories in a non-ethnic approach with tens of thousands of names recorded in the display. Although on show are NDH orders that set the genocide in context, the exhibition does not shine the light on perpetrators. Violence at Jasenovac was extreme but there is only a small display of the weapons used to kill the victims – axes, hammers and knives – though, this is deliberate so as not to generate further inter-ethnic hatred. The exhibition pulls back from describing the horrors of daily life in Jasenovac and portrays the NDH as a Nazi puppet state.

Since the end of the war over 100 mass graves have been located here but there may be more.

Donja Gradina Memorial Site (Javna ustanova Spomen-područja Donja Gradina; **w** jusp-donjagradina.org; ⊕ museum: 07.00–15.00 Mon-Fri, memorial site: 24hrs daily) The memorial site at Donja Gradina is signposted just after the border crossing. There is a small visitor centre and memorial by the road but most of the mass graves are in the adjoining wood. Paths lead to the various pits. It includes vats from which soap was allegedly made from victims' bodies. The myth that the Nazis made soap from their victims was widely believed in World War II, but it is possible that an attempt to do this was indeed carried out here as survivors have testified to it.

In summer, be sure to wear insect repellent and take a bottle of water as the site covers a large area.

Further afield

Sisak Approximately 7,000 Jewish, Roma and Serbian children forcibly removed from their parents were held in Sisak, 70km northwest of Jasenovac, in an old salt factory. Some 1,660 of them died of starvation. A plaque was placed on the building in 1960 and in the cemetery in 1974 – but both were destroyed in 1991. Not far from the building is a park with a memorial fountain, *Unfinished Games*, designed by Gabriel Kolar in 1964, which at the time of writing was in a state of disrepair.

Zagreb The Holocaust memorial, a 12m-tall wall of suitcases, to the left of the entrance of the main station, was erected in 2022. Before it was finished, it was criticised by the Jewish community, which had not been consulted about the memorial either by the mayor or the city authorities, because the initial dedication was to be for victims of the Holocaust in general, thus ignoring the role of Croatia's Ustasha. In the event, the dedication does recall the 'victims of the Holocaust and the Ustasha regime' and notes that 'from this place around 800 Zagreb Jews were deported to the Nazi camp Auschwitz in August 1942'.

There is a small memorial plaque at the site of Zagreb's synagogue at ulica Praška 7, which was destroyed by the Ustasha in 1941. Since a fire in 1980 destroyed the department store later built on the site, nothing has replaced it and so it remains a car park. The land was given back to the Jewish community in 1999 but quarrels about money, financing and the design for a new Jewish centre and synagogue there have stymied any development to date.

Dalmatian coast A reign of terror was also carried out along the coast. In July 1941, many of the Jews arrested in Croatia were sent to a camp at **Jadovno**, 20km from Gospić, 151km south of Rijeka. Jadovno was the first of the NDH camps and the first death camp in Europe. Between May and August 1941, some 21,500 Serbs and 2,500 Jews were killed here, many thrown alive into the deep ravines in the Velebit mountains. A small memorial plaque was put up in 1975, but it was destroyed in 1991. A replica was rededicated at the site in 2010.

On the barren island of **Pag**, the Ustasha established a concentration camp in Slana Bay about 5km from the village of Metajna, where a women's subcamp was also set up. From June to August 1941, Jews, Serbs and Croat communists were held at the camps. Historians estimate that between 4,000 and 13,000 people died here including 1,500 Jews. The small, originally Yugoslav-era memorial here has been vandalised and replaced twice. A bust of Canon Josip Felicinović, who, according to Documenta (a Croatian NGO dealing with history and the truth), 'participated in the planning of the Slana camp and often visited it, is today located on the main square in the town of Pag.'

After the Italian capitulation in August 1943, Yugoslav partisans rescued just over 2,000 Jews who had been held by the Italians at Kampor on the island of **Rab**. Many of them then joined the partisans. The 500 who were too weak to leave the camp were deported by the Germans to Auschwitz. The **Spomen Groblje Kampor** (Kampor 18; w ua-rab.hr/index.php/spomen-groblje-kampor; ⊕ 10.00–dusk daily; free) is notably larger than other memorials from the communist period, as it fitted the narrative of Yugoslav heroism and memorialised a camp that was run by Italians. It was built by the Slovenian architect Edvard Ravnikar and erected in 1953. A plaque dedicated to the Jewish partisans was put up by the Croatian Jewish community.

Osijek Two concentration camps in Đakovo and **Tenja** near Osijek are marked with memorials. In 2004, the Jewish community added a specific plaque to remember the Jewish victims here to a restored Yugoslav-era memorial which had not mentioned them. It is on the road to Tenja, halfway between there and Osijek. The municipality in Osijek renovated the entire obelisk and memorial in 2016. There is a petrol station on the site of the **Đakovo camp** but the Jewish community erected a memorial in the Jewish cemetery on Vladimira Nazora ulica 10 in 2013. The cemetery is unique in that it is the only burial site in Europe where victims of the Holocaust were interred under their first and last names.

BOSNIA AND HERZEGOVINA

The devastating 1991–95 war in Bosnia and Herzegovina dominates historical memory. Bosnian Muslims, now called Bosniaks, make up just over half the population, Serbs account for just over 30% and Croats just over 15%. The country is divided into two 'entities' and one autonomous region. It has three education systems, three presidents (a Serb, a Bosniak and a Croat) and the Bosniak–Croat Federation half of the country is divided into ten cantons. There is limited Holocaust education.

Most of the Jews who lived in Bosnia and Herzegovina left during the 1990s. Despite years of wrangling between Bosnia's Serb, Croat and Bosniak leaders, it has not been possible to resolve one of the legacies of the peace agreement that ended the war in 1995, which is that anyone who declares themselves to be a Jew, a Roma or indeed any other nationality apart from one of the big three, cannot serve as a member of the presidency of Bosnia, or be elected to certain other jobs.

GETTING AROUND The simplest way to get around Bosnia and Herzegovina is by car. There is a good bus service, but it takes time to get from one place to another. The centre of Sarajevo can be explored on foot. To visit the Vraca Memorial Park and the old Jewish cemetery take bus 101 from Trg Austrije.

HISTORY The Nazi quisling Independent State of Croatia (Nezavisna Država Hrvatska; NDH), established by the fascist Ustasha movement, annexed Bosnia after the Axis invasion of Yugoslavia in 1941. Persecution of Jews, Serbs and Roma began immediately. Serb villages were destroyed and their inhabitants either murdered or deported to Serbia. In June the mass arrest of the Jewish population of some 14,700 began. Reported numbers vary but, according to Marko Attila Hoare in his *The History of Bosnia: From the Middle Ages to the Present Day* (Saqi, 2007), 12,000 were murdered, 11,000 of whom died in concentration camps in the NDH. Some of those who survived did so because they joined the partisans, but some Jews were helped and hidden by their neighbours, including Muslims. The NDH's Roma population of 25,000–40,000 'was almost wholly exterminated by the Nazis and Ustashas' Hoare also notes. There were many cases of Bosnian Serbs, Croats and Bosniaks risking their lives to save Jews and others. Some Bosniaks, however, followed the call of Jerusalem's Mufti Haj Amin Al-Husseini, who came to Sarajevo to call on Bosniaks to join the 13th SS Volunteer Bosnian-Herzegovinian Division known as the Handžar Division, which was established in May 1943. Some Croats also joined, while its officers were mostly Volksdeutsche, local Yugoslav Germans.

SARAJEVO Before World War II, some 11,400 of Sarajevo's population of 90,000 were Jewish, though figures are not exact. In 1981 a commission created by the city's veterans' organisation concluded, according to historian Robert J Donia in his *Sarajevo: A Biography* (Hurst, 2006), that 10,961 Sarajevans died of violence during the war of whom 7,092 were Jews – 65% of all of the city's war deaths and 68% of the city's pre-war Jewish population.

Many of the survivors left for Israel in 1948. From the remnant population there was another wave of emigration during the 1992–95 war and siege of Sarajevo.

Where to stay and eat Hotel Europe (Vladislava Skarića 5; w hoteleuropegroup. ba; €€) is the best situated with good views of the Ottoman old town, Baščaršija. Baščaršija is the place to eat the famous Bosanska pita – pies filled with meat, cheese or spinach. The **Marriott Residence Inn** (Skenderija 43; w marriott.com; €) has kitchenettes.

What to see The **Jewish Museum** (Muzej Jevreja BiH; Velika avlija 33; w muzejsarajeva.ba; ⊕ 10.00–15.00 Mon–Fri, 10.00–13.00 Sun; BAM3) is a small Jewish museum in the 16th-century Old Synagogue which explores the rich pre-war Jewish life of Bosnia, as well as the history of the Holocaust.

No trip to Sarajevo is complete without seeing the **Sarajevo Haggadah** in the National Museum of Bosnia and Herzegovina (Zemaljski muzej; Zmaja od Bosne 3; w zemaljskimuzej.ba; ⊕ exhibited noon–13.00 Tue, Thu & 1st Sat of the month; BAM8). The Haggadah is a text that sets out the order of the Passover Seder and tells the story of the Jewish exodus from Egypt. The Sarajevo Haggadah was probably made in Barcelona in around 1350 and was acquired by the museum in 1894. During World War II it was hidden in a Bosniak village on Mount Bjelašnica; during the siege of Sarajevo in 1992–95 it was again hidden, this time in the vault of the National Bank.

Sarajevo's Holocaust monument is in the central part of the large **Old Jewish Cemetery** on the lower slopes of Mount Trebević. The main, but not only, gate is on Urijan Dedina ulica. The memorial is a few minutes' walk up from the gate. It was designed by architect Jahiel Finci and built in 1952. The huge cemetery, founded in 1630, was on the frontline during the 1992–95 war and was badly damaged as was the memorial itself. The cemetery was cleared of mines and ordinance in 1998.

The **Vraca Memorial Park**, on Husinjska ulica also on Mount Trebević, is 20 minutes' walk from the cemetery. The Austro-Hungarian fortress was used as a place of execution during World War II. The names of the 9,091 victims from Sarajevo are inscribed in stone on the walls of two inner atria, including the names of 7,262 Jews, victims of the Holocaust. During the Bosnian War of 1992–95, the complex was badly damaged and the museum building totally destroyed. Owing to a lack of funds, restoration has not been completed.

Further afield For information on the mass graves at Donja Gradina, once part of Jasenovac concentration camp in Croatia, see page 44.

Brčko The entire 157-strong Jewish community of Brčko was slaughtered by the Ustashas, reportedly with hammers, on 7 December 1941 on or close to the bridge over the Sava River, which here forms the border between Bosnia and Croatia. History repeated itself on 30 April 1992 when the bridge was blown up, killing some 100 civilians and refugees. A Yugoslav-era plaque to the Holocaust victims was replaced after the 1995 Dayton Accords which ended the Bosnian War. It is located on the Bosnian side of the bridge. There is another memorial to them in the Serbian cemetery. On 10 December 1941, between 150 and 300 Jewish refugees from Austria, Poland and elsewhere were also murdered in Brčko. The names of 99 are known; a memorial for them is located at Braće Ćuskića 10 near where they were murdered.

Mostar Jews settled in Mostar in the Middle Ages as the town lay on important trading routes leading to and from Dubrovnik and Italy. During the Holocaust, 138 Mostar Jews lost their lives. Mostar's Holocaust memorial is in the Jewish cemetery in the northern Sutina district, some 5km from the centre on the Sarajevo road. The key is kept with the cashier at the INA petrol station opposite and you can ask for it.

Kruščica A transit camp was set up in Kruščica, near Vitez in which the Ustasha held 3,000–5,000 prisoners, 90% of them Bosnian Jews, after the Italians closed down the Jadovno–Pag Island system of Ustasha death camps. Most of these prisoners were later transferred to the Djakovo, Loborgrad and Jasenovac concentration camps. The museum has been abandoned since the 1992–95 war when the site was damaged, but the memorials remain standing.

SERBIA

The German occupation of Yugoslavia in 1941 opened the door for the persecution of the Jews in Serbia. By the time the timetable for the murder of Europe's Jews was set at the Wannsee Conference in January 1942, the majority of Yugoslavia's Jewish community had already been murdered. It was a key step along the road to genocide.

GETTING AROUND Many of the sites in Belgrade city centre are in walking distance of each other. To get to the Museum of the Banjica Concentration Camp, take bus E9 from Terazije and change to bus 59 at Franše d'Eperea. To get to Jajinici take the E9 to Voždovac and change for bus 408. The E9 also stops at Topovske Šupe. To see the Stratište Memorial Complex, you will need your own transport.

HISTORY On the eve of World War II, about 33,500 Jews lived in what is now Serbia, 11,000 of them in the capital, Belgrade. In the 1930s, antisemitism was on the rise but limited to right-wing intellectual circles.

On 25 March 1941 the Regent, Prince Paul, declared that Yugoslavia was joining the Axis pact. The Serbian-dominated officer corps then launched a coup, toppling the government. On 6 April, Germany, Italy and Hungary invaded Yugoslavia, with Bulgaria joining in on 17 April. Much of Serbia came under direct German occupation and a Nazi-controlled Serbian government was installed; Bulgaria seized parts of what is now south Serbia including a part of Kosovo; and the NDH was awarded parts of Serbia up to Zemun, part of Belgrade on the right bank of the Danube. Persecution of the Jews began immediately, and Jews were made to register in the field below the Kalemegdan fortress.

Partisan resistance movements were immediately formed by the Communist Party, but, unlike in other eastern European countries, Tito's partisans welcomed Jewish fighters. As resistance increased, so did German reprisals. In August and September 1941, all Jews from the northern Banat region, today part of Vojvodina, Serbia's northern province, were deported to Belgrade. Jews, Roma and Serbian military officers were arrested in September. By the end of 1941 nearly all Jewish men had been shot.

Hungary occupied a large part of Vojvodina, where, before the war, about 20,000 Jews were living. Only 4,000 survived. In 1944, most of Vojvodina's Jews were rounded up by Hungarian police and deported to Auschwitz. Beside the Danube, a monument honours the memory of Novi Sad's 1,400 Jewish and Serbian inhabitants, shot down or thrown in the river by Hungarian militias on 23 January 1942, in revenge for an assassination committed by the resistance.

BELGRADE Belgrade was one of the centres of Sephardi life in the region but also had an Ashkenazi community. Belgrade's yeshiva was famous across the world. After the 1878 Congress of Berlin required all the Balkan states to grant complete equality to all ethnic groups, the Jewish community in Belgrade began to prosper. Most Jews lived in Dorçol, which was badly bombed by the Luftwaffe in April 1941.

🏠 **Where to stay and eat** The small boutique hotel **SuperB Luxury Suites** (Rajićeva 12; w superb.rs; €) next to the Kalemegdan fortress has large rooms. There are lots of restaurants nearby. Popular is the trendy rooftop café and restaurant in the **Mama Shelter** hotel (Kneza Mihaila 54a; w mamashelter.com/Belgrade/eat-drink; ⊕ 07.00–midnight daily; €€) on the fourth floor of the Rajićeva Shopping Centre on Kneza Mihaila.

History In July 1941, the first concentration camp in Belgrade opened in the city's southern suburb of Banjica. Some 24,000 prisoners, among them Jews and Roma, were held here.

In August 1941 a transit camp for Jewish and Roma men was also established at Topovske Šupe – meaning 'canon sheds' – in a former Yugoslav army base, and guarded by the Serbian gendarmerie. It was in the Autokomanda district, in what was then a populous area on the southern outskirts of the city. Normal life continued right outside the camp. Some 5,000 Jews and 1,500 Roma are believed to have passed through here before being shot at other sites around the city following the German order to shoot 100 for every German killed and 50 for every wounded. Some 2,200 Jewish men from Topovske Šupe were shot at Jabuka north of Belgrade. Women and children brought here were then moved to Sajmište. The camp closed in December 1941.

The Semlin (the German name for Zemun) concentration camp was set up in September 1941 in the Belgrade fairground Sajmište, also now called Staro Sajmište – literally Old Fairground – which had been earmarked for exhibitions and trade fairs. The camp that became operational in October 1941 was in full sight of the relatively normal life that continued in the city under the occupation. As most of the Jewish men had already been murdered, the prisoners held here were nearly all Jewish women, children and elderly but included some Roma and Sinti. Conditions were extremely squalid. There was little food and many people froze to death in the winter. Although it was on territory nominally controlled by the Croatian NDH, the camp was run by the Gestapo.

In March 1942, a mobile gas van sent from the Chełmno extermination camp in occupied Poland arrived in Belgrade. Over the course of the spring all the Jews in the Semlin camp, about 6,300 people, were killed as the van drove 50 at a time through the streets of the city. They were buried in mass graves in Jajnici. The camp then held Jews from Dalmatia and partisans. During this period an estimated 32,000 people, mostly Serbs, passed through the camp. The gas van was then transferred to Minsk in Belarus.

What to see Across the Sava River from Belgrade city centre, there is a large post-Yugoslav Holocaust monument on the riverbank right beside the former Semlin concentration camp at **Staro Sajmište** (off Zemunski put). There is a smaller Yugoslav-era one inside the camp area too. After the war, the site became an artists' colony and has been in a sorry state of repair for decades. The former Spasić pavilion, one of several built as part of the Sajmište complex, became a nightclub used for rock concerts and hosted Boy George in 2006. During the war it had been the camp infirmary. In June 2021, Belgrade's mayor announced reconstruction of the complex. So far, the central tower has undergone restoration and discussions are ongoing about creating a museum. Delays to memorialising the site have been widely attributed to the fact that it is opposite the new Belgrade Waterfront development of condominiums, hotels, offices and shops.

The **Museum of the Banjica Concentration Camp** (Muzej Banjičkog Logora; Generala Pavla Jurišića Šturma 33; w mgb.org.rs/visit/details/3; ⊕ 10.00–17.00 Thu–Sat; RSD100) is on the site of the first concentration camp in the south of the city. The army shooting range at **Jajinici** on the road to Mount Avala (cnr Bulevar JNA & Jajinici-Kumodraž), where an estimated 65,000 Jews, Serbs and Roma were killed, has a well-maintained memorial park which was laid out in 1951.

Two of the original barracks of the former Topovske Šupe concentration camp can be seen on ulica Tabanovačka in the Voždovac district in the south of Belgrade. The first commemorative plaque to those who died at the camp was put up in 1951. A new plaque was erected on the perimeter wall of one of the barracks in 2005. It was stolen in 2017 and replaced in 2019. For years controversy has raged about what to do with the site which was bought by Miroslav Mišković, one of Serbia's richest men, but remains derelict and rubbish-strewn. Mišković planned to build a shopping mall and two office blocks here along with partners from Israel. This divided the Serbian Jewish community and in 2020 the site received official recognition along with the Sajmište complex. The website set up in the campaign has useful information and a database of victims (w topovskesupe.rs).

The **Stratište Memorial Complex** at Jabuka (⊕ 24hrs daily), which commemorates 10,000 Jewish, Roma and Serbian victims, was inaugurated in 1981 and restored in 2019.

In the **Jewish Sephardic Cemetery** (Mije Kovačevića 1), adjacent to Belgrade's main New Cemetery, there is a moving memorial put up by the Jewish community in 1952. It includes pieces of stone debris from houses demolished in the Dorćol neighbourhood and fragments of tombstones from a destroyed Belgrade Jewish cemetery. There is also a monument here to some 800 Austrian Jewish refugees murdered in Zasavica in 1941 and reburied here in 1959. Just below Dorćol, on the banks of the Danube, is the 1990 *Menorah in Flames* memorial by the Yugoslav sculptor Nandor Glid (1924–97), a Holocaust survivor. It is almost identical to his memorial in Thessaloniki in Greece (page 59). There are also monuments to the Austrian and other murdered refugees in Zasavica and Kladovo.

NORTH MACEDONIA

North Macedonia is home to the only Holocaust museum in the Balkans, which makes it an important stop on any tour of Balkan Holocaust sites. Jews have lived in Macedonia since antiquity. The Jews of what is now North Macedonia were closely related to those of Thessaloniki, the biggest city in historic Macedonia.

GETTING AROUND All sites are walkable in Skopje and Bitola. There are a few trains from Skopje to Bitola daily and frequent buses.

HISTORY After the Balkan Wars in the early 20th century, what is modern-day North Macedonia was incorporated into Serbia and, after World War I, into

Yugoslavia. Although during the interwar years many Jews emigrated, in 1941 the country still had a vibrant, if small, Jewish community – they were predominantly Sephardi and lived in the capital Skopje, as well as in Bitola and Štip.

Most of the territory of today's North Macedonia was occupied by Bulgaria from 1941 to 1944. The mostly Albanian-populated west was incorporated into the Italian-controlled Greater Albania. During this period, Bulgarian police and military units deported their territory's Jews to Nazi German-held territories. On 10 March 1943, some 7,200 Jews – its whole Jewish population – were rounded up and taken to the Monopol tobacco factory in Skopje. After enduring five days without food and being subjected to violent beatings and rape, they were deported to the Treblinka extermination camp in occupied Poland. March of the Living (w motl.org; page 18) events mark the March 1943 deportation.

SKOPJE   About 200 Jews live in Skopje today, though there is almost no trace of the vibrant Sephardi community that once lived here. Although much of the city centre has been redeveloped in a kitsch style, visitors can get a feel for pre-war Skopje in the old Čaršija area, a few minutes' walk from the city's 15th-century Stone Bridge.

Where to stay and eat   The **Ibis City Centre** (Orce Nikolov Br 55; w all.accor. com; €) in the city centre is a good place to stay. Restaurants in the Čaršija, near the Holocaust museum, serve authentic local food.

What to see   The **Holocaust Memorial Centre for the Jews of Macedonia** (Memorijalen centar na holokaustot na Evreite od Makedonija; Samoilova 2; w holocaustfund.org.mk; ⊕ 09.00–19.00 Tue–Fri, 09.00–15.00 Sat–Sun; MKD110) opened in 2011 on the banks of the Vardar River in the heart of Skopje. Funded by restitution money paid to the Jewish community by the government in 2000, it was built in a long-dilapidated area which was a Jewish part of town until the Holocaust. Recently refurbished, the museum charts the history of Jews in the region and has multimedia displays which are also in English. In an installation at the entrance of the museum, dozens of digital frames display some 3,200 photographs, many of them recovered from the records of the Jews detained in the Bitola Ghetto. In the central atrium, the *Burning Bush* light sculpture has 7,144 strands, one for each deportee. As you progress through the museum you walk through a freight wagon similar to the ones used by the Bulgarians in which Jews were transported to Treblinka. The centre also displays urns containing ashes from the extermination camp.

Visitors can see two films, one on the Jews of Macedonia and the other about the Jewish partisans, especially Beno Russo and Roza Kamhi, who married after the war.

A 2004 memorial replaced a plaque erected in Yugoslav times in the former Monopol tobacco factory, where the Jews from Skopje and the surrounding area where held prior to deportation – it is now **Imperial Tobacco Skopje** (11 Oktomvri 125; ⊕ visits by appt – email e imptob.tks@mk.imptob.com – or possible during the 11 March commemoration).

Further afield

Bitola   Close to the Greek border, 170km south of Skopje, Bitola, known as Monastir during the Ottoman era and hence also among many Jews whose family roots are here, was the centre of Jewish life in this part of historic Macedonia. Dozens of Jewish businesses once lined the main commercial street Širok Sokak, known by locals as the Korzo.

Bitola was on the frontline in the Balkan Wars of 1912–13 and again during World War I, when it lay on the Salonica Front. The Jewish community went into decline in the 1920s not only because the town had been devastated by the wars but because it was now part of Yugoslavia and hence had been cut off from its economic hinterland which was now in Greek territory. For Bitola's Jews, this meant that a border also now lay between them and the much bigger Jewish community of Thessaloniki. There was an active Zionist movement in the city and many Jews left for Palestine.

At dawn on 11 March 1943, the Jewish community of Bitola were given an hour to leave the ghetto. They were taken by train to Skopje and from there to their deaths in the Treblinka extermination camp. There is a **Holocaust memorial** at Pande Nikolov 1 next to the site of the former Aragon Synagogue, on which now stands the Medical Centre Haim Abravanel. Also located here is the statue of **Estreja Ovadya**, the only Jewish woman declared a national hero in the former Yugoslavia. She was part of the Zionist left-wing youth movement Hashomer Hatzair, many of whom, including Ovadya, joined the partisans. They had their HQ at **Ruzveltova 24**.

The former Monastir Military Academy, where Kemal Atatürk, the father of modern-day Turkey studied, is now the **NI Institute and Museum Bitola** (Музеј Битола; Kliment Ohridski 18; w muzejbitola.mk; ⊕ 08.00–18.00 daily, closes 20.00 in summer; MKD120). In the archaeological exhibition, a case displays objects from a Bitola synagogue which include parts of a Torah scroll dating to the 15th century, a silver Torah finial and a votive hand. The museum also exhibits a partial list of the city's deported Jews, an urn with ashes from Treblinka and photographs of Jewish partisans.

Founded in 1497, the **Jewish cemetery**, the Beit Haim (Home of the Living), on a steep hill in the Ušici neighbourhood, is one of the oldest Jewish cemeteries in the Balkans. The gateway with Gothic-style arches dates from 1929. As this is a Sephardi cemetery, the gravestones are laid horizontally. The cemetery was badly damaged in the fighting in 1912–13, and during World War II gravestones were taken and used by the Bulgarian Army to pave their camp. Much work has gone into renovating the cemetery in recent years.

ALBANIA

The story of Albania's Jews during the Holocaust is completely unique. Although Albania, the only European country with a Muslim majority, was occupied by both fascist Italy and subsequently Nazi Germany, its Jewish population grew dramatically during World War II. It is the only country in Europe to have had a larger Jewish population in 1945 than in 1939.

Until the end of 1938, according to Robert Elsie, in his *Historical Dictionary of Albania* (Scarecrow Press, 2010), the Albanian embassy in Berlin issued visas to Jews when other countries were unwilling to take them. The records show that most of the Jews who were protected were not Albanian, probably because Albanian Jews needed less protection. This does not mean, however, that Holocaust memory among Albanians as a whole is without issues. This is the story that Albanians choose to remember, while little is said about the fate of many Jews in Kosovo, which was part of wartime Greater Albania (page 54).

GETTING AROUND Sites in Tirana are accessible on foot. The best way to get around Albania is by car.

HISTORY The first recorded Jewish presence in Albania is in the 12th century but the remains of a 5th- or 6th-century synagogue have also been found in Saranda. Primarily Romaniote and Sephardi, the Jewish community in what is now Albania has always been small in number.

In 1937, some 300 Jews lived in Albania. In April 1939, before the outbreak of World War II, Italy invaded and occupied the country and applied its 1938 racial laws; yet Jews from Yugoslavia, Greece and elsewhere fled to Albania as it was safer to be in a zone controlled by the Italians than the Germans. By 1945 Albania would be home to around 2,000 Jews.

After Italy surrendered to the Allies in 1943, Albania was occupied by Germany. When the Germans demanded lists of Jews, the Albanian authorities refused to hand them over; and when the occupiers attempted to arrest the Jews of Vlora, partisans stopped the operation. Only one family, the Arditis from Shkodër, were arrested during the period of the German occupation; the family was subsequently deported and killed.

After World War II Albania was sealed off from the world and ruled by the communist dictatorship of Enver Hoxha.

TIRANA The Albanian capital has a tiny Jewish community numbering between 50 and 200.

🏠 **Where to stay and eat** The **Hotel Rogner** (Bulevardi Dëshmorët e Kombit; w hotel-europapark.com; **€€**) has a large garden and swimming pool. Treat yourself at **La Vita e Bella** (Rruga Jul Variboba 21; 🅵; ⏰ noon–23.00 daily; **€€€**), the capital's best fish restaurant.

What to see In 2020, a **Holocaust memorial** was placed in the Grand Park, south of the city centre, close to the entrance near the Canadian consulate. The three black marble monuments remember the victims and honour those Albanians who helped the Jews.

Tirana's new **Besa Museum** was in the planning stage at the time of writing. Besa means 'oath' or 'word of honour' and embodies the principles of hospitality and protection of guests that motivated Albanians to protect Jews during World War II – between 600 and 1,800 Jewish lives were saved. The museum will be in the historic 19th-century house that once belonged to the Toptani family, a prominent Albanian noble family in the early 20th century.

There is an exhibit devoted to Albanian Jewish history in Tirana's **National Historical Museum** (Muzeu Historik Kombëtar; Sheshi Skënderbej 7; w mhk.gov. al; ⏰ 09.00–16.00 Tue–Sun; ALL150).

Further afield
Berat The **Solomon Museum** (Muzeu Solomoni; Rruga Mihal Komnena 5001; 🅵; ⏰ 09.30–16.30 daily; donation requested), which opened in 2018, is a private initiative set up by a local historian and Albania's only Jewish history museum. The exhibition features the 60 local Muslim and Christian families who hid Jews during the Holocaust.

KOSOVO

In 1910 there were some 3,000 Jews in Kosovo, but many left when the country came under Serbian rule in 1912. In 1941 there were known to be 551 Jews in

Kosovo, then part of Yugoslavia, but that number was soon swelled by an unknown number of Jewish refugees from German-occupied areas further north. Jews had lived in Kosovo since at least the 15th century.

HISTORY After Germany and Italy invaded Yugoslavia in April 1941, modern-day Kosovo came under German control before the Italian Army took its place. Most of Kosovo was then incorporated into an Italian-controlled Greater Albania, while a small part of eastern Kosovo came under Bulgarian control, and northern Kosovo and Mitrovica, with its valuable mines, remained under German military occupation. Exactly what happened during the Holocaust in Kosovo is extremely unclear not least since no-one knows how many Jews were there. Not only were there many refugees from Nazi-occupied areas, but people could move with relative ease to Albania itself. 'Most of the local Jewish men', writes Noel Malcom in his *Kosovo: A Short History* (Pan, 2002), were also sent by the Italians for internment in central Albania. After the Italian collapse, many then joined the partisans or were 'given refuge by Albanian villagers'. Stevan K Pavlowitch in his *Hitler's New Disorder: The Second World War in Yugoslavia* (Hurst, 2008) writes that, in November 1941, 300–400 Jewish refugees from Serbia arrived who had been given papers by the Italian legation in Belgrade, 'some of whom went on to Dalmatia'. Malcolm notes that Italian-controlled Kosovo was a place of 'relative safety' for Jews. 'Racial laws were proclaimed but not enforced: there was no curfew for Jews and no wearing of yellow stars.' In 1942 Jews from German-controlled Mitrovica were sent to Sajmište in Belgrade and killed.

While the Italians normally did not co-operate with the Nazis over the Final Solution and gave protection to Jews, in March 1942 the Carabinieri arrested 51 Jewish refugees and handed them over. They were to die in Sajmište. In the wake of the Italian collapse in 1943, Germany took control of the region and an Albanian Skanderbeg volunteer SS division was recruited, which rounded up 281 Jews, who were then deported to Sajmište and then Bergen-Belsen, where more than 200 were to die. Of Kosovo's 551 Jews from 1941, Malcolm writes that 210 were dead by the end of the war. Most of the survivors emigrated to Israel between 1948 and 1952.

PRISTINA Pristina is Europe's youngest capital and has a mixture of Ottoman- and communist-era buildings and memorials to the recent conflict but also has an interesting Holocaust story.

⌂ **Where to stay and eat** The **Garden Downtown Prishtina** (Meto Bajraktari Prishtina 53; w gardendowntown.com; €) is a modern hotel with a good restaurant and parking located close to the city centre.

What to see Virtually the only trace of Pristina's Jewish community is the old Jewish cemetery on Dëshmorët e Marecit street, a 30-minute hike uphill in Taukbashqe park which overlooks the city. There are several flat Sephardi-style tombs. There are also a handful of Jewish tombstones outside the Kosovo Museum on Hamdi Mramori 1 in the town centre.

In 2013, a **stele** was erected beside parliament to commemorate victims of the Holocaust. The inscription in Albanian, English, Hebrew and Serbian reads: 'This is the place where the last synagogue of Kosovo stood until 1963. This plaque is raised in memory of the Kosovo Jews who perished in Nazi camps during the Holocaust. The people of Kosovo will never forget them.' The synagogue was demolished when the whole Ottoman-era part of town here was cleared away.

In 2023 a memorial bearing the names of 23 Kosovo Albanians who rescued Jews from the Holocaust during World War II was inaugurated in the centre of the City Park. Among them is Leke Rezniqi, who in 2008 was the first Kosovar to be named as Righteous Among the Nations.

BULGARIA

Bulgaria was an Axis power and ally of Germany – but all of its 48,000 Jews survived World War II. On the surface it looks like a success story but, as in many other European countries, it depends on what you like to remember and what you choose to forget.

GETTING AROUND The centre of Sofia, Bulgaria's capital, is easy to get around on foot or by metro. To get to Nedelino in the Rhodope Mountains, 328km southeast of Sofia, take a bus. There is a train to Kyustendil, 103km southwest of Sofia.

HISTORY After World War I, Bulgaria lost territory it had briefly gained in the Balkan Wars and, as a result, as a revanchist power it grew closer to Germany. Tsar Boris III established a royal dictatorship in 1935. When war began, Bulgaria declared its neutrality but profited from agreements with the Nazis. German diplomacy forced the Romanians to hand over Southern Dobrudja to Bulgaria whose relations with Germany now tightened. In 1941, Bulgaria joined the Axis and took part in the invasion of Yugoslavia and Greece. Anti-Jewish legislation was introduced and foreign Jews expelled. In March 1943, after the deportation of Jews from territory occupied by Bulgaria, Boris III was about to deport the Jews of the country itself to the death camps when he faced opposition from members of the National Assembly, the Orthodox Church and the general public. He halted the deportation but interned much of the Jewish population in the countryside in appalling conditions. Bulgaria also refused to take part in the invasion of the Soviet Union. Boris III died of heart failure after a visit to Berlin in 1943.

When in September 1944 the Soviet Army swept down through Romania and liberated Bulgaria, the country switched sides and declared war on Germany. It then fought alongside Soviet and Yugoslav partisan forces until the war ended in May 1945.

Bulgaria's Jews had survived the war, but the anti-Jewish legislation had left them in dire poverty. Nearly half were dependent on soup kitchens. By 1950 most of Bulgaria's Jews had left for the newly declared state of Israel or elsewhere. Bulgaria was part of the Soviet bloc until 1990.

SOFIA Jews have lived in Sofia for over 2,000 years. The original community were Greek-speaking Romaniotes. Ashkenazi Jews then arrived in the region from Bavaria and Hungary. In the 15th century Sephardic Jews fleeing the Spanish Inquisition settled in Sofia. The city's synagogue is the largest in southeastern Europe but only a handful of Jews still live here.

Where to stay and eat The **Rosslyn Central Park Hotel Sofia** (Vitosha Bd 106; w centralparkhotel.bg; €€) is opposite Sofia's central National Palace of Culture (NDK) and within walking and metro distance of the main sights and restaurants.

What to see When Simeon, the son of Tsar Boris III, was elected prime minister in 2001, he began to rehabilitate his father. Outside the **Saint Sofia Church** on Moskovska ulica in the heart of the capital, a memorial thanks Tsar Boris III for saving

Bulgaria's Jews. The plaques are copies of those placed in the Bulgarian Forest near Jerusalem in 1999 but removed in 2000 at the request of the surviving descendants of the 11,343 Thracian and Macedonian Jews deported to the death camps. There are numerous memorials to Boris III across the city and one to the Jews of Bulgaria who were not deported, in the garden between Parliament, the National Academy of Arts and Sofia University. There are identical memorials in Plovdiv and Varna.

There is a small Jewish History Museum at **Central Sofia Synagogue** (ul. Exarch Joseph 16; ⊕ 08.30–12.30 & 13.00–16.30 Mon–Fri; €1), which was dedicated in 1909.

Further afield

Nedelino In the Rhodope mountains, Nedelino was one of ten forced labour camps in Bulgaria. A memorial in the main square put up in 2019 commemorates the Jewish men forced to build the roads from Nedelino to Byal Izvor and Zlatograd.

Kyustendil The saving of the Bulgarian Jews is remembered at the reconstruction of the former home of Dimitar Peshev, now the **Dimitar Peshev House Museum** (11 Tsar Simeon I; ⊕ 09.00–17.00 Wed–Sun; guided tours in English by appt). Peshev was the Deputy Speaker of the Bulgarian National Assembly, and in March 1943 he put together a petition against the deportation of Bulgaria's Jews. Trains to deport them were already waiting in Kyustendil station. The events in Kyustendil were not unique. In Plovdiv, Metropolitan Kiril sent a telegram to Tsar Boris as the Jews were gathered in the station awaiting deportation saying that if they were deported, he would go with them. Peshev was awarded the title of Righteous Among the Nations in 1973. The three-room exhibition tells the history of Jewish life in Bulgaria since 1878, when Jews were granted civil rights; the life and times of Peshev and events of March 1943.

GREECE

Jews have lived in Greece since the 4th century BCE. The most important Jewish city was Thessaloniki in the north of the country. Most Jews in Greece are Sephardim, but Greece is also home to a unique group, the ancient Greek-speaking Romaniote community. Some 60,000 Greek Jews died in the Holocaust, more than 80% of the total Jewish population.

Recent surveys have found alarming levels of antisemitism in Greece although violent attacks are rare. Holocaust denial and revisionism is most visible in the far-right party, Golden Dawn.

After years of oversight, the 2023 mini-series *To Vrahiolo tis Fotias* (*The Fire Bracelet*), which tells the story of a Jewish family in 20th-century Thessaloniki, has finally got Greeks talking about Holocaust. The series is based on the book of the same name by Béatrice Saias-Magrizou (Kastaniotis, 2006).

GETTING AROUND Intercity buses are the most efficient way to travel. There are frequent flights between Athens and Thessaloniki and also a rail connection. The best way to get to Rhodes from within Greece is to fly from Athens.

HISTORY Greece was ruled by the Ottomans until they began to lose control of it in the Greek War of Independence in 1821. The Ottomans had welcomed Jews who had fled from the Inquisition in Spain as they boosted the economy and brought skills. Most Jews were loyal to the Ottomans and when Tripolitsa, the Ottoman administrative centre of the Peloponnese, fell to the revolutionaries in 1821, its Jews were massacred alongside its Muslims. Ottoman rule in northern Greece came to an end in 1912–13.

In 1940, Italy invaded Greece but soon got bogged down, which served as a catalyst for the German invasion of southeastern Europe on 6 April 1941. Germany occupied western Macedonia, eastern Thrace, the region around Athens, western Crete and the Greek islands in the northern Aegean close to Turkey. Bulgaria occupied western Thrace. Italy took control of the rest of the Greek mainland, eastern Crete, and the islands in the eastern Mediterranean, the Ionian and Adriatic seas. Athens was jointly occupied by Germany and Italy.

In 1941, approximately 72,000 Jews lived in Greece. Italian forces did not engage in the mass murder of Jews and, as in Yugoslavia, many Jews fled from German-controlled areas to Italian ones.

After the Italian surrender in September 1943, the Germans occupied all of Greece and began deporting Jews from Athens in April 1944.

THESSALONIKI The maritime gateway to the Balkans and southeastern Europe was once one of the most cosmopolitan places on the continent. For hundreds of years, the Ottoman city of Salonica, as Thessaloniki was then known, was one of the few Jewish majority cities in Europe. The Jews who lived in Thessaloniki were Sephardi and spoke Ladino.

Jews made up just over half the population at the end of the 19th century. The city was also home to Greeks, who made up about 25% of the population, Turks, Bulgarians and Roma. So many Jews worked as stevedores in the port that it closed on Saturday for Shabbat and on Jewish holidays.

Where to stay and eat For a treat, stay at the **Electra Palace Hotel** (Aristotélous 9; w electrahotels.gr/hotels/electra-palace-thessaloniki; €€€), a city landmark. A more budget option is **Gatto Perso Luxury Studio Apartments** (Mitseon 10; w gattoperso.gr; €). Inspired by *A Taste of Sephardic Thessaloniki* (Fytrakis Editions, 2002), a book of family recipes by the late Nina Benroubi, one of the city's few Holocaust survivors, Kostas Markou, the chef at **Akadamia** (Ag. Mina 3;

w akadimiarestaurant.gr; ⊕ noon–02.00 Tue–Sun; €€), has introduced Sephardic dishes on to the menu.

History Jewish Thessaloniki began to disappear after the Greeks took control of it in 1912. However, disaster struck in 1917 when the heart of the city, which was also the heart of Jewish Salonica, was destroyed in a catastrophic fire. Homes, synagogues, businesses and livelihoods were all lost. A large proportion of the city's Jews relocated to the outskirts but many now emigrated. In the wake of the Greco-Turkish war of 1919–22 some 100,000 Greeks were resettled here during the population exchange between the countries. This drastically reduced the Jewish proportion of the city's population to some 20%. From 1686 until the population exchange, the city was also home to a significant community of 'Dönme' or heretical Jews.

A process of Hellenisation was rolled out in the interwar years that turned Salonica into a Greek and Christian city, which in 1937 was renamed Thessaniki. Greek, which most local Jews did not initially speak, was now the official language.

In 1941, the city was still home to Greece's largest pre-war Jewish community made up of around 43,000 people – 98% of whom were murdered in the Holocaust, the largest loss inflicted on any single community in Europe. Between 20 March and 19 August 1943 some 40,000 Jews were deported to Auschwitz from the railway station in the Baron de Hirsch neighbourhood in the west of the city. The

---

MOSHE HA-ELION'S STORY

Moshe Ha-Elion was born in Salonica (Thessaloniki) in 1925 into a middle-class Sephardic family. His father, a bookkeeper, died six days after the German occupation.

In 1943, the family was forced into the ghetto, where life was so difficult that Ha-Elion along with his grandparents, mother, sister and uncle, with his wife and baby, volunteered to be resettled in Poland. They had no idea what would happen to them.

When the family arrived in Auschwitz, Ha-Elion was separated from them and taken for forced labour.

When Ha-Elion and I met in 2018, he said, 'You could not comprehend the place. I was there for weeks and I did not know what was going on until one day a friend pointed at the smoke and told me my family were dead. I thought he had lost his mind. I simply could not believe the Germans could do this.' Ha-Elion leaned forward, the shock

and bewilderment still clearly evident on his face. 'You cannot understand the unimaginable.'

This is the problem with the story of the Holocaust as it fades into history. It is so unfathomable that it can easily be disbelieved. After his retirement in 1996, Ha-Elion became a tireless campaigner against Holocaust denial and sat on the board of Yad Vashem, Israel's official Holocaust memorial, for ten years.

After his liberation from the Ebensee concentration camp in Austria, in a displaced persons camp in Italy he began to record dates and notes of what had happened to him but soon abandoned the project 'as the task of building a new life took over'. Ha-Elion met and married a fellow Auschwitz survivor and left for Palestine. He fought and was wounded in the 1948 war but went on to serve in the Israeli Defence Force (IDF) for over 20 years, after which he worked in the Ministry of overcrowded freight wagons took eight days to get to Auschwitz, but by the time the trains reached Belgrade water had already run out. Most of the Jews on the transports were murdered on arrival. During the deportations, the smaller of two ghettos in the Baron de Hirsch quarter functioned as a transit camp.

There were so few survivors that the memory of what happened faded in the post-war years and conveniently there was no discussion of collaboration and profiteering from the murder by the remaining part of the city's population. It was only in the 1990s that interest in the annihilation of Thessaloniki's Jews began to develop.

What to see The modern city centre, opposite the seafront, was the heart of Jewish Salonica, though what exists today is the city that was rebuilt after the fire of 1917. In July 1942, thousands of Jewish men were rounded up in Plateia Eleftheria and humiliated in the blazing heat before being signed up for forced labour. Since 2007, the *Menorah in Flames* Holocaust memorial has stood at the southeastern corner of the square facing the sea and the busy seafront boulevard. It is by the Yugoslav sculptor and Holocaust survivor Nandor Glid and very similar to his Belgrade memorial (page 50).

Four minutes' walk away, the **Jewish Museum of Thessaloniki** (Agiou Mina 11; w jmth.gr; ⊕ 09.00–14.00 Mon–Fri, also 17.00–20.00 Wed, 10.00–14.00 Sun; €5) is housed in a former Jewish bank, one of the few buildings that survived the

Defence. Keeping his family safe was a priority.

In the 1980s, Ha-Elion decided that he must try once more to write down what he had seen and experienced. His memoir, *The Straits of Hell* (Harrassowitz, 2009), partly tells his story through poetry written in Ladino.

As we chatted, through his large glasses he studied his enormous computer screen looking for a file that contained a poem he had written about his sister Nina which he had set to music. He clicked on a video of a beautiful young Israeli soldier singing it in Hebrew. When the film finished, he opened an English translation. There was a pause, then he started to sing in a shaky frail voice:

'Her soul can hardly fathom, the terror she feels,
seeing guards and soldiers, fences and barbed wire,
the troops with dogs and weapons.

The circumstance was dire.
She knew, from now onwards, her life had changed forever,
her world had been destroyed, she would never be free.
With evening came the darkness. She felt a sadness like no other.'

Out of the window the lights of Tel Aviv, its skyscrapers and beachfront, twinkled in the distance. In the sitting room he had told me that when he and his wife, Hanna, arrived in Israel, he built them a lean-to shack behind a laundry where they worked on Levinsky Street.

I asked Ha-Elion if I could take his photograph. When I showed him the picture on my phone, he laughed, 'I didn't look that old even yesterday.'

It was time to leave. 'We must never stop talking about the Holocaust,' Ha-Elion said as he held my hand as I bid him farewell, 'never.' He stood by the door waving as I called the lift.

Ha-Elion died in 2021.

1917 fire. Its permanent exhibition explores the life and culture of the Sephardic community since the 15th century. The museum was expanded in 2019.

The **Villa Mehmet Kapandji**, the home of a Jewish merchant, at 108 Leoforos Vasilissis Olgas, was used as the Nazi headquarters. In December 1942, SS Hauptsturmführers Dieter Wisliceny and Alois Brunner were despatched to Thessaloniki to organise the deportation of the city's Jews. The Germans demanded that the Jewish community pay a ransom for the release of the men detained in Plateia Eleftheria. When it failed to do so, with the agreement of local authorities they destroyed the Old Jewish Cemetery, the largest in Europe. The Aristotelous University campus now occupies the site. The gravestones were used in reconstruction. In 2014, a memorial to the Greek victims of the Holocaust was erected at the campus.

Since 1951 the station in the Baron de Hirsch quarter on Stathmous Street from where the city's Jews were deported, has been used for freight only. Plans to build a Holocaust museum here have been dogged by issues over land ownership and a change of mayor has led to the fears that the project will be watered down.

Further afield

Ioannina This beautiful Ottoman-era lakeside town, 260km southwest of Thessaloniki, was the centre of Greece's ancient and unique Romaniote community (w jewishcomioannina.gr). Jews lived here since the 8th century. In April 1941 it came under Italian control but after their collapse in 1943 the Germans arrived. On 25 March 1944, helped by the Greek police, they gathered and then despatched 1,960 Jews, almost the entire community, to Auschwitz. Of them 1,850 did not survive.

Today, the large synagogue, whose origins date from the Byzantine period, is only used for services on Yom Kippur when members of the Ioannina Romaniote diaspora gather. There is a 1994 steel **Holocaust memorial** representing Torah scrolls at the little square at the intersection of Karamanli and Soutsou streets just outside the old city walls. To visit the synagogue, message the keeper on ↳30 265 102 5195.

Kavala The port city of Kavala, 153km east of Thessaloniki, was at the heart of the area occupied by Bulgaria. Kavala had the largest Jewish community in Thrace numbering some 1,650 members. They were deported to Lom, a port on the Danube, and then taken by boat to Vienna. In the Austrian capital, they were loaded into freight wagons and taken to the Treblinka death camp. A **monument** in the Jewish cemetery on Amerikanikou Erythrou Stavrou commemorates those who were murdered. The cemetery is the only trace of this once vibrant community.

Larissa Larissa, 151km south of Thessaloniki, nor far from Mount Olympus, was one of the gathering points for deportations to Auschwitz. Jews from across northern Greece were brought here and held in a camp prior to deportation. Thanks to tip-offs, about 500 of the town's Jews escaped to the mountains and joined the partisans. Today Larissa is again home to a large Jewish community, which has its own primary school, cultural centre and cemetery. In 1987, a Holocaust memorial was erected on the **Square of Jewish Martyrs of the Holocaust** (Platia Evreon Martiron Katoxis). The bronze sculpture, depicting a stele and a woman, whose head is bowed in mourning, was designed by sculptor Giorgos Hoularas.

Athens The Greek capital does not have a Holocaust museum but there are two Holocaust **memorials**. The first was unveiled in the 1950s and is located in the

Jewish cemetery in the suburb of Nikaia. The second was put up near the Beth Shalom Synagogue at Melidoni 5 in 2010 after a long campaign by the Greek Jewish community. On the eve of Passover 1944, Jews were trapped in the synagogue by the Germans by a ruse of matzo being handed out for the festival. They were taken to a transit camp in Haidari in the army barracks in the western suburbs of Athens. The site still belongs to the Greek Army. It is possible to visit the infamous Block 15, where prisoners were held in solitary confinement, when the site is opened for commemorations.

Thousands of Jews in Athens tried to find places to hide and among those who have been recognised as Righteous Among the Nations is Princess Alice, who hid Jews in the royal palace. Princess Alice was the mother of Britain's Prince Philip and grandmother of King Charles III.

Rhodes The Dodecanese island of Rhodes in the southeastern Aegean was an Italian possession from 1912 to 1947. Hence, Italy's 1938 racial laws were applied, prompting some islanders to be expelled and others to flee. After Italy's collapse in 1943, all of the Dodecanese were occupied by the Germans and in July 1944 the 1,700 Jews left were deported to Auschwitz via the Haidari transit camp near Athens. In 1912 there were some 4,500 Jews on Rhodes but by 1947 there were only 50. Jews had lived on the islands for over 2,000 years.

Today, **Rhodes Town** has a well-preserved Jewish Quarter, where there is a memorial on the Square of Jewish Martyrs. Built in 1577 the **Kahal Shalom Synagogue** (Dosiadou και; w jewishrhodes.org; ⊕ Apr–Oct 10.00–15.00 Sun–Fri, Nov–Mar 10.00–15.00 Mon–Fri by appt only; €6; downloadable app guide) is the oldest in what is now Greece and has a small Jewish Museum.

4

THE BALTIC STATES

N

Bradt

| 0 | 100km |
| 0 | 60 miles |

FINLAND

GULF OF FINLAND

TALLINN ③ ①

②

Narva

Hilumaa

Saaremaa

Pärnu

ESTONIA

Tartu

BALTIC SEA

Gulf of Riga

Ventspils

RUSSIA

RIGA ⑥

⑦

LATVIA

⑤ Liepāja

Jelgava

Rēzekne

Daugava

Šiauliai

④ Daugavpils

Klaipėda

⑨

Panevėžys

LITHUANIA

Neman

Kaunas ⑧

Neris

⑫ **VILNIUS**

⑩

⑪

Vilija

BELARUS

Kaliningrad (RUSSIA)

POLAND

■MINSK

○ **Memorial sites and museums**

Estonia
1. Kalevi-Liiva sand dunes *p77*
2. Klooga Concentration Camp & Holocaust Memorial Site *p77*
3. Tallinn *p76*

Latvia
4. Daugavpils *p75*
5. Liepāja *p75*
6. Riga *p72*
7. Salaspils Memorial *p75*

Lithuania
8. Kaunas *p70*
9. Lost Shtetl Museum (Šeduva) *p71*
10. Paneriai Forest *p68*
11. Rudnicki Forest *p69*
12. Vilnius *p67*

5

The Baltic States

The Holocaust erupted in Estonia, Latvia and Lithuania when Germany invaded the Soviet Union on 22 June 1941 and the territories it had seized under the 1939 Nazi–Soviet Pact, which included the modern-day Baltic states.

In the months that followed, local Jews along with thousands of others deported from the Reich died in a hail of bullets in the region's beguiling forests and on its beautiful sand dunes. The mass murders were carried out by both German forces and local collaborators. As Christopher Browning has shown in *The Origins of the Final Solution: The Evolution of Nazi Jewish Policy 1939–1942* (Arrow, 2005),

GOOD TO KNOW

Holocaust denial began with the German invasion. As historians like Christoph Dieckmann and Andrew Ezergailis have shown, while the Germans orchestrated the violence of local far-right militias, they sought to portray events as locally inspired pogroms – not that this reduces the moral questions left in their wake. Across the Baltic states, Holocaust memory is work in progress that has been led by government initiatives and scholarly research, but all three countries have struggled to come to terms with this aspect of their past.

After the war, the Soviet authorities did not recognise the specificity of the Jewish genocide and did not permit official memorialisation of Jewish victims. Under communism, the Jewish heritage of the Baltic states was erased from the history books and rarely discussed.

In the post-independence period, although Holocaust memorials have been created, the main focus has been on the communist era, which is presented as on a par with the German occupation, and memorials that honour local perpetrators as freedom fighters have been erected. The organisation Defending History (w defendinghistory.com), run by historian Dovid Katz, campaigns against Holocaust distortion in Lithuania.

One of the most controversial books published in Lithuania in recent years is Rūta Vanagaitė's *Our People: Discovering Lithuania's Hidden Holocaust* (Rowman and Littlefield, 2020). Vanagaite, the daughter of perpetrators, travelled across her homeland with Nazi hunter Efraim Zuroff, director of the Simon Wiesenthal Center's Israel office, and set out to prove that Lithuanians were an integral part of the Nazi killing machine. Zuroff's family were originally from Lithuania.

In *Come to This Court and Cry: How the Holocaust Ends* (Bloomsbury, 2022), Linda Kinstler tells the story of discovering her grandfather was subject to an ongoing criminal investigation in Latvia.

these murders turned German antisemitic policies into genocide and make the Holocaust sites in the region vital to understanding the Shoah and intensely moving to visit.

Before World War II, the Lithuanian capital, Vilnius, was one of Europe's most important Jewish cities, a centre for Jewish political, intellectual and religious thought. Although this culture was lost amid the destruction of the Holocaust, Vilnius is rapidly becoming a Jewish heritage hub and is the place to start a tour of the Baltic countries.

After World War II, parts of eastern Poland and the Baltic states were annexed by the Soviet Union. The Baltic states became independent countries in 1991, but it was only in 1998 when the states began the formal process of joining the European Union that any proper discussion of the Holocaust took place.

GETTING THERE AND AROUND

Budget airlines fly from London and many European cities to all three Baltic capitals, but Vilnius is undoubtably the main tourist hub with train connections to Warsaw and Riga and a regular bus service to Daugavpils. Buses and trains run between Tallinn and Riga. There are also ferries from Stockholm to Riga and Tallinn and from Helsinki to Tallinn.

The easiest way to see the Baltic states is by bus or car. Many of the memorial sites are very remote and there is no police presence. Only the Paneriai massacre site in Lithuania has a visitors' centre, which is only open in summer. There is often thick fog in autumn and winter and the forests turn to icy bogs when the snow melts. Solo travellers may feel more comfortable taking a taxi and asking the driver to wait. At grassroots level there is little knowledge of the Holocaust and many taxi drivers have not heard of the memorials, especially in rural areas.

ONLINE RESOURCES

ESTONIA
Estonian Jewish Museum w muuseum.jewish. ee/holocaust_en. Has a useful online database of documents & testimonies.

LATVIA
Latvian State Historical Archives w lvva-raduraksti.lv. Holds the 1897 Russian Empire census.
University of Latvia's Centre for Judaic Studies There are about 150 mass graves in Latvia. While some have new memorials, many are still marked by Soviet memorials that do not mention the specific suffering of the Jews. The University of Latvia's Centre for Judaic Studies has compiled a full list of memorials: w memorialplaces.lu.lv. They also have a database of Jews who lived in Latvia before World War II: w names.lu.lv.

LITHUANIA
Jewish Heritage Lithuania w jewish-heritage-lithuania.org. If you want to dig deeper into Jewish history in Lithuania, this website has a series of heritage maps & specialised routes.

HISTORY

Before the 1917 Russian Revolution, the Baltic states were part of the Russian Empire but only the Latgale region of Lativia and Lithuania was part of the Pale of Settlement, the Tsarist area of restricted Jewish settlement. In the interwar years, Estonia, Latvia and Lithuania were independent states with increasingly nationalist regimes. In 1939, as part of the Molotov–Ribbentrop Pact between Germany and the Soviet Union, eastern Poland and the Baltic states were occupied by Soviet forces. This is the seminal moment in historical memory in the region.

Antisemitism had always been prevalent but was now fed by the myth that Jews were supporters of communism, which was encouraged by Nazi-supported nationalist émigré groups based in Berlin. Some Jews welcomed the Soviet occupation for political reasons or in face of the danger of falling under German control, but Jews also suffered disproportionally during the Soviet occupation. Religious practice was banned, Hebrew outlawed (although Yiddish was tolerated) and Jewish businesses were nationalised. Thousands of Jews were among those deported to Stalin's Gulag.

Many Balts welcomed the German invasion in the false belief that the Germans would restore their independence. After the invasion, Latvia, Lithuania, Estonia and part of Belarus were united by the Germans into the Reichskommisariat Ostland administered from Riga. The Einsatzgruppen had an unambiguous order to murder the Jews and the Riga massacres in the late autumn of 1941 were, after Odesa and Kyiv, the largest in Europe. The overstretched German forces co-opted local collaborators in the mass murder of Jews. German propaganda fanned the flames of the Judeo-Bolshevik myth.

LITHUANIA

The question that is most commonly asked about the Holocaust is why Jews allowed themselves to be murdered. This question not only shifts the blame on to the victim but shows a misunderstanding of what actually happened during World War II. There were Jews who fought back, and resistance was far more widespread than is understood. Lithuania is a good place to discover that story.

The United States Holocaust Memorial Museum estimates that 90% of Lithuania's Jews were murdered during the Holocaust; some estimates go even higher. Most of those victims, some 190,000 people, were shot between June and December 1941.

Make time to read Grigory Kanovich's moving novel set during World War II, *Shtetl Love Song* (Noir Press, 2018); and watch *Izaokas* (2019), the first Lithuanian film to deal with the role Lithuanians played in the Holocaust.

GETTING AROUND Vilnius can be explored on foot. Take a train from Vilnius to the Paneriai Forest, which is just past the airport, 16km southwest of the city, and to visit Lithuania's second city, Kaunas. The site of the Jewish partisan bunker in the Rudnicki Forest, 19km south of Vilnius near the border with Belarus, no longer appears on maps. If you want to visit you will have to hire a driver – ask at the Jewish Cultural and Information Centre in Vilnius (page 67).

HISTORY Jews have lived in Lithuania for hundreds of years. Historically, the Grand Duchy of Lithuania extended over a vast territory and formed a union with Poland from the 14th century until the partitions of Poland in the late 18th century. At that time Lithuania came under Russian rule. It became an independent country after World War I, but Vilnius, known as Wilno in Polish, the present-day capital, was part of Poland in the interwar years.

Jews in Lithuania were Litvaks, who had a distinctive Yiddish dialect. Many Litvaks were proponents of the Haskalah, a Jewish cultural and educational movement that emerged in the late 18th century. The movement propagated secular education and the integration of Jews into Western culture, but in Lithuania they opposed spiritual assimilation. More than 80% of Lithuanian children, the highest proportion in the world, were enrolled in Jewish elementary schools.

Before the war, Lithuania's main towns were at least 30% Jewish and in small towns Jews made up 70–80% of the population.

When Hitler and Stalin divided Poland between them in 1939, Vilnius and Lithuania fell under Soviet control. The city then became part of Lithuania. After the German invasion of Poland in September 1939, refugees pushed Lithuania's Jewish population up to about 250,000. When Hitler invaded the Soviet Union on 22 June 1941, German forces took just five days to reach Vilnius and antisemitic violence began immediately.

VILNIUS The Lithuanian capital is like a stage set in which new actors play their roles after the previous ones have departed, never to return. Today, the city is overwhelmingly Lithuanian but until 1941, 45% of the population were Jews. Vilnius, known as Vilna in Russian and Yiddish, was one of the iconic Jewish cities of eastern Europe.

Famed as the home of the 18th-century rabbinic sage, the Vilna Gaon, Vilnius was the first base of YIVO (w yivo.org), the global centre for the study of Yiddish language and culture; the city was the birthplace in 1897 of the Socialist Jewish Bund movement but also an important Zionist centre.

In the interwar years, the Jews of Vilnius were engaged in a major debate about where their future lay.

⌂ **Where to stay and eat** The stylish **Rooma Apartments** (Aušros Vartų gatvė 11; w rooma-apartments.business.site; €€) in the Old Town are within walking distance of the Holocaust sites. Buy local produce in the nearby **Halės Market**. Vilnius claims to be the birthplace of the bagel. Taste them at **Beigeli Krautuvelle** (Pylimo 4; K; €) in the Lithuanian Jewish Community headquarters (w lzb.lt).

History In the autumn of 1941, two ghettos were set up in Vilnius. The Little Ghetto, which held 11,000 people, existed for a month before it was liquidated in October 1941.

About 29,000 Jews were held in the Great Ghetto, where there was an important underground armed resistance, the United Partisan Organisation (FPO; Fareinikte Partizaner Organizacie). At its inaugural meeting, 24-year-old Abba Kovner delivered his famous speech, calling on the audience: 'Let us not go to the slaughter like sheep. We are not strong, but the butchers can be answered in only one way: Self-defence.' Kovner and members of the unit fled into the forests when the ghetto was eventually liquidated in September 1943 and fought as a partisan unit.

Kovner was convinced that there was no future for the Jews in Europe and spent hours after the liberation in July 1944 pouring over maps, planning to lead the survivors to the Palestine Mandate. The Jewish Soviet journalist Ilya Ehrenburg warned Kovner that there was no future for Zionists in the Soviet Union and that he would be in danger if he stayed. Kovner was forced to flee to Poland in the late summer of 1944. He and his fellow partisans helped to create an escape route for the survivors who chose to follow him.

Lists of the survivors' names were drawn up at the Choral Synagogue, and at the Jewish Committee office on Gedimino Prospeckt (above the present-day McDonald's at No. 15), where there was a wall where people could write their names and leave messages. Testimonies were taken down according to a set questionnaire with the intention that they would be used at future trials.

The Germans appropriated the Strašūnas Library's rare collections to place them in an Institute for the Investigation of the Jewish Question. Not sufficiently versed in Jewish culture to know what was of value, they recruited a group of intellectuals to sort through the material.

Dubbed 'The Paper Brigade' by ghetto inmates, they risked their lives to save rare books and manuscripts, hiding them in at least ten secret caches. After the war, surviving members of the brigade retrieved much of their treasure and immediately set up a museum in the former ghetto library. During the Soviet era, the collection was smuggled out of Lithuania and taken to YIVO's new headquarters in New York.

Find out more in David E Fishman's The Book Smugglers: Partisans, Poets, and the Race to Save Jewish Treasures from the Nazis *(ForeEdge, 2018).*

What to see The entrance to the former **Little Ghetto** was located at the beginning of Stiklių gatve to the right if facing Vilnius Town Hall, where there is a map and memorial plaque. The area was the 16th-century Jewish Quarter and has been carefully restored. The buildings were connected by a network of courtyards, now home to restaurants and shops.

The former **Great Synagogue** was on Žydų gatve. Take the second left turn on Stiklių gatve. Next to it stood the famous Strašūnas Library. The complex was damaged in World War II, though not irrevocably, yet it was nevertheless demolished in the 1950s. An abandoned kindergarten now stands on the spot, but the foundations of the synagogue remain – when it was originally built in 1630–33, in order to comply with restrictions on the height of synagogues, the main part of the building was below street level. Important archaeological finds have prompted the local authorities to plan a restoration of the site which should be completed by 2026.

From Žydų gatve, walk across Vokiečiu gatve into the former **Great Ghetto**. Vokiečiu ran between the two ghettos. Now far wider than originally laid out, this was the heart of the Jewish Quarter and once bustled with shoppers and peddlers.

Stop at the **Jewish Culture and Information Centre** (Žydų Kultūros Ir Informacijos Centras; Mėsinių 3a/5; ⊕ noon–18.00 Mon–Fri, noon–16.00 Sat) to pick up a map of Jewish Vilnius. In the basement there is a fascinating recreation of a malina, a hiding place. Outside there are information panels, as well as an example of the 'Walls That Remember' graffiti art initiative and one of the city's talking statues. Use the QR code you'll find there to activate it.

The **Judenrat** was located at Rūdninku 8, a few minutes' walk away. The entrance to the Great Ghetto was at No. 18, where there is a memorial plaque. After the liquidation of the Great Ghetto in September 1943, around 1,250 Jews were transferred to a **labour lamp** on Subačiaus gatve (Bldgs 47 & 49), 2km east of the city centre. There is a memorial between the two buildings and an information plaque. The former **library** on Žemaitijos gatve was the meeting place of the underground armed resistance organisation. After the liberation, survivors set up a museum of Jewish artefacts here (see above) – but the Soviet authorities closed it in 1949. Currently derelict, the building is due to be turned into a Holocaust museum but work has yet to start.

It is a short walk to the **Choral Synagogue** (Choralinė Sinagoga; Pylimo g. 39; w jewishheritage-lithuania.org; ⊕ 10.00–15.00 Mon–Fri; €6; ring the bell on the gate for admission), where the partisan leader Abba Kovner made his famous rousing speech after the liberation at Jewish New Year 1944. Do not miss the fascinating old matzo-making machine on display in the women's gallery.

Vilna Gaon Museum of Jewish History (Vilniaus Gaono Žydu Istorijos Muziejus; w jmuseum.lt) The Vilna Gaon Museum of Jewish History covers a number of important museums. The closest to the Choral Synagogue is the **Samuel Bak Museum** in the Tolerance Centre (Tolerancijos Centras; Naugarduko g. 10/2; ⊕ 10.00–18.00 Tue–Fri, 11.00–18.00 Sat–Sun; €6) in the former Yiddish theatre. Much of the museum is dedicated to the artist Samuel Bak, but it also hosts an extremely moving exhibition about children who were saved during the Holocaust. A child's singing guides visitors to a memorial for the murdered Jewish children of Lithuania. Visitors are asked to place a stone, in the Jewish tradition, on the memorial.

The new **Museum of Culture and Identity of Lithuanian Jews** (Lietuvos Žydų Kultūros Ir Tapatybės Muziejus; Pylimo g. 4A; w jmuseum.lt/en/museum-of-culture-and-identity-of-lithuanian-jews; ⊕ 10.00–18.00 Tue–Fri, 11.00–18.00 Sat–Sun; €6) is a short walk north along Pylimo in the Lithuanian Jewish Community headquarters in the former Tarbut School. It also exhibits the work of Rafael Chvoleso (1913–2002) in the separately named **Rafaelio Chvoleso Muziejus** and other Jewish cultural figures. It tells the story of Jewish life in Lithuania, notably of Jewish secular schooling.

The **Holocaust Exhibition** (Holokausto Ekspuzicija; Pamėnkalnio str. 12; w jmuseum.lt/en/holocaust-exhibition; ⊕ 10.00–18.00 Tue–Fri, 11.00–18.00 Sat–Sun; €6) is in a wooden building known as the Green House. It is a short walk from the Museum of Culture and Identity of Lithuanian Jews. The museum is rather old-fashioned but is due to be replaced by the new museum in the former ghetto library (page 67).

Museum of Occupations and Freedom Fights (Okupacijų ir Laisvės Kovų Muziejus; Auku 2; w genocid.lt/muziejus; ⊕ 10.00–18.00 Wed–Sat, 10.00–17.00 Sun; €6) Ten minutes' walk from the Green House, the former district court building was the Gestapo HQ during the German occupation, after which it was used by the Soviet secret police. It is now a museum which looks at the Soviet period and the Lithuanian nationalist partisans who fought against the Soviets. The walls of the building are engraved with their names, among them some of those responsible for murders during the Holocaust, which are clearly visible on the Gedimo Prospeckt side of the building. Gedimo Prospeckt, the city's main shopping street, leads back to Vilnius Cathedral, the heart of the city and located 15 minutes on foot north of the Town Hall.

Further afield
Paneriai Forest Paneriai (Ponar in Yiddish) was and still is popular with day-trippers from Vilnius hunting berries and mushrooms, but it is also the site of one of the Shoah's horrific killing fields, which are now a memorial, the **Paneriu Memorialas** (Agrastu g. 17; w jmuseum.lt/lt/paneriu-memorialas-2; ⊕ 24hrs; free). It is an extremely atmospheric place, where trains clank by, eerily hidden by the trees in the dank forest.

During the Soviet occupation, the Red Army dug several huge round pits in which to store aircraft fuel outside the village of Aukštieji Paneriai, 14km southwest of Vilnius. The Germans used them as ready-made death pits. They hold the remains of 75,000 people, mostly Jews but also Soviet prisoners of war and Poles murdered by the Germans and Lithuanian collaborators between 1941 and 1943. The main chronicler of the murders was Polish journalist Kazimierz Sakowicz, who lived nearby and buried the records he kept. He was killed in 1944 and his diary only discovered in 1952. It was published in English as *Ponary Diary, 1941–1943: A Bystander's Account of a Mass Murder* (Yale University Press, 2006).

There are death pits across mile upon mile of eastern Europe, but Paneriai is one of the most important because of the eyewitness accounts that partisan leader Abba Kovner heard of the massacre, which not only convinced him that armed resistance was the only way forward, but sowed the seeds in his mind that there was no future for any Jews in Europe.

In June 1945, survivors erected a monument here which was replaced in 1952 with a simple obelisk adorned with a red star and which commemorated victims of fascism. The events are well documented in the Visitors Centre (⊕ 09.00–17.00 Tue–Wed, 09.00–16.00 Fri & Sun summer only unless by prior appt; donation requested).

Rudnicki Forest After the liquidation of the Vilnius Ghetto in 1943, Abba Kovner and his partisans hid out deep in the Rudnicki Forest, south of Vilnius near the border with modern-day Belarus. The partisans, because they had fought with the Red Army, were heroes in Soviet times, and every Soviet schoolchild visited the old partisan bunkers. Since the present Lithuanian government does not celebrate Soviet heroes, Kovner's hideout no longer appears on maps. If you decide to visit, pack mosquito repellent as the forest is infested.

KAUNAS Lithuania's second city is 103km northwest of Vilnius. Known in Yiddish as Kovne, or Kovno in Polish, it was an important centre of Jewish culture. In the interwar period the city was the capital of independent Lithuania. Its 32,000 Jews made up a quarter of the population.

Where to stay and eat In Kaunas the best budget accommodation option is the **Ibis** (Vytatuto pr. 28; w ibis.accor.com; €), which is centrally located near the bus station. Alternatively, **Moxy Kaunas Center** (Maironio g. 19; w marriot.com; €€) close to the university is a modern, vibrant hotel with a cocktail bar. Kaunas's best bakery is **Motiejaus Kepyklėlė** (Vilniaus gatvė 7; ⨍; ⊕ 08.00–18.00 Mon–Thu & Sat, 06.00–18.00 Fri, 09.00–18.00 Sun; €) and a good option for breakfast or a light lunch.

History The Germans entered Kaunas on 24 June 1941. A few days later, on 27 June, violence broke out at the Lietūkis Garage (Miško 11), where several dozen Jews were beaten to death by Lithuanians with crowbars. There is now a memorial.

Over 30,000 people were detained in the Kovno Ghetto in July and August 1941. From 1942 births were not permitted in the ghetto and pregnant women faced death. Despite this, a number of babies were smuggled out of the ghetto in potato sacks and hidden in non-Jewish homes. On 27–28 March 1944, some 1,600 children aged 12 and under were murdered.

When the ghetto was liquidated in July 1944, survivors were taken to Stutthof, where women and children were ordered off the train. The men were then transferred to subcamps of Dachau near Landsberg-am-Lech, where they would later play an important role in the Zionist revival in the displaced persons camps.

FANIA BRANTSOVSKAYA'S STORY

In the Ghetto Survivor's Office at the Jewish Centre in Vilnius, Fania Brantsovskaya takes a photograph of her family out of a small, plastic H&M bag designed for shoppers buying hair clips and socks. There are 16 people pictured in the sepia-toned photo, which was sent to relatives who had emigrated to the Palestine Mandate before the war, who finally managed to give it to her in 1990.

Next to 17-year-old Fania is her sister Riva, a delicate child, on whose lap sits a cousin with pigtails called Hinda. Brantsovskaya's father died in the Klooga concentration camp in Estonia; her mother was one of a group of women drowned in the Baltic Sea; Riva was murdered at Stutthof concentration camp; Hinda was shot at Paneriai.

During the war, Brantsovskaya was a member of Abba Kovner's partisan unit. 'Us girls would go to the labour camps and bring people to the partisans. We brought news to the partisans and engaged in sabotage,' she says. Food was often taken by force from peasants in the villages and Brantsovskaya has, since independence, been on a list of those that the Lithuanian government have considered prosecuting for war crimes. Lithuanian nationalists regard the Jewish partisans as communist collaborators because they fought alongside the Soviets.

In July 1944, fighting with the Red Army towards Vilnius, Brantsovskaya remembers the bodies of dead Soviet and German soldiers scattered along the road; their boots had all been stolen by the peasants.

Vilnius was liberated on 13 July 1944. Just 200 Jews remained in hiding. Brantsovskaya says that, when she saw a woman with a Jewish face, she would go up and kiss her. The caretaker of the building where her family had lived gave her photographs, which she had salvaged from their apartment. Brantsovskaya went around the city day after day with the pictures, asking if anyone had seen her family.

'One day I met a woman who told me Riva had survived, so every day I went to meet the trains. I had a ration card for a winter coat. I did not trade it in but waited to buy it for my sister. But a month later I met the woman again and this time she told me she had made a mistake and my sister was dead. It was terrible – it was the second time I lost my sister. I cried so much.'

Brantsovskaya fell in love with a fellow communist partisan and their marriage, on 27 July 1944, was one of the first to be celebrated after the liberation. They were both allocated jobs in the government ministries. She is proud that they attended the victory parade in Moscow's Red Square in May 1945, but lets her guard down when she says, 'We waited and hoped that our relatives would come. That is why we stayed in Vilnius.' After that the walls went up and for decades it was too late to leave, even if she had wanted to.

What to see Polish Jews fled to Lithuania after the German invasion in 1939. Thanks to visas issued by the Japanese diplomat Chiune Sugihara, the lives of 6,000 Jews were saved in the summer of 1940. Sugihara worked with the Dutch consul Jan Zwartendijk, who issued visas to the Dutch colony of Curaçao. Sugihara provided the transit visas. The **Sugihara House** (Sugiharos Muziejus; Vaižganto g. 30; w sugiharahouse.com; ⊕ Apr–Oct 10.00–17.00 Mon-Fri, 11.00–16.00 Sat–Sun, Nov–Mar 11.00–15.00 daily; €6), the museum in Sugihara's former home, tells the story. It also functions as a research centre.

The **Choral Synagogue** (Choralinė Sinagoga; Ožeškienės g. 13; ☎370 614 03100; ⊕ by appt only) is still a working synagogue. After the liberation, lists of survivors were compiled here. *The Children's Torah*, a memorial for the Jewish children killed in Lithuania during the war, was sculpted by Robertas Antinis.

The city's defensive fortifications built during the Russian Empire were transformed by the Germans into a place of mass murder. More than 50,000 people, mostly Jews, were murdered in mass shootings at the Ninth Fort, now the **Kaunas IX Fort Museum** (Kauno IX Forto Muziejus; Žemaičiu pl. 75; w 9fortomuziejus.lt; ⊕ Apr–Oct 10.00–18.00 Tue–Sun, Nov–Mar 10.00–17.00 Wed–Sun; €6). The most striking site inside the fort is graffiti on the walls made by prisoners brought from the Drancy transit camp in France. Names and dates are followed by the words 'Nous sommes 900 français' (We are 900 French). Details on the convoy from Drancy can be found on w convoi73.org. The museum, which opened in 1958, also provides insight into life in the ghetto. Buses to the fort on the outskirts of the city run from the centre. The **Kaunas Ghetto monument** is a small stele on Kauno geto vartai located on the site of the former ghetto gates. It has a map of the ghetto.

Further afield

Šeduva The architects of Warsaw's award-winning POLIN Museum of the History of Polish Jews (page 254) have designed a state-of-the-art Jewish museum outside the former shtetl of Šeduva, 107km north of Kaunas. Jews once made up half of the population of Šeduva but not a single Jew lives there today. Due to open in 2025, the privately funded **Lost Shtetl Museum** (w lostshtetl.lt) will tell the story of Lithuania's shtetl towns, a way of life that ended with the Holocaust.

LATVIA

The Holocaust in Latvia unfurled at such a pace that half of Latvia's Jewish community had been murdered before the creation of the ghetto in Riga, the capital, in October 1941. In a key turning point in the Holocaust, thousands of Jews from the Reich were then deported to the city.

GETTING AROUND Central Riga can be explored on foot. The simplest way to visit the memorials is by taxi. Alternatively, to visit the former ghetto in the southern suburbs, take bus 50 from Merķeļa iela to Krustpils iela. To see the former Kaiserwald labour camp, take tram 11 from the Opera to Brāļu kapi, then bus 48 to Saules dārzs. For the Jungfernhof concentration camp and the Rumbula Forest, take a bus from the bus station. For Salaspils take a train.

There are regular trains from Riga to Daugavpils and buses to Liepāja.

HISTORY Jews have lived in Latvia since the 16th century. Their diverse community was made up of Baltic Jews, Litvaks and Courlanders. Those in Riga and western Latvia were German-speaking and came from East Prussia, while in eastern Latgale they were Yiddish-speaking and migrated from western Ukraine. Granted equal rights in the 1920s their freedoms were eroded under the nationalist dictatorship from 1934.

After Germany's invasion of the Soviet Union many Jews fled to Russia but at least 70,000 remained on Latvian soil. The invasion forces were followed by mobile killing units, which murdered most of Latvia's Jews with the help of local collaborators. A Latvian SS legion was formed in 1943.

The 1935 census identified 3,839 Roma and Sinti living in Latvia, the largest community in the Baltic states. After the German invasion, the SS and the German military murdered Roma who fell into their hands but they did not seek them out, as was the case with Jews. When the mobile killing units were transformed into fixed security police units, systematic murder of Roma, with support from local civilian authorities, began. At least half of Latvia's Roma and Sinti were killed.

In Estonia, more than 90% of the Roma population, between 750 and 850 people, were murdered in mass shootings that began in October 1942. Figures for Lithuania are less precise but it is believed the vast majority of Lithuania's Roma were murdered. In addition, in 1944, 2,000–3,000 Roma from Lithuania and Belarus were deported to Auschwitz.

RIGA Jewish life in Latvia centred on the capital. In 1939, some 40,000 Jews (10% of the city's population) lived in Riga, where they played a major part in the city's economic and cultural life. Jews from Russia relocated here during the Soviet period, during which Riga was a hub of the refusenik dissident movement. Today, Riga has a small Jewish population of about 7,500 people.

Where to stay and eat Riga's old town with its pretty cobbled streets and impressive Art Nouveau buildings is the only part of the city that caters to tourists. **Neiburgs Hotel** (Jauniela 25/27; w neiburgs.com; €€) is a boutique aparthotel with a good restaurant (€€€). Riga's **Central Market** is the place to buy local cheeses – eat them with Latvia's famous black bread.

Trips to Liepāja and Daugavpils require an overnight. In **Liepāja** stay at the Promenade Hotel (Veca Ostmala 40; w promenadehotel.lv; €), which has a restaurant (€€), and in **Daugavpils** at the sparklingly clean Homelike Hotel (Mihoelesa iela 66; w homelikehotel.lv; €).

History When German troops arrived in Riga on 1 July 1941, many Jewish men were immediately shot. In October 1941, the Riga Ghetto was set up in the southern suburb of Latgale and enclosed with a barbed wire fence. On 29 November residents were told they were being moved to a new ghetto, but instead were taken on foot to the Rumbula Forest, 6km away, where they were shot in a two-day massacre that began the following day.

The ghetto was then used to house German and Austrian Jews. When they arrived in the ghetto the rooms were covered in blood from the round-up and littered with the bodies of more than 2,000 people who had been killed or had committed suicide. In the months that followed, thousands of newcomers were massacred in a hail of bullets in the forests that surround the city. There was a considerable Jewish resistance, but by the time the Red Army arrived in Riga in October 1944 nearly all of the city's Jews had been murdered by the occupying German forces and local collaborators.

What to see In the city centre, start at the **Museum of the Occupation of Latvia** (Latvijas Okupācijas Muzejs; Latviešu strēlnieku laukums 1; w okupacijasmuzejs.lv; ⊕ 10.00–18.00 Sat–Wed; €5). Opened in 2021, it equates the Soviet occupation with the Holocaust with the emphasis on the communist period. That said, it is worth a visit to understand how many Latvians regard the history of the 20th century.

Then, get a taste of pre-war Jewish life in Riga at the beautiful Art Nouveau **Peitav Synagogue** (Sinagoga Peitav; Peitav iela 6–8; w jews.lv/en/riga-synagogue; ☉ 10.00–17.00 Sun–Fri; €5), built in 1905. It is the centre of the Jewish community and was saved from destruction by the intervention of a local priest. The building was then used as a warehouse by the German authorities.

Across town, the Riga Jewish Community centre has a small, old-fashioned museum founded by survivors in 1989, the **Museum of the Jews of Latvia** (Muzejs Ebreji Latvijā; Skolas iela 6; w ebrejumuzejs.lv; ☉ 11.00–17.00 Sun–Thu, also Fri in summer; free), which tells the story of Latvia's Jews.

The main Holocaust sites are southeast of the station. And there are three mass killing sites in Riga's suburbs. All three are, despite their urban setting, relatively unknown and remote.

Riga Ghetto and Latvian Holocaust Museum (Rīgas Geto un Latvijas Holokausta Muzejs; Maskavas iela 14a; w rgm.lv; ☉ 10.00–18.00 Sun–Thu, 10.00–14.00 Fri; suggested donation €5)

Close to the Central Market, this privately funded museum opened in 2010. It features two memorial walls with the names of the murdered Latvian and foreign Jews. Among the exhibits is an unusual tiny 19th-century house which once stood in the former ghetto. It was originally built for a small family, but in the ghetto period it housed 30 people. On the first floor of the house there is a fascinating recreation of living quarters in the ghetto, and on the ground floor models of synagogues destroyed in the Holocaust. In the courtyard the copper tree remembers Latvians who saved Jews.

Great Choral Synagogue (Dzirnavu iela 124)

Ten minutes' walk from the museum are the ruins of the Great Choral Synagogue. Here, hundreds of Jews were locked inside the building on 4 July 1941 before it was burned to the ground by local collaborators. Jews were also burned alive in the synagogue at Stabu 63, where a plaque recalls the event.

Under communism, the Great Choral Synagogue site was for years a rubbish dump, but since 1988 it has been the city's main Holocaust memorial (☉ 24hrs). There is a ceremony every year on the anniversary.

The ruins are overshadowed by another memorial, dedicated to Latvians who saved Jews during the war and dominated by the name of Žana Lipkes, a former docker.

Žanis Lipke Memorial (Žana Lipkes Memoriāls; Mazais Balasta dambis 9; w lipke.lv; ☉ noon–18.00 Tue, Wed & Fri, noon–20.00 Thu, 10.00–16.00 Sat; donation requested)

Despite the historical distortion created by giant monuments like the one by the Great Choral Synagogue, precisely because so few people helped the Jews in Latvia, it is worth visiting the Žanis Lipke Memorial, across the Daugava River. The modern, atmospheric museum is dedicated to Lipke and has a recreation of the bunker where he hid 55 Jews in his back garden. The memorial is located next to his former home, where his descendants still live, and was paid for by the Jewish community.

The ghetto

The Riga Ghetto was in the then poor and still run-down suburb of Maskavas Forštate. Many of the original buildings, many wooden, still stand, notably on Ludzaz iela, the ghetto's main street. The Riga Ghetto Council was situated in the former Jewish school building at Lāčplēša 141, a short walk from the former Choral synagogue. The dead were buried in the Old Jewish Cemetery on Virsaišu, which was turned into a park in 1960. In 2007, a memorial stone was unveiled on the junction of Ebreju and Lïksnas. The first major selection of Reich Jews took place outside Mazā Kalna 2, on 5 February 1942.

Šķirotava railway station Deportation trains from Germany and Austria arrived at Šķirotava railway station not far from the ghetto. The deportees were forced to buy their train tickets and told that they were to be resettled on arrival at their destination. Approximately 2,000 sick and elderly Jews were instead murdered at the station and are buried in three large mass graves now covered by the railway tracks. The station was also used by the Soviets for deportations to Siberia, in 1941 and 1949, which are commemorated by a memorial.

Another memorial is located just north of Šķirotava station, a short walk off Meirānu iela. It remembers the 13,000 people who were murdered in March 1942 and during the summer of 1944, in **Dreiliņi Forest** in the northeast of the city, among them Jews deported to Riga and prisoners from Kaiserwald.

Rumbula Forest The most significant Holocaust memorial in Latvia is at Maskavas iela 47 in what remains of the Rumbula Forest, 12km south of the centre. The site of one of the biggest mass shootings of the Holocaust, its significance takes some believing as it is located on what is now the edge of the A6/E22 dual carriageway and surrounded by industrial units. The memorial in the shape of a menorah stands on the site of five mass graves.

On 29–30 November and 8 December 1941, approximately 25,000 Jews were murdered here by Germans and local collaborators in pits that were so vast the machine guns had to be positioned inside them. Only three people survived the massacre. First to be shot were the German Jews who had arrived at Šķirotava Station. The column of Jews from Riga arrived on foot the following morning. The blood-soaked clothes and possessions of the victims were sorted and sold to local residents. A memorial ceremony is held here every November.

Rumbula became an important protest site during the Soviet period, when a makeshift memorial, later taken down by the authorities, was erected. Eventually, an official black stone monument was put up to 'victims of fascism', though it did not mention that the victims were Jewish. Nevertheless, it was a considerable victory for the Jewish community.

Biķernieku Forest There are 55 mass graves in Biķernieku Forest east of Riga city centre. This is where most of the Reich Jews were murdered. A monument, located on the forested southern side of Biķernieku iela, was unveiled in 2001.

Jewish men from Riga were the first to be murdered here in July 1941. So far, 31,000 victims, among them Latvian Jews, 12,000 Jews from Germany, Austria and Czechoslovakia, Soviet prisoners of war and political prisoners have been identified. In 1943, the Germans dug up and burned some of the corpses to hide the evidence. Maintenance of the memorial, which has been vandalised several times, is paid for primarily by the German government.

Concentration camps There were three concentration camps in or around Riga. In 1943, the **Kaiserwald Labour Camp** was set up in Mežaparks, a suburb in the north of the city. About 12,000 surviving Latvian Jews, as well as those from Czechoslovakia, Germany and the Vilnius Ghetto, were held here. When the camp was dismantled in September 1944, prisoners were transferred to camps in Poland and Germany. During the Soviet era, a residential neighbourhood was built on the site. A monument was erected at Meža prospekts 11 in 2005.

A lush park stands on the site of **Jungfernhof concentration camp**, in Mazjumpravas muiža, 4km south of Riga centre. From the winter of 1941, about 4,000 Jews were imprisoned here. There are plans to mark the site with a series of memorials designed by the Massachusetts-based public art expert Karen Frostig, whose grandparents were deported from Vienna to Latvia in 1942. There is an online memorial at w lockerofmemory.com.

Just outside Salaspils, 10km southwest of Rumbula, the **Salaspils Memorial's** (Salaspils Memoriāls; w salaspilsmemorials.lv; ⊕ Apr–Oct 10.00–17.00 daily, Nov–Mar 10.00–15.00 daily; free) giant statues and museum commemorate the Kurtenhof concentration camp. Kurtenhof was the German name for Salaspils. The camp was built in late 1941 by Jewish prisoners deported from Austria, Czechoslovakia and Germany. At least a thousand Jews were transported from the Riga Ghetto to join the construction team in January 1942. The camp went on to hold 23,000 political prisoners and Baltic dissidents, among them many children. The park opened in 1967.

Further afield

Liepāja Liepāja, also known as Libau in German, 212km southwest of Riga, was a major port when Latvia was part of the Russian Empire and was later home to the Soviet Baltic Fleet. The city's Jewish community played an important role in its economic life.

In June 1941, about 6,500 Jews remained in Liepāja, which then became a German naval base. The synagogue that once stood at 11 Kuršu iela was demolished. Jews, mostly men, were shot at the lighthouse and fish-processing factory in the **harbour**, both of which are now marked with plaques, and in **Raina Park** north of the canal, where there is a small memorial. There is also a memorial wall in the **Jewish Cemetery** on Cenkones iela in the south of the city. It took decades of research to discover the 6,423 names of Liepāja's Jewish victims. The former ghetto is marked by a boulder in a yard between Kongu 29 and 31/33.

The most moving Holocaust memorial in the Baltics is 15km north of Liepāja on the **Šķēde Dunes**, a remote, flawless, white-sand beach surrounded by pine forests. In the freezing cold winter, over 15–17 December, 2,749 Jews, mostly women and children and elderly men, were stripped and shot at the edge of pits dug into the sand. In February 1942 a further 150 Jews were shot on the dunes. The **Memorial to Liepāja Jews – Victims of the Holocaust** (Memoriāls Liepājas Ebrejiem-Holokausta; ⊕ 24hrs daily) by sculptor Raimonds Gabaliņš was unveiled in 2005. (Sadly it is next to a water treatment plant.) It is laid out in the shape of a menorah. The **Alley of the Righteous Among the Nations** pays tribute to 26 non-Jews who helped save Jewish lives, among them Roberts and Johanna Seduls, who hid 11 Jews for nearly two years in a cleverly disguised hideout in the basement of their home on Tirgoņu iela 22.

The memorial is financed by the **Liepāja Jewish Heritage** (w liepajajewishheritage. lv) foundation. The website has a useful map of the ghetto and a full list of memorials in the area.

Daugavpils Also known as Dvinsk, Daugavpils is Latvia's second largest city and is located 226km southeast of Riga. Its pre-war Jewish community numbered just over 11,000, a third of the city's population. More than 55,000 Jews lived here in 1913. Today it is the place to understand how the legacy of the Soviet era was a poisoned chalice for its surviving Jewish community.

There is a small museum in the **Daugavpils Synagogue** (Cietokšņa iela 38; ☏371 2954 8760; ⊕ by appt; donation requested) which was renovated by the family of

Daugavpils' most famous son, the artist Mark Rothko. Today Josif Rothko, who runs the museum, is the youngest member of its 25-strong congregation; though they have no rabbi and understand hardly any of the Hebrew prayers as religious practice was supressed under communism. Rothko, the son of Holocaust survivors who returned to Daugavpils, is nevertheless a mine of information. 'The clever ones didn't come back,' he jokes. Rothko has written a guidebook to Jewish Latgale which is available in the museum.

The Germans set up a ghetto, which was more like an improvised prison, in the bridgehead **fortress** (Daugavas iela 38; ⊕ 24hrs daily; free) on the left bank of the Daugava River opposite the main citadel. Surrounded by a wall and moat, it had been badly damaged in the fighting in June 1941. There is a memorial on the southeastern side of the fortress on Lielā iela, which remains a prison.

Most of the Jews held here were shot near the village of Mežciems in the **Poguļanka Forest** by German and Latvian police and militia. In August 1941 children were buried alive here, and the victims' bodies were later burned to hide the evidence. Massacres like this were a crucial step on the road to genocide. There is a memorial at Ceriņu ilea 13 off the P67 north of the city.

ESTONIA

In 1941, Estonia had a small Jewish population of less than 5,000. Nevertheless, the country played an important role in the Holocaust as the Nazis established a series of labour camps here to which Jews were deported from as far away as France.

GETTING AROUND To visit the former Klooga concentration camp, 45km west of the capital, take a train from Tallinn to Klooga-Aedlinn. Visiting the mass graves at Kalevi-Liiva, 31km east of Tallinn, is easiest by car; but it is possible to take a train and then a bus from the capital. The dunes are on Route 264, a track about 450m off Route 263, north of the village of Ruu.

HISTORY The dogged resistance of the Red Army to defend the road to Leningrad (now St Petersburg), gave most of the Jewish community time to escape into Russia. When the Germans arrived, about 1,000 Jews remained, mostly the elderly and the sick, who were immediately murdered by German forces. Even before the Wannsee Conference in January 1942, Estonia was declared *judenfrei* – free of Jews. Only 12 of those Jews who remained in the country survived the war.

An estimated 12,500 Jews were deported to Estonia from other parts of occupied Europe to be shot or to work as forced labourers. Between 7,000 and 8,000 died here. As the Red Army advanced, more than 4,600 were taken to camps in other countries, where most of them perished. Estonian militia took part in running the camps and carrying out mass murder.

TALLINN Jews were given permission to settle in Tallinn only in 1865. They were a small community and there was little antisemitism.

🏠 **Where to stay and eat** The **Swissôtel** (Tornimae Street 3; w swissotel.com; €€) has great views across the city, an indoor swimming pool and is Jewish-observant-friendly. The trendy place to eat is in the **old factories** in Kalamaja and Kopli.

What to see Tallinn can be explored easily on foot. Visit the **Estonian Jewish Museum** (Eesti Juudi Muuseum; Karu 16; w museum.jewish.ee; ⊕ 11.00–17.00

Mon–Thu, 11.00–15.00 Sun; donation requested; visitors must register before their visit) next to the modern synagogue for an overview of Jewish life. In 2022, a memorial to the murdered Jews of Estonia was unveiled in the **Liiva Cemetery** (Kalmistu tee 34; ⊕ 09.00–16.00 Mon–Fri; free) in the south of the city, where between 300 and 600 Estonian Jews are buried in mass graves.

The **Patarei Prison Site** (Kalaranna 28; w patareiprison.org) in a former sea fortress was used as an execution site. In 1941, 207 Jewish Estonian men were killed here. There are memorials to the French Jews brought to the prison via the Ninth Fort in Kaunas. A new museum, the International Museum for the Victims of Communism, is due to open on the site in 2026.

Further afield

Klooga Near the beautiful Lake Klooga and Lahepere Bay, **Klooga Concentration Camp and Holocaust Memorial Site** (Klooga Koonduslaager Ja Holokausti Memoriaal; Klooga alevik 3, Lääne-Harju vald, Harju maakond; w klooga. nazismvictims.ee; ⊕ 24hrs daily; free) marks the location of a brutal forced labour camp set up by the Germans in 1943. It held primarily survivors of the Vilnius Ghetto in Lithuania, who formed a resistance movement. They managed to acquire weapons and had planned an uprising but were taken by surprise by the liquidation of the camp on 19 September 1944, as the Red Army drew near. Nearly 2,400 Jews and 100 Soviet prisoners of war were then executed in the forest surrounding the camp by the Germans and Estonian collaborators. The bodies were burned on pyres, which were still smouldering when the Soviet troops arrived on 28 September. Only 82 prisoners managed to escape. The SS destroyed the camp before retreating and the area is now covered in forest. Three monuments dating from 1951, 1994 and 2005, located along a dirt track road that runs north of Klooga-Aedlinn railway station, commemorate the victims.

Kalevi-Liiva The sand dunes on the Baltic Coast east of Tallinn were the main killing grounds in Estonia. An estimated 6,000 Jewish and Roma were shot here by German forces and Estonian collaborators. Many of the victims were German and central European Jews. Commemorative ceremonies take place each year on 5 September. The small Jägala concentration camp was located nearby but is not marked by a memorial.

6

Belarus and Russia

World War II – known in Russia and Belarus as the Great Patriotic War and in which the Soviet Union lost an estimated 27 million people – is a linchpin of Russia's national identity, even though the territory Russia controls today no longer covers the entirety of the former Soviet Union. Belarus was one of the Soviet Union's founding constituent republics. In the decades that followed the collapse of the Soviet Union, Belarus found it difficult to find an identity free of its Soviet past.

Holocaust distortion began immediately after the end of World War II in the Soviet Union, where the unique suffering of Jews was downplayed and rarely mentioned. Instead the emphasis was placed on the collective suffering of all Soviet citizens. Since the fall of communism, this trend has continued. Nevertheless, there is an increasing amount to see in Belarus.

GETTING THERE AND AROUND

Owing to the current political situation and ongoing war in Ukraine, it is necessary to check the most up-to-date information on which border crossings are

> ### GOOD TO KNOW
>
> Although Russia was among the states of the United Nations which initiated the effort to establish an International Holocaust Remembrance Day, it has been party to Holocaust distortion. Significantly, neither Belarus nor Russia is part of the International Holocaust Remembrance Alliance (IHRA) since all members must have a democratic government.
>
> In 2014, Russia enacted a law that made it a criminal offence to glorify Nazism or to spread information contradictory to the government's official stance on the role played by the Soviet Union in World War II. This law contributes to the government's efforts in shaping public memory of the Holocaust. Furthermore, the Russian leader, Vladimir Putin, justified his invasion of Ukraine as a war against 'neo-Nazis' – despite Ukraine having a Jewish president, who lost relatives in the Holocaust, and who heads a Western-backed democratically elected government.
>
> The Law on the Genocide of the Belarusian People adopted in 2022 equates Jewish Holocaust victims with all victims of the German occupation of Belarus, subsuming the genocide into the wider narrative of World War II. Belarus is an authoritarian state, and the political situation has been further complicated by the government's support for Russia's 2022 attack on Ukraine.

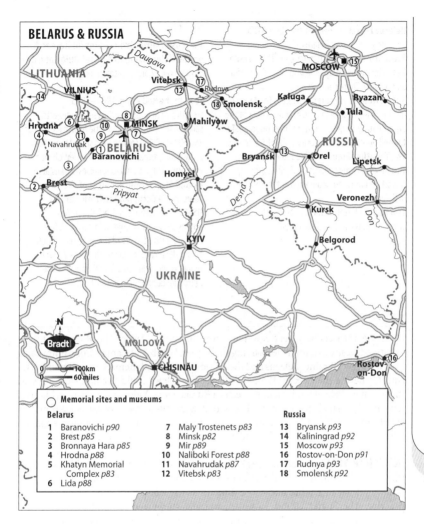

BELARUS & RUSSIA

○ **Memorial sites and museums**

Belarus

1 Baranovichi *p90*
2 Brest *p85*
3 Bronnaya Hara *p85*
4 Hrodna *p88*
5 Khatyn Memorial Complex *p83*
6 Lida *p88*
7 Maly Trostenets *p83*
8 Minsk *p82*
9 Mir *p89*
10 Naliboki Forest *p88*
11 Navahrudak *p87*
12 Vitebsk *p83*

Russia

13 Bryansk *p93*
14 Kaliningrad *p92*
15 Moscow *p93*
16 Rostov-on-Don *p91*
17 Rudnya *p93*
18 Smolensk *p92*

open. Normally, there are trains from Warsaw to Minsk and Moscow and good international connections by air.

Kaliningrad, a Russian exclave surrounded by Lithuania and Poland, is usually the easiest part of Russia to visit while on a trip to the Baltic states.

ONLINE RESOURCES

BELARUS

There are 3 useful **audio guides** to Navahrudak: 1 to the Jewish Resistance Museum (w izi. travel/en/b997-jewish-resistance-museum/en#af914fd4-1cea-4718-941d-7deb40660350); 1 to the memorial sites surrounding Navahrudak (w izi.travel/en/browse/73c4e1ff-1a80-40f9-82ff-298f80c58188); & another to Jewish

Navahrudak (w izi.travel/en/cf95-jewish-novogrudok/en#/browse/b232c694-c16b-4f2d-8da5-46625cc1256f/en).

Belarus Holocaust Memorials Project

w belarusmemorials.com. The goal of this charity is to place memorials on 500 massacre sites.

Belarus Travel w belarus-travel.com. Offers genealogical tours of Belarus.

Brest Stories w breststories.com. This website has an interactive map of Jewish Brest & a useful audio guide. There's also an app.

Shtetl Routes w shtetlroutes.eu. The Museum of Jewish Resistance in Navahrudak is part of the Shtetl Routes project, a tourist-orientated guide to the borderlands of Belarus, Poland & Ukraine.

The Together Plan w thetogetherplan.com. This UK charity runs educational youth projects & works on the memorialisation of the Holocaust in Belarus.

Tsal Kaplun Foundation w tkfshtetl.org. Shtetl stories from the former Soviet Union.

RUSSIA

The **Moshe Mirilashvili Center for Research on the Holocaust in the Soviet Union** at Yad Vashem runs 2 online research projects:

Jews in the Red Army, 1941–1945

w yadvashem.org/research/research-projects/ soldiers. This project explores the Jewish identity of 350,000–500,000 soldiers who served in the Red Army during World War II, as well as Jewish women who were Red Army doctors, nurses & translators.

Untold Stories: Murder Sites of the Jews in the Occupied Territories of the USSR w collections.yadvashem.org/en/ untold-stories. This project aims to provide a comprehensive picture of the more than 2,600 killing sites scattered across the former Soviet Union, where more than 2 million Jews were murdered during the Holocaust.

HISTORY

Until the 18th century very few Jews lived in Russia, but as the Russian Empire expanded westwards many Jews living in the then Polish-Lithuanian Commonwealth (modern-day Ukraine, Belarus and the Baltic states) found themselves under imperial rule. Catherine the Great (r1762–96) decreed that Jews could live and work only in the so-called Pale of Settlement in western Russia. Here, Yiddish-speaking Ashkenazi Jews lived in small towns and villages that were often majority Jewish, known as shtetls. In the 19th and early 20th centuries, there were a number of pogroms against Jews, which prompted many Jews to emigrate or join radical political parties.

INTERWAR YEARS After the 1917 Russian Revolution and the establishment of the Soviet Union in 1922, the Pale of Settlement was abolished and free practice of religion became more and more difficult as the Bolsheviks suppressed religious practice. The Soviet Union, however, initially supported its ethnic cultures and Yiddish was encouraged. As the country industrialised, many Jews moved from the countryside and small towns to the big cities. Jews had played a significant role in revolutionary movements and the early government of the USSR, but despite the enduring Judeo-Bolshevik myth that all Jews were communists, by the late 1930s they had little influence.

After the signing of the Treaty of Riga following ongoing hostilities between Poland and Russia, from 1921 to 1939 the territory of the Belorussian Soviet Socialist Republic, as it was then, was divided between the two countries. In the Soviet part, Yiddish was one of Belarus's four state languages and became an important conduit of Jewish identity. In the western, Polish, part, secular education in Hebrew and religious education in Yiddish, as well as all kinds of Jewish political parties and cultural institutions, were active, and Jews were part of the Polish administration of most cities and shtetls.

In 1939, as part of the Molotov–Ribbentrop Pact between Germany and the Soviet Union, eastern Poland and the Baltic states were occupied by Soviet forces.

WORLD WAR II The German invasion of the Soviet Union was the largest land offensive in history. The Germans occupied territory west of the frontline which ran from Leningrad (now St Petersburg) to Moscow and south to Stalingrad (now Volgograd).

As the Red Army retreated, many Jews fled eastwards and survived behind the Soviet frontline. Those who remained in parts of modern-day Russia and Belarus were murdered by the Germans in a hail of bullets or in mobile gas vans. The occupation was extremely violent as the Nazis regarded Slavs as a subhuman race.

Belarus was quickly overrun by German forces and became part of the new Eastern Reichskommissariat. But it also became a hub of partisan activity, including a major Jewish resistance movement, whose actions in turn fuelled German reprisals.

In July 1944, the Red Army liberated Belarus, and then fought the Germans all the way to Berlin.

At the end of World War II, 3 million Belarusians lay dead, among them 800,000 Jews, and Belarus did not reach pre-war population levels until 1971.

AFTERMATH As World War II drew to a close, Stalin initiated an antisemitic campaign. It culminated in the so-called Doctor's Plot, in which a group of doctors, who were nearly all Jewish, were subjected to a show trial and accused of plotting to assassinate Stalin. Repression in the USSR eased after Stalin's death in 1954, but persecution of Jews continued until the late 1980s.

BELARUS

Belarus was part of the former Jewish Pale of Settlement. Before World War II, the country was home to 1 million Jews, 90% of whom were shot by German mobile killing units which included Latvian, Lithuanian and Ukrainian volunteers. However, the local population, though mostly indifferent to the fate of their fellow Jewish citizens, did not take part in the killings. There was a significant and prolonged Jewish resistance movement.

MINSK Minsk was an important centre for Yiddish culture, but Yiddish schools and other institutions were closed down in the late 1930s, leaving the Jewish community without leadership when Germany invaded the Soviet Union in June 1941.

Getting around The metro is the best way to get around Minsk. To visit the former concentration camp at Maly Trostenets, it is best to take a taxi. Use the train to visit Brest and Vitebsk; but you will need a car to see the memorial at Khatyn.

Where to stay and eat There is a good choice of chain hotels in the city, and these are the best options. Local dishes can be tasted at **Kukhmistr** (Karla Marx 40; w kuhmistr.by; ⏱ noon–23.00 daily; €€). Belarusian cuisine has many potato dishes, of which the most Jewish are *draniki*, also known as latkes.

History The Minsk Ghetto was the largest in the German-occupied Soviet Union and held about 100,000 people. Established in July 1941, it was located in the Rakovskaya suburb in the west of the city, an area that had been badly bombed during the German invasion. Yubileinaya Square was the heart of the ghetto, and the location of the headquarters of the Jewish Council – the Judenrat – which ran the administration. Mass killings began in August.

In November 1941, the Germans needed to make room for 25,000 Jews deported from Austria, Bohemia and Moravia, and Germany. Some 19,000 Jews were shot; many of the new arrivals were later murdered in Maly Trostenets. More mass killings followed in March and April 1942. After a fifth round-up, which took place over 21–23 October 1943, the Minsk Ghetto – where an estimated 80,000 Jews died – ceased to exist.

There was a significant Jewish resistance movement in Minsk which included seven partisan units. Many Jews escaped and joined the partisans in the forests to the southeast and northwest of the city. Unfortunately, many Jewish partisans were killed during the war, but 7,442 in Belarus survived.

What to see Get to grips with the way Belarusians and Russians see World War II at the **Belarus State Museum of the History of the Great Patriotic War** (Музей Гісторыі Вялікай Айчыннай Вайны; 8 Pobeditley Av; w warmuseum.by; ⏱ 10.00–19.00 Tue–Sun; BYN11). Then visit the **Museum of Jewish History and Culture in Belarus** (Музей гісторыі і культуры яўрэяў Беларусі; vul. Khoruzhey 28; w jewishmuseum.by; ⏱ 14.00–18.00 Mon–Fri; free), which opened in 2002.

Yama (*The Pit*) on vulica Melnikajte is a moving sculpture depicting a line of men, women and children descending into a pit. It remembers the events of 2 March 1942, when approximately 5,000 Jews were executed near where the memorial now stands. Children from the ghetto orphanage were also buried alive here after the murderers had tossed them sweets. Much of the ghetto, including the synagogue, was then set on fire. There is a further memorial in the former Jewish cemetery, now a park, on vulica Kaliektarnaja. The only buildings that date from the ghetto period are on vulica Rakaŭskaya.

The **Holocaust Workshop** (Историческая мастерская; vul. Sukhaya 25; w gwminsk.com) opened in 2003 but was closed at the time of writing owing to lack of government funding. The research centre is in a house that formerly belonged to a Jewish family and is over 100 years old. Across the street from the museum, the old Jewish **cemetery** has several Holocaust memorials.

A plaque installed in 2005 at vulica Gebelev 5 commemorates **Mikhail Lievovich Gebelev**, one of the leaders of the resistance movement. In August 1942 he was handed over to the Gestapo by Belarusian collaborators. Brutally tortured, he was eventually hanged but did not reveal the names of his comrades.

Further afield

Maly Trostenets The little-known Maly Trostenets labour and extermination camp was the largest Nazi concentration camp in the occupied Soviet Union. Today a memorial complex stands on the site of the former camp, in what are now the suburbs of Minsk.

History In the summer of 1941, a forced labour camp was opened at the Karl Marx collective farm situated in the village of Maly Trostenets, 10km southeast of Minsk. It was originally used to hold Soviet prisoners of war, but from May 1942 it was used as an extermination camp for Jews. In November 1941 the nearby Blagovshchina Forest was the site of mass shootings of Jews from the Minsk Ghetto. From May to October 1942, Jews deported from the Reich were also shot at Blagovshchina. Shootings also took place in the Shashkova Forest, where the victims' bodies were afterwards burned in a makeshift crematorium. From June 1942, gas vans were also used for mass murder here. In June 1944 the surviving forced labourers were burned in a barn on the former collective farm.

Between spring 1942 and summer 1944, it is estimated that 60,000–200,000 people were murdered at Maly Trostenets, among them 22,000 Austrian and German Jews. Historians have not been able to agree on the death toll as the Germans destroyed all the camp's records and with them any evidence of the mass murders, though most believe that the Soviet-era figure of over 200,000 victims still used by the Belarusian authorities is an over-exaggeration. The majority of Belarusian Jews killed here have not been identified.

For decades, what happened at Maly Trostenets was forgotten, and memorialisation only began here in 2014. The memorial park at the site of the camp inaugurated in 2018.

What to see The **Trostenets Memorial Complex** (Мемориальный Комплекс Тростенец; Bd Sialichkaha; ⏱ 24hrs; free) is located southeast of Minsk city centre near the intersection of the M1 and M4 motorways. There is a useful guide to the site at w izi.travel/ru/4f73-maly-trostenets-a-culture-of-memory/en#aa88ae59-6589-4461-95e1-1571d2f17ab7. More information can be found on w trostenez.org.

The complex stretches over a large area and includes three distinct parts: the site of the former labour camp and the execution sites in Blagovshchina Forest and the Shashkova Forest.

The memorial's focal point is the site of the former camp. From the Gate of Memory, which comprises two 15m-tall columns, the Path of Memory leads to two freight wagons. At the northern end of the path a panel gives an overview of the site.

South of the Path of Memory the 2018 Massif of Names Memorial remembers the 9,735 Austrian Jews murdered here. This is the only memorial at the site that recognises that the victims were Jewish. From here a path leads past some reconstructed buildings and a guard tower to the Shashkova Forest.

The memorial in the **Blagovshchina Forest** was inaugurated in 2018. It is located 4.5km east of the main memorial complex north of the M4, and is best reached by car. A walkway symbolising a freight train leads up to the memorial. There are also yellow plaques tied to trees in what has become known as the Forest of Names; organised by an Austrian organisation, they remember the Austrian Jews murdered here.

Khatyn The **Khatyn Memorial Complex** (Мемарыяльны комплекс Хатынь; w khatyn.by; ⏱ 24hrs daily; free, museum BYN8), 75km north of Minsk, gives visitors an understanding of the brutality of the German invasion, which complicates the memorialisation of the Holocaust in Belarus. In March 1943, 149 villagers who lived in Khatyn were murdered in retaliation for the partisan attack in which the German Captain Hans Wölke – who had won a gold medal in the 1936 Olympics – was killed. The villagers were herded into a barn, which was set on fire, and those who tried to escape were shot. Just five children and one man, Iosif Kaminsky, survived. At the entrance to the complex, there is a 6m-tall statue of Kaminsky holding the body of his murdered son. 'I crawled over, lifted him slightly, but saw that bullets had ripped him in half,' Kaminsky recalled in 1961. 'My son Adam managed to ask, "Is Mummy still alive?" and then he died on the spot.'

Built in 1969, the site spreads across an area the size of ten football pitches on which there are memorials to the 216 Belarusian villages wiped out by the Germans to pave the way for the resettlement of the territory by German civilians.

Vitebsk The elegant city of Vitebsk in northern Belarus was the birthplace of surrealist painter Marc Chagall (1887–1985). Chagall's paintings encapsulate the world that was lost when Germany invaded the Soviet Union.

In 1939, about 37,000 of Vitebsk's 170,000 inhabitants were Jewish. When the Germans attacked the Soviet Union in June 1941, part of the population was evacuated further into the Soviet Union, among them thousands of Jews. In July, a ghetto was established on the right bank of the West Dvina River near the station, and those Jews remaining in the city were given just two days to move there; many were drowned crossing the river as they were forced into the ghetto.

After the war, many Jews returned to Vitebsk – as many as 17,000 Jews were living in the city in the 1970s. Most subsequently emigrated, but today there is a small Jewish community of 1,000 and after decades the ruined Great Synagogue at vulica Revolutiyonnaya 14 has been restored and was reopened in 2023.

What to see The Marc Chagall Museum and Art Centre (Арт-центр Марка Шагала; vul. Putna 2; ◷ 11.00–18.00 Tue–Sun; BYN2.50) houses a collection of the artist's graphic art and **book illustrations**. Among them is a series of sketches for Nikolai Gogol's novel *Dead Souls* and a series of coloured lithographs named *The Bible* and *12 Tribes of Israel*. Opened in 1992, the centre also runs the exhibition in the **House of Marc Chagall** (Дом-музей Марка Шагала; vul. Pokrovskaya 11), a classic redbrick Jewish building. Little of the original interior has survived, but the atmosphere has been accurately recreated using Chagall's drawings of his home. Chagall was brought up in a Hasidic family and was one of ten children. He left to study art in St Petersburg in 1906 and in 1910 moved to Paris. He returned to Vitebsk after the Russian Revolution but left again in 1922 never to return. He continued to paint pictures of Vitebsk, and his paintings of his hometown can be seen in the Paris Opera, and his stained-glass windows are in the Jewish Museum in Paris. Left along vulica Pokrovskaya, in the market square where his father worked as a fishmonger, there is a statue of the artist.

The **ghetto** area encompassed Ilyinsky, Kirov, Komsomolskaya and Engels streets and held about 16,000 people. Many of those who died in the ghetto were reburied in the Old Ulanovichskoye cemetery – the grave is unmarked. A memorial to an estimated 8,000–11,000 victims who were shot or died in the ghetto is on the junction of Inyinlsky Street and vulica Engels. The exact number of victims is not known.

There is also a memorial, erected in 2010, at the **Tulovsky Ravine** between the villages of Sebyakhi and Tulovo, now in the suburbs of Vitebsk in the east of the city. In August 1941, 500–600 Jewish doctors, teachers and students were shot here. The murder was followed by the shooting of 200 Soviet Jewish prisoners of war in December 1941. A further 8,419 Jews were taken by truck from the ghetto between August and December 1941, forced to strip naked and shot in the ravine. The massacre was carried out by Einsatzkommando 9 and the SS Division Das Reich.

Brest In 1939, 20,000 Jews – about 40% of the local population – lived in the then Polish city of Brest, also known as Brest-Litovsk, and as Brisk to the Jews who lived there. The city was the birthplace of former Israeli prime minister Menachem Begin (1913–92); there is a bust of him outside the house where he was born at vulica Kuibyshev 49.

History Brest was captured by the Germans on the first day of the invasion of the Soviet Union on 22 June 1941. One of the first mass murders in what is now Belarus took place here between 7 and 13 July 1941, when 4,000 Jewish men were rounded up and shot.

In November 1941 two ghettos were set up in the city. Jews from the Brest Ghettos were required to complete a questionnaire, which, in addition to each person's full name, age, marital status and children, included a photograph and a fingerprint. Some of these documents survived the war, and preserve the names of the 22,000 victims. Only 19 Jews from Brest survived the Holocaust. The ghetto lists are held in the regional archives.

The ghettos were liquidated in October 1942. More than 15,000 Jews from the ghetto were taken to the Brest Thermal Power Plant and from there to the nearby Tovarnaya railway station. They were moved by freight train to Bronnaya Hara, 120km northeast of Brest, where they were shot.

What to see The gate of the Main Ghetto was at vulica Sovietskaya 62, where the Belarus Cinema now stands. The cinema is built into the former **Choral Synagogue**, which was used by the Germans to store personal belongings confiscated from the ghetto inmates. It is possible to see part of the foundations in the basement by the toilets. Nearby, also on Kuibyshev Street, there is a **memorial** to the 34,000 Jews from the city and surrounding area who were imprisoned in the ghetto. The monument dates from 1992, replacing an earlier one erected in 1974, and stands on the site of a house where Jews were killed in a mass shooting during the liquidation of the ghetto.

In November 2010, the remains of 350 Jews shot by the Nazis in September 1941 on the outskirts of the former village of Gershony were reburied in the cemetery on the northern outskirts of the city. The remains of 1,214 people executed in the Brest Ghetto, discovered in 2019 during construction work, are also buried here.

The former **Jewish cemetery** was destroyed by the Germans in 1941–42. In the Soviet era a running track and the Lokomotiv Stadium were built on the site, and the headstones used in construction and to make roads. Over recent years, hundreds of the headstones and fragments have been discovered and catalogued by the Jewish community – with the help of UK-based charity The Together Plan (page 86) and its American arm, the Jewish Tapestry Project – to make a database of the Jews of Brest. The headstones will form part of a memorial designed by American artist Brad Goldberg, which is due to be completed at the site in 2024.

Bronnaya Hara The village of Bronnaya Hara, known in Polish as Bronaya Gora, 120km northeast of Brest, was the site of a mass murder of Jews. The village was chosen for its proximity to the main Brest–Minsk railway line.

In May 1942, hundreds of local civilians were conscripted to dig eight vast pits, each 60m long, up to 6m wide and about 4m deep. Later the same year, between June and November, Jews from Brest and other ghettos in the region were brought by train to Bronnaya Hara. They were told that they were to be resettled, but instead were murdered upon arrival. The exact number of Jews shot at Bronnaya Hara is not known and there is little documentation relating to the murders, but the size of the pits and the estimated number of trains involved in the transport of Jews here has led historians to conclude that 50,000 men, women and children were murdered.

In March 1944, about 100 local people were forced to open the mass graves and burn the decaying bodies to hide any trace of the atrocity. They themselves were then murdered and their bodies burned. After the war the area was abandoned.

It was not until the end of the 1980s that a number of Jewish and non-Jewish activists joined forces to establish a memorial. The first memorial stone was dedicated in 1992. It is located next to the disused side-track where the mass graves are located, 1km west of Bronnaya Hara's railway station. About 100m further on, another, larger, memorial was dedicated in 1994, which states that the victims were Jewish.

NAVAHRUDAK Known as Nowogródek in Polish, Navahrudak was part of Poland in the interwar period and had a Jewish community of about 6,000. Jews had lived in the city since the 16th century and were an integral part of economic, cultural and religious life here.

About 11,000 Jews from the town and the surrounding region were murdered in Navahrudak during the German occupation; but about 600 people, 10% of the town's pre-war Jewish community, survived the Holocaust. It was the highest survival rate in Belarus, thanks to the Jewish resistance. Navahrudak was an important centre of Jewish resistance and today has the only museum in the world dedicated to it.

Most of the survivors emigrated to Israel or the USA after the war, and only a handful of Jewish people live in Navahrudak today.

Getting around Buses run from Navahrudak to Hrodna via Lida and to Minsk via Mir. To see the Naliboki Forest, you need your own transport.

Where to stay and eat The **Hotel Grazhina** (vul. Pochtovaya 5; w hotel-grazhina-novogrudok.booked.net; €) is centrally located and in walking distance of the memorials and museum. The best coffee and cakes are served at **Kaviarnia** (pl. Lenina 4; ⌗; ⏲ 10.00–22.00 daily; €). It is famous for its poppyseed cake. Eat sushi at the **Samson** (vul. Mitskevicha 65; w samsona.by; ⏲ noon–01.00 Sun–Thu, noon–03.00 Fri–Sat; €).

in Israel. At university in Minsk, he studied Human Rights Law and began to get involved with Jewish communities in Belarus.

'The state allows us to function and gives administrative support, so times are less challenging,' he explains, 'but Belarus does not have the most advanced economy and looking for support outside is currently very difficult. In 2008, the financial crisis cut the aid given to the Jewish community by international charities and that has been compounded by the war in Ukraine and more recently in Gaza.'

Livshyts says the biggest challenge that The Together Plan faces is that 'a freebie culture has developed in the Jewish community. They were given fish by aid agencies that was already fried but they were not taught how to catch the fish themselves. It means people see involvement in the community only in terms of how it will benefit them. Added to this is the legacy of Soviet times that still makes people nervous of being openly Jewish.'

Brunner and Livshyts initiated a youth summer camp programme in Belarus run by volunteers from London. 'It taught our young people a lot,' she says 'and I saw that it was through their history that young people were able to explore their identities. Building on that history is a way to help a post-Soviet Jewish community to grow organically.'

The Together Plan has now taken on the challenge of building a Jewish Cultural Heritage Route with the European Association for the Preservation and Promotion of Jewish Culture and Heritage (AEPJ; w jewisheritage.org), as Jewish heritage tourism is a way to strengthen the community. A new Jewish life has begun to grow holistically out of the remembrance of the mass graves and atrocities.

History The German occupation of Navahrudak began in July 1941, and in the following winter a ghetto was established on vulica Przesieka. On 6 August 1942, some 500–600 ghetto inmates were selected for forced labour and taken to a camp on vulica Korelicka, now vulica Minskaya. The ghetto was liquidated in February 1943.

On 26 September 1943, there was a mass escape from the Korelicka labour camp. Of the around 230 escapees, about 130 made it to the forest of whom about 100 joined the Bielski partisans (page 88). The others were either caught or died on the way to the partisan units.

About 10,000 Jews from the town and surrounding area were murdered between December 1941 and May 1943.

What to see
Jewish Resistance Museum in Navahrudak (Музей еврейского сопротивления на Новогрудчине; 68/5 vul. Minskaya; f; ⊕ 09.00–18.00 Tue–Sun; BYN2) This museum, which opened in 2007, tells the story of the mass escape from the Korelicka labour camp and the remarkable rescue operation run by the Bielski brothers. The museum is located at the site of the former camp in the old Navahrudak Agricultural Lyceum. The exhibition is housed in the original barracks where the prisoners dug their 200m-long escape tunnel and includes a reconstruction of the interior living spaces, the entrance to the tunnel and a series of outdoor memorials.

The museum was created with the support of Jack Kagan, a former prisoner in the Navahrudak Ghetto and a Bielski partisan, and with the financial assistance of the International Task Force, now the International Holocaust Remembrance Alliance.

The swamps and forests of Belarus were ideal for partisan activities. Among the most famous Jewish partisans were Tuvia, Asael, Zus and Aron Bielski. The four brothers from the village of Stankevichi, 15km from Navahrudak, hid out in the Naliboki Forest, 65km northeast of Navahrudak. There are no remains of the dugouts but it is worth visiting to understand the hardship that those who hid out in these wild, primaeval forests endured. There is an information board at the site of the Bielski partisans' camp 3.5km from the village of Kletishche.

Unlike other Jewish partisan groups, the Bielski brothers took their family with them when they fled into the countryside. Eventually they moved through the forest with a 'tribe' of up to 1,230 people, making it the largest Jewish partisan group in Europe. After the liberation, Tuvia and Zus Bielski led those who wanted to follow them westward to find a way to flee the continent. Their story was told in the film *Defiance* (2008) based on the book of the same name by Nechama Tec.

In 1944, Asael Bielski joined the Red Army and died in the Battle of Königsberg. Aron, Tuvia and Zus Bielski emigrated to Palestine and later settled in New York. Tuvia died in 1987 and is buried on Mount Herzl in Jerusalem.

Kagan also financed and organised the construction of several monuments in and around Navahrudak, replacing Soviet memorials that did not mention that the victims were Jewish. Kagan lived in London and died in 2016.

Other memorials On the P10 highway that heads southwest from Navahrudak, a monument commemorates the 18,000 citizens, among them 5,100 Jews, who were shot in December 1941 by Germans and Lithuanian collaborators behind the military barracks in Skrydlevo.

On the P5 that leads north to Vselyub from Navahrudak, another memorial, inaugurated in 2022, marks the site of the former home of František and Františka Bobrovský. The couple were murdered by the Nazis for helping Jews. The monument is dedicated to the 11 families of Navahrudak and the region's residents who have been awarded the title of Righteous Among the Nations.

Further along the P5 near the village of Litovka, a memorial remembers 4,000 Jews shot here by Estonian police in August 1942 and a further 500 Jews who were also shot here in February 1943, during the liquidation of the Navahrudak Ghetto.

On the P11 road that heads east out of Navahrudak in the direction of Selets, just past the petrol station, there is a memorial on the mass grave where in May 1943 more than 250 Jews from the Korelicka labour camp were murdered.

Further afield

Lida There are two mass graves in Lida. One is in the forest, 25m from the bypass, where more than 12,000 Jews were murdered on 8 May 1942. The second is in the outskirts of Lida near the military training field, Borki. Both memorials were privately funded.

Hrodna Known as Grodno in Polish, the city was part of Poland in the interwar period. Half the population, about 21,000 people, were Jewish. The Germans set up two ghettos in Grodno in November 1941: one for those Jews assigned to forced labour and a second for those considered 'unproductive'. When the ghettos were liquidated in November 1942, those not chosen for forced labour were taken to Auschwitz, where they were gassed. When the Red Army liberated the town in mid-July 1944, there were only about 200 Jews left in Grodno. There is a memorial at the entrance to the former ghetto on vulica Zamkovaya.

The **Grodno State Museum of History and Archaeology** (Гродненский государственный историко-археологический музей; vul. Zamkovaya 20; w history.grodno.museum.by; ⊕ 10.00–18.00 Tue–Sun; BYN6) has an interactive exhibition on the Grodno Ghetto which forms part of an exhibition on the murder of the Belarusian people. The **Great Synagogue** (Vialikaja Trajeckaja vulica 59A; w jewishgrodno.com; ⊕ 10.00–18.00 daily; donation requested), which dates from the 16th century, was vandalised by the Germans and then closed under communism. After a catastrophic fire in 2013, it has now been renovated. A stadium stands nearby where a plaque, installed in 2008, reminds passers-by that it is built on the site of a former Jewish cemetery.

In the autumn of 1942, some 20,000 Jews from Hrodna and the surrounding area were taken to the former prisoner-of-war and transit camp at Kiełbasin, which was located at the junction of vulica Voľhi Solamaaj and Repina in the southwest of the city, before being transferred to Auschwitz. A memorial is dedicated to 14,000 Soviet victims, but no mention is made that they were Jews.

Mir The town of Mir was an important Jewish centre before World War II. Many of the Jews who lived here were fur traders.

After the German invasion of the Soviet Union, the town's Jews were nearly all murdered in two mass shootings, in November 1941 and in August 1942 when the ghetto was liquidated. The murder sites are marked by memorials. The memorial on vulica Tankistov, not far from the building of Technical School No. 234, marks the mass grave of 1,700 Jews. Another monument, on vulica Oktabrskaya, between numbers 12 and 14, remembers 700 Jews buried there who were killed in the November 1941 mass shooting.

Before the final mass murder, the surviving Jews were held in a ghetto in **Mir Castle** (Мірскі замак; vul. Krasnoarmeyskaya 2; w mirzamak.by; ⊕ 10.00–18.00 Fri–Wed, 13.00–18.00 Thu; BYR16), a 16th-century castle, now a UNESCO World Heritage Site. The museum has a permanent exhibition that tells the story of how Oswald Rufeisen managed to warn the Jews in the castle of a coming massacre. As a result, 200 of them managed to escape on the night of 9 August 1942 and join the partisans in the Naliboki Forest (page 88). Rufeisen was a Jew but he had concealed his identity and was working for the Germans as an interpreter. Rufeisen was denounced by a Jewish informer and then also joined

THE MIR YESHIVA

Mir was famous for its yeshiva which opened in 1815. After Mir was incorporated into the USSR in 1939, the yeshiva was relocated to Vilnius. Its students managed to escape the Holocaust, fleeing to Shanghai with visas issued by the Japanese Consul in Kaunas, Chiune Sugihara. After World War II, branches of the yeshiva were founded in New York and Jerusalem. The Jerusalem-based Mir Yeshivah has over 8,500 students and is the largest yeshiva in the world.

the partisans after hiding in a monastery. He later converted to Catholicism and became a priest.

Those Jews who remained in the castle were taken to the Jablonovchina Forest, 1km to the southeast of Mir, on 13 August 1942 and shot.

The only **synagogue complex** that has been preserved in Belarus is located on vulica Kirava. There is an interesting privately run museum, **Mirskij Posad** (Усадьба "Мирский Посад; Kirova 2; visits by appt – call **m** +375 29 929 4268) nearby, housed in a former inn. One of its rooms is entirely devoted to the history of Mir's Jews. It has a collection of Jewish religious items, books and magazines in Yiddish, musical instruments and everyday objects.

Baranovichi There are four memorials to the murdered Jews of Baranovichi. One, at the site of the former ghetto at the intersection of vulica Gritsevets and vulica Tsaryuk, remembers the 12,000 Jews who were imprisoned in the ghetto. After the liberation, the Jewish partisans who returned to Baranovichi buried the victims' personal possessions next to the memorial.

An obelisk was erected by the survivors and their families in 1992 in the Jewish cemetery, on vulica Chernyshevskogo, where the remains of Jews killed in the massacres in Baranovichi were reburied after the war. A plaque also commemorates the 7,000 Jews killed in December 1942–January 1943 on the Zielony Most, the Green Bridge, on vulica Kostelnaya.

The fourth memorial, erected in 1972, is in the Gai Forest, on vulica Kolpenitskaya in the northeastern part of the town, where a mass murder took place in July 1942. A transport carrying 3,000 Czech and Austrian Jews had been heading for Minsk, but was delayed because of a partisan attack in the locality. As its arrival would have coincided with the mass murder of 10,000 people in the Minsk Ghetto (between 28 and 31 July), the transport did not continue to Minsk. Instead, the Jewish deportees were murdered, initially in mobile gas vans (known to the local Jews as *dushegubka*, which translates as 'soul killer'), but later shot in the forest, as this proved quicker.

RESCUE AND RESISTANCE IN BARANOVICHI

There was a considerable Jewish resistance movement in the Baranovichi Ghetto which wanted to stage an uprising. There were three different groups, one of which was led by Eliezer Lidovsky, who would play a major role after the liberation leading the survivors out of eastern Europe.

But the uprising was opposed by many ghetto inmates and never took place, though many of the underground managed to escape and join the partisans in the forests that surround Baranovichi.

On the website w jewishpartisancommunity.org you can find out more about the partisans and read the story of Rachel Pinchusowitch Litwak, who was a young teacher before the war broke out. She was the sole survivor of her family.

Hugo Arman (1917–89), a German officer in charge of travel arrangements for soldiers and the security police, used his position to protect and provide food for some of the Jews in the ghetto and saved 46 people from the death squads. He was helped by a Polish partisan Edward Chacza (b1918). Arman and Chacza also provided the partisans with weapons. Their help enabled about 250 Jews to survive in the forests. Both men were recognised as Righteous Among the Nations.

After the German invasion of the Soviet Union in June 1941, the Wehrmacht pushed forward from Belarus and the Baltic states towards Leningrad and Moscow. Halted on the outskirts of both cities in the winter of 1941, the epicentre of the war on the eastern front shifted. In the summer of 1942, German and Axis forces launched an offensive in the Volga and Caucasus regions, the main aim of which was to reach the oil fields that lay beyond.

GETTING AROUND Train is the best option in Russia because of the vast distances involved. At the time of writing Rostov-on-Don was part of a no-fly zone and under martial law.

ROSTOV-ON-DON The north Caucasus in southern Russia, not far from the Ukrainian border, is a good place to learn about the Nazis' crimes against the Jews but also to explore the powerful national narrative of the Great Patriotic War. The defining battle of World War II in the European theatre of war was the Battle of Stalingrad, now Volgograd 472km northeast of Rostov-on-Don, where the huge statue of Mother Russia, *The Motherland Calls*, looks out over the city. Pack a copy of the journalist Vasily Grossman's (1905–64) novel *Stalingrad* (Vintage, 2020) – it is a stunning account of the battle, which he covered for *Krasnaya Zvezda*, the Red Army newspaper.

Where to stay and eat The best option is a chain hotel like the **Radison Blu** (Beregovaya ul. 25G/4; w radissonhotels.com; €) on the banks of the river Don. Drink *kalmyk* tea, a local speciality brewed with butter, milk, salt and nutmeg; and eat *bortsoki*, a doughnut-type bread snack.

History Rostov was part of the Pale of Settlement, but Jews who had settled there were allowed to remain when it was taken out of the Pale in 1888. In 1905 there was a major pogrom in the city. A Jewish self-defence force tried to resist the Cossacks but, nevertheless, 50 people were killed.

In 1939, just over 27,000 Jews lived here but by 1941 the city was overflowing with refugees. During September to November 1941, the Soviet authorities organised a large-scale evacuation, in which about 10,000 Jews managed to leave the city. Rostov fell to the Germans on 23 July 1942 and mobile killing squads soon arrived.

The German Army occupied Rostov twice, in November 1941 and from July 1942 to February 1943. In the summer of 1942, when the Germans approached Rostov-on-Don for the second time, another evacuation began. This evacuation was poorly organised and only a few Jews succeeded in escaping before the city was reoccupied by the Germans on 24 July.

After the war, many Jews returned to live in Rostov, but after the fall of communism, there was yet another mass emigration. Today, Rostov-on-Don has a Jewish community of 5,000 (see w jewishrostov.com).

What to see Since 1975, a striking monument has stood on the lonely grassy hillside in the west of the city. This cluster of stone figures with arms outstretched, terror, despair and sorrow etched in their faces, marks the **Zmievskaya Balka**, the Snake Ravine, where 15,000–18,000 Jews were murdered in what are considered the worst Holocaust-era crimes on modern-day Russian territory. Local Rostov men joined German Army soldiers in pushing families towards two large pits dug

Mountain Jews are believed to be descended from Persian Jews who left Israel after the destruction of the First Temple. They speak Tat, a western Iranian language. While they are neither Sephardi nor Ashkenazi, in recent centuries, the Mountain Jews have adopted Sephardic Judaism.

On the eve of World War II, there were 35,000 Mountain Jews living in the USSR. About 5,000 lived in the area under German occupation, many in collective farms in the North Caucasus. Initially, the Germans murdered Mountain Jews alongside their Ashkenazi counterparts, but by mid-October 1942, the Mountain Jews were able to convince the Germans that they were a separate ethnic group unrelated to Jews. The Germans then decided to halt their murder pending investigation.

In Nalchik, the capital of Kabardino-Balkaria, in particular, Mountain Jews had developed close relations with their Muslim neighbours, primarily the Kabardians, who came to their defence when questioned by SS officers. The Germans concluded that Mountain Jews did not look Jewish, and since they practised polygamy they were influenced by Islam. But the debate was not finalised before the Red Army advanced and began to push the Germans back. The delay of the investigation spared the Mountain Jews from annihilation. About 1,000 Mountain Jews were murdered in the Holocaust.

towards the edge of the ravine, where they were shot. Once the war ended, the KGB arrested ten men for collaborating with the Nazis in Rostov. They were convicted and executed for treason. Although the number of victims at Zmievskaya Balka approaches that of the infamous mass murder at Babyn Yar in Ukraine (page 329), the events here have received scant attention from historians.

Further afield

Kaliningrad Formerly Königsberg in German East Prussia, this small semi-exclave tucked in between present-day Poland and Lithuania (see map, page 248) was annexed to the Soviet Union in 1945 and renamed. Most of the Jews living in the main city – now also called Kaliningrad – had left before World War II. By 1939 only 1,000 Jews remained; they were deported to Auschwitz, Maly Trostenets and Theresienstadt.

The original **synagogue** on ulitsa Oktyabrskaya was destroyed during Kristallnacht in 1938 but has now been reconstructed. A memorial plaque to victims of the Holocaust is attached to the red building next door, a former Jewish orphanage. The synagogue complex has an exhibition on the Holocaust.

On the coast 50km from Kaliningrad city, **Yantarny**, then known as Palmnicken, was, in late January 1945, the culmination of a death march for some 3,000 women and children from concentration camps in the region. Here they were forced into the ice-covered water and mown down by machine gun fire. Only 13 people survived. There is a memorial on the seafront north of the town off ulitsa Sovetskaya. The monument, by Frank Meisler, features three hands, upturned, reaching to the sky.

Smolensk In western Russia not far from the border with Belarus, Smolensk was home in 1939 to 14,812 Jews, around a tenth of the local population. The city was occupied by the Germans on 16 July 1941. Many Jews had already left or were evacuated before, but several dozen Jewish residents, mostly members of the intelligentsia, were murdered during the first week of the occupation.

A ghetto was created in August 1941 in the suburb of Sadki near the Jewish cemetery, where there was also a labour camp. The ghetto was surrounded with barbed wire and its original inhabitants evicted. In the winter of 1941–42, more than 200 people, mostly children and old people, perished from starvation, cold, or disease. The killing of Jews in Smolensk continued throughout the entire period of the ghetto's existence: Jews were shot for attempting to escape, for not wearing the Star of David, and for being outside of the ghetto without permission. On 15–16 July 1942 the ghetto was liquidated. The Germans took 2,000 of the inmates to a trench near the village of Vyazovenka and shot them with the help of Lithuanian collaborators. There is a monument at the site. The remaining Jews were murdered in mobile gas vans.

From the 19th century the area around Smolensk had a sizeable Roma community, who during the late 1920s and 30s settled in special collective farms. One of these was at the village of Alesandrovka. In April 1942, the Roma residents were rounded up and the men forced to dig pits, where 176 men, women and children were later shot. Those Roma who had fled as the Red Army retreated returned to the village after its liberation, where they continued to make up the majority of the inhabitants. The village became a major site of remembrance for Soviet Roma and in 1982 a memorial was erected on the hill at Tabornaya Gora. In line with all Soviet memorials, the ethnicity of the victims was not mentioned.

Rudnya Rudnya is located 68km west of Smolensk. Before 1941, 80% of Rudnya's population was Jewish. The *Mourning Mother* memorial, unveiled in 1965, commemorates the victims of mass shootings carried out here by the SS in 1941. The plaque reads: 'Here, the remains of more than 1,200 people – women, children and elderly – were buried, after they were shot by the German fascist occupiers in anti-tank trenches outside of Rudnya in the area of Smolensk on October 20, 1941. Some of those who were not fatally injured were buried alive.'

Bryansk Before World War II, about 5,000 Jews lived in Bryansk, which lies 250km south of Smolensk. Many managed to flee the city which was overrun with refugees. A memorial to 'Victims of Fascism' erected in the 1990s remembers the thousands of civilians murdered between 1941 and 1943. The exact number of victims is not known but is estimated to be 7,500.

Moscow The **Jewish Museum and Tolerance Center** (Еврейский музей и центр толерантности; ul. Obraztsova 11; w jewish-museum.ru; ⏰ noon–22.00 Sun–Thu, 10.00–15.00 Fri; RUB400) opened in Moscow in 2012, the result of a multimillion-dollar project supported by Jewish and non-Jewish benefactors, foundations, and local authorities. The museum is dedicated to the history of Russian Jewry from the 18th century and housed in the former Bakhmetevsky Bus Garage, a constructivist building erected in 1927. In June 2019, President Putin opened the first monument in Moscow to the victims of the Holocaust at the museum. It commemorates Jewish resistance fighters. The museum also has a children's centre.

The **Holocaust Memorial Synagogue** (Мемориальная синагога; Kutuzovsky pr. 53; ⏰ 10.00–17.00 Tue–Thu, 10.00–15.00 Fri, 11.00–17.00 Sat; by appt only – call ☎499 148 1907; free), on Poklonnaya Hill near the open-air museum of the Victory Park in western Moscow, was built in 1998 and paid for by the charitable organisation Russian Jewish Congress. The synagogue has a small museum.

7

Belgium, the Netherlands and Luxembourg

Belgium, the Netherlands and Luxembourg huddle together in the north of Europe sandwiched between France and Germany. Each of these country's wartime experiences was unique as has been the way each has remembered its role in the murder of Europe's Jews. Belgium and the Netherlands share the challenges of the demographics of migration and a fading memory of the Holocaust, as is the case in many European countries.

GETTING THERE AND AROUND

Brussels and Amsterdam's Schiphol Airport are European transport hubs. There are high-speed train links to Brussels and Amsterdam from Cologne, Frankfurt, London, Paris and Strasbourg. There is a sleeper between Brussels and Berlin. Luxembourg also has an airport and is connected to Brussels by train.

ONLINE RESOURCES

BELGIUM
Kazerne Dossin - Memorial w kazernedossin. eu/en/research-centre. The research centre at the former transit camp has an important online archive of documents & images that includes those submitted by individuals & from other Belgian museums & archives.

LUXEMBOURG
MemoShoah w memoshoah.lu. This organisation has identified 3,997 of the Jews living in Luxembourg in May 1940 & the locations to which these people fled after the Germans invaded.

THE NETHERLANDS
Joods Monument w joodsmonument.nl. A digital memorial to the Jewish victims of the Holocaust resident in the Netherlands who were deported. It is maintained by the Jewish Cultural Quarter (page 101).

BELGIUM

Belgium is a federal state divided into three distinct regions: Dutch-speaking Flanders in the north, French-speaking Wallonia in the south and a small German-speaking region in the east. The growing divide between Flanders and Wallonia has meant that Belgium has undergone a belated reckoning with its role in the Holocaust. Formal admissions of guilt were delayed by the fact that there were significant regional differences in the way the Holocaust played out.

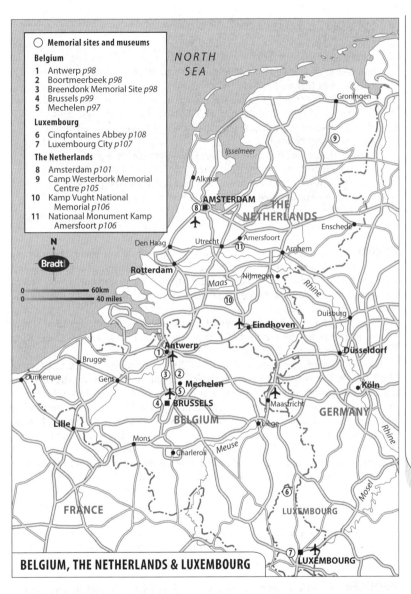

In Antwerp in Flanders, 67% Jews were deported to the death camps, while in Brussels the figure was only 37%; in Liege in Wallonia it was as low as 35%. There was widespread antisemitism in the Flemish-speaking north and some Flemish non-Jews felt an Aryan affinity with Germany. Most Jews lived in Brussels or the French-speaking south where resentment of the German occupation in World War I discouraged collaboration and there was also the possibility of escape to France.

GETTING AROUND To visit Antwerp, Brussels and Mechelen, you can take the train, but to see the sites at Boortmeerbeek and Breendonk you will need a car.

HISTORY In the interwar years, Belgium's Jewish population was comparatively small – approximately 70,000 people of an overall population of 8 million – but significantly only 10% of them were Belgian citizens. The vast majority were recent immigrants from eastern Europe and Nazi Germany, who had arrived in the country after World War I.

Those years saw the rise of fascist antisemitic parties and, although their stance was condemned by the authorities, many leading Belgians, among them King Leopold III, were widely believed to hold antisemitic views.

After the German invasion in May 1940, Belgium and the French territory of Nord-Pas-de-Calais were put jointly under German military administration, and the Belgian government fled into exile in London. Without any prompting from the Belgian authorities anti-Jewish legislation began to be introduced in October 1940 and Jewish businesses were confiscated. Nevertheless, the Germans left the enactment of the decrees to the Belgian civil service and police. Despite orders from their superiors that they must not assist the German authorities in anything other than routine maintenance of law and order, there were numerous incidents in which individual policemen or local officials assisted in the German arrest of Jews.

The Belgian civilian government made significant efforts to protect its Jewish citizens, but no attempt was made to prevent the deportation of immigrant Jews. When the deportations to the death camps in the east began in summer 1942, non-Belgian Jews were deported first; a year later the Belgian Jews were rounded up. Despite their vulnerability, many immigrant Jews survived thanks to their involvement in the resistance and the help given by ordinary people.

MECHELEN The little-known Flanders city of Mechelen (Malines in French) is a pretty peaceful place with some fine Baroque and Gothic buildings, as well as good restaurants and bars. At first glance it seems an unlikely place to be the ideal base from which to explore the history of the Holocaust in Belgium. Yet Mechelen was the site of an important transit camp, which was the antechamber to Auschwitz. The city, midway between Brussels and Antwerp, was conveniently situated between the country's two largest Jewish communities and was close to the railway and the junction towards Louvain, and Germany.

Detainees were treated to violent abuse on arrival at the camp, and while Jews were allowed to receive food packages, the Roma and Sinti were isolated and received no assistance from outside, and suffered severe malnutrition. Between

1942 and 1944, 25,852 people were deported from Mechelen to their deaths in the east. Only one in 20 survived.

Where to stay and eat VixV **Hotel** (Muntstraat 11; w vixxhotel.be; **€€**) in Mechelen has large self-catering suites in the city centre and provides secure parking. There is a **food court** in the meat market, De Vleeshalle (Huidevetterstrat 7). Kosher food is readily available in both Brussels and Antwerp.

What to see

Dossin Barracks (Kazerne Dossin; Goswin de Stassartstraat 153; w kazernedossin.eu; ⊕ 09.00–17.00 Mon–Tue & Thu–Fri, 09.30–17.00 Sat–Sun; €12) Kazerne Dossin was the site of the transit camp at Mechelen and is Belgium's main Holocaust memorial centre. The Jewish community of Antwerp acquired a small part of the building – which until 1970 had been used by the army, and then developed into luxury flats – and opened a small museum inside the barracks in 1996. A much larger state-funded museum was opened opposite the barracks in 2012. The barracks themselves are now an upmarket apartment complex and the bleak camp courtyard has been transformed into a pretty garden.

Start your visit at the original museum (situated on the right of the entrance to the barracks), which is now a moving memorial (free). Visitors are introduced to pre-war Jewish life in Belgium, before a staircase leads down to the basement, where the first room focuses on the destruction of a single family; in a short film Emiel Vos describes how his wife Rebecca and three tiny children were murdered in Auschwitz. (The testament is in Flemish with French subtitles, but a version with English subtitles on the third floor of the main museum is well worth watching.) The focus on one story contextualises the experience of the vast number of people

RESISTANCE AND RESCUE

The deportations sparked considerable public resistance, largely thanks to the work of the Jewish resistance. Although a fifth of the Jews rounded up in Belgium were arrested by the police, most policemen refused to take part. The introduction in May 1942 of a compulsory yellow star to be worn by Jews, with a black letter 'J' for *Juif* in French and *Jood* in Flemish, sparked widespread public outrage. The authorities in Brussels and Liege refused to distribute the badge, a move that gave many Jews the time to go into hiding. It was an act unparalleled in occupied Europe. A similar attempt to introduce armbands in Antwerp in 1940 was also dropped when non-Jewish citizens began to wear the armbands.

In early 1943, Belgian sociologist Victor Martin used his pre-war academic contacts to gather vital information for the underground Comité de Défense des Juifs which had been set up the previous summer. He travelled to Poland, where he gathered important intelligence on the Auschwitz extermination camp and the use of poisoned gas. News of his discoveries disseminated in the resistance newspapers changed public opinion, which until now had been relatively indifferent to the German anti-Jewish policy. As a result, the Jewish underground and the resistance were able to hide 4,000 children and 10,000 adults, providing them with food and false papers. The church played an important role hiding Jews, while the non-Jewish resistance encouraged ordinary Belgians to show their solidarity with Jews.

who spent the last days of their lives in the barracks. The visit then leads to the main memorial, over which the names of the victims are read aloud on a continuous reel. Visitors are then shown the letters thrown from the trains; a selection of the ID cards and certificates that deportees had to leave behind are also on display. They are for some people the only proof that they ever existed. The research team at the Dossin Barracks used these cards to make the list of names read aloud over the memorial and to create the wall of faces in the main museum opposite the barracks. The **main museum** is housed in a building constructed using 25,000 bricks, which represent the 25,843 Jews and Roma who were sent to their deaths from Mechelen. The permanent exhibition presents an unsparing look at Belgian collaboration, notably the role played by the Flemish SS.

Further afield

Boortmeerbeek A short 8km drive southeast of Mechelen, a memorial at the station in Boortmeerbeek recalls the daring 1943 attack on Convoy 20 that was bound for Auschwitz. It is the only known mass escape by deportees from a Holocaust train engineered by the resistance. Convoy 20 was an exceptionally large transport of 1,631 Jewish men, women and children and was the first in Belgium to use freight wagons. Prior to this deportation, trains were made up of third-class carriages. Three young students and members of the Belgian resistance, among them a 20-year-old Jew, Youra Livschitz, armed with a single pistol, a lantern and red paper, created a makeshift signal that stopped the train on the tracks between Boortmeerbeek and Haacht. The convoy was guarded by one officer and 15 men, yet the rescuers managed to open one wagon and free 17 people. The train driver then drove deliberately slowly so that more people had time to jump to safety. Of the 236 people who escaped, 26 were killed, 90 were later recaptured and sent to Auschwitz, but 120 escaped. It is an interesting memorial, for unusually it focuses on the survivors. It is believed that when Convoy 20 arrived in Auschwitz, in revenge for the escape, a higher proportion of the prisoners were gassed. Livschitz was captured and executed in 1944. His two comrades survived.

Breendonk Fort Breendonk, an early 20th-century concrete fortification 16km east of Mechelen, was used by the SS as a prison between September 1940 and 1944. The **Breendonk Memorial Site** (Brandstraat 57, 2830 Willebroek; w breendonk. be; ⊕ 09.30–5.30 daily; €11) commemorates the 3,600 Jews, resistance fighters and political opponents of the Nazi regime who were held here, of whom less than half survived the war. A trail leads through the cells, the wooden barracks, yard, shower room and latrines, torture chamber and execution ground. Before the opening of the Dossin Barracks in 1942, about half of the prisoners held here were Jews and many of the prisoners were deported to Auschwitz and concentration camps in Germany. The site became a museum in 1947.

Since 1944, a ceremony on 24 September has remembered the former prisoners. Today, that ceremony is held every three years, with the next due to take place in 2026.

ANTWERP Antwerp is the home to one of Europe's largest Jewish communities and one of the last in the world where Yiddish is the primary language. After a screening of the Nazi propaganda film *Der Ewige Jude* (*The Eternal Jew*; 1940) at Easter 1941, Flemish right-wing paramilitaries armed with iron bars attacked the home of the city's chief rabbi and burned two synagogues. The police and fire brigade were prevented from intervening by the German authorities. In 1942, there were three major round-ups of Jews, in which about 60% of the city's Jewish population were deported. The **Monument to the Deported Jewish Population** (Monument Gedeporteerde Joodse Bevolking) is at Belgiëlei 3 in the Jewish Quarter. There is more information and a useful digital walk through the main sites on w antwerpcommemorates.be.

BRUSSELS The **National Memorial to the Jewish Martyrs of Belgium** (Mémorial National aux Martyrs Juifs de Belgique) stands on Square des Martyrs Juifs in the Anderlecht district southwest of the Gare du Midi, an area which was home to many Jews before the war, and today remains home to a large immigrant community. When it was created in 1970, Belgium was one of the first countries to inaugurate such a memorial. Inscribed with 23,838 names, the monument is dedicated both to the Belgian Jews who were deported to their deaths and to those killed in action or as resistance fighters. It is a depressing place not just for the history it commemorates. The monument is permanently closed and has no security guard or police presence to protect it. The nearby **Resistance Museum of Belgium** (Musée de la Résistance de Belgique; w museumresistance.be) was also closed for renovation at the time of writing. After several delays the reopening is scheduled for 2024.

The **Jewish Museum of Belgium** (Musée Juif de Belgique; Rue des Minimes 21; w mjb-jmb.org; ⊕ 10.00–17.00 Tue–Fri, 10.00–18.00 Sat–Sun; €10) in the Sablon district has a small permanent exhibition on the Holocaust in Belgium. The museum was the site of a terrorist attack in 2014. The Gestapo headquarters were at nearby Avenue Louise 453.

THE NETHERLANDS

The Holocaust devastated Dutch Jewry, killing 75% of the country's Jews – the highest proportion in western Europe. Immediately after the war, the national narrative concentrated on the country's 'heroic national resistance' and the Holocaust was largely ignored. Today, the Holocaust is remembered by some important memorials, but cultivating a memory of the fate of the country's Jews has been and remains a challenge.

GETTING AROUND Amsterdam can be easily explored on foot. The former transit camp of Westerbork is complicated and expensive to visit without a car: take

GOOD TO KNOW

Although the Netherlands was the home of arguably the Holocaust's most famous victim, Anne Frank, a survey by the influential New York-based organisation the Claims Conference, published in 2023, found that almost a quarter of adults under the age of 40 in the Netherlands believed the Holocaust was a myth or the number of deaths exaggerated. The figures were higher than in other countries in Europe they have surveyed. Although 89% of 2,000 Dutch respondents had heard of the teenage diarist Anne Frank, who hid from the Nazis with her family in a house in Amsterdam, some 27% did not know she died at the Bergen-Belsen concentration camp shortly before the war ended in 1945. Only half of the respondents supported the 2020 official apology by Dutch Prime Minister Mark Rutte for the Netherlands' failure to protect the Jews during the Holocaust.

the train from Amsterdam Zuid to Beilen, then go by taxi (ordered in advance) to Westerbork. It is just over 9km and takes about 15 minutes; or take a bus to Hooghalen, and then walk the 1.5km to the museum. Budget €50 return, and note that taxis will only pick you up at Beilen station. Be aware, if you are on a journey to remember deported relatives, that deportation trains passed through Beilen. The complications and cost of getting to Westerbork mean that, unless you have a good reason to go, you might want to think twice about making the trip as there is little to see at the former camp and the museum is rather disappointing.

HISTORY Sephardi Jews from Spain and Portugal settled in the Netherlands in the 16th century fleeing the Inquisition. Ladino speakers, they were attracted by the religious tolerance of the Dutch provinces that had broken away from the Spanish Habsburgs. Ashkenazi Jews, who arrived in the 17th century, were distinctly different from the Sephardim. They were poor and spoke Yiddish and lived mainly in the Waterlooplein area. Some, however, made fortunes as diamond traders.

On the eve of World War II, 140,000 Jews lived in the Netherlands, accounting for 1.41% of the country's population, of whom about 25,000 are thought to have fled from the Reich. The entire community was highly integrated into Dutch society.

World War II After the German invasion in May 1940, a German civil administration was established to oversee the Dutch civil service. As the Nazis viewed the Dutch as an Aryan race, they were given a level of autonomy. Queen Wilhelmina and the government went into exile in London but did little to try to help the Jews, while the civil administration collaborated without protest in their persecution. Jews were required to register with the local authorities, excluded from certain professions and in 1942 forced to wear a yellow star. They were banned from public transport and from riding bicycles. Much of the administration of the persecution was carried out by the Jewish Council, who hoped that working with the Germans would save lives.

Deportations to the death camps in the east began in the summer of 1942 and ended on 3 September 1944. Dutch police and local authorities collaborated with the Germans in rounding up and deporting Jews. The geography of the Netherlands and the speed of the occupation made escape difficult. However, around 25,000 or 30,000 Jews managed to evade deportation by hiding with assistance from Dutch partisans. About two thirds of those in hiding survived.

Although only a small percentage of the Dutch population was active in the resistance, it is still widely believed that the role played by the Netherlands in World War II was commonly one of opposition towards the German occupiers, but this resistance only really got going in 1943. It was a widely held view in the decades after the war that Dutch society as a whole, not just the Jews, had been the victim of Nazi oppression.

Aftermath Although in 1945 the Netherlands set up special courts to process war crimes and had sentenced a total of 14,562 people by 1950, when the courts ceased operations, the experiences of Dutch Jews were marginalised by the task of rebuilding the country and the war in Indonesia. There was also an unwillingness in official circles to talk about the role that the Dutch authorities had played in the Holocaust as many officials were still in the same jobs.

In the 1960s, Jewish community groups and victims' organisations began to push for proper commemoration, but it was only in the 1970s and 80s that the Netherlands began to confront Dutch complicity and collaboration with the Nazi regime. Dutch railways apologised in 2005 for their role in the deportations and in 2017 the Dutch Red Cross recognised their failure to protect Dutch Jews during the German occupation.

Sources estimate that today there are between 30,000 and 50,000 Jews in the Netherlands, with a sizeable proportion living in and around Amsterdam. Although the community is overwhelmingly Ashkenazi, there are about 270 Sephardic Jewish families who form part of the Spanish and Portuguese Jewish community.

AMSTERDAM The Jews of Amsterdam called their city Mokum, Yiddish for 'place'. In 1940, half the Jewish population of the Netherlands lived in the capital, making up approximately 9% of the city's population. Today Jewish life in the city is concentrated in the southern suburbs of Amstelveen and Buitenveldert, and the community is mostly Ashkenazi.

Amsterdam has some significant Holocaust memorials and a brand new Holocaust museum.

Where to stay and eat Amsterdam is a major tourist hub and hotels are expensive, so it is worth booking well in advance. **Novotel** and **Ibis** hotels at various locations (w allaccor.com; €€) are Jewish-observant-friendly. **Sal Meijer's sandwich shop** (Bavincklaan 5; w sal-meijer.com; ⊕ 11.00–22.00 Sun–Thu, 11.00–15.30 Fri; K; €) is an Amsterdam institution famous for its salt beef, and ginger cupcakes. Once in the Old Jewish Quarter, it is now located in south Amsterdam not far from Anne Frank's former home on Merwedeplein. There is a kosher café in the **Jewish Museum** (see below). The **Dignita** (Nieuwe Herengracht 18a; w eatwelldogood. nl; ⊕ 09.00–18.00 daily; €€) restaurant in the garden by the National Holocaust Memorial has indoor and outdoor seating and serves an excellent all-day brunch.

What to see The Old Jewish Quarter, **Jodenbuurt**, centres on Jodenbreestraat and the Waterlooplein east of the river Amstel, an area that in the interwar years was dilapidated and rundown. Most of the Jews who lived here were Ashkenazi and made a living as peddlers and market stall holders or in the tobacco and diamond factories. The diamond business was hit by the 1930s depression and many Jews lost their jobs.

The urban geography here tells a sad tale. In the bitterly cold winter of 1944–45 anything that could be taken from the houses in the Jewish Quarter was looted and the area was redeveloped in the 1950s and 60s. The town hall and opera house have replaced the old quarter, and during the development of the metro system many of the original buildings were knocked down.

Before World War II, the area to the south of the Jodenbuurt was known as the **Jewish canals**. Here, the elegant houses of the Plantage are among Amsterdam's finest, and some of Europe's best Jewish museums, synagogues and memorials are to be found here.

The National Holocaust Museum, Dutch Theatre, Jewish Museum and Portuguese Synagogue are operated under one umbrella organisation – the **Jewish Cultural Quarter** (Joods Cultureel Kwartier; w jck.nl; combined ticket €30, valid 1 month). Start your visit at the Jewish Museum.

Jewish Museum (Joods Museum; Nieuwe Amstelstraat 1; w jck.nl/en/location/jewish-museum; ⊕ 10.00–17.00 daily except Jewish holidays; €20 inc Portuguese Synagogue, ticket valid 1 week) The Jewish museum's permanent exhibition is housed in a complex of four former Ashkenazi synagogues. The buildings had stood empty for 40 years before the museum opened in 1987. The exhibits tell the story of Amsterdam's Jewish community and the basics of Jewish beliefs. There is an exhibition especially for younger visitors. In May 1943, 3,000 people were rounded up and registered in the Great Synagogue and were held overnight in the square outside the Portuguese Synagogue.

Portuguese Synagogue (Portugese Synagoge; Mr Visserplein 3; w jck.nl/en/location/portuguese-synagogue; ⏰ 10.00–17.00 Sun–Fri; see Jewish Museum for admission) The elegant 17th-century Portuguese Synagogue stands opposite the Jewish Museum and is still a functioning place of worship. It also houses the Ets Haim Library, one of the finest Jewish book collections in the world. During the day, the building's vast windows let in an incredible natural light. The synagogue has neither heating nor electricity, making evening services especially moving. Visitors can get a chance to experience the occasional candlelit concerts held here. The Nazis considered using the synagogue as a deportation centre but decided against it due to the lack of electricity.

In February 1941, hundreds of Jewish men were arrested and rounded up in the square in front of the synagogue. The round-up prompted a short-lived strike by the city's dock workers remembered by the statue *De Dokwerker* by Mari Andriessen, a sculptor who during the war refused to join the Nazi-led artist union and hid Jewish friends in his home. The Germans suppressed the strike killing nine of the protesters.

Dutch Theatre (Hollandsche Schouwburg; Plantage Middenlaan 24; w jck.nl/en/location/hollandsche-schouwburg; ⏰ 10.00–17.00 daily; free) The Dutch Theatre is the most important Holocaust site in Amsterdam. The theatre had been designated as a Jewish theatre in 1941 but was transformed into an insanitary prison. From the summer of 1942, Jews were brought here and sometimes held for weeks before being taken by tram to Muiderpoort station to be transported on to the Westerbork transit camp. Today, only the façade of the building remains and there is a moving, modern memorial in the courtyard behind the entrance. Along the wall are 19 'forget-me-not' installations – photographs in the shape of small disks that tell individual stories. Also on display are photographs taken in 1942, by the teenager Lydia Riezouw from her home which overlooked the theatre. Among the prisoners was her friend Greetie Velleman, who was murdered in Auschwitz at the age of 17. The trees in the courtyard were planted by some of the Jews rescued from the Hollandsche Schouwburg nursery school.

National Holocaust Museum (Nationaal Holocaustmuseum; Plantage Middenlaan 27; w jck.nl/en/location/national-holocaust-museum; ⏰ 10.00–17.00 daily; €20 timed ticket) Across the street from the Dutch Theatre is the first museum dedicated to the Holocaust in the Netherlands in its entirety. The emphasis of the exhibition is on individual stories. Among the objects on display are items excavated at the former Sobibór extermination camp in Poland. The museum opened in 2023 and is located in the Hervormde Kweekschool, a former nursery school, where Jewish children, who were separated from their parents, were held. Hundreds of the children were smuggled out of the building and taken into hiding.

Auschwitz Memorial The Auschwitz Memorial in Wertheim Park, a short walk from the National Holocaust Museum, was designed by the writer and sculptor Jan Wolkers and unveiled in 1977. It is made up of six large, cracked mirrors under which is buried an urn containing ashes of victims from the camp. A memorial ceremony takes place here on 27 January.

National Holocaust Names Memorial (Nationaal Holocaust Namenmonument; Weesperstraat) The memorial located south across the canal from the Portuguese Synagogue was unveiled in 2021 after years of legal disputes over its location. Partly financed by crowdfunding, it was designed by Polish-American architect Daniel Libeskind, and is unusual in that it is made up of 102,000 bricks that form a series of 2m-high walls. Each brick bears a name of one of the victims, with 1,000 more bricks left blank to memorialise those who remain unknown. The memorial is the first in the Netherlands to name all 102,000 Dutch Jews, Sinti and Roma who were deported or killed by the Germans during World War II. According to Jewish tradition, stones at the bottom of the walls are left in remembrance.

In the garden across the road from the National Holocaust Names Memorial on Hortusplantsoen there is an unusual, tiny **Monument to Jewish Deaf Victims**. The monument is opposite the former School for the Deaf, where deaf Jewish prisoners were gathered before deportation.

Monument of Jewish Gratitude (Monument van Joodse Erkentelijkheid) Not long after the end of World War II, a Dutch artist named Jaap Kaas was asked by leaders of the country's surviving Jews to design a monument. He wanted it to show all the names of those deported but his plans were rejected as provocative. The Monument of Jewish Gratitude was put up by the Jewish community in 1950 on the spot where the National Holocaust Names Memorial now stands, but is now located further along Weesperstraat. Survivors hoped that the monument would alleviate their situation. Dutch Jewish survivors were often met with suspicion and hostility and there was discrimination when it came to obtaining homes and jobs. They were also charged back taxes and many parents were denied custody of their children who had been placed in hiding.

Monument to Jewish Resistance (Joods Verzetsmonument) Located on the north side of Waterlooplein, a memorial service is held at the Monument to Jewish Resistance every 9 November, the anniversary of Kristallnacht. The nearby **Walter Süskind Bridge** (Walter Süskindbrug) is named after a German Jewish member of the resistance, who manged to save the lives of 600 Jewish children being held in the Hervormde Kweekschool (see opposite), after their parents had been deported. Süskind, also a member of the Jewish Council, was caught and sent to Auschwitz. He died on a death march in 1945. The film *Süskind* (2012) tells his story.

There are some other notable addresses in the area. At 58 Nieuwe Keizersgracht, the former head office of the **Jewish Council** is marked by a plaque. By getting the council to implement much of the anti-Jewish legislation, the Germans limited opposition in the Jewish community. **Lippman Rosenthal & Co** was a Jewish bank located at 47–55 Sarphatistraat, where the Germans kept the assets stripped from the Jews. The money was used to pay for the deportations. In the late 19th century, **Traansvaal**, south of Muiderpoort station, became a working-class Jewish area. There are memorials to the deportees at the corner of Transvaalplein and in the square in front of the station.

Anne Frank House (Anne Frank Huis; Westermarkt 20; w annefrank.org; ⏰ 09.00–20.00 daily; €16 inc audio guide – tickets must be booked in advance & sell out quickly) The Anne Frank House welcomes more than 1 million visitors a year and is located in the western part of the city just north of the trendy shopping area of De Straatjes.

After Anne Frank and her family fled Germany in 1933, they settled in southern Amsterdam in Merwedeplein, where many other German Jews also lived. The family found themselves trapped in Amsterdam after the German invasion. In line with the Nuremberg Laws, they were stripped of their German citizenship in 1941 and became stateless. When the deportations began in 1942, the family went into hiding in a 'secret annex' concealed behind a bookcase in the building were Anne's father worked. The teenage Anne hid with her family and four friends in a series of small rooms at the top of the house on Westermarkt from 1942 to 1944 before they were captured and deported to Auschwitz. During this time, Anne, who was ambitious and wanted to become a journalist, kept a diary, which was found by her father, Otto, in 1947. Otto Frank was the sole surviving member of the family.

The *Diary of a Young Girl* was first published in 1947 and has since been translated into 70 languages and has sold more than 30 million copies.

The museum is well worth visiting for the unusual perspective it gives of Jewish life during the Holocaust. The rooms are preserved as they were but are unfurnished. It is an intimate and moving visit, which brings home the Jewish experience in a way former concentration camps cannot. So many Holocaust museums and memorials concentrate the mind on the death of victims rather than the struggles they fought to stay alive. It is also a good place to introduce teenagers to the subject of the Holocaust.

If the Anne Frank House is one of the reasons for your visit to Amsterdam, be sure to check availability before you make your travel arrangements. The museum can get very crowded, so consider booking for the evening when it is quieter. The visit takes about an hour. Please note that the original hiding place is not suitable for those with impaired mobility and has some very steep stairs.

South of the Rijksmuseum The affluent area south of the Rijksmuseum – the Netherlands' national museum at Museumstraat 1 – had a large Jewish population in the 1930s. The Central Office for Jewish Emigration (Zentralstelle für Jüdische Auswanderung) on Adama van Scheltemaplein, was where the deportation plans were drawn up. A row of tiles in the square remembers those Jews rounded up here. Etty Hillesum lived at Gabriël Metsusstraat 6. She kept a diary during the war years right up until the moment she was deported to Auschwitz, aged 28. Her diaries and letters were discovered by chance almost 40 years after they were written and published as *An Interrupted Life* (Persephone, 1999) which has been translated into more than 20 languages.

Further afield
Westerbork Dutch Jews were deported from the Westerbork transit camp located near the village of Hooghalen in a remote rural area in the north of the country, close to the German border. More than 100,000 people were deported from Westerbork in 93 transports.

History Westerbork was originally built in 1939 to house several hundred German Jewish refugees fleeing persecution in the Reich and was paid for by the Jewish community. After the Germans invaded and occupied the Netherlands in 1940, it remained under the control of the Dutch Jewish Council until the deportations began in the summer of 1942, when the SS assumed control. The Nazis treated the original German inmates as a preferred prisoner population who were responsible for drawing up the lists of deportees, confiscating valuables and taking people to the trains. Because of this, there were considerable tensions between the German and Dutch Jews, although ultimately both groups were to die in large numbers.

As there was a large semi-permanent community in Westerbork, unlike the other main transit camps in western Europe, Drancy in France or Mechelen in Belgium, it functioned like a deceptive miniature city, with a café, offices, a registry, canteen, kindergarten and hospital. Only the street names – the Boulevard of Misery, Suffering Alley and Worry Street – hinted at the internee's fears. There was a lively cultural life that included a symphony orchestra with some of the country's best musicians and a world-class cabaret, whose cast changed regularly due to the deportations. Performances ceased in October 1943.

The first transports left on 15–16 July 1942. In the months that followed, trains left twice a week, most headed for Auschwitz, but others for Sobibór. Having left Hoolhagen, the deportation trains – a mixture of freight wagons and passenger cars – were then attached to another train in Beilen 9km from Westerbork. At this point many letters would be thrown from the train. Initially the same train shuttled back and forth between Westerbork and the extermination camps.

When Westerbork was liberated by Canadian troops on 12 April 1945, there were 876 prisoners left in the camp. The commandant, Albert Gemmeker, was sentenced to ten years' imprisonment, but was released on account of good behaviour in 1951.

After the war the camp was used to hold suspected collaborators and then to house Indo-Dutch refugees from Indonesia after the colony became independent in 1949. It subsequently fell into disrepair and was demolished in 1971.

What to see The **Camp Westerbork Memorial Centre** (Herinneringscentrum Kamp Westerbork; Oosthalen 8, Hooghalen; w kampwesterbork.nl; ⊕ 10.00–17.00 Mon–Fri, 11.00–17.00 Sat–Sun & holidays (closed 9–26 Jan); €13.50) opened in 1983. Note that the permanent exhibition is at present in Dutch only with a limited translation booklet for English speakers.

The tour starts with a showing in Dutch and English of the propaganda film shot at the camp in May 1944. It was made by Rudolf Breslauer, a German Jewish inmate, and is a rare documentation of the sophisticated trickery used by the Nazis to establish a sense of calm. At the heart of the deception was the hospital, which was one of the best of its kind. It is believed that the commandant Albert Gemmeker ordered the film to portray Westerbork primarily as a work camp and he hoped it would support his defence in a future trial. The film also shows the deportation of 74 Sinti and Roma and includes the iconic shot of nine-year-old Settela Steinbach who was murdered with her family in Auschwitz. About 2,000–2,500 Sinti and Roma lived in the Netherlands in 1939; 245 passed through Westerbork. Breslauer was sent to Auschwitz with his wife and three children in 1944.

The former camp is 3km west of the museum and is connected by a shuttle bus which runs every 20 minutes and is included in the memorial centre admission price. Note that the site is next to the Dutch Institute for Radio Astronomy and because of this the use of electronic devices is prohibited and subject to a fine. The only part of the original camp that still exists is the former house of Commandant Albert Gemmeker. Until 2007, the house was a private residence; it is now protected by a glass cover. The rest of the site is grassy flatland, containing information plaques and memorials. Two freight wagons stand where the railway once ran through the middle of the camp, where the names of the deported Jews, Sinti and Roma are read out on a recording.

On the old Appellplatz there is a moving memorial in the shape of a map of the Netherlands made of 102,000 stones – one for each person deported, each decorated with a Star of David. The 215 stones with flames on them represent Roma and Sinti victims. A Roma and Sinti commemoration service is held here each year on 19 May.

Other transit camps Two smaller concentration camps were also used as transit camps. On the site of the Herzogenbusch concentration camp in Vught, 100km south of Amsterdam, is the **Kamp Vught National Memorial** (Nationaal Monument Kamp Vught; Lunettenlaan 600; w nmkampvught.nl; ⊕ memorial: 10.00–17.00 Mon–Fri, noon–17.00 Sat–Sun; 1B Barracks exhibition: varies; €12). Jews from the provinces, political prisoners, Sinti and Roma, and resistance fighters were held here as forced labourers. The memorial is located in the former cemetery. There is a reconstructed barracks, the 1B Barracks exhibition, watchtower and barbed wire fence. At the back of the complex, there is a moving memorial to the 1,260 children deported from here via Westerbork to Sobibór.

Near the city of Amersfoort, 60km southeast of Amsterdam, Kamp Amersfoort held prisoners prior to their deportation to Buchenwald and Mauthausen and served as a holding centre for local Jews. The barracks were demolished in the 1960s but the memorial centre, **Nationaal Monument Kamp Amersfoort** (Loes van Overeemlaan 19, Leusden; w kampamersfoort.nl; ⊕ 11.00–17.00 Tue–Sun, school holidays from 10.00; €12) includes a new museum, and visitors can see the rifle range which was an execution site. It became a memorial in 1953.

LUXEMBOURG

Luxembourg, one of the smallest countries in the world, was home to approximately 3,500 Jews in 1939, most of whom had fled from Nazi Germany and persecution in eastern Europe. An estimated 1,200 Jews live there today, primarily in Luxembourg city and Esch.

GETTING AROUND The walking route in the capital only takes about 2 hours. Luxembourg is an expensive place, so if you are on a budget just make this a pit stop.

HISTORY When Germany occupied Luxembourg in May 1940, the government fled to London and the German military administration extended the Nuremberg Laws to cover the territory. Synagogues across the country were desecrated and, from September 1941, Jews were required to wear a yellow star. Before emigration from the Reich was banned in October 1941, many Jews living in Luxembourg fled to southern France. Luxembourg was eventually annexed to Germany in August 1942.

It is believed that between 1,000 and 2,500 Jews were murdered, including those who fled to France. Only a handful were hidden by Luxembourgers. The Jewish community was largely made up of immigrants who were not integrated into local society, and as a result had no-one to turn to for help. Luxembourg was also a staunchly Catholic society in which antisemitism was prevalent.

During the war, Luxembourg's government-in-exile passed decrees guaranteeing the restitution of private and communal property, but after the liberation those laws were applied only to citizens of Luxembourg and those who had arrived in the country before 1931, which excluded at least 70% of the pre-war Jewish population.

LUXEMBOURG CITY Luxembourg's Holocaust sites are concentrated in the capital.

Until recently, commemoration of World War II in Luxembourg centred on the story of the 10,000 Luxembourgers conscripted into the Germany Army. The first World War II monument erected in 1971 did not mention the Jews who had also been deported. Yet, since the government made an official apology to the Jewish community for its collaboration with the Nazis in 2015, Luxembourg has made major strides in Holocaust commemoration. When the government signed a major restitution agreement with the Jewish community in 2021, it was the last country in western Europe to settle outstanding restitution claims.

Where to stay and eat If you want to stay, there is a good selection of chain hotels in the city. Most of the restaurants and cafés are near the site of the Old Synagogue and the Kaddish Memorial.

What to see Deportation trains left from the **Gare Centrale** on Place de la Gare. Inside the station's main entrance on the right are two plaques: one remembers the 658 Jewish deportees, of whom only 45 survived; the other is in honour of those deported as forced labourers. The first deportation took place on 16–17 October 1941, when 323 Jews were transported to the Łódź Ghetto in third-class carriages. Deportees had to pay for their tickets. There were a further six deportations to the death camps and ghettos in the east. The last train left in June 1943.

From the station walk up **Avenue de la Liberté**. The former offices of the ARBED steel company at No. 19 were used by the German authorities. It was here that legislation aimed at excluding Jews from civil society were drawn up and Jewish shops and businesses, many of them on what is now Grand-Rue and Rue Philippe II, were Aryanised.

At the top of Avenue de la Liberté, turn left into **Boulevard de la Pétrusse**. The Gestapo headquarters were in the Villa Pauly, at No. 57. The villa was confiscated from the surgeon Dr Norbert Pauly and used as an interrogation centre, and it was here that the registration and deportation of the Jewish community was organised. After the war, 16 members of the Gestapo were sentenced for war crimes in Luxembourg. Today, Villa Pauly is the headquarters of the Committee for the Remembrance of World War II (Comité pour la mémoire de la Deuxième Guerre mondiale), the National Foundation of the Resistance (Fondation nationale de la Résistance; FONARES) and the Luxembourg Foundation for Holocaust Remembrance (Fondation luxembourgeoise pour la Mémoire de la Shoah) and is used for temporary exhibitions.

In November 1940, Jewish children were excluded from public schools. A Jewish school was set up at Boulevard de la Pétrusse 72, which had been used as a cultural centre and place of prayer by east European Jewish immigrants during the 1930s. In public schools, French was forbidden and German was compulsory, but the pupils at the Jewish school were still taught in French. This exception was granted as it was assumed that the Jews would leave for France. The school closed in October 1941 after most of its teachers and pupils were deported to the Łódź Ghetto.

Across Pont Adolphe at 29 Rue Aldringen stood the **Old Synagogue**. It was built in 1823, and in 1938 was the target of antisemitic attacks. In May 1941, a group of local Nazi supporters stormed the building during a service. The German authorities used the attack as a pretext to demolish the synagogue.

Albert Nussbaum, a clothing manufacturer, lived at nearby **13 rue du Marché**. He managed to organise the official emigration of 1,000 Jews to North and South America via Portugal. He accompanied the groups to Lisbon, where he made contacts with Jewish organisations and embassies to facilitate further emigration. Nussbaum emigrated to the Dominican Republic and then the USA in May 1940.

Take the narrow **rue de la Congrégation**, the site of another former synagogue at No. 6, which leads back to Boulevard Roosevelt. Luxembourg's national Holocaust memorial, the **Kaddish Monument**, at 41a was unveiled in 2018. It was designed by the Polish-born Franco-Israeli sculptor Shelomo Selinger, who survived nine concentration camps and two death marches. The memorial is located on the site of the city's first synagogue.

Further afield The tiny village of **Troisvierges** near Cinqfontaines in the north of the country is set to become an important centre of remembrance in Luxembourg. **Cinqfontaines Abbey** on rue Massen is home to a new educational centre and memorial that will become a museum open to the public.

Cinqfontaines was used a transit camp from 1941 to 1943, during which time 300–400 people were kept here in terrible conditions. Although the internees were issued with passes to move around the immediate area, the locals did nothing to help them. Nevertheless, the transports were carried out discreetly. The train tracks that led up to the building can still be seen.

8

The British Isles

Before World War II, 70,000 Jewish refugees from German-occupied Europe were granted entry into the UK, among them 10,000 children brought on the Kindertransport. As part of the Allied powers, the British Armed Forces played a crucial role in the defeat of Nazi Germany, and it was the British Army that liberated the Bergen-Belsen concentration camp in northern Germany in 1945, shortly before the end of the war in Europe. These are the heroic stories that the nation likes to remember.

Often forgotten, however, is the fact that Britain controlled the Palestine Mandate from 1920 to 1948 and severely restricted Jewish immigration into the territory on the eve of World War II, closing yet another door for Jews trying to escape from Europe. When the British government did not repeal those restrictions after the war, many survivors found themselves trapped in displaced persons camps.

GETTING THERE AND AROUND

London's four airports make the capital an important major international travel hub with connections to major cities worldwide and direct flights to nearly all European capitals. Regional UK airports also connect with many European cities. Britain is linked to the continent by ferries (**w** directferries.com), the Eurotunnel (**w** eurotunnel.com) and Eurostar rail services (**w** eurostar.com).

There are direct flights to Alderney from Southampton and Guernsey; and daily ferry connections from Alderney to Guernsey and Diélette in France in summer (see **w** alderneyferryservices.co.uk).

The best way to get around the UK is by train or car.

ONLINE RESOURCES

Recordings of interviews with survivors who came to the UK after the Holocaust can be heard online at both the **Imperial War Museum** (**w** iwm.org.uk/collections) and the **British Library** (**w** sounds.bl.uk/oral-history).

'45 Aid Society **w** 45aid.org. The '45 Aid Society, which represents the child survivors (& their descendants) who were brought to the UK between 1945 & 1948, has a useful history section on its website. The children's story was told in the BBC drama *The Windermere Children* (2020). The BBC documentary series *The Holocaust, My Family & Me* (2020) presented by broadcaster Rob Rinder, a grandchild of one of the survivors, has subsequently been used in many schools as part of their Holocaust education programme.

The Centropa Kindertransport Collection **w** podcast.centropa.org/collection/1. An excellent podcast from the Vienna-based organisation Centropa (page 340).

Holocaust Educational Trust **w** het.org.uk. A useful resource for teachers & students.

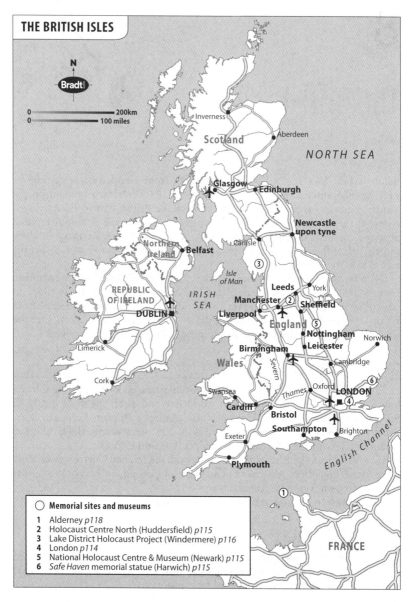

THE BRITISH ISLES

NORTH SEA

Inverness
Scotland
Aberdeen

Glasgow • Edinburgh

Newcastle upon tyne

Carlisle

Northern Ireland • Belfast

Isle of Man

③

Leeds • York

IRISH SEA

Manchester ② Sheffield

REPUBLIC OF IRELAND

Liverpool

DUBLIN

England ⑤

Nottingham
Leicester
Norwich

Limerick

Birmingham

Wales

Cambridge

Cork

Severn

Oxford

Thames

LONDON ④ ⑥

Swansea

Cardiff

Bristol

Southampton

Brighton

Exeter

Plymouth

English Channel

①

FRANCE

○ **Memorial sites and museums**
1 Alderney *p118*
2 Holocaust Centre North (Huddersfield) *p115*
3 Lake District Holocaust Project (Windermere) *p116*
4 London *p114*
5 National Holocaust Centre & Museum (Newark) *p115*
6 *Safe Haven* memorial statue (Harwich) *p115*

Holocaust Memorial Day Trust w hmd.org.uk. Another useful resource for teachers & students. There is information on both the memorial day itself as well as the Holocaust & other genocides.
Jewish Museum w jewishmuseum.org.uk. London's Jewish Museum left its premises in Camden Town in 2023 & is currently a virtual museum where some of the collection can be viewed.

National Anglo-Jewish Heritage Trail w jtrails.org.uk. Includes a useful Alderney Holocaust & Slave Labour Trail.
The Scottish Jewish Heritage Centre w sjhc. org.uk. The history of Scotland's Jewish community is held in the archive at the Garnethill Synagogue in Glasgow.
UK Holocaust Map w ukholocaustmap.org.uk. An extensive listing of all Holocaust-related sites

in the UK, curated by the Association of Jewish Refugees (w ajr.org.uk).

The Wiener Holocaust Library
w wienerholocaustlibrary.org. The Wiener Holocaust Library has an online exhibition 'On British Soil: Victims of Nazi Persecution in the Channel Islands' based on the research of Dr Gilly Carr of Cambridge University. Details of the latest archaeological digs can be found at w gillycarr.wordpress.com.

World Jewish Relief w worldjewishrelief.org. The Central British Fund, which organised the Kindertransport & looked after Jewish refugees before the war & survivors after, is now the humanitarian aid charity World Jewish Relief. They have files on the 65,000 people they helped to bring to the UK & the names of 315,000 people who contacted them in the 1930s & 40s. They are returning those files to the people they helped & their descendants.

HISTORY

Although between 80 and 90% of Jews in Britain are Ashkenazi, there is also a significant Sephardi community.

The Jews first arrived in Britain in 1070. William the Conqueror encouraged their settlement as he believed that their role as moneylenders was good for the economy since usury was not permitted for Christians. Widespread indebtedness to Jewish moneylenders who had amassed considerable wealth led to a series of deadly pogroms in the 12th century, notably in York on 16 March 1190. Edward I needed to tax the population more heavily in order to finance the Crusades, and to alleviate their debts he expelled the Jews from England in 1190.

In 1656 Oliver Cromwell announced that the ban would no longer be enforced, and in the 17th century Sephardi Jews, descendants of those Jews who had been expelled from the Iberian Peninsula in the Inquisition, formed the country's oldest Jewish community (w sephardi.org.uk).

Ashkenazi Jews began to arrive in the late 17th century, initially from Germany; but after the pogroms in the Russian Empire at the end of the 19th century, many more Ashkenazis sought refuge in Britain. Most of those refugees were poor and unassimilated. The Aliens Act of 1905 was designed to prevent the poor and criminals from entering the UK, but one of its objectives was to control Jewish immigration from eastern Europe as shown in the antisemitic debate that surrounded its introduction.

Many Yemeni, Baghdadi and Iraqi Jews settled in Britain after they were expelled from Arab lands after the decolonisation that followed World War II.

WORLD WAR I In 1917, in order to win Jewish support for the Allied war effort, the British government promised in a public statement, known as the **Balfour Declaration**, to establish a Jewish 'national home' in Ottoman-controlled Palestine. The phraseology was ambiguous, however, and did not promise a Jewish state. The declaration also pledged that this was on the understanding that 'nothing shall be done which may prejudice the civil and religious rights' of the communities already living there or 'the rights and political status enjoyed by Jews in any other country.' Britain had also already promised Arab nationalists a united Arab country covering most of the Middle East. Neither promise was kept after the defeat and collapse of the Ottoman Empire at the end of World War I.

INTERWAR YEARS The most significant developments were in the **Palestine Mandate**. After the collapse of the Ottoman Empire, in 1920 the League of Nations placed Palestine in its Mandates System under British control. The Mandate was meant to be a transitory phase until Palestine became a fully independent state.

THE RESCUE MYTH

The national narrative is that Britain is a liberal, tolerant country, but in regard to Jewish immigration in the 1930s, some of Britain's best-known historians have shown otherwise.

In the interwar years, the government maintained that Britain was not a country of immigration. It claimed that mass Jewish immigration would be a burden on the taxpayer, increase antisemitism – a fear echoed by Anglo-Jewry – and could threaten British jobs.

As a result, Jewish refugees were admitted only on a temporary basis, pending their re-emigration to a country of permanent settlement. They were not allowed to seek employment without permission and the Anglo-Jewish community was expected to find the funds to support them. Refugees who brought their businesses with them were prioritised, as were those who were willing to be domestic servants.

After the Kristallnacht pogrom in November 1938, the British government sped up the immigration process by issuing travel documents for children in lists. The Central British Fund, with the help of non-Jewish organisations like the Quakers, put together a unique humanitarian rescue programme known as the Kindertransport, in which about 10,000 Jewish children were brought to the UK. Kindertransport has come to symbolise Britain's willingness to help refugees and was the backstory to the creation of the character Paddington Bear. In reality, however, the visas given to the Kindertransport children were also subject to caveats and conditions.

After the fall of Norway in April 1940, a British press campaign resulted in the internment of 'enemy aliens' in the UK, which included many Jews who had fled the Nazis. In the year that followed the majority of those who had been interned were released.

After the war, the new Labour government continued the restrictive policies that had been introduced before the war. In addition, the 1947 European Volunteer Workers scheme, established to bring foreign labour into British industry, was primarily directed at east Europeans.

If you want to find out more about British refugee policy, a good place to start is by reading Louise London's Whitehall and the Jews, 1933–1948: British Immigration Policy, Jewish Refugees and the Holocaust *(Cambridge, 2000).*

In the two decades that followed, about 100,000 Jews settled in the Mandate. Arab groups opposed the mass immigration of Jews, and violence reached a peak in the Arab Revolt of 1936–39. In the 1939 White Paper the British government severely restricted Jewish immigration in an attempt to appease Arab opinion but also to secure access to Arab oil fields and the support of the Egyptians as conflict loomed in Europe.

In much of **Europe**, in the aftermath of World War I, there was little appetite for another war. Britain followed a policy of appeasement towards Nazi Germany, the height of which was the Munich Agreement in September 1938 (page 122).

WORLD WAR II The British Armed Forces fought in all theatres of the war. German plans to invade the British mainland in 1940 failed, but the Channel Islands – situated close to France – were occupied by the Nazis. The British government chose not to defend them. At the end of the war, the British 11th Armoured Division liberated the Bergen-Belsen concentration camp.

AFTERMATH Although it was one of the victorious Allied nations, Britain paid a heavy price for its involvement in the war, which ultimately led to decolonisation. In post-war Britain, there was considerable antisemitism. The terrible shortages were blamed on Jews, who were believed to be profiteers and black marketeers. Events like the Sergeants Affair (see below) were splashed over the tabloids and provoked a spontaneous anti-Jewish riot in the summer of 1947. In this story what played out in the Palestine Mandate – which fuelled much of the antisemitism in Britain at the time – is the most important element.

Palestine Mandate Despite their promises on the hustings to repeal the 1939 White Paper, once in office in the summer of 1945 the new Labour government chose not to do so. About 250,000 Jewish refugees were stranded in displaced persons camps after the war in Europe, many of them in the British-occupied sector of Germany. Unable to return home, many of the survivors came to regard Britain as their enemy for continuing to restrict immigration into the Palestine Mandate. Many of those survivors tried to reach the shores of Palestine on illegal immigrant boats, which were intercepted and boarded by the Royal Navy. In an attempt to stop the illegal immigration, from 1946 Jews who were captured on the boats were interned on the island of Cyprus. The most famous illegal immigrant ship was the *Exodus*, which set sail from the south of France in 1947. When the survivors on the ship were sent back to France but then forced to disembark in Hamburg, it caused a scandal that did much to change opinion in the USA and increased support for a Jewish state in Palestine.

The immigration policy also provoked an armed Jewish resistance against the British. By 1947, 100,000 British troops were stationed in Palestine. British soldiers, many of whom were national servicemen, were frequently targets of attacks and kidnaps. In July 1946 two major incidents occurred: first, the King David Hotel in Jerusalem was blown up and more than 90 people killed; then, in retaliation for the execution of three of their members, Jewish insurgents kidnapped and hanged two British Army sergeants in what became known as the Sergeants Affair.

As the Mandate slipped into a virtual civil war, the British referred the problem to the United Nations. In November 1947, the UN recommended the partition of Palestine and the establishment of separate Arab and Jewish states. On 15 May 1948, Britain gave up its mandate and the state of Israel was declared. War between Israel and the Arab states immediately broke out.

UNITED KINGDOM

LONDON London was the heart of the British Empire and it was in Whitehall that key decisions were made over the Palestine Mandate and how the country would react to the rise of the Nazi Party in Germany.

Getting around London is a very large city by European standards. The 'Tube' (London's underground railway network) is the fastest way to get around. If you are driving, be aware that there is a Congestion Charge (w tfl.gov.uk) for driving in central London, and parking is very expensive.

Where to stay and eat Jews fleeing from the Russian Empire at the end of the 19th century settled in the East End of London. Via the **Landmark Trust**

(w landmarktrust.org.uk), you can rent an elegant 18th-century house (sleeps 6; Princelet St, off Brick Ln; 🚇 Aldgate East; €€€€) in the heart of what was once the Jewish East End. The **London Marriot** (140 Park Ln, W1; 🚇 Marble Arch; w marriott.com; K; €€€€) offers a kosher breakfast. A more budget option is the **Croft Court Hotel** (44 Ravenscroft Av, NW11; 🚇 Golders Green; w croftcourthotel. london; K; €€; free parking) in Golders Green, the heart of Jewish London.

JW3 (341–351 Finchley Rd, NW3; 🚇 Finchley Road; w jw3.org.uk; ⊕ 10.00–22.00 Mon–Wed, 10.00–23.00 Sun & Thu; K; €) is London's Jewish Community Centre. It is a modern arts, culture and entertainment venue, which also has a café. **Beigel Bake** (159 Brick Ln, E1; 🚇 Liverpool Street; w bricklanebeigel.co.uk; ⊕ 24hrs; €) is London's best-known bagel shop. Also an institution is the **Carmelli Bakery** (126–128 Golders Green Rd, N11; 🚇 Golders Green; w carmelli.co.uk; ⊕ 07.00–22.00 Mon–Tue, 07.00–23.00 Wed–Thu, 07.00–13.30 Fri, 08.00–noon Sat, noon–23.00 Sun; K; €).

What to see

The small **Royal Park Victoria Tower Gardens** (🚇 Westminster) on the Embankment alongside the House of Lords has been since 2015 the contested planned site of the UK's proposed Holocaust memorial and learning centre (there is currently a rather puny one in Hyde Park, east of the Serpentine). The debate centres on the popularity of the park and the size of the memorial. In 2022, planning permission was refused because it had overlooked a 1900 law banning construction in the park. In 2023, the government introduced a bill to repeal the statute, which at the time of writing was at the Select Committee stage. Judge for yourself as you gaze out across the Thames.

Imperial War Museum (Lambeth Rd, SE1; 🚇 Lambeth North; w iwm.org.uk; ⊕ 10.00–18.00 daily; free) On the south side of the River Thames, the Imperial War Museum has a permanent exhibition on the Shoah in its Holocaust Galleries which provides a basic introduction to the Holocaust in an excellent multimedia display. Some critics say it is too theatrical. It focuses on Nazi Germany and events in the Third Reich and eastern Europe. There is also a detailed look at the Kindertransport (page 112), and one room is devoted to the Holocaust by Bullets that began in the east after the German invasion of the Soviet Union in 1941. The exhibition ends with a series of films of survivors and their descendants talking about their experiences.

The Wiener Holocaust Library (29 Russell Sq, WC1; 🚇 Russell Square; w wienerholocaustlibrary.org; ⊕ 10.00–17.00 Mon–Fri; free) This is the oldest Holocaust library in the world and opened in London on 1 September 1939. It was founded in Berlin in 1933 by Alfred Wiener, a German Jew, who spent years documenting the rise of antisemitism in Germany. Initially it informed Jewish communities and governments about the persecution of the Jews in Nazi Germany, becoming a research institute and public library after World War II. Today, it also hosts temporary and online exhibitions (page 111). Alfred Wiener's story is told by his grandson Daniel Finkelstein in *Hitler, Stalin, Mum and Dad: A Family Memoir of a Miraculous Survival* (Collins, 2023).

Liverpool Street Station (Liverpool St, EC2M; 🚇 Liverpool Street) The children who arrived on the Kindertransport at Liverpool Street Station are remembered by a memorial statue, *The Arrival*. It was designed by Frank Meisler, who was one of the children, and commissioned by Jewish organisations. The statue replaced another sculpture by Flor Kent which is now on the lower level of the station. Kent also sculpted the Kindertransport memorial at Westbahnhof in Vienna (page 27) of a boy sitting on a suitcase and one of Nicholas Winton in Hlavni Nádraži station in Prague (page 125).

Further afield

Harwich Almost all the 10,000 Kindertransport children arrived in Britain between December 1938 and May 1940 in the port of Harwich. The last transport left the Netherlands on 14 May 1940 after the Dutch surrendered to the Germans. A bronze memorial statue, *Safe Haven* (w kindertransport-memorial.org), unveiled in 2022, depicts children walking down the gangplank. Nearly 2,000 of the Kindertransport children spent their first weeks at the Dovercourt holiday camp 2 miles from the docks.

Huddersfield The **Holocaust Centre North** (University of Huddersfield Schwann Building, Queensgate; w hcn.org.uk; ⊕ 10.00–16.00 Mon–Thu, 11.00–15.30 Sun; suggested donation £4) has a permanent multimedia exhibition, 'Through Our Eyes', which tells the story of 16 children and young Holocaust survivors who settled in the north of England. Poignant personal objects and artefacts from Buchenwald and Mittelbau-Dora concentration camps are on display. Visitors can listen to recordings of survivors talking about how they rebuilt their lives in the UK.

Newark The permanent 'Journey Exhibition' at the **National Holocaust Centre and Museum** (Acre Edge Rd, Laxton, Newark; w holocaust.org.uk; ⊕ 10.00–16.30 Sun–Fri; £10) is aimed at schoolchildren over the age of nine. It tells the story of a fictional German Jewish boy living in Berlin. The story of the Holocaust is told in the main exhibition.

ISLE OF MAN

The Isle of Man is a self-governing British Crown Dependency located in the Irish Sea off England's northwest coast. From 1940 to 1945 enemy aliens were interned at Peveril Camp in Peel on the west coast of the island, Mooragh Camp in Ramsey on the northeast coast and in the capital, Douglas.

In Douglas and Ramsey, the internees lived in boarding houses and hotels on the seafront, which were cleared of guests. It is still possible to see the holes made by the posts for the barbed wire fences along the promenade. In Douglas's Hutchinson Square some of the barbed wire that surrounded a camp of 39 houses still remains. The Hutchinson camp was so severely overcrowded that internees had to share beds. Families were separated and women and children were held at a camp in Rushen. This camp's boundaries encircled both villages of Port Erin and Port St Mary.

Although some of those held on the Isle of Man were Nazi sympathisers, Jews who had fled the Reich, among them older children from the Kindertransport, along with many famous artists, musicians and intellectuals, were also interned here. Their story is told in the **Manx Museum** (1 Kingswood Gr, Douglas; w manxnationalheritage.im; ⊕ 09.30–16.30; suggested donation £10) and there is a database of names on w imuseum.im.

By the end of 1940, the plight of the refugees had become a political scandal and the government organised a programme of gradual release, although some internees were held on the island until the end of the war.

Windermere A group of child Holocaust survivors arrived in Windermere in the Lake District in August 1945. Among them were some of the youngest children to survive the Shoah. Many were teenagers who had endured life in the ghettos and forced labour. The **Lake District Holocaust Project** (Ellerthwaite Rd; w ldhp.org.uk; ⊕ 09.30–13.00 Mon, 09.30–17.00 Tue & Thu–Fri, 10.00–13.00 Sat; free) has its headquarters in Windermere Library, where there is a permanent exhibition about the group known as 'the Boys'. Guided tours of the former Calgarth Estate site where they stayed are available on request. At the time of writing there were plans to build a museum and education centre at the location.

CHANNEL ISLANDS

The Channel Islands, a tax haven and British Crown Dependency, just off France's Normandy coast, were the only part of the British Isles to be occupied by the Germans during World War II. In 1940 before the occupation, about 30 Jews lived on the islands, among them British citizens. Anti-Jewish legislation was introduced, and the Jewish population interned. Foreign Jews were deported but, Jewish British nationals remained on the islands until the end of the war. The Channel Islanders were told to collaborate with the Germans and the antisemitic legislation introduced was administered by British civil servants.

ALDERNEY Alderney, the most northerly of the Channel Islands, is a remote island, 1½ miles wide and 3½ miles long, which is home to just over 2,000 people. It is a charming place with stunning beaches and sea views. Ideal to explore on a short break, it is a good place to introduce older children to the Holocaust.

Strategically positioned just 10 miles from the French coast, near the port of Cherbourg, Alderney played a key role in German military strategy. During the occupation thousands of prisoners were brought to Alderney to build massive concrete defences known as the Atlantic Wall, designed to make an invasion of German-occupied Europe all but impossible. Concrete remains of bunkers and gun emplacements are dotted all over the island. Alderney has always been heavily fortified and existing Roman, Tudor and 18th- and 19th-century fortifications were reinforced by the Nazis.

Getting around Alderney can be explored on foot or by bike but it is hilly so a car can come in useful. There is car hire at the airport and bike hire in St Anne. A railway built in 1854 runs from Braye to Mannez Station just below the Odeon from May to September.

 Where to stay and eat The **Blonde Hedgehog** (6 Le Huret; w blondehedgehog. com; €€€) offers boutique accommodation in St Anne. The hotel has a restaurant (€€€€) that specialises in dishes using locally produced ingredients. The **Braye Beach Hotel** (Braye St; w handpickedhotels.co.uk/brayebeach; €€€), however, is unmissable for its fantastic views across the beach and is perfect for children.

History On 23 June 1940, Alderney's 1,500 residents were evacuated by the Royal Navy, though a handful remained on the island to care for the farms, which were an important supply of food for the Channel Islands.

About 6,000 people, including French Jews from the Drancy transit camp, prisoners of war and political prisoners from eastern Europe, Germany and Spain were deported to Alderney and detained in four camps run by Organisation Todt, a Nazi civil and military engineering organisation. The two labour camps, Borkum and Helgoland, and two concentration camps, Norderney and Sylt, were named after places in the Frisian Islands in the North Sea.

Helgoland was the first of the four camps created by the Germans in 1942. It was located at Platte Saline beach and held about 1,500 prisoners. It was the main camp

8

for Jewish prisoners, who were then moved to nearby Norderney, where they were segregated. Conditions were worse in the Jewish section of the camp. The Jews here – most of them French – wore civilian clothing but had a Star of David painted on their backs, and a white stripe down the side of each trouser leg.

Sylt was the only SS camp on British soil and the most westerly camp in Nazi-occupied Europe. The camp was set up in 1942 to hold Jewish and Russian prisoners, with Jewish prisoners segregated in a special section. In 1943 it became a subcamp of the Neuengamme concentration camp in Hamburg.

The environment on Alderney was extremely violent. Many prisoners were thrown into the sea, dead or alive, while others were moved to mainland Europe to be killed, which makes it difficult to ascertain exactly how many people died here.

What to see Evidence of all four camps is still visible on Alderney. The best way to explore the island is on a circular tour, starting in St Anne, where there is a large water tower and observation post built by prisoners, which dominates the skyline. Then visit the site of the former Sylt camp and follow the circular road around the island.

Lager Sylt concentration camp was located south of the island's tiny airport. The site can be reached by a track on the left of the road near the Napoleonic-era Telegraph Tower. Three gate pillars where Russian prisoners of war and at least one Muslim North African were crucified remain standing; a plaque was attached to one of the pillars in 2008 by survivors and their families. Stones traditionally placed by Jews on graves and memorials rest on the top of the plaque. The huts at Sylt were dug 1.5m into the ground for protection against the wind and possible attack. The site has been partially excavated but is overgrown and the ruins are not visible. A tunnel which led to what is thought to have been the camp commandant's house was found by archaeologists but is not accessible by the public. The house which stood overlooking the sea was moved near to Longis Common after the war and is now a private residence.

At the point where the dirt track joins the tarmacked road is a path which leads to the viewing point for the off-shore gannet colony. This path passes a number of gun emplacements built by prisoners.

Now follow the tarmacked road north. Just past the pig farm, a path leads to the most westerly tip of the island, **Fort Clonque**, refortified by the Germans during the occupation. Today, it is used for holiday accommodation but in World War II was used as an execution site where prisoners were hurled into the sea.

The **Helgoland** labour camp was located opposite **Platte Saline beach**, north of St Anne. Today the site on Route de Picaterre is covered by modern houses, one of which has the stone-clad gateposts of the former camp on each side of its driveway. They are clearly recognisable by their moulded concrete bases. The Platte Saline Gravel Plant on the beach opposite was also used during the war as an execution site. Bullet marks are visible on the wall. The road then continues to Braye Beach, where the harbour jetty was extended by forced labour in 1942. Now follow rue de Beaumont eastwards.

The **Hammond Memorial** stands on the brow of the hill with commanding views across the island to Saye Bay and Longis Common and was dedicated to victims in 1951. There are memorial plaques in various languages including Hebrew. This is the main point for commemoration services on the island. Here the road forks. Take the left turn.

The site of **Norderney concentration camp** was just inland of **Saye Beach**. In the summer, the fields where the former camp once stood are now used as a camping site. West of Saye Bay at Bibette Head, the fortifications for the Atlantic Wall are well preserved and infantry and gun positions are clearly visible.

The Odeon (⊕ 10.00–16.00 daily, weather permitting; free) east of Saye Beach is a massive naval range-finding tower built by forced labour in 1943. There are four floors to explore with information boards, and on a clear day there are stunning views across the sea to France.

Head south to **Longis Bay**. A gigantic concrete anti-tank wall was built by prisoners to prevent an amphibious assault on the beach here. Longis Common opposite the beach is believed to be the site of mass graves of prisoners who died on Alderney, known as the 'Russian cemetery'. The German War Graves Commission has exhumed 381 bodies here. Most were taken to the ossuary at Mont de Huisnes in France.

The fourth camp on the island was **Lager Borkum**, situated east of St Anne off the Longis Road. The gateposts are still standing on Impot Road opposite Kiln Farm. To the southeast of the gate the foundations of the huts are visible.

IRELAND

In the 1930s, Ireland closed its doors to Jewish refugees and did not take part in the Kindertransport. In Berlin the Irish ambassador Charles Bewley was virulently antisemitic and determined no Jews would enter Ireland. He was dismissed in 1939 but remained in Germany where he wrote propaganda for Joseph Goebbels.

Ireland was officially neutral in World War II but many Irish Jews were among those who volunteered to fight in the British Armed Forces. Its tiny Jewish community of 5,500 largely escaped the Holocaust. There are just six *Stolpersteine* (page 170) in memory of Irish victims of the Holocaust, at St Catherine's National School in Dublin, in the south of the city. They were living in continental Europe when they were arrested and deported to Auschwitz. Their biographies can be read on the website of the Holocaust Education Trust Ireland (w hetireland.org).

Although Ireland leaned towards co-operation with the Allies, Prime Minister Éamon De Valera notoriously went to sign the condolence book at the German embassy after Hitler's suicide in 1945. There has never been an official apology.

After the war, Jewish groups faced difficulty in bringing child survivors to Ireland, although the Irish Red Cross managed to bring over 500 Christian children, mainly from the Rhineland. De Valera was persuaded by his friend Chief Rabbi Isaac Herzog to allow into the country 100 Jewish child survivors, who had been rescued from war-torn Europe by British rabbi Dr Solomon Schonfeld on the condition they would spend only a year in Ireland. The children were looked after at Clonyn Castle in County Westmeath. In 1948, De Valera again intervened to permit 150 more refugee Jewish children to be brought to Ireland. The Jewish community in Dublin had close ties with its sister community in Belfast and looked after the children at Clonyn Castle, as well as at Millisle Farm in County Down near Belfast.

Today, Ireland's Jewish community remains small at about 2,500. Dublin's first kosher café since the 1960s opened in 2013 – located in the southern part of the city, **Deli 613** (89 Rathmines Rd Upper; w deli613.ie; K; €) serves beef sandwiches and chopped herring, alongside Israeli comfort food. It is named after the number of mitzvot (commandments) in the Torah.

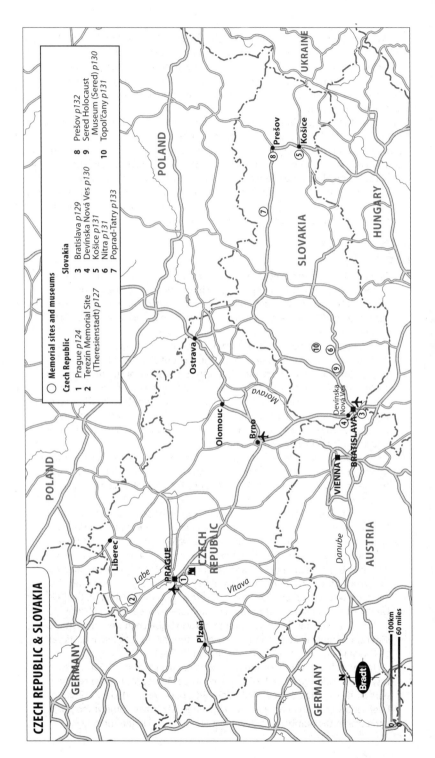

CZECH REPUBLIC & SLOVAKIA

○ **Memorial sites and museums**

Czech Republic
1 Prague p124
2 Terezín Memorial Site
  (Theresienstadt) p127

Slovakia
3 Bratislava p129
4 Devínska Nová Ves p130
5 Košice p131
6 Nitra p131
7 Poprad-Tatry p133

8 Prešov p132
9 Sered Holocaust
  Museum (Sered) p130
10 Topoľčany p131

100km
60 miles

Bradt

9

Czech Republic and Slovakia

At the heart of central Europe, the Czech Republic and Slovakia have a rich Jewish history. Jews first settled here in the 10th century. Both countries emerged from World War II relatively unscathed and, as a result, Prague in particular has some of the richest and best-preserved Jewish heritage sites on the continent. North of the Czech capital, Terezín (Theresienstadt in German) was the site of one of the most unusual ghettos.

GETTING THERE AND AROUND

Prague, the Czech capital, has excellent air and train connections. Most European and many international airlines fly to the city. It is 4 hours by train from Berlin, and is also easily accessible by car and bus from most continental capitals and major cities.

Bratislava, the Slovak capital, has a relatively small airport, but is conveniently just over an hour by train from Vienna. It is 4½ hours by train from Prague.

In both countries, you must buy a vignette to drive on the motorways.

ONLINE RESOURCES

CZECH REPUBLIC
Czech Route of Jewish Cultural Heritage w jewisheritage.org. Includes the Revitalization of Jewish Monuments in the Czech Republic project, which has preserved 15 important buildings in 10 towns across Bohemia, Moravia & Silesia.
Czech Torah Network w czechtorah.org. Dedicated to preserving Czech Torah scrolls that have been rescued & are on display across the world.
w holocaust.cz A full database of victims & documents relating to the persecution of Jews & Roma in the territory of today's Czech Republic.

Post Bellum w postbellum.cz. An NGO devoted to recording & providing access to eyewitness testimonies.
w stolpersteinecz.cz A useful record of memorial stumbling stones in the Czech Republic.

SLOVAKIA
The Nation's Memory Institute (UPN) w upn. gov.sk. Has an online register of liquidated & 'Aryanised' Jewish assets from the Holocaust era.
Slovak European Route of Jewish Heritage w slovak-jewish-heritage.org. Curated by the Slovak Jewish heritage database.

HISTORY

Until the end of World War I, the Czech Republic, and Slovakia, as we know them today, were both part of the Austro-Hungarian Empire. In the interwar period, they were united in the new state of Czechoslovakia along with Subcarpathian Rus that had also been part of the Austro-Hungarian Empire. Subcarpathian Rus was annexed by the Soviet Union after World War II and is now part of Ukraine (page 322).

Jewish life in the so-called Czech lands of Bohemia and Moravia, part of the Kingdom of Austria, was markedly different to that in Slovakia and the Carpathians, which were part of the Kingdom of Hungary. In Bohemia and Moravia, most Jews spoke German as well as Czech. They were highly assimilated, and Bohemia had the highest rate of mixed marriage in Europe. By contrast, in Slovakia, Jews were Orthodox and spoke primarily Hungarian. Before World War I, Slovak nationalists associated them with Hungarian control and in the interwar period with the new Czechoslovak state.

INTERWAR YEARS Between the two world wars, Czechoslovakia was a comparatively stable, liberal democracy in which Jews were recognised as a distinct ethnicity in the census. A Czech Jewish identity began to emerge. In the 1930 census, 356,830 people identified themselves as Jews by religion: 117,551 in Bohemia and Moravia, 136,737 Slovakia and 102,542 in Subcarpathian Rus.

In 1918–20 during the Paris Peace Conference, anti-Jewish riots broke out across the country as nationalists attacked Jewish communities they regarded as pro-Austrian or pro-Hungarian; and again in Slovakia in the 1930s encouraged by the Slovak People's Party. Jewish boxers and wrestlers took to the streets to defend their communities, a move that prompted the wrestler Imi Lichtenfeld (1910–98) to set up the Krav Maga movement, a form of simple martial arts, so Jews could defend themselves.

In 1938, Hitler threatened to launch a war in Europe when he demanded that the Sudetenland, the mountainous borderland region marking a natural boundary between Czechoslovakia and Germany, was handed over to the Reich. The area was home to 3 million ethnic Germans, but Hitler was also keen to get his hands on Czechoslovakian industry to boost Germany's economy in preparation for war. Although France had a military pact with Czechoslovakia, at the Munich Conference in September Britain and France, wanting to avoid war, allowed Germany to annex the territory. In the aftermath of the Munich Agreement, territories that Hungary had lost in the 1920 Treaty of Trianon in southern Slovakia and southern Subcarpathian Rus were ceded to Hungary, and a small portion of territory in Slovakia was also given to Poland.

In March 1939, Germany invaded Czechoslovakia. The remaining part of present-day Czech Republic became the Protectorate of Bohemia and Moravia, and German anti-Jewish laws were applied. Subcarpathian Rus was occupied by Hungary. Slovakia became an independent state under the leadership of Jozef Tiso (1887–1947), a Catholic priest and Slovakian politician. Significantly, Slovak state propaganda blamed the Jews for the territorial losses.

WORLD WAR II In June 1939, Adolf Eichmann arrived in Prague to create a Czech Central Agency for Emigration (Zentralstelle für jüdische Auswanderung), similar to the one he had already set up in Vienna (page 5). He intended to force the Jews to emigrate and appropriate their wealth and property. More than 26,000 left the Protectorate before emigration was banned in 1941.

In October 1941, Reinhard Heydrich was appointed as acting Reichsprotektor. Heydrich was at the same time put in charge of the 'Final Solution'. The Czech Jews were then deported to the Theresienstadt Ghetto.

Slovakia joined the Axis powers in 1940. A 'Jewish Code' similar to the Nuremberg Laws was proclaimed in September 1941 and the country became the first Axis partner to agree to the deportation of its Jews, for which it was paid. Between March and October 1942, the Hlinka Guard (the paramilitary wing of the Slovak People's Party), alongside Slovak police and military personnel, concentrated 58,000 Jews in labour camps, mainly in Novaky, Sered and Vyhne. They then transported them to the border with the General Government in occupied Poland, where they handed them over to the SS. The vast majority were murdered in Auschwitz, Majdanek and Sobibór in present-day Poland. Only 300 survived. Among them were Alfred Wetzler and Walter Rosenberg, who escaped from Auschwitz and informed the Jewish authorities in Slovakia of the mass extermination at the camp. Their story is told by Jonathan Friedland in *The Escape Artist: The Man Who Broke Out of Auschwitz to Warn the World* (John Murray, 2023).

When it emerged that the deportees had been murdered, the Slovak authorities suspended the deportations. Some 6,000 Slovak Jews fled to Hungary. In August 1944 Germany invaded Slovakia, prompting the resistance to stage the Slovak National Uprising against the invading forces and the regime of Jozef Tiso. The fighting and counter-measures taken by the Germans devastated the country. A further 12,600 Jewish people were deported to Auschwitz and the Theresienstadt Ghetto. Thousands of Jews remained in hiding when the Red Army occupied Slovakia in April 1945.

Watch *Bardejov* (2024), which tells the story of how Jewish leader Rafuel Lowy found an ingenious way to save Bardejov's Jewish population from being sent to Auschwitz.

AFTERMATH After World War II the two countries were reunited in the new state of Czechoslovakia. Post-war Czechoslovakia expelled its entire ethnic German population, as well as tens of thousands of Hungarians.

Jews who had identified as such in the 1930 census experienced discrimination. Antisemitism was rife and at least 36 Jewish survivors were killed and more than 100 seriously injured between 1945 and 1948. Much of the violence, in the form of riots, was sparked by restitution claims, conspiracy theories that Jewish doctors were plotting to murder non-Jews by poisoning, and the passage of Jewish refugees

GOOD TO KNOW

As in other communist countries there was little discussion of the Holocaust until after the collapse of the Berlin Wall in 1989. The Czech Republic has a good track record of remembering the Holocaust but has a long way to go in recognising the persecution both historical and contemporary of the Roma community.

Slovakia has faced issues coming to terms with its past as an ally of Nazi Germany. How the wartime state is viewed is a matter of debate in Slovakia. The far-right Our Slovakia party says Tiso's regime was the first independent Slovak state and should be celebrated. The Church has also refused to censure Tiso.

Antisemitism is no longer a vote winner in Slovakia, but many Slovak politicians use inflammatory language about the country's 400,000-strong Roma community and some right-wing groups, blaming Roma for rising crime, have created anti-Roma vigilante brigades. Locked out of education and the workplace, many of Slovakia's Roma are trapped in a spiral of disenfranchisement and poverty.

from Poland and Hungary through Czechoslovakia. The most significant riots took place in 1945 in Topol'čany and Kolbasov. There were also riots in Bratislava in 1946.

After the Soviet annexation of Subcarpathian Rus, most of the surviving Jews fled to western parts of Czechoslovakia. Yiddish speaking, and far more religious than their Bohemian and Moravian counterparts, they were greeted with hostility. Many Jews tried to leave the country.

Czechoslovakia came under communist control in 1948. After the Velvet Revolution in 1989, the two states parted ways in 1993.

CZECH REPUBLIC

The capital Prague dominates the country's tourist scene, but it is worth taking some time out of the city to visit Terezín, where the former Theresienstadt Ghetto was located.

GETTING AROUND Terezín can be visited as a day trip from Prague. There is a direct bus from Prague's Holešovice train/bus station (bus platform 7 direction Litomerice). It is just under an hour's drive from Prague to Terezín. Park in the car park at the Jewish cemetery.

PRAGUE Prague was one of medieval Europe's most important Jewish centres and its old town is remarkably well preserved. According to legend, the body of the Golem, an animated creature made from clay by the famous Rabbi Judah Loew ben Bezalel to defend the Jews from attack, lies in the attic of the Old New Synagogue.

In the 1930s, about 35,000 Jews lived in Prague. That number rose to 56,000 as refugees fled from Germany, Austria and Sutedenland. At the end of the war, Prague became a major centre through which survivors passed on their way home from the camps in Germany and then as they fled from eastern Europe.

Where to stay and eat Chain hotels abound in Prague. The **Ibis** (Na Poříčí 5; w allaccor.com; €) is a good bet in the city centre. Prague is one of Europe's busiest tourist hubs, so it pays to book in advance. There is an abundance of restaurants.

What to see The heart of Jewish Prague is the Josefov district, named after the Austro-Hungarian Emperor Joseph II, who passed the Edict of Tolerance in 1782 abolishing some of the discriminatory measures against Jews.

A Jewish Museum was originally founded in Prague in 1906. When it was shut down after the German invasion, the Nazis intended to turn its collection into a museum of the 'extinct Jewish race'. Those artefacts became a museum under Communism, but since 1994 Prague's Jewish Museum has been run by the local community and is spread across several buildings, among them the oldest surviving synagogues in Europe.

Pinkas Synagogue (Pinkasova Synagoga; Široká 23; w jewishmuseum.cz; ⊕ 09.00–18.00 Sun–Fri, closes 16.30 winter; CZK500) The synagogue is the second oldest in the city and functions as a memorial to the almost 80,000 Czech Jews who were murdered in the Holocaust. Their names are engraved on the walls. The list of victims was compiled using card files discovered shortly after the war, as well as transport schedules, registration lists and lists of survivors. In the 1950s it became a memorial to Jews from Czech lands murdered in the Holocaust but was closed from 1966 to 1989. On the first floor there is an exhibition of pictures drawn by children in the Theresienstadt Ghetto. Artist Friedl Dicker-Brandeis (1898–1944) encouraged the children to grapple with the harsh realities of the world they lived in through their art. Most of the children and Dicker-Brandeis were murdered in Auschwitz.

Prague Main Station (Praha hlavní nádraží) Prague's main station, known as Wilsonova Station, was a scene of heartbreak as parents said farewell to their children who left the country on the Kindertransport (page 6). About 10,000 of the children came to Britain, while smaller numbers were taken into other European countries. Most of their parents did not survive the war.

There are two important memorials to the Kindertransport inside the station. On Platform 1 there is a statue of the British humanitarian **Sir Nicholas Winton**, who on the eve of World War II, arranged eight trains that enabled a total of 669 Jewish children to escape Nazi-occupied Czechoslovakia, an operation now known as the Czech Kindertransport. His accomplishments remained unrecognised until in 1988 the BBC programme *That's Life!* reunited him with the children he had saved, as well as their children and grandchildren. His story is told in the 2023 film *One Life* and on w nicholaswinton.com. The Fantova café in the original entrance to the station is further along the platform. The **Farewell Memorial** is directly underneath. It is designed to look like a train door with the hands of children on one side and those of their parents on the other.

THE BELGICKA ORPHANAGE

The Jewish community's Lauder school on ulice Belgicka in Vinogrady was originally a home for Jewish orphaned boys and opened in 1898. Girls were cared for at another orphanage not far away. It was an orphanage for Jewish children from all over the Austro-Hungarian Empire. Both Czech and German was spoken in the home so all the boys could make themselves understood. After the Nazi invasion, more and more children crowded into the orphanage, which was also a hub for the now illegal education of Jewish children.

It was here that the children's opera *Brundibar* (*The Bumblebee*) was first performed after the start of the German occupation but before the mass transportations of the Bohemian and Moravian Jews to the Theresienstadt Ghetto. The score was then smuggled into the ghetto where it was staged in the Magdeburg Barracks in September 1943, after which the opera became a symbol of hope. The Nazis closed the orphanage in 1943, after which it was used by the German security services. During the occupation, 429 orphans were deported on 40 different transports. Only 63 of them survived.

After the liberation, the orphanage was returned to the Jewish community and reopened in June 1945. Halm Frantisek, the former lead violinist in the Prague Philharmonic Orchestra, at this point in his late 50s, was put in charge. He would entertain the children by playing the violin. Education played an important role in the rehabilitation of child survivors, as it was crucial to help them to stand on their own feet and to return to a normal life. It was here that hundreds of child survivors who were brought to Britain after the war were gathered before their departure, among them some of the youngest children to survive the Holocaust. Find out more at w 45aid.org.

From the end of war until 1950, 637 youngsters lived in the orphanage. After the orphanage closed it was nationalised and only handed back to the Jewish community after the fall of communism.

Bubny Railway Station Deportations were carried out at Bubny Station in the Holešovice area of Prague. The transports began on 16 October 1941, when the first of five trains departed for the Łódź Ghetto in Poland. Trains then left for the Theresienstadt Ghetto. In all, 50,000 Jews were deported from Bubny, of whom fewer than 300 survived. A striking sculpture, the ***Gate of Infinity*** by Aleš Veselý, erected in 2015, remembers the victims. It resembles Jacob's ladder and is in the form of a railway track. There are also plans to turn the dilapidated station into a Holocaust memorial and educational centre, the **Memorial of Silence** (w pamatnikticha.cz). Prior to deportation Jews were held in the nearby Holešovice exhibition hall at Dukelských hrdinů 47, where there is a memorial on the roadside wall of the hotel on Veletržni.

Vinogrady Tourists surge into Prague's Old Town but few make it to Vinogrady, a residential district not far from the National Museum. Vinogrady was a centre of Jewish life in Prague in the first half of the 20th century. Before World War II, it was home to the city's largest synagogue, which was destroyed in a bombing raid. A memorial marks the spot on ulice Sázavská.

Further afield

Terezín The most important Holocaust site in the Czech Republic is 61km north of Prague. Terezín, known in German as Theresienstadt, is a former garrison town, built in 1780 by Emperor Joseph II to resist a Prussian attack on the Austro-Hungarian Empire. It is surrounded by huge earth fortifications and high walls, and served the Nazis perfectly as a ghetto and transit camp for Czech, German and Austrian Jews.

History Approximately 150,000 Jews were held in Theresienstadt between 1941 and 1945, among them 15,000 children. Nearly 90,000 were deported to almost certain death further east. Roughly 33,000 died in the ghetto itself.

Initially, children under 12 years of age stayed with their mothers but in the summer of 1942 a system of children's homes was set up to care for orphans whose parents had been deported but also to shield children from the difficult existence in the adult barracks. The children were secretly educated in the homes and there was a Zionist sense of communal living and group identity.

The arrest and deportation to Theresienstadt of 481 Danish Jews in October 1943 caused an outcry in Scandinavia, prompting the Nazis to invite the International Committee of the Red Cross to visit Theresienstadt in an attempt to dispel rumours of the concentration and extermination camps in the east. Thus, in April 1944, Theresienstadt was transformed into a model ghetto with playgrounds, libraries and schools. Up until this point, schooling had taken place surreptitiously.

As part of the preparations for the planned deception, thousands of prisoners were deported to Auschwitz to reduce overcrowding before the Red Cross arrived. There was a second beautification process in March 1945, when leading Nazis tried to negotiate a separate peace deal with the USA. The ghetto was then completely transformed in the closing months of World War II as thousands of prisoners on death marches were brought to Theresienstadt. In the overcrowded insanitary conditions, a typhus epidemic broke out.

When the ghetto was liberated by the Red Army on 8 May, there were about 2,000 teenagers and just under 100 small children still there. Three hundred of them, now known as the Windermere Children after the BBC drama of the same name, were chosen to come to Britain in August 1945. After the repatriation of Theresienstadt's inmates, the ghetto was used as a holding centre for ethnic Germans prior to their expulsion from Czechoslovakia; and later it reverted to its original function as a garrison.

Modern-day Terezín is a down-at-heel place largely because, when the military moved out in 1996, the town lost 3,000 of its inhabitants and much of its purpose. It still looks the way large swathes of eastern Europe did in the early 1990s. Many of its buildings are in a state of decay.

What to see The **Terezín Memorial Site** (Památník Terezín; w pamatnik-terezin. cz; ⊕ 09.00–17.00 daily, Small Fortress and crematorium close 16.00 in winter; CZK310 inc guided tour – book in advance) comprises two main areas, the Small and Large fortresses, which are surrounded by a star-shaped wall and fortifications. The Large Fortress takes 2 hours to explore, but budget 3–4 hours to include the Small Fortress. Admission times apply to the Ghetto Museum and Small Fortress, otherwise Theresienstadt can be visited any time. Your visit will be greatly enhanced by taking a tour with one of the museum's knowledgeable guides. Including Terezín on a tour itinerary from Prague can be very expensive.

The **Large Fortress** is essentially the town itself and is where ghetto inmates lived during the Nazi occupation. In the early years of the ghetto, the **Marktplatz** (main square) was fenced off and filled with workshops, but in advance of the Red Cross visit in 1944, it was laid out and looked much as it does today. The building on the corner of Neue Gasse and Hauptstrasse once housed a shop selling underwear and clothing that had come from luggage brought on the transports. Alongside it was a café with live music. The first building on the eastern side was a home for Czech-speaking girls. The last building on the east side beyond the church was the headquarters of the SS until August 1942. Afterwards it was used as a home for German-speaking children.

The north of Marktplatz is dominated by the town hall, which was the Red Army's headquarters after the liberation. A plaque records their efforts to deal with the typhus epidemic. The corner of the building, now a post office, was also a children's home.

The **Ghetto Museum**, to the right of the town hall, opened in 1996. During the ghetto period, the museum building was a barracks for boys aged 10–15 years. The exhibition details the story of the camp. Copies of the children's art – the originals are housed in Prague's Pinkas Synagogue – are on show. There are some moving artefacts on the first floor including dolls of ghetto characters and a display of yellow stars. Despite the terrible living conditions and the constant threat of deportation, Theresienstadt had a highly developed cultural life, which reflected the prisoners' will to live and their need for distraction from their plight, which is reflected in the museum. Opposite the Ghetto Museum is the Stadtpark. A children's playground was built here in 1944. There is a reconstruction of a ghetto dormitory and rooms devoted to the cultural life in the ghetto, notably art works, in the **Magdeburg Barracks** on Hauptstrasse, which was also the seat of the Council of Elders.

From June 1943, transports to the Auschwitz-Birkenau concentration camp left from Theresienstadt's Sudstrasse. Railway tracks still run alongside the road, where there is an exhibition on the transports to and from the ghetto. The road leads to the cemetery, where many of the victims of the death marches are buried.

A short walk across the Ohre River – in which the ashes of 22,000 victims who died in the ghetto were dumped by the Germans – brings you to the **Small Fortress**. This fortress was a Nazi prison for political opponents. The exhibition here centres on the non-Jewish Czech experience of the occupation.

PITTER'S CASTLES

Přemysl Pitter (1895–1976), a Christian humanitarian and pacifist who cared for orphaned children in Prague in the 1930s, ran an after-school club in the working-class Žižkov quarter of Prague. Despite the dangers, Pitter and his life-long companion, Swiss-born Olga Fierz (1900–1990), continued to help Jewish children after the Nazi occupation. They delivered food parcels and provided families with the supplies they needed for the deportation.

After the liberation, Pitter was appointed to the Czech National Council. He went straight to Theresienstadt to look for 'his' children. They were no longer alive, but he discovered there were hundreds of other small children and adolescents whose lives were threatened by a typhus epidemic. To save the youngest, Pitter organised the removal of all those capable of travelling.

On 15 May 1945, Pitter requisitioned four castles, which had been confiscated from their former German owners in Aktion Zamek (*zamek* means castle in Czech). The castles were in a cluster of villages – Kamenice, Lojovice, Olešovice and Štiřín – 25km south of Prague. Just one week later, Pitter brought the first 40 Jewish children to their new home in Olesovice. A supper of white rolls, butter, eggs and sweet semolina was served in the dining room which was illuminated by huge chandeliers. The children, many of whom had been filmed in the Nazi propaganda film made in Theresienstadt, were frightened that the whole thing was a Nazi trick.

By July 1945, Pitter was caring for 150 children who had been liberated in the ghetto, and many more orphans soon joined them. Pitter was a controversial character, as he cared not only for Jewish children but also for children orphaned in the brutal expulsion of the country's German population. It was a move that cost him his seat on the Social Commission.

All four castles were within walking distance of each other, and the children were in close contact. There were daily lessons, even in Latin, walks across the beautiful countryside meadows and frequent Bible sessions. Despite the emphasis on Christian teaching, correspondence in the archives in Prague shows that Pitter wanted his Jewish children to remain as a group, growing up surrounded by those who had had similar experiences. He agreed to allow 40 of his children to leave for Britain in August 1945 because he believed they would spend only a short time there before being sent to British Mandate Palestine. In the UK, Pitter's wishes were either not known, or simply ignored. After their arrival, the youngest children were placed under the care of the child psychologist Anna Freud, daughter of Sigmund Freud, and put up for adoption by British or American families. The remaining children from Theresienstadt went to Israel and were brought up together on a kibbutz.

After the communist coup, Pitter and Fierz fled Czechoslovakia. He died in 1976 in Switzerland.

For more information see w pitter.eu and w 45aid.org.

SLOVAKIA

Slovakia once had an important Jewish community which was all but wiped out in the Holocaust – of the 90,000 Jews living in Slovakia in 1938, 70,000 were murdered. Like the Czech Republic, the country has some significant Jewish heritage sites, not to mention some of Europe's most beautiful mountainous regions.

GETTING AROUND To see the former Sered concentration camp, take the train from Bratislava's Hlavna (main) station to Galanta and then a bus to Sered. The museum is on the edge of town about 20 minutes' walk from the centre. There are tours from Bratislava, but they are expensive. To reach Devínska Nová Ves, take bus 21 from the main bus station.

Trains run between Bratislava and Košice. To explore the rest of Slovakia, it helps to have a car.

BRATISLAVA Bratislava is a good place to start a trip to Slovakia, and it is in easy reach of Vienna. Known as Pressburg until World War I, Bratislava was a centre for Austro-Hungarian Orthodox Jewry, and home to one of its great yeshivas, the Pressburg Yeshiva, which closed in 1941. In 1940, about 18,000 Jews lived in the city.

Today, Bratislava is a relaxing place to be a tourist – a place where you can while away the hours in the cafés along the Danube and exploring the streets of its pretty old town. Sadly much of the old Jewish Quarter was demolished in the 1960s during a communist-era development programme and is now covered by the bus station.

Where to stay and eat Chain hotels abound in Bratislava. The **Radisson Blu** (Hviezdoslavovo námestie 3; w radissonhotels.com; €€) is a good bet. There is an abundance of restaurants in Bratislava's old town. The banks of the Danube are a good place to escape the bustle and there are some nice cafés and restaurants.

What to see The **Museum of Jewish Culture** (Múseum Židovskej Kultúry; Židovská 297; w muzeum.sk/muzeum-zidovskej-kultury-snm-bratislava; ⊕ 11.00–17.00 Sun–Fri; €7) has 7,000 objects in its collection and focuses on everyday life and Jewish festivals. It is located in the Zsigray mansion, one of the surviving buildings from the original Jewish Quarter.

A **Holocaust memorial**, erected in 1996, stands in Rybné Square on the site of the former Neolog Synagogue, which was demolished in 1969. The memorial consists of a black wall etched with the silhouette of the destroyed synagogue, and a sculpture topped by a Star of David. On the black granite platform are the Hebrew and Slovak words for remember: *Zachor* and *Pamätaj.*

Bratislava has one functioning **synagogue** (Heydukova 11–13), built in the 1920s in a Cubist design. A plaque on the house of Aron Grünhut also on Heydukova, opposite the synagogue, remembers the Orthodox businessman who chartered two Danube steamships and transported 1,350 Slovak Jews to Mandate Palestine. He survived the war and was active in re-establishing the Pressburg Yeshiva in Israel.

Two other interesting plaques are on **Ventúrska**. At No. 20 there is a memorial to 16 members of the Steiner family, who had run a bookselling business in the city since 1847. Their shop was Aryanised and taken over by the writer Ludo Ondrejov, who informed on them to the authorities, which led to their deportation. The artist Adolf Frankl lived at No. 16. After surviving deportation to Auschwitz, he began to paint his work *Art against the Oblivion*. He lived in Vienna after the war.

The Jewish cemetery was destroyed in 1943. The only part that was saved was the **tomb of Moses Sofer** (1762–1839), a pilgrimage site on the Ludvíka Svobodu Embankment. Why this was the case is not known but among the theories are a fear of being cursed by the sage. Sofer, known as the Chatam Sofer, was one of the most important Orthodox rabbis in the early 19th century and founder of the Pressburg Yeshiva.

Further afield

Devínska Nová Ves Bratislava sits on the border with Austria. As a result, it was an important stopping point for Jewish refugees from eastern Europe in the immediate aftermath of the Holocaust. Once the survivors arrived in Bratislava, many of them were taken to Devínska Nová Ves, 14km northwest of the city. The town is separated from Austria by the pretty Morava River, and in 1946 thousands of Jews were among the 100,000 who walked across the border here. The survivors streamed across a small wooden bridge, which spanned the river at that time. It was wrecked by ice floes in the harsh winter of 1946, but the charity the American Jewish Joint Distribution Committee paid the authorities to build a new one. They also paid for a hostel in town that could accommodate 300 survivors a night.

The new bridge did not last long as Devínska Nová Ves was on the frontline of the Cold War and the Morava River formed part of the Iron Curtain. As the Russians took control of eastern Europe, the area became a no-go zone with watchtowers and barbed wire, making it inaccessible for a generation. This is one of the reasons that today the banks of the Morava have such an old-world charm about them and are home to rare wildflowers. It is a popular spot for day-trippers.

Today, there is a cycle route, the Cyklomost Slobody, the Freedom Cycle Bridge which leads into Austria. It was built in 2012 to celebrate the newfound liberty of the post-Soviet world. Sadly, though, you will find no mention of the Jewish refugees who passed this way after the war. They have been forgotten.

Sered Slovakia has only one Holocaust museum, in Sered, 67km northeast of Bratislava, at the site of the former Sered concentration camp.

History The camp was established in 1941 as a labour camp on the initiative of the Jewish Council in the hope that proving Jews were useful workers would stave off the threat of deportation. Nevertheless, by the time the camp opened in the spring of 1942, deportations had begun and the camp, which was run by the Slovakian Hlinka Guard, also became a transit camp. During the summer of 1942, some 4,500 Jews were sent from Sered to occupied Poland on five transports.

After the last transport, the conditions at Sered improved. The remaining prisoners produced an impressive number of quality goods, and as a result received more food and even leave passes. There were school services for the children and cultural activities.

During the August 1944 Slovak National Uprising, many prisoners escaped to take part in the revolt. However, after the Germans quashed the uprising, Sered passed into the hands of the SS. One of the most important of Adolf Eichmann's assistants, the Austrian Alois Brunner, who had deported Jews from Vienna, Berlin, Greece and France, took control of the camp in the October and remained in charge until March 1945. During this time, a further 13,500 Jews were deported to Theresienstadt and Auschwitz. When the camp was liberated by the Soviet Army in April 1945, Brunner went into hiding. He died in Syria decades later.

After the war, the camp at Sered was used as a military barracks. A plaque was installed in 1998.

What to see The **Sered Holocaust Museum** (Múzeum holokaustu v Seredi; Kasárenská 1005/54; w snm.sk/en/museums/museum-of-jewish-culture/sered-holocaust-museum; ⊕ Sep–Jun 08.00–15.00 Mon–Fri, 09.00–16.00 Sun, Jul–Aug 09.00–16.00 Mon–Fri, 10.00–17.30 Sun; €7) opened in 2016, and the exhibition is modern and informative. Five of the original barracks have been reconstructed, the first dedicated to the years 1938–45, during which Jews were persecuted by the independent Slovak state. The names of victims deported in 1942 are engraved on glass panels. There is a section of the exhibition dedicated to the Slovak National Uprising and the role played by the Jews.

Between the first and second barracks is an original freight wagon which was twice used in transports to Auschwitz. The museum bought it from a private owner, who had used it as a garden shed having inherited it from his father who worked on the railways. There are original carvings inside.

The remaining barracks have exhibitions on forced labour, life in the Sered camp and the extermination camps to which Slovakia's Jews were sent. One of the most remarkable objects on display is Alois Brunner's wooden military suitcase. The exhibition ends with a look at those who chose to protect the Jews and have been recognised as Righteous Among the Nations.

Nitra In Nitra, 30km west of Sered, the **synagogue** (Pri synagóge 3; w nitra.sk/ synagogal; ⊕ 13.00–18.00 Tue & Sat–Sun, 09.00–noon & 13.00–18.00 Wed–Thu; €3), built in 1911, stood derelict after the war until 2003, but is now a concert hall. In what was the women's gallery, there is an exhibition about the Jews of Nitra. A plaque outside remembers the 6,000 Jews who were deported from the town and the surrounding area.

Topoľčany Before the war, the Jewish community of Topoľčany – a city located 33km north of Nitra – had been one of the wealthiest in the country and accounted for 25% of the local population. The Jewish community was Orthodox and did not mix with the rest of the population, but there was little antisemitic violence before the war. In 1938, however, the city became a bastion of the right-wing Slovak People's Party.

After the war, about 750 survivors, some entire families, returned to Topoľčany having hidden out with partisans in the mountains. In September 1945 Topoľčany was the scene of a serious pogrom, in which 47 survivors were injured and 15 seriously hurt. The riot was probably caused by fears that returning survivors would reclaim their property, which had been confiscated. A documentary shown on Slovak television in 2004, *Love Thy Neighbour*, prompted the mayor of Topoľčany to offer an apology. Walter Fried, who had survived the violence, erected a plaque on the former synagogue in 1998. As with the pogrom in the Polish city of Kielce, the violence prompted survivors to leave the country. No Jews live in Topoľčany today.

Košice Slovakia's second largest city, Košice is 438km east of Bratislava. Jews have lived here since the 15th century, and Košice still has a small Jewish community of about 800 people. In the city centre, there is a small but interesting Jewish district centred on ulica Zvonarska, where the synagogue, built in 1899, has an impressive Moorish interior.

In 1938, Košice was annexed by Hungary. In 1941, those Jews who did not have Hungarian citizenship were deported to Kamianets-Podilskyi, then in German-occupied territory of pre-war Poland and today in Ukraine, where they were shot. Then, in 1944 after Hungary was occupied by the Germans, the remaining Jews in Košice were deported to Auschwitz. There is a memorial plaque in the synagogue at Puškinova 3 where Jews were held before they were deported.

Košice was the first seat of the new post-war government, and in the immediate aftermath of the Holocaust it was an important centre where survivors could find assistance. The Jewish Committee was supported by United Nations Relief and

Rehabilitation Administration (UNRAA) and the American Joint Jewish Defence Committee. Pre-war youth movements played an important role in helping survivors, as did the Orthodox community. Nevertheless, the first anti-Jewish riots in Slovakia broke out in the city in May 1945.

Prešov In 1938, Prešov, which lies 38km north of Košice, was home to 4,300 Jews. Like other towns in Slovakia, it would become the scene of post-war anti-Jewish riots.

Before the war, in 1928, the Orthodox synagogue set up a museum. After it was shut down during the Tiso regime, its collection was given to the Jewish Museum in Prague. It was returned in 1993, when the **Museum of Jewish Culture** (Múzeum židovskej kultúry; Okružná ulica 32; w synagoga-presov.sk; ⊕ 11.00–15.00 Tue–Wed, 09.00–13.00 Thu–Fri, 14.00–16.00 Sun; €3) reopened in the newly renovated synagogue. In the courtyard there is a memorial to the 6,000 Jews who were deported from Prešov and the surrounding areas. There is also a memorial plaque on the town hall.

ROMA AND SINTI

After the German occupation, anti-Romani laws already in place in the Reich were applied in Bohemia and Moravia. The entire Roma community in what is now the Czech Republic was annihilated after deportation to Auschwitz. Slovak Roma were not deported to Auschwitz, but instead killed in Slovakia in detention camps like Dubnica nad Váhom, in the south, which was among the most brutal.

Today, Slovakia has one of the largest Roma communities in Europe and numbers approximately 450,000, and those Roma who now live in the Czech Republic originally came from Slovakia. Roma and Sinti in both countries still suffer severe discrimination and are a target for far-right groups. A recent survey revealed that 86% of Czechs aged under 36 have negative perceptions of Roma.

In Brno in the Czech Republic, the **Museum of Roma Culture** (Muzeum Romské Kultury; Bratislavská 67; w rommuz.cz; ⊕ 10.00–18.00 Tue–Sun; CZK120) is a state institution that documents the country's Roma genocide, which has been slowly recognised since the fall of communism. It holds 200 survivors' testimonies and has an extensive collection of artefacts that explain the history and culture of the Romani people.

In 2022, the pig farm that had stood for decades on the site of a Roma concentration camp at **Lety**, 70km south of Prague, was finally demolished. A memorial and replica of a barracks are accessible to visitors (⊕ 24hrs; free) via an educational nature trail that starts in the village next to the town hall. At time of writing an exhibition hall was under construction. A hotel sits on the site of another Roma camp at **Hononín**, where a small memorial remembers its existence.

There is a memorial at Dubnica nad Váhom in the memorial park on the main street, Hlavná. Remembrance ceremonies take place here on 2 August, marking the day in 1944 when nearly 3,000 Roma men, women and children died in the gas chambers at Auschwitz.

There is also a small exhibition on the Roma Holocaust at the Holocaust Museum in Sered (page 130).

Poprad-Tatry The first transport of Jews from Slovakia destined for Auschwitz left from the railway station in the holiday resort town of Poprad-Tatry in the High Tatra Mountains. Poprad is 112km northwest of Košice. The transport that left the station on ulica Wolkera on the morning of 25 March 1942 was unique as it was made up of 999 unmarried Jewish young women aged between 16 and 36. There was one single man in the transport. They had volunteered for government service and left home dressed in their best clothes, confidently waving goodbye to their families, believing they were being sent to work in a factory. In Poprad, they were held in the transit camp for almost a month, where they were fed starvation rations and forced to clean the barracks on their hands and knees. Only a handful of the women would survive the war.

Heather Dune Macadam told their story in *The Nine Hundred: The Extraordinary Young Women of the First Official Jewish Transport to Auschwitz* (Citadel Press, 2019). During her research, Macadam left a list of the women's names at the memorial in Poprad in 2012. One of those names was that of Adela Gross, who was 18 when she boarded the train. She was later gassed in Auschwitz. Until her family saw her name on the list, they had no idea what had happened to her. A memorial ceremony is held at the railway station every year on 25 March.

10

France

The Holocaust unfurled in different ways across Nazi-occupied Europe. Nowhere was that more so than in France. Unlike in Belgium and The Netherlands, the French government did not go into exile and continued to function. It had autonomy over its internal policy and, most importantly, its police force. As a result, the persecution of the Jews and the death of 75,000 Jewish men, women and children deported from France is deeply entwined with the political debate that surrounds the fall of France in June 1940 and the politics of the Vichy government led by Marshal Philippe Pétain which governed France in its wake. Exactly what happened in France between 1940 and 1944 has been a matter of contentious debate ever since.

Above all, a journey into the French history of the Shoah reveals that the Nazis were not all-powerful and nothing was predetermined during World War II. In France, public opinion mattered. Even during the occupation, people and politicians had a choice in the way they acted and how far they would collaborate with the Nazis. As the war turned, widespread indifference turned into sympathy for the Jews' plight.

GETTING THERE AND AROUND

Paris has three international airports and is France's central hub for transcontinental travellers. The city is linked to many major European cities by high-speed rail links. Bus networks offer cheaper but longer alternatives.

Travellers to France need to be aware that a ban on short-haul flights means that travel within France is simpler by car or train. If travelling by car, factor road tolls into your budget.

ONLINE RESOURCES

Commission des victims de spoliations
w civs.gouv.fr. The Commission is responsible for examining individual requests by victims or their beneficiaries for compensation for the spoliation of property.
Fondation pour la Mémoire de la Shoah
w fondationshoah.org. An informative website about the Holocaust in France & beyond.
Klarsfeld Foundation w klarsfeldfoundation. org. The driving force behind Holocaust memorialisation in France has been the Nazi hunter Serge Klarsfeld & his wife, Beate.

You can find out more about them on their website.
Mémorial de la Shoah w memorialdelashoah. org. The main online portal for information on the Holocaust in France, this website has a mass of online archives & a database of victims. The memorial in Paris also has a documentation centre if you are trying to trace or register a relative. The museum itself (page 144) has an excellent bookshop that sells books in English.

Jews have lived in France since the time of the Roman Empire. In the medieval period, France was a centre of Jewish learning but the community's fate waxed and waned with expulsions and returns until the French Revolution, when the process of emancipation began. Full equality was granted in 1831. Jews then achieved an affluence and distinction that was without parallel in Europe.

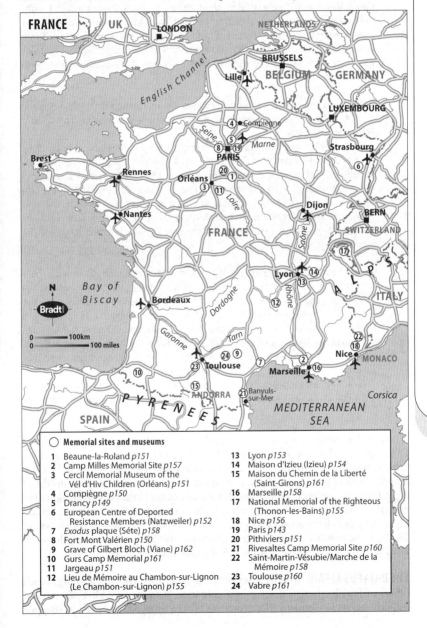

○ **Memorial sites and museums**

1 Beaune-la-Roland *p151*
2 Camp Milles Memorial Site *p157*
3 Cercil Memorial Museum of the Vél d'Hiv Children (Orléans) *p151*
4 Compiègne *p150*
5 Drancy *p149*
6 European Centre of Deported Resistance Members (Natzweiler) *p152*
7 *Exodus* plaque (Séte) *p158*
8 Fort Mont Valérien *p150*
9 Grave of Gilbert Bloch (Viane) *p162*
10 Gurs Camp Memorial *p161*
11 Jargeau *p151*
12 Lieu de Mémoire au Chambon-sur-Lignon (Le Chambon-sur-Lignon) *p155*

13 Lyon *p153*
14 Maison d'Izieu (Izieu) *p154*
15 Maison du Chemin de la Liberté (Saint-Girons) *p161*
16 Marseille *p158*
17 National Memorial of the Righteous (Thonon-les-Bains) *p155*
18 Nice *p156*
19 Paris *p143*
20 Pithiviers *p151*
21 Rivesaltes Camp Memorial Site *p160*
22 Saint-Martin-Vésubie/Marche de la Mémoire *p158*
23 Toulouse *p160*
24 Vabre *p161*

The political debate over exactly what happened in France during the years 1940–44 centres of a series of **myths**:

- **The defeatist French Army simply collapsed in 1940** The stereotypes of 'stupid generals' and 'cowardly soldiers' still endure. Although the French Army had suffered initial defeats after the German invasion, French forces fought back as the Germans advanced on Paris. Many soldiers were shocked when they were given orders to retreat, and an armistice was announced. There was no rout. The Germans were too exhausted to take advantage of the gains they had made – but the window of opportunity to resupply and regroup was missed.

- **Pétain was the shield protecting France** Pétain claimed that, while General Charles de Gaulle was the sword in exile in London, he was the shield protecting France and its citizens.
  In the 1970s, historian Robert O Paxton showed in his seminal book *Vichy France: Old Guard and New Order 1940–1944* (Norton, 1972) that the National Revolution and collaboration were deeply entwined, and that the Vichy regime had actively sought collaboration with Nazi Germany. Paxton brought the fate of the Jews to the forefront of public attention just after the 1968 riots that had prompted a new generation to question the narratives they had been brought up with. He made the case that the antisemitic legislation introduced by Vichy was home grown.

- **Pétain protected the Jews** In 1942, the spin doctors in Vichy invented a story that has now turned into a myth – by arresting stateless Jews, they argued they were sheltering French Jews. It is a fact that foreign-born Jews made up the majority of those who were deported from France during the Holocaust and that politicians in Vichy were unsure how the public would react to measures taken against Jews who were French nationals and had been for generations, so as a result tried to prevent their deportation – but that does not mean that he protected them.
  The 1940 Statut des Juifs (Jewish Law) was not only aimed at foreign Jews, it hit French citizens just as hard. The teachers, the lawyers and the university

Yet in the 1880s an antisemitism based on racist ideology emerged. Édouard Drumont, founder of the Antisemitic League of France and the newspaper *La Libre Parole*, drew on traditional Catholic beliefs that Jews had murdered Christ, a violent antipathy towards the values of the French Revolution and a dislike of capitalism and socialism, both of which were associated in the popular imagination with Jews. Added to this toxic mix was a scientific racism that attributed certain highly negative characteristics to Jews. The turmoil of the Franco-Prussian War in 1870–71, the hostility in right-wing circles to the Third Republic which followed it, and the economic depression of the 1880s popularised his ideas.

THE DREYFUS AFFAIR In November 1894, Captain Alfred Dreyfus, a young French officer of Jewish Alsatian descent, was convicted of treason for allegedly passing military secrets to Germany. His sword was broken by an officer as he was stripped professors, who all lost their jobs, were mostly French Jews. The only way to protect French Jews would have been to refuse to deport any Jews at all.

In 2022, the right-wing TV star and pundit Éric Zemmour stood in the presidential elections. One of his controversial beliefs is that Pétain and his government did everything they could to protect French Jews. Zemmour chooses to ignore the fact that a copy of the draft of the *Statut des Juifs*, discovered in 2010, now held in the archives at the Mémorial de la Shoah in Paris, was marked up in pencil by Pétain. It shows how closely he was involved in every step of drawing up the statute, which began, '*Nous Maréchal de France, chef de l'Etat français*' ('We, the Marshal of France, head of the French state'). At the bottom is his signature. The paragraph intended to spare Jews born as French citizens from the prohibitions is crossed out with a wavy pencil line – much like an item might be removed from a shopping list. Despite the claims he made after the war, Pétain had no intention in his domestic policy of distinguishing between French Jews and Jews who had been born as foreign nationals.

When Pétain and the French prime minister, Pierre Laval, were pressurised by Germany in 1943 to denaturalise all foreign-born Jews, they refused, not because they wanted to save their lives but because they wanted to do things their own way. If the denaturalisation commission withdrew a foreign-born Jew's citizenship according to French law, they had no objection to their deportation.

- **France was a country of resisters** In June 1940, de Gaulle left for London where he claimed he alone spoke for France and the true government of France was in exile. When he returned to power after the war, he invented what became known as the 'Gaullist myth' of France as a nation of resisters.

- **The Vichy government was an aberration** The Gaullist narrative was that between 1940 and 1944 the French Republic had been in exile in London and that Vichy was not the government of France. For de Gaulle, that illegitimacy stemmed from the armistice and that the government had at that moment stopped being the guarantor of the national interest. A legitimacy of a government is also based on its support which Pétain undoubtably had in 1940 even if by 1944 that support had moved to the resistance. France was in Vichy long before it was in London.

of his rank and title, and he was sent to a penal colony in French Guiana. Two years later, the real spy was revealed but was acquitted in a military court. The army then falsely accused Dreyfus of further crimes. After the novelist Émile Zola wrote the editorial *J'accuse!*, France was divided into factions of those who supported Dreyfus's release and those who opposed it. The affair marked a fundamental break in the integration of Jews into western European society. Although Dreyfus was eventually pardoned and set free, the divisions embittered French politics and cast a shadow over the new century. Antisemitism, however, declined during World War I as it was widely recognised that Jewish soldiers were fighting for their country.

INTERWAR YEARS Most French Jews lived in Paris and were highly assimilated into French culture. After World War I and the Russian Revolution, many Jewish refugees and immigrants from eastern Europe, who were far less assimilated, settled

THE HOLOCAUST IN FRENCH CINEMA

French directors have addressed the Holocaust in a number of important films and documentaries. The following films are among the most important.

Claude Lanzmann's 1969 film *Le chagrin et la pitié* (*The Sorrow and the Pity*) exposed the Gaullist myth that France was a country of resisters. His extraordinary film *Shoah* (1985) is notable as it used no archive footage. Louis Malle's *Lacombe, Lucien* (1974) addressed collaboration in the story of an 18-year-old boy from a small French town who joins the Milice but then falls in love with a Jewish girl. In *Au revoir les enfants* (*Goodbye, Children*; 1987) Malle recalled his own experiences in a tale of Jewish children hidden in a French school. Both *La Rafle* (*The Round-Up*; 2010), directed by Roselyne Bosch, and *Elle s'appelait Sarah* (*Sarah's Key*; 2010), directed by Gilles Paquet-Brenner, about the Vél d'Hiv round-up played a crucial role in France in bringing the Shoah to public attention in a similar way to *Schindler's List* in the English-speaking world.

in the capital and became the majority of the French Jewish population. After 1933, Jewish German refugees also fled to France.

World War I had led to a shortage of labour and conscripts, so immigrants were initially welcome. Yet after the Great Depression as unemployment soared, a hatred of foreigners who could 'steal' jobs rippled through all layers of society. In the language of the time, foreigners were synonymous with Jews and immigration restrictions were imposed.

Antisemitism increased in the 1930s. It was heightened by tensions in French politics when the Popular Front government led by the Jewish politician Léon Blum took power in 1936. The economic downturn and the deteriorating international situation fuelled widespread dislike of the Third Republic. As war threatened, Jews were blamed as warmongers.

WORLD WAR II

1940 War broke out in September 1939 but in the period known as the phoney war there was little action in France until the Germans invaded the country in May 1940. As the Wehrmacht moved across northern France, 6 million people abandoned their homes. Laden down with pets and children, they crowded along the roads pushing bicycles and prams crammed with what was left of their lives. Nazi planes repeatedly bombed the columns of refugees and bodies were left scattered along the roadside. There was no-one to help the wounded. It is hardly surprising that, when an armistice was signed with Germany, ordinary people felt an overwhelming sense of relief. The armistice divided France into five zones. A small area in the northeast was annexed to the German military government of Belgium. A corner of southeastern France was handed over to the Italians and Alsace-Lorraine was annexed by Germany. Germany took control of the north of the country, including Paris and the Atlantic coast. This zone was known as the Occupied Zone. The rest of the country, the Free Zone, was governed by an administration led by Marshal Pétain. The new French government based itself in the spa town of Vichy. Pétain, the heroic commander at the Battle of Verdun in February 1916, appeared to have saved France's honour and prevented an all-out occupation. A small handful of French formed the kernel of a resistance movement and General de Gaulle fled to London where he became head of the Free French.

On 9 July, parliament granted Marshal Pétain extraordinary powers and dissolved the Third Republic. The État Français, the French State, that took its place was antisemitic, xenophobic and highly conservative. In the 'National Revolution', the national motto of *'Liberté, Egalité, Fraternité'* became *'Travail, Famille, Patrie'* – work, family, homeland. *Patrie* meant 'France for the French', *La France aux Français*. While a handful of society opposed the Vichy government and a larger group actively supported it, most French were indifferent and lived in a grey zone between the two.

1942 Deportations began in March. While Adolf Eichmann, the SS officer in charge of logistically organising the Holocaust, and his team pushed for mass deportations, Carl Oberg and Helmut Knochen, the heads of the German Security police, knew that they simply did not have the manpower to carry out mass arrests. They were also worried about the impact German troops arresting Jews on the streets of Paris would have on public opinion. Their top priority was to keep the

VICHY'S ANTISEMITIC POLICIES

Without any pressure from Germany, restrictions on the publication of antisemitic literature were lifted and key homegrown anti-Jewish legislation was immediately introduced.

DENATURALISATION In 1939, France had a Jewish population of 330,000, of whom fewer than half had French citizenship. Of the 150,000 French Jews, 30,000 of those were foreign-born and had been granted citizenship after the 1927 change in the naturalisation law. A new legal commission, the Commission de révision des naturalisations, was set up to review all naturalisations granted since 1927 and to strip unworthy foreigners of their citizenship. In the reality of 1940, foreigners were synonymous with Jews. Few people raised objections and the press, now muzzled, did not protest. Some 16,000 immigrants, over one-third of whom were Jews, lost their citizenship. From 1942 onwards, Vichy did not oppose the deportation of denaturalised Jews.

STATUT DES JUIFS The law promulgated on 3 October 1940 reversed the emancipation of the Jews in France, making them second-class citizens. It defined a Jew as someone with three Jewish grandparents. Jews were banned from working in a range of professions including the military, education, the civil service and the media. For Jews in France, it came as a bolt from the blue, and was a shock on par with the armistice. The next day a new law gave *préfets* the powers to detain 'foreigners of the Jewish race in special camps or under house arrest'. Harsher legislation was introduced in 1941 as Vichy sought greater collaboration with Germany.

YELLOW STAR On 29 May, the Germans ordered that all Jews in the Occupied Zone would have to wear a yellow star. Pétain, however, refused to follow suit in the Free Zone, concerned that it might provoke a sympathetic reaction among the general public. Nevertheless, all Jews in the Free Zone had 'Juif' stamped on their *carte d'identité*. What mattered about Pétain's opposition is that it showed that Vichy could say no to the Germans.

country calm and malleable so its economy could be exploited for the German war effort. The only way to carry out mass round-ups was with the help of the French police.

In September, a new law, the Service du Travail Obligatoire, or STO, required all able-bodied men aged 18–50 and all single women aged 21–35 to be subject to work as the government deemed necessary in both France and Germany. To evade the STO, thousands of young people joined the resistance. The STO and deportation of resistance members turned public opinion against the German occupation, but it also relegated the fate of the Jews into second place.

In November 1942, after the Allied victory in North Africa, Germany occupied the Free Zone. Pétain and the Vichy government chose not to go into exile in North Africa but to remain in France. The occupation further alienated public opinion. In response to the German invasion, Italy occupied Alpes-Maritimes and parts of the French Alps.

1943–44 Although the French police collaborated with the Germans in a major round-up in Marseille in January, Vichy continued to oppose the deportation of French Jews. In the same month the government founded the Milice, a political paramilitary organisation whose job it was to hunt down members of the resistance. Led by Prime Minister Pierre Laval, its de facto head was Joseph Darnand, whose aim was to turn the movement into a single fascist party in control of the French state. Yet, as the war turned in the Allies' favour, Vichy politicians began to think twice about how far they were willing to collaborate with the Germans.

JEWISH RESISTANCE

Over 75% of the Jews in France survived the Shoah. Public sympathy was just one element in their survival. Geography also played a part. France is a huge country, much of which is sparsely populated, and there are significant mountain ranges which provided places to hide. France is also bordered by Spain, Switzerland and Italy, all of which offered the possibility of escape. Often overlooked is the importance of the Jewish resistance in France, which was one of the most organised Jewish resistance movements in Europe.

In the summer of 1942, the youth section of the Union Générale des Israélites de France, an organisation that had been set up by Vichy at the Nazis' insistence, went underground. The youth movement was the organisation's sixth department, the Sixième, and the resistance movement they formed was also known as the Sixième. In May, the leaders of the Sixième met secretly in the university town of Montpellier with the Mouvement de la Jeunesse Sioniste, the Young Zionist Movement. They had also gone underground and formed a resistance movement.

From now on the two groups would work in tandem, forging identity papers and documents, hiding Jewish children and taking them secretly across the border into Spain or Switzerland. They also created an armed partisan movement, the Armée Juive, which was a proper militia of almost 2,000 armed men and women. Oddly, in most of the Holocaust and resistance museums in France there is no mention of the Armée Juive.

The Jewish resistance collected deliveries of cash from Switzerland that came from the charity the American Joint Jewish Distribution Committee to support their activities.

Liberation In June 1944, the Allies landed in Normandy. Resistance networks had been united and trained by secret agents dropped behind enemy lines and who played a significant role in the liberation. On 25 August, General de Gaulle entered Paris with his Free French forces and walked triumphally down the Champs Élysées.

The liberation was followed by a period of retribution known as the *épuration*, which in French carries the meaning of not simply revenge but purification. Pétain and other leading members of the Vichy government were put on trial. Despite Pétain's conviction, Vichy apologists soon began to emerge.

The Holocaust was largely overlooked, as was the case elsewhere in Europe, until the Eichmann trial in 1961. French Jews, shocked by de Gaulle's criticism of Israel during the Six Day War in 1967, began to press for recognition of France's role in the Holocaust. Student protests in 1968 prompted the new generation to question what they had been told.

PARIS

Paris is the centre of French Jewish life and has a Jewish population of 277,000. France has the largest Jewish population in Europe and the third largest in the world, after Israel and the USA.

GETTING AROUND In central Paris it is easiest to walk but use the Métro system for longer trips. Paris is no longer an easy city to visit with a car, but if you do street parking is extremely expensive – so budget €30–35 for 24 hours in a car park.

To visit the former Drancy internment camp, if using public transport take the Métro to Bobigny–Pablo Picasso then bus 251 to the stop Place du 19 mars 1962 or the RER B to Le Bourget then bus 143 to the stop Square de la Libération. There are free shuttles from the Mémorial de la Shoah in central Paris on Sundays (for details, check w drancy.memorialdelashoah.org). There is a car park by the museum.

To get to Fort Mont Valérien take the RER train to Mont Valérien then bus 360. The easiest way to see the sites that are further from Paris is by car. Trains run to Compiègne from the Gare du Nord. Bus 106 from the centre goes to Le Francport-Château from where it is a 20-minute walk to the Armistice Memorial. Trains leave for Orléans from the Gare d'Austerlitz. RER trains run from Paris to Pithiviers. There are buses from Orléans to Beaune-la-Roland, Jargeau and Pithiviers.

The Natzweiler-Struthof concentration camp is a full day trip from Paris and is located in Alsace. It can be visited by public transport if you are prepared to walk or take a taxi from the station in Rothau, which has connections to Strasbourg about 1½ hours away by train. An 8km hiking path signposted the Chemin des déportés leads from the station in Rothau to the camp.

WHERE TO STAY AND EAT There is no shortage of hotel accommodation in Paris. The challenge is finding a room that is not going to break the bank. Look for hotels in less touristy areas like the 17th and 20th arrondissements. Paris is far smaller than London and easy to get around. For kosher hotels, w totallyjewishtravel.com has a good selection. The **Hotel Rochechouart** (55 Bd Marguerite de Rochechouart; 9th; 🚇 Anvers; w orsohotels.com/hotel-rochechouart.com; €€€) is the trendy choice for something special and has a beautiful rooftop bar.

The French capital is one of the easiest cities in Europe to be kosher and eat well. In the post-war period Sephardic Jews from the former French colonies in North Africa arrived in France in large numbers, bringing with them their own cuisine. As the Marais district (🚇 St Paul) has turned into a trendy shopping district, it

KEY ROUND-UPS

MAY 1941 Some 4,000 foreign Jews were arrested in the Rafle du billet vert, the green card round-up after French police delivered a green card to 6,694 foreign Jews living in Paris, instructing them to report for a status check.

DECEMBER 1941 In what became known as the Rafle des notables, on 12 December, the French police, accompanied by German soldiers, in a significant development arrested 743 Parisian Jews, among them middle-aged doctors, lawyers and university professors, all of whom were veterans of the 1914–18 war. Fifty-five of them held the Légion d'Honneur, the country's highest order of merit.

JULY 1942 In May 1942, René Bousquet became head of the Vichy police. His brief was to secure Vichy sovereignty over the police in both the Free and Occupied zones. To do this, he agreed to arrest 20,000 foreign-born French Jews living in Paris. On 16–17 July, 13,000 Jewish men, women and children were arrested in the Vél d'Hiv Round-up. Outraged, many Parisians tried to help their neighbours; as a result, Bousquet was 7,000 short of his target.

The round-up came in the wake of a broadcast on 22 June, in which Laval had shocked the nation when he had said he wished for a German victory otherwise Bolshevism would establish itself everywhere. This outright support of Germany had already alienated many French people.

AUGUST 1942 Some 6,500 Jews were arrested in the Free Zone. The round-up prompted 72-year-old Archbishop Jules-Géraud Saliège to break the silence of the Catholic Church issuing a statement that said: 'Jews are real men and women. Foreigners are real men and women...They are part of the human species. They are our brothers, like anyone else. A Christian cannot forget that.' His words were published in underground newspapers, broadcast back to France on the BBC and read out from pulpits across the Free Zone. It reminded many of those in the grey zone of indifference where their moral compass should lie.

JANUARY 1943 In the southern port city of Marseille, in a violent round-up 12,000 French police officers assisted the Germans in arresting 6,000 Jews.

SEPTEMBER 1943 After the capitulation of Italy, Alois Brunner, one of Eichmann's key assistants, was sent to Nice to round up the 25,000 Jews who had taken refuge in the Italian zone. The round-up failed as the French police and the general population refused to co-operate.

After the liberation, no attempt was made by the French state to find out and catalogue the names of the victims or the survivors. A Jewish lawyer, Serge Klarsfeld, would eventually do this in the 1970s when he managed to find the lists of the deportation convoys. His seminal 1978 book Mémorial de la Déportation des Juifs de France *(Memorial of the Deportation of the Jews of France) was the first to list the names of the Jewish deportees.*

has sadly lost many of its Jewish shops and cafés, but **L'As du Falalfel** (34 rue des Rosiers; 🔲; ⊕ 11.00–23.00 Sun–Thu, 11.00–15.00 Fri; €€) remains a favourite lunchtime spot and is the top place to eat falafels in Paris. Both **Florence Kahn** (24 rue des Ecouffes; ⊕ 10.00–18.30 Thu–Sun; €) and the bakery **Sacha Finklesztajn** (27 rue des Rosiers; w laboutiquejaune.fr; ⊕ 11.00–18.00 Mon, 10.00 Tue–Thu, 10.00–19.00 Fri–Sat, 10.30–19.00 Sun; €) are the places to try Ashkenazi cakes and bread. There is also a branch of the Israeli chain **Miznon** (22 rue des Ecouffes; 🚇 Richelieu-Drouot; w miznonparis.com; ⊕ noon–23.00 Sun–Thu, noon–16.00 Fri; €€). **Chez Bob de Tunis** (10 rue Richeris; 9th; 🚇 Cadet; ⊕ 08.00–18.00 Sun–Fri; €) is cheap and cheerful and the place to eat Sephardi North African food. There are plenty of kosher shops in the 20th arrondissement. Israeli chef Assaf Granit has a modern take on Ashkenazi cuisine in his new restaurant **Boubalé** (6 rue des Archives; 🚇 Hôtel de Ville; w boubaleparis.com; ⊕ 12.30–14.30 & 19.00–01.00 daily; €€€€). It is not kosher and is pricey, but it is the place to go for a treat.

HISTORY About 175,000 Jews lived in or had found refuge in Paris in 1940. After the German invasion, many Jews fled the capital alongside its other residents but by early autumn many had returned to the capital even though it was under German occupation. The German census of Jews in September 1940 registered 150,000, among them 64,000 foreigners, as living in Paris. About 50,000 would be murdered during the German occupation.

In October 1941, the Germans bombed six synagogues in the city. In the aftermath Jewish organisations were centralised, Jewish businesses were Aryanised and several other anti-Jewish measures were introduced.

In June 1942, Jews in Paris were ordered to wear a yellow star. The following month, 13,000 Jews were arrested by the French police in the Vél d'Hiv Round-up (page 145). By mid-1943, 60,000 Jews remained in the city. The Germans began to deport Jewish residents of orphanages, nursing homes, and hospitals. Early in 1944, the Germans also began to deport Jewish French citizens.

On 25 August 1944, Allied forces liberated Paris.

WHAT TO SEE
Nissim de Camondo Museum (Musée Nissim de Camondo; 63 rue de Monceau; 8th; 🚇 Monceau/Villiers; w madparis.fr/Musee-Nissim-se-Camondo-125; ⊕ 10.00–17.30 Tue–Sun; €13) Here, visitors can see just how high it was possible for a Jew to rise in French society. Moïse de Camondo was from a Sephardic family who founded the largest bank in the Ottoman Empire. He modelled his house on the Petit Trianon in Versailles and filled it with an extraordinary collection of 18th-century art and furniture. After his son Nissim was killed in World War I, he gave the house and his collection to the nation. Yet, despite their influence, Camondo's daughter and her family were murdered in Auschwitz. Many of the capital's most assimilated and wealthy Jews lived in the 8th and 16th arrondissements.

Le Marais The Marais district was one of the principal Jewish quarters of Paris in 1940. Marais means 'swamp' in French. The area was developed as an aristocratic area but fell into decline after the French Revolution. Known colloquially as the Pletzl, it was home to immigrant families from eastern Europe. While in recent years the area has become one of the city's trendiest shopping areas, traces of its Jewish past still remain.

Stop off at the **Museum of Jewish Art and History** (Musée d'art et d'histoire du Judaïsme; 71 rue du Temple; 4th; 🚇 Rambateau; w mahj.org/en; ⊕ 11.00–18.00 Tue

LA GRANDE MOSQUÉE DE PARIS

The rector of the Grand Mosque in Paris, Si Kaddour Benghabrit (1868–1954), was the organiser of a resistance movement that saved North African Jews by providing them with false identities, offering them shelter in Muslim homes and hiding them in the cellars of the mosque, from where they escaped via the sewers to the Seine. From there they were smuggled out of the city by boat.

In the 1940s, Paris was home to a large community of North Africans, among them thousands of Sephardi Jews, who spoke Arabic and shared traditions and customs with the Arab community. Both Muslim and Jewish men were circumcised. Muslim and Jewish names were often similar and neither group ate pork. These factors made it possible for a Jew from North Africa to pass as an Arab. Many of those who attended the mosque lived alongside Jewish immigrants in the northeast of the city, notably in Belleville.

The exact number of Jews helped has not been established by historians, but some witnesses have claimed the number to be as high as 1,700.

Benghabrit was arrested and interrogated by the Gestapo several times, but higher German command ordered his release as the Germans could not risk Algerian riots in North Africa or Paris. Benghabrit was given the Grand Croix de la Légion d'Honneur after the war but has not been recognised as Righteous Among the Nations as no survivors have come forward to verify the story.

There is nothing to see that relates to this period in the mosque (2 place du Puits de l'Ermite; 5th; 🚇 Place Monge; 🕘 09.00–18.00 Sat–Thu; €3), but it is a tranquil place to consider a story that today seems exceptional but was not unique during the Holocaust. Muslims in the Balkans also helped to save Jews while just as in France some collaborated. In 2013, Mohammed Helmy, a doctor, became the first Arab in history to be awarded the title of Righteous Among the Nations for rescuing one of his Jewish patients in Berlin.

& Thu–Sat, 11.00–21.00 Wed, 10.00–19.00 Sun; €10) not only to discover the rich history of Jewish culture in France but to see the statue of Captain Alfred Dreyfus (page 136) in the courtyard. The permanent exhibition in the museum covers the Dreyfus Affair and its polarising impact on French politics.

In the heart of the Marais a plaque on the **École élémentaire des Hospitalières-Saint-Gervais** (10 rue des Hospitalières Saint-Gervais) is a reminder of a shocking moment in French history, when the Vichy authorities decided that Jewish children would be deported without their parents. After which, families from the school turned to the principal, Joseph Migneret, for help. As 260 of his pupils had been arrested, he joined an underground network that helped the children and their families who had not yet been caught, to get false papers and to cross into the Free Zone. He even hid Jews in his own home until they could leave Paris. Migneret was declared Righteous Among the Nations in 1990. Look out for plaques on schools all over the city recording the names of the deported children.

The **Holocaust Memorial** (Mémorial de la Shoah; 17 rue Geoffroy l'Asnier; 4th; 🚇 Saint Paul/Hôtel de Ville; w memorialdelashoah.org; 🕘 10.00–18.00 Sun–Wed & Fri, 10.00–22.00 Thu; free) began life as the Centre de documentation juive contemporaine in 1943. Like Oyneg Shabes in the Warsaw Ghetto (page 256), the French Jewish resistance began to gather documentation during the occupation. The modern museum traces the history of antisemitism in France and the events of the Shoah period. When the museum and memorial opened in 2005 it was a clear break with the past and the final admission of state culpability in the murder of 75,000 Jewish men, women and children. Visitors step into a courtyard where the moving Wall of Names towers overhead. Twenty years on, it is difficult to convey quite how extraordinary it was for relatives to be able to point at the names of their family members on the wall.

Inside, in the dark, cavernous crypt opposite the eternal flame, are the police files compiled in Paris and the department of the Seine during the Nazi occupation. Also in the crypt, the fighters of the Warsaw Ghetto are remembered, but oddly not France's own Jewish partisans.

Outside the complex, and always accessible, is the Wall of the Righteous on which are recorded the names of French citizens recognised as Righteous Among the Nations.

Rothschild Hospital (Hôpital Rothschild; 5 rue Santerre; 12th; 🚇 Picpus) The red-brick hospital, founded by Baron Edmond de Rothschild in 1912, was turned into a prison from 1941 to 1944, where Jews, often the elderly or new mothers, waited to be transferred to Drancy. Women who gave birth at the hospital had to register their children with the Gestapo. A resistance network in the hospital registered many babies as stillbirths to protect them. There is a plaque on the building, which is still a functioning hospital, on rue de Picpus.

Memorial to the Martyrs of the Deportation (Mémorial des Martyrs de la Deportation; Sq de Île de France, quai de l'Archevêché; 1st; 🚇 Cité/Saint Michel; ℹ️; ⏱ Apr–Sep 10.00–19.00 Tue–Sun, Oct–Mar 10.00–17.00 Tue–Sun; free) This memorial was unveiled in 1962 by General de Gaulle, then President of France, and reflects the Gaullist myth of a nation of resisters. It remembers the 200,000 people deported from France between 1940 and 1944.

A vast, hexagonal, dimly lit crypt opens on to the gallery covered by luminous rods representing the deportees killed in the camps and the ashes of an unknown deportee from Natzweiler-Struthof camp in Alsace, the only Nazi concentration camp on French soil. On either side of the crypt, two small galleries contain earth from the different camps and ashes brought back from the cremation ovens, enshrined in triangular urns. On the last Sunday of April, there is a commemoration service.

The deportees were symbols of the national martyrdom and the resistance fighters, the heroic image of France. As a result, the Jews were subsumed into the general victim narrative and their specific experience went unrecognised. Even in 1956, Alain Resnais's famous documentary film *Nuit et brouillard* (*Night and Fog*) did not explain the difference between a concentration camp or an extermination camp, blurring the specific experience of the Holocaust, and emphasising deportation for forced labour and resistance activities. A quote engraved on the memorial references the Night and Fog Directive (Nacht und Nebel in German). On 7 December 1941, Hitler announced the policy that targeted political activists and members of the resistance in territory occupied by the Germans. They were to disappear into the dark leaving families and colleagues unsure of their fate.

Memorials of the Vél d'Hiv Round-up In the shadow of the Eiffel Tower are a series of monuments that remember the Vél d'Hiv Round-up. They are important as they not only commemorate the horrific arrest of 13,000 men, women and children but also chart how the Shoah has been remembered in France since 1945.

For those arrested a nightmare began to unfold. Adults without children were moved to the Drancy internment camp north of the city. Families were taken to the Vélodrome d'Hiver, the Winter Cycling Track, on **rue Nélaton** (🚇 Bir-Hakeim) in the 15th arrondissement. The stadium gave its name to the round-up. For days, 8,160 men, women and children were crammed into the stands without food and water. The ventilation flaps were closed to prevent escapes and in the heat, the stadium was like a furnace. The families held here were transferred to internment camps at Pithiviers and Beaune-la-Rolande, near Orléans. There the police separated the children from their parents, who were moved to Drancy to await deportation.

In 1946, a small plaque was put up inside the stadium by families and friends of the victims and the first private commemorations took place. The vélodrome itself went back to entertaining the crowds until it was damaged by a fire in 1959 and demolished. In the 1960s Jewish groups began to petition the government for an official memorial to be built at the site.

In 1985, Claude Lanzmann's film *Shoah* increased the pressure for recognition of Vichy's crimes and in 1986, a stele was placed in a tiny garden at **8 Boulevard de Grenelle**. Most people walk past it without stopping, but the small stone steps that run up to a plaque on the wall symbolise the mountain that the state had just begun to climb to overcome the myths of the Gaullist era. The monument reminds us of the horrors of July 1942 but still names the perpetrators as the 'Nazi Occupiers'. As a result, it did not put an end to the campaign for the Fifth Republic to take responsibility for Vichy's crimes. President Mitterrand's silence and ambiguity over his own career under the Vichy government only deepened the rift. Eventually, in 1993, Mitterrand agreed that France would introduce a day of commemoration for 'Racist and Anti-Semitic Persecution'.

In the **Place des Martyrs Juifs du Vélodrome d'Hiver**, a small public garden on Quai de Grenelle on the banks of the Seine, a bronze-and-stone monument designed by Auschwitz survivor Walter Spitzer shows a family awaiting deportation with a pervading sense of sadness and resignation. It is rather banal like so many Holocaust memorials. It gives no sense of the fear and sheer panic of the moment. Nevertheless, this monument matters for what is inscribed on it. The words in inverted commas in the inscription are crucial: *The French Republic in homage to the victims of racist and antisemitic persecutions and crimes against humanity committed under the de facto authority the 'Government of the French state' 1940–44. Let us never forget.* Mitterrand had made an important step forward in accepting French culpability, even if he still held to the myth that the perpetrator, the French government, was not legitimate.

It was only in 1995, that newly elected President Jacques Chirac put an end to decades of equivocations over France's wartime role and admitted in a speech he gave at quai de Grenelle that it was indeed the French state who had committed the crime.

A short walk from the deportation memorial at 7 rue Nélaton is the **Jardin d'Enfants de Vél d'Hiv**. Inaugurated in 2017, the monument has a wall of remembrance where the names and ages of 4,000 children are inscribed. Nearly all the children in question had been born in France and had French citizenship. Although the Germans had not requested the children's deportation, it was decided at a Vichy cabinet meeting, at which Pétain was present, that the children would also be deported for 'humanitarian reasons', so families could be reunited. There was, however, nothing humanitarian about it at all. Deportation solved the problem of caring for thousands of children, who might one day ask what happened to their parents, most of whom had already been gassed in Auschwitz.

As 75% of the Jews survived in France, there is a temptation to say that the persecution cannot have been as bad as in the east but the children's deportation was key evidence at the 1961 Eichmann trial.

The children were deported with Jewish adults moved to Drancy from the Free Zone not to alleviate the children's suffering but to trick the railway workers so they would assume they were families. To find out more, read Serge Klarsfeld's *French Children of the Holocaust* (NYU Press, 1996).

Hôtel Lutetia (Bd Raspail; 6th; 🚇 Sèvres-Babylone; w hotellutetia.com) The luxury Hôtel Lutetia on the Left Bank was requisitioned after the liberation as a reception centre for deportees returning to Paris. Endless trucks and buses brought over 500 every day, both Jews and non-Jews, from the Gare d'Orsay. Crowds gathered outside desperate for news of their relatives. Inside the hotel, in the elegant corridor between the restaurant and the bar, the survivors studied noticeboards covered in photos left by the families of the missing in their life 'before', smiling at weddings or on holiday. But could the survivors identify any of the faces? Joseph Bialot, a Jew from Belleville, who was just 18 years old when he was deported to Auschwitz, looked at the pictures in disbelief as 'the photos exhibited were of normal people with chubby faces, with hair, and we only recalled empty faces and shaved heads.' Although the hotel nowadays belongs to an Israeli company, there is no memorialisation inside, but a plaque on the outside of the hotel remembers what happened here.

OPERATION FURNITURE

In October 1940, a special taskforce was charged with collecting looted artwork from France and Belgium, which was gathered in the Jeu de Paume gallery in the Tuileries just off the place de la Concorde; but the theft carried out by the German occupiers was far more systematic than gathering in priceless artworks. It was aimed at obliterating traces of entire families.

Not content with arresting and deporting Jews, the Germans embarked on systematic requisition of everything they owned – their sheets, towels, kitchen utensils, right down to underwear. The contents of 38,000 Parisian houses and apartments were taken in hundreds of trains to Germany.

The theft was highly organised and named Aktion Möbel, Operation Furniture. Its commander, Colonel Kurt von Behr, kept meticulous records and photographs of his work. Although he committed suicide in 1945, in 1948 American soldiers found some of the pictures he had commissioned. They then lay gathering dust in a German archive in Koblenz until 2004 when they were rediscovered. The photographs show baskets full to the brim with light bulbs and trestle tables laden down with everything from stolen plates to toys.

From 1943 onwards, some of the stolen furniture was taken to Lévitan department store on rue du Faubourg Saint-Martin in the 10th arrondissement. The elegantly designed shop had been closed in July 1941, as its owner was Jewish. Here items were polished, cleaned, repaired, and put on sale for Germans to browse and buy. The furniture was laid out in show rooms – empty rooms that had lost their owners – one after the other. The shop was staffed by 795 Jewish prisoners from the Drancy internment camp north of Paris, who slept on the fourth floor. After the war, the shop was returned to its owners but soon sold.

FURTHER AFIELD

Drancy The former Drancy internment camp, 12km northeast of Paris, is France's most significant Holocaust site. Of the 74 deportation convoys that left from occupied France, 62 went from Drancy. Of those, 57 went to Auschwitz-Birkenau, four to Sobibór and one to the Baltics. Yet for a place so symbolic, Drancy is a surprise. Despite its importance, it gets few visitors.

The former internment camp is a now a low-rise housing estate, but the memorial and museum, as well as the newly refurbished Bobigny station, from which many deportation trains left, are significant sites and well worth visiting.

History Construction of the concrete five-storey U-shaped building was begun in the 1930s. The Cité de la Muette, the Silent City, was to be a model housing estate but in 1938 the money ran out and the project was abandoned.

After war broke out, the complex was initially used as a prisoner-of-war camp until it was turned into an internment camp for Jewish prisoners in 1941. It later became a transit camp where Jews were held before deportation to extermination camps in eastern Europe. The unfinished buildings were divided into 22 sections, each with its own stairwell, which made them easy to police. The apartments had no running water and conditions in the camp were abominable.

From August 1941 to June 1943 the camp was run by the Gestapo, but with the complicity of the French authorities, notably the police and the gendarmerie – without which the camp would not have been able to function. Deportations began in 1942. Between 27 March 1942 and 23 June 1943, 42 trains carrying 40,450 Jews left from nearby Le Bourget-Drancy station. The first convoy headed for Auschwitz.

GOOD TO KNOW

Drancy is a place that still retains a sense of urgency and the ability to expose the fault lines in French society. In post-war France there was a housing crisis, so the local municipality quickly completed the construction work that had begun at Drancy in the 1930s and, in 1948, the first residents moved in. It is, however, far from the only place that people in Europe live in former Nazi camps.

Today, the former internment camp is home to more than 500 people, mostly immigrants from Africa and nearly all of them single or single parents. There are now modern PVC-framed windows but little else has changed. The state of disrepair shows a callous indifference to the memory of what once happened here but more important than that, a disregard for the lives of those who live here now.

The run-down suburbs, or *banlieues*, of France's 93rd department grew up around 19th-century factories conveniently situated at arm's length from the elegant Parisian boulevards. Now home to a large immigrant Muslim community, many of whom face discrimination and marginalisation, Drancy faces a unique problem on top of the predictable, the challenge of remembering the past when the present is so fragile. Radicalisation is an issue – Samy Amimour, a Muslim of Algerian origin, a local bus driver and resident of nearby Bobigny, joined the Islamic State in Syria in 2013. In 2015, he took part in the attack on the Bataclan nightclub in Paris that cost 130 people their lives.

In the summer of 1943, Alois Brunner was sent to run the camp and speed up deportations. He revolutionised the way the camp was run, streamlining the deportation machine, so it no longer needed to rely on the help of the French police. To make prisoners more compliant Drancy was refurbished. Brunner moved the deportations to a goods station at nearby Bobigny, as it was easier to access and fed quickly into the main east–west railway junction. It was also significantly less conspicuous as it was located on what was then a quiet tree-lined street. Deportations were now to be carried out on a regular basis. In 13 months, 21 convoys left from Bobigny, taking 22,500 people to their deaths.

When the prisoners arrived at the station the train would already be waiting. They were lined up in front of the wagons in rows of five, one after the other, and violently forced on board by guards with whips and ferocious dogs. Prisoners deported from Drancy who were selected for slave labour in Auschwitz were ordered to send postcards from Poland to their family and friends. They all followed an almost identical format: 'I am in a labour camp and am well' or 'I am healthy. Kisses.'

The Germans abandoned Drancy on 17 August 1944. The SS tried to burn the camp records but in the confusion the prisoners managed to hide vital documents in the cellar. The card index files were concealed under packages on a supply truck leaving the camp and were hidden in a nearby butcher's shop. It was a vital testament which means we know the name of each person who was deported. Brunner resurfaced in Slovakia as the commander of the Sered concentration camp.

What to see Although there is no access to the buildings, it is possible to walk around the courtyard of the housing complex which is open to the street. The lawn and driveway laid out by Alois Brunner in 1943 still exist. Opposite the former camp are suburban roads of small, early-20th-century houses – what happened here was no secret.

On the edge of the estate is a memorial designed by Holocaust survivor Shelomo Selinger in 1976. The central block represents the ten men needed to say Kaddish, the mourning prayers; the wavelike pattern at the foot of the sculpture evokes the fire of the crematoria; and two stairs, each with seven steps, recall the seven degrees of suffering and the seven degrees of the elevation of the soul. On the right side, the man's beard forms the letter *lamed*, ל, and the woman's hair a *vav*, ו. The Hebrew letters have a numerical value of 36 and so recall the 36 righteous individuals who, according to Jewish tradition, support the world.

The freight wagon behind the monument has been vandalised on numerous occasions. Despite the few metres of railway track that lead up to it, there was no station here. Prisoners were taken in green-and-white buses on loan from the Paris Métro to the nearby station of Le Bourget and then Bobigny.

The housing complex became a national monument in 2001 and a small museum, the **Drancy Holocaust Memorial** (Mémorial de la Shoah Drancy; 110–112 av Jean Jaurès; w drancy.memorialdelashoah.org; ⊕ 10.00–18.00 Sun–Thu; free), opened opposite the estate in 2012. When it was built, residents complained that the past was of more interest than their present problems and as a result the memorial is discreetly signposted and easy to miss. It was designed not to intrude and for visitors to look down on the former camp through large glass windows, a step away from reality. There is an excellent exhibition on the history of the camp.

The main deportation memorial is at the former station in **Bobigny**, which looks almost exactly as it did during World War II. After years of neglect, a campaign by survivors saved the building from demolition in the 1980s, and the **Former Bobigny Station Deportation Memorial** (Mémorial de la Ancienne Gare de Déportation de

Bobigny; 151 av Henri Barbusse; w garedeportation.bobigny.fr; ⊕ 09.30–12.30 & 14.00–17.00 Wed–Sun; free) eventually opened in 2023.

The memorial garden is planted symbolically with trees from the Mediterranean and eastern Europe. It contains 75 stelae, one for each of the convoys that left from France.

Fort Mont Valérien
One of 16 forts built around the French capital in the 19th century, Mont Valérien (Av du Professeur Léon Bernard, 92150 Suresnes; w mont-valerien.fr; ⊕ for guided tours only: Mar–Jun & Sep–Oct 15.00 & 16.00 Tue–Fri, 14.30 & 16.00 Sun, winter & Jul–Aug 15.00 Tue & Sun; free) in the western suburb of Suresnes, 13km from the centre of Paris, was the main execution site used by the Germans during the occupation. Among the victims were hundreds of Jews who had joined the resistance. After the war, General de Gaulle chose the site as the main monument to those who lost their lives in the resistance.

Compiègne
Compiègne, 85km north of Paris, is the place to start a tour of Holocaust memorials in France. There are two excellent museums that explain the fall of France in 1940, as well as the Vichy regime's antisemitic policies and collaboration with Nazi Germany, events that are deeply entwined in the story of the Shoah.

The **Armistice Memorial** (Mémorial de l'Armistice; Route de Soissons; w armistice-museum.com; ⊕ 10.00–18.00 daily, Dec until 17.30; €8) is just outside Compiègne in the forest clearing where the armistice that brought an end to the fighting in World War I was signed in a railway dining car. Hitler chose the same spot for the armistice between France and Germany to be signed on 22 June 1940. The railway wagon was removed from the museum and placed at the exact place where the French and German delegations had met in 1918. After the ceremony, the site was cleared and ploughed up and the wagon taken to Berlin. Hitler ordered that the statue of the French military commander Marshall Foch, the Supreme Allied Commander on the Western Front in 1918, was left untouched so he could survey the disaster that had befallen France. The armistice of 1940 was one of the most important moments in the history of 20th-century France and framed public opinion in the years to come, creating the backdrop to the stage on which the Holocaust played out in France.

The original dining car had been destroyed by the end of the war, but a similar wagon is on show inside the museum. The informative exhibition charts the failure of the Treaty of Versailles that followed the 1918 armistice.

There is an excellent museum at the **Royallieu Internment Camp and Deportation Memorial** (Mémorial de l'internement et de la déportation Camp de Royallieu; 2 av des Martyrs de la Liberté; w memorial-compiegne.fr; ⊕ 10.00–18.00 Wed–Mon; €5, inc English audio guide). A French Army barracks, it was used after the 1940 armistice as a prisoner-of-war camp for French and British soldiers. After the December 1941 round-up, known as the Rafle des notables, the Jews who had been arrested were taken to Royallieu, which then became a transit camp. Royallieu was the only internment camp entirely under the control of the Wehrmacht. About 45,000 people – political prisoners, members of the resistance, Russians, Americans and Jews – were held here. Conditions in the Jewish part of the camp were the harshest and some prisoners starved to death.

The tour starts at the Wall of Names. The exhibition in the remaining barracks then picks up the story after the armistice was signed with a close look at the repression and persecution under the Vichy government led by Marshal Pétain and the German occupying forces. The exhibition details the fate of all the prisoners held in the camp, putting the deportation of the Jews in the contemporary context of the deportation of political opponents of the Vichy government and of the forced labour programme. The remains of an escape tunnel are next to the temporary exhibition hall. The camp remained a military base until the memorial was created in 2008.

The convoys that left from here mainly carried resistance fighters, but the first convoy of Jews destined for Auschwitz left from Compiègne station in March 1942. A memorial path leads from the museum to the station, where there is the **Deportation Wagon Memorial** (Mémorial du Wagon de la Déportation).

Orléans There were three important internment camps near Orléans, 133km southwest of Paris: Jargeau, Pithiviers and Beaune-la-Roland. The **Cercil Memorial Museum of the Vél d'Hiv Children** (Cercil-Musée Mémorial des enfants du Vél d'Hiv; 45 rue du Bourdon Blanc; w musee-memorial-cercil.fr; ⊕ 11.00–20.00 Tue, 11.00–18.00 Wed–Fri, 14.00–18.00 Sun; €4) remembers the 4,700 children interned in the camps of Beaune-la-Roland and Pithiviers between 1941 and 1943, the overwhelming majority of whom were murdered in Auschwitz.

The camps were under the jurisdiction of the prefecture du Loiret and Orléans and guarded by the French police. The first Jews brought to the camps were foreign Jewish men who were arrested in May 1941. After the Vél d'Hiv round-up in July 1942, 8,000 Jews, mostly women and children, were interned in the two camps. The children were separated from their parents, who were deported to Auschwitz. The camps at Pithiviers and Beaune-la-Roland were closed in 1943 when Drancy became the focal transit camp. The museum also has a small exhibition on the Roma who were held in the former prisoner-of-war camp at nearby Jargeau.

Pithiviers and Beaune-la-Roland Pithiviers, 50km northeast of Orléans, has a new museum dedicated to the fate of the Jews deported from the internment camp at the **Gare de Pithiviers** (Place de la Gare; w memorialdelashoah.org/pithiviers; ⊕ 14.00–18.00 Sat–Sun; free). Eight deportation convoys left from the station taking 6,000 Jewish men, women and children to Auschwitz-Birkenau. The exhibition also covers the internment camp at Beaune-la-Rolande and the persecution of Jews in France. The Pithiviers camp was destroyed after the war but is marked by a memorial (Sq Max Jacob) with the names of all those who were interned there.

Among those deported from Pithiviers was the novelist Irène Némirovsky, the author of *Suite Française* (Random House, 2012), a novel that describes the fall of France and the German occupation up until 1941. It is a remarkable account as it was written as events unfurled and was only discovered by her daughter among her papers in the 1990s. The book was made into a film in 2014.

The memorials at **Beaune-la-Roland**, 22km southeast of Pithiviers, are at the site of the former camp (5 routes des Déportés) and at the old train station (Place de la Gare). Convoys 5 and 15 left from here in the summer of 1942.

Jargeau Some 1,200 Roma were interned between April 1941 and December 1945 in appalling conditions in Jargeau, 24km east of Orléans. Its history was forgotten until in 1991 a plaque was placed on the school that now occupies the site (3 rue Albert Serin-Moulin).

Alsace Alsace and Lorraine were annexed to the Reich in 1940. It had been a disputed territory before the Franco-Prussian War of 1870–71 when it was annexed by Germany until it was returned to France after World War I.

In the Vosges mountains on Mont Louise the **Natzweiler-Struthof concentration camp** was the only concentration camp on French soil. Between 1941 and 1944, 52,000 people were deported to the camp and its subcamps, where they worked in a pink granite quarry. Pink granite was needed for Albert Speer's construction of a new capital city in Berlin. The internees were mainly political prisoners and members of the resistance but included Jews, Jehovah's Witnesses and Roma. Medical experiments were also carried out at the camp and 86 Jews were murdered in these experiments in the gas chamber. Their skeletons were sent to Strasbourg University, where a large collection of Jewish skeletons was amassed as part of a study aimed at establishing Jewish racial inferiority. The camp was entirely German-run and for this reason has been memorialised since the 1950s.

You can visit the former camp at the **European Centre of Deported Resistance Members** (Centre européen du résistant déporté; Route départmentale 130, Natzweiler; w struthof.fr; ⊕ 09.00–18.30 daily, closes 17.30 in winter; €8). It takes about 2 hours to visit the site, but beware it is a tricky place if you have limited mobility as it cascades down a mountainside. It is an imposing site with the original barbed wire fence, watchtower and gallows. There is also an informative museum. The gas chamber is located 1.5km downhill from the camp.

LYON

Lyon was a hub of resistance in the Free Zone. An industrial and university city, it was home to a cosmopolitan immigrant workforce, many of whom supported the communists and were among those Vichy sought to exclude.

The city's dramatic topography and confusing layout made it a natural birthplace for an underground movement. Two major rivers run through Lyon: the Rhône and Saône. In 1940, it had 17 bridges and was surrounded by hills covered in forest. Crucially, the city is close to the Swiss border. It is also surrounded by vast flood plains that were perfect for parachute drops.

GETTING AROUND The city centre can be explored on foot. Taxis are pricey but Lyon also has a public bicycle service, Vélo'v (w velov.grandlyon.com), with more than 300 pick-up/drop-off points around the city. To visit Montluc prison, take tram T or buses C7, C25 and 69 to the Manufacture-Montluc stop.

The former children's home in Izieu is extremely difficult to reach by public transport. You will need a car to get there as it is a remote rural spot. There are trains from Lyon to Thonon-les-Bains but you have to change at Bellegarde. Le Chambon-sur-Lignon is 88km southwest of Lyon in the heart of the wild and lonely Auvergne. If using public transport, take the train from Lyon to Saint-Etienne and then a bus.

WHERE TO STAY AND EAT Lyon is a major European city so has the full range of accommodation options, but the hotels are mostly chains and expensive. The best budget option is **Mama Shelter** (13 rue Domer; w fr.mamashelter.com/lyon; €) which has a good restaurant. Traditional restaurants are called *bouchon*. It was in such restaurants that the resistance would meet under cover. Most *bouchon* are found in the central 2nd arrondissement. They serve rustic cuisine, principally offal.

HISTORY The first resistance groups in Lyon were spontaneous grassroots movements that countered Vichy's propaganda machine with underground newspapers, which the Nazis and the French police both took seriously from the very start. The Germans relied on a network of thousands of French informers, who quickly infiltrated the resistance groups. Yet, despite the dangers, within six months Lyon's fledgling resistance networks turned to sabotage.

When Hitler invaded the Soviet Union in 1941, the communists, who until now had refrained from anti-German action because of the 1939 Nazi–Soviet Pact, suddenly became an underground force to be reckoned with. Resistance became increasingly violent and was supported by Britain's Special Operations Executive (SOE), who parachuted in agents and weapons.

The new communist presence in the resistance challenged de Gaulle's authority over what had become an important domestic pressure point. It prompted him to despatch an envoy, Jean Moulin, to Lyon to unify the movement under his control.

In November 1942, after the Allied landings in North Africa, the Germans occupied the Free Zone; Lyon was to pay the price for its defiance. Klaus Barbie, a sadistic 29-year-old SS officer, became the Gestapo chief. He personally tortured and executed many of his prisoners, among them Jean Moulin, who subsequently died of his injuries. It was not long before the entire resistance operation was compromised by infiltrators and SOE's secret agents fled the city. After the war, Barbie went into hiding in South America but was extradited and put on trial in Lyon in 1987.

WHAT TO SEE Start your visit with the excellent exhibition at the **Centre for the History of Resistance and Deportation** (Centre d'Histoire de la Résistance et de la Déportation; 14 av Berthelot; w chrd.lyon.fr; ⏲ 10.00–18.00 Tue–Sun; €6). Housed in Klaus Barbie's former Gestapo headquarters, the museum outlines the special role played by the city during World War II. Much of this resistance activity was centred on Lyon's **Old Town** on the banks of the Saône, which in the 1940s was an insanitary and rundown working-class district. The Renaissance houses, that once belonged to wealthy silk merchants, are built into the hillside with narrow passageways, or *traboules*, running between them. It is possible to enter on the ground floor of one building and leave by the higher floor of another. From the top of the hill, there is a panoramic view across the city, perfect for watching out for approaching police vans.

The Hôtel Terminus, Barbie's HQ is now the **Mercure Lyon Centre Château Perrache** (Esplanade de la Gare, 12 Cr de Verdun Rambaud), its history hidden behind a splash of primary colours. On the third floor Barbie plunged prisoners into scalding and then freezing water and hung them upside down. In his 1988 documentary, *The Life and Times of Klaus Barbie*, Marcel Ophuls interviewed Barbie's victims, who described how in the blink of an eye he turned from a calm interrogator into a raving sadist.

A memorial plaque at 12 rue Sainte-Catherine pays tribute to the 80 Jews arrested on 9 February 1943 and deported to extermination camps. The UGIF, the central Jewish organisation created on German orders, had their headquarters in the building. The UGIF became part of the Jewish resistance and handed out false papers as well as assistance. As people arrived Klaus Barbie's men picked them up one after the other. The arrests were one of the charges levelled against Barbie at his trial in 1987.

Further out of town, **Montluc Prison National Memorial** (Mémorial National de la Prison de Montluc; 4 rue Jeanne Hachette; w memorial-montluc.fr; ⊕ Sep & Jun 14.00–17.30 Wed–Sat, Jul–Aug 09.00–noon & 14.00–17.30 Wed–Sat; free) built in 1921, was used as a military prison by Vichy until it was requisitioned by the Germans in January 1943. Run by the Gestapo, it became the main transit camp for deportations in the region. About 10,000 people were held here, among them the children of Izieu (see below) and the resistance leader Jean Moulin. After the war it was used as a women's prison until 2010.

FURTHER AFIELD

Izieu Jewish children were hidden by the Jewish and non-Jewish resistance across France. The work was led by the Oeuvre de Secours aux Enfants (OSE), a French Jewish humanitarian agency that managed to legally or secretly liberate children from Vichy's internment camps, care for them and help them avoid deportation, sometimes moving them clandestinely to neutral Switzerland.

The most famous of these homes was in the village of Izieu in the foothills of the Alps, 88km southeast of Lyon. The **Maison d'Izieu** (70 route de Lambraz; w memorializieu.eu; ⊕ Jul–Aug 10.00–17.00 daily); €12, inc English audio guide) is one of the most moving Holocaust sites in France. The home was run by Sabine and Miron Zlatin, both Jews from eastern Europe who had settled in France before the war. From the spring of 1943 until April 1944 more than 100 children fleeing Vichy and the Nazis took shelter in the house and were helped by the local population.

On the morning of 6 April 1944, as the children were eating breakfast, the Gestapo drew up outside. The 44 children aged between four and 17, as well as seven of the adults looking after them, were arrested. It is not clear if Klaus Barbie was actually present at the arrest, but he had given the order for it to take place. Most Gestapo leaders overlooked the existence of such homes. Five of the adults and 42 of the children were gassed in Auschwitz. Two of the teenage boys and Miron Zlatin were shot in Estonia. The abduction of the children by the Gestapo motivated Serge and Beate Klarsfeld to hunt down Barbie in Bolivia in the 1970s.

The exhibition in the barn charts the antisemitic laws introduced by the Vichy government and the story of the children who came from across German-occupied Europe. In the house itself you can see the children's drawings and their school room. It is a good place to introduce older children to the Holocaust as not only is it a beautiful spot with extraordinary views, it is an intimate tale that children can relate to. It takes less than an hour to visit. The bookshop has an excellent selection of children's books in French.

Thonon-les-Bains

Thonon-les-Bains On the banks of Lake Geneva, Thonon-les-Bains is just 23km from the Swiss border and was the centre of an important resistance network.

The **National Memorial of the Righteous** (Mémorial National des Justes; Maison forêstière de Ripaille, 10 chemin de la forêt, **w** thononlesbains.com/patrimoine-culturel/memorial-national-des-justes-la-clairiere-des-justes-thonon-les-bains; ⊕ 10.00–16.30 daily, closes 19.00 in summer; free), in a glade in the Ripaille Forest near the Château de Ripaille, pays homage to the Righteous Among the Nations, who hid, helped and saved the Jews during World War II. The memorial is surrounded by 70 trees from the five continents which represent the 70 nations mentioned in the Bible. Designed by the sculptor Nicholas Moscovitz, the monument was inaugurated in 1997.

Le Chambon-sur-Lignon

The 5,000 villagers of Le Chambon-sur-Lignon in Haute-Loire saved 3,000–5,000 Jews from the Nazis. Under the leadership of the local Protestant minister Pastor Andre Trocmé, the villagers risked their lives to hide foreign-born Jews and children in the village and on the surrounding plateau. It was an extremely dangerous thing to do and some villagers were deported. In 1990, Yad Vashem declared Le Chambon a Village des Justes. The **Lieu de Mémoire au Chambon-sur-Lignon** (23 route du Mazet; **w** memoireduchambon.com; ⊕ Mar–Apr & Oct–Nov 14.00–18.00 Wed-Sat, May–Sep 10.00–12.30 & 14.00–18.00 Tue–Sun; €5) is a museum dedicated to the Righteous Among the Nations, known as Justes in French.

NICE

The Côte d'Azur is not the first place that springs to mind when the Holocaust is mentioned, but even before the German invasion in 1940, the French Riviera had become the temporary home of many political and Jewish refugees who had fled from Austria and Germany. After the fall of France, they were joined by thousands of Parisian Jews. The wealthiest bunkered down in the city's luxury hotels and the poor and impoverished crowded into the boarding houses near the station. Their story was captured in Joseph Joffo's classic memoir, *Un sac de billes* (*A Bag of Marbles*; Lerner, 2013), which was made into a film in 2017. Most French schoolchildren have read the book.

The Jewish refugees' presence was widely resented and there was initially considerable support for Vichy's antisemitic policies. Marshal Pétain was a local hero and had a holiday home at nearby Villeneuve Loubet. But in 1943 Nice became a city that resisted mass Nazi deportations.

GETTING AROUND Nice city centre can be explored on foot. Take the train to see Marseille and the former Camp des Milles, which is 10 minutes by taxi from the TGV station at Aix-en-Provence. Saint-Martin-Vésubie is 67km north of Nice. Bus 90 runs from the Grand Arénas.

WHERE TO STAY AND EAT Nice has a good choice of chain hotels but be aware they are pricey. **Le Doirtoir Boutique Suites** (11 rue de Paradis; **w** ledortoir.net; €€) is a small boutique hotel in the heart of the city. **AC Hotel Nice Marriot** (59 promenade des Anglais; **w** marriot.com; €€€), a large modern hotel with swimming pool, is Jewish-observant-friendly.

Nice is an easy city to eat in on a budget. Its market is one of the most colourful in the south of France and the tasty local snack *socca*, a chickpea pancake, is sold in the market. **Chabrol** (12 rue Bavastro; **w** le-chabrol-restaurant-nice.com; ⊕ 19.00–22.00 Mon–Sat, also noon–13.30 Sat; €€€) serves classic French food in a bistro-type atmosphere in the trendy port area of town. **Falafel Sahara** (39 av de la République; w falafel-sahara.com; ⊕ 11.00–17.00 Mon–Thu, 11.00–15.00 Fri, 11.00–22.00 Sun; K; €€) serves typical Levantine cuisine with excellent hummus.

HISTORY Nice is a city with an Italian feel and was until 1860 part of the Kingdom of Piedmont-Sardinia. It was also the birthplace of Giuseppe Garibaldi, the Italian nationalist leader, a key player in the unification of Italy. In return for French support for unification, Nice, its surroundings and the parts of the Duchy of Savoy in the Alps were ceded to France in a rigged plebiscite. Mussolini invaded France in 1940 in the hope he could seize the territory back and annexed the border town of Menton.

Italian occupation After the Allied victory in North Africa in autumn 1942, as the German Army occupied the Vichy controlled Free Zone, Mussolini took control of the Côte d'Azur and parts of Savoy. The nine months that followed provided the Jews in the Italian occupied zone with a moment of reprieve, as the threat of arrest and deportation disappeared. The Italians' attitude was driven first and foremost by the desire to make the area as separate from France as possible but the Fascist government in Rome was also keen to assert its independence from Germany.

The occupation also had an important effect on the rest of the population, for whom the period was far from an idyllic reprieve. Food shortages were acute. After the liberation of North Africa, ships no longer sailed into Nice's harbour loaded with olive oil and wheat. Salted fish, vegetables, wine and eggs simply disappeared from the shelves. The occupation bred a bitterness and resentment that fuelled resistance and polarised society, but it also prompted a change in public opinion that made ordinary French people sympathetic to the plight of the Jews.

In the late summer of 1943, a Jewish banker, Angelo Donati, drew up a plan to evacuate the 25,000 Jews who had crowded into the city by boat to North Africa. Before he put his plan into action General Eisenhower announced that Italy had capitulated. The SS were waiting in Marseille.

German occupation At daybreak on 9 September, a convoy of German tanks rolled eastwards along the Promenade des Anglais. The following morning in the bright sunshine, SS Hauptsturmführer Alois Brunner stepped down from the train at the Gare de Nice-Ville.

As in the rest of France, the French civil service and the police remained in their posts but to Brunner's surprise they refused to co-operate with him. There were also far fewer whistle-blowers than he had expected, although he found collaborators in the white Russian émigré community, who were happy to track down Jews in hiding and simply arrest people who looked Jewish. The Jewish resistance, however, launched an emergency operation. Forgers were brought into the city to make false papers; children were hidden, and collaborators intimidated and in some cases assassinated.

Brunner remained in Nice until December 1943. Although 1,820 Jews were deported to Drancy, the operation was a humiliating failure. After his departure, a further 1,129 people were sent to Drancy, among them one of France's most famous Holocaust survivors, Simone Veil, who was then 15 years old. Veil later became a lawyer, campaigner for women's rights and a government minister.

WHAT TO SEE Start outside the pretty Belle Epoch **Hôtel Excelsior** on 19 Avenue Durante, which was requisitioned by the SS as a transit camp. A huge swastika flag hung in the elegant white hallway. Alois Brunner would watch the prisoners arrive from the balcony on the first floor. There were violent interrogations and the conditions inside the hotel were appalling especially in the first few months of the German occupation. Not surprisingly, the hotel's owners have refused to let the local council put up a plaque on the hotel but across the road the municipality has erected a small memorial.

Arno Klarsfeld, the father of the Jewish Nazi hunter and campaigner Serge Klarsfeld, was arrested in Nice. The Klarsfeld family lived at nearby 15 rue d'Italie. Klarsfeld, his mother and sister escaped the round-up by hiding behind a false partition. His father was sent to Auschwitz on *convoi* 61.

From the Excelsior, walk across to the square in front of the station, the **Gare de Nice-Ville**. Groups of prisoners left the Excelsior three times a week. As soon as Brunner had 50 Jews in the hotel, he dispatched them to the Drancy internment camp outside Paris. Local people wrote letters to the town hall to complain how badly the Jews were treated as they made this short journey and travellers hurled insults at the German soldiers. On the platform there is a memorial plaque. The prisoners travelled in a sealed third-class carriage. The journey took 48 hours and they were given no food or water.

In the hilltop suburb of **Cimiez** the former **Hôtel Hermitage** (today a private apartment block) that dominates the Nice skyline was used as an interrogation centre by the Gestapo. The inauguration ceremony for the Vichy militia, the Milice was held at the nearby Roman amphitheatre (184 av des Arènes de Cimiez; ◷ 08.30–18.00 daily; free).

Situated behind the Christian cemetery on Castle Hill, the **Israelite Cemetery** (Allée Francois Aragon; ◷ 08.00–16.30 Sun–Fri; free), established in 1783, is one of the most beautiful in Europe. There is a stunning view across the rooftops of the old town towards the seafront Promenade des Anglais and the sweeping Baie des Anges. Inside the cemetery by the gate are two memorials to victims of the Holocaust. One contains ashes from Auschwitz. Another claims to contain soap made from human remains. The Nazis in fact never made soap out of Jewish corpses. The **Wall of the Deported** (Mur des Déportés; ◷ 24hrs daily) was unveiled in January 2019. The names of 3,486 Jews arrested along the Côte d'Azur and deported to their deaths in Auschwitz are engraved on the memorial. It is situated on one of the external walls of the Jewish cemetery close to a monument to the Justes Parmi Les Nations, the Righteous Among the Nations of Alpes-Maritimes inaugurated in 2014.

FURTHER AFIELD

Les Milles The most important Holocaust site in the region is the **Camp Milles Memorial Site** (Le Site Mémorial Camp des Milles; 40 chemin de la Badesse, Aix-en-Provence; w campdesmilles.org; ◷ 10.00–19.00 daily; €9.50) just outside the small town of Les Milles near Aix-en-Provence. The former tile factory was used as an internment camp, which opened in September 1939. Germans and Austrians living in Provence, who were now considered enemy aliens, were interned here, among them many artists and intellectuals including the Surrealist Hans Bellmar and the painter Max Ernst. In 1942, the factory was used as a transit camp for Jews arrested in the region who were deported to Drancy and then to Auschwitz.

The site has a moving and informative museum which opened in 2012. Visitors enter a rabbit warren of former kilns where the prisoners lived and can see the murals painted by many of the artists interned here. Outside there is a freight wagon at the siding from which the trains departed for Drancy.

Marseille In January 1943, in a violent round-up 12,000 French police officers assisted the Germans in arresting 6,000 Jews. At the time Marseille was full of Jewish refugees. Since the Allied invasion of North Africa in November 1942, an invasion of Europe's Mediterranean and Adriatic coasts had become a real possibility. The last thing the Nazis wanted was vital ports like Marseille brimming with what they regarded as a dangerous fifth column living in the old run-down streets along the portside.

The round-up began around the opera house on the evening of 22 January. At dusk the following day buses began moving through the gloomy streets towards the portside slums of **Le Panier**, the oldest part of the city. The police ordered everyone out of their homes telling them to bring with them the barest minimum for an overnight stay. They were given the impression that they would be away for a matter of hours. When the thousands of residents, most of whom were not Jewish, were finally released, they returned to find that their homes had been dynamited. They received no help from the town hall and no compensation. The operation was the pinnacle of Franco-German co-operation during the war and an event that oddly few people outside of Marseille remember.

The **Deportation Memorial** (Mémorial des Déportations; 1 quai du Port; ⊕ 09.30–12.30 & 13.30–18.00 Tue–Sun; free) is located at the foot of the Fort Saint-Jean on the Vieux Port in a bunker built by the Germans.

Séte After the defeat of Germany, the former Jewish underground turned its hand to clandestinely removing survivors from the British and French occupied sectors of Germany and taking them to Marseille. Those fit to fight in the nascent Israeli-dense forces were trained in secret camps dotted around the surrounding countryside. In 1947, the Haganah, an underground Jewish military organisation, acquired a worn-out passenger boat, the *President Warfield*. Renamed the *Exodus*, in July 1947, it set sail from the fishing port of **Séte** with more than 4,500 survivors on board. But even before the ship reached Palestine territorial waters, it was surrounded by Royal Navy destroyers. In the struggle that followed three people were killed, and dozens wounded. The ship was towed into Haifa and the passengers were transferred to three navy transports and taken back to France. When the ships docked at **Port-de-Bouc** west of Marseille, the refugees refused to disembark and the French authorities refused to forcibly remove them. The passengers staged a 24-day hunger strike before the ships were taken to Hamburg, then in the British-controlled zone in Germany, where the British Army forced the passengers off the ship.

The story of the *Exodus* was headline news across the world and played a major role in increasing diplomatic sympathy with the plight of the survivors and international support for the recognition of a Jewish state. In Séte a small plaque on the quayside commemorates the event.

Saint-Martin-Vésubie Saint-Martin-Vésubie was one of many remote villages in Alpes-Maritimes that sheltered Jews. Believing that the US Army had reached Piedmont, between 9 and 13 September 1943 over 1,000 of them fled into Italy on foot across the mountains. Unfortunately, the Nazis had already occupied northern Italy. When they arrived in Piedmont at least 330 of them were arrested and deported to their deaths. The **Marche de la Mémoire** (w ame43.org), a memorial walk organised by the Association pour la Mémoire de l'Eté 1943, is held every September and follows the old salt road across the Col de Fenestre. The names of the victims are read out at the highest point on the walk.

In New York and Washington, American Jews lobbied for visas and raised funds to help celebrity writers and artists but there were limits to what they could achieve. The Emergency Rescue Committee managed to acquire 200 visas for prominent anti-Nazi intellectuals to be brought to the United States. **Varian Fry**, a New York journalist, was sent to Marseille to help to get them out. He managed to save 2,000–4,000 prominent celebrities using illegal paperwork, among them the painter Marc Chagall, before he was expelled from France in 1941.

Fry was not well received by the State Department when he returned home to the United States, nor by the Emergency Rescue Committee, who disapproved of his highly illegal methods. He was ostracised and died without his work being acknowledged. He is now one of the handful of Americans to be recognised as Righteous Among the Nations. His story inspired the 2023 Netflix mini-series *Transatlantic*.

TOULOUSE

Toulouse, France's fourth city, was an important resistance hub. Its close proximity to the Spanish border defined the nature of that resistance much as it does the atmosphere in the city today. Toulouse has a Spanish feel about it and after Franco's victory in the Spanish Civil War, Republican refugees fled over the border into France. They were interned in two of France's most notorious internment camps, Gurs and Rivesaltes, both in the southwest of France.

The southwest was also an important escape route as Vichy's opponents and Jews tried to make their way over the Pyrenees into Spain and then Portugal.

GETTING AROUND Central Toulouse is easily explored by foot. The local branch of the Mémorial de la Shoah offers guided tours of Toulouse. The walking tour takes an hour (e antennesud@memorialdelashoah.org; €6).

Public transport options are available to visit the sites in the region, but it helps to have a car. The memorial at the former internment camp of Rivesaltes is 200km southeast of Toulouse near Perpignan. Rivesaltes station is 7km from the memorial. Bus 503 goes to Salses-le-Château.

The memorial at Gurs is 241km southwest of Toulouse. The nearest stations are Orthez and Puyoô. There are bus connections to nearby Salies and Sauveterre.

To explore Vabre and the surrounding area, you need a car.

WHERE TO STAY AND EAT Base yourself in the Capitole de Toulouse, the historic heart of the city, or the trendy Carmes district. There is a wide variety of hotels and rental accommodation. Of the chain hotels **Mercure Centre Saint Georges** (Rue Saint Jérome; w mercure.com; €) is a good option, or try the boutique hotel **Villa du Taur** (62 rue du Taur; w villadutaur.com; €€). In summer, picnic on the riverfront or enjoy tapas in Place Saint Pierre or Place de la Daurade.

HISTORY In the autumn of 1942, a significant resistance movement grew in the southwest as Jews took up arms, and young men and women fled into the remote countryside to evade being sent to work in Germany under the STO, the forced labour scheme.

After the Allied landings in Provence, the 220,000 German troops stationed in the southwest were effectively trapped and the battles were fierce. There were major reprisals such as that at Oradour-sur-Glane as the forces retreated to the northeast.

Spanish Republicans played a major role in liberating Toulouse on 19 August 1944, as did the communists and the Jewish resistance.

WHAT TO SEE The **Holocaust Memorial** (Mémorial de la Shoah; 29 square Boulingrin; ⏱ 24hrs daily) in the Grand Rond park was designed by the architect Mikaël Sebban. Erected in 2008, it is in the form of six metal doorways and inscribed with the words 'Where are you?' and 'Where is your brother?', evoking the notion of responsibility for the well-being of others.

The **Memorial to the Righteous Among the Nations of the Midi-Pyrenees** (Mémorial en hommage aux Justes des Nations de Midi-Pyrenées; Allée Jules Guesde; ⏱ 08.00–20.00 daily; free) in the nearby Jardin des Plates is engraved with the names of 131 non-Jews recognised by Yad Vashem as Righteous Among the Nations.

Near the Jardin des Plantes on the junction between Allée Frédéric Mistral and Allée Serge Ravanel the **Monument to the Glory of the Resistance** (Monument de la Gloire de la Resistance; ⏱ 11.00–18.00 Sat–Sun; free) opposite the former Gestapo headquarters is an unusual underground network of tunnels and crypts. On 19 August at 11.00, a ray of sunlight illuminates a plaque on the ground where the words are engraved: 'August 19, 1945, Liberation of Toulouse'. Serge Ravanel, who was Jewish, was the leader of the resistance in Toulouse.

The **Departmental Resistance and Deportation Museum** (Musée departmental de la Résistance et de la Déportation; 52 Allée des Demoiselles; w musee-resistance. haute-garonne.fr; ⏱ 10.00–18.00 Tue–Sat; free), a 10-minute walk from the memorial, traces the history of the resistance in Toulouse but oddly does not mention the important local Jewish resistance movement.

FURTHER AFIELD

Rivesaltes The **Rivesaltes Camp Memorial Site** (Le Mémorial du Camp de Rivesaltes; Av Christian Bourquin, Salses-le-Château; w memorialcamprivesaltes. eu; ⏱ Apr–Oct 10.00–18.00 daily, Tue–Sun in winter; €9.50) is one of the most important sites to visit in the southwest of France. The former internment camp held foreign Jews, Roma and Spanish Republicans from 1939 to 1944. In 1942 around 2,400 Jewish men, women and children were deported from the Rivesaltes camp to Drancy and from there to Auschwitz. After the German occupation of the Free Zone in November 1942, Rivesaltes became a German Army barracks and the internees were moved to other camps. After the war, the camp was used to hold collaborators and Axis prisoners of war from 1944 to 1948. Rivesaltes also housed *harkis*, Muslim Algerians who served as auxiliaries in the French Army during the Algerian War from 1954 to 1962.

The camp was built on an exposed windy plain which is cold in winter and extremely hot in summer. The skeletal remains of the barracks surround a comprehensive underground museum, which opened in 2015. It looks at not only the Spanish Civil War but also the issues of decolonisation. For years, the history of Rivesaltes was not well known but a scandal that erupted after the camp archives were found in a nearby rubbish dump catapulted it back into public consciousness. The Nazi hunter Serge Klarsfeld was the driving force behind the creation of the museum.

Irish aid worker Mary Elmes (**w** holocausteducationireland.org/mary-elmes) saved more than 200 children from Rivesaltes. She hid them in the boot of her car and drove them high into the Pyrenees, where they crossed the border illegally.

There is a café on site and a picnic area.

Gurs At the foot of the Pyrenees in southwestern France, Gurs Camp (Camp de Gurs), just south of the village of Gurs on the D936, was the first and largest internment camp set up in pre-war France. It opened in April 1939, as a detention camp for political refugees and members of the International Brigade fleeing Spain after the Spanish Civil War. German Jewish refugees were interned here as 'enemy aliens', as well as French left-wing politicians who opposed the war with Germany. In October 1940, 6,500 Jews from southwestern Germany were deported to Gurs.

Conditions in the camp were primitive and hundreds of prisoners died of contagious diseases. Between August 1942 and March 1943, Vichy handed over 3,907 of its Jewish internees to the Germans. The majority were transferred to Drancy and from there deported to Auschwitz. The camp was closed in November 1943 by which time 22,000 prisoners, including 18,000 Jews, had passed through the camp. The camp was then used briefly to hold members of the resistance and political prisoners. After the liberation of France, it was used to hold German prisoners of war and collaborators. After the camp closed in December 1945, a forest was planted on the site.

The **Gurs Camp Memorial** (Mémorial du Camp de Gurs; **w** campgurs.com; ⊕ 24hrs daily; free), designed by the Israeli artist Dani Karavan and inaugurated in 1994, is a mix of wood and concrete sculptures that depict the contours of the overcrowded barracks which held 60 people. A 180m-long railway track symbolises the ultimate journey to the death camps. A permanent outdoor exhibition documents the camp's history.

The memorial trail runs 2km parallel to the D936 and leads to the cemetery, where there are two monuments. One is dedicated to the Spanish Republicans and the other to the Jews expelled from southern Germany in October 1940. Towns in the German province of Baden pay for the upkeep of the cemetery.

Vabre This remote grey-stone town in the hills of the Haut-Languedoc was a tight-knit community united in its opposition to the Vichy regime, which was led by its Protestant pastor, Robert Cook. Far from insular, Vabre was an industrial town that made its living weaving cloth that it sold to Jewish tailors in Paris. In July 1942, after the mass arrest of Jews in the capital, many tailors arrived with their families seeking sanctuary.

THE CHEMIN DE LA LIBERTÉ

A unique hiking path across the Pyrenees into northern Spain marks the route taken by hundreds of Allied soldiers and airmen, French and Jews escaping Vichy France. Not a hike for the faint-hearted, it crosses the mountain peaks of Ariège. A four-day commemorative hike takes place every July. The high mountain route was carefully chosen to avoid all official checkpoints and any likely contact with German patrols.

The Chemin de la Liberté starts in Saint-Girons, where there is a small exhibition in the **Maison du Chemin de la Liberté** (Av Aristide Bergès; **w** chemindelaliberte.fr; ⊕ 13.30–17.15 Mon–Fri; free).

The people of Vabre had not forgotten how the state had mistreated their forebears, the Protestant Huguenots in the 17th century, and did everything they could to help the Jewish fugitives, especially after the Vabre police were ordered on 26 August to the nearby resort of Lacaune to arrest foreign-born Jews, who had been interned there. Ninety were taken into custody, among them 22 children, all of whom were later murdered at Auschwitz. The gendarmes from Vabre returned home in tears, and police chief Hubert Landes decided it was the last time he and his men would follow that kind of order. A year later he warned Jewish refugees of an impending overnight round-up, urging them to hide. Yad Vashem recognised Vabre as a Town of the Righteous in 2015, and Hubert Landes and Pastor Robert Cook as Righteous.

Many of the surviving Jews in the area joined the local maquis as the Compagnie Marc Haguenau. They took part in a dramatic attack on a German supply train heading for Castres on 19 August 1944. The story of the maquis is remembered in the small **Resistance Museum** (Musée Résistance; Rue du Suquet; e sivabre@voila. fr; w maquisdevabre.fr; ⊕ by appt Jul–Aug; free). The **Vieux Lacaune Museum** (Musée du Vieux Lacaune; Place du Grifoul; w museeduvieuxlacaune.fr; ⊕ 10.30– 12.30 & 14.30–18.00 daily) 30km east of Vabre tells the story of the Jews interned in the town. Those arrested and sent to their deaths are remembered by a memorial in the town centre.

The local people also cared for the Jews in death. In the cemetery in Lacaune, there is a collection of Jewish graves. They belong to elderly people who remained in the town after the liberation. They were the sole survivors of their families and had no-one else to bury them.

In the tiny village of **Viane**, 23km east of Vabre, is the neatly fenced **grave of Gilbert Bloch**, one of the leaders of the Compagnie Marc Haguenau. He was killed in action in August 1944. He had no family to claim his body. His father had died before the war and his mother had been deported to Auschwitz, so the locals decided that he would be buried in Viane.

11

Germany

The Nazi policies that gave rise to the genocide of World War II were drawn up in the German capital, Berlin. For tens of thousands of Jewish survivors, the Holocaust also ended on German soil, as they found themselves among many other prisoners brought on death marches to Bergen-Belsen and Dachau concentration camps in the north and south of the country respectively.

Germany has faced up to its guilt as a perpetrator of the Holocaust like no other – there is even a word for it, *Vergangenheitsbewältigung*, which means 'struggle to overcome the past'. Not that this acceptance of guilt is without issues: the reactionary populism in the form of the Alternative for Germany Party (AfD) claims the Holocaust is over-remembered.

The country has thousands of memorials and museums. This chapter, therefore, more than any other in this guide, offers the visitor a selective introduction. The sites have been chosen as they offer an understanding of the key developments in the Nazi persecution of the Jews.

GETTING THERE AND AROUND

Airports at Berlin, Munich and Frankfurt have connections to most of the world's major cities, while Hamburg and Nuremberg have links to European destinations. High-speed train services as well as buses (see w flixbus.co.uk) link to most European cities. To travel between cities within Germany, the train is the best option (w bahn.de). From Berlin, Hamburg can be reached in 2 hours and Munich in 4 hours. Most major sites on the outskirts of the cities are accessible by public transport, but to explore smaller sites it helps to have a car. Germany has no road tolls.

ONLINE RESOURCES

A helpful interactive map of Holocaust memorials in Germany can be found at w deutschland.de/en/topic/politics/holocaust-memorials-in-germany-aninteractive-map.

Arolsen Archives – International Center on Nazi Persecution w arolsen-archives.org. The most comprehensive archive on the victims of Nazi persecution, these archives hold some 30 million documents from the concentration camps, details of forced labour & files on displaced persons. Of these, 13 million are accessible online.
Bundesarchiv w bundesarchiv.de/gedenkbuch. Search for names in the Memorial Book.

Dokumente zum Nationalsozialismus w ns-archiv.de. A useful resource on the history of the Nazi period.
European Association for the Preservation & Promotion of Jewish Culture & Heritage w jewisheritage.org/european-routes# national. Details Jewish heritage routes in Germany.

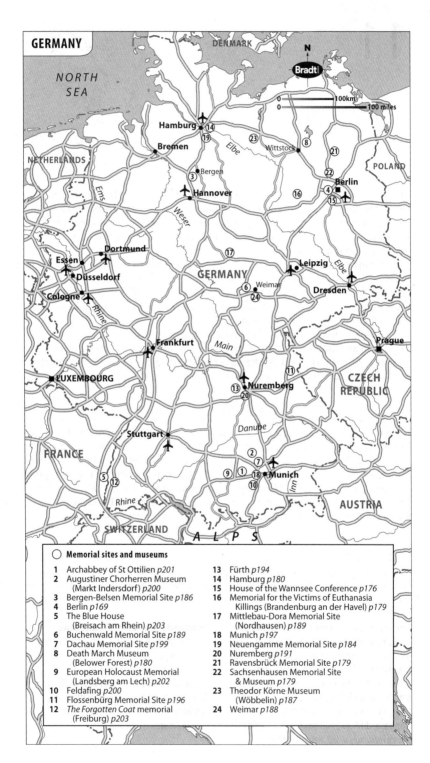

GERMANY

NORTH
SEA

DENMARK

NETHERLANDS

Hamburg (14)
(19)
Bremen
(23) Wittstock (8)
Elbe
(21)

POLAND

(3) Bergen
(22)
Hannover
Berlin
(4)
(16)
(15)

Weser

Ems

Dortmund
(17)
Essen
Düsseldorf
GERMANY
Leipzig
Elbe
Cologne
(6) Weimar
(24)
Dresden

Rhine

Frankfurt
Main
Prague

LUXEMBOURG
(11)
CZECH
REPUBLIC
(13) Nuremberg
(20)

Stuttgart
Danube

FRANCE
(2)
(7)
(5) (12)
(9) (1)
(18) Munich
(10)

Rhine
Inn
AUSTRIA

SWITZERLAND
A L P S

⭕ **Memorial sites and museums**

1 Archabbey of St Ottilien *p201*
2 Augustiner Chorherren Museum
   (Markt Indersdorf) *p200*
3 Bergen-Belsen Memorial Site *p186*
4 Berlin *p169*
5 The Blue House
   (Breisach am Rhein) *p203*
6 Buchenwald Memorial Site *p189*
7 Dachau Memorial Site *p199*
8 Death March Museum
   (Belower Forest) *p180*
9 European Holocaust Memorial
   (Landsberg am Lech) *p202*
10 Feldafing *p200*
11 Flossenbürg Memorial Site *p196*
12 *The Forgotten Coat* memorial
   (Freiburg) *p203*

13 Fürth *p194*
14 Hamburg *p180*
15 House of the Wannsee Conference *p176*
16 Memorial for the Victims of Euthanasia
   Killings (Brandenburg an der Havel) *p179*
17 Mittelbau-Dora Memorial Site
   (Nordhausen) *p189*
18 Munich *p197*
19 Neuengamme Memorial Site *p184*
20 Nuremberg *p191*
21 Ravensbrück Memorial Site *p179*
22 Sachsenhausen Memorial Site
   & Museum *p179*
23 Theodor Körne Museum
   (Wöbbelin) *p187*
24 Weimar *p188*

Jewish Museum Berlin w jmberlin.de. Has information on past exhibitions that illuminate German Jewish history & contemporary issues.
Leo Baeck Institute w lbi.org. Offers an understanding of Jewish heritage in Germany.
Memorial to the Murdered Jews of Europe Foundation w stiftung-denkmal.de. Set up by the German Bundestag, the foundation promotes understanding of the Holocaust across Europe & is partnered with the United States Holocaust Memorial Museum (w ushmm.org).
Memorial Museums Department at the Topography of Terror Foundation w gedenkstaettenforum.de. A useful site to keep abreast of news & events at memorials & museums across Germany.

HISTORY

Jews have lived in the area that is now Germany since Roman times, and in the Middle Ages Mainz and Worms were important centres of Talmudic study. In the late 19th century, the Jewish Enlightenment created a highly assimilated community deeply loyal to the new country. The German Jewish community was one of the most well integrated in Europe and excelled in science, literature and the arts, accounting for 24% of the country's Nobel prize winners.

In 1866, Prussia emancipated all its Jews. Other states followed suit after unification in 1870; but almost immediately their position was undermined by the depression of the 1870s. In the 1890s, antisemitic parties were represented in the Reichstag. A racial antisemitism was on the rise that saw Jews as alien to a distinctive German Christian culture.

In 1933, there were approximately 525,000 self-identifying Jews in Germany, less than 1% of the population. About 100,000 were recent immigrants from the east, known as Ostjuden. They spoke Yiddish and were Orthodox, unlike the highly assimilated German-speaking Jews who lit Hanukkah candles but simultaneously put up Christmas trees.

WORLD WAR I Although most German Jews supported Germany's entry into World War I, after suffering more than 600,000 German casualties in the Battle of the Somme in 1916, antisemites in the army and the Reichstag blamed Jews for the defeat and singled them out as shirkers. In October 1916, a census of Jewish soldiers was ordered to assess their commitment to defending the Fatherland. The dead and the wounded as well as the living were to be counted. Although the statistics compiled by the War Ministry failed to uncover any evidence that Jewish soldiers had evaded the frontline, the exact findings were never made public.

In 1918, the German Empire collapsed and the defeat plunged Germany into social chaos and economic ruin. Jewish veterans faced accusations of cowardice and dereliction of duty, and a myth rapidly gained ground that Germany had been stabbed in the back by a conspiracy of socialists and Jews.

INTERWAR YEARS The atmosphere in the years after the 1918 defeat was toxic and disastrous for German Jews. The Spartacists, a radical group of communists, called a general strike and demanded that factory owners hand over control to workers' councils. Several of their leaders, like Rosa Luxemburg, were Jewish. In Bavaria, a left-wing government led by the Jewish journalist Kurt Eisner took power.

Germany became a republic. But it looked to many Germans as if the Jews had overthrown the German Empire – Hugo Preuss, one of the group who drew up the Weimar constitution, was Jewish. Germans felt victimised and antisemitic groups moved from the margins to the mainstream.

In addition, there was deep resentment over the severity of the Treaty of Versailles, in which Germany lost territory and was forced to pay reparations that undermined the German economy further. The period 1919–23 was one of economic and political turmoil which culminated in hyperinflation in 1923. It was the perfect breeding ground for radical right-wing antisemitic groups. Jewish politicians were assassinated and food riots in Berlin turned into a pogrom when Jewish shops were looted.

In 1919, former soldier Adolf Hitler joined the tiny and unimportant German Workers' Party (later to become the National Socialist German Workers' Party) and became their leader. After trying to seize power in a coup d'état in 1923, Hitler was imprisoned. During his time in Landsberg Prison, he began to write *Mein Kampf*, in which he set out his racial theory and plans for global domination. After his release in April 1924, the party tried to gain popularity by legal means. The party was elected to the Reichstag but made little gains against the backdrop of economic stability in the country at that time.

After the Wall Street Crash of 1929, the Nazis received 18.3% of the vote in the 1930 elections. In July 1932 they became the largest party in the Reichstag.

1933–39 Hitler became Chancellor on 30 January 1933. At nightfall his supporters held a vast torchlight parade through central Berlin that converged on the Brandenburg Gate. Although it looked as if the Nazis were fulfilling their destiny, there was nothing certain in German politics and no indication that Hitler would remain in office for very long.

But within months the country became a one-party state. In March 1933, the concentration camp of Dachau was opened to hold anyone considered an enemy of the state, among them communists, socialists and liberals. Persecution of the Jews began immediately, and German Jews, under little illusion of the danger they were in, began to leave the country. Others stayed, some believing Hitler could not last, others to protect their property and businesses, or because they were fearful of becoming refugees or simply because they did not have the means to leave.

Nazi Jewish policy was designed to cut Jews out of society to avoid a second alleged 'stab in the back'. The drive to make Germany the dominant power in Europe meant that Jews were stripped of their citizenship and property in a series of racial laws.

The 1938 Anschluss with Austria saw a spike in antisemitism. It was followed by a radicalisation of Nazi Jewish policy as Jews were expelled from Austria's Burgenland, as were Polish Jews living in the Reich.

On 7 November 1938, a Polish immigrant in France, Herschel Grynszpan, whose parents were among the Polish Jews who had been expelled, shot an official at the German Embassy in Paris (page 5). It prompted an orgy of violence against Jews across the Reich, which was orchestrated by the Nazi Party and became known as Kristallnacht. Synagogues burned, Jewish shops were looted, and Jews killed; thousands of Jewish men were imprisoned in concentration camps. After the pogrom, 10,000 children were brought to the UK on the Kindertransport scheme. German Jews had a high survival rate as many emigrated before 1939.

WORLD WAR II AND ITS AFTERMATH For a full description of the evolution of Nazi antisemitic policies and how they changed during World War II, see page 2.

Deportation Jews from the Reich began to be deported in late 1941, against a backdrop of widespread indifference and apathy among the general population

Remembering the Holocaust has passed through several phases in Germany. As Germans initially confronted what had happened after the war, a culture of victimisation was reinforced by the fact that hundreds of thousands of German soldiers remained missing in action or were held in Soviet prisoner-of-war camps until 1956. And at first, in both East and West Germanies, there was an emphasis on collective German suffering which was not conducive to recognising the fate of the Jews, about which there was a general amnesia.

Each of the two new German states drew on different historical narratives: in West Germany, Nazism was portrayed as an alien idea that had been imposed on the German people; in East Germany, fascism was blamed on capitalism and the emphasis was on both communist resistance and Soviet liberation, and no differentiation was made between victims of the Nazis.

Denazification was difficult and complex, and never fully completed. The first West German Chancellor, Konrad Adenauer, who came to power in 1949, was opposed to the process of denazification and opted for a strategy of integration in order to move forward. The developing Cold War meant that Britain and America saw West Germany as a useful ally against the Soviet Union, and therefore the former Nazis who returned to their positions in society were viewed as less of a threat than communists. On top of this, even the process of establishing who was and who was not a Nazi was challenging and often relied on citizens providing information about themselves.

In West Germany, acceptance of its perpetrator role was driven by the need for international acceptance and an agreement was reached with Israel to pay survivors reparations. West Germany officially apologised to Israel for the Holocaust in 1952. In response, East Germany adopted an anti-Zionist stance, allied itself with Arab states and arrested citizens who were suspected of sympathetic leanings towards 'cosmopolitan', ie: American and Jewish, influences. Antisemitic stereotypes soon re-emerged.

Yet, in the 1960s the next generation of Germans began to ask questions, prompted by the publication of Anne Frank's diary in 1955, the trial of Adolf Eichmann in Jerusalem in 1961 and that of 22 former Auschwitz personnel in Frankfurt in 1963–65. The election of the Social Democratic Party, with Germany's former resistance fighter Willy Brandt as Chancellor, in 1969 continued this trend. Yet, the greatest impact on the way Germans saw their past was the broadcast in 1979 of the NBC miniseries *Holocaust*, which became the most widely watched television programme in the history of the Federal Republic. The publication in 1996 of Daniel Goldhagen's *Hitler's Willing Executioners* (Abacus, 1997) generated greater awareness of the role played by ordinary Germans in the Holocaust. The travelling exhibition, the 'Wehrmachtsausstellung', which focused attention on the crimes committed by the Wehrmacht, opened in Hamburg in 1995. It challenged the hitherto sanitised version of the German Army's wartime behaviour.

Since unification, the state's recognition of its responsibility has been unwavering.

towards Nazi Jewish policy. As historian Ian Kershaw has written, 'the road to Auschwitz was built by hatred, but paved with indifference.'

1945 Germany was ruined by the war. The country was devastated, parts of it destroyed, and overrun with refugees. In the German context, the refugees that mattered to the general public were Germans expelled from eastern Europe and from the former territories now given to the new state of Poland. Germany was occupied by the Allies and split into four zones of Allied occupation. The northeast was controlled by the Soviet Union, the southeast by the Americans, the northwest by Britain and the southwest by France. In the wake of the liberation of the camps, American, British and French forces tried to expose Germans to the reality of the Nazi regime, with forced tours of the concentration camps.

Germany divided and reunited In 1949, Germany was divided into two states: the Federal Republic of Germany (FRG), made up of the Western occupation zones, and the communist German Democratic Republic (GDR) in the east. The country's division soon took on the tensions of the emerging Cold War. The FRG joined NATO and the GDR the Warsaw Pact. In 1961, the construction of the Berlin Wall cemented the division between the two states. The country was reunited in 1990, after the fall of the Berlin Wall the previous year.

In the 1990s many Soviet Jews settled in the country. Today, Germany's Jewish community numbers 100,000 and is the eighth largest in the world.

BERLIN

Germany's capital was the beating heart of the Third Reich, which Hitler's architect, Albert Speer, hoped to turn into a new glittering city called Germania. Badly destroyed by bombing raids in the closing days of World War II, however, Berlin became a city divided by the Cold War until reunification in 1992.

Today, Berlin is a vibrant place. At its centre is the Brandenburg Gate. In the 1930s the area around it was the administrative hub of the Third Reich. To the east was the manufacturing quarter of Prenzlauer Berg, where many Jewish immigrants from eastern Europe lived and worked. To the west, the area around Kurfürstendamm is the commercial heart of the city, home to its shops and theatres. To the south and southwest are the elegant middle-class suburbs, where many of Berlin's Jews lived in 1933. Berlin is a city with two stories: that of the persecutors and the victims who lived right on their doorstep.

GETTING AROUND Both the U-Bahn (underground rail) and S-Bahn (commuter train) systems are the best way to get around but can be confusing, so it helps to have a good transport map. As well as giving discounted entry to museums, the Berlin Welcome Card (w berlin-welcomecard.de; €26) gives free travel on the city's public transport. Berlin is a surprisingly easy city to visit by car. It has no congestion charge and, compared with other western European cities, parking is easy to find and moderately priced. Use the EasyPark app.

To see the former Sachsenhausen concentration camp 30km north of Berlin, take S-Bahn 1 to Oranienburg, then walk 20 minutes; or take bus 804/821. To get to the former Ravensbrück camp, take the RE 5 train from Berlin to Stralsund/Rostock which stops at Fürstenberg and runs every hour. The memorial is a good 30-minute walk from Fürstenberg station. The Death March Museum in the Belower Forest is quite remote and you need a car to visit.

WHERE TO STAY AND EAT Berlin has a good selection of chain hotels and apartments. The nicest place to stay is in the west around Kurfürstendamm, as there are plenty of shops and restaurants in the area. This was the heart of 1920s Berlin. The best hotel is the **Hoxton Charlottenburg** (Meineckestr. 18–19; w thehoxton. com; €€€). After some heavy sightseeing, especially if you are tracing family roots, it is good to escape into modern Germany. The hotel has an excellent Indian restaurant, the **House of Tandoor** (⊕ 07.30–22.30 daily; €€€), and there are plenty of alternative places within easy walking distance. The **Crowne Plaza City Center Hotel** (9 Nürnbergerstr. 65; w ihg.com/crowneplaza; €€€) offers kosher meals for an additional fee. The websites w berlin.de and w kosherberlin.de have lists of kosher restaurants in the city.

If you are visiting the Oranienburgerstrasse area with children, it's useful to know there is a large park with a playground near the synagogue. If you are combining your sightseeing with the museums on the nearby Museum Island, the area around the New Synagogue has lots of places to eat, notably in the **Hackesche Höfe** (Rosenthalerstr. 40–41; w hackesche-hoefe.de), a series of interlinking Art Nouveau courtyards and tenements where there are plenty of restaurants, bars and shops. The theatre in the complex puts on klezmer concerts.

HISTORY Berlin was the centre of Jewish life in Germany in the 19th and early 20th centuries. In 1933 it was home to about 160,000 Jews, 32% of the country's Jewish population. At the time, 4.2 million people lived in Berlin. There were effectively two Jewish communities: the assimilated, comfortably-off middle class and the immigrant working-class Jews mostly from eastern Europe.

After the collapse of the German Empire in 1918, Prenzlauer Berg in the east became the centre of the Spartacist left-wing revolt. Before long, the government called in the Freikorps, a militia made up of former soldiers, to crush the rebellion. There was fierce fighting in Berlin's working-class areas.

The Berlin municipality introduced 55 anti-Jewish measures in the first two years of the Nazi regime. By 1939, the city's Jewish population had fallen to 80,000 as many fled the country, often in difficult circumstances and with considerable loss of assets. By the end of World War II, more than 50,000 Jewish Berliners had been deported to ghettos in Minsk, Riga, Kaunas, Łódź and Theresienstadt. From July 1942, trains went directly to Auschwitz. A few thousand Jews managed to survive in the city but German Jewish Berlin was destroyed.

At the end of the war the city, like the country, was occupied by the Allies and divided into four sectors. East Berlin became the capital of the GDR, but the West German capital was moved to Bonn. Berlin was a physically divided city after the Berlin Wall went up in 1961. Since its fall in 1989, the city has made great strides in remembering its once lively Jewish community. Most Jews who live in Berlin today come from the former Soviet Union.

WHAT TO SEE
Around the Brandenburg Gate The area around the Brandenburg Gate, once part of the Berlin Wall which divided the city from 1961 to 1989, was the heart of Hitler's government and is a fitting place to begin a tour of Berlin's memorials.

Designed by American architect Peter Eisenman, the **Memorial to the Murdered Jews of Europe** (Denkmal für die Ermordeten Juden Europas; Cora-Berliner-Str. 1; 🚇 Mohrenstr; w stiftung-denkmal.de; memorial ⊕ 24hrs daily; information centre ⊕ 10.00–18.00 Tue–Sun; free) was unveiled in 2005. Made up of 2,711 grey stelae of various sizes, symbolising Europe's Jewish communities destroyed during the

Holocaust, it covers an area the size of three football fields. Allow time to walk among the stelae to get a feel for its artistic merit; though many of the stelae have developed severe cracks and the site was undergoing restoration at the time of writing. The memorial receives 4 million visitors a year but has been dogged by controversy and has been the background of numerous inappropriate selfies. Be prepared to see people jumping from stele to stele or sitting on them drinking wine or having a snack. Nothing seems to be done to prevent this sort of behaviour. The **information centre** below the memorial was not part of the original design and was created in response to concerns that the memorial would otherwise be too open to interpretation and needed historical grounding. The exhibition inside documents the persecution and mass murder of Europe's Jews in four thematic rooms. In the height of the season, you will have to queue for security reasons, but it is worth the wait.

A memorial to the Roma and Sinti and another to homosexuals persecuted under Nazism, both in the **Tiergarten**, were added in 2008 to offset further criticism. The Romani memorial is not far from the Reichstag. That to homosexual victims is across the road from the main memorial. The Nazis' euthanasia programme known as T4 (page 7) was based at **Tiergartenstrasse 4**, where there is a memorial at the site to its victims. All three monuments are looked after by the Murdered Jews of Europe Foundation.

On the southern side of Unter den Linden east of the Brandenburg Gate, in **Bebelplatz**, opposite Humboldt University, a memorial glass window looks down on to a set of empty bookshelves. This is the spot where, on 10 May 1933, 25,000 books written by authors considered to be enemies of the Third Reich were burned. This event was the culmination of a weeks-long, student-led campaign against 'un-German spirit', which saw authors blacklisted and denounced. Next to the monument is a plaque bearing the words of the poet Heinrich Heine, written in 1820: 'Dort wo man Buecher verbrennt, verbrennt man am Ende auch Menschen' ('Where books are burned, in the end people will burn too').

Friedrichstrasse Station (Friedrichstrasse Bahnhof) Outside the Friedrich-strasse railway station, at the junction of Georgenstrasse and Friedrichstrasse, a bronze memorial remembers the 20,000 children who left the Reich between 1938 and 1939 and those who were deported to their deaths. The British charity the

STOLPERSTEINE

Embedded in pavements in towns and cities all over Europe, you might see small brass plaques that remember a victim of Nazi extermination or persecution. They are also shown on the cover of this book (page 172). The plaques, each measuring 10cm x 10cm, are called *Stolpersteine*, or stumbling blocks. The idea is that they stop you in your tracks and make you reflect on the individuals named on them who lost their lives. The project was set up in 1992 by the German artist Gunter Demnig, who frequently quotes the Torah when he says, 'a person is only forgotten when his or her name is forgotten'.

Most of the stones commemorate Jewish victims, but there are also Stolpersteine who remember Sinti and Roma and other victims. Stones are placed outside the last place the person voluntarily lived. Find out more about the project at w stolpersteine.eu; and about Stolpersteine in Berlin at w stolpersteine-berlin.de. There are small biographies of the people remembered.

Central British Fund, now World Jewish Relief, brought 10,000 children to safety in Great Britain before the German invasion of Poland and another 10,000 children went to the Netherlands, Belgium, France, Switzerland and Sweden. Entitled *Trains to Life - Trains to Death*, the privately funded memorial was erected in 2008. It was designed by the Israeli artist Frank Meisler, who himself fled Danzig, now Gdansk in Poland, on the Kindertransport. The bronze sculpture is composed of seven figures – children, with yellow stars on their coats (though the wearing of stars was not a legal requirement yet at the time of the Kindertransport). There is a similar memorial at London's Liverpool Street Station (page 114).

Across the Spree River, the area around Oranienburgerstrasse was 10% Jewish before World War II. Many of the Jews who lived here in tenements were immigrants from eastern Europe.

The New Synagogue (Neue Synagoge; Oranienburgerstr. 28–30; 🚇 Oranienburgerstrasse or Hackescher Markt) The Moorish New Synagogue was built in 1866 and was the largest synagogue in Germany, seating 3,200 people. Religious practice here corresponded with liberal Judaism, which was the dominant trend in Germany in the late 19th century. Partially destroyed during Kristallnacht in 1938, the synagogue survived thanks to the intervention of a courageous Berlin policeman, and services continued to be held here until it was eventually closed in 1940. It was then used as a warehouse. Damaged by Allied bombing in 1943, the main synagogue hall was demolished in 1958. After the war, Jewish survivors in East Berlin used the adjacent building, the former premises of the Jewish community council, as a meeting place. Reconstruction of the façade and entrance lobby began in 1988.

Today the building houses the **Centrum Judaicum Foundation** (w centrumjudaicum.de; ⊕ Apr–Sep 10.00–18.00 Mon–Fri, 10.00–19.00 Sun, Oct–Mar 10.00–18.00 Sun–Thu, 10.00–15.00 Fri; €7), which is a museum, archive and research centre. On show are Torahs and scrolls discovered during the restoration. A guided tour is available to see the open space behind the restored façade, but it is no longer possible to visit the Dome.

The Old Jewish Cemetery and nearby The **Old Jewish Cemetery** (Alte Jüdische Friedhof) on Grosse Hamburgerstrasse, a short walk from the New Synagogue, was the city's oldest Jewish cemetery, used between 1672 and 1827; today, the site is a small park. The philosopher Moses Mendelssohn (1729–86), a central figure in the Jewish struggle for equal rights, was buried in the cemetery, and a replica gravestone marks the spot where he is believed to lie. In 1943, the cemetery was turned into an air-raid shelter, and the gravestones used to reinforce its walls. It was also used for mass burials of civilians and soldiers killed in the air raids. A heartrending collection of sculpted figures, the *Monument to Jewish Victims of Fascism*, was placed by the entrance in 1985.

The **Jewish School** was at Grosse Hamburgerstrasse 27, just north of the cemetery. The number of pupils doubled after the Nazis took power, reflecting the problems Jewish children faced in regular schools. After the school closed in 1942, it and the adjacent old people's home (destroyed in a bombing raid) was used as a transit camp for Jews prior to deportation. The building is once again a Jewish school; and a relief portrait and memorial plaque on its façade honour Moses Mendelssohn. A bust of Mendelssohn, which stood in the front garden of the school, was destroyed by members of the SA in 1941. Opposite the school, *The Missing House* sculpture at No. 15/16 lists the names of former residents, most of whom were not Jewish,

Pictured on the cover of this book are five *Stolpersteine* ('Stumbling Stones'; page 170) in remembrance of Max Sommerfeld, his brother-in-law Max Kessler, his sister Rosalie Kessler, his nephew Phillip Kessler, and a woman named Johanna Schöneberg. These Stolpersteine were embedded in 2010 in the pavement outside Friedrichstrasse 105 in Mitte – about 10 minutes' walk from the New Synagogue – where the family had lived since 1935.

Max Sommerfeld was born in 1885 in the town of Gniezno, 50km east of Poznan, in what is modern-day Poland but until World War I was part of the German Empire. His sister Rosalie was three years younger. After the death of their father, Philip, the siblings moved to Berlin with their mother, Johanna. Rosalie ran a shop at Reinickendorferstrasse 24. Virtually nothing is known about Max. We have no idea how he made a living or if he ever married.

Before World War I, Rosalie met Max Kessler, a watchmaker who had a shop on the same street that Rosalie ran her business. He was six years her senior and came from what is now the Polish city of Opole in Upper Silesia, then also part of Germany. The couple married in June 1917. Rosalie became a housewife and the following year their son Philip was born. On 25 April 1921, twins Eleonore and Klara followed.

The family was hit badly by the boycotts of Jewish shops and the anti-Jewish measures introduced by the Nazis. There was little or no chance of further education for the Kessler children and Max Kessler lost his businesses in the Aryanisation process. Max and Rosalie and their son were taken as forced labourers after the war broke out in 1939.

On 1 October 1941, Berlin's Jewish community was informed that their 'resettlement' was about to begin. Max Sommerfeld was taken to Grunewald station (page 175) 7km away across the city. Older adults and the sick were moved by truck, while others were made to walk. They were then forced aboard third-class

who were killed when the building was hit during the aerial bombardment of February 1945.

Five minutes' walk north along Grosse Hamburgerstrasse, on **Koppenplatz**, Karl Biedermann's bronze sculpture *The Deserted Room* depicts a table and two chairs, one of which has been overturned in a round-up.

The nearby Hackesche Höfe is made up of eight public courtyards (*höfe*) that were former tenements and are now lined with cafés and boutiques. In the complex, the **Otto Weidt's Workshop for the Blind Museum** (Museum Blindenwerkstatt Otto Weidt; w museum-blindenwerkstatt.de; ⏲ 09.00–18.00 Mon–Fri, 10.00–18.00 Sat–Sun; free) documents the extraordinary bravery of Otto Weidt, who ran a broom and brush workshop which supplied the German Army and employed many blind and deaf Jews. In 1942, when they were threatened with deportation, Weidt succeeded in rescuing his workforce from the nearby transit camp on Grosse Hamburgerstrasse after he bribed the Gestapo. Weidt managed to procure false papers for his staff and hid several in the back room of his workshop, which is preserved in its original condition.

The **Anne Frank Centre** (Anne-Frank-Zentrum; w annefrank.de; ⏲ 10.00–18.00 Tue–Sun; €8), also in the complex, tells the story of perhaps the Holocaust's most famous victim. The museum is aimed at teenagers and school trips.

Not far from the Hackesche Höfe, the **Rosenstrasse Women memorial** (Die Frauen der Rosenstrasse; w visitberlin.de/de/1943-die-frauen-der-rosenstrasse), passenger cars, with no idea where they were being taken. They were deported to Riga on 27 November 1941. On the night of 30 November, the mass murder of 25,000 Jews from the Riga Ghetto began in the Rumbula Forest (page 74). Max Sommerfeld arrived at Šķirotava station south of the Riga Ghetto in a transport of 1,000 Jews from Germany. Some of the older adults, who could have included Max, who was by now 56, were shot at the station. The rest were massacred in the Rumbula Forest.

In early December 1942, Rosalie and Max Kessler and their son Philip were interned in the transit camp at Grosse Hamburgerstrasse not far from the New Synagogue. They were deported on Transport 24 from Putlitzstrasse Station in Moabit which left for Auschwitz on 9 December 1942. At the selection, 137 people were taken as slave labourers and the remaining 898 were immediately gassed. It is believed that only two people survived from the transport. The Kesslers were probably among those selected to be gassed. Also on the transport was Rosalie and Max's daughter Eleonore Caro, who was also gassed. At the time of deportation, Rosalie was 53 years old, Max 59, Philip 24 and Eleonore 21. Eleonore's twin sister Klara had been deported to Auschwitz on 29 November 1942, a few days before her parents and siblings.

Nothing is known about Johanna Schöneberg who is remembered on another Stolperstein. She was born in 1895 in Mirosławiec, now in modern-day Poland. If in any way she was related to the Sommerfeld/Kessler family, we do not know. She was deported to Auschwitz on 1 March 1943 and gassed.

The information that we have about the Sommerfeld/Kessler family comes from official records. No-one has registered their deaths at Israel's Yad Vashem memorial, so it is highly probable that they had no direct descendants, if any. There are no photographs of them. If you know anything about the family, please let us know at e info@bradtguides.com.

erected in 1995, recalls the 1943 demonstrations by Christian women outside the Gestapo headquarters on Rosenstrasse after the arrest of their Jewish husbands. The husbands were eventually released, which shows that it was possible to resist Nazi terror.

Around Potsdamer Platz During the war, the German High Command was housed to the west of Potsdamer Platz at Stauffenbergstrasse 13, a building that is still part of the Ministry of Defence. It is here that Count von Stauffenberg, who had attempted to assassinate Hitler in the doomed July Bomb Plot of 1944 in the Wolf's Lair, was executed. Now it is home to the **German Resistance Memorial Centre** (Gedenkstätte Deutscher Widerstand; 🚇 Potsdamer Platz; w gdw-berlin. de; ⊕ 09.00–18.00 Mon–Fri, 10.00–18.00 Sat–Sun; free). The commemorative courtyard is dedicated to the memory of Stauffenberg and the other officers executed here on the night of 20 July 1944. The permanent exhibition on the second floor covers anti-Nazi resistance, detailing the growth of resistance and the groups within which it emerged, as well as how the Nazi state reacted to it. On the third floor the **Silent Heroes Memorial Centre** (Gedenkstätte Stille Helden; w gedenkstaette-stille-helden.de) is part of the same museum and commemorates Jews who resisted Nazi persecution and those who helped them. The example of the helpers, often referred to as 'silent heroes', shows that it was possible to support the persecuted even in the Reich. The exhibition addresses the conditions of life in hiding as well as the actions and motives of those who helped the persecuted.

South of Potsdamer Platz on Niederkirchnerstrasse, a stone's throw from Checkpoint Charlie, the **Topography of Terror Documentation Centre** (Dokumentationszentrum Topographie des Terrors; ⓠ Potsdamer Platz; w topographie.de; ⊕ 10.00–20.00 daily; free) has a permanent exhibition in German and English that focuses on the central institutions of the SS and police in the Third Reich and the crimes they committed across Europe. It is an important and rare site that looks at the perpetrators. The street, formerly Prinz-Albrechtstrasse, was the centre of the Nazi terror machine. The Neoclassical Prinz Albrecht Palais on the corner of Wilhelmstrasse was the headquarters of Reinhard Heydrich and the Reich's security services. Prinz-Albrechtstrasse 8 was the Gestapo HQ. Hotel Prinz Albrecht at No. 9 was the headquarters of the SS. Damaged in World War II, the buildings were later pulled down and during the Cold War the area was a barren wasteland; today it is one of the few places the Berlin Wall is still visible. There are two exhibitions, one in the information centre and the other below the remains of the Berlin Wall in the former foundations.

The **Jewish Museum Berlin** (Jüdisches Museum Berlin; Lindenstrasse 9–14; ⓠ Kochstrasse; w jmberlin.de; ⊕ 10.00–18.00 daily; free), also a short walk from Checkpoint Charlie, was designed by the architect Daniel Libeskind, who was born in Łódź in Poland in 1946 to survivor parents. The museum, a zinc-clad modernist building, opened in 2001 and is the biggest Jewish museum space in Europe. It is easy to forget more than 25 years on what an enormous breakthrough the opening of this museum was. Libeskind deliberately created a dark tunnel that leads visitors to three routes: the Axis of Continuity, the Axis of Emigration or the Axis of the Holocaust. The Axis of the Holocaust leads to a dark tower, a dead end symbolising the fate of so many German Jews. The Axis of Emigration leads to a garden of trees with a slanting pavement, the Garden of Exile. If travelling with small children be aware that they are likely to lose their footing. The Axis of Continuity leads up a steep flight of stairs to the main exhibition. The first section of the exhibition traces the history of the Jews in Germany, while the second floor concentrates on the Nazi period and its aftermath. The children's museum, **Anoha** (w anoha.de; ⊕ 09.00–16.00 Tue–Fri, 10.00–17.00 Sat–Sun; free; book online), is on the opposite side of the road.

The remains of the entrance of **Anhalt Station** (Anhalter Bahnhof) on Möckernstrasse, southeast of Potsdamer Platz, are a ghostly reminder of what much of this part of Berlin looked like in the Cold War. Before World War II, it was Berlin's principal railway station, and it was from here that Hitler set off on his trip to Italy to meet Mussolini in 1938. From 1936, special trains ran to help Jews leave for Palestine. The first Kindertransport left from Anhalter on 1 December 1938. The train was destined for the Hook of Holland from where the children sailed to the UK.

More than 9,600 people were deported from Anhalter in 116 transports, which usually took place in the morning during the normal commuter bustle, with one or two third-class passenger cars attached to scheduled trains. After the war, the station was in the Western sector but few trains left from here. It was closed in 1952 and, despite public protests, was demolished in 1959–61.

A new **Exile Museum**, due to open in 2027 on the site of the former station, will tell the story of the 500,000 people who fled Germany after the Nazis took power in 1933 and what was lost to the country. It will also focus on the contemporary experience of exile. In the meantime, it is possible to visit the temporary exhibition at Fasanenstrasse 24 (w stiftung-exilmuseum.berlin; ⊕ 15.00–18.00 Thu; free).

The nearby **German Museum of Technology** (Deutsches Technikmuseum; Trebbinerstr. 9; 🚇 Gleisdreieck; w sdtb.de; ⊕ 09.00–17.30 Tue–Fri, 10.00–18.00 Sat–Sun; €12, free 1st Sun of the month) has an interesting exhibition on the role of the Deutsche Reichsbahn, the German Reich Railway, in the Holocaust. The deportation of the Reich's Jews, as well as those from western Europe, was organised by the Berlin-based Reich Main Security Office in close co-operation with the Reich Ministry for Transport. At first, the Reichsbahn used older passenger trains for the deportations; however, from 1942, it increasingly began deploying freight trains. The trains could carry up to 1,000 people on each transport. The Reichsbahn granted a discount for transports carrying more than 400 people. For years the complicity of the German railways was not discussed but the issue is now addressed in the exhibition in **Locomotive Shed 2**, which opened in 2005. It tells the story of 12 of the deportees. A freight car is also on display.

Kurfürstendamm and around Kurfürstendamm, Berlin's main shopping street, was the scene of serious anti-Jewish riots in the summer of 1935. It was the most brutal anti-Jewish manifestation since Hitler had come to power. Eventually, Jews were forbidden from walking along the street.

The Story of Berlin (Kurfürstendamm 207–8; 🚇 Kurfürstendamm; w story-of-berlin.de; closed at time of writing for renovation until winter 2024/25) gives an excellent overview of the history of Berlin. It is a good museum to visit with teenage children. Adolf Eichmann, whose job it was until the war broke out to oversee forced Jewish emigration, ran the **Central Office of Jewish Emigration** at Kurfürstendamm 115/116. He had already opened a similar office in Vienna in 1938 before returning to Berlin. The building was demolished in 1961, but there is a memorial built into a bus stop near to the site. The British, who controlled Palestine at the time, restricted immigration but the Palestine Office run by Zionist officials at Kurfürstendamm 10 was nevertheless besieged by Jewish Berliners looking for an escape route. The bureau was closed down in 1941.

Schöneberg South of Kurfürstendamm, there are some interesting memorials in the affluent suburb of Schöneberg. After the foundation of the German Empire in 1871, Berlin grew rapidly and spread into adjoining rural areas. Schöneberg, a small village, became an affluent middle-class suburb where 16,000 Jews lived in 1933, more than 7% of the district's inhabitants. Most opted for emigration, but 6,000 who remained in Schöneberg were deported to ghettos and extermination camps in the occupied eastern territories.

An exhibition 'We Were Neighbours' ('Wir Waren Nachbarn'; John-F-Kennedy-Platz 1; 🚇 Rathaus Schöneberg; w wirwarennachbarn.de; ⊕ 10.00–18.00 Sat–Thu; free) in the town hall explores the stories of 170 Jews who lived in the area. On the walls are 6,000 handwritten file cards with the names, addresses and biographical data of the deported.

Eighty panels called *Orte des Erinnerns* (*Places of Remembrance*), by American artists Renata Stih and Frieder Schnock, were put up in 1993. Attached to lampposts around Schöneberg, they recall the successive steps the Nazis took in the persecution of the Jews. One outside a radio shop recalls the ban on Jews owning radios. While at Wittenbergplatz U-Bahn station a striking memorial lists the names of concentration and extermination camps as if they were a schedule for commuter trains.

Platform 17 (Gleis 17; w deutschebahn.com/en/group/history/topics/platform17_memorial-6929106; ⊕ 24hrs daily) The most moving of all of Berlin's

Holocaust memorials is Gleis 17, or Platform 17, at Grunewald S-Bahn station. It was from here, in the heart of a wealthy, leafy suburb in the west of the city, that the first train left for the Łódź Ghetto on 18 October 1941. The pretty, timbered station built at the end of the 19th century is surrounded by large villas and apartments, which remain exactly as they were in the early 1940s. The memorial, on a disused platform on the right inside the station, provides a harsh reminder of the complicity of bystanders – there is no record of any protests when the Jews were deported. Plaques next to the tracks list the transports that left Berlin between 1941 and 1945, the number of people, and their destinations – Auschwitz, Riga and Theresienstadt. Each transport consisted of roughly 1,000 people.

Other deportation memorials There are four smaller memorials that remember the deportations.

In the southern suburb of **Steglitz** near the Botanical Gardens on Herman Ehlers Platz, a mirrored wall lists 1,723 names of Jews from the deportation lists, among them 229 from Steglitz. The memorial stands on the site of the former synagogue which has been rebuilt and now stands at Düppelstrasse 41.

A memorial with a Star of David on **Putlitzbrücke**, the bridge that connects the districts of Moabit and Wedding, remembers the 30,000 Jews who were deported from the Moabit Freight Depot. There is another memorial at Levetzowstrasse 7/8, the site of **Levetzow Synagogue**, which was damaged in the bombing raids and demolished in the 1950s. Jews were gathered here, 2km away from the depot on the northern side of the Spree across the river from the Tiergarten. Until 1960, the site went unmarked. The current monument, put up in 1988, is in the form of a stylised freight car. Metal plaques remember the city's destroyed synagogues and list the transports.

Auerbach Orphanage (Schönhauser Allee 162) was until 1942 a sanctuary for Jewish children. In 1942, 60 children and three staff were deported to Riga, where they were shot in the forest. In November, 75 children aged between ten months and 16 years were deported to Auschwitz and gassed. The building was destroyed in Allied bombing raids in 1943. Since 2014 the names of the murdered children and staff have been inscribed on the only remaining wall of the building on Schönhauser Allee 162 in Prenzlauer Berg.

House of the Wannsee Conference (Haus der Wannsee-Konferenz; Am Grossen Wannsee 56; 🚉 S1 or S7: Wannsee, then bus 114; w ghwk.de; ⊕ 10.00–18.00 daily; free) On Tuesday 20 January 1942, in the middle of a freezing cold winter, an extraordinary meeting took place in the southwestern suburbs of Berlin. A number of top Nazi officials arrived in the Villa Marlier (now known as the Haus der Wannsee-Konferenz) on the banks of the frozen Wannsee to attend the meeting, called by the director of the Reich Main Security Office, SS Obergruppenführer Reinhard Heydrich. On the agenda was a plan to 'evacuate' all of Europe's Jews to occupied Poland, where they would be killed.

At the meeting, Heydrich spoke for nearly an hour. Then there were 30 minutes of questions and comments, followed by informal conversation. The emphasis was on setting a clear timeframe for the murder of Europe's Jews which would be the most efficient and cost effective. The mass murder of Jews had begun after the invasion of the Soviet Union the previous summer, but using a bullet per person was expensive and mass graves not only took time to dig and cover up but retained the possibility of revealing their secrets. In the 2001 film *Conspiracy*, SS Brigadeführer Dr Wilhelm Stuckart, State Secretary of the Interior Ministry, who had drawn up the Nuremberg

Laws, and Friedrich Kritzinger, the Permanent Secretary at the Reich Chancellery, were portrayed as dissenters. In reality, it was a chillingly bureaucratic meeting in which the participants were all in agreement.

Adolf Eichmann, Heydrich's assistant, had drawn up a list of European countries which were divided into 'A' and 'B'. 'A' were those occupied by the Nazis and 'B' were countries that were allied, neutral or at war with Germany. The 'B' list included Great Britain, Switzerland, Sweden and Turkey. The number of Jews in each country were totalled at the bottom of the page. The men who attended the meeting committed themselves to the murder of 11 million people,

As the Allies advanced on Berlin, the participants were told that they should destroy their copy of the minutes. Martin Luther was unable to carry out the order and his copy was discovered in 1947 – it is a crucial document as it is the only piece of physical evidence that proves the meeting took place.

In 1944, Luther was caught conniving to oust his boss, Foreign Minister Joachim Ribbentrop; he was sent to Sachsenhausen concentration camp and died of heart failure soon after being liberated by the Red Army. Eichmann survived the war and went into hiding in Argentina. He was eventually tracked down by Israeli agents, who took him back to Jerusalem where he was put on trial in 1961. The trial was televised and caused a sensation. For many people, it was the first time they discovered the extent of the atrocities committed by the Nazis and their collaborators. Eichmann told the court that the participants at the Wannsee Conference discussed the subject 'quite bluntly', and there was 'talk about killing and eliminating and extermination'.

After the war the villa was used as a school. Holocaust survivor Joseph Wulf campaigned to have the house turned into a documentation centre. He died in 1974, before the house became a memorial in 1992. The most striking thing today is how peaceful and sophisticated the house is, a million miles from the horror of the mass shooting and the extermination camps. Two stone cherubs stand on either side of the driveway.

The exhibition here documents the systematic process which led to the Holocaust and shines a spotlight on the desk perpetrators. The meeting is believed to have happened in the large room to the right attached to the conservatory. The 14 men seated around the table represented the state and Nazi organisations over which Heydrich needed to assert his authority. Most had met before and worked on joint projects in the decade since the Nazi Party had come to power.

The museum also has interesting online exhibitions, one of which uses 1,000 photographs and 380 diaries and letters by Wehrmacht soldiers who took part in the invasion of Poland in 1939.

Marzahn Two weeks before the Berlin Olympic Games in 1936, a camp for Roma and Sinti was established in the suburb of Marzahn, 15km northeast of the city centre. Between 1,000 and 1,200 people were held here in terrible conditions with little sanitation or water. In 1943 most of the inmates were deported to Auschwitz. After much of the camp was destroyed in an air raid in 1944, the 24 Sinti and Roma who remained there had to live together in a single barracks. At the end of April 1945, the Red Army liberated the camp, but the inhabitants were forced to live there for several more years as there was no other accommodation. The former camp was then forgotten. The site is so marginalised even in contemporary Berlin that this is little surprise. The East German authorities erected vast housing estates in the district, but the former camp is where the tower blocks give way to small industrial sites and a McDonald's. The first memorial was put up in 1986. Today on

A permanent exhibition in the university town of Heidelberg in western Germany, the Dokumentations- und Kulturzentrum Deutscher Sinti und Roma Heidelberg (Bremeneckgasse 2; w sintiundroma.de; ⊕ 09.30–19.45 Tue, 09.30–16.30 Wed–Fri, 11.00–16.30 Sat–Sun; free) is dedicated to the Romani genocide. The centre opened in 1997 and tells the story of the half a million Sinti and Roma murdered in the Porajmos, the Holocaust that befell the Romani people.

Sinti and Roma had lived in Germany for about 600 years. Sinti immigrated to German-speaking regions in the Middle Ages; members of the minorities that immigrated to eastern Europe are called Roma. For centuries they have been persecuted as 'gypsies'.

In the Weimar Republic Sinti and Roma were discriminated against and heavily policed. The National Socialists tightened these measures in 1933, and in 1934 they were subjected to forced sterilisation. The following year, special camps were established, where hundreds of Romani were interned. Romani were subject to racial laws similar to the Nuremberg Laws that applied to Jews.

In 1940, about 2,500 men, women and children were deported to concentration camps and ghettos in the east. In December 1942, Heinrich Himmler ordered the deportation of all remaining Sinti and Roma from the Reich to Auschwitz-Birkenau. It was only in 1982 that the German Chancellor Helmut Schmidt acknowledged the genocide.

The exhibition's focus is on the 600 years of history and culture of the Sinti and Roma in Germany as well as information on the persecution and murder of Sinti and Roma during National Socialism.

Otto-Rosenberg-Platz there is a small **open-air exhibition** (🚊 Raoul Wallenberg Str.; w sinti-roma-berlin.de; ⊕ 24hrs daily; free).

FURTHER AFIELD
Sachsenhausen The former concentration camp of Sachsenhausen near Oranienburg, 30km north of Berlin, is now a museum and memorial site.

History The camp built in 1936 originally held high-profile political prisoners, but after Kristallnacht 5,000 Jews were imprisoned here. Many of the Jews interned after Kristallnacht were released on the condition they would emigrate. In 1942 many Jewish prisoners were deported to Auschwitz from Sachsenhausen, among them Polish or stateless Jews from Berlin. Around 200,000 prisoners are thought to have passed through Sachsenhausen, and an estimated 30,000 people died here, of whom 10,000 were Soviet prisoners of war. Some Soviet prisoners were murdered in experimental gas vans but most were shot. Sachsenhausen also served as an SS training base and was the administrative centre for the concentration camp system.

At the end of the war, death marches arrived in Sachsenhausen, notably the march from Auschwitz which left the camp in November 1944. Prisoners walked 600km in the freezing winter weather and on arrival at Sachsenhausen were forced to sleep naked on the stone floor before marching 650km south to Mauthausen in Austria.

Afterwards Sachsenhausen was used as a camp by the Soviet secret police, the NKVD. The site became a memorial in 1961. In line with other memorials in the GDR it centred on the victory of anti-fascist coalition over fascism.

What to see Few original buildings remain but much has been done at the **Sachsenhausen Memorial Site and Museum** (Gedenkstätte und Museum Sachsenhausen; Strasse der Nationen 22; 🚊 Oranienburg; w sachsenhausen-sbg.de; ⊕ 08.30–18.00 daily, closes 16.30 mid-Oct–mid-March; free) to bring the history of the camp to life. Each area of the camp hosts an exhibit. In the former infirmary there is an exhibition on medicine and Nazi policies.

Visitors approach the camp along a road that separated the main camp from the SS barracks. To the left of the entrance before the main gate is the commandant's house. The exhibition here looks at the perpetrators. The new museum on the right of the gate traces the story of the memorial in the GDR period.

The main gate leads to the roll call area. The 1961 obelisk rises up in the distance. Behind it is the Soviet camp. The exhibition in Barrack 38 tells the story of the camp's Jewish prisoners including Operation Bernhard, a scheme that produced counterfeit British banknotes intended to destabilise the British economy. The story of the Jews who were forced to make the counterfeit notes was made into a film, *The Counterfeiters* (2007).

Ravensbrück

Ravensbrück concentration camp, 90km north of Sachsenhausen, was the largest women's camp in Germany's pre-war borders. It initially held political prisoners, criminals and 'a-socials'; the guards were women, but the administrative staff were men. Of the 130,000 people held here 15% were Jewish and 5% Roma, and about 90,000 people died. Many Jewish prisoners arrived in the camp as those further to the east were evacuated in 1945. There was also a forgotten camp for men at Ravensbrück. After the war, the site became a Soviet military base until the 1990s. It is now a museum, the **Ravensbrück Memorial Site** (Gedenkstätte Ravensbrück; Strasse der Nationen, Fürstenberg; w ravensbrueck-sbg.de; ⊕ 10.00–16.00 Tue–Sun; free). The exhibition, which was opened in 2013, is displayed across two storeys of the renovated former SS headquarters building. There is another exhibition that looks at the female guards in their barracks. In

THE T4 PROGRAMME IN BRANDENBURG

Brandenburg an der Havel, 85km west of Berlin, was a killing site where more than 9,000 patients from psychiatric hospitals, among them children, were murdered in the gas chambers as part of the Nazis' T4 euthanasia programme. Experiments carried out in Brandenburg confirmed that large numbers could be killed by carbon monoxide in a sealed space. The murders, sanctioned by Hitler and backdated to 1 September 1939, took place in a former poorhouse used as a prison in the centre of the town. The crematoria smoke filled the centre of Brandenburg and opposition to the project grew. The building is now home to the **Memorial for the Victims of Euthanasia Killings** (Gedenkstätte Opfer der Euthanasie-Morde Nicolaiplatz 28; w brandenburg-euthanasie-sbg.de; ⊕ memorial: 24hrs daily, museum: 13.00–17.00 Thu–Fri, 10.00–17.00 Sat–Sun; free) where there is a small museum. A memorial event is held here every year on 1 September.

the cell block it is possible to see where the prisoners were held. Exhibitions cover everyday life in the camp and slave-labour textile production.

Belower Forest (Belower Wald) The **Death March Museum** (Gedenkstätte Todesmarsch; Belower Damm 1, Wittstock; w below-sbg.de; ☉ 24hrs daily, visitors centre 10.00–16.00 Mon–Fri; free) in the Belower Forest is 128km northwest of Berlin and commemorates a series of death marches from Sachsenhausen. Just before the Red Army liberated the camp on 21 April 1945, 33,000 prisoners were sent on a series of death marches. Some 16,000 prisoners camped in the forest in late April 1945. Without food or water, they ate bark, roots and weeds to stay alive. The open-air museum opened in 2010.

HAMBURG

Hamburg is Germany's second largest city, on the broad river Elbe, and is an important port that attracted Jews escaping persecution in Spain to settle in the city in the 16th century. The city had a significant Jewish population before the Holocaust who played an important role in its cultural and economic life. Hamburg is a good place to understand how Germans felt a sense of victimhood in the post-war era which meant that, until the 1960s, the country's role in the Holocaust was forgotten in a national amnesia. The city was a target of numerous bombing raids in World War II which targeted not only the shipyards, U-boat pens and oil refineries but also civilians and civic infrastructure. A raid at the end of July 1943 created a massive firestorm that killed thousands.

GETTING AROUND Hamburg has an efficient U- and S-Bahn system. The memorial at the former Neuengamme concentration camp is 30km southeast of Hamburg. If you do not have your own transport, catch the train from Hamburg Central Station to Bergedorf, then take bus 127 or 227. The Bergen-Belsen Memorial Site is 102km south of Hamburg in Lower Saxony. Take a train from Hamburg Central Station to Celle and then bus 100 or 110. To see Wöbbelin you will need your own transport.

🏠 **WHERE TO STAY AND EAT** Hamburg has plenty of chain hotels but avoid those in Hafen City away from the tourist area of Speicherstadt, which is a soulless modern development. If you have your own transport, opt for the **Landhaus Flottbek** (Baron Voghtstr. 179, Gos Flotbek; w landhaus-flottbek.de; **€€**) in the western suburbs, a boutique hotel with lots of atmosphere and a better deal than the city's chains. It also has an excellent **restaurant** (**€€€**) with a full vegetarian menu. It is very popular, so book a table when you make the reservation.

HISTORY In 1933, about 20,000 Jews lived in Hamburg. Many left after the Nazis came to power but, in a pattern repeated across Germany, the Jews who remained in the city were deported (on 17 transports) to Łódź, Minsk, Riga, Auschwitz and Theresienstadt. About 7,800 Hamburg Jews were murdered in the Holocaust.

WHAT TO SEE On the **Town Hall** (Rathaus) in Hamburg's Old Town, there are relief portraits carved in to columns honouring the citizens who contributed to building the city, among them seven Jews including the banker Salomon Heine, the composer Felix Mendelssohn Bartholdy and the entrepreneur Albert Ballin. On the Mönckebergstrasse side of the town hall square there is a statue commemorating the 19th-century romantic poet Heinrich Heine, who spent time in the city with his uncle Salomon and whose famous *Germany: A Winter's Tale* was published in 1844 after a visit to Hamburg. Erected in 1982, the statue replaced an earlier one that once stood in Hamburg's Stadtpark but was demolished and melted down by the Nazis. The original statue's destruction in 1933 and Nazi book burnings are recalled in relief on the statue's base.

The **port** in the heart of the city is Europe's second largest after Rotterdam. In Hafen City, the Hamburg America Company had many warehouses in the tourist area of Speicherstadt. The company was owned by an Orthodox Jew named Albert Ballin who converted one of his warehouses into a hostel for Jewish refugees from Russia, complete with a kosher kitchen. It is now home to the **BallinStadt Emigration Museum** (BallinStadt Auswanderermuseum; Veddeler Bogen 2; w ballinstadt.de; ⊕ Mar–Oct 10.00–18.00 Tue–Sun, Nov–Feb 10.00–16.30 Tue–Sun; €13.90), where it is possible to view emigration lists.

In the middle of eastern Hafen City is the site of the former **Hannover Station** (Hannoverscher Bahnhof). Between 1940 and 1945, more than 8,000 Jews, Sinti and Roma from Hamburg and northern Germany were deported from the station in 20 transports to ghettos and extermination camps in the German-occupied areas. The station was badly damaged by bombing in 1945 and demolished. Most of the area was destroyed in Allied air raids and is today covered in modern buildings, many of which are still under construction.

A small park, Lohsepark, on the site of the former platform 2, serves as a memorial, the **Hanover Station Memorial** (Denkmal Hannoverscher Bahnhof; Uberseeallee (next to the Holiday Inn); 🚊 Hafen City Universität U4; w hannoverscher-bahnhof.gedenkstaetten-hamburg.de; memorial ⊕ 24hrs daily, visitors centre ⊕ noon–18.00 daily, visits in Nov–Mar by appt; e amina.edzards@gedenkstaetten.hamburg.de; free). The park was landscaped in 2017. A new documentation centre is due to open at the site in 2026, which will hopefully give the memorial more gravity. It will also show the fate of those 1,000 or so people persecuted mostly on political grounds who were forced into the Wehrmacht's Probation Battalion 999 and deployed into military service from Hannover Station. A plaque at **Hamburg Central Station** by the Mönckebergstrasse exit also recalls the deportations from the Hannover Station.

Across the river on **Landungsbrücken**, near where the ferries depart and the museum ships are docked (Bridge 3), there are monuments to two Jewish refugee ships, the *St Louis* and the *Exodus*. On 13 May 1939, more than 900 Jews boarded the SS *St Louis*, a luxury cruise liner, at the Hamburg docks. They had visas for Cuba from where they hoped to travel on to the USA, but when the ship docked in Havana, they were turned away. Refused entry to the US, the ship was forced to return to Europe – it docked in Antwerp in Belgium. The passengers were taken in by Belgium, France, Holland and the UK. In the years that followed 250 of them would be murdered in the Holocaust.

In 1947 the *Exodus* docked in Hamburg with 4,530 Jewish refugees on board. The ship had secretly set sail from the south of France and had tried to break through the British Royal Navy blockade of the Palestine Mandate, which was then part of the British Empire. The ship was captured and turned back to France, where the refugees refused to disembark. The British took the ship to Hamburg, then under British control, where British soldiers used water canon to force the survivors to leave the boat, among them many women and children. The plight of the *Exodus* and its passengers caused an international outcry that accelerated the foundation of the State of Israel.

Ten minutes' walk to the north, the **Museum for Hamburg History** (Museum für Hamburgische Geschichte; Holstenwall 24; w shmh.de/museum-fuer-hamburgische-geschichte; closed for modernisation at time of writing) has a permanent exhibition on the Jews of Hamburg which covers in detail the persecution and deportation of Hamburg's Jewish residents.

A striking new monument installed in 2022 by the entrance to the Hamburg Building Authority at Stadthausbrücke 8 reminds passers-by that this was once the **Gestapo HQ**. Called *Stigma*, it is made up of red paving stones that look like bloodstains on the pavement.

At Hamburg's **Dammtor Station** (Dammtor Bahnhof), 25 minutes' walk to the northwest, there is a moving bronze memorial called *The Final Parting* dedicated to the 1,000 children who left from Hamburg on the Kindertransport. It is situated on the south side of the station. The sculpture by Frank Meisler and Arie Ovadia was privately funded and erected in 2015. Most of the children were the sole survivors of their families. In 1942, prior to deportation from the station at Dammtor, Jews were gathered at the **Platz der Jüdischen Deportierten** in Moorweide park just to the north of the station. A monument marks the spot.

In **Grindel**, 15 minutes by foot from Dammtor station, the **Great Synagogue** on Bornplatz was destroyed during Kristallnacht in 1938 and demolished in 1939. It stood on the square now named after the then chief rabbi of Hamburg, Joseph Carlebach, who was killed in Riga in a mass shooting in 1942. Dedicated in 1906, the synagogue once held 1,200 people. After World War II, the plot served as a car park for the adjacent Hamburg University. Fifty years after Kristallnacht, the square was paved with grey concrete stones. Dark granite marks the contours of the synagogue which was the largest in northern Germany. This is currently a controversial spot as there are plans drawn up by local government officials and the Jewish community to rebuild the synagogue. The initiative was sparked by the terrorist attack on a synagogue in nearby Halle in 2019 and uses the slogan 'No to antisemitism, yes to the Bornplatz Synagogue'. Critics say the construction will erase Nazi crimes.

In the suburbs North of Grindel, on **Meerweinstrasse** there is a good example of how many memorials in Germany are the result of grassroots initiatives. The local school at 26–28 has commemorated two of its Jewish former teachers, Julia Cohn and Hertha Feiner-Asmus. Cohn was able to send her son to Britain before the war started, but she was deported from Hamburg in 1941 and murdered in Riga. Two of Hertha Feiner-Asmus's daughters survived in Switzerland. She died on a transport to Auschwitz in 1943. There is a freight wagon memorial outside the school.

Ohlsdorf Jewish Cemetery (Ilandkoppel 6; w jfhh.org; ⊕ 08.00–15.00 Sun–Fri; free), established in 1883, was closed in 1943 and makeshift housing for those who had lost their homes in the bombing was put up on the site. It reverted to being a Jewish cemetery in 1945, and in 1951 a memorial stone with an inscription in German and Hebrew was placed here, dedicated to the Jews murdered in the Holocaust. An urn containing the ashes of prisoners from Auschwitz was placed in front of it in 1957.

The **Poppenbüttel Prefabricated Building Memorial** (Gedenkstätte Plattenhaus Poppenbüttel; Kritenbarg 8; 🚉 Poppenbüttel; w poppenbuettel.gedenkstaetten-hamburg.de; ⊕ 10.00–17.00 Sun; free), 17km north of Ohlsdorf, was the Sasel satellite camp of Neuengamme (see opposite). The camp was for women brought into the city to clear rubble from the bombing and to build prefab accommodation. It functioned from September 1944 to May 1945 and was one of eight such camps holding in all 2,800 women. The camp at Poppenbüttel held 500 women, among them survivors of the Łódź Ghetto in Poland who were brought to Hamburg from Auschwitz. It is thought that they were evacuated to Bergen-Belsen in April 1945. The exhibition in the only remaining prefab building commemorates the destruction of Jewish life in Hamburg and the persecution of women under the Nazi regime. It is also possible to see one of the original apartments built by the prisoners.

Altona in the west of Hamburg was one of the city's Jewish districts. Near Altona S-Bahn station outside the town hall at Platz der Republik, there is a memorial to the local Jewish community: a black rectangular monument, which was designed by the American minimalist sculptor Sol LeWitt. In 1987, a memorial stone was erected by the U-Bahn exit for Museumstrasse to commemorate more than 800 Polish Jews who were deported from Altona. On 28 October 1938, they were taken from their homes to the station, from where they were deported to Poland by train. Following Austria's incorporation into the Reich in 1938, the Polish parliament revoked the citizenship of all Polish citizens who had lived abroad for more than five years. The German government, which did not want to be stuck with tens of thousands of stateless Jewish Poles, passed legislation in August that allowed it to deport any foreigner who had lost their citizenship from their home country. As a result the 50,000 Polish people living in Germany became stateless.

Further to the west, in **Blankenese** a simple birch-wood roofed structure remembers the Jews held at Steubenweg 36, now Grotiusweg 36. There were no ghettos in Germany, but Jews were held in 'Jewish houses' under supervision by the security services. The names of the 17 victims are engraved in the memorial. They were deported between October 1941 and July 1942 from the Hannoverscher Bahnhof. Two residents of the house on Steubenweg took their own lives to avoid deportation.

In **Rothenburgsort** east of the centre, the **Bullenhuser Damm Memorial** (Gedenkstätte Bullenhuser Damm; Bullenhuser Damm 92; 🚇 Rothenburgsort; w bullenhuser-damm.gedenkstaetten-hamburg.de; ⊕ 10.00–17.00 Sun; free) is one of the most important memorials in Hamburg. It remembers 20 Jewish children and 28 adults who were hanged by the SS on the night of 22 April 1945. The children had been brought from Auschwitz to the nearby Neuengamme concentration camp (see below). From there they were taken to a school in the Rothenburgsort that had been used as a subcamp of Neuengamme. The children, ten girls and ten boys aged between five and 12, were subjected to medical experiments and deliberately infected with tuberculosis bacteria rubbed into open wounds. Fearful of being convicted for war crimes, the SS killed the children.

The story only entered into public memory in the late 1970s when the journalist Günter Schwarberg discovered the children's identities. Schwarberg founded the Children of Bullenhauser Damm Association with relatives of the victims and set up a memorial, which since 1999 has been a branch of the Neuengamme Concentration Camp Memorial Site.

The biographies of the children and their carers are presented in 24 symbolic suitcases. A corridor leads to the basement where the murders were committed.

In the suburb of **Harburg** 15km south of the city centre, there is a memorial plaque to Hamburg's 1,264 **Sinti and Roma** who were deported to Bełżec and Auschwitz at the former police station on Nöldekestrasse, which was the assembly point for more than 500 of those arrested.

FURTHER AFIELD
Neuengamme Neuengamme on the outskirts of Hamburg opened as a concentration camp in 1938. Originally a satellite of Sachsenhausen, Neuengamme

became a camp in its own right in 1940. It held political prisoners from across occupied Europe and Soviet prisoners of war, who were forced to dig canals, produce bricks, work in clay pits and manufacture arms. Some 80,000 men and 13,500 women were imprisoned in the main camp and its 85 satellite camps. Just under 43,000 people died here in the appalling conditions.

During the death marches, several thousand prisoners were loaded on to ships in the Bay of Lübeck 70km northeast of Hamburg, two of which were hit by bombs in an RAF raid in May 1945. The camp was liberated by the British, who used it as a displaced persons camp and then held suspected Nazis here until 1948. A prison built on the site in 1949 was demolished in 2002–06, allowing visitors access for the first time.

What to see The former camp is now the **Neuengamme Memorial Site** (Gedenkstätte Neuengamme; Jean-Dolidier-Weg 75; w kz-gedenkstaette-neuengamme.de; ⊕ 09.30–16.00 Mon–Fri, 10.00–17.00 Sat–Sun, until 19.00 in summer; free). Allow at least 2 hours for your visit. There is a useful app, in German and English, which it helps to download in advance, or be sure to use the audio guide. There are also free guided tours in English. Visitors looking for information about relatives can search the memorial's records for names of prisoners.

The memorial site spans an area of 600,000m^2 and is over 1km long, some parts of which are always accessible. There are parking spots along the road, which runs along a field on the opposite side from the camp.

Stop first at the Mahnmal bus stop on Jean-Dolidier-Weg, to see the House of Remembrance, where 23,395 of those identified victims' names are recorded and the obelisk stands that marks the site where the SS buried ashes from the crematorium.

Then drive or walk to the main gate, which leads into the former roll call area, the Appellplatz. The site was reconstructed after the demolition of the prison as 1950s post-war buildings covered the northern part of the Appellplatz.

On the site there are 17 of the original buildings but only the outlines of the wooden barracks are still visible. The main exhibit, 'Traces of History', is located in a former cell block, where the introductory film gives a quick overview of the camp. An exhibition about the crimes of the SS is housed in the former SS garages; and a further two exhibitions on slave labour are located in the former brickworks and the site of the Walther factory. In the remains of the prison there is a further small exhibit.

Bergen-Belsen The former concentration camp is now a memorial site. It lies 102km south of Hamburg in Lower Saxony.

History Bergen-Belsen was originally an army training camp, but after the outbreak of war it was used to hold prisoners of war. Although the British and French prisoners were treated according to the Geneva convention, the Soviet prisoners were treated as sub-humans. Between 1941 and 1943, 20,000 of them died here. Bergen-Belsen was also used as a special detention camp for Jews who the Nazis hoped to exchange for Germans held by the Allies. In the final months of the war thousands of prisoners, mostly Jews, were transferred to the camp. In the six weeks before 15 April 1945, when the British Army arrived at Bergen-Belsen, 27,000 inmates died in the camp, among them Anne Frank.

The British soldiers of the 11th Armoured Division who entered the camp found 60,000 prisoners dying of disease and starvation; half of those would die in the weeks that followed. The story soon became a media sensation in the UK and the footage was shown on newsreels in cinemas across the Western world. The images of mounds of corpses shocked the public. That said, they soon forgot about the story and for decades Belsen became a neglected place.

After the liberation, the British soldiers battled to eradicate a severe outbreak of typhus and the concentration camp was burned to the ground. SS guards, who had still been in the camp when it was liberated, were assigned the task of burying the dead. The survivors were taken to the nearby Wehrmacht barracks at Hohne, just to the north, which had been a panzer training school. The barracks already housed prisoners who had been brought from the Mittelbau-Dora labour camp in the weeks before the liberation.

Urgent medical care was the top priority, and a hospital was set up in the new displaced persons camp. At first, German prisoners who had medical training were used as staff, as were survivors, who worked alongside the British Army Medical Corps and the Red Cross. Ninety-seven medical students were also sent from the UK. The first aid workers to arrive in Belsen were Quakers. They were followed by volunteers from the Jewish Committee for Relief Abroad's Jewish Relief Unit. A key

THE CHILD SURVIVORS

A significant number of children and teenagers were liberated at Bergen-Belsen. After the war they were taken to Britain, Palestine, Sweden and Switzerland for recuperation.

As the Belsen-Hohne displaced persons camp was the largest in the British-occupied zone of Germany and the British government had offered 1,000 visas to the Central British Fund to bring Jewish orphans from the concentration camps to the UK, it is logical to assume that most of those children should have come from Belsen, yet only 47 child survivors from the camp were brought to Britain.

Despite the offer from the British government, opinions in the leadership of the Jewish survivors and among aid workers were divided as to where the children would build a new life. The Zionists believed that the children should be taken to the Palestine Mandate. They regarded Britain as the new enemy for the visa restrictions the British had imposed in 1939. The religious leadership objected to children coming to Britain as many of those who came on the Kindertransport had been placed in non-Jewish homes. Eventually, it was agreed that 47 children would be flown from nearby Celle to Southampton in southern England.

The children stayed in a children's home in the displaced persons camp run by a volunteer working with the British Jewish Relief Unit, 22-year-old Sadie Rurka. The night before the children were due to leave for the UK, Rurka, who was in favour of her charges being taken to the UK, argued late into the night with the head of the Central Committee of the Liberated Jews, Josef Rosensaft. Rosensaft, a staunch Zionist, wanted the children to settle in Palestine. He only agreed to let the children leave after David Ben-Gurion, the leader of the Jews in the Palestine Mandate, who was on a visit to the camp, personally interceded on their behalf. He promised Rosensaft that the children would be resettled in the Palestine Mandate. This did not happen largely because on arrival in the UK the children refused to be sent to Zionist training farms in Scotland and Northern Ireland. Find out more at w 45aid.org.

role in caring for Jewish survivors was played by the British Army chaplains Rabbi Leslie Hardman and Rabbi Isaac Levy.

What to see At the **Bergen-Belsen Memorial Site** (Gedenkstatte Bergen-Belsen; Anne Frank Platz, Loheide; **w** bergenbelsen.stiftung-ng.de; ⊕ 24hrs daily; Documentation Centre & exhibition: Apr–Sep 10.00–18.00 daily, Oct–Mar 10.00–17.00 daily; free), in a large clearing in the forest where the camp once stood, you will find 17 information stelae with short texts and photographs which provide information about the history of the camp and mark the site of the buildings. Allow at least 2 hours to see the exhibition and the memorials, more if you intend to walk

ALTER WEINER'S STORY

On 9 May 1945, 19-year-old Alter Weiner was among the prisoners in Wöbbelin waiting for the roll call to be counted, but no guards showed up. It felt like an ominous trick he recalled. 'A Russian tank approached the gate of our camp. An officer stepped down and told us: "We have come to liberate you!" We couldn't understand his Russian language, but we obviously understood that Germany had indeed been defeated.' The camp residents were then told they had three days to rape, rob and even kill Germans. Weiner was unable to move and had no inclination for revenge. 'I looked at the Russian soldiers as my heroic liberators. We expected them to remove our mountains of despair.'

All Weiner owned in the world were the prison clothes he stood in. He had no money nor a slice of bread to call his own. He had no idea where he was or how to get home to Chrzanów in Poland.

Local Germans were brought into the camp to see what the Nazis had done and on one occasion Weiner heard an ambulance. He imagined it was coming to help the survivors – but it was on its way to care for a German visitor who had fainted.

Weiner managed to return home but recalled: 'I knocked at the front door and told the Polish occupant that I had survived the war, and would like to look at my former home. The man slammed the door in my face. I was dumbfounded. I did not know where to turn.'

His mother had died before the war and his father had been shot by the Germans in 1939. He had no idea where his stepmother and stepbrother were. He never saw them again. He toyed with the idea of starting a new life in Chrzanów but, 'Poles who noticed me turned their heads. Some of them threw hostile glances at me.'

Finally, Weiner made his way to Kraków. He lived briefly in Israel but then moved to New York where he became an accountant. He retired to Oregon on America's Pacific coast and after years of silence wrote a book about his life called *From a Name to a Number; A Holocaust Survivor's Autobiography* (AuthorHouse, 2007).

Weiner was a man who lived in the present and it was the act of telling that mattered to him and the impact that conveying his story had. Weiner received more than 88,000 letters from people who had heard him speak or read his book. Many were from high school students, some of whom told him his story had stopped them contemplating suicide. He was a witty and engaging speaker.

In 2017, Weiner was run over by a car on the way to the grocery store. The police report said he had been wearing too many dark clothes.

to the Soviet prisoner-of-war cemetery. The camp is exposed, so come prepared for the weather. There is a café (w heidekueche.de) in the exhibition hall.

The permanent exhibition is excellent: it has 45 video points and covers the history of the camp and the story of the displaced persons camp in the Hohne barracks. About 12,000 people passed through the displaced persons camp which operated until 1950. This is still a military site and not accessible to the public, but the original buildings can be clearly seen from the road.

There is a series of memorials, of which the largest is the Soviet memorial put up in 1945. In September 1945, Jewish former prisoners of Bergen-Belsen concentration camp built a wooden memorial to commemorate the Jewish victims. On 16 April 1946, the wooden memorial was replaced by a monument made of stone. This is still there. Not long after the liberation, a Polish camp committee was established in the displaced persons camp with the aim of keeping alive the memory of the Poles who had been murdered. On 2 November 1945, a large wooden cross was dedicated to them in the presence of several thousand survivors as well as representatives of the Vatican and the British military government.

There are 13 mass graves and 15 individual graves. The gravestone memorial to Anne Frank and her sister is symbolic. No-one knows where her remains lie.

North of the camp on the L298 there is a memorial at the ramp where prisoners were transported to and from the camp.

Wöbbelin Near Ludwigslust in Mecklenburg, Wöbbelin was a satellite camp of Neuengamme used to collect prisoners from death marches from the Neuengamme concentration camp and its satellites. Others came from Auschwitz. The camp, 92km southeast of Hamburg, was still under construction when 5,000 prisoners arrived in the freezing spring of 1945; the barracks had no windows or doors. Food supplies were desperately short and survivors reported cases of cannibalism.

When the camp was liberated by the Americans on 2 May 1945, about 3,500 prisoners were left alive. The stench of rotting bodies filled the air. The camp was then destroyed. There is little to see here today, but this is an important story and it is worth stopping here if you are driving from Hamburg to Berlin.

The first memorial was placed at the camp in 1960. The site was vandalised by right-wing extremists in 2002. The visitors centre, the **Theodor Körne Museum** (Ludwigslusterstr. 2; ⊕ noon–16.00 Tue–Fri, 11.00–16.00 Sun; free), hosts small exhibitions and events. It is just past the memorial and is signposted.

WEIMAR

Weimar in central Germany is one of the country's loveliest cities. Famous as a centre for German culture, it was the home of the towering figures of German literature Johann Wolfgang von Goethe (1749–1832) and Friedrich Schiller (1759–1805), as well as the cradle of the humanistic cultural movement. The Bauhaus was founded here in 1919 and the city gave its name to the democratic Weimar Republic which lasted from the end of World War I until 1933.

It is a tranquil, relaxed city with beautiful parks and squares, yet nowhere is it more clear than in Weimar that one of the most advanced countries in the early 20th century was the perpetrator of one of the most horrific crimes ever committed.

GETTING AROUND The centre of Weimar can be explored on foot. To see the former Buchenwald concentration camp, take bus 6 from the main station. To visit the memorial at Mittelbau-Dora by public transport, take a train to Nordhausen and then a bus or taxi. The memorial is 6km north of Nordhausen.

WHERE TO STAY AND EAT Despite its past Nazi connections, **Hotel Elephant** (Markt 19; w hotelelephantweimar.de; **€€**) remains the best hotel in Weimar. Weimar is known for its onions and holds an **Onion Fair** every October. The Weimarer Zwiebelkuchen is an onion tart with a bread base topped with onions, eggs and sour cream. Try classic local dishes at the **Erbenhof Café and Restaurant** (Brauhausgasse 10; w erbenhof.de; ⊕ 07.00–18.00 daily, dinner 17.00–23.00 Mon–Sat; café **€€**; restaurant **€€€**), which has a pretty terrace in summer.

HISTORY Weimar was one of the first Nazi strongholds and Thuringia, the region surrounding Weimar, lifted its ban on Hitler's political activities in 1924. As early as 1932, the Nazi Party achieved a governing majority in Thuringia. The city was of key interest to the Nazis not only because they opposed the Weimar Republic but as a centre of German culture Weimar had important propaganda potential. The entire city and its cultural activities were redesigned in order to correspond to the Nazi ideal of a 'German culture' for the 'national community', the Volksgemeinschaft.

WHAT TO SEE The city has a useful app which traces how Weimar was converted into a Nazi model city.

Hitler was a regular visitor to Weimar and stayed at the **Hotel Elephant** on Marktplatz. Crowds would gather beneath the balcony of his room. Just 5 minutes' walk away, the **German National Theatre** (Deutsches Nationaltheater) on Theaterplatz is where the Weimar Republic was proclaimed, and where the Hitler Youth Movement was also founded in 1926.

The **Gauforum** on Jorge Semprún Platz between the Old Town and the railway station was the only government complex outside of Berlin. Although there were plans to build similar complexes in other German cities, this was the only one that was ever completed. A public park and numerous private and commercial buildings were demolished to make way for the buildings and the residents were forcibly resettled. Today, it is home to the Thuringian government and a shopping centre. The **Marstall building** on Kegelplatz opposite the castle was the Gestapo headquarters.

Elisabeth Förster-Nietzsche, the sister of the philosopher Friedrich Nietzsche, ran the former Nietzsche archive at **Humboldtstrasse 36a**. It became a shrine for Nazi sympathisers as she twisted her dead brother's writing to support Nazi ideology.

Memorial plaques at the east entrance to **Weimar's main railway station** remember the arrival of prisoners taken to the nearby Buchenwald concentration camp. In full view of the public, they were transferred to the camp from 1937 to 1943, after which a railway was built that went directly to the camp. There is another memorial in front of the former freight depot. The story of forced labour under the Nazis is told in the brand-new **Museum of Forced Labour under National Socialism** (Museum Zwangsarbeit im Nationalsozialismus; Jorge-Semprún-Platz 2; w museum-zwangsarbeit.de; ⊕ 10.00–18.00 Tue–Sun; €7).

In 1941, Jewish people were forced to wear a yellow star and Jews were interned in '**Jewish houses**'. Two of these were located at Belvederer Allee 6 and at Brühl 6. They were monitored by the Gestapo and the residents constantly harassed. Both houses belonged to Jewish families.

FURTHER AFIELD
Buchenwald The former Buchenwald concentration camp is Weimar's most important Holocaust memorial and was located on Ettersberg Mountain, 10km north of the city.

History The concentration camp at Buchenwald was built in 1937. It originally held men who were political prisoners, so-called asocials, criminals, homosexuals, Jehovah's Witnesses, Jews, Sinti and Roma. Prisoners were initially from the Reich but after the outbreak of war they came from across occupied Europe. Between 1937 and 1945 more than 280,000 people from over 50 countries were held here, among them the French politician Léon Blum. An estimated 54,000 people, among them 8,000 Soviet prisoners of war, were killed in the camp and its 139 subcamps, where in 1944 women and girls were also held as forced labourers in the armaments industry.

In 1945 many mass transports of prisoners from further east arrived here, among them many teenage boys, but in April 1945, 28,000 people left here on death marches. There was a significant resistance movement run by communists in the camp. The camp was liberated by the Americans but later used as an internment camp by the Soviet secret police.

What to see Download the free app and audio guide before visiting the **Buchenwald Memorial Site** (Gedenkstätte KZ-Buchenwald; w buchenwald.de; ⊕ 09.00–18.00 Tue–Sun, closes 16.20 in winter; free). The access road to the camp was built by inmates in 1938–39 and is known as the Blood Road.

The visit starts with a 30-minute introductory film shown in the visitor's centre, where there is also a café. The entrance to the former camp is a few minutes' walk to the north of the information centre. In the iron work of the gates are the words 'Jedem Das Seine' (to each his own). The clock above it is stopped at the moment the Americans liberated the camp. One wing of the gatehouse was used as a prison.

The route leads to the Appellplatz. Until the 1950s, the rows of prisoners' barracks stood behind. Visitors can see the crematoria, where the furnaces were specially designed for the SS by the Topf und Söhne company in nearby Erfurt.

There is a fascinating museum in the former depot originally used to store inmates' clothing and personal possessions. Behind it is an exhibition about the Soviet-era camp.

The Little Camp originally set up as a quarantine zone was used to house the children who arrived at the camp in January 1945. Kinderblock 66 was run by the communist underground, who managed to persuade the SS to let them look after more than 1,000 children. Among them was the writer Elie Wiesel.

The railway memorial, the GDR memorial, the SS living quarters and the remains of the SS zoo are all outside the perimeter fence.

There is a moving walk along the **Commemorative Buchenwald Railway Path** (request stop Bus 6 Gedenkweg). Since 2009 individual stones commemorate 2,000 children and teenagers deported to Buchenwald.

Nordhausen Outside Nordhausen, 131km northwest of Weimar, the former Mittelbau-Dora concentration camp is now the **Mittelbau-Dora Memorial Site** (Gedenkstätte Mittelbau-Dora; Kohnsteinweg 20; w dora.de; ⊕ 10.00–18.00 Tue–Sun, closes 16.00 in winter; free). The camp had a system of 39 subcamps, but here prisoners were used as slave labourers on the V1 and V2 rocket programme. They constructed underground tunnels – a small part of which visitors may see – in the

11

Hartz mountains for use as aircraft factories and fuel plants. But the work was never completed. Of the more than 60,000 prisoners held here, a third did not survive. Download the app before visiting.

NUREMBERG

Nuremberg (Nürnberg in German) is a picturesque city in the Franconia region of northern Bavaria. It is a strange place, where the tourist attractions are a mixture of gingerbread, Christmas markets and giant Nazi monuments. Famous for the vast annual searchlight rallies held here by the Nazi Party, it was also the site of the post-war trials of senior Nazis.

GETTING AROUND Nuremberg has a good public transport system – buy the Nürnberg + Fürth Card (w tourismus.nuernberg.de/en/booking/nuernberg-card-city-card; €33) valid for 50 museums and free transport. Buses 36, 45, 55 and 65 (bus stop: Dutzendteich Bahnhof) and trams 6, 8, 36, 45, 55, 65 or 🚊 2 Nürnberg-Dutzendteich go to the Rally Grounds. Take the U-Bahn to the Palace of Justice. You can explore the city centre on foot.

To visit the former concentration camp at Flossenbürg, you need a car, as public transport is complicated and time consuming.

WHERE TO STAY AND EAT There are plenty of chain hotels in Nuremberg. The **SORAT Hotel Saxx Nürnberg** (Hauptmarkt 17; w sorat-hotels.com/en/hotel/nuernberg; €) next to the Hauptmarkt is a basic hotel with parking. There is a small supermarket, daily market and plenty of restaurants and cafés in the Hauptmarkt. Pack a picnic if visiting the Rally Grounds, which are in a huge parkland and recreation area. The former Restaurant Wanner on the edge of Lake Dutzendteich, now the **Gutmann** (Bayernstr. 150; w gutmann-am-dutzendteich. de; ⊕ 10.00–23.00 daily; €€€), has been popular with day-trippers to the park since the 19th century.

HISTORY Jews have lived in Nuremberg since the 12th century. Following a pogrom in 1298 in which 562 Jews were murdered, the Jews were expelled from the city; the synagogue was demolished, and in its place the Frauenkirche church was built. Jews were allowed back into the city at the end of the 17th century. The present-day Jewish community is made up of Jews from the former Soviet Union.

Between the two world wars, Nuremberg was a Nazi Party centre. Julius Streicher set up one of the party's first branches here in 1922 and was, for a time, a rival of Hitler's for the leadership. Streicher also edited the notoriously antisemitic newspaper *Der Stuermer* and was crucial in drumming up support for the Nationalsozialistische Deutsche Arbeiterpartei (NSDAP), or National Socialist German Workers' Party, in Bavaria. In 1933, Streicher became the Gauleiter of Franconia, an important post; after the war, he was among those convicted at the Nuremberg trials.

Attacks on Jews and Jewish property and boycotts of Jewish businesses were regular occurrences after the Nazis came to power in 1933, but the situation took a turn for the worse when, on 30 July 1933, 400 wealthy and distinguished Jews were arrested and publicly humiliated – some were forced to trim the grass in public parks with their teeth. In August 1938, the synagogue and community centre were demolished. Three months later during Kristallnacht the two remaining synagogues and numerous shops were burned to the ground; 91 Jews were killed. In the wake of Kristallnacht, between 2,000 and 3,000 Jews left Nuremberg. In 1941, only 1,800 Jews remained in the city.

During World War II, Nuremberg was an important site for armaments production, and in January 1945, it was badly bombed by the RAF. Ninety per cent of the city was destroyed, 1,800 residents killed and 100,000 people left homeless. Although much of the city centre was later reconstructed, the bombing left a deep psychological impact on the local population and bred a sense of German victimhood in the years after the war. It was only in the 1960s that interest in Nuremberg's Nazi past emerged. Neil Gregor's *Haunted City: Nuremberg and the Nazi Past* (Yale, 2008) looks at how Nuremberg has dealt with the memory of its complex and difficult history.

WHAT TO SEE The original Jewish Quarter was in the area around the main market, **Hauptmarkt**, which was renamed Adolf Hitler Platz under the Third Reich and used for mass meetings and parades, including Hitler's famous motorcade.

The **main synagogue** was on the banks of the pretty Pegnitz River a short walk from the Hauptmarkt just before the Spitalbrücke bridge. A memorial marks the spot. In front of it there is a stone pillar reminiscent of a cantor's pillar, on which sits a sooty stone from the original synagogue wall. The bell tower erected in Nuremberg in the 1950s in memory of the city's civilians killed in World War II was built with stones from the synagogue.

A second monument marks the site of the **Adat Yisrael Synagogue** on Essenweinstrasse. On it is written the verse from Deuteronomy 25:17: '*Remember what Amalek did unto thee*'. Amalek was the first enemy to attack the Israelites after the Exodus from Egypt, who was set on eradicating them as a people. Jews believe that Amalek has returned in many guises throughout their history.

At the **Memorial of the Nuremberg Trials** (Memorium Nürnberger Prozesse; Bärenschanzstrasse 72; 🚇 1 Bärenschanze; w museen.nuernberg.de/memorium-nuernberger-prozesse; ⊕ Apr–Oct 09.00–18.00 Mon & Wed–Fri, 10.00–18.00 Sat–Sun, Nov–Mar 10.00–18.00 Wed–Mon; €6) in the **Palace of Justice** (Justizpalast) the tour begins in Courtroom 600, where the trial of 22 leading Nazis began on 20 November 1945. It is smaller than it originally was as the press gallery is now part of the slightly wordy but informative museum on the floor above. Courtroom 600 is still used for trials so access is not always possible.

After the end of World War II, the victorious Allies held trials of war criminals in Nuremberg's Palace of Justice. These trials played a pivotal role in shaping human rights law.

Although the Soviet Union wanted the trials to be held in Berlin, Nuremberg was chosen for its symbolic value. The Palace of Justice was also one of the few in the country that remained intact and was next to a large prison. The courtroom had also been used by the Nazis to try political offences.

The trial of 22 primarily high-ranking Nazis, who had been captured by the Allies at the end of the war, took place between October 1945 and October 1946. Among the defendants were Hermann Göring, one of the most important Nazi leaders, Wilhelm Frick, Hans Frank, Joachim von Ribbentrop, Hitler's architect Albert Speer, who was the wartime Armaments Minister, and Julius Streicher, the local Nuremberg politician. They were accused of three charges: crimes against peace; war crimes, including murder, ill treatment or deportation to slave labour of civilian populations, killing hostages and plundering property; and crimes against humanity, namely murder, extermination, enslavement and deportation of civilian populations. The murder of Europe's Jews was laid out before the court. The tribunal was made up of American, British, French and Soviet judges and prosecutors. Twelve of the defendants were sentenced to death. Göring committed suicide before the sentence was carried out.

Between 1946 and 1949, 12 additional trials were held before US military tribunals. The Nuremberg Principles form the basis for today's International Criminal Court in The Hague.

The Nazi Party Rally Grounds The site of the Nazi Party rallies, the Ort Reichsparteitage, is in the southeast of the city in the vast Volkspark Dutzendteich (⏲ 24hrs; free). The remains of the enormous structures used in the rallies are dotted around the 4km² park.

History From 1933 to 1939, the Nazis constructed a series of buildings around Lake Dutzendteich, an artificial lake created in the 14th century. The parkland that surrounds it had been used for mass national events since the end of the 19th century. In 1927 and 1929 the first NSDAP rallies were held here, but from 1933 the rallies became annual events, held each September until 1938. As the scale of the rallies grew, a series of huge complexes were designed by Hitler's architect, Albert Speer, of which only the Zeppelinfeld, Luitpoldarena and Grosse Strasse were finished before the war broke out in 1939, when the rally was cancelled.

Up to 1 million people attended the rallies, while film and radio broadcast them to all corners of the Reich. Crucial in this propaganda campaign was Leni Riefenstahl's 1934 film *Triumph of the Will*.

Today the park is used for sporting events and concerts and is a recreational area.

What to see Start your visit at the Congress Hall, where there is an exhibition that tells the history of the Rally Grounds, which originally covered an area of 12km². There is a useful map of the site on **w** museums.nuernberg.de.

Congress Hall Part of Lake Dutzendteich was drained prior to construction work on the Congress Hall which began in 1935. The hall was modelled on the Colosseum in Rome and was planned to hold 50,000 people – but, like all the structures here, it was built in haste and was left unfinished. Construction was halted when war broke out in 1939. Today the hall has no roof, and is in a state of decay. The building is in the shape of a U flanked by two head buildings, one of which is now the Documentation Centre. The large empty space that was to have been used as the heart of the arena was until recently a car park and is accessed through the gateway between the two wings of the structure. There are plans to turn part of the Congress Hall into an arts centre. It is a controversial move which will transform the half-finished structure which, in its current state, is a unique commemoration of the Nazis' failure.

The **Documentation Centre** (Dokumentationszentrum Reichsparteitsgelände; Bayernstrasse 110; w rebuilding.documentaion-centre-nuremberg.de; ☉ 10.00–18.00 daily; free) was closed for renovation at the time of writing and is due to reopen in 2025. In the meantime, a small exhibition in part of the Documentation Centre provides a compact history of the rallies and the site.

Luitpoldhain The first Nazi rallies in the 1920s were held in the Luitpoldhain, across the road from the Documentation Centre. This park was named after Luitpold, the Prince Regent of Bavaria, and was originally laid out in 1906. The Nazis reconfigured the park into a massive, paved arena with seats for 50,000 spectators, the Luitpoldarena. The SA and SS held rallies here involving 150,000 participants. The rallies ended with rituals to commemorate the dead in which the flag carried by the Munich Beer Hall Putsch rebels and stained by their blood played a central part. Speer's Luitpold Hall, the Luitpoldhalle, stood at the top of the Luitpoldhain but was damaged in a bombing raid in 1942 and demolished in 1945 (it's now a car park). The park was then laid out once again. Today, the extent of the lawns gives visitors a sense of the size of the rallies held here. The foundations of the main grandstand are still visible, and the Memorial Hall still stands. Today, it commemorates the victims of World War I and World War II, along with the victims of the National Socialist tyranny (1933–45).

Zeppelin Grandstand (🚊 2 Frankenstadion; ☉ 24hrs daily) The Zeppelin Grandstand was built between 1935 and 1937, as the Nazi rallies outgrew the Luitpoldhain. The 360m-long grandstand was designed by Albert Speer and modelled on the Pergamon Altar. It is southeast of the Documentation Centre in an area of the park known as the Zeppelinwiese, the Zeppelin Meadow, which gets its name from the moment in August 1909 when Ferdinand Graf von Zeppelin landed one of his airships here. The giant swastika that once stood on top of the grandstand was blown up by the American military in 1945, after their victory parade. In 1967, the pillar galleries were demolished.

Great Avenue The Great Avenue (Grosse Strasse), measuring 60m wide and 1.5km long, cuts through the grounds west of the Zeppelin Grandstand. Completed in 1939, it was designed by Speer to be the central axis of the rally grounds but was never used as a marching ground as the Nazi rallies stopped with the outbreak of war. After the war, the road was used as a temporary airfield by the US Army. The avenue runs past Lake Silbersee, which was created when the foundations of the **German Stadium** flooded. The stadium was to hold 400,000 people and was to have been the biggest arena in the world. The views from the avenue back across Lake Dutzendteich of the Congress Hall give visitors an appreciation of its sheer size.

The term 'genocide' was coined by the Polish Jewish lawyer Raphael Lemkin (1900–59). Lemkin was born in what is present-day Belarus but was then part of Poland. After the German invasion in 1939, he fled to the United States.

In 1933, Lemkin published a pamphlet proposing that the League of Nations create new international laws relating to the mass murder of groups of people, in the hope that atrocities such as the mass killings of Armenians in 1915 could be prevented. The idea was rejected, but later, after investigating the fate of Jews in the Holocaust, Lemkin decided to use the term 'genocide', which he defined in his 1944 book *Axis Rule in Occupied Europe*.

The International Military Tribunal at Nuremberg used the term 'genocide' to describe the fate of Jews and others under Nazi rule but did not charge the defendants with it as a specific crime. Lemkin lobbied the United Nations to adopt the term. On 9 December 1948, the UN established genocide as a crime in international law.

Those interested in finding out more about Lemkin should read Phillipe Sands's East West Street: On the Origins of Genocide and Crimes against Humanity *(Weidenfeld & Nicholson, 2016).*

Märzfeld (Langwasser; 🚊 1 Scharfreiterring; 50mins' walk from the Zeppelin Grandstand) In 1938, construction began of a station in the area southeast of the Great Avenue known as the Märzfeld, the March Field. The area was named to commemorate the re-introduction of conscription in March 1935. It was to have a capacity for 250,000 but was never finished. After the war, the area was developed into the Langwasser suburb as there was an urgent need for housing in the city. The station at Märzfeld was the departure point for the deportation of Jews from the region – the first train left for Latvia on 29 November 1941. Next to it, barracks-style accommodation was originally used for visiting Hitler Youth and Nazi organisations; but between 1939 and 1945 the barracks were used to house prisoners of war. Conditions were appalling and thousands, especially Soviet prisoners, died here. After years of neglect, the city is now in the process of designing a memorial to the deportees.

FURTHER AFIELD

Fürth Fürth, 7km northwest of Nuremberg, had a Jewish population of 1,990 in 1933, of whom 1,068 were murdered in the Holocaust. Jews had lived in the city for 500 years. A memorial to the Jewish community stands on Geleitsgasse, just off Königstrasse. One of the most well-known Jews who lived in Fürth before the war was the former US Secretary of State Henry Kissinger. His family fled the city in 1938, as did hundreds of others.

The **Jewish Museum Franconia** (Jüdisches Museum Franken; Königstrasse 89; 🚊 1 Fürth Rathaus; w juedisches-museum.org; ⊕ 10.00–17.00 Tue–Sun; €8) provides a flavour of Jewish life in southern Germany before 1933 and is housed in an 18th-century building with a ritual bath. The museum café serves a lemon cake, a local Jewish speciality, which is made from a recipe kept in the museum's archives.

Flossenbürg Flossenbürg concentration camp, 80km east of Nuremberg, opened in May 1938 in a remote forested area known for its granite quarries. Granite was in high demand for the construction of the Nazis' monumental buildings. The camp held political prisoners until August 1944, when approximately 10,000 Jews, mostly from Hungary and Poland, arrived in Flossenbürg and its subcamps. Some 13,000 more came in the winter months of 1945, as the SS evacuated other camps to the east. At least 7,000 prisoners died on route before reaching Flossenbürg. Living conditions were appalling and about 30,000 prisoners died. As the Americans advanced across Bavaria in April 1945, the camp was evacuated. Between 16,000 and 20,000 people were forcibly moved in a series of death marches and in open-top freight wagons. The camp was liberated by the 90th Infantry Division on

AN EYE FOR AN EYE

The partisan Abba Kovner, who fought in the forests around Vilnius, now in Lithuania, plotted with his fellow Jewish partisans and members of the Kraków Jewish underground to take revenge for the murder of 6 million Jews in the Holocaust. They had seen the Hebrew word *Nakam*, meaning 'revenge', written on the walls of abandoned ghettos, concentration camps and bunkers.

Kovner had a biblical world vision and retained a deeply religious way of thinking after the war, even if he no longer believed in God. His thoughts were framed in terms of the Old Testament's vengeance and justice. He planned to inflict on Germany not the targeted killing of guilty men but the same fate the Nazis had inflicted on the Jews – indiscriminate killing on a massive scale.

Kovner had two plans. Plan A was to murder 6 million Germans by poisoning water supplies; Plan B was to murder a smaller number of high-ranking Nazis awaiting war crimes trials, again through poisoning.

Plan A involved infiltrating the water systems of Munich, Berlin, Weimar, Nuremberg and Hamburg. The idea was that the partisans would shut off the valves that led to those neighbourhoods where foreigners lived but elsewhere death would flow out of the taps killing without discrimination both young and old, sick and healthy. Kovner made his way to Tel Aviv, where his plans were not well received, but after a month of frustrating meetings, he found his way to a biophysicist who provided him with the poison. Kovner set sail for France with the poison hidden in two canisters of dried milk. It was unlikely he had enough to kill 6 million people, but before the ship arrived in Toulon he was tipped off that he was about to be arrested and threw the poison overboard. Kovner spent four months in a British prison. He always believed he had been betrayed by the Jewish Agency in Tel Aviv, but the experience changed him. Kovner returned to Palestine and abandoned the idea of revenge as he too started to look to the future.

However, the team he left behind in Europe were determined to carry on with Plan B. Their target was a group of SS prisoners at Stalag 13 prisoner-of-war camp, not far from Nuremberg. The plan was to poison hundreds of loaves of bread that were designated for the SS. Three of them managed to get a job at the bakery that supplied the prison with bread and spread white arsenic powder, which looked like flour, on the bottoms of two thousand loaves.

On 23 April 1946, the *New York Times* reported that 2,283 German prisoners of war had fallen ill from poisoning, with 207 hospitalised and 'seriously ill'. Officially no-one died, but the partisans, who then left for the Palestine Mandate, always maintained that there had been a cover-up.

11

23 April, who then used it to intern SS and displaced persons. The SS and prisoner barracks were demolished in 1955. Housing and commercial developments were built on part of the site.

The remaining parts of the concentration camp at Flossenbürg are now, since 1995, the **Flossenbürg Memorial Site** (Gedenkstätte Flossenbürg; Gedächtnisallee 5–7; w gedenkstaette-flossenbuerg.de; ⊕ Mar–Nov 09.00–17.00 daily, Dec–Feb 09.00–16.00 daily; free).

Visitors enter through the former Appellplatz. The former laundry building on the right houses a small museum. Further on, visitors see the crematoria. In the memorial chapel there are ashes recovered from the campgrounds. The white Jewish memorial contains one single Hebrew word *Zakhor*, remember. The camp commandant's headquarters is not accessible to the public and houses the memorial administration. Another part of the site is now a park which contains the mass graves of 5,000 victims of the death marches. The quarry, where so many of the inmates were worked to death, is still in use.

MUNICH

Munich is one of Germany's finest cities and the capital of Bavaria, one of the country's most scenic regions. In the wake of Germany's defeat in World War I, Bavaria was plunged into chaos, communist revolution and political violence. It was the perfect breeding ground for right-wing militia groups and it was here, in 1918, that Adolf Hitler began his political career. The Nazi Party was born in Munich and the city was given the honorary title of Capital of the Movement in 1935.

The city is also famous for its Oktoberfest beer festival, which has an important Jewish heritage – Jews played a major role in the brewing industry after a ban allowing them to own breweries was lifted in 1868.

GETTING AROUND The city centre can be explored on foot. There is a large car park near the Jewish Center Jakobsplatz.

To see the former Dachau concentration camp, take the S-Bahn 2 from Munich's main railway station (München Hauptbahnhof). The journey takes about 25 minutes. On arrival in Dachau, take bus 726 or walk to the site. Parking on site is cash only. The S-Bahn 2 continues on to Kloster Indersdorf.

To visit Feldafing, take the S-Bahn 6. For Sankt Ottilien take the S-Bahn 4 to Geltendorf. Trains also run from Munich to Landsberg am Lech.

 WHERE TO STAY AND EAT The best budget accommodation option is the **Mercure Hotel München Altstadt** (Hotterstr. 4; w all.accor.com; €€€). Eat in and around the **Viktualienmarkt**. The Jewish Community Centre near the Jewish Museum has an excellent restaurant, **Einstein** (w einstein-restaurant.de; ⊕ noon–14.30 & 18.00–22.30 Mon–Thu, noon–14.30 Fri; K; €€€).

HISTORY The German Workers' Party, which was renamed the National Socialist German Workers' Party (NSDAP), was founded in Munich in the 1920s and had its national headquarters in the city until 1945. After World War I, Adolf Hitler began his political career in Munich. In 1919, he joined the German Workers' Party and in 1921 was appointed leader of the NSDAP. In 1923, inspired by Mussolini's March on Rome, Hitler decided to stage a coup d'état, the Beer Hall Putsch, but the plan failed when the army withdrew support. The Nazis then turned to democratic

In 2015, Bavaria banned the brass cobblestones known as *Stolpersteine* (page 170) that mark the last voluntary residence of Jewish and Roma victims of the Nazis – the Stolpersteine were considered disrespectful as, embedded in the ground, they are walked on and get dirty. A series of new memorials, often a stainless-steel post or memorial on a wall, commemorates the 10,000 victims at their former homes.

means to gain power. Hitler's trial for his role in the coup which was held in Munich made him famous across Germany. He was sentenced to five years in prison but the right-wing bias of the court meant he served just over a year of his sentence.

Although Munich was the birthplace of the NSDAP, Munich University was the home of a student resistance movement known as the White Rose, which spoke out against the Nazi regime and the persecution of Jews. Its leaders, Hans and Sophie Scholl and Christoph Probst, were executed in Munich's Stadelheim Prison in 1943.

Before the war the city had a population of 9,000 Jews, 3,500 of whom emigrated before 1939. In 1938, 1,000 Jewish men were imprisoned in the Dachau concentration camp. Munich played an important part in the immediate post-Holocaust story of many of the survivors liberated in Dachau and its subcamps and of the thousands who arrived in the city by train, fleeing from eastern Europe. The beating heart of post-war Jewish Munich was the Deutsches Museum. The US Army chaplain Rabbi Abraham Klausner, who had drawn up a list of 25,000 survivors known as the Sharit Ha-Platah, set up an information office in the building, which buzzed with people searching for relatives. Survivors wrote their names on the wall and where they intended to go next. You can read more about it in my book *The People on the Beach: Journeys to Freedom after the Holocaust* (Hurst, 2020).

WHAT TO SEE Start your visit at the heart of Nazi Munich in Königsplatz, which was used as a Nazi parade ground and was surrounded by Nazi administrative buildings. The grand Classicist ambience of Königsplatz made the square the ideal backdrop for staging Nazi spectacles. The **Munich Documentation Centre for the History of National Socialism** (NS-Dokumentationszentrum München; Max-Mannheimer-Platz 1; w nsdoku.de; ⊕ 10.00–19.00 Tue–Sun; free), a six-storey modern cube, stands on the site of the former Brown House (Braunes Haus), formerly the Palais Barlow, which was the Nazi Party headquarters. The centre, which opened in 2015, has an excellent permanent exhibition on the history of National Socialism. The website has a useful downloadable Nazi history trail. Next to the documentation centre is the **Führerbau**, where the 1938 Munich Accords were signed.

There are two important memorials on the way back to the city centre and one crucial site. The 1983 memorial on **Platz der Opfer des Nationalsozialismus** near the former Gestapo HQ remembers Nazi victims, and there is a plaque recognising the murdered Sinti and Roma. Just 5 minutes' walk away is the 19th-century **Feldherrnhalle** on Odeonsplatz, modelled on the Loggia dei Lanzi in Florence, which was the scene of Hitler's failed 1923 putsch. The loggia had a cult status under the Nazis and is not marked. Retrace your steps to Platz der Opfer des Nationalsozialismus, from where it is a 10-minute walk to the memorial at Herzog-Max-Strasse 4, which marks the site of the **Hauptsynagoge** destroyed in June 1938.

On **Marienplatz**, at the heart of Munich, there are two important memorials. On the southern side of the **Old Town Hall** (Altes Rathaus) a plaque reminds passers-by that in the ballroom the Nazi propaganda minister initiated the pre-planned Kristallnacht pogrom on 9 November 1938. A commemoration takes place here each year on the anniversary.

In the entrance to the **New Town Hall** (Neues Rathaus), under the clock tower on the stairs leading up to the first floor, on the right (through the glass doors), there is a memorial to the Jews deported on the first deportation train to Kaunas in Lithuania in November 1941, who were all shot on arrival.

It is a short walk from here to the **Jewish Center Jakobsplatz** (Jüdisches Zentrum Jakobsplatz; Sankt-Jakobs-Platz 16; w ikg-m.de/juedisches-zentrum; ⏲ 10.00–18.00 Tue–Sun; €6) which is home to the Jewish Museum, the Jewish Community Centre and the modern Ohel Synagogue. The original synagogue was destroyed on Kristallnacht.

North of the Olympic Park, on Troppauerstrasse in Milbertshofen, the former site of the **labour and transit camp** for Jews is marked by a memorial.

FURTHER AFIELD

Dachau Twenty kilometres to the northwest of Munich, Dachau, now a suburb of Munich, was home to one of the most notorious Nazi concentration camps. It is now a memorial site.

History The Nazis' first concentration camp, Dachau operated from 1933 to 1945. It began as a detention centre for political prisoners and was a model for subsequent camps. Along with its 140 satellite camps, it became a prison for all the groups considered 'undesirable' – Jews, Roma and Sinti, homosexuals, political opponents and anti-Nazi clergy – as well as many Poles. New SS camp guards were also trained at Dachau.

In the last months of World War II, the camp was transformed by the arrival of thousands of prisoners on death marches. When the camp was liberated by the US Army on 29 April 1945, bodies lay in freight wagons in the sidings and spilled out of the open railway cars on to the ground. Besides the dead, the American troops were met by 30,000 starving and disease-ridden prisoners crammed into infested barracks.

BAYERN MUNICH'S JEWISH STORY

The foundations of football team Bayern Munich's success were laid by its Jewish president Kurt Landauer, who was one of the pioneers of professional football in the first half of the 20th century. The Nazis considered professional football a 'Jewish plot' and condemned Bayern Munich as a 'Jewish club'. Fearing that his role would adversely affect the club, Landauer resigned as the club's president but remained in Munich. He was arrested the day after Kristallnacht and interned in the Dachau concentration camp.

He was released after 33 days and fled to Switzerland in May 1939. His family were murdered in the Holocaust. Landauer returned to Munich in June 1947, and less than two months later he again became president of FC Bayern Munich.

In 2015, the team renamed the plaza in front of the stadium Kurt-Landauer-Platz and a statue of him was erected at the club's headquarters, overseeing the training grounds, in May 2019.

In the spring of 1946 during the first Passover since the liberation, Rabbi Abraham Klausner, a young American army chaplain who had arrived in Dachau with the US Army, used the festival to give the survivors a psychological boost. On the evenings of 15–16 April 1946, 200 survivors and GIs gathered in Munich's **Deutsches Theater restaurant** to celebrate the traditional Seder meal. An elegant spot, it had been popular with Nazi grandees and was one of the few restaurants still working in the city.

Long tables were covered with white tablecloths, silver cutlery and neatly folded white napkins, each set with flowers and bottles of sweet kosher wine. For the survivors, the symbolism and the luxury was breathtaking.

Klausner had discovered a radical rewriting of the Haggadah, the text that relates the Exodus from Egypt, written in Hebrew and Yiddish by Yosef Sheinson. Sheinson was a survivor of the Kovno Ghetto, modern-day Kaunas in Lithuania, who had been in the nearby Kaufering camp. It retold the story of Exodus through the experience of the Holocaust. The opening page starkly rewrote the text's most echoing words as 'We were slaves to Hitler in Germany.' It reflected the feelings among survivors that their experiences in the camps were a calamity darker than slavery in Egypt.

The Survivors' Haggadah was given further terrifying majesty by seven haunting woodcuts by the artist Miklos Adler, a survivor from Debrecen in Hungary. One image showed a hard-faced Nazi officer separating a boy from his mother as Jews trudged off towards smokestacks. To this day there is still something shocking about the Survivor's Haggadah, in its simplicity and its terrifying woodcuts.

A copy is held at the United States Holocaust Memorial Museum (w ushmm.org). On their website it is possible to watch a short film about the Haggadah in the Curators Corner.

The first American rabbi to enter the camp was 30-year-old Abraham Klausner, who was the first outsider to draw up a plan to help the survivors. Once Kaddish was said and the dead were buried, Klausner vowed he would reunite the survivors with what families and friends they had left. He would play a crucial role in the Jewish revival that happened in the American-occupied sector.

What to see The original complex was a vast site with massive warehouses and storerooms, much of which is not accessible to the public. Before visiting the **Dachau Memorial Site** (Gedenkstatte Dachau; Alte Romerstrasse 75; w kz-gedenkataette-dachau; ⊕ 09.00–17.00 daily; free), it is worth looking at the website, which also has a selection of audio guides.

Tourists enter through a small gateway in the larger main gate, in which, worked into the metal, are the infamous words *Arbeit Macht Frei*, Work Sets You Free. The gate leads into the roll call area where prisoners were counted and made to stand for hours in terrible conditions. Many of the prisoners brought to Dachau on the death marches died on the square.

Much of the original camp still stands and two barracks have been restored to their wartime condition. The main exhibition housed in the camp's farm buildings, laundry and supply rooms is extensive. It documents the history of the camp, the rise of the Nazis and the 'Final Solution'. Visitors can also see the crematoria, the

11

gallows and gas chamber (built in 1942 but never used for mass murder), and the necropolis.

At the back of the campgrounds are four chapels, Catholic, Protestant and Jewish, which date from the 1960s. The Jewish chapel is built underground, symbolising the underground life of Jews during the Nazi period. There is also a Russian Orthodox chapel erected in 1994.

Since the establishment of the memorial site at Dachau in 1965, the exhibitions have focused on the fate of those who were imprisoned in the camp. But there are plans for a new exhibition, due to open in 2025 in buildings previously inaccessible to the public, which will examine how SS officers and Nazi prison guards became perpetrators.

Outside the parameters of the memorial there are a number of other sites including the mass graves and the Death March memorial on the junction of Theodor-Heuss and Sudetenland streets.

Markt Indersdorf The convent Kloster Indersdorf in the town of Markt Indersdorf, 15km north across the beautiful Bavarian countryside from Dachau, played a remarkable role in the rehabilitation of child survivors. The United Nations Relief and Rehabilitation Administration (UNRRA) opened a children's home in the cloister on 7 July 1945, where orphaned children, both Jews and non-Jews, were cared for.

The UNRRA team spent time listening to the children's stories and asked not only about their wartime experiences but also their life before the war, which the older children later reported did much to restore their strength. They were encouraged to express their experiences through art and drama and re-enacted scenes from the camps in a play performed in front of General Eisenhower. One survivor, Erwin Farkas, who went on to become a psychologist, said that he benefitted from telling his story repeatedly as it allowed him to distance himself from the trauma.

Farkas was one of 50 children selected to be taken to Britain for rehabilitation under a scheme run by the Central British Fund. You can read their stories on the website of the charitable organisation they set up, the '45 Aid Society (w 45aid. org). In October 1945, before they left the convent, photographs were taken of the children by the well-known American photographer Charles Haacker and published in newspapers across the world in the hope that relatives might be found. Salek Benedikt from Łódź, one of the children who would come to Britain, had the idea of writing each of the children's names in chalk on a piece of wood so that their names featured clearly in each of their photos; the resulting photographs are deeply impactful. Benedikt would later become a successful graphic artist.

There is a small exhibition at the convent, the **Augustiner Chorherren Museum** (Marienplatz 1; 🚂 2 from Munich; w augustiner-chorherren-museum.de; ⊕ 13.00–17.00 Sun; €5). The final room tells the children's story and displays copies of the photographs, which can also be viewed on the United States Holocaust Memorial Museum website (w ushmm.org). The children's story is told in Anna Andlauer's *The Rage to Live* (Create Space, 2018).

Feldafing On the northwest shore of Lake Starnberg (Starnberger See), 36km southwest of Munich, Feldafing is an extraordinarily important place in Jewish history which has been virtually forgotten. After the war, a former Nazi school here became the first displaced persons camp that was exclusively Jewish. Until the summer of 1945, displaced persons camps had been categorised by nationality, and by granting the Jews a separate camp the American occupying forces took an important step in

When 12-year-old Ivor Perl, then Izak Perlmutter, was deported with his family from Hungary to Auschwitz, it felt like an adventure. During the journey he would crouch down in the freight wagon and watch the wheels and the train tracks through the cracks in the floorboards.

'When the train stopped in Auschwitz, people shouted in Yiddish telling us to say we were older than 16. I spoke Yiddish and it saved my life. When we got off the train, we were divided into rows of men and women and children. I ran to my mother, but she sent me back to my brother. We were selected as slave labourers.'

The brothers were sent with their father to build a vast underground concrete bunker in a subcamp of Dachau near Allach, where the Nazis were going to build aeroplanes. The brothers then survived a death march to Dachau, where they were liberated.

Perl and his brother tried to return home. 'Some people who knew us from the camp stopped us and persuaded us to go back to Dachau and ask the Red Cross to see if our family were alive.' Not long after, Perl discovered no-one had survived – he had lost his parents and seven siblings. He does not remember how he reacted.

In July the brothers were moved to Feldafing Jewish Displaced Persons camp. There they spent much of the time messing about on the edge of the lake.

On the Eve of Yom Kippur, Perl was one of 5,000 survivors who attended the service at Feldafing. 'It was in an old barracks. The atmosphere was charged. The room was full of wailing, screaming and crying. Everyone there had lost the people they loved. Then it hit me that I would never feel my mother's arms around me or see my father and the rest of my brothers and sisters ever again. I ran out of the room.'

The Yom Kippur service was led by Rabbi Yekusiel Yehidah Halberstam of the Sanz dynasty. He had lost his wife and 11 children but became a surrogate father figure to the child survivors. When Perl and his brother heard that a group of youngsters were to be taken to Britain, they went to ask his advice. Until this moment they had been set on going to Palestine.

'He told us, "Leave Germany. Leave this horrible place." I knew nothing about England but decided that it must be paradise. Britain was a world power, and somehow, I ended up at the centre of the modern world!'

Perl became a blouse cutter, then set up his own business. He married and had four children. He now lives in north London.

recognising Jews as a nation. Although there is nothing to see at the camp today, the lake is a beautiful place to contemplate this important piece of history.

Archabbey of St Ottilien (Erzabtei Sankt Ottilien; Erzabtei 1, Eresing; w dphospital-ottilien.org; ⊕ 08.00–18.00 daily; free) Sankt Ottilien is a large Baroque monastery surrounded by lush farming land 45km west of Munich. It was the unlikely setting for a Jewish cultural and nationalist revival after the Holocaust.

In May 1945, a train carrying 3,500 mostly Jewish prisoners from the Kaufering concentration camp, a satellite of Dachau, drew into the station in the nearby sleepy village of Schwabhausen. After it was strafed by American fighter planes, the SS fled. The 800 survivors were gathered together by a young doctor from Kaunas in Lithuania, Dr Zalman Grinberg, who, with the help of an American gentile from St Louis, Captain Otto B Raymond, concocted a plan to take over the nearby military hospital in the monastery of St Ottilien where the injured survivors could recuperate. The monastery became the first Jewish hospital in Bavaria.

A few weeks after the liberation, Grinberg organised a concert on the monastery lawn where survivors, among them members of the former Kovno Ghetto Orchestra, played music which the Nazis had banned. Grinberg stepped on to the stage to deliver a game-changing speech, in which he described the odyssey they had endured, and instilled in the survivors a sense of self-confidence and a determination that they would settle in the Palestine Mandate.

When the Central Committee of Liberated Jews held its first conference at St Ottilien on 25 July 1945, Grinberg was elected chairman. The establishment of the Central Committee of the Liberated Jews of Germany was a highly significant event as it turned the survivors into a political body that the authorities had to deal with, especially after the US Army recognised them as the representatives of Jews in occupied Europe in mid-1946.

The monastery was also home to a maternity hospital, where, between 1946 and 1948, 427 babies were born. Pregnancy was a major challenge for displaced women suffering from malnutrition, typhus, tuberculosis and other ailments. Survivors were also fearful of German doctors, and rumours abounded, some true, of doctors and midwives wilfully murdering Jewish babies. When as adults some of those born at St Ottilien began to return to see their birthplace, the monks decided to commemorate the events that took place here. There is a small exhibition and plaques across the site. There is also a restaurant (€€) and bierkeller.

Landsberg am Lech

On the 'Romantic Road' from Würzburg to Füssen, 19km southwest of St Ottilien, this picture postcard town was once a Nazi pilgrimage site. Hitler started to write *Mein Kampf* while imprisoned here after the failed Munich Putsch of 1923.

The prison (which remains a prison and cannot be visited) across the river from the Old Town was also the scene of an important post-war trial of Nazi war criminals. In a small graveyard near the prison, rows of crosses mark the graves of the 300 Nazi war criminals executed here.

Although prisoners from the nearby concentrations camps were used for all types of forced labour, even in the town's restaurants, after the war they were forgotten. The late Manfried Deiler, a local man, was told by his parents and teachers that nothing had happened in Landsberg during the war, and he grew up believing this. But, on a trip to Dachau in 1988, he discovered that 23,000 Jewish prisoners had been brought to Landsberg to produce the Messerschmitt ME262 aircraft, Hitler's secret weapon with which the German leader hoped he would sweep the American and British planes out of German skies.

Deiler then set out to remind his fellow citizens what had actually happened on their doorstep in World War II. He founded the **European Holocaust Memorial** (Europäische Holocaustgedenkstätte; Erpftingerstrasse; w kaufering-memorial.de/en; ⊕ by appt, ask in the tourist office in Landsberg for details), which now owns part of the former Kaufering concentration camp. The site, which has extensive information boards, can be seen from the perimeter fence.

Landsberg was also the site of another exclusively Jewish displaced persons camp.

Breisach am Rhein and Freiburg

Two memorials in the southwest of Germany are interesting as they remember the approximately 6,500 Jews from the region deported in full sight of their neighbours to Vichy France in October 1940. The French authorities had not been informed about the plan. Disguised as Wehrmacht army transports, the trains passed the demarcation line that divided France undetected. When the Vichy government discovered who was on the train, the Jews were interned at the Gurs camp near the Spanish border as enemy aliens. The camp was completely unprepared to take the new inmates. Within months, many of those interned at Gurs fell ill and died due to the insufficient food and medical supplies.

In **Breisach am Rhein**, near the French border, a small museum in the former Jewish school, **The Blue House** (Das Blaue Haus; Rheintorstr. 3; w blaueshausbreisach.de; ⊕ 14.00–17.00 Wed & Sun or by appt; donation requested) tells the story of the former Jewish community.

In **Freiburg**, since 2017 a mirror of water on Platz der Alten Synagoge has marked the site of the former synagogue which was destroyed in 1938. It is a controversial memorial as many children play in the water in summer. A memorial, *The Forgotten Coat,* on the Wiwilí Bridge over the railway line near the station remembers the 350 men, women and children who were deported to Gurs. Surviving photographs taken in nearby Lörrach show people watching as the Jewish deportees are loaded into trucks, and crowds of non-Jewish residents queuing to buy the belongings the Jews left behind – glasses, chairs, coffee grinders, and a whole variety of household items – showing considerable popular co-operation and consent in the deportation.

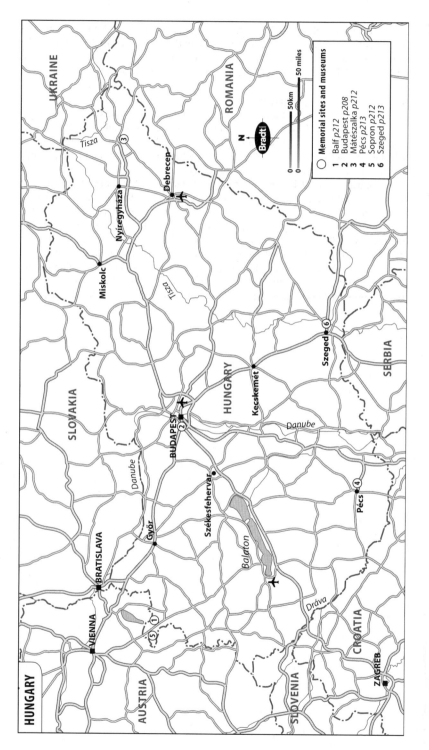

12

Hungary

The 1944 deportation from Hungary of almost 440,000 Jews in just 56 days was the deadliest extermination campaign in the Holocaust. It was extremely well documented by the Germans, and many of the images that we have of the ramp at Auschwitz show the arrival of Hungarian Jews. Although two ghettos were established in Budapest in 1944, most of the city's Jews survived the war. But life in the country's small towns and villages was eradicated.

Today Hungary has a large Jewish population of around 100,000, most of whom live in Budapest, which is home to Europe's largest synagogue. But the distortion of historical memory in the country makes it important to get to grips with some historical facts before visiting its memorials and museums.

GETTING THERE AND AROUND

Budapest is well connected by low-cost airlines to most major European cities. There are regular rail services between Berlin, Vienna and Prague and the city's three train stations. Bus links are also good. To drive on Hungary's motorways, you must buy a vignette (**w** hu-vignette.com). To visit the towns mentioned in this chapter you can use the train, but for more rural sites in Sopron you need your own transport.

ONLINE RESOURCES

The Vienna-based organisation **Centropa** (**w** centropa.org/en/hungary; see also page 340) has an extensive archive on Hungarian Jewry.

HISTORY

Hungary's Jewish population played a significant part in the development of the country's political, cultural and economic life after emancipation in 1867. It was, however, divided by a schism which created three religious denominations: Neolog (a form of Reform Judaism), the Status Quo traditionalists and the Orthodox. Although most Jews were integrated into Hungarian society, there was also a large Hassid community.

In the early 20th century there was widespread resentment of the level of success Jews had achieved in Hungarian society; 60% of Hungarian doctors, for example, were Jewish. In areas of the Kingdom of Hungary where Hungarians were not in the majority, Jews were associated with Magyarisation.

INTERWAR YEARS The 1920 Treaty of Trianon stripped Hungary of two thirds of its territory. A sense of grievance and shock fed a fanatical nationalist movement which soon acquired an authoritarian nature, which in turn fuelled growing antisemitism. Soon Jews, who had become the largest single minority left in the country, became a scapegoat for the ills that had befallen Hungary. The 1919 communist uprising, which had had many Jewish leaders, also had a serious impact on the way Hungarian Jews were viewed by their countrymen and fostered the Judeo-Bolshevik myth.

After Hungary tried to reclaim Transylvania and Slovakia, the Romanian Army invaded and the Hungarian Soviet Republic was suppressed. It was followed by two years of violence, known as the White Terror in which members of the reactionary forces of the National Army under the command of the former Austro-Hungarian admiral Miklós Horthy carried out counter-reprisals. The National Army took control of Budapest and Horthy was named regent in 1920. Horthy's role in the violence is still a matter of debate.

Horthy, an avowed antisemite, was personally responsible for anti-Jewish legislation and introduced quotas for Jews at universities, making Hungary the first interwar state to pass such legislation. Horthy's desire to overturn the Treaty of Trianon drew him into the orbit of Nazi Germany. The interwar years also saw the emergence of the far-right Arrow Cross Party.

Hungary's 1938–41 racial laws were modelled on Germany's Nuremberg Laws. By reversing the equal citizenship laws of 1867, the government excluded the Jewish community from Hungarian society. Jews then found themselves impoverished and marginalised.

The German invasion of Bohemia and Moravia in March 1939 sparked the dismemberment of Czechoslovakia. Hungary occupied Subcarpathian Rus

GOOD TO KNOW

Memorialisation of the Holocaust in Hungary has been subject to historical distortion since the end of World War II. After the communist takeover in 1949, Jews were not recognised as having suffered uniquely both in the interwar period and during the war itself, and the Holocaust slipped into the black hole of history. It re-emerged after the fall of the Berlin Wall, when some important steps were taken to remember the fate of Hungary's Jewish community, notably in the capital.

This continued during the first term of the Viktor Orbán government (1998–2002). Orbán was re-elected as prime minister in 2010, 2014, 2018 and 2022. In recent years under his leadership, Hungary has gained the dubious distinction of rewriting history, downplaying the responsibility of the Hungarian government and local officials, to rehabilitate war criminals and diminish its own guilt. Hungarians are presented not as allies of the Germans but victims of a Nazi occupation. Attention has also been deflected from the Holocaust by emphasising Jewish emancipation in 1867, rescue activities and the fact that Horthy halted deportations in early July 1944. There is also a move to equate the Holocaust with the Soviet Gulag. In 2014, the main Jewish community broke from the government over Holocaust revisionism.

A visit to the **House of Terror** (Terror Háza), one of Budapest's most controversial museums, is a step into the dangerous world of memory politics and historical distortion. The museum, which opened in 2002, is located inside the building that served first as the headquarters of the fascist collaborationist Arrow Cross Party, and later by the Soviet-supported secret police, and seeks to equate the communist and Nazi totalitarian regimes.

and parts of southern Slovakia, increasing its Jewish population. The January 1941 census would show that 846,000 people were classified as Jewish under the racial laws.

WORLD WAR II In August 1940, Transylvania – home to 160,000 Jews – was occupied by Hungary. Hungary then took part in the invasion of Yugoslavia in 1941, annexing sections of Baranja, Bačka, Međimurje and Prekmurje, again increasing the country's Jewish population. Later that year the country joined Germany in invading the Soviet Union. Thousands of Jewish men were sent to forced labour battalions attached to the armed forces. In April 1941, 20,000 Jews who could not prove legal residency were deported to Ukraine, where they were shot by the Einsatzgruppen. This was a serious step in the escalation towards genocide. Nevertheless, Horthy resisted German pressure to deport the country's Jews.

After Stalingrad, Horthy began to look for a way out of his alliance with Germany and tried to negotiate a separate armistice with the Allies. It prompted Germany to occupy Hungary in March 1944, an act known formally as Operation Margarethe.

Adolf Eichmann was despatched to oversee the destruction of the country's Jewish population. Between 19 May and 9 July 1944, almost 440,000 Hungarian Jews mostly living in small towns and the countryside were rounded up in 170 ghettos and sent on 147 trains to Auschwitz-Birkenau. The trains were escorted by Hungarian gendarmes to Košice then in Hungary, although now in Slovakia, from where SS guards took them over the border. All but 15,000 of the 440,000 were sent

This distortion has continued and surrounds the debate over a project known by its temporary name, the **House of Fates** (Sorsok Háza), whose head is the controversial Mária Schmidt, also head of the House of Terror. The unfinished museum stands in the Józsefvaros district at the site of the former railway station, from where several trainloads of Budapest Jews left for Auschwitz. Construction began in 2015 and has so far cost over €20 million. Critics, among them the Israeli Holocaust memorial Yad Vashem and the United States Holocaust Memorial Museum, say the museum will present Hungary as a victim not a collaborator by concentrating on events after March 1944 and ignoring Hungarian antisemitism and anti-Jewish legislation.

The 2014 **Memorial to the Victims of the German Occupation** (A Német Megszállás Áldozatainak Emlékműve) in Freedom Square (Szabadsag ter) has been criticised for representing Hungary as an innocent victim of Nazi Germany. It shows a German eagle swooping down on the Archangel Gabriel, who represents Hungary. It has been condemned by Jewish organisations and is the object of protest.

Over the past few years, Orbán has supported thinly veiled antisemitic campaigns, particularly against the Hungarian-born financier George Soros. The government-funded Centre for Gypsy History, Culture, Education and Study of the Holocaust, which opened in 2014, was closed in 2017.

There has been little memorialisation in the rest of the country. Statues of Horthy and streets named after him are commonplace. Nevertheless, Hungarian cinema has produced two excellent films about the Holocaust: *Saul fia* (*Son of Saul*, 2015) about a Jewish Hungarian prisoner in Auschwitz, and the 2017 film *1945*, a tale of two Jewish Hungarian survivors who return home.

to Auschwitz. With only 150 people under his command, Adolf Eichmann could not have run the operation without the help of the Hungarian authorities.

Yet on 7 July 1944, following a private intervention by Pope Pius XII, Horthy stopped the deportations, saving the Jews of Budapest. News of the mass murder had been brought to international attention by two Jews who had escaped from Auschwitz, although some historians have said that Horthy knew of the genocide and had already seen their report.

Horthy was deposed in October 1944 in a coup staged by the far-right ultranationalist Arrow Cross Party. In December 1944 and January 1945 approximately 20,000 Jews were shot on the banks of the Danube and two ghettos were set up in the 7th District and the so-called International Ghetto near Szent István Park. About 100,000 Jews were still alive when the Red Army occupied Budapest. Many of the survivors chose to emigrate to Israel in the early post-war years, and after the failed 1956 revolution.

BUDAPEST

Budapest was and remains the centre of the Jewish community in Hungary. The city is home to some moving memorials and important stories. It also has a vibrant Jewish Quarter which is the city's cool hipster place to hang out. Budapest hosts several Jewish cultural festivals, notably the Jewish Cultural Festival (Zsidó Kulturális Fesztivál; **w** zsidokulturalisfesztival.hu), which is held at the end of summer.

GETTING AROUND Most of the main sites in Budapest are walkable. If you are using a car in Budapest, download the Vox app to pay for parking.

WHERE TO STAY AND EAT Choose a hotel in downtown Pest, so you can walk to the main sites, though budget for high prices. There are a number of Jewish-observant-friendly hotels on **w** totallyjewishtravel.com.

Budapest has undergone a Jewish renaissance in recent years especially in the restaurant scene. **Mazel Tov** (Akácfa u. 47; **w** mazeltov.hu; €€) serves Israeli cuisine and **Rosenstein Vendéglő** (Msonyi u. 3; **w** rosenstein.hu; €€€) specialises in traditional Hungarian Jewish food. **Gozsdu Court**, once the heart of the Jewish Quarter, is a series of interconnected courtyards running from Király utca to Dob utca, lined with cafés, bars and restaurants.

Blintzes (pancakes with fillings) are traditional in Hungary and local Jews eat cream cheese pancakes at the festival of Shavuot, when it is customary to eat dairy dishes.

WHAT TO SEE
Holocaust Memorial Centre (Holokauszt Emlékközpont; Metro 2 or tram 4/6 to Corvin Negyed; IX Páva u. 39; **w** hdke.hu; ⏰ 10.00–18.00 Tue–Sun; HUF3,600) Budapest's Holocaust Memorial Centre is outside the traditional Jewish Quarter and as a result is often sadly overlooked by tourists. The memorial and museum is in the former Páva Street Synagogue, once the second largest in the city. The complex was used as an internment camp in 1944 and is the best place to start to understand the Holocaust in Hungary.

The museum was the first Holocaust memorial centre in central Europe founded by the state and, despite the atmosphere in current Hungarian politics, remains honest about the role played by Hungarians in the murder of its Jewish citizens.

It is part of the Holocaust Documentation Centre and Memorial Collection, a government foundation.

The museum is underground and entered via a staircase in the Tower of Lost Communities on which are engraved the names of 1,441 Jewish settlements that ceased to exist after the 1944 deportations. The modern permanent exhibition 'From Deprivation of Rights to Genocide', holds no punches in its description of Hungary's role in the Holocaust and the persecution of its Jewish population, which began long before the German invasion in March 1944. Visitors are met with the sound of marching jackboots, while the sloping floor reflects the country's descent into genocide. There are plenty of English translations, so it is highly accessible if you do not speak Hungarian. The exhibition also details the Roma genocide. The tour finishes in the restored synagogue, which is now used for cultural events.

In the courtyard on the 8m-high Wall of Names are inscribed the names of 60,000 victims who have so far been identified. If you would like to register a name, you need to make an appointment in advance.

Dohány Street Synagogue (Dohány utcai Zsinagóga; w dohany-zsinagoga.hu; ⏲ Jan–Feb & Nov–Dec 10.00–16.00 Sun–Thu, 10.00–14.00 Fri, Mar–Apr & Oct 10.00–18.00 Sun–Thu, 10.00–16.00 Fri, May–Sep 10.00–20.00 Sun–Thu, 10.00–16.00 Fri; closed Jewish holidays; HUF9,000) The Dohány Street Synagogue is the largest synagogue in Europe. Designed by the Viennese architect Ludwig Förster and built between 1854 and 1859, its Moorish style was unique at the time but has subsequently been copied across the world. (The Central Synagogue in New York is an almost exact replica.) The street on which it stands is named after a snuff and tobacco vendor, Anton Prinder, who had a shop here in the early 19th century – *dohány* is the Hungarian word for tobacco.

In 1939, the synagogue was attacked by the pro-Nazi Arrow Cross Party. It was then used as a stable and was damaged during the siege of Budapest at the end of the war. Renovations began in 1991.

A centre of Neolog Judaism, the synagogue can hold almost 3,000 people. Inside, surprisingly, it resembles a church, and there is no bimah in the centre. The ark contains Torah scrolls from synagogues destroyed during the Holocaust. Highly unusual for a synagogue, it also sells fridge magnets and postcards. The synagogue is unusual too in that it has an organ, once played by Hungarian composer Franz Liszt, and a mass grave in the courtyard. Jews are never normally buried in the grounds of a synagogue, but during the winter of 1944–45, when the synagogue was part of the ghetto, Jews who died of hunger, cold and disease were buried here. The grave contains the remains of at least 2,281 people, whose identities are for the most part unknown. There is a wordy but highly informative exhibition in the basement of the synagogue about the Budapest Ghetto.

Theodor Herzl, the Jewish journalist and political activist, who was the father of modern political Zionism, was born next to the synagogue. The **Jewish Museum** now stands on the spot and is part of the synagogue complex. Its arcaded building was constructed in 1931 and contains a collection of Judaica that underpin daily Jewish life, which are shown in an exhibition called 'Tamid', meaning 'always' in Hebrew. Archivists in the museum can help with family research, if emailed in advance (e familiy@milev.hu).

In the courtyard behind the synagogue stands the **Emanuel Tree Memorial** – a silver-coloured weeping willow made of metal with the names of 30,000 Hungarian Holocaust victims engraved on its leaves. The American actor Tony Curtis, whose Jewish parents were born in Hungary, paid for the statue.

In 2015, 6,300 documents from the May 1944 census, a precursor to the planned liquidation of Budapest's Jewish community, were found hidden in the wall of their apartment by a couple as they were redecorating. The census allowed researchers to identify almost 2,000 apartment buildings which had been used as holding locations for some 220,000 Jews who had been identified and forced to wear a yellow Star of David the month before. Each of these buildings was also marked with a yellow star. Inside, as many as 25 people were crammed into a single apartment.

Miklós Horthy had suspended the deportations as the course of the war went in the Allies' favour, but in the second half of August 1944 gave permission for the deportation of Jews from Budapest's 'yellow-star houses'. The deportations were cancelled at the last minute when Romania declared war on Germany. Those in the yellow-star houses were then confined to the ghetto in November 1944.

The buildings that were once yellow-star houses are now private residences, but an interactive map on the informative Yellow-Star Houses website (w yellowstarhouses.org) marks their locations.

The synagogue complex also contains a symbolic headstone for **Raoul Wallenberg**, the Swedish diplomat who issued life-saving diplomatic passports and papers to thousands of Hungarian Jews. Wallenberg delivered papers to Jews on the banks of the Danube about to be shot and those in the railway station about to be deported. He even warned the commander of the German troops that he would see him prosecuted for war crimes if the ghetto was liquidated. Once the Jews had protective papers they were housed in an international ghetto. The Arrow Cross Party permitted this as it meant Jews would be taken out of Hungary. Wallenberg disappeared in January 1945 and is believed to have been taken to Moscow by the Soviet secret police, accused of spying for the Germans.

Wallenberg was not the only diplomat to help the Jews. There are also memorials in the synagogue complex to Italians Giorgio Perlasca, Angelo Rotta and Gennaro Verolino, as well as to Portuguese diplomats Carlos de Liz-Teixeira Branquinho and Carlos Sampaio Garrido.

Budapest Ghetto The Budapest Ghetto was enclosed by today's Király, Kertész, Dohány and Rumbach streets in the Jewish Quarter. In November 1944, some 70,000 Budapest Jews were herded into the ghetto, where they lived 14 people to a room. The **Ghetto Memorial Wall** at Dohány utca 34 shows a map of the confined area, and there are bullet-shaped peep holes through which visitors can see images of the ghetto. A reconstructed part of the ghetto wall can be seen from a distance at Király utca 15 in the courtyard of a private apartment building. Several thousand people died in the ghetto before the Soviet Army liberated it in January 1945. A memorial to those who died in the ghetto was at time of writing under construction in Klauzál tér, where corpses were dumped in the winter of 1944–45. The memorial will be in the shape of a bronze plate with the marks of 3,000 nails which symbolise the unburied dead.

Of additional interest is Eleanor Dunai's account of her deaf father's survival as a child in the Budapest Ghetto: *Surviving in Silence: A Deaf Boy in the Holocaust* (Gallaudet University Press, 2002).

Memorials to foreign diplomats The foreign diplomats who tried to save Budapest's Jews are remembered across the city. The diplomats were financially supported by the charity the American Joint Jewish Defence Committee.

In 1946, a monument was put up by survivors in St Stephen's Park (Szent Istvan Park) to honour **Raoul Wallenberg** (page 244). It depicted him as a mythological hero fighting a serpent. In 1949, the night before the monument was to be unveiled, the communist authorities removed it. It was then placed outside a pharmaceutical factory in the eastern city of Debrecen without any reference to Wallenberg. A copy of the statue was reinstated in 1999 and a ceremony is held here annually on 4 August, Wallenberg's birthday. There is another monument to Wallenberg at Erzsébet tér 11–13. Raoul Wallenberg utca, renamed in 1989, is in the heart of the former International Ghetto, which he set up with his diplomatic colleagues. There is a plaque on the safe house in the International Ghetto, at Pozsonyi út 10. Another statue marks the spot in Buda where Wallenberg's abandoned car was found. If you would like to find out more about Wallenberg, a useful website is **w** walkwithraoul. hu.

The bravery of the Swiss diplomat **Carl Lutz** has been overshadowed by the fame of Raoul Wallenberg. The **Glass House** (Üvegház; Vadasz u. 29; **w** uveghaz. org; ⊕ 13.00–16.00 daily; free), which he declared neutral territory and where he provided a safe haven for some 3,000 Jews, is now a small but excellent museum and should not be missed. A former glass factory, it is not far from the Hungarian Parliament, in the former international ghetto. The building was also used by the Jewish youth underground movement. A memorial at Dob utca 12, not far from the Dohány Street Synagogue, depicts Lutz as a golden angel, descending from the heavens to help a fallen victim. He saved an estimated 60,000 Hungarian Jews.

There is a plaque to the 'Spanish Schindler', diplomat **Ángel Sanz Briz**, on the Spanish Embassy at Eötvös utca 11. Acting independently of General Franco's fascist government, he managed to save 5,000 Jewish lives. He even rented accommodation where they could live safely. He was helped by the Italian **Giorgio Perlasca**, who is often credited for acting alone. Sanz Briz never said a word about what he had done, even to his family. Eleven years after his death he was recognised as Righteous Among the Nations.

Other memorials The pure simplicity of the *Shoes on the Banks of the Danube* (*Cipők a Duna-parton*) makes it one of Europe's most moving Holocaust memorials. You'll find the 60 cast-iron men's, women's and children's shoes on the embankment between the parliament building and the Chain Bridge. Approximately 20,000 Jews were shot on the banks of the river by the Arrow Cross militia, who ordered them to remove their shoes before the execution took place.

The **Memorial to the Jewish Labourers** (A zsidó munkaszolgálatosok emlékműve; Bethlen tér 2) commemorates the thousands of Jewish Hungarian men who were taken into forced labour service units, *munkaszolgálat*, during World War II. Most of them were condemned to brutal physical work or sent to the front without proper clothing and equipment. The monument of two converging walls of caged stones is outside the former Jewish school for the deaf.

In the Trefort Garden opposite the Astoria Hotel, the Faculty of Humanities building of the **ELITE University** bears a memorial, installed in 2014. Along the walls of the building, once used as the German Army headquarters, runs a narrow bronze band, 250m long, on which are listed the names of the students and teachers who died in the Holocaust.

FURTHER AFIELD

Sopron In March 1944, several small ghettos were set up in and around Sopron, 217km west of Budapest near the Austrian border. The main ghetto was in the city's old town, which is full of narrow alleyways. The entrances to many through-houses, which allowed a public passage between streets, were bricked in. On 29 June, the Hungarian constabulary dissolved all the ghettos and brought the Jews to an industrial area on the outskirts of the city.

On 5 July, approximately 3,000 Jews from the ghettos were deported to Auschwitz. The exact number of Jewish victims from Sopron is not known, but it is believed that all the Jewish children under the age of 16 were murdered.

On the square in front of the former Orthodox Synagogue on Új utca, at No. 22, there is an evocative **memorial** designed by Hungarian sculptor László Kutas. It depicts victims' clothes left hanging on pegs outside a gas chamber; lying on the floor are shoes, spectacles and children's toys.

There are plans to renovate the abandoned medieval Orthodox Synagogue.

Balf In the winter of 1944–45 tens of thousands of prisoners, mostly Jews from Budapest, were forced to build a series of anti-tank defences known as the Southeast Wall along Hungary's border with Austria. These were intended to slow down the advance of the Red Army. At least 30,000 Jewish forced labourers from the Budapest Ghetto were taken to work on the project. The camp at Balf, 7km from Sopron, which housed them, was one of the largest in the area. Of the 2,000 men in Balf at least half died in the inhuman conditions, among them the well-known Hungarian writer and literary critic Antal Szerb – he was beaten to death. In March 1945, the camp was closed and the prisoners transferred on a death march to Mauthausen in Austria, 227km away.

The original **memorial** to the victims of the Balf camp, inaugurated in 1948, was funded by private donations from Jewish organisations. Designed by Sopron architect Oszkár Füredi (1890–1978), it is in the form of an obelisk and stands next to the Sopron-Balfi Szent Farkas-vártemplom church, on the northern edge of the village, near a mass grave which contains the remains of about 100 men.

Another monument at the same spot was inaugurated in 1968. The central element, a bronze relief depicting the death march, was stolen in 2005. Its theft prompted the construction of a **National Memorial** inaugurated in 2008. It consists of several symbolic gravestones, which incline towards the obelisk and finally fall to the ground.

Mátészalka Near the Slovak, Ukrainian and Romanian borders, 281km northeast of Budapest, Mátészalka played a central role in the deportation of the Jewish communities of Transcarpathia, now part of Ukraine. Jews had played a major role in the modernisation of the Mátészalka in the late 19th century, and by 1941, 1,555 Jews lived in the town making up about 15% of the population.

A ghetto was set up here in March 1944, where prior to deportation the inmates lived in appalling conditions. Hungarian police tortured Jews in the cellar of the synagogue and many women and girls were raped. Five transports left from Mátészalka for Auschwitz between March and June 1944.

The Orthodox synagogue, built in 1857, on Kossuth utca 44, stands as a memorial to this lost Jewish community. Shortly after the war, the 150 survivors placed a memorial plaque with 1,700 names of murdered Jews from Mátészalka and its surroundings inside the synagogue. In 2004, another plaque was added on the synagogue's outer façade.

American film star Tony Curtis was born in the USA shortly after his parents emigrated from Mateszalka. Private visits made by him and his daughter Jamie Lee Curtis, who has paid to renovate the synagogue, have brought attention to the Jewish history of the city. On the renovated façades of some houses graffiti from the ghetto period can be seen.

Szeged
The university city of Szeged, 176km south of Budapest, is located in the border triangle with Serbia and Romania and is the third largest city in Hungary. It was home to 7,000 Jews in 1944, 5.8% of the population.

In the late 19th century, Szeged was dominated by the Reform-oriented Neolog movement, whose members preferred the path of assimilation and identified strongly with Hungary. The community opened its magnificent New Synagogue in 1903. After the German invasion in March 1944, two ghettos were established in Szeged: a large one for about 3,800 Jews of Jewish religion, and a smaller one for about 500 Christians considered as Jews under the racial laws. On 20 June, the inhabitants of both ghettos had to move to a collection camp, in which a total of 4,800 people were crammed together. On 25 June, the first transport left for Auschwitz. Further trains followed.

During the Holocaust almost half of the Jews living in the Szeged region were murdered. Despite these losses, in 1949 the Jewish community counted about 1,800 members. The community is still one of the most active in Hungary today.

On a wall inside the **New Synagogue** (Új Zsinagóga; ⊕ Apr–Sep 09.00–noon & 13.00–17.00 Sun–Fri, Oct–Mar 10.00–15.00 Sun–Fri; HUF2,000), the first memorial plaque for 2,400 victims known by name was inaugurated in 1948. In 2004, a monument in the form of an obelisk with a Star of David as its base was put up on the former entrance to the ghetto. In 2014, a large menorah in the courtyard of the New Synagogue was erected in memory of the murdered Jews from Szeged.

A controversial monument in front of the cathedral represents the Jews and Christians as two brothers. While the older, Jewish, brother falls out of the boat into the water, the Christian brother desperately prays to God instead of coming to his brother's aid.

Pécs
Near the Croatian border, 236km southwest of Budapest, Pécs is one of Hungary's oldest cities. The story here followed a similar pattern to other towns across the country after the German invasion in March 1944. In May, a ghetto was established; and in June, the Jews were relocated to an army barracks, where many died of disease before an estimated 5,000 people were deported to Auschwitz. Between 750 and 950 survivors returned to Pécs but left the country soon after.

In 1988, a memorial plaque was affixed to one of the central buildings of the former ghetto. There is a memorial wall in the cemetery and a relief dedicated to the memory of the murdered children on the Jewish community building on Mária Úz. In 2010, when Pécs was European Capital of Culture, a memorial was unveiled at the main railway station. It depicts silhouettes of five figures evoking the void created by the Holocaust.

13

Italy

Italy was a key player in the history of the Holocaust. Fascism was invented here and became a model emulated by Hitler and other right-wing European governments in the interwar period. From 1938 onwards Italy persecuted its Jewish community under the draconian *leggi razziali*, racist antisemitic laws; and, by allying with Hitler and taking part in the invasion of former Yugoslavia, Greece and the Soviet Union, Italy endorsed the Nazis' genocidal policies. It was also a move that led to the loss of 500,000 Italian lives. Not to forget Mussolini's colonial ambitions that killed several hundred thousand Africans in the territories of present-day Libya, Eritrea, Somalia and Ethiopia.

The memory of the Holocaust was always present in Italian culture, and Italy has produced some of the most powerful Holocaust literature and cinema. Of the films the best known is the controversial *La vita è bella* (*Life Is Beautiful*; 1997). Among the list of famous writers who chronicled the Holocaust are Giorgio Bassani and Primo Levi. Equally important is the fascist journalist Kurt Erich Suckert, who wrote under the pseudonym Curzio Malaparte. In 1941 he was sent to cover the eastern front as a correspondent for *Corriere della Sera*. His novelistic accounts of the murder of Jews in Iași in Romania and an encounter with the Croatian fascist leader Ante Pavelić are among the most memorable descriptions in his most famous book *Kaputt* (New York Review Books Classics, 2007), which was first published in 1944.

Yet despite its presence in popular culture, the role Italy itself played in the Shoah is often overlooked. Italy's Jewish community had the third highest survival rate after Denmark and Bulgaria, with 15–20% of Italian Jews murdered in the Holocaust. Nevertheless, the Holocaust is an important part of Italian history that shines a spotlight on the way that Italians regard their complicated 20th-century past.

GETTING THERE AND AROUND

Milan's airports, Malpensa and Linate, and Rome's Fiumicino and Ciampino all have good international connections. Trieste has direct flights to London. The closest airport to Ferrara is in Bologna. International trains link Milan and Trieste with Geneva, Paris, Marseille, Munich, Vienna and Zurich.

SHOAH OR HOLOCAUST?

The Italian for Holocaust, Olocausto, is used on war memorials meaning the supreme sacrifice – *offrirsi in olocausto per la patria*. The word is of Greek origin and implies a sacrificial offering burned in a temple.

The Holocaust in Italy is referred to by the Hebrew Shoah meaning 'catastrophe' or 'disaster'. It is also the term preferred by many Jews.

ITALY

AUSTRIA
HUNGARY
SWITZERLAND
LJUBLJANA
ZAGREB
SLOVENIA
Trieste ⑮
Venice
CROATIA
Milan ⑨ ⑦ ⑭
Verona
Turin
Po
Bologna ⑪ ⑧ ① ②
Genoa
Le Spezia ⑥
SAN MARINO
Florence ③④
BOSNIA & HERZEGOVINA
SARAJEVO
FRANCE
MONACO
ITALY
Adriatic Sea
Corsica
⑬ ROME
Bari
Naples
⑩
Tyrrhenian Sea
⑤
Palermo
Ionian Sea
Sicily
Catania
N
Bradt!
0 —— 100km
0 —— 100 miles

○ Memorial sites and museums
1 Bologna *p231*
2 Ferrara *p229*
3 Florence *p226*
4 Gino Bartali Cycling Museum *p228*
5 International Memory Museum of Ferramonti – Tarsia *p222*
6 La Spezia *p225*
7 Meina *p225*
8 Memorial Museum to the Deported (Carpi) & Campo di Fossoli *p229*
9 Milan *p223*
10 Museum of Memory & Acceptance (Santa Maria al Bagno) *p222*
11 Nonantola *p230*
12 Passage of Remembrance (Bolzano) *p236*
13 Rome *p220*
14 Selvino *p225*
15 Trieste *p233*

The best way to get around Italy is by car or train. If travelling by car, factor road tolls into your budget. Also be aware that you cannot drive in most town centres. If you do get a parking fine, you must pay it at the post office.

ONLINE RESOURCES

Fondazione Centro di Documentazione Ebraica Contemporanea w cdec. Based in Milan, the foundation runs a project called 'Names of the Shoah', which publishes online a list of Italian Holocaust victims. It includes the list of Jews deported between 1943 & 1945 compiled by Liliana Picciotto in *Il Libro della Memoria* (Ugo Mursia, 2002), as well as individual lists of Jews interned in Italy between 1940 & 1943, those

arrested in Milan & Rome, as well as Jews killed in the Fosse Ardeatine massacre.
Fondazione per I Bene Culturali Ebraici in Italia w visitjewishitaly.it. A site that details Jewish heritage sites in Italy. Italy is full of Jewish history & there are many more sites to discover than those covered in this guide.
Museo della Comunità Ebraica di Trieste Carlo e Vera Wagner w museoebraicotrieste.it. This

website includes a section on the Stolpersteine memorials to those who were deported from the city of Trieste. The stumbling stones, designed by German artist Gunter Demnig, were first laid in Trieste in 2018. The website also has a series of suggested walking routes.

HISTORY

Jews have lived on the Italian peninsula for more than 2,000 years and are one of the oldest communities in the Western diaspora. The core of the community is made up of Italkim, Jews who have lived in Italy since Roman times, who were joined by both Sephardi and Ashkenazi Jews over the centuries. Italy has a rich Jewish history, of which the Holocaust is just a part. Although the Jewish community has always been small in number, Jews have played an important role in Italian society. Jewish influence on Italian culture is found every time you sit down to eat. Jews who fled the Inquisition in southern Italy brought with them their love of aubergines, now a staple in the Italian kitchen.

Italy's Jewish community was emancipated in 1870, during the Risorgimento (1861–71) when the country was unified into one state. Many Italian Jews were elite, educated and highly assimilated. Giuseppe Ottolenghi became the minister of war in 1903 and both Alessandro Fortis and Luigi Luzzatti served as prime minister, Fortis from 1905 to 1906 and Luzzatti from 1910 to 1911.

INTERWAR YEARS In 1922, King Victor Emmanuel III appointed Benito Mussolini, the leader of the Italian Fascist Party (Partito Nazionale Fascista), as prime minister. Over the seven years that followed, Mussolini created a one-party dictatorship. Political opposition was suppressed, and many opponents were sent into internal exile. Antisemitism was not as entrenched in Italy as in many other European countries and the Fascist Party had many Jewish members.

Although the conquest of Abyssinia had already led to racial legislation, the 1938 Racial Laws came like a bolt out of the blue for Italian Jewry. More draconian than the Nuremberg Laws enacted in Nazi Germany, they forbade Jews from working at or attending Italian schools and universities and excluded them from public office. Mixed marriages were banned, Jews were dismissed from the armed forces and foreign Jews, mostly refugees from Austria and Germany, were interned.

The Delegazione per l'Assistenza degli Emigranti Ebrei (DELASEM) was set up in 1939 to help foreign Jews in Italy to emigrate. Jewish emigration through Italy was encouraged by Mussolini as it was good business for Italian shipping companies. After the German invasion in 1943, DELASEM went underground.

WORLD WAR II Italy became an ally of Nazi Germany in 1939, declaring war on Britain and France in June 1940. Mussolini wanted to create a new Roman Empire in the Mediterranean. He invaded Albania in 1939 and took part in the German invasion of Greece and Yugoslavia in 1941. Italy was Nazi Germany's principal ally and carried out anti-Slavic and antisemitic acts often with extreme violence in some of the territories it occupied, but not in others.

The Italian people were not in favour of entry into the war. The defeats and failure of the Axis offensive in North Africa undermined the legitimacy of the Fascist regime. After the Allied landings in Sicily in July 1943, the Fascist Grand Council issued a vote of no confidence in Mussolini and negotiated a ceasefire. Mussolini was arrested.

The Germans then invaded Italy and occupied northern and central Italy, as well as the Italian zones of Albania, France, Greece and Yugoslavia. Mussolini was

THE FORGOTTEN HERO

Raffaele Cantoni, a well-known Jewish anti-fascist and socialist, was one of the most important Italian Jews of the 20th century. In 1945, he was the man of the moment who had both the energy and a vast array of contacts to help not only his community and his country but also the survivors flooding into Italy across the Alps.

Born in Venice, Cantoni was brought up in Padua but always spoke with a Venetian accent. Cantoni was a difficult man to pigeonhole. He was also a freemason with friends in the clergy. He was neither an intellectual nor religious but was above all a man of action. An accountant by profession, he had excellent management and negotiating skills and an astonishing capacity for fundraising.

In 1933, he was appointed director of the Comitato di Assistenza profughi ebrei, the Jewish Refugee Assistance Committee, which was set up in Milan in 1933. As director, he found himself working with the international organisations that were trying to help the German Jews, among them the American Joint Jewish Defence Committee and the World Jewish Congress.

During the early years of the Fascist regime Mussolini presented himself as a friend of the Jews and met with Chaim Weizmann and Nahum Goldmann, the founder of the World Jewish Congress. Italian universities were open to foreign students and many Jews came to study there. Cantoni was also a leading figure in the Delegazione per l'Assistenza degli Emigranti Ebrei (DELASEM), an official body set up in 1939 to help Jewish emigrants. Under Fascism it was a legal organisation until in 1943, when it went underground. It received funds from the charities the American Joint Jewish Defence Committee and the Hebrew Immigrant Aid Society. As a result of his experience and contacts, Cantoni was in the perfect position to swing into action the moment the war came to an end. Like many other leading Jews and anti-fascists, Cantoni had fled to Switzerland but only after he had been arrested and had escaped by jumping from a train heading for Auschwitz.

freed by SS paratroopers and became the head of the pro-German Italian Social Republic based in Salo on Lake Garda. Although the Germans held military power in the Salo Republic, the Italians had independent control over the police. The Salo Republic's 1943 Manifesto of Verona deprived Jews of their Italian nationality and classified them as enemies of the state. The republic also collaborated in the round-up and deportation of Jews to the death camps.

Deportations After the German invasion of Italy in 1943, there were major Jewish and anti-fascist round-ups. There was a strong anti-fascist resistance movement and tens of thousands of Italians were deported. Transit camps were set up in Bolzano, Fossoli di Carpi and Borgo San Dalmazzo near Cuneo. Deportation trains left from Bologna, Bolzano, Cuneo, Florence, Fossoli di Carpi, Genoa, Mantua, Milan, Rome, Trieste and Verona.

The unwillingness of some policemen to assist in the round-up of Jews and the sympathy of the general population meant that only 4,733 Jews were deported to Auschwitz, of whom only 314 survived. A further 506 Jews were sent to Bergen-Belsen, Buchenwald, Ravensbrück and Flossenbürg, most of whom were Libyan Jews who had been brought to Italy before the German occupation. The 328 Jews

Italy HISTORY

13

held in Borgo San Dalmazzo were deported to Auschwitz via the Drancy transit camp in France.

Still, it is important to remember that half of Jews sent to their deaths were seized not by Germans but by Italian police and informing was commonplace. The Fossoli transit camp was run by Italian forces between December 1943 and February 1944. After that, guarding and supplying the camp remained in Italian hands, as did transportation of prisoners.

The role of the Vatican during World War II is also a matter of fierce debate. It was only in 1998 that Pope John Paul II finally acknowledged that the Church should have intervened more forcefully to defend the Jews during the Holocaust.

It is also important to note that the racial laws were not immediately revoked after the fall of Fascism in Italy in July 1943. It was only in October 1944 that they began to be repealed, a process that would not be completed until 1947.

AFTERMATH In April 1945, communist partisans captured and murdered Mussolini and his mistress Clara Petacci in Giulino on Lake Como. The National Liberation Committee (CLN), made up of anti-fascist parties, was set up in Rome on 8 September 1943 and took control of the rest of the country as the Germans

GOOD TO KNOW

There is a tendency, not just in Italy, to see Mussolini as a benign dictator, who did many good things but made one fatal mistake in allying with Nazi Germany.

The fact that the deportations began only after the German invasion in 1943 allowed a story that Italians were a *brava gente*, good people, not capable of holding antisemitic prejudices, to grow in the post-war years. That the Italian government had excluded Jews from society and identified them in registers is often ignored. Although in some places occupied by Italy, the Italians did not hand over the Jews to their German allies, it was not out of benevolence but as part of a game of power politics between the two countries.

After the fall of Fascism, Italian Jews were happy to emphasise the story of those who had helped them as they were keen to reintegrate themselves into Italian society. The fact that Italy changed sides in the middle of the war has also confused the way the Holocaust in Italy is perceived. Nor were there any trials of Fascist officials akin to the Nuremberg trials to focus public attention on crimes committed by the Italian state. Many Fascist officials continued to work in public office. Gaetano Azzariti, who served as the president of the special tribunal overseeing the racial laws, was appointed as Minister of Justice after the fall of Mussolini and went on to become President of Italy's Constitutional Court in 1957.

As a result, Italy has accepted little responsibility for the persecution of the Jews. Commemoration events tend to focus on German responsibility and highlight Italian resistance and the help given to survivors after the war. Simon Levis Sullam's important book *The Italian Executioners: The Genocide of the Jews of Italy* (Princeton University Press, 2018) did much to balance Italians' understanding of the Holocaust.

Although there are now plans to build a Holocaust museum in Rome, there is still no documentation centre that addresses the crimes of Fascism.

retreated. The CLN was to rule Italy until 1946, when Italians voted for a republic in a referendum.

In the post-war period, Italians helped over 70,000 desperate Jewish refugees who arrived in the country. The help given to the survivors by the left-wing former partisans and trade unions is a story that has only recently been rediscovered in Italy. Many former partisans helped more than 25,000 Jewish refugees leave for Palestine in the run-up to 1948, and they also illegally trafficked arms that were used in the battles against Arab forces. This story is a central theme in my book *The People on the Beach: Journeys to Freedom after the Holocaust* (Hurst, 2020). Some of those who helped the Jewish refugees forgot this story, as after 1967 sympathy for the Palestinians and criticism of Israel grew.

ROME

Rome is the home of one of Europe's oldest Jewish communities, who first settled in the city during the Roman Empire. It is one of the oldest continuous Jewish settlements in the world. Today, the city is home to half of the country's 35,000-strong Jewish population.

For Italians the round-up of Jews in the Old Ghetto in Rome on 16 October 1943, the largest single round-up and deportation in Italy, and the massacre of resistance leaders at the Fosse Ardeatine in March 1944 have come to symbolise the German occupation.

It has nevertheless taken 20 years of discussion and bureaucratic wrangling for the green light to build a Holocaust museum to be given. The project was given the official go-ahead by Prime Minister Giorgia Meloni in March 2023.

Rome's new Holocaust museum will be in the grounds of the Neoclassical Villa Torlonia, the former residence of Benito Mussolini on Via Nomentana, a kilometre from Porta Pia. Locating the museum in the Fascist leader's former residence links the regime inextricably with the Holocaust, a connection many Italians did not recognise until the late 20th century. The fact that the villa includes Roman-era Jewish catacombs underscores the two millennia of Jewish presence in the city. Designed by Italian architects Luca Zevi and Giorgio Tamburini, the cuboid-shaped museum will have high black walls bearing the names of all the Italian Jews deported from the country.

GETTING AROUND Central Rome can be explored on foot. Much of the city centre is covered by a *zona traffico limitato*, ZTL or a limited traffic zone, which means it is inaccessible to private cars. There is a substantial fine for drivers who flout the rules.

To see the museum and memorial at the Fosse Ardeatine massacres site, near the Via Appia, take bus 118 from the San Callisto catacombs. To get to Santa Maria al Bagno take a bus to Salerno and change.

WHERE TO STAY AND EAT Rome can be extremely busy in the summer months, so if you can, book accommodation well in advance. Good hotels tend to be very expensive. The Jewish community in Rome (**w** romaebraica.it) can recommend kosher bed-and-breakfast accommodation.

There is an abundance of high-quality **kosher restaurants** in the ghetto. Although they are touristy, this is the place to eat the classic fried artichokes. Artichokes are a controversial topic in the kosher world as outside of Italy they are considered non-kosher.

Libyan Jews were evacuated by the Italian navy and settled in Rome after the 1967 Six Day War. They settled near Piazza Bologna in the north of the city. They brought with them a unique cuisine, rich in spices, nuts and grains. Try it at **Little Tripoli** (Via Polesine 16–18; ▮f; €€).

HISTORY In September 1943, when Italy capitulated, there were about 12,000 Jews living in Rome. When the Germans occupied the city in early September, they demanded a ransom of 50kg of gold from the Jewish community in exchange for their safety. The moment is captured in Carlo Lizzani's classic film *L'Oro di Roma* (*Gold of Rome*; 1961), which was filmed in and around the Great Synagogue.

Although the ransom was delivered by the Jewish community, on 16 October the former ghetto was sealed by German forces, as local police were considered unreliable. More than 1,000 Roman Jews were deported to Auschwitz. The names of those to be arrested were supplied by Demorazza, the General Directorate for Demography and Race of the Italian Ministry of the Interior. A further 800 were also later deported.

Many Jews went into hiding. Among them were the Italian writer Giacomo Debenedetti (1901–67) and his family. A year later, after the liberation, he wrote a stunning essay, '16 Ottobre 1943', describing the round-up. It was one of the first eyewitness accounts of a single event during the Holocaust. It is published in English alongside the essay 'Eight Jews', written after the Fosse Ardeatine massacre (*October 16, 1943/Eight Jews*; Notre Dame, 2001).

The German military commander in Rome was initially wary of conducting a round-up as he was nervous that the Vatican would condemn the move, but the Church remained silent. Although Pope Pius XII failed to condemn the round-ups, many Catholic institutions provided aid and shelter and Chief Rabbi Israel Zolli was hidden in the Vatican itself. As a result, 10,000 of the city's Jews survived to see the Americans liberate Rome on 4 June 1944. Zolli then claimed at the Yom Kippur service in 1944 that he had seen a vision of Jesus and controversially converted to Catholicism.

WHAT TO SEE A Jewish ghetto was established in Rome in 1555, an area centred on four cramped blocks near the Tiber River and the Portico d'Ottavia. Today, it remains a hub of Jewish life in the city.

The current Holocaust Museum, run by the **Fondazione Museo della Shoah** (Via del Portico d'Ottavia, 29; w museodellashoah.it; ⊕ 10.00–17.00 Sun–Thu, 10.00–13.00 Fri; free) is in the Casina dei Vallati on the eastern edge of the former ghetto. The small but highly informative permanent exhibition includes a virtual interactive map, which reconstructs the arrests and deportations that took place on 16 October 1943, when before dawn the SS sealed off the area and began rounding up local families. The square in front of the **Portico d'Ottavia** commemorates the event with various plaques.

A few steps from the portico, in the **Great Synagogue** (Tempio Maggiore; Lungotevere de' Cenci; w romaebraica.it; ⊕ 10.00–17.00 Sun–Thu, 09.00–14.00 Fri; €11; guided tours of the ghetto available), the **Jewish Museum of Rome** (Museo Ebraico di Roma) tells the story of the city's Jewish community, their persecution under Fascism and the round-up of 16 October 1943. The massive wooden entrance doors facing the Tiber are flanked by two plaques. One lists the names of Jews killed in the massacre at the Fosse Ardeatine in March 1944, the other remembers the 6 million Jews who were murdered in the Holocaust. The synagogue was the scene of a terrorist attack in 1982.

K-SYNDROME

On the island in the Tiber next to the ghetto, Jews were hidden in the Fatebenefratelli hospital. When the SS arrived at the hospital on the evening of 16 October 1943, the doctors met them in masks and deterred the Nazis from checking on their Jewish patients, informing them that everyone had been suddenly struck down by an illness, 'K-syndrome', and that it was highly contagious.

In truth, the anti-fascist doctors, among them the hospital's head physician, had invented the mysterious disease, naming it after Albert Kesselring, the commander in chief of the Mediterranean, and Herbert Kappler, the head of German security forces in Rome.

On **Via del Tempio** alongside the synagogue, there is a plaque to the 112 pupils from the Jewish school who were killed in the concentration camps. Look out for the brass **Stolpersteine** (page 170) in the pavement in front of the homes of those who were arrested in the 1943 round-up. These 'stumbling stones' have been placed in front of several doors on Via della Reginella, north of Via del Tempio. In addition, on the façade of Via della Reginella 15 hang ten small works of art, including a frieze that depicts the round-up of Jews in this neighbourhood.

The Jews who were detained, among them 200 children, were taken to the Military College in Palazzo Salviati, at Via della Lungara 82–83, in Trastevere (the building is now home to the Higher Institute for Defense Studies). A plaque commemorates the event. They remained there for two days until, on 18 October, they were taken to **Tiburtina Station** in the northeastern part of the city. The train took six days to reach Auschwitz. A plaque remembers the deportation on platform 1, where there is also a new multimedia memorial, the Memory Track (Binario della Memoria).

The SS headquarters was in the San Giovanni part of the city and now houses the **Museum of the Liberation – Rome** (Museo storico della Liberazione – Roma; Via Tasso 145; w museoliberazione.it; ⊕ 09.00–19.00 daily; free). The museum documents the persecution of the Jews and the Italian resistance figures interrogated there, with particular focus on the Fosse Ardeatine massacre. Visitors can see the original torture chambers and cells.

The quarries known as the Fosse Ardeatine, near the Via Appia in the southwest of the city centre, were the scene of a massacre carried out on 24 March 1944. In retaliation for a partisan attack in Via Rasella, 335 Italian civilians and soldiers, political prisoners, Jews and ordinary prisoners were brought here and shot. This event, the largest massacre of Jews carried out on Italian territory during the Holocaust, has become the symbol of the German occupation of Rome. The quarry was transformed into a national monument, the **Fosse Ardeatine Mausoleum** (Mausoleo Fosse Ardeatine; Via Ardeatina; w mausoleofosseardeatine.it; ⊕ 08.15–15.30 Mon–Fri, 08.15–16.30 Sat–Sun, museum 15mins earlier; free), in 1949 and has a small museum.

FURTHER AFIELD

Ferramonti di Tarsia South of Tarsia the A3 Salerno-Reggio Calabria motorway near the Tarsia Sud exit, runs over the site of what was the largest concentration camp in Italy. Set up between June and September 1940, more than 3,800 Jews were imprisoned in the camp, the majority of whom were foreign-born refugees. The camp was situated in malarial wetlands near a former land reclamation construction

Italy ROME

13

221

site, but despite the scant food supplies, the conditions at Ferramonti cannot be compared to those in German concentration camps. The prisoners were not abused or deported. The camp was abandoned by the Italian authorities after armistice, and the original 92 barracks later demolished during the construction of the motorway. The **International Memory Museum of Ferramonti – Tarsia** (Museo Internazionale della Memoria Ferramonti di Tarsia; Viale R Pacifici; e museomemoria.ferramonti@ virgilio.it; ■; ⊕ daily by appt via email; free) is on a plot of land that was originally outside the camp, in buildings that housed people who worked at Ferramonti.

Santa Maria al Bagno Previously known as Santa Maria di Bagni, in the heel of Italy, this seaside town was home to one of five post-war Jewish displaced persons camps that spread along the coast of Puglia. Relations between the survivors and the locals were close. Many of the buildings in the town still have Hebrew names and slogans written on them. There is also a small museum, the **Museum of Memory and Acceptance** (Museo della Memoria e dell'Accoglienza; Lungomare Alfonso Lamarmora; ■; ⊕ 09.00–13.00 Sun–Fri; €5), which is home to some extraordinary murals painted by Romanian Holocaust survivor and artist Zvi Miller. His pictures with images of menorahs, camps and the Jewish Brigade all mixed together are reminiscent of Soviet propaganda posters.

MILAN

The northern powerhouse of Milan is Italy's second city and has a lively Jewish community. Fascism was born in the city, when in 1919 Mussolini founded the National Fascist Party. Yet, it was in Milan that the story of the dark days of life in Italy between 1938 and 1945 combined with the dramatic years after the Holocaust. Although after the liberation in April 1945 Milan was in chaos, the city soon became a hub for the reception of the 70,000 Jewish refugees who arrived in Italy after the end of hostilities. Milan was also an important operational base for the Jewish underground (page 223), who helped thousands of survivors make their way illegally to the Palestine Mandate.

GETTING AROUND Milan has an efficient metro system and is famous for its trams, which are the best ways to get around the city. It is possible to take the train to Meina, between Arona and Stresa, 77km north of Milan, and La Spezia, 224km south of Milan in Liguria. Selvino is 70km from Milan. Take the train to Bergamo and change for Albino. In Albino catch the cable car to Selvino.

WHERE TO STAY AND EAT Room Mate Giulia (Via Silvio Pellico 4; ⛟ Duomo; w roommatehotels.com; €€€) is a boutique hotel close to the Duomo and the main synagogue. Try traditional Jewish dishes at **Ba'Ghetto** (Via Sardegna 45; ⛟ Wagner; w baghetto.com; K; €€€). **Snubar** (Via Giorgio Washington 13; ⛟ Wagner; w snubar. eu; K; €€€) specialises in Jewish Lebanese cuisine. Be aware that in August Milan tends to close down as locals head to the mountains and the coast.

HISTORY There were about 12,000 Jews living in Milan in 1938, about 5,000 of whom escaped to the Palestine Mandate or the United States before 1941. The community suffered under the German occupation and from December 1943 deportations began, with trains leaving from the Stazione Centrale, Milan's main station, for Bergen-Belsen, the Italian transit camps in Fossoli di Carpi and Bolzano, and Auschwitz. At the end of the war, fewer than 5,000 Jews remained in the city.

After liberation, many of the surviving Jews in eastern Europe felt that they could not rebuild their lives there and hoped to start a new life far away from Europe, preferably in Palestine. Palestine was at this point controlled by the British, who had restricted Jewish immigration in 1939 and continued to do so after the war.

The Jewish underground was run by Yehuda Arazi, a Haganah secret agent, and Ada Ascarelli Sereni. Under Arazi and Sereni's guiding hands between the end of World War II and the birth of the state of Israel in May 1948, of the 56 boats that smuggled Jewish refugees into Palestine, 34 set sail from the Italian coast.

Sereni was an unlikely leader of a secret underground. She had grown up in one of the richest Italian Jewish families in Rome. She married the Zionist Enzo Sereni and, unusually for Italian Jews, the couple moved to Palestine in 1927. In 1944, Enzo was parachuted into Italy behind enemy lines to participate in the resistance and organise help for the survivors. He was caught, and murdered in Dachau. Ada joined the Jewish underground in Italy partly to find out what had happened to her husband.

Sereni provided Arazi with the key contacts while he masterminded the black marketeering that funded the illegal immigration. Jewish Brigade soldiers in the British Army gave up their weekly ration of a bottle of whisky or rum to give Arazi valuable currency with which to operate.

When the Jewish Brigade was moved out of Italy in August 1945, Arazi audaciously invented a phantom British platoon that had its headquarters in Milan at Via Cantù 3, right under his enemy's nose above the British officers' club. The platoon's lorries were used to move the survivors, weapons and supplies to the illegal immigrant ships that sailed from Italy's ports.

Outside the upmarket little town of Magenta, 33km west of Milan, the Jewish underground had an operations site in a villa, called La Fagiana, known by its code name Camp A. The site, which operated from 1945 to 1948, was where everything that was needed to kit out the illegal immigrant ships that tried to break through the Royal Navy blockade of the Palestine coast was prepared. Primo Levi described the 'farm' in his novel *If Not Now, When?* (Penguin, 2000).

Today, the house is still known as La Casetta di Ebrei, the Jewish House. It is located on a dirt track road off the SP11 just before the bridge over the Ticino River leads to an area known as Boffalora sopra Ticino.

Milan was liberated on 25 April 1945, an event that is now marked by a national holiday. In Milan itself, it is celebrated by a big parade which also commemorates the participation of the Jewish Brigade in the liberation of the city.

After the Six Day War in 1967, many Jews expelled from Arab lands settled in Milan.

WHAT TO SEE Milan's Holocaust Memorial is one of the most interesting Holocaust memorials in Italy.

Milan Holocaust Memorial (Memoriale della Shoah di Milano; Piazza Edmond Jacob Safra 1; 🚇 Centrale FS; w memorialeshoah.it; ⏲ 10.00–16.00 Mon–Fri,

10.00–18.00 Sat–Sun; €10, last Fri of the month free) Tucked away underneath the city's monumental Central Station, the unassuming entrance to the Milan Holocaust Memorial is in a side street to the right if you are facing the station.

It was here that more than 2,000 Jews and political prisoners were gathered before being despatched to their deaths via the infamous Binario 21, a platform located under the station designed as a cutting-edge way of loading mail and other goods on to trains. Away from the bustle of the elegant station, parcels and letters were brought in by a side entrance, then loaded on to trucks, which were raised by an elevator on to the wagons. These wagons were then coupled to trains about to depart between platforms 18 and 19, just outside the enormous canopy of the station.

While Jews and political prisoners were awaiting deportation under the station, above people were catching trains and getting on with their ordinary lives. Today, trains rumble noisily overhead. When the deportees were brought here, they would have heard the same terrifying noise. Snarling dogs were used to ensure obedience as they were hastily pushed into the awaiting wagons.

Out of the 169 people deported on the first train on 6 December 1943, only five survived the war. On 30 January 1944, a second train loaded with Jewish prisoners left the Central Station bound for Auschwitz–Birkenau. Only 22 of the 605 people on board survived. In the entrance of the memorial, the word *Indifferenza* is written on the wall. It was chosen by Liliana Segre, who was 13 when she was deported to Auschwitz. This word, in her opinion, encapsulates the attitude of the public to their neighbour's fate – indifference. Nevertheless, one of the reasons that the Nazis chose the site for deportations was that it was out of the public gaze.

On the platform there is an original freight wagon and a list of names on the wall. The memorial is also an educational centre and library. In 2023, murals of characters from *The Simpsons* dressed in concentration camp clothing and wearing yellow stars appeared on the wall of the memorial. They were painted by the well-known Italian pop artist aleXsandro Palombo. The artist's use of pop culture helps people overcome what he calls a 'visual stumbling block to force us to see what we no longer see'. The murals have been defaced numerous times and the decision has been taken that the graffti will no longer be cleaned, but will remain as a testament to the dangers of antisemitism.

Before arriving at the station many of the political prisoners and partisans would have been tortured at the SS headquarters in the Hotel Regina, which was situated behind the Galleria Vittorio Emanuele and is now a bank. Jews were held in the San Vittore prison.

Palazzo Erba Odescalchi (Via Unione 5; 🚇 Missori; closed to the public) The
Palazzo Erba Odescalchi, a grand 16th-century palace in one of Milan's tiny medieval streets a few minutes' walk from the city's magnificent cathedral, was used after the liberation as a reception centre to help Milan's Jewish community, as the main synagogue had been bombed. Having been used as a billet for fascist militias, this large, imposing building – with four wings surrounding a central elegant courtyard with an arched loggia – was now standing empty.

As soon as it opened, streams of survivors were already walking across Alpine passes knee deep in snow trying to find a way out of Europe. They had little luggage, just a knapsack and the odd suitcase. The *palazzo* became the pulsating heart of what is known in Hebrew as the Bricha, the Jewish escape from Europe. Between 1945 and 1947, 35,000 people would pass through its doors.

On his return to Italy, Primo Levi, the young chemist who had been in Auschwitz, was a frequent visitor and described it in his novel *If Not Now, When?* (Penguin, 2000).

Jewish Brigade National Study Centre (Centro Studi Nazionale Brigata Ebraica; Corso Lodi 8; 🚇 Porta Romana; e info@brigataebraica.it; w brigataebraica. it; ⏱ by appt only via email; free) The Jewish Brigade played a crucial role in the liberation of Italy and helping survivors after the end of the war. Here, an interesting exhibition tells their story.

FURTHER AFIELD

Meina On the western side of Lake Maggiore, 70km northwest of Milan, the SS arrested Jews in nine nearby localities, among them the uncle and cousin of author Primo Levi. In the 1940s there were two hotels in Meina, which has a stunning view across the water to Switzerland. One, the Hotel Meina, was the site of the first collective massacre of Jews in Italy carried out by the SS.

Several Jewish families, some refugees from Greece who had escaped with the help of the Italian consuls in Athens and Thessaloniki during the round-ups of February 1943 (page 58), had been interned by the SS in the Hotel Meina. During the night of 22–23 September, they were taken into the woods around the village and shot in the back of the neck. Their bodies were placed in sacks weighed down with stones and dumped in the lake. Two bodies were discovered by local fishermen and another in Switzerland, where the massacre was widely reported in the Swiss press.

The hotel was abandoned in the post-war period and demolished in 2009. On the lakeside, a memorial and 17 Stolpersteine (page 170) remember the victims. The memorial – a sculpture of a head without eyes to see, without a mouth to talk or cry, by Israeli sculptor Ofer Lellouche – was inaugurated in 2022. The memorial brings home the fact that the Holocaust wiped out entire families, in this case the Fernadez-Diaz family, who owned factories and the Olympus brewery in Thessaloniki.

La Spezia The port of La Spezia, on the Liguria coast 224km southeast of Milan, was the scene of an extraordinary clash between survivors and the British Royal Navy in the spring of 1946. A new monument and outdoor exhibition on the former Pagliari pier marks the spot where more than 1,000 Holocaust survivors went on hunger strike when the occupying British forces blocked their illegal ship, the *Dov Hoz*, from sailing to Palestine. The pier is alongside the Marina del Levante.

When the British demanded that the survivors immediately disembark, the leader of the Haganah, Yehuda Arazi, who was hiding on the ship under the guise of a survivor, shouted back that he would blow the ship sky-high if the British tried to remove them forcibly. As the British sealed the port off with tanks, the news of the Holocaust survivors' plight made headlines across the world. Arazi sent radio messages to world leaders, including President Truman, informing them that the 1,000 survivors were crowded into a small ship in an Allied port being besieged by the greatest navy in the world.

The affair had a major impact on American policy, moving it in favour of an Israeli state. Eventually, the Labour government in London agreed to let the ship set sail. Before they left, the survivors celebrated a hasty Passover on the pier.

After 45 days in La Spezia, in front of a huge crowd of local well-wishers, the survivors finally set out to sea. Surprisingly this drama was immediately forgotten in La Spezia until 1996. The city now awards the annual Exodus Prize for intercultural co-operation.

These events inspired the historical novel *Exodus* (Turtleback, 1999) by Leon Uris and a 1960 Hollywood blockbuster, starring Paul Newman.

Selvino After World War II, 800 Jewish child survivors were cared for in Selvino, 70km northeast of Milan in the foothills of the Alps. They were among the most vulnerable Jewish refugees to arrive in Italy. The newly formed children's home, known as Jewish Sciesopoli, was based in an imposing four-storey fascist-era former boarding school on the outskirts of the town, on Via Cardo 64. It is currently in a state of dereliction and therefore closed to the public; but there is a campaign to turn the building into a museum and conference centre.

The **museum** (MuMeSE: Museo Memoriale di Sciesopoli Ebraica Casa dei Bambini di Selvino; Corso Milano 19; w comunediselvino.it – search 'Sciesopoli'; ⊕ Jul–Aug 10.00–noon & 15.00–17.00 Sun; €5), based in the town hall, tells the story of the children of Selvino. Life at Jewish Sciesopoli was highly ordered and the sense of community and working together lay at the core of the institution. The children who spent time at the house described it as a fairy-tale palace with dormitories, classrooms, a cinema, a gymnasium, a heated swimming pool, a spacious modern kitchen, craft rooms, clinics and bathrooms. There were luxuries that children had not seen for years – white sheets, blankets and food.

The children in Selvino were trained for a new life in Palestine. They were allowed only to speak Hebrew, which they had to learn – Yiddish was not allowed – and they were taught to reconnect with Jewish culture. Nearly all the children from Selvino settled on the same kibbutz in Israel and their families have remained close friends.

FLORENCE

The Jewish community of Florence is one of the oldest in Europe. Jews have lived in the city for more than 900 years. In 1939, Florence was home to about 3,000 Jews.

GETTING AROUND Florence can be explored on foot. Buses run up to Fiesole. To see the Museum and Documentation Centre of the Deportations and Resistance in Prato, take the train to Prato then take a bus to Cantagallo and walk for 20 minutes or call a taxi.

 WHERE TO STAY AND EAT The **Pensione Bencista** (Via Benedetto da Maiano, 4; w bencista.com; €€€) in Fiesole was used to house teenage Jewish survivors from eastern Europe and is described in detail in my book *The People on the Beach: Journeys to Freedom after the Holocaust* (Hurst, 2020).

WHAT TO SEE There is a moving **Holocaust memorial** to the city's 243 deported Jews at the main railway station, Firenze Santa Maria Novella, at platform 16. Only 13 returned after the end of the war. The sculpture consists of a length of railway track obstructed by several large stone blocks split with a metal spike.

The imposing neo-Moorish **Great Synagogue and Jewish Museum** (Tempio Maggiore; Via Farini 6; w jewishflorence.it/synagogue; ⊕ Jun–Sep 10.00–18.30 Sun–Thu, 10.00–17.00 Fri, Oct–May 10.00–15.00 Sun–Fri; €6.50), built between 1874 and 1882, was used as a storehouse during the German occupation. Before they withdrew from the city, the Germans made a failed attempt to blow the building up. Bayonet marks are still visible on the doors of the Great Ark. The museum tells the story of Florentine Jewry and has a room dedicated to the Holocaust. The Jewish Brigade (page 231) of the British Army helped survivors in the city, and in the synagogue garden there is a memorial to one of them, Arie Avisar, who did much to care for child survivors in the city and in the children's home in Fiesole. There is also a memorial to the city's 243 deportees.

Around 20km north of the city in Prato, the **Museum and Documentation Centre of the Deportations and Resistance** (Museo e Centro di Documentazione della Deportazione e Resistenza; Via di Cantagallo, 250; w museodelladeportazione. it; ⊕ 09.30–12.30 Mon–Fri, also 15.00–18.00 Mon, Thu, Sat & Sun; free) is the

YECHIEL ALEKSANDER'S STORY

Immediately after World War II, the Villa Bencista in Fiesole, just outside Florence, was used to house teenage Jewish survivors from eastern Europe. They left for Palestine on the illegal immigrant ship the *Josiah Wedgewood* that sailed from Vado Ligure in Liguria in June 1946. The Simoni family, who had bought the villa in 1925, were connected to the anti-fascist resistance, and have been hoteliers here ever since.

One of the boys who found themselves at the Villa Bencista was Yechiel Aleksander, a teenager from Łódź in Poland.

Aleksander was deported to Auschwitz in August 1944. There he became an apprentice builder. One of the first and most bizarre jobs that he was given was to convert a water reservoir into a swimming pool for camp guards. The day after he arrived at Auschwitz the Germans had abandoned Paris and the Red Army was moving towards Warsaw.

Aleksander endured a death march to Mauthausen in January 1945 and another to the camp at Gunskirchen (page 33). Throughout the whole experience he remained with a group of friends from Łódź. Aleksander's mother had died in 1941 and his father had been shot.

When I met him in his home in Israel in 2018, Aleksander, then a sprightly 91-year-old, said that in the ghetto he and his friends ran wild, stealing and finding any way to survive.

'To have friends was to live. If you had friends, you were not alone in the struggle to survive. This I tell you from my heart,' he said.

After liberation, he and 15 other boys took refuge in Wels train station in Austria. 'I was just 27kg but we were bad, very bad. We stole and swore and were very, very violent and went out in groups of eight to ten. We were out of control. We did not listen to anyone until one day soldiers from the Jewish Brigade came and saved us.'

The Brigade took them to Graz in Austria, and then to Italy. He crossed the border at Tarvisio and from there he was eventually taken to Fiesole. As he described the mountains to me, he broke into Italian. When asked what Italy meant to him, he did not hesitate and replied, 'Amore! Civilizzazione!' (Love! Civilisation!).

When I asked him about the Jewish Brigade officer, Arie Avisar, who was in charge of the Villa Bencista children, he jumped up from his chair in amazement. Regaining his composure, he told me that Avisar was extremely kind and took time to learn Yiddish to find out what had happened to the young people in his care. 'He taught us to be people. He even took us to see the opera *La Bohème*.'

Aleksander did not talk about his experiences until he returned to Poland for a visit in 1994. He then dedicated his life to telling his story and returned to Auschwitz with the March of the Living educational programme (page 18).

Aleksander died in Israel in 2022.

Gino Bartali was an Italian cycling legend who won the gruelling Tour de France twice, first in 1938 and again ten years later in 1948.

Born outside Florence in rural Tuscany in 1914, Bartali grew up in poverty. He was a devout Catholic with strong moral convictions, and after he won the 1938 Tour de France refused to dedicate his win to Mussolini, despite the fact that another prominent cyclist, a vocal critic of Fascism, was found mysteriously murdered at the same time. When war broke out in Europe in 1939, Bartali was conscripted into military service as a bike messenger. After the German invasion, at the request of the Catholic Cardinal of Florence, a close friend, Bartali transported false papers to Florence from Assisi where they were forged, hiding his cargo in the frame and handlebars of his bicycle. He would also pick up money from a Swiss Bank account in Genoa to distribute to Jewish people hiding in Florence. He also hid his Jewish friend Giacomo Goldenberg and his family. His actions saved many Jewish lives.

Bartali kept his story secret and it was only revealed after his death in 2000. Bartali was recognised as Righteous Among the Nations in 2010.

The **Gino Bartali Cycling Museum** (Museo del Ciclismo Gino Bartali; Via Chiantigiana 177; w ciclomuseo-bartali.it; ⊕ 10.00–13.00 Fri & Sat, 10.00–16.00 Sun; free) in his birthplace of Ponte a Ema, 10km southeast of Florence, tells his story. To get there, take bus 365a from Florence.

place to get to grips with a crucial part of Italian history – anti-fascist resistance and the subsequent deportation of tens of thousands of Italians. Following the general strike proclaimed in northern and central Italy in March 1944, hundreds of Tuscans and more than a hundred from Prato were deported to the Mauthausen concentration camp and its subcamp Ebensee (page 32) in Austria. Prato is twinned with Ebensee. The Holocaust as a result is seen by many as a part of this wider event. The exhibition covers resistance and deportations in general, as well as the Shoah and Roma Holocaust in Italy.

FERRARA

Ferrara is a beautiful Renaissance city in the Po valley in Emilia-Romagna. It is a good place to take a long view of the Holocaust in Italy and put it in the context of the acceptance and rejection of the country's Jewish community over the centuries.

Before the war, Ferrara was home to one of Italy's most important Jewish writers, Giorgio Bassani (1916–2000), who immortalised the city in his novel *The Garden of the Finzi-Continis* (Penguin, 2018), first published in 1962. It is the story of a wealthy Jewish family who live in genteel seclusion in their luxurious villa as the 1938 Racial Laws exclude them from society. For Bassani it was that betrayal that formed the core of his work rather than the horror of the death camps. The book was made into an Oscar-winning film by the director Vittorio De Sica in 1971. Many tourists visit Ferrara hoping to see the Finzi-Continis' garden, but it existed only in Bassani's imagination.

Ferrara is a gem off the beaten track. It can be visited on a day trip but it pays to stay and read Bassani's novels in one of the city's cafés and rent a bike to explore the area. Ferrara is an interesting place to visit in winter when it is clouded in fog. Fog is often invoked by Italian writers as a metaphor for the country's 20th-century history.

GETTING AROUND Ferrara can be easily explored on foot. Take the train to see Bologna, 48km south of Ferrara. Trains run from Bologna to Carpi, 70km west of Ferrara. To see Nonantola and Piangipane, it helps to have your own transport.

WHERE TO STAY AND EAT There is a good choice of apartments for rent in the former ghetto on w airbnb.com. Many of the restaurants in the area serve classic Jewish dishes, although they are not kosher. Look out for *burriche* pastries, spelt soup and *ricciolini* pasta which were traditionally eaten at Yom Kippur. Pumpkin mash is also typical of the region and was eaten during the autumn High Holidays. Pumpkins were introduced to Italian cuisine by Sephardic Jews.

HISTORY When Ferrara was controlled by the d'Este family, it was a medieval centre of Jewish life. Their castle dominates the city centre. Italian Jews were joined by Ashkenazim from Germany and Sephardim who had fled the Spanish Inquisition, and they were free to live where they wished until Ferrara came under the control of the Papal States in the 17th century. Jews were then confined to living in a ghetto until their emancipation in 1859. The former Jewish Quarter of Ferrara is one of the largest and best preserved in Italy.

Anti-Jewish violence erupted in Ferrara in September 1941. In 1944, during the German occupation of northern Italy, the Jewish population was transferred to the transit camp at Fossoli di Carpi.

WHAT TO SEE The **National Museum of Italian Judaism and the Holocaust** (Museo Nazionale dell'Ebraismo Italiano e della Shoah; via Piangipane 81; w meis.museum; ⊕ 10.00–18.00 Tue–Sun; €10), which opened in 2017, is a lively multimedia museum in the former prison, which was used during World War II to detain anti-fascist partisans and Jews prior to their deportation.

The permanent exhibition focuses on Rome and the southern regions of Sicily, Puglia, Campania and Calabria, where most Jews settled during the first millennium. There is a replica of the Arch of Titus, commemorating Rome's victory over Jerusalem. Today, however, there are few Jews in southern Italy, as they were forced out during the Inquisition.

There is also a film and small exhibition on the racial laws and the Holocaust. The museum is still expanding. The complex when finished will include Ferrara's only kosher restaurant.

A short walk from the museum, **Via Mazzini**, once the main street in the old ghetto, is now dotted with cafés and shops. Until World War II, most of the shops here were run by Jewish families. Two plaques on the outside of the synagogue at No. 95 remember the persecution of the Jews.

The writer Giorgio Bassani was brought up at Via Cisterna del Follo 1, now a private house. He is buried in the **Jewish cemetery** (Via delle Vigne 12; ⊕ 09.00–13.00 Sun–Fri; free).

FURTHER AFIELD
Fossoli and Carpi Campo di Fossoli (via Remesina Esterna 32; w fondazionefossoli. org/i-luoghi/campo-di-fossoli; ⊕ Apr–Jun & 15–30 Sep 10.00–13.00 & 15.00–19.00 Sun & public hols, Oct–Nov & Feb–Mar 10.00–13.00 & 14.00–18.00 Sun & public hols; free), a former transit camp, is in the village of Fossoli, 6km north of Carpi, which is 20km north of Modena. Built as an Allied prisoner-of-war camp in 1942, in December 1943 it was turned into a transit camp for Jews by the Italian Salo Republic due to its strategic location close to the Modena–Verona railway.

On 19 and 22 February 1944, the first Jews were deported from Fossoli to Auschwitz-Birkenau, among them the author Primo Levi. He had been interned at Fossoli in January that year. The first pages of his novel *If This Is a Man?* (Penguin, 1996) recall his brief detention in the camp at Fossoli, which was then under the control of the Italian police. Of the 650 Italian Jews in his transport, Levi was one of only 20 who left Auschwitz alive.

From March 1944, Fossoli was taken over by the SS. Under their regime, eight transports left from the camp carrying a total of 5,000 people of whom 2,802 were Jews. After the war the site was used to hold fascists and Italian refugees from Yugoslavia, as well as Jewish survivors, until 1947 when the site was abandoned. Some five decades later, volunteers began to renovate the former camp and, in 2004, one of the barracks that used to house Jewish inmates was reconstructed.

In Carpi itself, the **Memorial Museum to the Deported** (Museo Monumento al Deportato; Via Manfredo Pio 2; e info@fondazionefossoli.it w fondazionefossoli. org/i-luoghi/museo-monumento-al-deportato; ⊕ 10.00–13.00 & 15.00–19.00 Fri– Sun & hols, on Thu by request (Oct–Mar closes 18.00); app guide downloadable; €3) in the Palazzo dei Pio tells the story of the camp.

Nonantola In Nonantola, 30km east of Carpi, a memorial, *Davanti a Villa Emma* (w davantiavillaemma.org), is currently in the planning stage. As its name in Italian suggests, it will be located in front of (*davanti*) the **Villa Emma** (Via Giuseppe di Vittorio 31; w fondazionevillaemma.org; villa: not open to the public) and will remember a moving story of Jewish resistance and the help given to Jewish refugee children from the former Yugoslavia. When German troops occupied the Croatian capital Zagreb in 1941, a Young Zionist from Osijek, Josef Indig, led 43 Jewish children, who had already fled from Austria and Germany, into a part of Slovenia annexed by Italy. In July 1942, the underground Jewish organisation DELASEM rented the Villa Emma to house them as partisan activity in Slovenia was endangering their safety. They were then joined by another group of children, mostly Bosnian Jewish orphans.

Within 24 hours of the German invasion in September 1943, doctor Giuseppe Moreali and the young parish priest Don Arrigo Beccari organised for the children to be hidden by local families. All but one, a boy who was ill in a sanitorium and was deported to Auschwitz, escaped to Switzerland. They left for the Palestine Mandate in May 1945. The **Museo di Nonantola** (Via del Macello; w museodinonantola. it/contenuto/luoghi/museo.ashx; ⊕ 09.30–12.30 & 15.30–18.30 Sat–Sun, guided tours by appt; free) has a small exhibition that tells the story of the children of the Villa Emma and the daily life at the house where the children were trained for kibbutz life in the Palestine Mandate.

Bologna The city of Bologna has an impressive Holocaust memorial built in 2016. The **Memoriale della Shoah** stands at the intersection of Via de' Carracci and

SOLDIERS OF THE STAR

The Jewish Brigade, which was part of the British Army and recruited from the Jewish population in the Palestine Mandate, landed in Italy with the Allied invasion forces in summer 1943. Its khaki-coloured army jeeps were emblazoned with painted yellow Stars of David and the soldiers wore similar insignia and armbands. They then spent months in Fiuggi, a pretty spa town southeast of Rome, before fighting near Bologna in the Battle of the Senio.

Fiuggi was once a popular aristocratic resort famous for its *acqua di Fiuggi* mineral water. The water-bottling plant was taken over by the Jewish Brigade and became their headquarters. Outside, the sign identifying the building as the Fiuggi Bottling Works was replaced by one in large Hebrew letters, announcing it was now the HQ of the 'Jewish Fighting Brigade'. Signs on the officers' mess, billet, dining room, washroom, latrines and storeroom were also in Hebrew. As many of the officers were British Jews, English was spoken by all HQ staff, but on the parade ground all orders were given in Hebrew.

Times were tough in the spa world and the soldiers' arrival in town offered a good business opportunity for the locals. It was not long before Fiuggi's children greeted the Brigaders with a cheery 'Shalom!'. Every morning, in the main square, the blue-and-white flag with the Star of David was raised. Soon Fiuggi was dotted with signs in Hebrew and at Hanukkah a giant 6ft menorah was erected on a hill above the town, visible for miles around.

Not only did the Brigade have a clear and striking Jewish identity but it had its own agenda. In Fiuggi, the men began to hear eyewitness reports of the events in the concentration and extermination camps. A voluntary cut in rations by all ranks enabled a store of food to be accumulated in anticipation of finding refugees. A Brigade Refugee Committee was set up to which members all contributed part of their pay.

At first the Brigade helped Jewish survivors in Italy, but, after they were billeted in the northeastern town of Tarvisio on the Austrian border, against army orders they crossed into Austria and began to bring survivors back to safety in Italy. As a result, this tiny inconsequential town became a staging post for thousands of desperate Jewish refugees who arrived in the valley, many still wearing their concentration camp uniforms.

The soldiers of the Jewish Brigade killed in the Battle of the Senio are buried in the Commonwealth War Graves cemetery in the hamlet of **Piangipane**, 70km southeast of Ferrara. The assault opened up the road to Bologna.

Ponte Matteotti, close to the high-speed train station. It comprises two 10m-tall blocks of Corten steel facing each other yet positioned at a slight angle. The path between them narrows to a gap of just 80cm, creating a sense of oppression and disorientation. On the inner surfaces, a grill of rectangular cells evokes the cramped barracks in the camps.

TRIESTE

Trieste in the northeastern corner of Italy is the capital of Friuli-Venezia Giulia. All too often we think in the confines of modern maps, but Trieste is a city defined by its fluctuating borders. Here it pays to think out of the box, as this is the only way to understand how Trieste became the epicentre of the Holocaust in Italy.

GETTING AROUND There are buses from the station to the city centre. The main sites in the centre are accessible on foot or by bus. For those travelling by car, there is parking on the seafront.

To visit the Risiera di San Sabba memorial, take bus 10 from Piazza Goldoni. You can reach Bolzano by train from Trieste.

WHERE TO STAY AND EAT Everything is about the sea in Trieste so, if you can afford it, stay at the **Savoia Excelsior Palace** (Riva del Mandracchio 4; w collezione. starhotels.com; €€€), a 19th-century hotel opposite the port which has rooms looking out over the bay. Accommodation in Trieste in summer is expensive and it pays to book in advance if you can.

Coffee and cakes keep Trieste ticking over. Indeed, coffee arrives in the port every day, and the city is home to the Italian coffee company Illy. The **Caffè San Marco** (Via Cesare Battisti 18; w caffesanmarco.com; ⏰ 08.30–23.00 Mon–Fri, 08.30–23.45 Sat, 09.00–21.00 Sun; €€) near the Grand Synagogue has a beautiful turn-of-the-century Viennese-style interior and was in the early 20th century a meeting place for writers and intellectuals. **La Bomboniera** (Via XXX Ottobre 3A; f; ⏰ 07.00–19.00 Mon–Thu, 07.00–20.00 Fri–Sun; €) was until the 1930s a kosher pastry shop. It also has a beautiful interior and sells traditional Austrian cakes and marzipan treats for the Jewish festival of Purim in the early spring. Kosher food products, including locally produced smoked turkey, are sold at the **synagogue** (page 234).

HISTORY Once the principal port of the Austro-Hungarian Empire, Trieste, in the late 19th and early 20th century, had more in common with Vienna than the Italian cities to the west. The city was then part of the Austrian Riviera, which included the now Croatian city of Rijeka and the once elegant resort of Opatia. Home to Slovenes, Croats and Serbs, and a large, influential, Jewish community, it was a multi-cultural city, as is captured in Daša Drindić's extraordinary, eclectic novel *Trieste* (Maclehose, 2011).

Italy's northeastern borders were the scene of fierce fighting in World War I, notably at Caporetto, now in Slovenia. Italy entered the war on the side of the British and French in 1915, in the hope that it would be granted control of Habsburg territory in the Adriatic with predominantly Italian populations. The limitations of those gains in the post-war settlement bred resentment and sparked an international crisis in the city of Fiume, now Rijeka in Croatia, which was occupied in 1919 by the poet and flamboyant right-wing activist Gabriele D'Annunzio. His actions inspired Mussolini and were the first steps on the road to a fascist Italy.

In 1922, Trieste was incorporated into Italy, along with Istria, and the islands of Cres, Krk and Lošinj, after which a drive to Italianise the region began. Fascism was from the start anti-Slav and the area embarked on a period of ethnic intolerance which lasted until Trieste once again became part of Italy in 1954.

In 1931, about 5,000 Jews lived in Trieste, making it the third largest Jewish community in Italy. By 1938, the community had grown to 7,000. Trieste is known to Jews as 'the Gateway to Zion'. Indeed, from the late 19th century until Italy joined the Axis in 1940, thousands of Jews fled here to escape the pogroms in the Russian Empire and then Nazism.

It was in 1938, in Trieste, that Mussolini announced the anti-Jewish Racial Laws. More than 150,000 people and black-shirts crowded into Piazza Unità d'Italia to hear Mussolini declare that Jews were the 'irreconcilable enemies' of Fascism. The crowd cheered and applauded the announcement. It was a media event beamed across the country. Mussolini's adoption of a racial policy – which included a ban on mixed marriages and excluded Jews from Italian society – was a key part of the development of an imperial foreign policy.

After the Italian capitulation in 1943, Udine, Trieste, Gorizia, Pola, Fiume and Ljubljana were placed under the direct control of the Third Reich. Policing, political and racial repression and anti-partisan activities fell under the control of the SS commanded by Odilo Globocnik. Born in Trieste, Globocnik had overseen the mass murder of Polish Jewry during Operation Reinhard. During the Nazi occupation the city was a centre for deportations to Auschwitz.

After the war, Trieste was under Allied military control until 1954, when it was handed back to Italy.

Today, the city's Jewish community has about 700 members.

WHAT TO SEE At the heart of Trieste is **Piazza Unità d'Italia**, a spectacular square that opens out on to the sea. It was here in 1938, that Mussolini announced the anti-Jewish Racial Laws. A small plaque on the town hall commemorates the event. The fountain of the Four Continents at the centre of the piazza was moved for the occasion so that a vast platform could be erected, emblazoned with the word DUX, the Latin for leader. Mussolini used the phrase to link his regime

FOIBE

Foiba means 'sinkhole' in Italian, but it is a word that is commonly associated with the massacres committed mainly by Yugoslav partisans at the end of World War II, who threw their victims into *foibe*, although many of the massacre sites were in fact old quarries and mines.

The victims included Germans, fascist Italians and Slovenes, and anti-fascists opposed to the Yugoslav occupation. The atmosphere of terror created by the murders prompted 350,000 Italians to leave Istria and the Dalmatian coast which had been incorporated in the new communist state of Yugoslavia. There is a memorial to one of the most well known of these massacres at Basovizza, above Trieste near the Slovene border. Historians have not been able to put an exact figure on the number of people killed in the *foibe*.

In the Trieste region it adds just one more ingredient to the minestrone of post-war memory and the positioning of the Holocaust in the narrative of this mix. There is a tendency on the right to equate the *foibe* and the Holocaust.

to the Roman Empire. (The fountain was only returned to its original position in 2000.)

Facing the sea, the building on the left of the square is the former headquarters of **Lloyd Triestino**. Approximately 15,000 Jews, mostly from Vienna, boarded Lloyd Triestino ships in Italian ports destined for Shanghai after the 1938 Anschluss – the Shanghai International Settlement was the only port in the world that allowed visa-free access. Umberto Beniamino Steindler, a ship's captain who, during the 1930s, brought thousands of Jews to safety in Haifa, is buried in the **Jewish cemetery** (Via della Pace 4; ⊕ 08.30–noon & 15.30-18.00 Sun–Thu, 08.30–noon Fri; free) where there is also a Holocaust memorial.

Still facing the sea, to your right is **Piazza della Borsa** (*borsa* is the Italian for stock exchange). To the right of Piazza della Borsa is the arched entrance to the old ghetto on Via Portizza. In 1696, Jews were confined to the ghetto, which marginalised them from the rest of the city's population. But in 1782, the Austro-Hungarian Edict of Tolerance allowed Jews to work in the stock exchange and in the liberal professions and in 1784 the doors of the Trieste ghetto were opened. From then on, Jews played an important role in the city's business and cultural life. The ghetto was once a thriving busy place.

From here it is a 15-minute walk to the vast **synagogue** (Via S. Francesco d'Assisi 19; **w** triestebraica.it/it/siti-ebraici/la-sinagoga; ⊕ 10.30–11.15 Tue, 17.00–17.45 Wed & Mon, 16.00–16.45 Thu, 10.00–10.45 & 11.30–12.15 Sun; €7, joint ticket with the Museo della Comunità Ebraica €10) built in 1912. The building was desecrated several times during World War II, and the Germans used it as a warehouse to store requisitioned Jewish possessions.

A 10-minute walk eastwards from the synagogue takes you to the **Carlo and Vera Wagner Museum of the Jewish Community of Trieste** (Museo della Comunità Ebraica di Trieste Carlo e Vera Wagner; 5 Via del Monte; **w** museoebraicotrieste.it; ⊕ 10.00–13.00 Mon, Wed & Fri, 16.00–19.00 Tue, 10.00–16.00 Thu; €6, joint ticket with the synagogue €10). The building it occupies was once the Jewish hospital. From the end of the 19th century until 1940, it was used to house Jewish refugees fleeing Tsarist Russia and later the Third Reich. Also here were once the offices of the Jewish Agency that helped Jews wanting to settle in Palestine. The museum has a large collection of Judaica and charts the history of the Jewish community of Trieste. One room is dedicated to the Holocaust. On display are jewellery and other items that were confiscated by the Nazis, each tagged with its value in Reichsmarks. The exhibition is in Italian and English.

The **Risiera di San Sabba** (Via Giovanni Palatucci 5; **w** risierasansabba.it; ⊕ Oct–Mar 09.00–17.00 daily, Apr–Sep 09.00–19.00 daily; free) in the southern suburbs of Trieste is one of Italy's most important Holocaust museums. This former industrial rice-processing plant was built in 1898, but closed in the early 1930s. It was then used as a military barracks before the occupying German forces turned it into a temporary prison camp for captured Italian soldiers. It was then used as a detention centre for Croatian, Italian and Slovenian partisans and political prisoners, and as a transit and extermination camp for Jews.

Visitors can walk around the complex, which became a museum in 1975, in a silence that pushes away the sounds of the past – the barking dogs, the stomp of the SS boots, the screams, the cries in Croatian, Italian and Slovenian and the music from the Germans' entertainment hall. The Death Cell on the left as you enter the complex was where prisoners were held before execution. Bodies of the dead awaiting cremation were also stored here. An estimated 2,000–3,000 prisoners were executed in the prison.

When the Red Army scouts arrived at the gates of Auschwitz in January 1945, they found a group of tiny starving children, among them seven-year-old Tatiana Bucci and her five-year-old sister, Andra.

The sisters were born in the Italian port of Fiume, now the Croatian city of Rijeka. Their father was a Catholic Slovene merchant seaman, who was taken as a prisoner of war by the British. Their mother, Mira, was a Jewish dressmaker who had been born in the Russian Empire. Under Fascist laws, she was forced to choose an Italian name for her daughter, but nevertheless she always called her Tatiana.

After the Germans occupied Fiume, the Bucci sisters, along with their mother, grandmother, an uncle, two aunts and their cousin Sergio who was six years old, were taken to the Risiera di San Sabba prison, where they spent days in one of the prison's tiny cells.

On arrival at Auschwitz, their grandma and one aunt, Sonia, were gassed. Their mother, their aunt Gisella, their uncle and the three children passed the selection. When they had their arms tattooed, the girls' mother went ahead of them and, as a result, knew her daughters' numbers. The sisters and Sergio were then led to a children's block overseen by the notorious Dr Mengele, who carried out medical experiments on multiples. Bucci thinks Mengele probably thought they were triplets.

The female prisoner in charge of the block took a shine to the pretty little girls and allowed their mother to see them regularly. Crucially she reminded her daughters of their names – in Tatiana's case her official name, Liliana – until one day she disappeared. Bucci says they assumed she was dead. 'We were surrounded by death. That is what being Jewish in Auschwitz meant.'

One day the woman in charge of the block warned them a man was going to ask the children who wanted to see their mothers to step forward. 'She told us it was a trick. We told Sergio but he did not listen. When the SS doctor appeared in the barracks, Sergio stepped forward.' He was led away with 20 other children.

After the liberation, the Bucci were taken to Prague and then flown to the UK by the Central British Fund, the charity now known as World Jewish Relief (page 111). By this point they had forgotten most of their Italian and spoke a mixture of Czech and German.

Miraculously the girls' mother and aunt Gisella survived the war, and their father returned to Italy at the end of hostilities. That their mother knew their Auschwitz numbers and the girls remembered their names was the key to their parents tracking them down.

After Fiume was annexed by Yugoslavia, the family settled in Trieste. 'My father told us about being a prisoner…but my mother never discussed anything; but there was always the question of Sergio,' says Bucci.

Gisella was convinced her son was alive. 'Although Andra and I knew that in Auschwitz children who were taken away never came back, we did not mention it to the adults,' she says. It was only in the 1980s that she and Andra discovered that Sergio had been taken to Hamburg (page 183). 'He had thought he was going to be reunited with his mother but was subjected to a series of barbaric medical experiments and then hanged in the basement of a school. He was seven years old,' she adds bitterly.

Jews awaiting deportation were held in 17 tiny cells that each held up to six people and in the Sala delle Croci. The name, meaning 'Hall of Crosses', derives from the appearance of the pillars and wooden beams which in the past supported the attics of the three upper floors, eliminated during the renovation. The SS dormitories were on the upper floor of the building. Prisoners destined for deportation were taken in wagons to Trieste's Central Station from the former San Sabba station next to the Risiera.

The **exhibition** is housed in the former kitchen and canteen. The memorial in the prison courtyard marks the site of the only crematorium in Italy which was blown up by the Nazis in April 1945.

After the war, San Sabba housed Italian refugees from Yugoslavia. The 1976 war crimes trial brought the story of the prison into public discourse in Italy, though the commander of the Risiera, Joseph Obenhauser, never served his life sentence due to bilateral agreements between Italy and Germany that meant the Germans did not have to hand him over to the Italian courts.

At **Trieste Central Station** a small plaque remembers those who were deported from here between September 1943 and February 1945. The total number of deportees is thought to be 8,222, a figure that included an estimated 1,457 Jews, among them 708 from Trieste. The first transport of Jews left on 7 December 1943. Of the 159 people who boarded the freight wagons only nine returned at the end of the war. The trains left from the former grain silos adjacent to the station, out of the public eye. After the war, the silos were used to house refugees from Istria and Dalmatia; now part of the silos are a car park, but most are largely derelict. Their future has been a matter of fierce debate for some years.

Since 70% of the convoys that left Italy departed from Trieste, there is a campaign to turn part of the building into a National Auschwitz and Deportation Memorial, reminiscent of Milan's Binario 21. One of the leading campaigners is Liliana (Tatiana) Bucci, who was just seven years old when she was deported to Auschwitz with her family.

FURTHER AFIELD

Bolzano Along one side of Via Resia in the suburb of Gries is the remaining wall of one of the four German concentration camps set up in Italy. The camp was established in 1944 after the evacuation of the Fossoli di Carpi transit camp as the frontline approached. It was built to house 1,500 prisoners but reached a final capacity of 4,000. As a result, conditions in the camp were appalling.

Bolzano was the only German camp in Italy that had subcamps for forced labour. Among those held here were political prisoners, partisans, Jews, Roma and Sinti, Jehovah's Witnesses and Allied prisoners. Between the summer of 1944 and February 1945, numerous transports left Bolzano for Ravensbrück, Flossenbürg, Dachau, Auschwitz and Mauthausen.

The **Passage of Remembrance** on the remaining wall tells the story of the camp through panels. A memorial records the names of men, women and children held in the camp. Sculptures by the local artist Christine Tschager honour the victims at the Gries site, the Virgl Tunnel (Galleria del Virgolo) subcamp, on the SS12 and on Via Pacinotti where prisoners were sent to board the deportation trains.

14

The Nordic Countries

In recent years there has been an increase in active research and commemoration of the Holocaust in Scandinavia. However, the Jewish experience in Denmark, Finland, Norway and Sweden differed considerably. Finland joined the German invasion of the Soviet Union in 1941, and so Jewish soldiers in the Finnish Army fought alongside the Wehrmacht. In Norway hundreds of Jews were brutally rounded up and shipped across the North Sea to their deaths in Auschwitz. Denmark was the scene of a dramatic rescue that saved 99% of its Jews.

GETTING THERE AND AROUND

All four countries have good international air, ferry and rail connections. Take the train to travel between Norway and Sweden, and Denmark and Sweden. There are ferries to and from Stockholm to Denmark and Germany and between Britain and Norway. The journey across the Baltic Sea from Stockholm to Finland is unforgettable.

ONLINE RESOURCES

DENMARK
Danish Institute for International Studies w folkedrab.dk. Offers a wide range of educational materials about the Holocaust in general & the Danish experience, including information on Danish volunteers who fought for the Germans & other genocides.

SWEDEN
International Holocaust Remembrance Alliance w holocaustremembrance.com. Set up in the 1990s after manifestations of xenophobia, antisemitism & racism in Sweden prompted an

interest in Holocaust education at an official level. It was believed that widespread Holocaust education would put an end to prejudice. Former prime minister Göran Persson was at the forefront of the initiative.
The Living History Forum w levandehistoria. se. Promotes democracy, tolerance & human rights. Among its projects has been placing Stolpersteine (page 170) outside 3 houses in Stockholm where people lived after finding refuge here, but who were later expelled & murdered in the Holocaust.

NORWAY

The Holocaust is often reduced to numbers, which in turn gives prominence to the places where the largest number of people were murdered. As a result, there is a tendency to overlook the destruction of small communities. Before World War II, Norway had a Jewish population of about 1,900, of whom 773 were deported while hundreds fled to Sweden and the UK. Of those deported, only 24 survived.

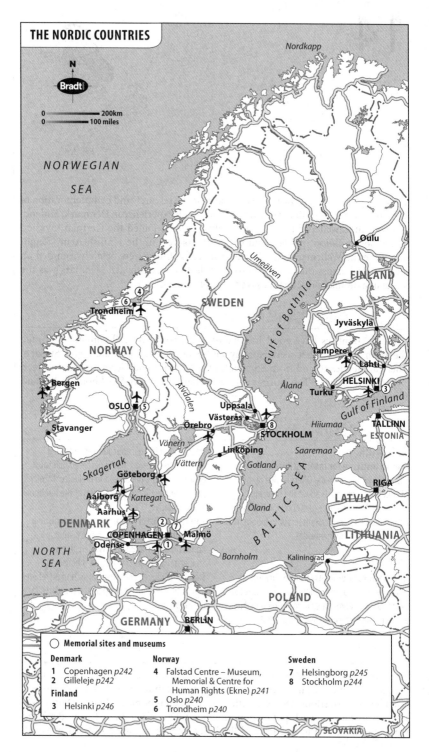

THE NORDIC COUNTRIES

N

Bradt

0 ——————— 200km
0 ——————— 100 miles

NORWEGIAN SEA

Nordkapp

NORTH SEA

FINLAND

Oulu

Jyväskylä

Tampere

Lahti

HELSINKI ③

Turku

Gulf of Finland

TALLINN

ESTONIA

Åland

Hiiumaa

Saaremaa

Gulf of Bothnia

Umeälven

SWEDEN

④
⑥ Trondheim

NORWAY

Bergen

OSLO ⑤

Stavanger

Älvdalen

Uppsala

Västerås

Örebro

Vänern

Linköping

STOCKHOLM ⑧

Gotland

Vättern

Göteborg

Skagerrak

Aalborg *Kattegat*

Aarhus

DENMARK

Odense

COPENHAGEN ② ⑦ Malmö ①

Öland

BALTIC SEA

RIGA

LATVIA

LITHUANIA

Bornholm

Kaliningrad

POLAND

GERMANY BERLIN

SLOVAKIA

⊙ **Memorial sites and museums**

Denmark
1 Copenhagen *p242*
2 Gilleleje *p242*
Finland
3 Helsinki *p246*

Norway
4 Falstad Centre – Museum,
   Memorial & Centre for
   Human Rights (Ekne) *p241*
5 Oslo *p240*
6 Trondheim *p240*

Sweden
7 Helsingborg *p245*
8 Stockholm *p244*

Norway's Jewish community was mostly wiped out, and received little sympathy and assistance when those who survived the war returned.

The figures are comparatively small, but the trauma inflicted was no less than in the mass killing fields of the east; nor was the question of moral responsibility diminished.

GETTING AROUND The best way to get to Trondheim, 491km north of the capital, is to take the night train from Oslo. The best way to get around Oslo is by bike (w oslobysykkel.no). Take bus 30 or the ferry to Bygdøy to see the Holocaust Centre.

HISTORY Jews were only permitted to settle in Norway in 1851. At that time, the country had a tiny Jewish population of about 25. After pogroms broke out in Tsarist Russia at the end of the 20th century about 1,000 Jews from the Baltic states, then part of the Russian Empire, sought refuge in Norway. In the 1930s, Jews from Austria and Germany also fled to Norway. Antisemitism was widespread in the first part of the 20th century and was a key part of the Norwegian far-right party Nasjonal Samling's platform, which was founded by former minister of defence Vidkun Quisling in 1933.

Germany invaded Norway on 9 April 1940. King Haakon VII fled to London, where he set up a government-in-exile, and Quisling declared himself prime minister – but his government lasted only six days. The Germans then appointed Josef Terboven Reich Commissioner of occupied Norway. Quisling was back in power when the main assault on Norwegian Jewry began in the autumn of 1942. Despite protests from the Church, deportations went ahead.

Jewish men were arrested in October 1942 and sent to a labour camp in Tønsberg, 101km south of Oslo; it was the only camp in Norway run entirely by Norwegians (it remains a prison today and cannot be visited). On 26 November, women and children were arrested and taken to the pier at Akershuskaia in Oslo,

14

where they were joined by the men who had already been interned. On the same day 530 Norwegian Jews, who had been arrested by the Germans with the help of the local police, boarded the SS *Donau*, a cargo boat that took them to Germany. From Germany, they were transferred on to Auschwitz, where nearly all were murdered. A smaller group sailed on the *Monte Rosa*. Some of the other Jews who had been arrested were delayed en route to Oslo, possibly by the Red Cross and sympathetic railway workers. They were then imprisoned under harsh conditions at the Bredtveit concentration camp just outside Oslo. On 24 February 1943, this group was deported by ship to Stettin, from where they too were taken to Auschwitz.

The Germans withdrew from Norway in May 1945. Quisling was later tried on several charges including high treason against the Norwegian state, and executed. In 2012, Norway's prime minister Jens Stoltenberg made an official apology for the deportations.

OSLO In the 1980s, Oslo's Jewish community underwent a small revival and the community of 800 is now centred around Mosaiske Trossamfund Synagogue.

Where to stay and eat It is advisable to book as far in advance as possible as hotels can be difficult to find, and prices are high. Aker Brygge waterfront has a good selection of restaurants and bars. For a treat, have a drink at the rooftop bar **Centropa Mezzanin** (Anne-Cath. Vestlys plass 1; w centropa.no; ⏲ 13.00–23.00 Wed–Sat, noon–18.00 Sun; €€€) at the Deichman Bjorvika public library.

What to see In 1948 a memorial was erected in the **Helfyr Jewish Cemetery** on Tvetenveien 7 to the Jews from Oslo and southern Norway who lost their lives in the Holocaust.

In 2000, a memorial was placed at the point where the *Donau* and *Gotenland* deportation ships departed, outside the walls of Akershus Fortress which looks out across the fjord. The *Place of Remembrance* memorial, designed by British sculptor Antony Gormley, is in the form of six chairs, seatless and rusted.

North of Carl Berners Plass the **Sukkertoppen Memorial Park** has several monuments honouring those who helped Jews escape to Sweden. The park is located on a small hill at Hekkveien 8. At the top of the hill is a stone Star of David with a short history of the refugee effort.

The **HL-Senteret** (Villa Grande, Huk Aveny 56; w hlsenteret.no; ⏲ mid-May–mid-Sep 10.00–18.00 daily, mid-Sep–mid-May 10.00–16.00 daily; NOK120), the Norwegian Centre for Holocaust and Minorities Studies, has three permanent exhibitions on the Holocaust and racism in Norway. The centre is housed in the Villa Grande, Quisling's former residence.

Further afield

Trondheim Most of Norway's Jews lived in the capital but about 300 lived in the northern city of Trondheim.

The most moving memorial in Trondheim is to Cissi Klein, who was 13 years old when she was deported to Auschwitz and murdered. Her parents, who ran a shop, were originally from the Baltic states. In 1995, a statue of her was erected in a small park close to her home on what is now called Cissi Kleins gate. Every 6 October, the day local police arrested her at school, pupils from the Kalvskinnet Primary School visit the park to lay flowers.

The main Holocaust memorial, from 1947, stands in the **Lamedoen Cemetery** on Thomas von Westens gate and remembers the 130 Jews from Trondheim who died in the Holocaust. The **Jewish Museum Trondheim** (Jødisk Museum Trondheim; Arkitekt Christies gate 1B; **w** jodiskmuseum.org; ⊕ Jun–mid-Aug 10.00–16.00 Mon–Fri, mid-Aug–May noon–15.00 Tue–Thu, noon–16.00 Sun; NOK100; guided tours in English on Sun) is housed in Europe's northernmost synagogue – the building was once a railway station. On display is the concentration camp shirt of Julius Paltiel, who was deported from Norway on the transport ship *Gotenland* in 1943. Paltiel was liberated from Buchenwald concentration camp in 1945.

Ekne In October 1941, the former Falstad school for delinquent boys in Ekne, 71km north of Trondheim, became an SS prison camp and was used to hold Jews from Trondheim before deportation to Auschwitz. At least 230 Soviet prisoners of war, members of the Norwegian resistance and Yugoslav partisans were shot in the surrounding forest. The **Falstad Centre – Museum, Memorial and Centre for Human Rights** (Falstadvegen 59; **w** falstadsenteret.no; ⊕ noon–16.00 Tue–Fri, noon–17.00 Sun; NOK100) opened in 2000 and has a permanent exhibition.

DENMARK

In 1943, the moment news was leaked of an impending round-up of Denmark's Jewish population, the Danish people pulled off an incredible feat, helping nearly all of the country's 7,700 Jews escape to Sweden. Denmark was unique in occupied Europe in that here the Holocaust failed despite the fact that there was little initial resistance to the German occupation. That the king wore a yellow star in solidarity with the Jews is, however, a myth.

GETTING AROUND Most sites in Copenhagen are accessible on foot. Gilleleje is 1 hour 15 minutes by train from Copenhagen.

HISTORY Prior to the German invasion, there had been minimal antisemitism in Denmark, where the Jewish community was integrated and accepted. As early as 1814, Jews had been given equal citizenship.

During the occupation, the Germans were keen to cultivate good relations with the Danes whom they regarded as 'fellow Aryans', and the Danish people were given an autonomy that was unparalleled in other areas of occupied Europe. In return, the government collaborated with the Germans and until October 1943 the Jewish community lived relatively normal lives.

The Danes' attitude towards the occupation changed as the course of the war turned in favour of the Allies. By the summer of 1943, resistance activities brought the relationship between the German occupiers and the Danes to breaking point, and when the Germans demanded that saboteurs were handed over to German military courts, the Danish government resigned. Martial law was imposed and the order given to deport Denmark's Jews.

German officials, however, warned non-Danish Jews of the plan. It is widely believed that SS leader Werner Best decided to leak news of the round-up as he was concerned it would provoke a national uprising in Denmark. He believed the fate of the Danish Jews could wait until the war was won. Labour leaders and Lutheran clergy in turn alerted Jewish community leaders.

The Danes quickly organised a nationwide effort to smuggle the Jews by sea to neutral Sweden, and within weeks fishermen ferried some 7,200 Danish Jews and 680 non-Jewish family members to safety across the straits separating Denmark from Sweden. The passage was a terrifying ordeal and children were given sleeping pills to keep them from crying. Some boats were boarded by Gestapo patrols.

The Germans caught 481 Jews, who were deported to Terezín, or Theresienstadt in German (page 126), in the present-day Czech Republic. The Danes' rescue of their Jewish community deterred the Germans from sending them on from the Theresienstadt Ghetto to Auschwitz. As a result, a high number of Danish Jews in the ghetto managed to survive the war. In all, 120 Danish Jews died in the Holocaust either in Theresienstadt or escaping across the sea to Sweden.

COPENHAGEN An estimated 6,000–7,000 Jews live in Denmark, most of them in the capital city, Copenhagen. This is the oldest Jewish community in Scandinavia. The remarkable story of their rescue means that the community is roughly the same size as it was before the German occupation.

Where to stay and eat Coco Hotel (Vesterbrogade 41; w coco-hotel.com; €€) is a smart boutique hotel that won't break the bank. **Gils Deli** (Lyngbyvej 87; w gilsdeli.dk; ⊕ 10.00–17.30 Tue–Wed, 10.00–19.30 Thu, 08.00–13.00 Fri; K; €), a stalwart of the local Jewish community, sells kosher products and Israeli salads. There is a kosher restaurant, **Taim** (w chabadenmark.com; ⊕ 17.00–20.30 Thu–Sun; K; €€), in the Chabad House at Ole Suhrs Gade 10.

What to see In a dramatic service at the **Great Synagogue** at Krystalgade 12 on the eve of Rosh Hashanah 1943, Rabbi Marcus Melchior told the congregation to go home and go into hiding. The synagogue is open by appointment only – email e mt@mosaiske.dk.

The **Danish Jewish Museum** (Dansk Jødisk Museum; Proviantpassagen 6; w jewmus.dk; ⊕ Jun–Aug 10.00–17.00 Tue–Sun, Sep–May 11.00–17.00 Wed–Sun; DKK100), designed by the Polish-born American Jewish architect Daniel Liebeskind, opened in 2004. The exhibitions tell the story of the rescue of the Jewish community and are dedicated to the 481 Jews deported to Theresienstadt. On display are Torah scrolls and manuscripts that were hidden during the war.

Further afield
Gilleleje The small port of Gilleleje, 62km north of Copenhagen, played a central role in the rescue of the Danish Jewish community. An exhibition in the **Gilleleje Museum** (Vesterbrogade 56; ⊕ 13.00–16.00 Wed–Fri, 10.00–14.00 Sat; DKK40) tells the story. There is a useful guided walk of Gilleleje on w visitnorthzealand. com/north-zealand/events/when-jews-fled-self-guided-tour-gilleleje-about-october-1943-gdk908758.

On the night of 6–7 October 1943, after a tip-off, the Gestapo discovered one of the hiding places in the attic of the village church, where around 80 Jews were waiting for their escape boat to Sweden. They were arrested and deported to Theresienstadt. In 1997, the sculpture *Teka Bashofar Gadol*, Hebrew for 'Let the mighty Shofar proclaim', was unveiled on the lawn outside the Cultural Centre. The 6m-tall statue was a gift to the community of Gilleleje from Yuli Ofer, an Israeli ship owner.

SWEDEN

Jews were allowed to settle in Sweden in the early 18th century but only in small communities, and severe restrictions on employment were enforced. Jews were not granted full civil rights in Sweden until 1870. As Jews emigrated from eastern

Europe at the end of the 19th century, the Jewish population in Sweden swelled. In 1900, there were only 1,630 Jews in Sweden, but by 1920 that number had risen to 2,750. After 1933, Jewish immigration increased again.

Until 2000, when the government launched a Holocaust education programme, there was little interest in the Holocaust in Sweden and no recognition of the role the country had played in it. Swedes are rightly proud of the efforts they made to rescue Jews after 1942 and the help given to the survivors in the immediate postwar period. Yet, the national narrative overlooks the fact that, although Sweden was neutral during World War II, its foreign policy was initially pro-German.

In 2023, the World Jewish Congress estimated that 15,000 Jews lived in Sweden, making it the largest Jewish community in Scandinavia. As there is no ethnic registration in Sweden, the figure is a rough estimate.

GETTING AROUND Use the metro, the Tunnelbana, to get around Stockholm. Directions in the capital are often accompanied by the name of the closest subway stop, using T as an abbreviation. Helsingborg is just over 5 hours by train from Stockholm.

HISTORY The narrative in Sweden has centred on the sanctuary given to Jews fleeing from Finland, Norway and Denmark. Swedes also worked within occupied Europe to rescue Jews.

In Budapest, the Swedish diplomat Raoul Wallenberg saved tens of thousands of Hungarian Jews by providing them with documents and visas know as 'protective passports'. Their protective power rested on the implication that the carrier was a presumptive Swedish citizen on their way to Sweden.

In the last months of the war, in an operation known as the 'White Buses', the Swedish Red Cross negotiated the release of more than 15,000 concentration camp inmates in Germany and occupied Czechoslovakia. Although the operation was initially targeted at saving citizens of Scandinavian countries, those of other countries were also rescued.

Nevertheless, between 1934 and 1938, Sweden maintained a restrictive immigration policy regarding refugees from Nazi Germany. Many members of the upper and wealthy classes in Sweden were pro-German. Despite its neutrality, for the first half of the war Sweden had close economic ties with Germany. After Germany invaded Norway and Denmark in April 1940, the British sea blockade cut Sweden off from the rest of the world, forcing it to depend on Germany economically. Sweden supplied Germany iron ore, vital for the war effort, and Germany used Sweden's railroads and coastal waters to move soldiers and war materials to Norway and Finland. After the Allied victories at Stalingrad and in North Africa, in May 1943 Sweden reopened trade relations with the Allies, and in July, the Swedish government announced that it would no longer permit Germany to transfer soldiers or war materials across the country.

STOCKHOLM Jews have lived in Stockholm since the 17th century. Today most of the country's Jewish population live in the capital.

Where to stay and eat Restaurants in Sweden are expensive, so you may wish to opt for self-catering accommodation. The thing to eat is a *smörgåsbord*. The best in Stockholm is found in the **Veranda restaurant** (Södra Blasieholmshamnen 8; w grandhotel.se; €€€; dress code smart-casual) in the Grand Hôtel. There is a lovely waterfront view.

RAOUL WALLENBERG Few Swedes have received the international acclaim of Raoul Wallenberg (1912–56). As a Swedish diplomat in Hungary in 1944, he managed to save tens of thousands of Jews in one of the most successful rescue efforts of World War II.

Wallenberg, an architect and businessman, arrived in Budapest in July 1944. The Germans had occupied Hungary in March of that year and were deporting Hungarian Jewry to their deaths in Auschwitz. With the authorisation of the Swedish government, Wallenberg issued protective Swedish passports and rented safe 'Swedish houses' where they could seek shelter. After the Red Army liberated Budapest in January 1945, Wallenberg disappeared.

In 1956, the Soviet authorities said that he had died in the Lubyanka prison in 1947, but that has never been confirmed. In October 2016, Wallenberg was declared dead by the Swedish Tax Agency, which registers births and deaths. The date is a formality and exactly what happened to him has never been discovered. The Swedish government has been criticised for failing to press the Soviet authorities about Wallenberg's case and failing to support his family or give him the recognition he deserved. In recent years, however, the government has made an official apology. Wallenberg is now commemorated on 27 August, Raoul Wallenberg Day. This is the first national day in Sweden to commemorate and honour a civilian.

The **Army Museum** (Armémuseum; Riddargatan 13; Östermalmstorg; w armemuseum.se; 11.00–17.00 Wed–Sat, 11.00–19.00 Tue; SEK140) has a reconstruction of Wallenberg's office and papers belonging to him while he was in Budapest, among them his passport and driving licence which were returned to the family by the Soviet Union in 1989.

In 2022, the **Raoul Wallenberg Academy** (w raoulwallenberg.se) inaugurated a digital museum dedicated to Wallenberg.

COUNT FOLKE BERNADOTTE Lesser known is Count Folke Bernadotte (1895–1948), who as the Vice-Chairman of the Swedish Red Cross negotiated with the Germans to bring concentration camp prisoners to Sweden in special buses, known as 'White Buses'. Among them were 400 Danish Jews who had been held in Theresienstadt. Bernadotte also successfully organised the release of 10,000 women from the Ravensbrück concentration camp, including 2,000 Jews, most of whom were then brought to Sweden.

In May 1948, Bernadotte was asked to act as the United Nation's mediator in the Israel–Palestine conflict. He was assassinated a year later, most probably by members of a Jewish paramilitary organisation. His plan for a political solution died with him.

The **Folke Bernadotte Academy** (w fba.se) is an agency for peace, security and development.

What to see The Swedish Holocaust Museum (Sveriges museum om Förintelsen; Torsgatan 19; St-Eriksplan; w museumforintelsen.se; 11.00–20.00 Wed, 11.00–17.00 Thu–Sun; free) was established in July 2022. At the time of writing, the museum was housed at a temporary exhibition site and focused on the stories of seven survivors who came to Sweden, and had yet to find a permanent home.

There is an unusual Holocaust memorial at the entrance to the **Great Synagogue** (Wahrendorffsgatan 3B; 🚇 Kungsträdgården; w jfst.se; register on the website for a guided tour; donation requested). Inaugurated in 1998 by King Carl XVI Gustav and designed by sculptor Sivert Lindblom and architect Gabriel Herdevall, the monument is made up of 8,500 stone tablets. Each tablet bears the name of a victim, who was a relative of Jews living in Sweden.

Just outside the synagogue there is a monument to the Swedish diplomat **Raoul Wallenberg** (see opposite): a large granite globe inscribed in the 22 languages spoken by the victims of persecution by the Nazis and their allies. In front of the Jewish Community Centre on **Raoul Wallenbergs torg**, there is a sculpture by Willy Gordon representing a Jew fleeing with a Sefer Torah, a Torah scroll.

The **Jewish Museum** (Judiska Muséet; Själagårdsgatan 19; 🚇 Gamla Stan; w judiskamuseet.se; ⊕ 11.00–17.00 Tue–Wed & Sat–Sun, 11.00–20.00 Thu, 11.00–16.00 Fri; SEK100) in the old town is located in Sweden's oldest synagogue. It has an important collection of Judaica and hosts temporary exhibitions.

Further afield

Helsingborg Jews fleeing Denmark arrived in Helsingborg, 556km southwest of Stockholm. The **Raoul Wallenberg sculpture** in Ångfärje Park was inaugurated in 2022. The Jewish refugees were gathered in the park after their arrival in Sweden.

FINLAND

Finland has an unusual Holocaust history. When the country took part in the 1941 German invasion of the Soviet Union, Finnish Jewish soldiers found themselves fighting alongside the Wehrmacht. They were given Saturdays off for the Sabbath and also had a field synagogue. In 1942, the Germans demanded that the Finns hand over the country's Jews, but the government refused. Since they valued Finnish co-operation in the war against the Soviet Union, the Germans did not press the issue. Finland was the only Axis country where synagogues remained open throughout World War II.

HISTORY Finland was part of the Swedish Empire until 1809, when it was conquered by Russia. Only former Jewish conscripts to the Russian Army who had served in the Grand Duchy were allowed to settle there in specified places for a limited period and they could work only in certain occupations. In 1917, during the Russian Revolution, Finland became an independent country and Jews were granted equal citizenship.

In November 1939, the Soviet Union attacked Finland, and after fierce fighting Finland was forced to cede the province of Karelia in the east of the country. In an attempt to regain the territory, Finland took part in the German invasion of the Soviet Union in 1941.

In 1939 around 6,500 Roma lived in Finland. The Finnish Roma were not handed over to the Germans but interned in camps, and between 1939 and 1944, 1,000 Roma men served in the Finnish Army.

HELSINKI During the war, about 150 Jewish refugees from central Europe fled to Finland. At first, they were interned in villages in the countryside. About 100 men were taken for forced labour and about 40 were held in various labour camps in Sulla in Lapland, Kemijärvi and Suursaari, an island in the Gulf of Finland. At the

14

request of the Germans, the Finnish secret police designated up to 50 of the Jewish forced labourers for deportation.

Initially nine men were selected, among them Dr Walter Cohen, a German Jewish refugee. After he contacted Abraham Stiller, a distinguished member of the Jewish congregation in Helsinki, word spread, eventually reaching the press. A petition was signed by more than 500 people to support Cohen, who was not deported, although the remaining eight Jewish men were handed over to the Germans. They were taken to Tallinn in Estonia and then to Auschwitz. Only one survived. The deportation was condemned at the time by the church and many politicians.

 Where to stay and eat The Finnish capital has a range of chain hotels which are often cheaper at the weekend. The best time to eat out is at lunch when many restaurants offer deals.

What to see Finland's only Holocaust memorial, erected in 2000, is in Helsinki's **Tähtitorninmäki Park**. A slab of light Ylämaa granite, 1m high and showing raised hands begging for mercy, commemorates the deportation of the eight Jewish refugees in November 1942 (see above).

The Zeppelin Grandstand is one of several structures built between 1922 and 1939, still standing at the former Nazi Party Rally Grounds in Nuremberg PAGE 193

top
(U/S)

Crematoria at the Buchenwald Memorial Site in Weimar, Germany PAGE 189.

above left
(RW)

The entrance gate to the Dachau Memorial Site near Munich PAGE 199

above right
(CI/D)

The House of the Wannsee Conference, the lakeside villa near Berlin where the 'Final Solution' was organised in January 1942, today holds an interesting exhibition PAGE 176

below
(SP/D)

above
(OP/S)

The *Stone Flower* monument at the Jasenovac Memorial Site in Croatia, stands on the site of a former Roma camp PAGE 43

left
(RW)

The ruins of the Campo di Fossoli transit camp at Fossoli di Carpi, Italy PAGE 229

below
(RW)

Prison cells at the former Risiera di San Sabba detention centre in Trieste, in northern Italy PAGE 234

View over Sarajevo from the city's
Old Jewish Cemetery PAGE 47

above
(TH/D)

The *Menorah in Flames* memorial in
Thessaloniki by Yugoslav sculptor
Nandor Glid; there is an almost identical
monument in Belgrade PAGES 59 & 50

right
(R/D)

The Holocaust Memorial Centre for the
Jews of Macedonia in Skopje PAGE 51

below
(S/S)

above
(GK/S)
Dohány Street Synagogue in Budapest is Europe's largest synagogue and the model for the Central Synagogue in New York PAGE 209

below left
(DG/S)
The Holocaust memorial in Bratislava PAGE 129

below right
(RW)
A freight wagon used in deportations on display at the Sered Holocaust Museum in Slovakia PAGE 130

bottom right
(K/S)
The *Shoes on the Banks of the Danube* memorial in Budapest remembers the 20,000 Jews who lost their lives here PAGE 211

The graveyard at the former 'model ghetto' of Theresienstadt, now the Terezín Memorial Site, in the Czech Republic PAGE 127

above (IE/S)

The 17m-tall Memorial Column is one of several elements of Bucharest's Holocaust Memorial PAGE 296

below left (R85/D)

A statue of British humanitarian Sir Nicholas Winton, who enabled the escape of 669 children from Czechoslovakia in 1939, stands on Platform 1 of Prague's Main Station PAGE 125

below right (RW)

above
(R90/S)
At the Treblinka Museum, stones mark the path of the railway line that transported Jews to their deaths PAGE 259

top right
(RW)
Shoes collected at Majdanek Museum and Memorial Site near Lublin in Poland PAGE 267

above right
(RW)
The Bełżec Museum and Memorial Site at the former extermination camp in Poland PAGE 269

below
(RW)
The Sobibór Museum and Memorial Site in Poland PAGE 268

On Ghetto Heroes Square, at the heart of Kraków's former ghetto, a series of empty chairs stand as a memorial to the deportations that took place from here PAGE 280

above (A/S)

The Mirror Field installation at the Babyn Yar memorial park in Kyiv shows a new approach to remembering the Holocaust PAGE 329

below (RW)

above
(S/D)

The Pit memorial in Minsk stands near the site where 5,000 Jews were executed in March 1942 PAGE 82

below left
(SP/S)

A memorial at Yantarny, on the Kaliningrad coast, remembers the 3,000 women and children killed there in January 1945 PAGE 92

below right
(PD/D)

This Soviet-era memorial remembers the 27,000 Jews and Soviet citizens murdered in 1942–43 in the Zmievskaya Balka (Snake Ravine) near Rostov-on-Don in Russia PAGE 91

15

Poland

In 1939, Poland was home to the largest Jewish community in Europe and was the centre of the Jewish diaspora. During the German occupation, Poland instead became the centre of the genocide of Europe's Jews and, as a result, the country has some of the most important Holocaust sites in Europe. In recent decades Auschwitz has become the iconic symbol of the Holocaust and receives over 2 million visitors a year – but there is far more to Poland than Auschwitz.

Much of what happened in Poland during the Holocaust was unique, as its cities and towns reveal. During World War II, 90% of Poland's Jewish citizens were forced out of their homes and imprisoned in ghettos. Those that survived the ghettos spent years there before being murdered in one of the many death camps set up in the German-occupied territories or sent to work in the harsh conditions of the forced labour camps.

The destruction of Jewish life in Poland left behind a huge void in Polish society and over the last 20 years what are called 'traces' of their once vibrant culture have been and continue to be rediscovered by a new generation of Poles. Since the fall of the Berlin Wall in 1989, memorialising the country's Jewish past and associating oneself with Poland's Jewish heritage has become a trendy way of asserting an alternative to the country's increasingly nationalistic politics. As arguments rage about the role that Poles played in the Holocaust, it is important to remember that the current debate about the Holocaust in Poland is taking place in a country where, until the democratic transition in 1988–89, surprisingly little was known about its Jewish history despite the erection of some significant monuments in the decades after the war.

Poland is one of Europe's largest countries and the sites included in this chapter have been chosen to give a general introduction to the Holocaust in Poland, reminders of which can be seen in every village and urban centre.

GETTING THERE AND AROUND

Warsaw is a hub for air and rail travel and makes the logical starting point for travellers, although most Polish cities have international airports with flights to the UK. Train is the best way to travel between the main cities, but to see remoter sites it helps to have your own transport. If travelling by car, be aware that some motorways have tolls.

ONLINE RESOURCES

Jewish Historical Institute e familyheritage@ jhi.pl. The Jewish Historical Institute in Warsaw holds records dating back as far as the 17th century & which cover much of the country. The institute also helps people with genealogical research – contact them via email.

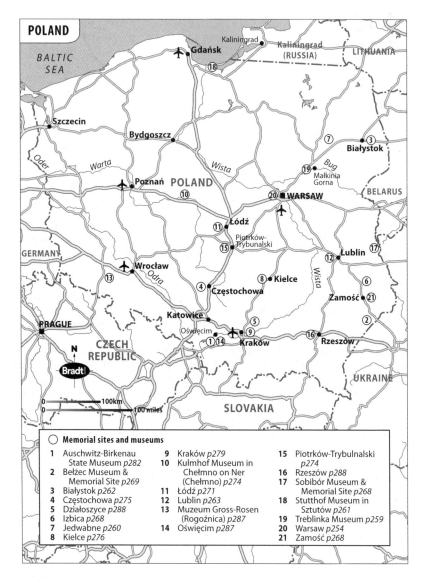

POLAND

BALTIC SEA

Szczecin

Bydgoszcz

Oder
Warta
Wisła

Poznań POLAND

GERMANY

Wrocław
Odra

PRAGUE

CZECH REPUBLIC

N

Bradt

0 ___ 100km
0 ___ 100 miles

SLOVAKIA

Gdańsk

Kaliningrad

Kaliningrad (RUSSIA)

LITHUANIA

⑱

⑦ ③
Białystok

Bug
⑲ Małkinia Gorna

BELARUS

⑳ ■ WARSAW

Łódź
⑪
Piotrków-Trybunalski
⑮

Lublin ⑰
⑫

⑧ ● Kielce
④ Częstochowa

Wisła

Zamość ● ㉑
⑥

②

Katowice
⑤
Oświęcim ⑨
①⑭ Kraków

⑯ ● Rzeszów

UKRAINE

○ **Memorial sites and museums**

1	Auschwitz-Birkenau State Museum *p282*	9	Kraków *p279*	15	Piotrków-Trybulnalski *p274*
2	Bełżec Museum & Memorial Site *p269*	10	Kulmhof Museum in Chełmno on Ner (Chełmno) *p274*	16	Rzeszów *p288*
3	Białystok *p262*	11	Łódź *p271*	17	Sobibór Museum & Memorial Site *p268*
4	Częstochowa *p275*	12	Lublin *p263*	18	Stutthof Museum in Sztutów *p261*
5	Działoszyce *p288*	13	Muzeum Gross-Rosen (Rogoźnica) *p287*	19	Treblinka Museum *p259*
6	Izbica *p268*	14	Oświęcim *p287*	20	Warsaw *p254*
7	Jedwabne *p260*			21	Zamość *p268*
8	Kielce *p276*				

Jri-poland w jri-poland.org. An online resource for Jewish genealogists looking for Jewish records for the current & former territories of Poland.
Taube Center for Jewish Life & Learning w taubecenter.org. The only American Jewish foundation to have an office in Poland.

It connects Jews from around the world with their heritage through educational & cultural programmes.
Virtual Shtetl w sztetl.org.pl. A useful tool if you want to dig deeper or are tracing family roots in Poland.

HISTORY

Jews first settled in Poland in the Middle Ages. Polish kings valued their contribution to the economic development of the country and so encouraged further immigration. At this time, Poland was a safe haven for Jews and Jewish culture flourished. It was also the birthplace of Hassidic Judaism, which emerged in the 18th century, and a centre of Reform Judaism and the Haskalah, the Jewish Enlightenment.

In the second half of the 18th century, Poland was divided between Austria-Hungary, Prussia and Russia, and 'disappeared' from the map. As a result, Poles have traditionally seen themselves as victims of their more powerful neighbours. The majority of Polish Jews found themselves in the Russian Empire and the Polish lands annexed by Russia became part of the Pale of Settlement, the area to which the freedom of movement of Jews was restricted. Tsarist antisemitic policies and violence in the late 19th century encouraged mass emigration to western Europe and the Americas.

INTERWAR YEARS In the 1930s, Poland was home to Europe's largest Jewish community of about 3.5 million Jews, who made up almost 10% of the population and were concentrated in cities and medium-sized towns. While there was a wealthy elite of businessmen, doctors and lawyers, most Polish Jews were extremely poor. Despite the poverty, Polish Jewry had a rich cultural life; the socialist Bund, Zionist organisations and Orthodox Jews all took part in the political life of interwar Poland.

Most Jews attended Polish schools and the middle and upper classes were highly Polonised. Yet, in the 1930s, Polish nationalism took on an antisemitic tone with restrictions on Jewish economic life and access to higher education, and there was widespread violence against Jews. Between 1935 and 1937, 79 Jews were killed and 500 injured, prompting tens of thousands of Polish Jews to emigrate.

WORLD WAR II Germany attacked Poland in September 1939, triggering France and Britain to declare war on Germany. The Polish Army – of which roughly 10% (about 100,000 soldiers) were Jewish – was soon crushed. The same month, the Soviet Union occupied eastern Poland, leaving the west to Germany. This was a turning point for the Jews who lived in the territories occupied by the Soviet Union. Even though they suffered under the occupation in the deportations to the Gulag and the nationalisation of businesses, Jews were widely seen as Soviet sympathisers, fuelling the widely held belief in the Judeo-Bolshevik myth.

The Germans incorporated part of Polish territory into the Reich and took control of an area known as the General Government, which was administered by the Nazi lawyer Hans Frank. The Polish government, which did not comply with German rule, went into exile and fled first to Romania, France, and then to Britain, from where it organised underground resistance efforts and the Polish forces' contribution to the Allied war effort.

Persecution of the Jews began immediately as the Germans burned synagogues across the country and introduced strict regulations that marginalised Jews from Polish society. Jews had to wear white armbands with a blue Star of David and were confined to ghettos in the principal cities and towns, where many died of starvation and disease. The Nazis enforced curfews, food rations and forced labour.

1941 The genocide began in Poland on 22 June 1941, when Germany invaded the Soviet Union. During the months that followed, in what is known as the Shoah by Bullets, the Germans massacred some 700,000 Jews living in the newly acquired eastern territory. In the December 'gas vans' began to be used at the Chełmno extermination camp.

The Holocaust is an inflammatory topic in Polish politics. From 2015 to 2023, Poland's government, led by the right-wing nationalist Prawo i Sprawiedliwość (PiS; Law and Justice) party, pursued a controversial approach to Holocaust remembrance. It claimed that Poland has been wrongly maligned as one of the perpetrators of the Holocaust and emphasised Polish victims of the Nazis over their Jewish counterparts.

In January 2018, an amendment to the Act on the Institute of National Remembrance prohibited the false attribution of blame for Nazi crimes to the Polish state or nation. Parliament modified the amendment in June of that year, changing it from a criminal to a civil offence. The publication in 2018 of *Night without End: The Fate of Jews in German-occupied Poland* (Indiana University Press, 2022) by Jan Grabowski and Barbara Engelking – a study outlining Polish responsibility for locating Jews in hiding, mass murder and looting – resulted in a storm of protest and law claiming the evidence was falsified and it had smeared the national character of the Polish people.

Poland's efforts to reframe history reflect a trend proliferating in other European countries, but what makes Poland so distinctive was the scale of state official involvement in redirecting the narrative. During the years PiS were in power, the Institute of National Remembrance, founded in 1998, was manipulated for nationalist purposes and a number of controversial new museums opened or were commissioned. In Ostrołęka, 120km north of Warsaw, a museum honours Jozef Kuras, a Polish partisan, although historians have documented cases in which partisans under his command murdered Holocaust survivors.

Memorials to Poles killed by the Nazis for hiding Jews also proliferated across the Polish countryside. The government-funded **Pilecki Insititute**, which researches the experiences of Poles under totalitarianism in the 20th century, has a programme dedicated to honouring Poles killed by the Germans for hiding Jews, of whom only a handful have been recognised by Yad Vashem. Those recognised as Righteous Among the Nations must have been nominated by Jews they helped, but the corroborating testimony for the institute's cases comes from Poles rather than Jews, as the Jews involved were summarily murdered or deported. Nor is it clear if many of these individuals profited from the assistance they gave. How far these trends will be corrected by the new government waits to be seen as Poland's PiS-aligned president, Andrzej Duda, remains in office until 2025.

1942–44 Jews from all over Europe were deported by train to occupied Poland and transported to the six death camps operated by the Germans: Auschwitz-Birkenau, Bełżec, Chełmno, Majdanek, Sobibór and Treblinka. During this period about 90% of all Polish Jews were murdered.

The United States Holocaust Memorial and Museum (**w** ushmm.org) estimates that at least 3 million Polish Jews were murdered during the occupation, along with 1.8 million to 1.9 million non-Jewish Polish citizens. Polish sources generally give a higher figure for non-Jewish Polish deaths – about 3 million. A further 1.5 million Poles were deported for forced labour. Non-Jewish Poles were also brutally treated, but anti-Polish measures never reached the genocidal extent of those against the Jews.

The Germans prohibited Poles from assisting Jews. Unlike in some other European countries, the penalty for helping Jews in Poland was death without trial for the individual and their entire family. Nevertheless, Poland is home to the greatest number of Righteous Among the Nations. Almost 7,000 Poles have been recognised for their role in protecting Jews.

Individual Poles were, however, also involved in the persecution of Jews. Many of these acts of murder were executed without German instruction or assistance, although in some cases German officers may have influenced and encouraged the local population. The Blue Police, a Polish police force, was set up by the Germans in October 1939 under the command of the SS.

Jewish resistance The Jewish youth movements of both the Bund and Zionist groups formed the basis of the underground resistance movement that developed in the ghettos during the German occupation. The 1943 Warsaw Ghetto Uprising confirmed the Germans' worst fears, and led, on grounds of security, to the liquidation of nearly all of the remaining 54 ghettos and Jewish labour camps on Polish soil. The uprising inspired resistance and in the months after there were revolts in the Treblinka and Sobibór extermination camps and in ghettos across the country.

AFTERMATH Initially, most survivors hoped they could return home and find family members who had survived, or at least some remnants of the lives they had lived before the Holocaust. But the stories of the return home are about Jews being rejected by their neighbours. Many survivors found that not only were their neighbours not happy to see that they had survived, but they had no physical home to return to – someone else was living in their house. Again and again survivors say that they left Poland because they feared for their lives and were not welcome in the towns and villages where their families had previously lived for generations.

In 1947, Poland became a communist state. Antisemitism sparked waves of emigration in the late 1950s and also after the 1967 Six Day War, prompted by Israel's victory over the Soviet-backed Arabs.

WARSAW

Before World War II, Warsaw was a hub of Jewish culture, and in 1939 a third of its population was Jewish. It was the second largest Jewish centre in the world after New York, with roughly 450,000 Jews living there among an overall population of 1.3 million people. Today, it is a city where the majority of people identify as Polish Roman Catholic. As a result, Warsaw is a place with two stories: one of loss and of the desolation that the murder of Warsaw's Jewish population left in its wake; the other of heroic resistance during the Warsaw Uprising of 1944 and of a city rising like a phoenix from the ashes. So, before setting off to discover Warsaw's Holocaust sites, visit its Old Town, which was completely rebuilt after the war, and the Warsaw Uprising Monument on Plac Krasińskich to understand how Poles see World War II.

GETTING AROUND Most of the sites in Warsaw in both the area of the former Small Ghetto and around the POLIN Museum can be reached on foot. Buses link the two areas, but taxis are readily available on apps like Uber. Parking is easy in the POLIN area and machines take credit cards.

It is possible to book a guided tour from Warsaw of the memorial site at the former Treblinka extermination camp – there are plenty of options online, but they are very expensive. The best option without a car, as well as the simplest and least costly, is to take a train from Warsaw Central Station to Małkinia Górna and then take a taxi for the remaining 7km. Be aware that this is the same route taken by the trains to the extermination camp. A visit to the memorial at the extermination camp, Treblinka II, takes less than an hour, so it is feasible to ask the taxi to wait.

There are train connections to Białystok and Gdansk, should you want to visit the former Stutthof concentration camp. To get there, take the 870 bus from Gdansk bus station. To see Jedwabne, you will need your own transport.

WHERE TO STAY AND EAT Warsaw has plenty of chain hotels that cluster around the Palace of Culture and Science, the giant Stalinist wedding-cake skyscraper in Świętokrzyski Park. The area is home to Warsaw Central Station for easy airport connections and there are plenty of shops and restaurants. It is a good spot from which to explore the former ghetto as the wall of the Small Ghetto ran through the northern side of the square.

The best hotel option is the **PURO** (Widok 9; w purohotel.pl; €). Part of a trendy small Polish chain, it has an Italian restaurant, parking and is pet friendly. The PURO is just around the corner from the Jewish Community Centre and a short walk from the Nosyk Synagogue. The **Warsaw Jewish Community Centre** (ul. Chmielna 9a; €) has a Sunday brunch, at which visitors are welcome. The area around Chmielna has plenty of bars and restaurants and a lively atmosphere.

HISTORY During the interwar years, the core of the Jewish community in Warsaw were merchants, workers and craftsmen, who lived predominantly in the north of the city, in the areas of Muranów and Nalewki, in crowded tenements. (This lost world was caught on camera by the Russian-American photographer Roman Visniac (1897–1990), who is best known for capturing scenes of Jewish life and culture in eastern Europe before the Holocaust. His pictures can be seen at w vishniac.icp.org.) Assimilated wealthy Jews lived in the southern part of Warsaw. The community was extremely diverse and made up of Zionists, socialists, communists, and religious and assimilated Jews. Yiddish was the everyday language, but assimilated Jews spoke predominantly Polish.

When the German invasion took place in September 1939, Warsaw was badly bombed. The city then became part of the General Government administered from Kraków.

The Warsaw Ghetto In the autumn of 1940, some 113,000 Poles were moved out of the area designated as the Jewish ghetto in the north of the city. The ghetto was sealed on 16 November 1940, and by March 1941 some 445,000 Jews from the city and surrounding area were imprisoned inside its 3m-high walls. Tens of thousands more were brought into the Warsaw Ghetto in the months that followed along with Jews from western Poland and from Bohemia and Moravia, now the Czech Republic. Penniless, they found themselves destitute and starving. Typically one room was inhabited by seven to eight people; typhus and tuberculosis were endemic. At least 100,000 people died within the ghetto. Smuggling was one of the few ways to survive – since Jews under 12 years did not have to wear armbands with the Star of David, boys would sneak out to find food.

The ghetto was divided in two sections: the Great Ghetto to the north of the busy Chłodna street (excluded from the ghetto) and the Small Ghetto to the south, where the richer inmates, intelligentsia and members of the Judenrat lived. In January 1942, a wooden footbridge was erected across Chłodna to link the two areas and to streamline the traffic flow that had previously been impeded by Jews crossing the road, under supervision, between the two ghettos. After the deportations in July (see below) the Small Ghetto was closed and the bridge became defunct. The bridge features in many memoirs of the ghetto, among them Adolf Rudnicki's story *The Great Stefan Konecki*. It is also depicted in the film *The Pianist* (2002), which portrays life in the Warsaw Ghetto.

There are remains of the ghetto wall at Złota 60 in Muranów and in the former Small Ghetto at ulica Waliców 11 and ulica Sienna 55. Iron slabs in the pavement mark its boundaries.

Deportations On 22 July 1942, the eve of Tisha B'Av, a major round-up began which lasted for 46 days. (Round-ups were often timed to coincide with important events in the Jewish calendar; page 16.) During this period, almost 300,000 Jews were deported and taken to their deaths at the Treblinka extermination camp. One escapee, Dawid Nowodworski, brought news of the mass murder back to the ghetto in late August 1942, which left the remaining 70,000–80,000 inhabitants under no illusions regarding their fate. Fewer than half had work permits which would allow them to remain in the ghetto. Across Poland, as the plans drawn up at the Wannsee Conference in January 1942, to murder all of Europe's Jews, were put into action, the Nazis kept young men and women who they considered strong enough as forced labourers. Many of the ghettos that remained then became forced labour camps. Many Jews, helped by the Polish resistance, went into hiding on the Aryan side, where there were more than 20,000 Jews living undercover.

Youth leaders of the left-wing Jewish Fighting Organisation (ZOB), and the right-wing Jewish Military Union joined forces and began to liaise with the Polish resistance. When deportations began again in January 1943, the resistance fought back. Nevertheless, a further 5,000 were deported and 1,200 shot inside the ghetto. Significantly, the resistance changed the attitude of the Polish underground, who until now had been reluctant to arm the Jewish fighters.

Warsaw Ghetto Uprising On 19 April 1943, on the eve of Passover, German soldiers entered the Warsaw Ghetto intent on its liquidation. They were greeted by a shower of Molotov cocktails, and street battles continued for two months. The uprising was the first large-scale civilian resistance in Europe and inspired Jews across the continent. But by 16 May the Germans had crushed it and the ghetto was razed.

Warsaw Uprising The Polish Resistance rose up against the Germans on 1 August 1944, expecting support from the Red Army who had arrived on the east bank of the Vistula; but Stalin halted the advance and did not come to their assistance. The

THE WARSAW GENUFLECTION

The main act of Holocaust remembrance during communist rule was an annual commemoration of the Warsaw Ghetto Uprising. In 1970, the West German chancellor Willy Brandt visited Warsaw and knelt in front of Warsaw Ghetto memorial. Brandt was a Social Democrat who had resisted the Nazis. It was a game-changer in the way Germans viewed their Nazi past, although in Poland it was not widely reported. A period of Ostpolitik followed in which Germany accepted the loss of its eastern territories and Polish–German relations warmed.

15

Germans crushed the revolt and razed the entire city. About 166,000 Poles lost their lives. As many as 17,000 Jews who had been in hiding fought alongside the Poles.

WHAT TO SEE The Jewish Historical Institute (page 256) publishes two useful maps of the ghetto and sites related to the Ringelblum archive. It is worth stopping by the institute to pick them up before setting off to explore the former ghetto.

The Great Ghetto area
The heart of the Warsaw Ghetto was the **Muranów** district, 1km east of the Old Town. Modern-day Muranów offers a haunting reminder of what the Holocaust was – destruction and devastation. The reality of what had happened to Jewish life in Poland was summed up in the rubble of the ghetto. There was to be no rising from the ashes for Poland's Jewish community; the ghetto area was not rebuilt like the Old Town – there was no-one left to do so. Today it is covered in modern apartment blocks.

POLIN Museum of the History of Polish Jews (Muzeum Historii Żydów Polskich; Mordechaja Anielewicza 6; w polin.pl; ⏱ 10.00–18.00 Sun–Mon & Wed–Fri, 10.00–20.00 Sat; PLN45 inc audio guide, Core Exhibition free on Thu) The once desolate area of Muranów is now buzzing, thanks to the ultra-modern POLIN Museum, which opened in 2013. The museum is the best place to start a tour of Poland's Holocaust sites as it tells the story of the Jewish community from their arrival in the country in the Middle Ages. Polin is the Hebrew name for Poland. The exhibition, divided into seven time themes, helps the visitor to focus not just on the destruction of Jewish Poland but also on what was lost and what came after. The permanent collection celebrates the rich and vibrant Jewish culture that played a central part in Polish life for a thousand years. The painted *bimah* from the Gwoździec Synagogue in southern Poland, is at the heart of this part of the exhibition. The exhibition explains the partition of Poland at the end of the 18th century and follows through industrialisation and World Wars I and II, and takes a hard look at Polish antisemitism in the aftermath of the Holocaust.

Outside the museum on a bench is a **statue of Jan Karski**, who was a leading member of the Polish resistance (see below).

Opposite the entrance to the POLIN museum stands the **Monument of the Ghetto Heroes**, designed by the sculptor Nathan Rapoport while he was in exile in the Soviet Union. Immediately after the war, the Jewish community set about raising money to build it and it was officially unveiled in 1948. Before the museum was built, the monument stood in a large empty park, bordered by the streets of Zamenhofa and Anielewicza, the gaping space in front of it like a vast wound. Today, the museum

---

JAN KARSKI

Karski was a leading member of the Polish resistance. He made two undercover visits to the Warsaw Ghetto and, dressed as an Estonian guard, also witnessed a deportation to the Bełżec extermination camp from Izbica. He then took the report of what he had seen to London and Washington; but his account had little effect on Allied policy, largely because he had no photographic evidence.

Karski wrote a highly readable memoir of his wartime life, *Story of a Secret State: My Report to the World* (Penguin, 2012). After the war, he taught at Georgetown University in Washington and spoke about his experiences in Claude Lanzmann's epic film *Shoah* (1985).

dwarfs the memorial, taking away much of its gravitas. The **Memorial Route of Jewish Martyrdom and Struggle** that begins here is marked by 16 granite blocks.

Other sites in the Great Ghetto North of the Monument of the Ghetto Heroes at Mila 18 is the **Anielewicz Mound**, located in a small park. Here, a group of ghetto fighters led by the charismatic 24-year-old Zionist Mordechai Anielewicz, hid in a bunker with about 300 other ghetto inmates. The bunker was the headquarters of the operations of the Jewish Combat Organisation. When the bunker was discovered by the Germans on 8 May 1943, Anielewicz and 120 other fighters committed suicide by blowing themselves up, while the others surrendered. The Central Jewish Committee of Poland placed a memorial on the mound, built from the rubble of nearby buildings, in 1946.

Before the war, the station north of the park at Stawki 10 had been used as a freight terminal. The Germans turned it into the **Umschlagplatz**, where up to 300,000 Jewish people were gathered prior to deportation to the extermination camps. Many families chose to stay together, so even those who had work permits exempting them from deportation joined the transports. A memorial, in the form of a 4m-long wall with a black stripe on the front like a prayer shawl, was unveiled here in 1988. On the wall are engraved the 400 most popular Polish and Jewish names, symbolising the coexistence of Jews and non-Jews in the city. A commemorative march begins here every year on 22 July marking the date of the first deportations.

The vast **Jewish Cemetery** is located at the end of ulica Niska on Okopowa. The mass grave of those who died of hunger, disease and exhaustion is in the southeastern corner.

In July 1943, nearby on ulica Gesia, now ulica Anielewicz 34, east of the intersection with ulica Okopowa, the Germans opened a concentration camp. They brought 4,000 foreign Jews to sort through the rubble after the Ghetto Uprising, retrieving 30 million bricks and 6,000 tonnes of scrap metal. Conditions were horrific and prisoners were often shot, and their bodies burned in funeral pyres on the top of the rubble.

South of the POLIN museum is the **Pawiak Prison Museum** (Muzeum Więzienia Pawiak; ul. Dzielna 24/26; w pawiak.muzn.pl; ⏱ 10.00–17.00 Tue & Thu–Sun, 11.00–19.00 Wed; PLN20). The prison was built in the 1830s, and during the German occupation it was used by the Gestapo, who detained over 100,000 people here, half of whom were executed or transported to concentration camps.

The suppression of the Ghetto Uprising ended in the symbolic destruction of the **Great Synagogue** on ulica Tłomackie on the eastern side of the ghetto. It was built in 1878 and could hold 2,000 people. Excluded from the ghetto in May 1942, it was used as a warehouse for furniture from Jewish apartments. The Blue Skyscraper now stands in its place.

St Augustine's Church on ulica Nowolipki survived the destruction of the ghetto and was one of the few buildings left standing after the uprising. It was used to store Jewish property stolen by the Germans after the deportations. To the south of Nowolipki, the former **Femina Cinema** on al. Solidarności 155 is now a supermarket but was, during the ghetto's existence, the centre of its lively cultural life, an important part of Jewish resistance.

To the south, on the site of the wooden bridge across Chłodna built by the Germans to link the two areas of the ghetto (page 252) is a luminescent **Footbridge of Memory**, which was created in 2011 by Tomasz Lec.

The Small Ghetto area
The **Nosyk Synagogue** (ul. Twarda 6; w warszawa. jewish.org.pl/en/community/religion), built in 1898–1902, was closed during the

One of the most important items to survive the Warsaw Ghetto is a milk churn. In it was hidden one of the most significant collections of documents relating to the destruction of Poland's Jewish community. The churn is on display at the **Jewish Historical Institute** (Żydowski Instytut Historyczny; ul. Tłomackie 5; w jhi.pl; ⊕ 09.00–18.00 Mon & Wed–Thu, 09.00–16.00 Fri, 10.00–18.00 Sun; PLN15) which was founded by survivors in 1947. The building dating to 1936 is original and was formerly the Main Judaistic Library, which had a collection of more than 30,000 volumes until it was plundered and the contents taken to Germany. It was included in the ghetto and housed the offices of a German-approved Jewish relief organisation, Aleynhilf (Self-Help).

One of its leaders was the social worker and historian Emanuel Ringelblum (1900–44), who believed that the Jewish people should tell their own story for themselves. As a historian of Polish Jewish history from the Middle Ages to the 18th century, he had been frustrated by the fact that, while the Jewish community's rabbis commented on and interpreted religious texts, there was little or no documentation of daily life from a Jewish perspective. He believed that at this dramatic moment in Jewish history it was vital that the Jews told their story in their own voices. In an act of intellectual resistance, Ringelblum and his colleagues created a secret group, calling themselves Oyneg Shabes (Yiddish for 'Joy of the Sabbath') as they met at the institute on the Sabbath. They documented all aspects of life in the ghetto by collecting documents, posters and decrees, and

German occupation but reopened in 1945. It was restored in 1977–83 and holds regular services. The annual Singer Warsaw Jewish Cultural Festival (w shalom.org. pl) is held on nearby ulica Prozna, where tenement buildings that survived the destruction of the ghetto still stand.

Plac Grzybowski was the site of the Judenrat office (pl. Grzybowski 26/28). The head of the Judenrat committed suicide here on 22 July 1942 after refusing to supply 6,000 Jews per day for deportation. Judenräte were set up by the Germans as administrative bodies run by Jews, who were responsible for carrying out their orders.

The last location of the children's home run by the writer and educator **Janusz Korczak** and Stephanie Wilczyńska was at ulica Sienna 16, now the northeastern wing of the vast Palace of Culture and Science. From here Korczak, his staff and 200 children were taken to the Umschlagplatz (page 255) and from there to their deaths at Treblinka. Korczak turned down a hiding place on the Aryan side in order to take care of the children. There is a plaque that remembers them at the entrance to the Laika Theatre and a monument dedicated to Korczak in the park north of the Palace of Culture and Science.

To the east on Prosta 51, the **Monument to the Evacuation of the Warsaw Ghetto Fighters**, marks the spot where some dozen ghetto fighters emerged from the sewers on the night of 8–9 May 1943 with the help of the Polish underground. Many of those evacuated joined the Polish resistance and fought in the Warsaw Uprising in 1944.

The **Warsaw Ghetto Museum** (Muzeum Getta Warszawskiego; ul. Śliska 51; w 1943.pl), which is due to open in 2026, has already been singled out by historians who are critics of Poland's right-wing nationalists who fear it will rewrite history to fit their political agenda. The museum's head, Daniel Blatman, who teaches Holocaust studies at Jerusalem University, has denied this. The museum will be keeping diaries and detailed descriptions of other ghettos in occupied Poland, as well as the extermination camps at Chełmno and Treblinka.

The permanent exhibition at the Jewish Historical Institute tells the story of the Oyneg Shabes group. At first, members hid their documents among the day-to-day paperwork of Aleynhilf. Ringelblum managed to smuggle news of the mass murders out of the ghetto in the hope that Allied leaders would help, but they did not react. When in July 1942 it became clear that the ghetto was about to be liquidated, part of the archive was buried in ten metal boxes in the basement of the Ber Borochov school at ulica Nowolipki 28/30. Two large metal milk cans with more documents were also hidden here in February 1943.

In 1946, two surviving members of the group retrieved the first part of the archive but the second part was only discovered by accident during construction work in 1950. A third cache of documents buried under the Brushmakers' Workshop, now the Embassy of the People's Republic of China at ulica Świętojerska 34, has never been found. Most of the members of Oyneg Shabes, including Ringelblum, did not live to see the end of the war.

You can find out more on the Yad Vashem website (w yadvashem.org/yv/en/exhibitions/ringelblum/index.asp) and in Samuel Kassow's book Who Will Write Our History: Emanuel Ringelblum, the Warsaw Ghetto and Oyneg Shabes Archive *(Indiana University Press, 2007).*

housed in the former children's hospital built in the 1870s. Most of its patients met their deaths in Treblinka. It was one of the few buildings to survive the war and was used as a children's hospital until 2014.

Warsaw Zoo (Miejski Ogród Zoologiczny; ul. Starzyńskiego; w zoo.waw. pl; ⊕ 09.00–18.00 daily, closes earlier in winter; PLN35) Warsaw Zoo, in Praga across the Vistula River from the Old Town, was an unlikely site of rescue. The zoo's then director, Jan Żabiński, and his wife, Antonina, hid hundreds of Jews who had escaped from the ghetto in the basement of their house inside the zoo. The Żabińskis were recognised as Righteous Among the Nations in 1965, and the zoo was renamed in their honour in 2023. Their story was turned into a film, *The Zookeeper's Wife*, in 2017. It is possible to visit the **Żabiński Villa** (⊕ 11.00–13.00 or by appt via e willa@zoo.waw.pl) on the first Sunday of the month.

FURTHER AFIELD
Treblinka Treblinka, 85km northeast of Warsaw, was the site of one of the Germans' deadliest extermination camps, and between 800,000 and 920,000 Jews from ten different countries were murdered here between 1942 and 1943. Close to the Bug River in remote countryside, Treblinka was chosen for the site of the camp as it was close to the main Warsaw–Białystok railway line. Today, it is a quiet, lonely place which gets few visitors. Surrounded by deep forests, the site is eerie and evocative and, given what happened here, surprisingly calm and peaceful.

History The camp was set up as part of Operation Reinhard, a plan to murder all the Jews in the General Government-controlled area of Poland. It was close to an existing labour camp, Treblinka I, a gravel mine where Polish prisoners were

Yossi Gerstein grew up on Krochmalna Street, home to some of Warsaw's poorest Jews. He can still taste the porridge he ate for breakfast, see the Hanukkah menorah on the windowsill and the boys playing football in the street. In the late 2000s, Gerstein returned but could no longer recognise his former home as Krochmalna was destroyed in the Warsaw Ghetto Uprising.

Gerstein's father was a warehouse manager, who was shot by the Germans when they looted the warehouse. In 1940, his mother realised that the ghetto was about to be sealed. Although Gerstein was just six years old, she packed his backpack and took him to the edge of the ghetto, where she told him to run away. For days before, she had reminded Gerstein of his name, her name and their address: Krochmalna 23. He still repeats it like a mantra. Her last words to her son were: 'Do not forget your name, your parents and that you are a Jew. If you run away perhaps you will stay alive.'

'My mother was forced to make a decision that no parent should ever have to face. It must have broken her heart,' he says. Gerstein had a sister, a toddler, whose name he cannot remember. 'She had to stay with her. She had no choice.'

From that moment onwards, Gerstein lived feral on the streets.

'I hid in attics and scavenged for food, but at night I would dream about my mother. She was tall with black hair that flowed down over her shoulders. Years passed but, eventually, I was drawn to the ghetto. I had to see my mother one more time…I was on my way home when a manhole cover in the street suddenly opened and two people who looked Jewish came out of the sewer. They looked at me and asked, "What do you want child?" I replied, "I want my mother."'

When Gerstein told them his address, they said everyone who lived there was sent away to Treblinka. He had no idea where it was.

Not long after, Gerstein was caught by two Polish policemen and handed over to the Germans. He was then put on a deportation train. But the train was bombed, and he managed to escape and was taken in by a farmer. Where the farm was, he has no idea. After the liberation he was found by other survivors and taken to the Slovakian town of Košice, a centre where Jewish survivors found help and assistance. It was when he got to Prague that he was told what Treblinka was. 'When they told me, I knew I was alone in the world.'

In 1946, Gerstein left for Britain on a scheme organised by the Jewish charity the Central British Fund, now World Jewish Relief. He later started a new life in Israel, where he married and had four children. He still dreams about his mother every night.

held. Prisoners and Jews from the surrounding area were forced to construct the extermination camp, known as Treblinka II. The camp was surrounded by barbed wire fences worked into the branches of the trees and was supervised by 30 SS and 100 Ukrainian guards.

Jews were transported to Treblinka in freight cars, a journey that often took days, with the first transport arriving from Warsaw on 23 July 1942. The platform could unload 20 wagons at a time. The first commandant, Irmfried Eberl, a veteran of the T4 euthanasia programme, accepted more transports than he could manage and the initial unloading process was chaotic. Thousands were kept in freight wagons for so long that the SS resorted to mass shootings. Dozens of Jews managed to escape, while many died of suffocation. The bodies were not always cleared away before further transports arrived.

From late 1942, the victims' first sight of Treblinka was a wooden barracks later painted to look like a railway station, with timetables and a clock. The station platform was intended to make victims believe they were arriving in a transit camp before being moved on to labour camps. From the ramp, victims were led into a barracks where men and women were separated. Their heads were then shaved. Those who were too weak to walk were taken to an 'infirmary', behind which they were shot in a large pit. The barracks opened into a barbed wire corridor that led to the gas chamber. The bodies were initially buried then cremated in mass graves. The process took 2–3 hours.

In April 1943, transports slowed. On 2 August 1943, the Sonderkommando initiated an uprising in the camp but failed to destroy the gas chambers but cut the telephone lines. About 300 of the 800 prisoners held in the camp managed to escape during the uprising, of whom 70 survived the war. After the last transport arrived from Białystok in August 1943, the camp was demolished and landscaped.

Immediately after the liberation, Treblinka was a scene of frenzied excavation as the local peasantry, convinced that Jews were richer than them, arrived with shovels and dug up the remains of the murdered in search of hidden treasure or at least a gold tooth. Some of the earliest photographs of the site show freshly dug holes with human bones scattered around.

The site became a memorial in 1964.

What to see The site at Treblinka is over 2km long. The main area which was once the extermination camp, Treblinka II, is a short walk from the car park. The labour camp, Treblinka I, is at the other end of the forest complex. It is possible to drive there, where there is a second car park. There is no need to book in advance, as access is 24 hours and free.

The **Treblinka Museum** (Muzeum Treblinka; Kosów Lacki; w muzeumtreblinka. eu; information centre ⏰ 09.00–18.30 daily; free) is next to the main car park. It is a simple, old-fashioned museum that can be skipped if time is short. There are plans to build a new museum at Treblinka but at time of writing work had not begun. The path from the car park takes you past the site of the SS camp, just before you arrive at the start of the clearing. In the forest to the left once stood the commandant's office, barracks, a doctor's surgery, the kitchen and the guard's zoo, which contained forest animals and peacocks.

The railway line is marked by stone slabs that lead to the ramp.

Nothing remains of the camp, which is now covered by 17,000 stones, 216 of which are marked with the names of communities destroyed by the mass murder in Treblinka. They stand on the site of the mass graves and buried ashes. The path continues behind the main monuments and curves back to the car park and visitors' centre.

A memorial on the road from Małkinia Górna at the village of Treblinka has raised concerns among Holocaust historians about how far Poland's former far-right government went in distorting history. Unveiled in November 2021 at the site of the former Treblinka train station, the memorial has a monument to a 21-year-old Polish railway worker named Jan Maletka, who was shot and killed at the station in August 1942 for trying to give water to Jewish people trapped in cramped wagons and dying of thirst. Many historians say the memorial paints a misleading, or even false, picture of the past and that Maletka's story is based on

In the summer of 1938, David Kurtz, a New Yorker visiting his hometown of Nasielsk 53km north of Warsaw, filmed the people who lived there. The footage sat in a closet in Palm Beach in Florida until it was found by Kurtz's grandson Glenn in 2009 – and just in time, as the film was about to be lost to the menace known as 'vinegar syndrome'. It was rescued by the United States Holocaust Memorial Museum.

In 2014, Glenn Kurtz wrote a book about his grandfather's experience, *Three Minutes in Poland* (FSG Adult). An hour-long documentary made out of the footage, *Three Minutes: A Lengthening* (2022), recreates the story behind the people in the film, nearly all of whom were murdered in Treblinka. Shot in colour, the film has a vivid immediacy that brings a lost world to life.

one single account. Gangs sold water for gold, money and jewellery. According to Jan Grabowski, an academic at the University of Ottawa who specialises in Polish–Jewish relations, there is no historical evidence to back up the memorial. Nevertheless, it is worth stopping here to appreciate the sheer number of trains that were backed up waiting to enter Treblinka II. In his documentary *Shoah* (1985), Claude Lanzmann interviewed the villagers who remembered how the shocking scenes became part of everyday life.

Jedwabne A grey, nondescript small town, 163km north of Warsaw, Jedwabne was until 2000 as obscure as it looks. It is surrounded by fields of corn and the road that leads to it from Lomza runs through small villages where the houses sit in a line along the road. The Polish historian Jan T Gross shot the town into the headlines, however, when he wrote *Neighbours: The Destruction of the Jewish Community in Jedwabne, Poland* (Arrow, 2003), an account of what happened here on a warm summer's day in July 1941 when 1,600 Jews were burned alive in a barn on the edge of the town, where today scruffy fields begin beneath the pylons. There is a small memorial that marks the contours of the barn which was shockingly small.

The people of Jedwabne then moved into the homes of the Jews they had murdered, ate off their dinner plates and slept in their beds. Even those neighbours who were not complicit in murder took advantage and helped themselves to their share of what the Jews had left behind. What made, and continues to make, Gross's revelations about the events that followed in Jedwabne so toxic is that, for decades, the locals claimed that the Germans carried out the massacre and a stone monument stated so for all to see.

Gross's book challenged the national myth of the Polish experience in the war of heroic martyrdom. When then-president Aleksander Kwaśniewski went to Jedwabne in 2001 on the 60th anniversary of the massacre to unveil a new monument and to apologise to the Jewish people, many of the town's residents stayed at home. It is easy to say Polish society was evil and rotten to the core, and many a Jew will tell you this, but, although antisemitism was rife and institutionalised in Poland in the 1930s, nothing like Jedwabne had happened before the Germans arrived.

In August 1939, when Hitler and Stalin divided Poland, Jedwabne was assigned to the Russians. Across those parts of Poland occupied by the Soviets, it was widely believed that Jews collaborated with the Red Army at the expense of the Poles. It was a sentiment that played into Nazi hands once the Germans invaded Soviet territory in June 1941 and Jedwabne fell under German control. The town's population had been subjected to a campaign of Sovietisation, and so all but the Jews welcomed the German soldiers.

Stutthof Stutthof, located 40km northwest of the port of Elblag, was established as a prison for Poles in September 1939, and later expanded into a concentration camp in 1942. In 1944, some 50,000 Jews from Estonia, Latvia and Lithuania passed through here as the Red Army advanced westwards. Hungarian, Czech and Greek Jews were also brought to the camp from Auschwitz. But the camp could not cope with the numbers, and thousands died of disease or were gassed. In addition, about 25,000 prisoners lost their lives on a series of death marches and evacuations by sea before the camp was liberated by the Red Army on 9 May 1945.

What to see The **Stutthof Museum in Sztutów** (Muzeum Stutthof w Sztutowie; Muzealna 6; w stutthof.org; ⊕ 08.00–18.00 daily, closes 15.00 in winter; free) opened in 1961. Much of the former camp is now forested over, but a significant section remains. It takes about 2 hours to see the terrain and the exhibitions.

At the entrance visitors pass the commandant's villa and the guard-doghouse (the purebred German Shepherds housed here weighed more than some of the starving inmates they were trained to guard). The visitor's centre is in the former SS guardhouse. Be sure to buy tickets to see the documentary film (PLN5), which is shown in the former administrative building. The political department building houses a collection of thousands of confiscated shoes. Next door is an exhibition dedicated to the Polish priests who were among the first rounded up and executed following the Nazi takeover of nearby Danzig, now Gdansk.

Visitors then pass through the main gate which is surrounded by a fence and watchtowers. There are varying exhibitions in the huts that detail the history of the camp. In the women's barracks there are moving personal items on display including children's drawings. The Star of David memorial by the crematorium remembers the 28,000 Jews who passed through the camp; exhibitions here detail Stutthof's role as an extermination camp and the death marches. There is a small brick gas chamber; and an original gallows stands outside, as well as freight wagons, which in Stutthof were converted into mobile gas chambers.

The circuit leads past the *Monument to Fight and Freedom*, which was designed by Wiktor Tolkin and unveiled in 1968. Much of Stutthof was razed to the ground as the Nazis sought to hide traces of their crimes, and as such the area known as

POLISH CINEMA AND THE HOLOCAUST

Polish filmmakers have gone a long way to tackle some of the taboos of the Holocaust. *Aftermath* (2012) fictionalises the story of what happened to those who tried to help the Jews of Jedwabne, who were shunned by local townspeople. In a contemporary setting, two brothers are threatened by fellow villagers when they try to find out what happened to the Jewish community who were once their neighbours. The film tackles issues of indifference and complicity depicting antisemitism in modern-day Poland.

Other films that have tackled difficult issues are: *Ida* (2013) set in 1962, which tells the story of an orphan raised by nuns who finds out she is Jewish; *Wesele 2* (*The Wedding Day*; 2021), a story of a modern wedding haunted by one that took place in World War II; and *W Ukryciu* (*In Hiding*; 2013), a tense thriller about a Jewish woman hidden by a Polish family.

'new camp' now has 21 concrete blocks placed in the area where the barracks once stood. In the forest to the north of the perimeter, prior to the construction of the gas chamber, thousands of Jews were shot and their bodies burned on pyres. A ring of symbolic stones marks the edge of the pit.

Białystok   On the eve of World War II, about 60,000 Jews, 43% of the population, lived in the textile manufacturing city of Białystok, 198km northeast of Warsaw. From 1939 until the German invasion of the Soviet Union, the city was in Soviet-occupied Poland and its Jewish population grew rapidly as Jews sought refuge in the Soviet sector.

When the Germans arrived in June 1941, in an orgy of killing more than 2,000 Jews were murdered or burned alive in and around the **Great Synagogue** at ulica Suraska 2. The memorial, erected in 1996, is in the shape of the synagogue's dome as if twisted by the fire. Two weeks later, 3,000–4,000 Jews were shot in the **Pietrasze Forest**. A memorial marked on maps stands on the execution site.

Key to an exploration of the city's Holocaust history and tracing roots is **Miejsce – The Meeting Place** (Malmeda 6; w jewishbialystok.pl; ⊕ 16.00–19.00 Mon–Fri; donation requested), which is run by the Association of the Museum of Białystok Jews. The street on which it is located takes its name from Yitzhak Malmed, who threw acid in the face of a German soldier. Malmed was hanged in front of the Judenrat office, at Malmed 10, where there is a plaque. In retaliation, 100 Jews, including Malmed's wife and child, were shot, mainly in the block where he lived at Kupieka 39.

The **Białystok Ghetto**, through which more than 50,000 Jews passed, was located in the northwest of the city. It stretched between present-day Lipowa, Przejazd, Poleska and Sienkiewicza streets. In February 1943, some 10,000 Jews were deported to Treblinka and 2,000 were murdered in the ghetto. There was a significant resistance movement in the ghetto, and in August 1943 an uprising took place – the second largest after the Warsaw Ghetto Uprising – which is marked by the **Ghetto Defenders Memorial** on Plac Tenenbauma (the square is named after the Zionist Mordechai Tenenbaum, one of its leaders). A few hundred Jews were able to escape to the vast Knyszyn Forest where they formed a partisan unit.

The remaining ghetto inmates were either killed in the fighting or taken from the Poleski station to Auschwitz, Majdanek or Treblinka. There is a memorial, but a new museum at the site, the **Sybir Memorial Museum** (Muzeum Pamięci Sybiru; Węglowa, 1; w sybir.bialystok.pl; ⊕ 09.30–17.00 Tue–Fri & Sun, 10.30–18.00 Sat; PLN25), remembers the Poles who were deported from Soviet-occupied Poland. It is an event that affected many Jews and played into the Judeo-Bolshevik myth, so it is worth a quick visit.

LUBLIN

Lublin, 170km southeast of Warsaw, is a small, unassuming place but there is something striking about its urban geography. Its unusual white neo-Gothic castle was built by the Russians when they controlled this part of Poland in the 19th century. It sits on the hill where the Polish kings once held court, but the buildings that normally huddle at the base of a castle are missing. Alongside the low rectangular castellated façade runs a dual carriageway, as straight as a die, and in front of the castle is a half-empty car park. Every day the city's commuters drive over the site of Lublin's 16th-century Great Synagogue.

GETTING AROUND Lublin can easily be explored on foot, but to visit the State Museum of Majdanek take bus 156 from Brama Krakowska.

The easiest way to explore the region around Lublin is by car. If you do not have your own transport, to visit the former Sobibór extermination camp, take the bus from Lublin to Włodawa. From there take a taxi to Sobibór, 18km away. Alternatively take a train to Chelm and then a taxi. To see the Bełżec Memorial Site take the bus (**w** bigbus.moj-bus.pl) from Lublin to Tomaszów Lubelski, then take a taxi.

The train from Lublin to Zamość passes through Izbica.

WHERE TO STAY AND EAT **Hotel Ilan** (Lubatowska 85; **w** hotelilan.pl; **K** on request; **€**) is in the former historic yeshiva building, which is the headquarters of the Jewish community. There are quite a few kitsch 'Jewish' restaurants in Lublin but **The Olive** (in Hotel Ilan; **K**; **€€**) serves Polish and Jewish dishes and kosher food on request.

HISTORY Before World War II, Lublin had a vibrant Jewish community, both religious and secular, Zionist and Bundist. The Jews were long-term residents of Lublin, having been allowed to settle below the castle outside the city walls in 1336. In 1939, some 43,000 Jews lived in the city among a population of 120,000. Only 300 survived the war. In March 1941, the Germans established a ghetto in Podzamcze, literally the area below the castle. It was the first ghetto to be liquidated as part of Operation Reinhard (page 264).

The first round-up took place during the night of 16–17 March 1942, and the Maharshal Synagogue was used as an assembly point. In the weeks that followed, 28,000 of the ghetto's 43,000 Jews were forcibly marched at night to the site of the former municipal slaughterhouse to await deportation. The Jews of Lublin were the first to be deported to the Bełżec extermination camp. The synagogue, built in 1567, was destroyed by the Nazis after the deportations in 1942.

After the ghetto's liquidation, Jews with work permits were transferred to a new ghetto in the suburb of Majdan Tatarski. The Poles who lived in the area were forcibly moved out. The 3,000 Jews without work permits, many of them children, were taken and shot in Krępiec Forest. It is believed that 30,000 corpses from Majdanek concentration camp were also burned in the forest in 1943. Evidence of what happened here, based on the accounts of Polish eyewitnesses, was collected by Soviet investigators after the liberation.

The new ghetto was liquidated on 9 November 1942. About 3,000 Jews were taken to Majdanek concentration camp, and several dozen to the labour camp on ulica Lipowa and to the prison at Lublin Castle. Approximately 260 people, including members of the Judenrat and the Jewish police, were shot on the spot.

Lublin was liberated by the Red Army in the summer of 1944. When the Soviets arrived in the city, they set up a left-wing provisional Polish government, the Polish Committee of National Liberation, which was to evolve into the Polish communist government. Lublin was also the headquarters of the Central Committee of Polish Jews, the only Jewish body that the communist government would deal with. It organised social care, helped survivors and lobbied the authorities.

WHAT TO SEE
The Old Jewish Quarter The car park and the curve of seemingly old houses that face Lublin Castle today were erected after the war on the area that was once Lublin's Jewish Quarter, which was destroyed in the war. It was also the location of the **ghetto**.

15

In 1942 Lublin became the base of Operation Reinhard (Aktion Reinhardt in German), the code name for the mass murder of Polish Jews living in the General Government area, which was the largest mass murder in history. Three extermination camps were set up, at Bełżec, Sobibór and Treblinka. The SS ran the operation from the city west of the Old Town. The university's law faculty on Spokojna 1 was where the deaths of 2 million Jews were orchestrated.

In charge of the operation was the Austrian Odilo Globocnik, who had his headquarters at Wieniawska 6/8. A native of Trieste then in the Austro-Hungarian Empire, Globocnik returned to the city in 1943 after Italy's capitulation. He then organised the deportation of the region's Jews. Globocnik committed suicide in 1945 after he was captured by Allied troops.

Its boundaries are marked by murals and 43 memorial tiles, which remember the 43,000 Jews who were imprisoned here. The memorial was organised by the NN Theatre (w teatrnn.pl/pamiec/en/the boundaries-of-the-podzamcze-ghetto).

On the southernside of al. Tysiąclecia opposite the bus station, a **memorial flagstone** marks the site of the Maharshal Synagogue. The flagstone is the first of 21 that lead to a memorial on ulica Zimna, east of the centre, the **Lublin Umschlagplatz** (Umschlagplatz w Lublinie; ⊕ 24hrs daily; free), where Lublin's Jews were gathered prior to deportation. The tiles are marked with random Hebrew letters, symbolising Lublin's lost Jewish culture. The 22nd and final letter of the Hebrew alphabet is cut into the roof of the memorial. This project was also organised by the NN Theatre, who used the testimonies of survivors and Polish eyewitnesses to recreate the route (w teatrnn.pl/pamiec/en/the-ghetto-in-podzamcze).

To the right of the stairs leading up to the castle, a plaque shows a map of the **former Jewish area**. The original well that was once on ulica Szeroka still stands, in the bus depot.

The **house of the famous Seer of Lublin**, Yakov Icchak Horowic – one of the spiritual leaders of the Hasidic movement – once stood at ulica Zamkowy 10. Horowic is buried in the **Old Jewish Cemetery** at ulica Kalinowszczyzna 5–7, a short walk to the east of the castle, which is in itself a moving memorial to the Jews of Lublin. Another plaque at the junction of aleja Tysiąclecia and aleja Unii Lubelskiej marks the place where the Yiddish poet **Jakub Glatsztejn** was born. He emigrated to the USA in 1921, but his work was dedicated to the memory of Jewish Lublin.

To the north of the castle, the only remnant of pre-war Jewish life in Lublin is at the former yeshiva, **Yeshiva Chachmei Lublin** (Lubartowska 85), founded by Rabbi Meir Shapiro in 1930 and renowned for its teachers and its important library. In 1939, the Germans turned the school into a hospital, and after the war the building became the Medical Academy. The yeshiva is now used as a hotel and is the headquarters of the Jewish community. In the rooms adjacent to the synagogue, you can see a permanent exhibition (w hotelilan.pl; ⊕ times vary; free) documenting its history. The former Jewish hospital is at No. 83.

The writer **Anna Langfus** was born at Lunartowski 24. After the war she settled in France. Langfus's novels deal with her wartime experiences, suffering and loss in Poland. Her *Les Bagages de Sable* (*Sandbags*; Gallimard, 1962) won the Prix Goncourt in 1962.

The Old Town Above the car park in front of Lublin Castle is the pretty beige-coloured **Grodzka Gate**, which dates from 1342 and leads to the Old Town. The gate is now home to the **NN Theatre Centre** (see below).

The **Lamp of Memory** at ulica Podwale 15 near the Grodzka Gate was lit in 2004 in the only surviving pre-war street lamp. The glowing lamp remembers Lublin's Jews and, like the eternal light hanging above the ark of every synagogue, it is never turned off. Further along at ulica Grodzka 11 is the **former Jewish orphanage**. Many parents had sent their children there in the hope they would be safe, but on 24 March 1942 more than 100 children and three of the staff were taken to a former sand mine where they were shot and buried in a mass grave. In 1948 they were reburied in the Jewish cemetery on ulica Waleczne, where a monument was erected in 1987.

Turn right on ulica Ku Farze. The building at **ulica Noworybna 3** was the most important address for Jewish survivors in the months after the liberation – it was

THE GRODZKA GATE – NN THEATRE CENTRE

The driving force behind memorialisation of the Holocaust in Lublin is the **Grodzka Gate – NN Theatre Centre** (Ośrodek Brama Grodzka – Teatr NN; ul. Grodzka 21; w teatrnn.pl; ⏱ 09.30–16.30 Mon–Fri; PLN18), a museum, educational centre and cultural institute. The museum has a permanent exhibition on the history of Jewish Lublin and holds temporary exhibits and theatre shows.

In 1990, the then derelict Grodzka Gate was taken over by a group of young actors who set about restoring it and learning about its history. Also known as the Jewish Gate, the Grodzka Gate connected the Christian area, now Lublin's attractive Old Town, to the Jewish sector that sat below the castle. It was the meeting place of Christian and Jewish Lublin, and the organisers of the NN looked upon the concept positively, seeing not a door that could be shut but a portal for understanding. Funded by the local authorities in Lublin since 1994, the NN project has taken on the enormous challenge of bringing alive the memory of Jewish Lublin which, under communism, slipped into the black hole of forgotten memories.

It is not easy to evoke a place that no longer exists and that no-one remembers. Undaunted, the young people of the NN began to research the stories of those who had once lived in the city. Those stories have been collected in files, which run along the walls of the museum. There are 43,000 thin brown files on the higher shelf, and on the lower shelves white files dedicated to each of the buildings. In between the files runs a strip of photographs, 2,700 of them, which were developed from glass negatives found in the attic of one of the city's former tenements when it was being restored. The team believe that they were taken by a single photographer who worked in the city between 1914 and 1939. The NN is more than an archive, it is also an imaginative educational centre. The Letters to the Ghetto project, held for the first time in 2001, is typical of their work. Schoolchildren are invited to send letters to randomly chosen addresses in the Jewish Quarter that have disappeared and to recipients who are long dead. The letters are returned marked 'recipient unknown' or 'no such address'.

The NN Theatre's website is an invaluable source of information for visitors interested in the Jewish history of the city and details the numerous projects, guided walks and events they organise.

Besides offering food and shelter, the most important task in hand for the Central Committee of Polish Jews after the liberation was to make a list of survivors. The earliest existing Holocaust testament was written at ulica Noworybna 3 on 29 July 1944.

The Central Committee set up a Historical Committee, which created a methodology and questionnaire for testimonies and began to train survivors, who were paid by the committee, to record them. Early in 1945, this committee also moved to Łódź and then to Warsaw, where it became the Jewish Historical Institute (page 256). There was no paper, so they wrote on the back of German documents, even on the back of a board game.

These testimonies were important because the survivors were looking for justice and wanted to provide material for possible trials. Local groups in the liberated areas also sent names to the committee in Lublin, which compiled a list of 2,393 names, which was printed as a 15-page booklet by the World Jewish Congress. This would later be expanded into the 58,000-name *Register of Jewish Survivors II*, which was published in Jerusalem in August 1945.

The new Polish authorities after the liberation permitted Yiddish broadcasts on the radio. They were the first of their type in Poland and their main purpose was to help survivors find their loved ones. The broadcasts were made from Lublin railway station at 21.00 every evening until early 1945, when it moved to Łódź and then on to Warsaw until the programmes were stopped in 1949 by the communist authorities.

headquarters of the Central Committee of Polish Jews (see above), which was to evolve into the Polish communist government. It was here that Jewish life began briefly to revive in Lublin. In 1944, Lublin became a meeting point for the Jews who had been liberated. The partisan leader **Abba Kovner** arrived from Vilnius in December 1944 and stayed at ulica Noworybna 3. Kovner was nurturing two ideas: one, that he must find an escape route out of Europe; the other, that he would not leave until he had taken revenge on the Germans for what they had done to the Jews.

The **Monument to the Victims of the Ghetto** (Pomnik Ofiar Getta Lubelskiego), unveiled in 1962, was moved from its original location between ulica Lubartowska and ulica Świętoduska because of construction works and now stands west of the Old Town at ulica Radziwiłłowska 4.

Outside the centre In the suburb of Bronowice in the west of the city on ulica Leszczyńskiego, there is a **memorial** to Jews murdered in November 1942 during the liquidation of the ghetto in the suburb of Majdan Tatarski.

There is a second memorial at the former **Flugplatz labour camp** at ulica Wrońska 2. Between 1942 and 1943, Jews from across Nazi-occupied Europe were brought here to work as forced labourers at the Emil Plage and Teofil Laśkiewicz factory. Established in 1921, it had produced the first aeroplanes in Poland.

On a service road parallel to the S17, the road to Zamość, 14km southeast of Lublin, is a memorial, the **Pomnik pamięci pomordowanych w Lesie Krępieckim**, to the 3,000 Jews without work permits, many of them children, who were murdered at **Krępiec Forest** in April 1942.

Majdanek Museum and Memorial Site (Muzeum I Miejzsce Pmięci w Majdanek; ul. Droga Męczenników Majdanka 67; w majdanek.eu; ⏰ 09.00–18.00 daily (Nov–Mar until 16.00); free) One of the most important concentration and extermination camps in Poland was in the modern southern suburbs of Lublin. The Majdanek concentration camp is now a museum and memorial site. Of the 150,000 people held prisoner here, 80,000 died. When the camp was liberated in August 1944, it dominated the headlines in Soviet papers. When the Soviet secret police arrived in Lublin, they immediately saw the potential of the camp and incarcerated the members of the Polish Home Army they had captured here, but they left the remains of the crematoria and the gas chamber untouched. Within days it was a ghoulish attraction for local sightseers. There are pictures of parents with small children staring at heaps of ashes and old men peering into ovens.

As early as 12 September 1944, the Polish-Soviet Commission for Investigating the German Crimes Committed at Majdanek turned the camp into a museum. The driving force behind the project came from the former Polish political and Soviet prisoners held here, as no Jews remained in Majdanek by the summer of 1944. The museum began functioning in early November and was the first in the world to commemorate the atrocities of World War II.

Today, few people visit Majdanek. You are likely to find yourself alone staring at the walls of the gas chambers stained a discoloured blue by the Zyklon B gas and at the 280,000 pairs of shoes brought form the nearby extermination camps of Bełżec and Sobibór. Watchtowers and barbed wire fences line the walkway to the huge concrete dome erected here in 1967 which covers a mountain of ashes. Scraps of bone are clearly visible. One of the first visitors here was the partisan leader, Abba Kovner. It is easy to see how it must have confirmed his fears about the extent of the Holocaust and reinforced his belief that the future of the Jews lay elsewhere.

FURTHER AFIELD

Sobibór The wild untamed Bug River slips into marshy woodland and forms a natural border between Poland and Belarus. Today this is a real political frontier where the EU comes to an end. Across the water, Belarus is in a world of its own, yet until the end of World War II much of it was part of the Polish heartland and there was no border here at all. An empty road winds through russet-trunked pines and sandy groves to the small village of Żłobek Duży, 96km east of Lublin, clustered around a lonely little siding. The station was built after the war, but the tracks that cut through the forest are original and come to an abrupt end at the site of the deadly Sobibór extermination camp.

History The camp at Sobibór opened in March 1942, but killings began in earnest in May. It was a surreal, systemised world where people were quickly herded from the cattle trucks, stripped naked, their heads shaved, and funnelled into the gas chambers which were pumped full of carbon monoxide. In their *Black Book of Soviet Jewry* (Transaction, 2003), journalists Ilya Ehrenburg and Vasily Grossman record the story of a German guard at Sobibór, a boxer from Berlin, who could slay a man with one hand, but patted the naked children on the head as they walked into the gas chamber and even gave them sweets.

The camp was surrounded by both a minefield and flocks of geese. Branches were woven into the perimeter fence and the geese would be stirred up to create a cacophony while the slaughter was carried out, in the belief these would hide the reality from the local population. They failed, and the Jewish underground soon had word of what was happening. By July, 100,000 Jews, mainly from the Lublin region, had lost their lives in this hellhole. Some of the 34,313 Dutch Jews brought in 19 trains also died here.

In all it is thought 170,000 people were murdered at Sobibór, until a Jewish rebellion prompted the camp's closure in the autumn of 1943. The gas chambers were quickly demolished by the Germans and covered by an asphalt road; trees were planted to disguise the site. When the Red Army arrived in this part of Poland, there was nothing to see and no reason to make a diversion into the lonely forests where few people lived.

In the post-war population exchange, which began in the months that followed and in which Ukrainians were sent east and Poles moved west, Ukrainians were housed in the former guards' barracks which were demolished in 1947. Until the 1960s the site was abandoned and forgotten.

What to see The Sobibór death camp is now the **Sobibór Museum and Memorial Site** (Muzeum i Miejsce Pmięci w Sobiborze; w sobibor-memorial.eu; ⊕ Apr–Oct 09.00–17.00, Nov–Mar 09.00–16.00; free) which has a new visitors centre. The central part of the exhibition space is a long showcase containing 700 objects discovered during archaeological excavations which have been going on since 2000. These objects include personal items belonging to the victims.

At the time of writing, the area where the murders took place was closed for the construction of a new memorial wall, which will run along the path to the gas chamber.

Izbica The small town of Izbica, 83km south of Sobibór, was unique in Poland as until World War I it was entirely Jewish. From 1940, Jews were resettled here from parts of western Poland that had been incorporated into the Reich and from March 1942 the town was used a transit camp for 24,000 Jews, among them 10,000 Bohemian, Slovakian, Austrian and German Jews, prior to their transportation to the Majdanek, Sobibór and Bełżec extermination camps. Many Jews died here from starvation and disease. On 2 November 1942, the camp was liquidated, and the remaining 2,000 Jews were shot in the Jewish cemetery, where there are several memorials. A path leads up the hill to the cemetery from a yard on the corner of Fabryczna.

Zamość When Poles talk about the Holocaust, especially those who are keen to record it and remember the Polish Jewish culture that thrived in their country for generations, they invariably talk about what they have lost. Zamość, 20km south of Izbica, shines a bright light on this part of Polish history.

Zamość was designed in 1580 by Italian architect Bernardo Morando for the nobleman Jan Zamoyski as the ideal Renaissance town – it would feel at home on the plains of Lombardy. It was his private fiefdom and sat on the important trading route between the Baltic and the Black seas; it had a cosmopolitan population including Armenians, Germans, Greeks, Italians, Jews and Scots. Records in the town hall show that officials were busy learning Hebrew in the 17th century, as it was important for trade. The radical socialist Rosa Luxemburg was born here in 1871.

In 1939, 45% of the people of Zamość were Jewish. Nazi occupation policy in the region, above and beyond ghettoising and then murdering 12,000 of Zamość's Jewish citizens, was to drive the Poles off their rich fertile fields and give them to German settlers. A few hundred Jews from Zamość survived the war in the Soviet Union and 50 in the city itself. Today, the town's beautiful Renaissance synagogue has been carefully restored but it is used as a visitors' centre as there is no *minyan*, the required ten men for worship.

An hour-and-a-half's drive westwards from Lublin through Tarnagrod takes you to the small town of Nisko on the San River. After the German invasion of Poland in September 1939, Adolf Eichmann devised a new plan to forcibly relocate Jews from the Reich and Poland to a reservation in a swampy area just outside Nisko. The plan drew on the Indian reservations in the USA as a model.

The first transport of 901 Jews left from the Protectorate of Bohemia and Moravia, now the Czech Republic, on 18 October. Approximately 95,000 Jews in all were sent to Nisko, many of whom died of hunger and disease. The project was not a secret and was reported in the world press. The plan was eventually abandoned in April 1940, when a policy of ghettoisation was adopted to gather Jews in one place before eventual resettlement. There are no traces of the former reservation.

Bełżec From Zamość, the main road to Ukraine leads south to Tomaszow Lubelski. In the suburbs on the 17/E72 just north of the Ukrainian border is the site of the Bełżec extermination camp, the first of the Aktion Reinhardt camps and a template for those to come. Without a bevy of survivors, the site of the former camp has found it hard to find a future and it receives few visitors. As a result, it does not figure in popular culture and, like many aspects of the Holocaust, is a forgotten story. Although Bełżec, like Sobibór, is nowadays relatively little known, knowledge of their existence was brought out of Poland by the underground agent Jan Karski (page 254) and the Allies were aware of both camps.

History The camp was built on the main road to Lviv, which was then in Poland, and located deliberately just next to the mainline between Lviv and Lublin. Local trains still pass this way. When experimental gassing was carried out here in February 1942, the victims had little idea of what awaited them. But as the weeks passed by, Jews arrived knowing their fate and the unloading and processing of new arrivals to the camp became increasingly frantic. There was often violence as they fought for their lives. By December 1942, 500,000 people had been consumed by the killing machine. It is thought that fewer than ten people escaped from Bełżec. Only two gave any testimony of what had happened there. One of them was murdered after the war and the other made it to the safety of Canada.

Just the size of a few football pitches, Bełżec must have been such a hive of intense activity that no-one passing by could have failed to notice. Although the Germans had at first made no attempt to hide the camp, at the end of 1943 it was decided that all evidence of its existence would be eradicated, and they replaced the camp with a new country house with landscaped gardens. Bełżec remained like this until the 1960s, when a small memorial was erected in what was by then a rundown park.

What to see In 2004, Bełżec edged back into the national consciousness when a striking memorial was built at the **Bełżec Museum and Memorial Site** (Muzeum i Miejsce Pmięci w Bełżcu; Ofiar Obozu Zagłady 4; w belzec.eu; ⊕ 09.00–17.00 Tue–Sun; free). The site rises up a small hill and is covered in twisted wire and industrial slag. A straight path cuts through the middle, tracing the original path to the gas chambers. It proved to be a design flaw as it was too easy for the victims to see where they were being taken; for this reason, at Sobibór the path twists in order to conceal the destination. The tracks at the left of the entrance gate are not from Bełżec but Treblinka. To the right of the entrance there is a fascinating exhibition. Note the concrete disks found in the excavations – one theory is that they were given to victims in return for valuables, playing into the illusion that they were being taken to a bathhouse. As in so many camp museums, there are crushed Nivea cream tins. The museum also has an excellent website with a series of online exhibitions.

ŁÓDŹ

Once a thriving industrial city known as 'the Manchester of Poland', modern-day Łódź has more in common with Detroit in the USA. It is a post-industrial, ugly yet edgy city, but an important place to visit if you are interested in Poland's Jewish history.

In the late 19th century Łódź and the surrounding area underwent rapid industrialisation and became the textile hub of the Russian Empire, which then controlled this part of Poland. Jews owned over half the businesses in the city, and many of them were manufacturing tycoons and lived in lavish palaces. Jews were well represented in the professions and local businesses but many lived in squalor in the tenements of Bałuty, which was almost 99% Jewish.

In 1939, a third of the city's 670,000 inhabitants were Jews, making Łódź Poland's second largest Jewish community. Today only a few hundred Jews still live in Łódź. The heart of the community is at ulica Pomoska 18, where there is a small functioning synagogue.

GETTING AROUND You can walk from the Manufaktura centre to the Bałuty area of the former ghetto. To visit the Radegast station memorial and the Jewish cemetery, you will need to take bus Z6 from the Zachodnia-Manufaktura stop. The two sites are 15 minutes' walk apart. Taxis in Łódź are relatively cheap.

If you do not have your own transport, to visit the site of the Chełmno extermination camp take the train to Kolo and then a taxi, a journey of about 15 minutes. It is worth asking the taxi to wait to take you on to nearby Rzuchowski Forest. It is still cheaper than taking a tourist guided tour.

The direct train from Łódź to Częstochowa passes through Piotrków Trybunalski. There are trains from Częstochowa to Kielce.

WHERE TO STAY AND EAT With plenty of restaurants and shops, the Manufaktura shopping centre – once a vast Jewish-owned textile factory – is the best base. The **Vienna House** (Ogrodowa 17; w wyndhamhotels.com; €), within the complex, is a modern hotel with a swimming pool. There is also an excellent **PURO hotel** (Ogrodowa 16; w purohotel.pl; €) with a pan-Asian restaurant. From here, it's a short walk to the city's main street, Piotrkowska, where there are restaurants and bars especially in the courtyard at No. 138/140 (w piotrkowskacenter.pl/en). Alternatively, **Linat Orchim** (ul. Pomoska 18; w linatorchim.pl/en; €) at the Jewish community centre offers inexpensive accommodation and has the city's only kosher restaurant, **Café Tuwin** (K; €).

HISTORY When the Germans invaded Poland in September 1939, Łódź was incorporated into the Third Reich in the administrative district of Wartheland, which had its capital in Poznań. Łódź was renamed Litzmannstadt. Wartheland had been annexed by Prussia in the Polish partition of the late 18th century and given to Poland after World War I. As a consequence, it had a local population of Volksdeutsche. The Nazis originally planned to ship the Jews out to the Baltic states and Aryanise the city, but this proved impossible as the Jewish population was too large.

After the invasion, 70,000 Jews were relocated, murdered or managed to flee to Soviet-occupied eastern Poland.

The Łódź Ghetto The 165,000 Jews who remained in the city after the German invasion were interned in a ghetto in the spring of 1940, part of which included the impoverished Bałuty neighbourhood. Jews were also brought in from surrounding towns and, from 1941, from Belgium, Germany and Luxembourg. More than 230,000 Jews would pass through the ghetto. Surrounded by barbed wire and covering a vast area of 4km^2, it was one of the largest in Poland.

Life in Litzmannstadt was a strange existence in parallel worlds. Tramline 41 continued to function as normal and ran through the ghetto so all could see it. Apart from this, the ghetto was completely cut off. It had its own money and postal service, but since the money was worthless outside the ghetto, it served to isolate the Jews further.

From 1942 onwards, Łódź Ghetto was effectively a forced labour camp, furnishing the Reich with elegant clothes, shoes and uniforms. Life inside was a daily routine of hunger, starvation, sickness and suicide. To make room for the arrival of new workers, children, the elderly and sick were deported to the Chełmno extermination camp. The ghetto had a controversial Jewish leader, Chaim Rumkowski, who believed that, by co-operating with the Germans and working for them, lives would be spared. His appeal for parents to hand over their children in May 1942 was one of his most controversial moves.

Łódź Ghetto was one of the last to be liquidated and the remaining 70,000 Jews in the city were deported to Auschwitz. As the Łódź Ghetto was liquidated only in the summer of 1944, a significant number of Jews from Łódź and the surrounding area survived the war. Many of these testimonies can be watched on the US Shoah Foundation website (w sfi.usc.edu). One of Britain's most well-known Holocaust survivors, Arek Hersch, spent time in the Łódź Ghetto. He speaks regularly about his experiences and has given talks that are easily accessible on the internet, and he has written a memoir, *A Detail of History* (Apostrophe, 2015), which is available on Kindle.

Aftermath After the end of the war Łódź became a hub for Jewish survivors. For women it was extremely dangerous as many were raped by the Soviet troops. Surviving children were also gathered here before being taken illegally across the border into Czechoslovakia. Most of the survivors decided to make their way out of Poland.

WHAT TO SEE To get a feel for pre-war Łódź, start your visit at the **Łódź City Museum** (Muzeum Miasta Łodzi; Ogrodowa 15; w muzeum-lodz.pl; ⊕ 09.00–17.00 Tue–Thu, 11.00–19.00 Fri–Sun; PLN22) located in the former neo-Baroque-style palace of the textile magnate Izrael Poznański. The museum offers guided tours and thematic walks, and there is a small exhibition about Łódź-born Jan Karski (page 254), the courier for the Polish underground who brought news of the murder of the Jews to leaders in London and Washington. Behind the museum, Poznański's former factory is now the **Manufaktura** shopping centre. Similar grand houses and factories are located all over the city and along Piotrkowska, Poland's longest street at 4.2km, many of the factory and tenement buildings have been converted into bars and restaurants.

In 2023 during restoration work on Północna 23, the street that runs east from the Manufaktura complex and was just outside the ghetto limits, an exceptional treasure trove hidden during World War II was unearthed. It contained hundreds of Jewish-owned items, including Judaica and household utensils wrapped in newspapers, among them candlesticks, cups, cutlery, serving dishes and storage containers, clothing and sacred texts. The items are due to be put on display in the **Archaeology and Ethnography Museum** (Muzeum Archeologiczne i Etnograficzne w Łodzi; plac Wolności; **w** maie.lodz.pl; ⊕ 10.00–18.00 Tue–Sun; PLN12).

Łódź Ghetto area
Łódź Ghetto began just north of the Manufaktura complex and extended to the Jewish Cemetery in the east of the city. Today, it is rather a drab and depressing place. The ghetto area to the east and north was redeveloped under communism although the orphanage remains at Marysińska 100. Yet, unlike in the former Warsaw Ghetto, some of the original buildings do exist and have explanatory plaques attached which are also in English. To see all the sites of the ghetto, you need to follow the walking tour on **w** lodz-ghetto.com. The trail is roughly 10km long, so if you are looking for specific sites the tour is especially useful. A leaflet with a shorter tour is available at the Radegast Station memorial (page 273).

Around Bałucki Rynek The key highlights are around Bałucki Rynek, the main marketplace, where both the German and Jewish administrations were based. Food, raw materials and fuel were unloaded here, and the area could only be entered with a special pass. Still standing, **Łagiewnicka 25** housed several Jewish administrative offices. The **Gestapo HQ** was at Limanowskiego 1.

There were seven hospitals in the ghetto, from which the patients were deported in 1942. To the north of the market, **Łagiewnicka 34–35** was Hospital No. 1. Rumkowski had an apartment here until the deportations. It was then used as an assembly point. During the liquidation, the head of the ghetto, Hans Biebow, gathered a group of 600 Jews here and placed them on a special train destined for Stutthof. The prisoners were taken to work as slave labourers in Dresden. Biebow was hoping that his rescue of the 600 from the gas chambers of Auschwitz would save him if he was captured by Allied forces. He was eventually caught and hanged in 1947.

South of the market in front of the fire station at **Zachodnia 14**, Rumkowski gave his infamous speech on 4 September 1942, calling upon the ghetto inhabitants to give up their children to save everyone else.

Zgierska just to the west of Bałucki Rynek cut through the ghetto. The buildings on either side of the thoroughfare were part of the ghetto, but trams and cars were free to pass along it. Many of the original buildings remain, but not the three wooden footbridges which were erected in the summer of 1940 allowing the people in the ghetto to move from one section to the other. One of those bridges next to the red-brick **Church of the Assumption of the Blessed Virgin Mary** on Plac Kościelny, which was used as a warehouse for stolen Jewish property, can be seen on many photographs from the time. In 1942, the clothes of the people murdered at Chełmno extermination camp were brought here – the forced labourers tasked with sorting the clothes began to realise that mass murder was taking place. The *Ghetto Chronicles* which recorded life in the ghetto from January 1941 to July 1944 were written by Jewish journalists and intellectuals at **Zgierska 4**.

Park Ocalałych The **Survivors Park** (Park Ocalałych) in the eastern section of the former ghetto has a monument to those who survived and 594 trees planted by survivors, as well as memorials to Jan Karski (page 254) and to Poles who helped save Jews. From the Mound of Memory, an artificial 8m hill, there is a view across the city. The park is also home to the **Marek Edelman Dialogue Center** (w centrumdialogu.com; ⊕ 11.00–18.00 Mon–Fri, noon–16.00 Sat–Sun; free), founded in 2010, which promotes the multi-cultural and multi-ethnic heritage of Łódź and hosts temporary exhibitions.

More than 5,000 Roma and Sinti, among them 2,689 children, were brought to Łódź from Burgenland in Austria in late autumn 1941. They were held in the nearby **Zigeunerlager** on Wojska Polskiego 84 at the junction with Głowackiego, a short walk from the park. The site is marked by a plaque and there is a small exhibition. The conditions in the camp were terrible: there was no sanitation or kitchens, and typhus was rampant. In January 1942, the camp was liquidated and the people confined there murdered in the Chełmno extermination camp.

Jewish Cemetery The Jewish Cemetery (public entrance on ul. Zmienna; ⊕ 09.00–17.00 Sun–Fri), one of the largest in Europe, was in the eastern limits of the ghetto. The industrialist Izrael Poznański is buried here, but the most moving part of the cemetery, known as the **Ghetto Field**, is in the southern part of the complex. An estimated 45,000 Jews, who died in the ghetto, are buried here. The 700 Roma and Sinti who died in the ghetto are buried in section PV and PV1.

From 1942, a camp for Polish children was at **ulica Bracka 23**, a 15-minute walk to the west of the cemetery gates. They were mostly orphans of political prisoners or those who had been trying to survive trading on the black market. The site became a park in the 1970s and a memorial in the shape of a broken heart was erected in 1977.

Radegast Station (al. Pamięci Ofiar; ⊕ 11.00–18.00 Sun–Tue, 10.00–16.00 Wed–Thu & Sat; PLN10) From the Jewish Cemetery, it's a 15-minute walk to the Radegast railway station, one of the most moving and significant memorials in Łódź. From here deportations were carried out first to the Chełmno extermination camp and then in the summer of 1944 to Auschwitz. The tunnel that leads to the station is lined by original deportation lists. These lists are of people deported to Chełmno; there were no lists of those deported to Auschwitz. The station was built in 1937 and before the deportations began was used to bring raw materials into the ghetto and to ship out goods that had been made in its factories. Transports of Jews, Roma and Sinti from other parts of occupied Europe also arrived here. There is a large model of the ghetto in the exhibition. This is the place to ask for help if you are looking for somewhere specific.

Three original cattle cars stand on the tracks by the platform with their doors open, so that visitors can see what it was like inside. The outdoor exhibition tells the story of the Łódź Ghetto. There are also plaques commemorating the Jews of Vienna and Luxembourg, who were transported to the death camps after first passing through the ghetto. On the anniversary of the ghetto's liquidation in August, the memorial service at the Jewish Cemetery is followed by a commemorative march to the station.

FURTHER AFIELD

Chełmno The former Chełmno extermination camp, 77km northwest of Łódź, was the site of the first Nazi extermination camp on Polish soil and the first place where Jews were gassed. They choked to death as gas vans drove into the Rzuchów

Forest along the road from Dabie to Kolo. In terms of numbers who died, Chełmno was the fifth most deadly extermination camp. Yet it gets few visitors, well under 20,000 a year and most of whom are local schoolchildren. The noise of the traffic on the main Berlin–Warsaw highway that was originally built by forced labourers rises up from the valley below but is drowned out by the cows' mooing in the barn next to the empty car park.

It is well worth booking in advance a museum run tour in English in order to understand the importance of the monuments in the nearby Rzuchów Forest.

History The first transport from the Łodz Ghetto arrived in December 1941. In the months that followed, more than 200,000 Jews, Soviet prisoners of war and Roma were murdered here. Chełmno closed temporarily in March 1943 but was reactivated when the Łódź Ghetto was liquidated.

Chełmno is one of the most sinister of the Nazi extermination camps because it was here that the Nazi teams led by those who had gained experience in the T4 euthanasia programme in Germany experimented with ways to carry out mass murder and dispose of the bodies.

Operations at Chełmno were top secret and, when the locals passed by the death pits in the forest, they were ordered to look straight ahead, or they would be shot. Even the postman who brought letters to the camp had to stand with his back to it. Nevertheless, the stench of rotting bodies could be smelt for miles around, so the Nazis began to burn the corpses. In the Rzuchów Forest they built the first crematoria. When the Germans noticed that the grass grew greener where the ashes were scattered, the camp started a side-line business selling bonemeal to Polish farmers, who scattered it on their land thinking it was from an abattoir.

What to see The **Kulmhof Museum in Chełmno on Ner** (Muzeum Kulmhof w Chełmnie nad Nerem; Chełmno 59a; w chelmno-muzeum.eu; ⊕ 09.00–15.00 Tue–Sun; free) uses the German name for the village, Kulmhof, as the area around the camp was annexed by the Reich in 1940.

The tour starts at the ruins of the country house, where in the cellar Jews from the neighbouring towns were stripped of their possessions and then loaded into mobile gas vans. There is a moving exhibition in the granary and a new museum. The testimony of Simon Srebnik, one of two people to survive the camp, is shown in the museum. He was featured in Claude Lanzmann's epic film *Shoah* (1985). Lanzmann devoted a large part of the film to Chełmno, interviewing a former Nazi guard, who testified that the Jews were naked and beaten into the vans in the most brutal fashion; and a German settler who described the screams and yells she heard coming from the camp. Also revealing are his interviews with the villagers, who believed that all the Jews who were murdered in the camp were extremely wealthy.

The **Rzuchów Forest** is 15 minutes away. The first monument here was put up in the 1960s but as with other memorials during the communist period it did not mention that most of the victims were Jewish. During the changing political climate of the 1980s, archaeological research began at the site and memorials were erected. Visitors can see the remains of the experimental crematorium.

Piotrków-Trybunalski
Known as Petrikev in Yiddish, Piotrków-Trybunalski is 55km south of Łódź. This historic town was the seat of the Polish parliament between 1354 and 1567 and home of the Polish Crown Tribunal.

In the 19th century it developed as an industrial base due to its position on the Vienna–Warsaw railway line. Jews had lived in Piotrków since the early 16th century and in 1939 the community numbered about 15,000 people, 27% of the population. It was Jewish families who established the city's first factories and most of its shops. Piotrków was a centre for timber, textiles and glass manufacturing, and also a major hub of the Jewish printing industry, which produced a wide range of publications including Yiddish newspapers, and secular and rabbinic literature.

The city was badly affected by the 1930s economic depression, and towards the beginning of World War II antisemitic attacks became frequent. When the German Army arrived on 5 September 1939, persecution of the Jews began immediately. A month later a ghetto was established, the first in occupied Poland. Eventually, almost 25,000 people were confined to the ghetto, which was an open ghetto without walls. There is a memorial in the main market square in the Old Town. On 14 October 1942 the ghetto was surrounded by SS and Ukrainian militia and in the days that followed approximately 22,000 people were deported to the Treblinka extermination camp. Three labour camps were set up in Piotrków, one at the Bugai wood factory on ulica Sulejowska, another at the Kara factory and a third at the Hortensia glass factory in the north of the town at ulica 1 Maja 21, where some of the original buildings have survived.

The **Great Synagogue** at Jerozolimska 29 is now the public library. The current building dates from the mid 19th century. The Small Synagogue on the right dates from 1775. In November 1942, those Jews who had hidden in the ghetto and did not have work permits were rounded up and held in the synagogue for some days before they were shot in nearby Raków Forest. Their bodies were later exhumed and are buried in the Jewish cemetery on ulica Spacerowa, where there is a second mass grave of Jews shot by the Germans on 21 April 1943.

The BBC series *My Family, the Holocaust and Me* (2020) is partly set in Piotrków and forms the basis of a Holocaust education programme, drawn up by University College London, used in many British schools.

Częstochowa

Częstochowa, 137km west of Kielce, is famous for the monastery of Jasna Góra, home to the icon the Black Madonna, but until the German invasion the city also had a significant Jewish population.

The city museum, **Muzeum Częstochowskie** (ul. Katedralna 8; ⊕ 11.30–17.00 Tue–Sun; PLN9), has a permanent exhibition on the city's Jewish history. Jews played a major role in the development of its industrial base. In the 1930s Częstochowa was the site of the largest Zionist agricultural training school in Poland. The website w czestochowa.pl/jewish-tour has an extensive list of Jewish memorial sites in the city.

When the Germans arrived in Częstochowa in 1939, they immediately murdered the city's intelligentsia, both Jews and Poles. It was a move that left both the Polish and Jewish community leaderless. A memorial at ulica Olsztyńska 28 commemorates the victims.

The **Częstochowa Ghetto**, set up on 9 April 1941, was the fourth largest in Poland and held 40,000 Jews on the eve of its liquidation. There was a significant Jewish resistance movement, which fought back when the ghetto was liquidated in June 1943. The commander of the Jewish resistance, Mordekhai Zylberberg, and many of the ghetto fighters were killed, but a handful managed to escape and join the partisans. There is a commemorative plaque at Bohaterów Getta, 1–3 and a memorial in the Jewish cemetery on Złota, 42-202. One of Częstochowa's roundabouts is named after Leon Silberstein, one of the resistance leaders.

After the liquidation of the ghetto and deportation of 40,000 Jews to the Treblinka death camp, the Germans established a forced labour camp for the survivors in which more than 5,000 people were imprisoned. Until January 1945, the German metallurgical company HASAG (Hugo Schneider AG) ran four forced labour factories in Częstochowa.

Kielce Situated 134km east of Częstochowa, this is the place to get to grips with the impact of the Nazi occupation on Poland.

The former synagogue sits on a traffic island in the middle of a busy dual carriageway, Aleja IX Wieków. A few minutes' walk eastwards a memorial marks the location of the former ghetto. It is a menorah that is either sinking into or rising out of the ground depending on which way you look at the story of what happened here. The money to erect it was raised by local activist Bogdan Białek, who has worked relentlessly for 30 years to get Poles to face up to what happened in Poland immediately after the Holocaust.

BOGDAN BIAŁEK'S STORY

When Bogdan Białek, a psychologist from Białystok, moved to Kielce in 1978 he was surprised by the silence that surrounded the events of July 1946. When communism fell in 1989, locals in Kielce held a memorial for the victims of the pogrom, but for Białek it was not enough. A devout Catholic, he decided that he was going to single-handedly force the town to acknowledge its past.

In the decades that have followed, he has endured death threats and had a hand grenade thrown into his office, but has never given up. He claims his educational campaign has worked. Kielce, he says, is devoid of antisemitic graffiti, has a low incidence of racist crimes and local football fans do not engage in racist chants, as they do in the rest of the country. But there are still plenty of locals who do not support him and voice their dislike.

So what went wrong in Kielce, and Poland as a whole for that matter? Why could Jewish survivors see no future in the country where their families had lived for hundreds of years? Białek is quick to point out that all of Europe was antisemitic in the 1930s; but by telling the tale of how 60 pregnant Jewish women were stripped and brutally murdered by the Nazis in Kielce for all to see, he explains the depth of horror inflicted on Poles during the war. 'Violence became an everyday thing in Poland and was normalised. We can see in veterans returning from Afghanistan and Iraq how exposure to violence changes behaviour, and in Poland we see this on a mass scale. Those veterans meet with psychologists, but there was no psychologist for the Polish people.'

He also points out that most of Poland's elite was destroyed by the war and were among the first victims of the Nazis. 'In 1946 there were 20 million people in Poland but only about 300,000 had finished high school. Not only this, but there was a famine in Poland in 1946 and the country was overrun with a gangster culture.' As if he is the nation's psychologist he says, 'Poland was a country in moral and material ruin.' Before I leave, he adds that it was not just the communists but the Church who refused to help the Polish people confront their past. He has a zeal that is unnerving and is keen to show me his own Wailing Wall, where locals can atone for their sins and leave messages that he sends on to be placed in the real wall in Jerusalem.

Białek could not have chosen a more difficult spot to fight his cause as Kielce was the site of a bloody pogrom in July 1946 which prompted an exodus of survivors from Poland. Rumours that Jewish survivors had kidnapped a child to use its blood to make matzo prompted a huge, frenzied crowd to surround the offices of the American Jewish Joint Distribution Committee at ulica Planty 7. The office ran a hostel for survivors. The crowd attacked the building and in the riot 42 Jewish men, women and children were murdered and 80 seriously wounded. Among the victims were pregnant women with their stomachs ripped open. Although most of the violence took place at the building on ulica Planty, Jews were attacked all over the city and even on passing trains.

At the former building on ulica Planty, Białek set up a museum and educational centre, **The Jan Karski Society** (w jankarski.org.pl; ☉ 12.30–16.30 Mon–Fri; free), named after the Polish underground courier. There is a documentary film about his work: *Bogdan's Journey* (2016).

KRAKÓW

Kraków, in the south of Poland, is one of Europe's leading Jewish heritage destinations. The city offers visitors a fascinating introduction to the story of Poland's Jews as, in stark contrast to the capital Warsaw, Kraków emerged from World War II unscathed and is one of Poland's most beautiful cities.

The former Jewish district of Kazimierz is now one of its big attractions. The area takes its name from Kazimierz the Great, who ruled Poland from Kraków in the 14th century. While other nations were expelling their Jews, Kazimierz, a tolerant and progressive king, actively welcomed them and granted them special privileges.

Tourists have flocked to Kraków since the film *Schindler's List* (1993) immortalised the story of the Kraków Ghetto and the concentration camp of Płaszów. The film, based on the novel *Schindler's Ark* by Thomas Keneally, tells the story of the German industrialist Oskar Schindler who saved the lives of 1,000 Jews by employing them in his factories. It was a ground-breaking movie that exposed millions of people to the Holocaust for the first time and prompted many survivors to tell their stories.

Kazimierz is at its busiest in late June/early July during the nine-day **Jewish Festival**. The event is bookended by an inaugural concert on the first Sunday and the final klezmer concert on the last Saturday both held in ulica Szeroka (w jewishfestival.pl/en). It is mostly non-Jews who are drawn to the event, regarding the country's Jewish history as alternative and trendy.

A good place to connect with present-day Jewish life in the city is at the **Jewish Cultural Centre** at ulica Miodowa 24. It was opened in 2007 by King Charles III, then the Prince of Wales, and Queen Camilla and was funded by the London-based charity World Jewish Relief, which was founded in 1933 and played a key role in the Kindertransport (page 6). Both Jews and non-Jews are welcome. The centre offers guided tours of Kraków and Auschwitz, a Shabbat dinner with the local community, and help tracing family trees; they also organise an annual cycling event, Ride for the Living (w friendsofjcckrakow.org), from Kraków to Auschwitz.

GETTING AROUND Sites in Kraków are all accessible on foot. It is possible to visit the Auschwitz-Birkenau complex, 60km to the east of Kraków, on a day trip. There are regular trains from Kraków to Oświęcim, where the former camp is located. There are buses from the station to Auschwitz I and Auschwitz II-Birkenau. If driving, it costs PLN20 to park at Auschwitz I and PLN40 at Auschwitz II. Guided tours leave from Kraków and are advertised in hotels but are expensive. To visit the museum at the former Gross Rosen concentration camp and Działoszyce you need a car. Trains run between Kraków and Rzeszów, but to see the Ulma Family Museum (page 288) in Markowa, you need a car.

WHERE TO STAY AND EAT On the edge of Kazimierz the **PURO hotel** (Halicka 14A; w purohotel.pl; €) is a stylish modern option with a café, restaurant and parking. Kazimierz is full of restaurants and cafés and is always busy in the evening. **Hamsa** (Szeroka 2; w hamsa.pl; ⊕ 10.00–22.00 Mon–Thu, 10.00–23.00 Fri, 09.00–23.00 Sat, 09.00–22.00 Sun; €€) is a Middle Eastern restaurant with vegetarian and vegan options. **Klezmer-Hois** (Seroka 6; w klezmer.pl; ⊕ 07.00–23.00 daily; €€) is a vintage hotel with a restaurant that serves traditional Jewish dishes and holds live concerts. The Jewish Festival runs the stylish **Cheder Café** (ul. Jozefa 36; ⊕ 10.00–21.00 Mon–Thu, 10.00–22.00 Fri–Sun; €), as a year-round venue for lectures, workshops and meetings. **Falafel Shelanu** (ul. Berka Joselewicza 9; ⊕ 10.30–18.00 Sun–Thu, 10.00–14.00 Fri; K; €) serves fast food and breakfast. The **Chabad house** (ul. Sebastiana 23; ⊕ 08.00–22.00 Sat–Thu, 08.00–14.00 Fri; K; €) sells kosher food.

HISTORY After the third partition of Poland in 1795, Galicia became part of the Habsburg lands. Kraków was one of central Europe's great cities and a meeting place for Poles, Germans, Czechs, Hungarians and, of course, Jews, who were granted equal rights in the 1860s. The city was a university town and important intellectual hub. The 1931 census recorded 55,515 Jewish residents, who made up about 25% of the population. Jewish life was a lively mixture of religious and secular.

The German Army took control of Kraków in the first week of September 1939. Initially, thousands of Jews were expelled from the city, but in March 1941 a ghetto was established in which 20,000 Jews were imprisoned. Under Operation Reinhard, Kraków's Jews were brutally murdered and imprisoned in forced labour camps.

A labour camp was established in the southern suburb of Płaszów in 1942. It was built on the site of two Jewish cemeteries. Both Poles and Jews were imprisoned here but in different sectors. Conditions were exceptionally brutal under the regime of the commandant Amon Göth and are depicted in the 1993 film *Schindler's List*.

THE POST-WAR POGROM

By the summer of 1945, about 4,000 Jews were living in Kraków, many refugees from elsewhere. The city was a tinderbox waiting to blow. Food was short and antisemitism rife. The streets were buzzing with the old blood libel tales. On 11 August 1945, Jews at the Kupa Synagogue in Kazimierz tried to catch a 13-year-old boy who was throwing stones at the congregation. The boy fled claiming that the Jews had tried to kill him. An angry crowd rapidly assembled, attacking the worshipers, and burning the Torah scrolls.

Riots broke out in the surrounding area. A hostel where survivors had taken refuge was also attacked and the Jews beaten up. Not satisfied with having hospitalised them, thugs followed their victims to hospital and beat them while nursing staff offered the minimum of care. A 56-year-old woman who had survived Auschwitz lost her life and many Jews were injured. Although the Polish intelligentsia were shocked that this could have happened in the historic university town of Kraków, the seat of Polish learning and sophistication, similar incidents took place across the country.

After the uprisings in the Warsaw and Białystok ghettos and at the extermination camps of Sobibór and Treblinka about 9,000 Jews were shot in Płaszów and the survivors deported to Auschwitz. Göth was executed for war crimes in 1946.

In October 1942, 600 Jews were murdered in the ghetto and 4,500 deported to their deaths at the Bełżec extermination camp. Escapees from the train brought news of their fate back to ghetto, where a resistance movement began. In March 1943, the ghetto was liquidated. Some 2,000 Jews were shot on the spot, a further 6,000 were taken to the labour camp at Płaszów and 3,000 were deported to nearby Auschwitz. On arrival, 549 were selected to work and the rest murdered in the gas chambers.

On 14 January 1945, Kraków was liberated by the Red Army.

WHAT TO SEE Any tour of Kraków starts at the **Wawel Castle** (Wawel 5; w wawel. krakow.pl/en; ⊕ 09.00–19.00 daily, closes 13.00 Mon; prices vary), one of the most culturally significant sites in Poland. It includes the cathedral where Polish monarchs were crowned. During the German occupation Kraków was part of the General Government and Hans Frank had his headquarters here. His office was in the present-day library. At the northern foot of the hill a 1920s apartment block at Straszewskiego 7 was home to Oskar Schindler.

The Old Jewish Quarter

A 10-minute walk along Stradomska leads to the Jewish district of **Kazimierz**, which was an island in the Middle Ages. It is a bustling tourist attraction that centres on ulica Szeroka, a large rectangular town square. Kazimierz is a strange place where the historic verges on kitsch. The area is unique as a preserved Jewish settlement and is home to some of the oldest surviving synagogues in Poland, but it bustles with tourists and the fridge-magnet sellers and tours that accompany them.

The 16th-century **Old Synagogue** (Seroka 24; w muzeumkrakowa.pl/en/branches/old-synagogue; ⊕ 10.00–14.00 Mon, 09.00–17.00 Tue–Sun; PLN18) houses a Museum of Jewish History that covers the Nazi period. There are various Holocaust memorials in the area but the most interesting is in the **Remuh Synagogue** (Seroka 40; w gwzkrakow.pl/services/synagogi; ⊕ 09.00–18.00 Sun–Fri, closes 16.00 in winter; PLN10, cash only), an active synagogue. Services are held here on the Sabbath and High Holidays. In the cemetery there is a wall made up of shattered tombstones known as the Wailing Wall.

Outside the Remuh Synagogue is a **statue of Jan Karski**, a leading member of the Polish resistance (page 254).

The **Jewish Museum of Galicia** (Dajwór, 18; w galiciajewishmuseum.org; ⊕ 10.00–18.00 daily; PLN24) is worth visiting if you wish to explore the Galicia region. On display is an exhibition of photographs by the British photographer Chris Schwartz. The catalogue *Rediscovering Traces of Memory: The Jewish Heritage of Galicia* by Jonathan Webber and Chris Swararz is an invaluable companion for a detailed tour of the region. Its ruined synagogues are ghostly memorials. On many of the ruins the Lion of Judah exhorting the Jews to be strong as a lion in the service of God is still visible. Jewish tombstones in Galicia are works of art. Among the best preserved are in the Jewish cemetery in the town of Lubaczów 254km east of Kraków. The museum also has a good bookshop and a quiet café away from the bustle of Seroka.

The Ghetto

The Jewish ghetto was in the suburb of Podgórze on the opposite bank of the Vistula River. The ghetto, established in March 1941, was far smaller than those in Łódź and Warsaw and held some 20,000 Jews. It was enclosed by barbed-wire fences and, in places, by newly built stone walls. The only surviving remnants of the ghetto walls are at ulica Lwowska 25–29 and behind the school building at ulica Limanowskiego 60/62. The latter is in the shape of Jewish tombstones.

The main memorial is in the large **Ghetto Heroes Square** (Plac Bohaterów Getta), which was the assembly point for deportations, mainly to Bełżec and Auschwitz-Birkenau. Deportation trains left from nearby Zabłocie station. The square, which was renamed in 1948, is dominated by a memorial to the deportations in the form of a series of empty chairs. A small pavilion with the dates 1941 and 1943 is designed as a point to leave remembrance candles but is often covered in beer bottles. After the ghetto was liquidated on 13–14 March 1943, about 6,000 survivors were moved to the Płaszów labour camp. Every year, the March of Remembrance follows the route they took from Plac Bohaterów.

A plaque at No. 6, put up in 1948, on the western side of Plac Bohaterów Getta, marks the headquarters of the ghetto's significant underground resistance movement, which radicalised after deportations to the Bełżec extermination camp began in June 1942. Before this it had centred on continuing education for children and cultural resistance. Their most famous attack was carried out on the **Cyganeria Café** in the city centre, killing 12 German officers. A plaque was placed at the site at Szpitalna 38 in 2022.

On the southwestern corner of the square is the **Eagle Pharmacy** (Apteka pod Orłem; Bohaterów 18; w muzeumkrakowa.pl/en/branches/eagle-pharmacy; ⊕ 10.00–17.00 Tue–Sun; PLN18). When the ghetto was created, the Polish pharmacist Tadeusz Pankiewicz and his staff were the only Poles allowed to live and work in the ghetto. The shop became an important centre of social life, as well as the place to access food and medicine and acquire false papers. The shop has been recreated to look as it did during the Nazi occupation and has a small museum. Pankiewicz wrote an account of the war years, *The Pharmacy in the Kraków Ghetto* (Wydawnictwo Literackie, 2017), and has been recognised as Righteous Among the Nations.

It is a short walk to the former industrial district of Zabłocie, where **Oskar Schindler's Enamel Factory** (ul. Lipowa 4; w muzeumkrakowa.pl/en/branches/oskar-schindlers-enamel-factory; ⊕ 09.00–14.00 Mon, 09.00–19.00 Tue–Thu (closed 1st Tue of month), 09.00–20.00 Fri–Sun, winter 10.00–18.00 daily; PLN36) was located. There are long queues at the museum, so it pays to buy a ticket in advance. It is very crowded in high season as most people access the exhibition on a guided tour which more than doubles the price. Schindler employed 1,000 Jews in the factory who, after the liquidation of the ghetto, were due to be moved to the Płaszów camp. He constructed a barracks in the factory at his own expense where they lived until August 1944 when the factory was closed. At this point the prisoners who had been moved to Płaszów were saved when he drew up his famous list which allowed them to join him in the Sudetenland rather than being sent to Auschwitz. Schindler is not the focus of the exhibition here; the building contains a multimedia exhibition on the German occupation and an art museum. After his death in 1974, Schindler was buried on Mount Zion in Jerusalem.

Little of the **Płaszów camp** remains and the area is now a public park. High on a hill above the former camp there is a vast communist-era monument on the site of one of the mass graves, from which there is a view over the commercial shopping district and the arterial roads that encircle it. To the right is the Jewish memorial and a statue that honours Hungarian women who were taken from Płaszów to Auschwitz. The quarry where prisoners worked is behind it. Amon Göth's house remains at ulica Heltmana 22 but is a private residence.

At the time of writing, work had begun to turn the area into a memorial museum. The development has been highly controversial: locals object to the loss of their open space and fear an influx of tourists into what is a residential area; Jewish groups are fearful that this could cause an antisemitic backlash. Two museums on Kamieńskiego and in the Grey House, which served as the SS living quarters at Jerozolimska 3, are due to open in 2026.

FURTHER AFIELD
Auschwitz/Oświcięm
Auschwitz is the most-visited site associated with the Holocaust in the world and receives almost 2.5 million visitors a year.

If you have been to the other extermination camps on Polish soil, which attract few visitors and remain places of memorial, Auschwitz will come as a shock. It swarms with tourists and in this respect is in a league of its own. It is not only the size of the place, the level of preservation and the magnitude of the crime that attracts visitors; Auschwitz has not been forgotten because, unlike Sobibór and Treblinka, where the mass murder was also an international event, there were a significant number of survivors left to tell the story of what happened here – among them the writers Primo Levi and Elie Wiesel.

Auschwitz is also unique as a historical site for the sheer number of personal items that remain. Scientists battle to preserve suitcases, keys and clothes, while archivists scan yellowing documents and work to preserve the crumbling paper that chronicles the horrors. Money is a constant challenge, but all the cash in the world cannot preserve the 7,000kg of victim's hair – saved by the SS to sell to textile factories – that is brittle and fading and will soon turn to dust.

There are many fictional and non-fiction accounts of Auschwitz; among the most famous are Primo Levi's *If This Is a Man…*(Penguin, 2000) and Elie Wiesel's *Night* (Penguin, 2006), both of which are on sale in the bookshop at the museum. The experience of the Sonderkommando was caught in the award-winning Hungarian film *Saul Fia* (*Son of Saul*; 2015), while *Zone of Interest* (2023) focuses on the daily life led by commandant Rudolf Höss and his family, who lived next to the camp.

History Auschwitz was a huge complex, a metropolis that swarmed with people. It was a society of its own with its own hierarchy and was made up of three large sites: Auschwitz I, the original camp, which was a political prison and labour camp; Auschwitz II-Birkenau, which was both a concentration camp and the

FACTS AND FIGURES

Historians estimate that 1.1 million people were murdered in Auschwitz, about 90% of whom were Jews, half of them women and children. The figure also includes 75,000 non-Jewish Poles, 21,000 Sinti and Roma and 15,000 Soviet prisoners of war. The exact figure will never be known as the SS destroyed much of the paperwork and the identity of those who were condemned to death was not recorded in the camp. The initial Soviet figure of 4 million deaths has been discredited.

During the Cold War the fact that the vast majority of the victims were Jews and that Romani were also selected on the basis of alleged biological difference was not acknowledged.

According to a national opinion poll published in 2020, nearly half of Poles today think Auschwitz was primarily a place of Polish suffering.

main extermination camp; and Auschwitz III-Monowitz, a labour camp attached to the IG Farben factory, one of the biggest chemical companies in Europe – the first concentration camp set up and paid for by a private company, it produced buna, a synthetically produced rubber made from coal, and by 1944, 90% of the labourers were Jewish (the site remains a factory today and access is restricted). Auschwitz also had 45 satellite camps which meant that it was the largest of the Nazi concentration camps.

The town of Oświcięm, Auschwitz in German, was part of western Poland annexed to the German Reich in 1939. The original Auschwitz I camp, which opened in June 1940 as a holding place for Polish political prisoners, was set up in a former Polish Army barracks. The site was chosen as Oświcięm was a major railway hub.

Auschwitz II-Birkenau, was built in 1941 on the site of the village of Brzezinka (Birkenau in German), originally to hold Soviet prisoners of war. Of the 10,000 Soviet prisoners who arrived in Birkenau in October 1941, by May the following year only 186 were still alive. Zyklon B gas was used initially on the Soviet prisoners in autumn 1941. Until 1942, very few Jews were interned in the camp, but when the invasion of the Soviet Union failed to proceed at a blitzkrieg pace, the idea of resettling Europe's Jews in Siberia was abandoned, and genocidal policies were adopted. The first Jews were gassed in the camp in February 1942, but Birkenau only became a centre of mass murder in 1943 after the closure of Bełzec, Sobibór and Treblinka. However, Birkenau was not just an extermination camp but also a labour camp. Prisoners fit for work were selected on arrival, and tattooed, but most died after three to four months in what was referred to in Nazi documents as 'extermination through work'. Auschwitz was the only place where tattooing was done, but from the summer of 1944 it was sometimes not carried out. (In other camps prisoners wore their number on their clothes or on metal discs around their necks.) By the end of the war, about 7,000 people attached to the SS had worked in the camp.

Despite the notoriety of Auschwitz today, the news of its liberation struggled to make it on to the front pages of the world's newspapers in January 1945. The liberation of Majdanek the previous summer had been covered in the Soviet press and a trial had quickly followed, but Auschwitz was largely ignored. The Soviets had no interest in highlighting Jewish suffering and so the Red Army's arrival in Auschwitz was treated as an incidental event in the push westwards.

Auschwitz was not built for posterity and, in the months after the war, 200 of the wooden barracks were taken down so that the materials could be used for reconstruction. Fearful that the evidence of what happened would disappear, Polish survivors took the initiative and set up a museum in June 1946 and a group of guards was organised to protect the former camp from looting. The museum centred on the original camp at Auschwitz I, where political prisoners had been held. It received 100,000 visitors in 1946 alone, mainly Poles. It was officially opened by a decree of the Polish parliament in July 1947 and since then 44 million people have been here.

What to see A visit to the **Auschwitz-Birkenau State Museum** (Miejsce Pamięci i Muzeum Auschwitz-Birkenau; Więźniow Oświęcimia 55, Oświęcim; w auschwitz. org; ⊕ Jan & Nov 07.30–15.00 daily, Feb 07.30–16.00 daily, Mar & Oct 07.30–17.00 daily, Apr–May & Sep 07.30–18.00 daily, Jun–Aug 07.30–19.00 daily, Dec 07.30–14.00 daily; free, tour PLN90) starts at the former Auschwitz I site. At the end of the tour, a bus takes visitors to Auschwitz II-Birkenau, the site of the extermination camp 2km away; but, if you have your own car, you can drive. If you take the bus, however, you will not see the **Old Jewish Ramp** (Alte Judenrampe), a former freight station in an open field 900m from Birkenau's main gate. From here, prisoners unable to walk were loaded into lorries and driven directly to the gas chambers. This memorial is moving but rarely visited. A plaque at the site remembers the French Jews who arrived at the ramp. If you want to see this, you will have to take a taxi or your own car.

Allow 4 hours to see Auschwitz I and II.

Auschwitz I Individual visits are possible at Auschwitz I, but at restricted times; otherwise you must join a guided tour. Although the website says that tickets must be bought online at **w** visit.auschwitz.org, you can purchase tickets at the gate, though you may have to wait some hours to be admitted. Tours are tailored to the interests of each national group, and the guide listened to via headphones.

The tour starts in **Block 4**. Visitors see an urn with ashes gathered near the crematoria in Birkenau after the war, archival photographs of the camp and a model of a gas chamber and Zyklon B cans. Zyklon B was stored in airtight metal tins. It was made by the Frankfurt am Main company, a subsidiary of IG Farben, Deutsche Gesellschaft für Schädlingbekämpfing (German Pest Control Company). It was first used in late summer 1941. The first victims were largely Soviet prisoners of war and sick forced labourers including Jews. Room 5 contains one of the most moving exhibits – 2 tonnes of women's hair.

On display in **Block 5** are personal items brought by victims to the camp, among them spectacles, Jewish prayer shawls, prosthetic limbs and the pans, bowls and everyday utensils brought by Jews believing they would start a new life in the east. Upstairs are their suitcases and shoes. **Block 6** outlines the story of the prisoners' experiences. **Block 7** continues this theme, looking at housing and sanitary conditions. **Block 10** is dedicated to medical experiments.

GOOD TO KNOW

The complex at Auschwitz swarms with tourists, which can come as a shock if you are visiting the memorial to remember family members who were murdered here. Some survivors say that they have found the place too commercialised.

The most shocking addition to the mass tourism at the site is an ice cream van that sells fridge magnets near the gate at Auschwitz II. It is not on land owned by the memorial, who have asked the local council to remove the van, but you will also encounter people eating sandwiches in the visitors centre at Auschwitz I which has a shop selling chocolates and snacks. If you are visiting because you lost family here it is best to avoid peak season and, if that is not possible, visit Birkenau first thing in the morning or late in the afternoon when the tour groups are less likely to be there.

Although there is intense security at Auschwitz I, there is none at Auschwitz II.

At Auschwitz II there is little shade in summer and the site can be extremely cold in winter. No food or drinks are available inside the site, but you can bring a small bottle of water.

If you take an individual ticket without a guide, there is a useful guide on sale in the shop *The Auschwitz-Birkenau Memorial: A Guidebook*. The memorial's website (**w** visit.auschwitz.org) also offers virtual tours.

Two Jewish prisoners, Alfred Wetzler and Rudolf Vrba (Watler Rosenberg), escaped from the camp and returned to their native Slovakia, where they warned the Slovakian Jewish Council of the mass murder they had witnessed.

Vrba had worked in Kanada, where victim's possessions were sorted, and at the Alte Judenrampe and had memorised the transports he saw arrive over a two-year period. Watching the Jews step down from the train, he soon became aware that Auschwitz relied on the Jews' ignorance of what awaited them to function efficiently. This realisation made him determined to warn the Jews of Hungary who were yet to be deported.

Wetzler and Vrba's report reached the World Jewish Congress in June 1944 and was seen by Churchill and Roosevelt. World leaders appealed to the Hungarian leader Horthy who stopped the transports. The two men thus saved 200,000 lives, even if all of those Jews did not survive the war. Vrba's story is told by Jonathan Friedland in *The Escape Artist: The Man Who Broke Out of Auschwitz to Warn the World* (John Murray, 2022).

The BBC broadcast some of the details as did the American and Swiss press. In June 1944, American reconnaissance flights took pictures of the complex that were so detailed it was possible to see people walking towards the crematoria. Public interest was however limited, and the Allies took no action. Incredulity, antisemitism and strategic considerations all played a part.

Block 11 was the camp jail and the courtyard a point of execution. Then follow the blocks dedicated to different nations. **Block 20** was where thousands of people were murdered by phenol injections into the heart. The tour continues to the roll call square, the gallows where the former commandant Rudolf Höss was executed and ends in the first gas chamber in the camp and Crematorium I.

Auschwitz II-Birkenau Birkenau is a vast site and the most significant part of the whole complex, and the heart of the killing machine.

Next to the main gate there is a car park and visitors' centre that looks like a motorway service station. Although it seems totally out of place here, visiting the camp is an emotional experience and can be exhausting in the cold of winter or the heat of summer and the café is a good place to warm up, cool down and gather yourself. But there are no queues at Birkenau, and you do not have to join a guided tour. Another surprise for visitors is the large black **memorial by the main gate** that remembers the Polish inhabitants of the village on which the camp is built, who were expelled from their homes.

To gauge the scale of the camp, climb up to the top of the gate tower. The gateway, used as the main SS guardhouse, and the spur of the **railway** that runs under it were built in the spring of 1944 to receive the Hungarian Jews due for deportation. The ramp sits between the two parts of the camp known as BI and BII. Half a million Jews, as well as 13,000 Poles captured in the Warsaw Uprising, arrived here in 1944. In the summer alone, 10,000 Hungarian Jews arrived every day.

As you walk along the main ramp, the remains of B1, the women's camp, are on your left. It was the original camp before it became the women's camp. Male prisoners were kept in the BII camp to the right of the tracks. Halfway along there is a **freight wagon** that was used to deport Hungarian Jews in 1944, placed here in 2009. The former **Roma and Sinti camp** and the site of Dr Mengele's medical experimentation block were located to the right at the top of the ramp. While some **barracks** remain, most have disappeared, the wood used in their construction taken by local people after the war. Only the ghostly brick chimneys have been left standing. Designed for 180 people, each barracks in reality housed 700; they had earthen floors, no heating or electricity and were crawling with vermin. Birkenau was built on boggy ground.

At the end of the ramp, 800m from the main gate, are the ruins of the **gas chambers** and **Crematoria II and III**. Crematorium II remains in ruins after it was blown up by the Germans in January 1945. Victims were led underground into an undressing room, where banal announcements about cleanliness were broadcast. They were told to leave their clothes on the pegs provided and proceed to the showers. The 'shower room' was then sealed. Zyklon B was released into the room via four installations. The SS then watched the people die through a peep hole. Ventilators then sucked out the gas and the doors leading out were opened. The whole process took 20 minutes. The corpses were then removed by the Sonderkommando. They were kept in strict isolation and had a life expectancy of only a few weeks.

The Sonderkommando, who were predominantly Jewish, were allowed to take what was left in the undressing room. The Polish Jews came with virtually nothing, but in the bags and pockets of the Jews from further afield there was often food. The Greeks brought olives that the Polish Sonderkommando ate thinking they were plums, only to be shocked by their bitter taste. They also brought cornbread. The Dutch brought dainty sandwiches made of white bread. Surviving Sonderkommando also testified that not all of the Jews went to the gas chamber without a fight, notably a group of boys who were gassed in October 1944.

The corpses were initially burned in the crematoria in the main camp or buried in mass graves covered in lime, but these bodies were exhumed in 1942 and burned.

Between the ruins of the gas chamber is the **International Monument to the Victims of Auschwitz**, erected in 1967. The text is written in the principal languages they spoke.

The main camp **bathhouse**, known as the 'sauna', was where new arrivals selected for work were taken. Here their personal possessions were taken from them, their heads were shaved, they were disinfected, tattooed and given prison clothing. The process was brutal and the nudity was shocking especially for observant Jews. A second selection sometimes took place here. The 'sauna' was also used to disinfect clothes.

SINTI AND ROMA IN AUSCHWITZ

By 1944, 22,600 Sinti and Roma had been brought to the camp, half of whom were women and children. Of these, 1,700 were murdered on arrival and the rest were given numbers beginning with Z for Zigeuner, gypsy in German. Conditions in the Roma camp were horrendous even by Auschwitz standards and 7,000 of the inmates died from starvation and disease. The camp was liquidated on 2 August 1944, when all the inmates were gassed in Crematorium V.

Roma People Association in Poland (Stowarzyszenie Romów w Polsce; ul. Berka Joselewicza 5; w stowarzyszenic.romowie.net) in Oświęcim has a library and archives that are open to the public.

DANI CHANOCH'S STORY

Dani Chanoch is a miracle survivor. He was born in 1933 in Kovno in Lithuania into a wealthy family. His father owned a factory and they lived on the pretty picture-postcard main square opposite the town hall of what is now known as Kaunas. His life was he says, 'like living in a candy box'.

He greets me outside his house with a warm handshake and reminds me that it is 18 January, the anniversary of the day he was death-marched out of Auschwitz. He is smiling and affable as he ushers me into his messy office at the top of the house. 'It's an archive,' he says pointing at the shelves. 'I have records of everything here.' The wind whistles round the building.

In the first days of the German occupation, which began in 1941, Lithuanians killed and murdered Jews at will. It was too dangerous for the family to go out, but Chanoch with his Baltic looks and blond hair was sent to collect food and run errands. The moment he was caught by a German soldier but managed to wriggle free changed his life. 'I realised that I had to fight to live,' he says.

When the Kovno Ghetto was liquidated in July 1944, the Chanoch family was deported. 'At Stutthof, they decided to hide me with the men as it would give me a chance to stay alive. This is the point that the family ended. I did not say goodbye to my mother,' he says. 'But if you want to survive, if you want to stay alive, there is no time for pain or sorrow.'

He was taken with his father and brother to a subcamp of Dachau but Dani was then transferred with 131 boys to Auschwitz. There he was put to work on the ramp emptying the freight wagons of the bodies of those who had died on the journey and the belongings that the people had been told to leave behind. He was 11 years old. One transport brought his father to be gassed, but at the time he had no idea of this.

Chanoch escaped two selections on Rosh Hashanah and Yom Kippur in which 90 of the boys in the group were murdered. 'The high holidays were the selection season. Once they came with a stick and, if you were shorter than the stick, that was it.' He tells me: 'We tried to hide those who were too short. We were all friends and we had a solidarity. You survive if you keep together.' The first thing I noticed about Chanoch was how tall he was.

Chanoch is feisty and a bit of a showman. 'I have a BA, you know! A Bachelor of Auschwitz,' he jokes. But it is not a joke – it is an explanation. In 2008, he retraced the route of his Holocaust experiences with his two grown children to make a film, *Pizza in Auschwitz*. It is a funny film about a terrible subject. When Chanoch insisted on spending the night on his old bunk, his daughter brought take-away pizza to make sure he ate something.

Chanoch now lives in Karmei Yosef in Israel, where he has selected a spot where he wants to be buried and has already held a mock funeral service. He likes shocking people but adds, 'I want to know exactly where I will be buried and what will happen to me. So many did not. My family did not have the luxury of a grave.'

The ruins of the **warehouse complex**, called Kanada, was where the prisoners' possessions were sorted prior to being sent to Germany. In February 1943, 824 freight cars departed full of goods. The warehouse was burned to the ground in January 1945 as the Germans tried to destroy evidence of their crimes.

The ruins of **gas chambers IV and V** are located on the edge of the woods, where the photographs of Hungarian Jews waiting to be gassed were taken. The gas chambers here functioned from the spring of 1943 and were at ground level. The chutes for the Zyklon B were located in the walls. Crematorium IV was set on fire during the Sonderkommando uprising in October 1944. At the site of Crematorium V are photographs taken in secret by the Sonderkommando in the summer of 1944. Human ashes were dumped in the pond next to Crematorium IV.

The cottage known as the **Red House**, which was used as a gas chamber in 1942, stood in the field beyond. It was destroyed in 1943. Walk back to the car park past Mexico, a planned expansion begun in the summer of 1944 which was never completed. At the top of the path is the former command building and the SS barracks.

Oświęcim Auschwitz was not just the site of the biggest mass murder in human history but the living enactment of the Nazi policy of Lebensraum. Oświęcim, at the confluence of the Vistula and Soła rivers, is an old Austro-Hungarian town typical of the Galicia region. Few Germans lived here but during World War II it was transformed into a model German eastern settlement. Today, it is a small industrial town that is worth visiting if you are in Poland only to see the former Auschwitz camp, as it is representative of hundreds of similar towns across the country.

When the Germans occupied Oświęcim on 3 September 1939, it was home to 5,000 Jews, 50% of the town's population, a notably high figure for western Galicia. Jews had lived in the region since the 10th century. The town was an intellectual centre for Orthodoxy but also had significant Zionist organisations. Jews worked in the professions and owned some of Oświęcim's main factories.

The main synagogue was destroyed in 1939 and is now a memorial park. The walls of the building are outlined in stone. Deportations began in 1940 when 1,000 Jews were sent to Lublin. At Passover 1941, the remaining Jews were marched to the station as Germans lined the streets to watch and taken by train to ghettos in nearby Będzin, Chrzanów and Sosnowiec. The Poles were moved into districts with poor infrastructure.

In the pretty old town square, the **Oshpitzin Jewish Museum** (Oszpicini Muzeum Żydowskie; Plac Księdza Jana Skarbka 5; w oshpitzin.pl; ⊕ 11.00–18.00 daily; PLN20; book online) is a museum and café complex in a former synagogue. Café Bergson was in the home of the last Jew to live in Oświęcim, Szymon Kluger, who died in 2000. Until 1998, the synagogue was a carpet warehouse.

There is also a new museum backed by the former PiS government, the **Remembrance Museum of Land of Oświęcim Residents** (Muzeum Pamięci Mieskańców Ziemi Oświęcimskiej; w muzeumpamieci.pl; ⊕ 10.00–18.00 Tue–Sun; PLN15), which details the history of the local population and the ways in which they helped prisoners in the Auschwitz concentration camp.

Gross Rosen Initially a satellite of Sachsenhausen, Gross Rosen became an independent camp in 1941. It held mostly Polish and German political prisoners, but between October 1943 and January 1945, some 57,000 Jewish prisoners, mostly women, were imprisoned here. Prisoners worked in the granite quarry. An estimated 125,000 people passed through the camp and its subcamps, of whom 40,000 died. The camp was evacuated in February 1945; some of the original buildings remain. The **Muzeum Gross-Rosen** (Muzeum Gross-Rosen w Rogoźnicy; Ofiar Gross Rosen; w gross-rosen.eu; ⊕ May–Sep 08.00–17.00 daily, Oct–Apr 08.00–16.00

daily; free) in the former concentration camp is 2km south of Rogoźnica, which was part of Germany until 1945. The visit takes 2 hours. Be sure to watch the explanatory film.

Działoszyce The tiny town of Działoszyce, 54km northeast of Kraków, has never recovered from the Holocaust and today's population, numbering just 3,000 people, is one-fifth of what it was before the war. In 1939, there were 7,000 Jews in Działoszyce who were joined by 5,000 Jews expelled from Lublin, Kraków, Poznan and Warsaw.

In September 1942, more than 1,200 Jews were shot in pits in the town's **Jewish cemetery**; the surviving Jews were deported to Bełżec extermination camp. Some Jews escaped to the forest but only 200 survived the war. The cemetery is located on the left side of the dirt road prolonging the ulica Skalbmierza, where a memorial marks the mass grave.

The **synagogue**, also on ulica Skalbmierska, was built in 1852 and considered one of the most beautiful in Poland. It now stands as a haunting ruin and is a striking memorial.

Rzeszów Rzeszów, 167km east of Kraków, was another scene of a post-war blood libel in June 1945. When a Polish girl was found murdered, local militia arrested the town's Jews, among them those simply passing through the town. As they were taken to the police station, crowds threw stones at them. A few days later, a rumour that Christian children were killed by Jews in an act of ritual murder was spread in Przemyśl, 92km southeast of Rzeszów.

Before the war 12,000 Jews lived in Rzeszów, accounting for just under a third of the population. The ghetto, which centred on the market square, held 20,000 Jews in 1941. Some 600 Jews from Rzeszów escaped to the Soviet Union, 100 survived in Poland, hiding in dense forests or in the homes of peasants brave enough to offer them sanctuary.

The **Ulma Family Museum of Poles Saving Jews in World War II** (Markowa 37-120; w muzeumulmow.pl; ⊕ Nov–Mar 10.00–16.00 Tue–Sun, Apr–Oct 10.00–18.00 Tue–Sun; PLN20, free Tue) in the village of Markowa, 26km east of Rzeszów, tells the story of the Ulma family who sheltered eight Jews during the German occupation. When they were denounced to the Germans by a Polish policeman in March 1944, the family, including their small children, were shot dead one after the other in the main square. The mother, who was pregnant, went into labour during the executions, but the baby was not saved. The museum, a modern minimalist glass structure, opened in 2016 and displays photographs, some still stained with blood, of the family taken by the father. The highlight of the exhibit is a reconstruction of the family home. The Ulma family were not the norm in Polish society, although some 20 Jews hidden in the surrounding area also survived the war. The family was recognised as Righteous Among the Nations in 1995. Critics say that the museum was part of the former nationalist government campaign to whitewash Polish history during World War II as the long-term plan for the museum is to turn it into an exhibition dedicated to all Poles who helped Jews. Although the exhibition mentions collaboration, such information is not easy to access.

16

Romania and Moldova

Few remember that Romania was an ally of Nazi Germany and that the country took part in the invasion of the Soviet Union in 1941. Independent of the Nazis' 'Final Solution', Romania also carried out its own genocide in which between 250,000 and 380,000 Romanian and Ukrainian Jews lost their lives.

Most of modern-day Moldova was part of Romania during the interwar period but it was taken over by the Soviet Union in 1940, and taken back under Romanian control again in 1941. The Romanians also recovered northern Bukovina and occupied territory in modern-day Ukraine.

Like other European countries, Romania has a complicated relationship with its past but it has made considerable strides in confronting its role as a perpetrator in the Holocaust.

GETTING THERE AND AROUND

It is possible to fly to Bucharest from all major European countries. There are international trains serving Bucharest from Chişinău, Istanbul, Sofia and Vienna. If you arrive by car, you must buy a vignette to drive on all of the country's roads, not just its motorways.

Moldova is surrounded by Romania to the southwest and Ukraine to the northeast. If you come by car, you will need to buy a vignette at the border. There are flights to Chişinău from Bucharest, Istanbul, several Italian and German cities, Tel Aviv and London's Luton Airport. There are daily train services to Chişinău from Romania and Ukraine. The night train between Chişinău and Bucharest is a comfortable way to travel, especially if you can afford a first-class sleeper.

ONLINE RESOURCES

MOLDOVA
Jewish Community of Moldova w jcm. md/en. An 87-page compilation called *Jewish Heritage Sites & Monuments in Moldova*, compiled by Samuel D Gruber in 2010, is invaluable & also available here online.
Jewish Memory: History of the Jews in Mondova w jewishmemory.md. Has details & pictures of all the main Jewish & Holocaust memorial sites in Moldova.
Maghid w maghid.org. An informative website on Moldovan Jewish heritage.

Transhistory Audiowalks w audiowalks. centropa.org/Chisinau. A useful audio guide created by Vienna-based Centropa (page 340).

ROMANIA
Centre for Historical Studies of the Jews of Romania 'Wilhelm Filderman' w jguideeurope.org/en/site/hasefer-publishing-house. A useful resource for academic information.
Federation of Jewish Communities in Romania w jewishfed.ro. Lists the contacts of active cultural clubs, hosts the community

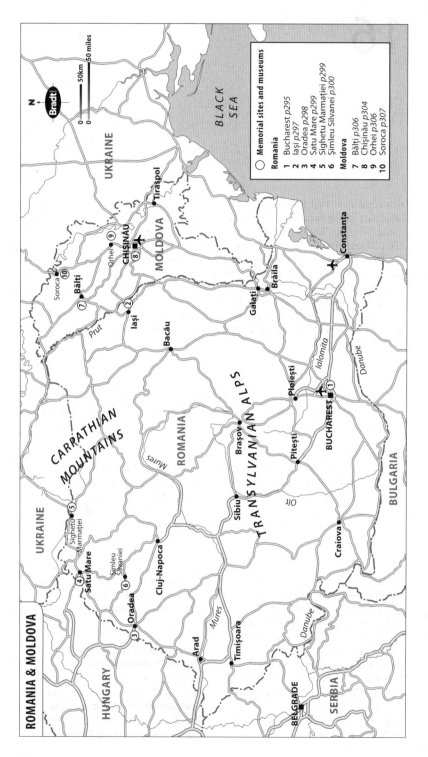

ROMANIA & MOLDOVA

Memorial sites and museums

Romania
1 Bucharest *p295*
2 Iași *p297*
3 Oradea *p298*
4 Satu Mare *p299*
5 Sighetu Marmației *p299*
6 Șimleu Silvaniei *p300*

Moldova
7 Bălți *p306*
8 Chișinău *p304*
9 Orhei *p306*
10 Soroca *p307*

newspaper (in Romanian) & runs schedules of various events & religious services.

Jewish Community Center w jcc.ro. In Bucharest, a great resource for current activities & networking is the website of the very active Jewish Community Center (JCC). It organises the Open Synagogues Night in Bucharest & lots of other informative & fun events open to both the Jewish & non-Jewish public.

Museum of the Holocaust in Northern Transylvania w holocausttransilvania.ro. A virtual museum.

The Tarbut Foundation Can help families trace their roots in northern Transylvania and Bukovina (w jewisheritage.org/maramures-bukovina-family-roots-journeys), and also offers guided tours of Sighet in northern Transylvania for those interested in discovering more of the town's Jewish past (w ftsighet.com). There is also a useful app: Jewish Sighet.

Virtual Museum of Roma Culture w romanomuseum.com. Launched in 2022, an online project designed to empower the country's Roma population.

ROMANIA

After World War II, Romania came under communist control. Political liberties were curtailed and dissent was crushed by the Securitate, Romania's secret police. But the communist dictator Nicolae Ceaușescu, who took power in 1965, followed a foreign policy that was not under complete control of Moscow. The country was cut off from the world and forgotten by many, its role in the Holocaust was suppressed at home and fell into the black hole of historical memory abroad. In 2023, after years of wrangling, the government approved plans to build a new National Museum of the Holocaust in Bucharest.

Be sure to pack a copy of Norman Manea's *October, Eight O'Clock* (Avalon, 1994), a series of stories that partly evoke the Holocaust. Manea is one of Romania's most famous writers and was just five years old when he was deported to Transnistria. His other most well-known work is *The Hooligan's Return: A Memoir* (Yale, 2013), in which he recounts his childhood in Bukovina, his deportation to Transnistria, communism, exile and then his return to Romania.

GETTING AROUND Oradea is just 8km from the Hungarian border and is a good place to start exploring Romania if you are arriving by car or train. Romania is a large country, so to travel to Oradea and Iași from the capital it's better to fly or take the train.

HISTORY Romania's Jewish community was relatively small until, in the mid 19th century, Jews fleeing from persecution in the Russian Empire settled in the country (much smaller than it is today). Laws were introduced limiting their civil rights and there were major anti-Jewish riots in Bucharest in 1866. After the infamous Kishinev Pogrom of 1903 (page 305), more Jews fled Bessarabia, then part of the Russian Empire, and sought refuge in Romania.

Interwar years The end of World War I saw the creation of Greater Romania. To pre-war Romanian territories were now added: Transylvania, which until then had been in the Hungarian part of Austro-Hungary; Bukovina, which had been in the Austrian part; Bessarabia, which had been part of the Russian Empire; plus part of Banat (which was divided with Yugoslavia), Crişana and Maramureş in the north. This doubled Romania's population, of whom almost one third was made up of minority ethnic groups. Especially with the addition of Bessarabia (most of which is now neighbouring Moldova), Romania had a Jewish population of about 730,000, the third largest in Europe after Poland and Russia. Although primarily

In Romania the Holocaust was swept under the carpet and little discussed during the communist period. After the fall of the communist dictator Nicolae Ceauşescu, the idea persisted that the Romanian state had protected its Jews because most of those who lived in what became known as the Old Kingdom, that is to say within its pre-1918 borders including southern Bukovina and southern Transylvania, survived. That was not the case in the areas Romania occupied during World War II nor in Hungarian-occupied northern Transylvania.

When Romania negotiated its entry into the European Union, it was required to come clean about its past. Romania responded like a star student. The government set up the Elie Wiesel National Institute for Studying the Holocaust in Romania and commissioned it to examine the country's role. Their report concluded that between 1940 and 1944 the dictatorship of Ion Antonescu was responsible for the death of between 280,000 and 380,000 Jews and 11,000 Roma in Romania and Romanian-controlled territory. This was officially recognised by the government in 2004.

While successive Romanian governments have made significant steps towards better Holocaust memory, the public seem to have lagged behind. The issues involved were addressed in Radu Jude's black comedy *I Do Not Care If We Go Down in History as Barbarians* (2018). The film follows the challenges faced by a young director when she tries to re-enact the 1941 massacre of 34,000 Jews in Romanian-occupied Odesa. The title is a quote from a speech made by Mihai Antonescu, the foreign minister, before the slaughter.

There have been moves to rehabilitate Ion Antonescu, Romania's wartime leader until his fall in 1944. There are statues to him in a number of towns. Streets have also been renamed after him. Despite a ban on symbols used by the fascist Iron Guard, they persist.

A survey commissioned by the Elie Wiesel Institute, released in October 2017, found that only 41% of adults believed the Holocaust had occurred in the country, while 44% considered Antonescu a hero. Football stadiums often echo to the sound of anti-Roma slogans. The chant 'one million crows [Roma], a single solution: Ion Antonescu!' is frequently heard.

Mandatory Holocaust education in secondary schools was only introduced in 2023.

Ashkenazi, there was also a significant Sephardi community which settled in the country in the 16th century when the Ottoman Empire held sway in the region.

Romania was politically unstable in the interwar period. The reign of King Carol II was dogged by controversy. In 1925 a scandal surrounded his affair with Magda (Elena) Lupescu and he went into exile. He returned to rule Romania again in 1930, and by 1938 he had established a royal dictatorship. Antisemitism permeated the political and aristocratic circles in Romania at the time, as Queen Marie of Romania's memoirs make clear – though King Carol II himself was not an antisemite. Lupescu, Carol's mistress and subsequent wife, was Jewish, albeit born to parents who had converted to Christianity. Antisemitic legislation began to be passed in 1934, leading to that of January 1938 which resulted in a loss of citizenship for at least 200,000 Jews.

World War II Post-World War I, Romania had strong ties to France. After the fall of France in June 1940, though, Romania was diplomatically isolated and opted for German protection. It came at a price, as in 1940 Germany obliged Romania to cede northern Transylvania to Hungary, southern Dobruja to Bulgaria and Bessarabia and northern Bukovina to the Soviet Union. This radicalised Romanian politics.

Looking for a scapegoat, Romanians attacked Jewish communities, whom they often tarred as communist sympathisers. On 8 August 1940 the government passed a decree-law stripping Jews of many of their rights. A category of 'Romanians by blood' was created to distinguish those people from a lesser category of 'Romanian citizens'. The new laws banned most Jews from a variety of careers in public service and the military. Jews were also mostly banned from being lawyers, or owning liquor shops, media outlets and so on. A process of expropriating Jewish-owned property began.

In September 1940, Carol II was forced to abdicate and fled the country. The extreme right-wing Iron Guard was brought into a right-wing military government led by the deeply antisemitic General Ion Antonescu. In November 1940, Romania officially joined the Axis alliance; and Antonescu took the title Conducător, the Romania equivalent of the German Führer.

Between 21 and 23 January 1941, the Iron Guard staged a rebellion against Antonescu, while at the same time carrying out a violent pogrom in Bucharest. Antonescu, with the help of German officials, defeated them and took complete control. Some 80 laws and regulations were passed in the period 1941–42, progressively stripping Jews of their property, their rights to work, study and so on. These mimicked many Nazi laws.

Invasion of the Soviet Union In June 1941, Romania took part in the invasion of the Soviet Union, with the aim of reoccupying the territories annexed by the Soviets in 1940. Between 29 June and 6 July the Romanian government instigated a pogrom in Iași, in which more than 13,000, some one third of the city's Jewish population, were killed. Many died after being forced into so-called 'death trains' made up of cattle wagons. The German and Romanian armies now pushed deep into the Soviet Union, and the Romanians recovered not only Bessarabia and northern Bukovina, but also took a large region between the Dniester and Southern Bug rivers where they created the so-called Transnistria Governorate. Unlike Bessarabia, where the majority of the population was Romanian, there were few Romanians here, but the area did have a large Jewish population, especially in the historic port city of Odesa. This region was administered by Romania from 1941 to 1944 but not formally annexed by it. Most of it lies in what is now Ukraine, but a small part is now the current de facto Russian-controlled breakaway part of Moldova also called Transnistria.

As soon as they took Bessarabia and northern Bukovina, the Romanian Army and the Einsatzgruppen massacred between 100,000 and 120,000 Jews. Approximately 155,000 Jews in Bessarabia and northern Bukovina plus 25,000 Roma were deported to Transnistria, to ghettos and transit and concentration camps, where they were murdered or died of starvation, illness, hypothermia and exhaustion. In only a few days in October 1941, Romanian troops and police along with the Einsatzgruppen murdered some 30,000 Odesa Jews and then 100,000 more during the period of their occupation (page 324). About 380,000 Jews were murdered in Transnistria, northern Bukovina and Bessarabia. Some estimates put that number at 400,000.

Plans were made to deport all of Romania's Jews by the end of the summer of 1942, but Antonescu cancelled the orders for a variety of reasons including a failure of Hitler to promise the return of northern Transylvania to Romania in exchange. As a result, most Jews in the so-called Regat or Old Kingdom, plus southern Transylvania and southern Bukovina survived the war. From this grew the myth that Antonescu had protected the country's Jews. Wilhelm Filderman, a Romanian Jewish leader, also played a role. Either because he was a former classmate of Antonescu or via other political channels, Filderman exerted some influence on the decision to save the Jews of the Old Kingdom and southern Transylvania, arguing that handing them over to the Nazis would harm Romania's post-war interests. Earlier he had failed in his attempts to save the Jews of the occupied territories. Between April and August 1944, in a series of battles, Soviet forces took control of Moldova. With the support of opposition politicians, King Michael, Carol II's young son, overthrew Antonescu and signed an armistice with the Soviet Union. In August 1944, Romania switched sides and fought alongside the Red Army as it drove on eastwards.

Antonescu was executed in 1946.

Aftermath After the war, Romania was part of the communist bloc until 1989. At least 290,000 Jews remained alive within its borders immediately after the war, though some reports put that number as high as 360,000. Mass emigration ensued and, by the end of 1951, some 115,000 Romanian Jews had left for Israel. In 1948 Filderman too had been forced into exile. Those who remained faced increasing persecution especially in 1952–53, the period of Stalin's antisemitic paranoia. Ana Pauker, the Jewish former foreign minister, was purged and arrested on charges relating to Zionism and Israel. Jews, sometimes accused of being Zionists, were prominent in a number of trials of 'traitors and saboteurs'. Despite this, throughout the communist era, Romania allowed large numbers of Jews to emigrate to Israel, mostly in exchange for cash payments. By 1987, there were only 27,000 Jews left in the country. Further emigration since the 1989 revolution has reduced numbers even more. In the 2021 census 2,378 people declared themselves to be Jewish although the 'core' Jewish population, that is those who identify as Jewish, has been calculated by the Institute for Jewish Policy Research as 8,700.

BUCHAREST After a trip to Pyongyang, Nicolae Ceaușescu returned to Bucharest and decided to remodel the city on the North Korean capital. He began a systematic destruction of the city centre, known colloquially as Ceaușima, a play on the dictator's name and the nuclear destruction of Hiroshima. A major earthquake in 1977 gave him both the justification and excuse to bring in the bulldozers as it was primarily pre-war buildings in the city centre that were damaged.

Despite the destruction, there are still important traces of pre-war Jewish life and some important memorials and museums. The construction of a new Holocaust museum has been endlessly delayed by bureaucratic wrangling.

Getting around Bucharest is a big city, but it has an efficient metro system. The old city centre situated between the two squares Unirii and Universitate can be explored on foot.

🏠 **Where to stay and eat** The **Hilton Garden Inn Bucharest Old Town** (Str. 12 Doamnei; **w** hilton.com; **€€€**) is in walking distance of the main sights in the city centre. Many of the main hotels in the city centre are Jewish-observant-friendly. The **Lev Or Bucharest Kosher Hotel** (Str. Occidentului 4; **K**; **€**) has a swimming pool.

Mămăligă – famously immortalised in the Barry Sisters' song 'Rumeine   is a boiled corn mix similar to polenta, and was a staple of the Jewish Romanian diet as it was for most Romanians. It will be on the menu in most traditional Romanian restaurants. **Avraham Kosher** (Bd Corneliu Coposu 4; ⛶; K; €) is a good option if you keep kosher.

History

Bucharest's peacetime Jewish population peaked at around 70,000 in 1930, equating to 10% of the city's population. However, by 1941 about 102,000 Jews were living in the city, many having sought refuge in the capital. The atmosphere was extremely violent and there was widespread antisemitism. The difficult situation in which Jews found themselves, even before the war, is described in the 1934 autobiographical novel *For Two Thousand Years* (Penguin, 2016) by Romanian Jewish writer Iosif Mendel Hechter, who wrote under the pen name Mihail Sebastian. He survived the massacres of World War II, documenting them in a diary later published as *Journal 1935–1944: The Fascist Years* (Pimlico, 2003), only to be killed in 1945 in a road traffic accident.

In January 1941, the paramilitary Iron Guard revolted against the government of Ion Antonescu. Horia Sima, their leader, was part of this government but the two had fallen out bitterly. During the rebellion, the Iron Guard carried out a violent pogrom in Bucharest, killing about 120 Jews. Angry mobs stormed Jewish homes and synagogues, many women were raped and, in a horrific act of torture, 15 Jews, including a five-year-old girl, were hung alive on meat hooks. The Sephardi synagogue was completely destroyed.

What to see

The old Jewish district centred on two main streets, Calea Dudeşti and Calea Văcăreşti. It was largely destroyed in the 1980s to make way for Bulevardul Unirii. The huge Malbim Synagogue, which was badly damaged in 1941 when it was attacked by far-right Legionaries, was one of hundreds of Jewish properties that were demolished. Three important synagogues remain standing.

Coral Temple (Templul Coral; Stara Sfânta Vineri 9–11; 🚇 Universitate; ⛶; ⏱ 10.00–14.30 Mon–Thu, 10.00–12.30 Fri; RON20) The largest of the few working synagogues in the country, the Choral Temple looks much like Vienna's Tempelgasse Synagogue, which was destroyed in Kristallnacht in 1938. Its façade of beige and brown bricks has four decorative turrets, and the Moorish-styled interior is a stunning mix of gold and patterned frescoes. Work began on the building in 1864, but just before it was completed in 1866, it was ransacked by an antisemitic mob. It finally opened in 1867. The synagogue was severely damaged during the 1941 pogrom and was renovated in 1945.

In 1991, after the collapse of the communist regime, the Jewish community erected a Holocaust monument in the shape of a menorah in front of the synagogue. It was one of the first Holocaust memorials in Bucharest. A number of memorial plaques on the nearby wall document the numbers of victims from the different regions of the country.

Great Synagogue (Sinagoga Mare; Str. Adamache 11; 🚇 Piaţa Universitatii; ⛶; ⏱ 10.00–14.00 Mon–Thu) The Great Synagogue was originally built in 1845 by the Polish Jewish community, but much of what you see today was designed in 1936. It was damaged by an earthquake in 1940, and then ransacked in the 1941 pogrom. It has a lavish Rococo interior and houses exhibits on the community and the Holocaust. There is a memorial to the 1941 pogrom outside.

The *Struma* was a 74-year-old once-luxury yacht that had latterly been used as a cattle barge on the Danube. On 12 December 1941, it set sail from the Romanian Black Sea port of Constanța. On board were 769 Jews despite there really being room for only 150. It was the last ship to leave Europe carrying Jewish refugees. They intended to anchor in Turkey, from where they hoped to reach safety in the Palestine Mandate.

The *Struma* took three days to cross the Black Sea, but the Turks refused the refugees entry. The ship then spent 70 days in quarantine in Istanbul harbour. Despite help from the local Jewish community, there was an acute shortage of food and drinking water. The Jewish Agency in Palestine and the American Jewish Joint Distribution Committee tried to convince the British authorities, who controlled the Palestine Mandate, and who had imposed strict controls on Jewish immigration two years earlier, to grant the refugees visas. When they refused, the Turks forcibly towed the ship into the Black Sea. The following day, 24 February 1942, the *Struma* was torpedoed by a Soviet submarine which had mistaken it for an enemy ship. Only one of the refugees survived.

Holy Union Temple (Templul Unirea Sfântă; Str. Mamulari 3; 🚇 Piața Unirii) The Holy Union Temple, built in 1850, is home to the **Jewish History Museum** (w museum.jewishfed.ro; ⏲ 10.00–17.00 Tue–Sat; free). The exhibition includes a room devoted to the Holocaust in Romania and a Holocaust memorial. The museum is also home to a large collection of Romanian Judaica collected by former Chief Rabbi Moses Rosen (1912–94).

Holocaust Memorial (Str. Anghel Saligny 1; 🚇 Izvor; w visitbucharest.today/holocaust-memorial; ⏲ 24hrs daily; free) Bucharest's Holocaust Memorial was unveiled in 2009. The memorial covers 3,000m² and is made of several elements. On each side of the 17m-tall Memorial Column is a single Hebrew letter, which taken together spell the word *zachor*, meaning 'remember' – but the letters are impossible to see. The Via Dolorosa monument beside the column is a symbolic railway track which recalls the 'death trains' of the Iași pogrom of 1941 and those which took Jews and Roma to their deaths in Poland and Transnistria. The overwhelming majority of Jews who died in the gas chambers were those deported from Hungarian-occupied northern Transylvania. A symbolic Roma wheel recalls the Roma and Sinti victims. The hall of remembrance resembles a gas chamber. Beside it are tombstones from desecrated Jewish cemeteries in Bucharest and Odesa.

Jewish Theatre (Teatrul Evreiesc de Stat; Str. Iuliu Barasch 15; w teatrul-evreiesc.com.ro) The Teatrul Evreiesc de Stat is the oldest continuous Yiddish-language theatre in the world and was established in Iași in 1876. It became a state institution in 1948. It recalls the vibrant world that existed before the Shoah, but its performances also fight against revisionism and play a part in Holocaust education.

Further afield

Iași In the 19th century, Iași, 414km northeast of Bucharest, was an important centre of Jewish learning and intellectual life. It was the home to *Korot Haitim*, one of the first modern Yiddish-language newspapers; the world's first professional Yiddish-language theatre, now based in Bucharest, was founded here in 1876 by Avram Goldfaden; and in 1877 the poet Naftali Herz Imber, while staying here, wrote the first version of the poem that would eventually become 'Hatikvah', the Israeli national anthem.

By 1930, about one third of Iaşi's population was Jewish: the city was home to more than 30,000 Jews and had 127 synagogues. It was also the cradle of several fascist and antisemitic movements. Once the German and Romanian invasion of the Soviet Union began, the Soviet air force bombed Iaşi, and the city's Jews, widely viewed as communist sympathisers, were targeted. Posters appeared across the city accusing Jews of guiding in the bombers.

In 1941, in a shocking but little-known chapter in Romanian history, 13,000 Jews were murdered in a bloody pogrom (see below).

What to see During the 1941 pogrom, a series of shootings took place at the police headquarters, which is now the **Iaşi Pogrom Museum** (Muzeul Pogromului de la Iaşi; Str. Vasile Alecsandri 6; w muzeulliteraturiiiasi.ro/muzeul-pogromului-de-la-iasi; ⊕ 10.00–17.00 Tue–Sun; RON30). The museum was created by the Elie Wiesel National Institute for the Study of the Holocaust in Romania, in collaboration with the United States Holocaust Memorial Museum, and opened in 2021, on the 80th anniversary of the pogrom. The exhibition is slightly text heavy but includes hologram survivor testimonies and there are many photographs of the pogrom on display.

The **Victims of the Iaşi Pogrom Monument** was unveiled in 1976. It is located outside the **Great Synagogue** (Sinagoga Mare din Iaşi; Str. Sinagogilor 7; ⊕ 08.30–13.30 Mon–Thu, 08.30–12.30 Fri; under restoration at time of writing), which was founded in 1671 in the old Jewish area of Târgu Cucului and today is the oldest surviving synagogue in Romania.

THE IAŞI POGROM

On 27 June 1941, Antonescu called the head of the Iaşi garrison and told him to 'cleanse' the city of its Jews. On the night of 28–29 June, a violent pogrom broke out organised primarily by police units. Soldiers, men of the Iron Guard who had just been released from prison, Romanian and German soldiers and mobs that gathered hunted, killed and arrested the city's Jews.

Those who were not murdered were forced to board two trains – one of which took six-and-a-half days to reach Călăraşi in southern Romania. It is believed that as many as 5,000 people were on the train when it departed. Only 1,011 survived the journey. Many of those who died of exhaustion or suffocated were thrown out of the train on the way. The second train took 8 hours to cover the 15km journey to Podu Iloaiei. Of the 2,700 people who were forced on to this train, 700 survived. After several months in exile, the survivors were eventually allowed to return to Iaşi.

There are two excellent documentaries about the pogrom: Romanian-born French filmmaker Nellu Cohn and William Karel's *La mort en face, le pogrom de Iasi* (*Death in the Face: The Iaşi Pogrom*; 2019) and Radu Jude's *Iesirea trenurilor din gara* (*The Exit of the Trains*; 2020). The Iaşi pogrom also features in the film *Train de Vie – Un Treno per Vivere* (*Train of Life*; 1998). There is also a useful website: w iasi1941.com.

Many of the victims of the 1941 pogroms were buried in the **Jewish Cemetery** (Cimitirul Evreiesc; Aleea Cimitirul Evreiesc; ⏲ 24hrs daily – in theory but in practice this can vary), located outside the city on Mountain Hill (Dealul Munteni), where more than 100,000 graves, some dating from the late 1800s, stretch across the hillside. There is a moving memorial there. In October 2010, another mass grave was discovered in the **Vulturi Forest**, in the village of Popricani, 14km north of Iași. The victims are also buried in the cemetery.

Oradea Oradea, in Crișana in northwest Romania, lies 642km northwest of Bucharest and close to the Hungarian border. Known as Nagyvárad in Hungarian, Oradea and the surrounding area was part of the Austro-Hungarian Empire until the end of World War I. It is one of the best places to discover the history of the Holocaust.

In 1940, up to 30,000 Jews, about one third of the population, lived in Oradea. The Jews of Oradea were culturally Hungarian and until this point, they had played an important part in the economic and cultural life of the city, though there were outbursts of antisemitism. In December 1927 there had been anti-Jewish riots, organised by Romanian students, in which several Jews were killed. In August 1940, Romania was forced by Germany and Italy to cede it to Hungary as part of a broadly defined northern Transylvania. With the Hungarian takeover, Jewish life in the

A HOLOCAUST STORY FOR SOCIAL MEDIA

Eva Heyman starts her Instagram account (@eva.stories) like so many teenage girls. She has just got her first pair of high heels, she has been eating ice cream in the park and has a crush on a boy. She lives in the Hungarian city of Nagyvárad (Oradea), which is now in Romania.

The account, created by Israeli tech executive Mati Kochavi and his daughter Maya, is based on the diaries kept by the real Eva Heyman in 1944, in which Eva gave vivid expression to her inner secrets, hopes and fears as her world shrank following the German invasion. In 70 short posts, 'Eva' tells the story of how her happy, secular, middle-class life collapses and she is forced into a ghetto. She eventually finds herself on a transport to Auschwitz, where the account abruptly ends.

Eva's real diary ended on 30 May 1944, a few days before her deportation. The Instagram stories from the train were recreated by the producers and are based on descriptions that Eva heard in the ghetto and included in her journal before she was deported.

Eva was killed in Auschwitz on 17 October 1944, one of 1.5 million children murdered in the Holocaust. Her mother, Agnes Zsolt, survived the Holocaust and found the diary when she returned to Nagyvárad after the war; she escaped from Hungary on the Kasztner train to Switzerland (page 34) with Eva's stepfather, Béla Zsolt, who wrote one of the first Holocaust memoirs, *Kilenc Koffer* (*Nine Suitcases*; Pimlico, 2005). After the war, Eva's mother eventually committed suicide.

Not surprisingly the project has its critics, who say it trivialises the horror. It is, however, extremely powerful and moving to see the story played out in such a modern format.

There is a sculpture of Eva Heyman in the eastern side of Nicolae Bălcescu Park on Evreilor Deportati.

city became ever more precarious and Jews were subject to Hungary's anti-Jewish legislation. In 1942, Jewish men were taken to serve in forced labour battalions; Jews were sacked from their jobs and Jewish businesses seized.

In May 1944, following the German invasion of Hungary in March, two ghettos were created in Oradea. The main ghetto, located near the Orthodox synagogue, was for the city's Jews and held 27,000 people; it was the second largest in Hungary. The second was for Jews from the surrounding countryside and held 8,000 people. Deportations began on 23 May. The vast majority of Oradea's Jews were murdered in Auschwitz.

The **Museum of Jewish History** (Muzeul Istoriei Evreilor din Oradea; Str. Primăriei 25; w oradeaheritage.ro/sinagoga-aachvas-rein; ⊕ 10.00–18.00 Tue–Sun; ROM15) opened in 2018 in the Aachvas Rein Synagogue and charts the history of the Jewish community of Oradea from the 15th century. The first floor of the museum has a permanent exhibition and Holocaust memorial.

Nowhere is the massive scope of Jewish life in the region more evident than in the overgrown **Jewish cemetery** in Velenta on Strada Războieni. The size of five football fields, it is one of central Europe's largest surviving cemeteries of its kind. It also contains a Holocaust memorial. The present-day Jewish community is based in the Sinagoga Neologă Sion (Str. Independenței 22; **f**).

Satu Mare An important pilgrimage site for some Haredi Jews, Satu Mare in northwest Romania, 140km northeast of Oradea, was once a bustling Jewish centre. Before the Holocaust, prayers were led in the synagogue by Rabbi Joel Teitelbaum, the late founder of the Satmar movement of Hasidic Judaism. Satmar is the Yiddish name for Satu Mare.

Satu Mare's Jews were imprisoned in a ghetto on 3 May 1944. The heart of what was the ghetto is now Strada Martirilor Deportați, known as Báthory Street during the Hungarian occupation.

In 2004, a monument was dedicated to the memory of the 18,000 Jews from the town and its surrounding area who were murdered in the Holocaust. On Strada Decebal, situated between the Great Orthodox Synagogue and the older Orthodox prayer house, the monument is an eight-tonne block of stone set on a pedestal. There is an earlier monument in the Orthodox cemetery, in the form of a chapel with the names of thousands of Holocaust victims.

Sighetu Marmației Known until 1960 as Sighet, Sighetu Marmației was the cultural heartland of Jewish Maramureş. It lies 109km east of Satu Mare in the beautiful Carpathian region on the Tisa River, which here forms the border with Ukraine. The region was annexed by Hungary in 1940. After the German occupation of Hungary, Sighet's 11,000 Jews, who made up half the population, were deported to Auschwitz. At the station on Strada Gării, a **plaque** commemorates the deportation.

There were just a handful of survivors who returned to Sighet after the liberation. They erected a **monument** to those who had been murdered, on Strada Gheorghe Doja 75 where the town's largest synagogue once stood.

The town was the childhood home of the 1986 Nobel Peace Prize winner Elie Wiesel (page 300). Like many other Jewish townspeople, Wiesel's parents were shopkeepers. The **Elie Wiesel Memorial House** (Casa Memorială Elie Wiesel; Str. Tudor Vladimirescu 1; w muzeulmaramuresului.ro/descopera/casa-memoriala-elie-wiesel; ⊕ Oct–Apr 08.00–16.00 Tue–Sun, May–Sep 09.00–18.00 Tue–Sun; RON20) is the house where Wiesel was born in 1928. The small museum is dedicated to the victims of the Holocaust and the Jewish way of life before World War II. In 1944, the family and the rest of the Jewish community were placed in one of the two ghettos in Sighet and then deported to Auschwitz.

Seven minutes by foot from the Elie Wiesel Memorial House is the **Sighet Memorial to the Victims of Communism and of the Resistance** (Memorialul Victimelor Comunismului şi al Rezistenţei; Str. Corneliu Coposu 4; w memorialsighet.ro; ⊕ 09.30–16.30 Tue–Sun; RON20). Housed in the former prison, the museum was founded in 1994 by the poet Ana Blandiana and her husband, the writer Romulus Rusan, both vocal critics of the Ceauşescu regime. A visit to the museum will contextualise how, in Romania, the story of the Holocaust sits alongside more recent injustices. It is a unique institution in Romania, where members of the Securitate and politicians, much as they had done after the fall of the Antonescu regime, effectively swept the past under the carpet and were not punished for their crimes.

Şimleu Silvaniei In the spring of 1944, 8,500 Jews who lived in Şimleu Silvaniei, 94km northeast of Oradea, and the surrounding area were taken to an abandoned brick factory. The old factory, located 5km south of the town in a marshy, isolated area, became the Cehei Ghetto. Conditions in the ghetto were appalling and any local non-Jews who tried to help the prisoners were shot. The site is located south of Şimleu Silvaniei station on road 108F, close to the railway line.

Among those held in the Cehei Ghetto were ten-year-old Eva Kor and her twin sister, Miriam. When they were deported to Auschwitz, the girls were selected to be part of Dr Mengele's medical experiments. In the 1980s, Kor began searching for other Auschwitz twins and founded the Indiana-based museum and educational organisation CANDLES (Children of Auschwitz Nazi Deadly Lab Experiments Survivors; w candlesholocaustmuseum.org). She was also famous for publicly forgiving the Nazis for what they had done.

The **Holocaust Museum of Northern Transylvania** (Muzeul Holocaustului din Transilvania de Nord; Piaţa 1 Mai; w holocaustmuseum.ro; ⊕ 09.00–17.00 Tue–Fri), opened in Şimleu Silvaniei in 2005, is the first Holocaust museum in Transylvania. It is housed in the former synagogue, which, after the war, was used as a warehouse before falling into disrepair.

MOLDOVA

The history of the Holocaust in Moldova is one of a vanished Jewish world, where ruined Jewish cemeteries lie untended and weeds grow in the ruins of destroyed synagogues. The country has numerous unmarked death pits and forgotten stories. Today there are barely 1,600 people left in the country of 2.5 million people who identify as Jewish, though there are a few thousand more if one includes people who have at least one Jewish parent. In 1930 there were 270,000 Jews in Bessarabia but its borders were somewhat different to today's Moldova.

GETTING AROUND The easiest and fastest way to get around within Moldova, if you do not have your own transport, is by minibus. They are also the easiest way to travel between Chişinău and Tiraspol, but take your passport if you are going to Transnistria as there are checks on the 'border' of the self-proclaimed breakaway state. In Chişinău use the Hip app if you need a taxi.

HISTORY From the 14th century much of the historic Principality of Moldavia was under Ottoman vassalage. In 1812, that part of the territory between the Dniester and Prut rivers was ceded to the Russian Empire and became known as Bessarabia. Before that only the area also known as Budjak (Bugeac/Budzhak) was commonly referred to as Bessarabia. In the wake of the Russian Revolution and World War I, Bessarabia became part of a Greater Romania, but following the Nazi–Soviet pact of 1939, in 1940 the Soviet Union seized Bessarabia back. To this they added a strip of territory on the east bank of the Dniester, which today is the breakaway region of Transnistria. The Romanian Army along with Germans reconquered Bessarabia in 1941, only for the Red Army to take it back again in 1944. Moldova was one of 15 Soviet republics until independence in 1991. The Soviets detached Budjak from Bessarabia in 1940 and it became part of Ukraine.

Jews have lived in Moldova since the 14th century. The Jewish population of the country increased in the 19th century when Bessarabia was part of the Pale of Settlement – Jewish immigration was encouraged by the Tsarist authorities in order to stimulate the economy. In 1901 almost 12% of Bessarabia's population was Jewish. Although there were many other minorities, including Ukrainians, Russians, Tartars, Gagauz, Albanians, Bulgarians and Bessarabian Germans, the vast majority of the population of Bessarabia, except for Budjak, was Romanian.

In the interwar period, Jewish communities had a well-developed cultural life and a system of philanthropic, political and religious institutions. On the eve of World War II, 275,000 Jews lived in present-day Moldova.

World War II Under Soviet rule from 1940 to 1941, national and religious institutions were closed and Zionist and Jewish youth groups dissolved. Many Zionist activists were sent to Siberia.

In June 1941, the German and Romanian armies seized Bessarabia back from the Soviets, who had occupied it for a year. Two thirds of the Jewish population had already fled as the armies advanced eastwards. Einsatzgruppen, which followed

The borders of historic Moldavia shifted throughout the ages. Today the Republic of Moldova comprises much of Moldavia's eastern part, while its western part is now Romanian Moldavia. Its southern region is now part of Ukraine. Together, Moldova and what is now in Ukraine in the south, used to be known as Bessarabia. Chişinău, which is the Romanian name of Moldova's capital city, was historically better known abroad as Kishinev, its Russian name.

Moldova was part of the Soviet Union until 1991. The Soviets insisted that Moldovan was a different language from Romanian, but in fact the 'two' languages are the same. In 2023 Moldova approved a law whereby the country's only official language was Romanian. Most Moldovans however are bilingual and speak Russian as well as Romanian. As everywhere in this region, places have different names in different languages and Jews whose family emigrated generations ago may know the Russian, Ukrainian or Yiddish names for places that today appear on maps with Romanian ones.

Recognition of the unique Jewish experience in the Holocaust was not a topic for discussion in the Soviet era, when all citizens were treated as equal victims. Although today Moldova is a parliamentary democracy and the government has worked to establish both Holocaust commemoration and that of the 1903 Kishinev pogrom, many Moldovan Jews still experience antisemitism at a community level. Jewish cemeteries and memorials have also been vandalised.

The documentary maker Matthew Mishory captured Moldova's relationship with its Jewish past in his 2015 film *Absent*. He returned to his father's village of Mărculeşti, where the entire Jewish population of 1,000 people were shot by the

the Wehrmacht, and the Romanian Army were involved in numerous massacres. German and Romanian military units are believed to have murdered between 150,000 and 250,000 Jews.

As the German Army advanced beyond Moldova, the Romanian Army was left in control. Approximately 110,033 Jews from Bessarabia and Bukovina were deported across the Dniester River to Transnistria, now in modern-day Ukraine, but which was under Romanian control from 1941 to 1944.

Aftermath In August 1944, the Soviets reoccupied the region and restored Soviet Moldova. In 1945–46 most Jewish survivors from Moldova returned, but under communism they met with increasing hardships and were forbidden to practise many Jewish traditions. Still, the number of Jews in Moldova increased significantly, peaking at around 98,000 in 1970. During the 1970s and especially the late 1980s, many Moldovan Jews emigrated to Israel. And between 1990 and 2005 many also settled in Germany as part of an initiative to increase the Jewish population there. Large numbers of Jews from elsewhere in the former Soviet Union also passed through Moldova as they left for Israel and elsewhere.

CHIŞINĂU Chişinău is the capital of Moldova and the largest city in the country. It was once a bustling multi-ethnic city of the Russian Empire, where Jews lived next to Russians, Ukrainians, Romanians, Poles, Germans, Armenians, Greeks and Roma. According to the 1897 census, 40% of Chişinău's population of 108,000 was Jewish. The Jewish community was represented in all walks of life, and it played an essential role in the development and the social and economic life of the city. Jews

Romanian Army in July 1941. He found the villagers were misinformed, denied the massacre or simply accepted it without thinking much about it.

Moldova has also been criticised by the Simon Wiesenthal Center, the global Jewish human rights organisation, which researches the Holocaust and hate in a historic and contemporary context. They, and others, have pointed out that there are also several monuments that honour antisemites and Nazi collaborators, among them one erected in 2000 to Octavian Goga, the Romanian prime minister who enacted laws in January 1938 that stripped many Jews of their citizenship. There is also an Octavian Goga Street in Chișinău which ironically intersects with a street named for Rabbi Yehuda Leib Tsirelson (Zirelson) who was Chief Rabbi of Bessarabia and a member of the Romanian parliament where he famously clashed with Goga, then minister of interior.

The Goga bust is in the Alley of the Classics in **Stephen the Great Public Park** (Grădina Publică Ștefan cel Mare și Sfânt). In **Valea Morilor Park**, there is a monument to Romanian soldiers of World War I who died fighting the Germans and those who died fighting the Soviets in 1941. This would not be controversial except that the plaque commemorates the 'liberation' of Bessarabia and northern Bukovina after which the Romanian Army, together with the Germans, unleashed the Holocaust, murdering the majority of the Jews of these regions.

One of the issues that has dogged Holocaust commemoration in Moldova is that this country is the poorest in Europe and, although authorities say they plan to erect a Jewish cultural and historical centre near the Chișinău cemetery, at the time of writing no clear schedule had been announced.

lived all over the city: poorer Jewish families lived in the lower town, wealthier ones in the upper town. Most of the shops on modern-day Bulevardul Ștefan cel Mare și Sfânt were owned by Jews.

However, antisemitism was rife. Before the Holocaust, no other word evoked Jewish suffering more than Kishinev, the Russian name for Chișinău; indeed the most famous of the pogroms that occurred in the Russian Empire happened in the city in spring 1903. But the violence and destruction of the Holocaust here overshadowed the persecution, pogroms and also the better times for Jews that preceded it.

Where to stay and eat Stay at the reasonably priced Zentrum ApartHotel (Str. 31 August 1989 103; w zentrum.md/en; €€). It has parking and the suites have cooking facilities and washing machines. Stop for a drink in the cafés on pedestrianised Strada Eugen Doga. The **Forshmak Restaurant** (Bd Constantin Negruzzi 2/4, ▮; €) is not kosher but offers Jewish regional dishes, among them *forshmak*, a herring paste that originates from nearby Odesa. **Laffa Israel Street Food** (Str. Alexander Pushkin 32; K; €) serves tasty plates of hummus and pita.

History The Kishinev Pogrom (page 305), which broke out in Chișinău around Easter 1903, was a turning point. There had already been antisemitic riots in the Russian Empire in the 1880s, but the extent of the violence that erupted in 1903 was the moment Jews realised that life in Europe had turned deadly.

In the first days following the 1941 German invasion of the Soviet Union, Chișinău was attacked by the Romanian Army. Many of the 70,000 Jews who lived

TRANSNISTRIA

Today what is now called Transnistria or Pridnestrovie – which means 'across the Dniester' – is a breakaway, Russian-controlled, sliver of Moldova. Between the two world wars, when Bessarabia was part of Romania, this sliver was an autonomous republic within Soviet Ukraine. In 1940 when the Soviets took back Bessarabia from Romania, they united Bessarabia and Transnistria to form the Moldovan Soviet Socialist Republic. When the Romanians reconquered this region with the Germans in 1941, the region west of the Dniester which had been in Romania until 1940 was reincorporated into the country, but the Romanians then created a huge area stretching from the Dniester east to the Bug River deep in Ukraine, including Odesa in the south and up to Zhmerynka in the north. This they called the Transnistria Governorate.

In the modern breakaway region of Transnistria, as in the rest of Moldova, there are several Holocaust monuments.

At **Dubašari** (Dubossary), 1 hour's drive north from the regional capital of Tiraspol, there is a memorial complex at a major mass execution site. It is on Zoya Kosmedimyanskaya Street close to the junction with Kosmonavtov Street. The first monument was erected in 1949 and the most recent, *Requiem*, a statue of a Jewish man with his head covered in a prayer shawl, was unveiled in 2017.

There are several Holocaust monuments in **Tiraspol's** Jewish cemetery, at the corner of Ukrainskaya and Stroiteley streets. Among them is a Soviet-era monument at a mass grave of Jews killed in and around the city. In 2018 a new Holocaust Memorial was erected on 25 October Street.

In **Rybnitsa**, in the north of Transnistria, there are several monuments including one at the site of the former ghetto. There are also memorials in **Bender** in the south, including one unveiled in 2002 on the bank of the Dniester, where some 2,000 Jews were executed in 1941.

in the city became victims of the intensive aerial bombardment; thousands of others escaped to the east. When the Romanians entered the city on 16 July 1941, they staged a pogrom that continued for several days.

The remaining Jews were held in a ghetto and then deported to what was to become the Transnistria Governorate. Chișinău's Jewish community was as good as annihilated.

What to see Close to the restaurant in **Alunelul Park** (Parcul Alunelul) in the northwestern part of the city, near to the site of a former synagogue, a memorial commemorates the 1903 pogrom. It consists of two parts: a red granite monument erected in 1993 and a lighter one in 2003. Information in Romanian, Russian and English is posted here along with the names of the victims who have been identified. There are inscriptions in Hebrew, Romanian, Russian and Yiddish. This part of the park was, until the late 1950s, part of the Jewish cemetery, and the victims were buried here.

The rest of the Jewish cemetery, 10 minutes' walk away, is one of the largest in Europe and a labyrinth of headstones, trees and weeds. The gate is opposite 28 Strada Milano. The Torah scrolls desecrated in the 1903 pogrom are also buried here next to Rabbi Tsirelson, who died in 1941 at the time of the Romanian invasion.

The red-brick shrine can be found by following the path immediately to the left of the gate. It is close to the ruined cemetery prayer hall.

There were once 60 synagogues in Chişinău. The **Anton Chekov Theatre**, on Strada Vlaicu Pircalab, is where the Choral Synagogue used to stand. Built in 1913, the synagogue was barely damaged in the war but was closed in 1945 and demolished to make way for the theatre in 1966. A small plaque commemorates this on the wall of the theatre next to the 1872 Talmud-Torah school building which was not demolished. The site of the former Lemnaria Synagogue is today the home of **Kedem** (Str. Eugen Doga 4–5; 🗹; ⏰ 10.00–20.00 Sun–Fri), the Jewish community centre and focal point of Jewish life in the city where you can find help in tracing family roots. There is a small exhibition here that tells the story of the local Jewish community. The façade of the original synagogue still stands.

On Strada Ierusalim, south of Bulevardul Grigore Vieru, stands the **Monument to the Victims of the Jewish Ghetto** (Monumentul Victimelor Ghetto-ului Evreiesc). It is close to the main entrance of the former ghetto established by the Romanians in 1941, where more than 11,000 Jewish men, women and children were forced to live. Several hundred of the ghetto's inhabitants were executed in August 1941 and many women raped. The area of the ghetto has changed little over the years and its buildings are themselves a haunting memorial. An information board shows its boundaries. Some parts of leafy low-rise old Chişinău are redolent of the city a century ago.

The **Memorial to the Victims of Fascism** (Memorialul Victimelor Fascismului), which commemorates those murdered throughout Bessarabia, was erected in 1982 at Strada Calea Orheiului 19, a busy main road in the city's northern Rişcani district. It stands by what is believed to be a mass execution site for Jews, Roma and others. A board lists the names of some 15,000 Jewish victims.

THE 1903 POGROM

On Easter Sunday in April 1903, an anti-Jewish riot broke out in Chişinău. The pretext for the pogrom, which lasted three days, were medieval-style accusations in the local newspaper *Bessarabets* of a ritual 'blood libel' murder. Jews were blamed for killing a boy in Dubăsari (Dubossary), a town now in the breakaway region of Transnistria, to use his blood to make matzo for the Passover festival. Synagogues were attacked, Torah scrolls desecrated and 1,350 Jewish homes and 588 businesses destroyed; 49 people were murdered and countless Jewish women raped. The riot, widely reported in the international press, shocked the world and had significant repercussions.

The Jewish poet Hayim Nahman Bialik condemned the Jews of Kishinev for their cowardliness. His Hebrew poem 'B'Ir HaHagira, Be-'Ir ha-haregah' ('In the City of Slaughter') became a rallying cry for Jewish self-defence. The pogrom also boosted support for the Zionist cause.

The Jews' enemies also drew conclusions from the pogrom. The editor of *Bessarabets*, Pavel Krushevan, went on to publish and disseminate the infamous antisemitic forgery *The Protocols of the Elders of Zion*. The exact origins of the text are not clear.

To find out more, read Steven J Zipperstein's Pogrom: Kishinev and the Tilt of History *(Liveright, 2019).*

16

The collection at the **National Museum of the History of Moldova** (Muzeul Național de Istorie a Moldovei; Str. 31 August 1989 121A; w nationalmuseum. md; ☉ Apr–Oct 10.00–18.00 Sat–Thu, Nov–Mar 10.00–17.00 Sat–Thu; MDL10) includes some Bessarabian Jewish artefacts.

Further afield

Bălți Before the German invasion of the Soviet Union in 1941, the northern Moldovan city of Bălți – immortalised for many by the Yiddish song 'Mein Shtetele Belz' – had the second largest Jewish population in Bessarabia. The Jewish community numbered about 14,000 and accounted for just under half of the city's population; they ran the city's flour mills and factories. The city was the largest sunflower-oil-producing centre in Bessarabia – sunflower oil was an important export.

In the interwar period the Romanian authorities tried to keep antisemitism in the city under control, but there were a number of violent incidents especially after the drop in grain prices in the 1930s, which were blamed on the Jews.

The Soviets occupied Bălți in 1940 and deported thousands of people of all ethnicities including Jews from the wider northern Bessarabian region to Siberia and elsewhere. On 9 July 1941, German and Romanian forces took back Bessarabia. Many Jews fled before they arrived, but Romanian soldiers killed several hundred who were still in the city. The remaining Jews of Bălți, as well as those in the surrounding area, were then deported across the river Dniester to the Romanian-created Transnistria Governorate. Most did not survive. It is not exactly known how many Jews from Bălți perished in the Holocaust.

The **Holocaust memorial** in the shape of a menorah at Strada Ștefan cel Mare 43 was erected in 1997. A further monument in the Jewish cemetery put up by the Jewish community in 2001 stands on the site of a mass grave where many of the victims are buried.

Orhei Known as Orgeyev in Russian, Orhei, 50km north of Chișinău, lies in a touristic region. Half an hour's drive away at Orheiul Vechi is a famous medieval monastery built into cliffs. Jews had lived in Orhei since the 16th century and in 1930 the 6,300 who lived in the town made up just under half of the population. Jews owned almost all the shops in the town centre, where Jewish doctors, lawyers and merchants lived. The first mayor and founder of Tel Aviv, Meir Dizengoff (1861–1936), was born in a nearby village.

Mass murders were committed when German and Romanian forces occupied Orhei in July 1941. A memorial on Strada Unirii commemorates the victims. Columns of Jews were driven from Chișinău to Transnistria through Orhei. They were met by Romanian police, who confiscated their carts and forced them to continue on foot. The old and sick were killed; valuables, documents and money were seized.

Traces of Jewish Orhei still exist. The building at Strada Scrisului Latin 15 was once a synagogue. Strada Vasile Lupu still has some original shtetl buildings. There are a number of Holocaust memorials at the large and generally unkempt **Jewish cemetery**, including one at its entrance. It is on a hill on the edge of the city and is one of the oldest in Bessarabia. Some victims of the Holocaust killed nearby were reburied here in 1944.

The new **Orhei Jewish History Museum** (Muzeul de Istorie a Evreilor din Orhei; Str. Vasile Lupu 62; by appt only – contact the Jewish community in Chișinău) opened in 2023 and is Moldova's first museum dedicated to the history of Jews in

Bessarabia. Run by the Jewish Community of Moldova, it is housed in a former synagogue, across two rooms, and looks at cultural and religious life.

Soroca In northern Moldova on the banks of the Dniester River, which here forms the border with Ukraine, Soroca was the oldest Jewish community in Bessarabia. The first mention of Jews settled here dates to 1499. When German and Romanian forces occupied the town in July 1941, they immediately murdered 200 Jews, and in August a camp was set up in Vertiujeni (Vertujeni, Vertuzhany), 35km southeast of Soroca, where some 26,000 Jews were imprisoned. Vertiujeni had been a Jewish agricultural colony, originally created in 1838. In the Jewish cemetery is a memorial to the many Jews murdered here. In Soroca the Germans and Romanians then rounded up about 5,000–6,000 Jews and transferred them across the Dniester to nearby Yampil' in Ukraine, where they were left to fend for themselves. The Germans eventually drove them back to Soroca on death marches during which many elderly and children died. Jews who refused to cross back over the river were shot and the women raped.

There are three **monuments** to victims of the Holocaust in Soroca. Two of them are in the Jewish cemetery. The first is dedicated to 41 Jews shot near the Bekirovsky (Bakirov) Bridge on 21 July 1941. The second is dedicated to the victims from Soroca and other towns in the north of Moldova who died in the nearby Cosăuți Forest. There is also a monument to the Victims of Fascism.

In the **Cosăuți Forest**, the two mass graves are marked by a memorial inaugurated in 2022. More than 6,000 Jewish people are buried in them.

Across the rest of Moldova and historic Bessarabia there are numerous other Holocaust memorials, mostly in small towns and villages where there are no more Jews. For further information, see w jewishmemory.md.

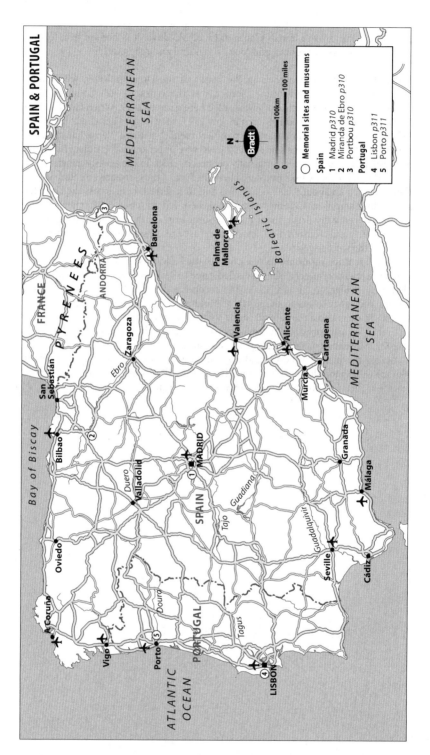

SPAIN & PORTUGAL

Memorial sites and museums

Spain
1 Madrid *p310*
2 Miranda de Ebro *p310*
3 Portbou *p310*

Portugal
4 Lisbon *p311*
5 Porto *p311*

0   100km
0   100 miles

MEDITERRANEAN SEA

Barcelona

ANDORRA

FRANCE

PYRENEES

San Sebastián

Zaragoza

Ebro

Palma de Mallorca

Balearic Islands

Valencia

Alicante

Cartagena

Murcia

MEDITERRANEAN SEA

Bilbao

Bay of Biscay

Valladolid

Duero

MADRID

SPAIN

Guadiana

Tajo

Granada

Málaga

Oviedo

Seville

Guadalquivir

Cádiz

A Coruña

Vigo

Porto

Douro

PORTUGAL

Tagus

LISBON

ATLANTIC OCEAN

Bradt

17

Spain and Portugal

Spain and Portugal are a good place to look at the Holocaust through the long view of the history of antisemitism. The introduction of the Inquisition to the Iberian Peninsula in the 15th century was a key moment in Jewish history. Thousands of Jews were burned at the stake, while many more fled in fear of their lives. Others went underground and practised their religion in secret until most lost their religious and cultural identity – they are known as Marranos. The Inquisition continued into the 19th century. In the late 1800s a small number of Jews settled on the Iberian Peninsula, principally in Barcelona and Madrid. Although very few Jews lived in Spain and Portugal on the eve of World War II, there was considerable antisemitism.

GETTING THERE AND AROUND

Madrid and Lisbon have major international airports. Barcelona is the closest airport to Portbou, and Bilbao is convenient for visiting Miranda de Ebro. Lisbon and Porto airports service intercontinental flights to/from Brazil, North America and many European destinations. International trains run from France to both Spain and Portugal.

Trains are both fast and efficient and are the best way to get around Spain and Portugal if you do not have a car.

SPAIN

At the outbreak of World War II, Spain had recently emerged from a three-year civil war. General Francisco Franco (1892–1975), who had taken control at the head of a coalition of fascist, monarchist and conservative factions, was a fanatical antisemite and was sympathetic to Nazi ideology. After Franco's victory, Jewish communities in Spain were dissolved and were to remain banned until 1945. But even after 1945, Jews could only practise their religion in private; in 1968 a new law guaranteeing freedom of religion was eventually passed.

Before World War II, an estimated 4,000 Jews lived in Spain.

HISTORY Officially neutral during World War II, Spain had strong economic ties with Nazi Germany. Between 1940 and 1941 it looked as if it might side with the Axis powers. During this period, a register of Jews was compiled and Jewish status was included on all official identity documents. The Blue Division, a group of Spanish volunteers who fought alongside Axis troops during the siege of Leningrad, are still memorialised in Spain today. Although Franco's government did not intervene to stop the deportation of Spanish Republicans from France, Spanish diplomats in some of Europe's capital cities took their own initiative and played an important role in facilitating the escape of thousands of Jews. Some 20,000–30,000 Jews travelled through Spain on transit visas heading for Gibraltar and Portugal; many others arrived illegally. Since Jewish relief organisations were banned, they were prevented from giving humanitarian aid to the refugees.

PORTBOU Once a tiny fishing village, the holiday resort of Portbou on Spain's Costa Brava is the last town before the French border. Many Jewish refugees fleeing from France during the German occupation made their way here, among them the German Jewish philosopher Walter Benjamin (1892–1940), who escaped over the Pyrenees in 1940. Benjamin had hoped to travel on to Lisbon and from there to the United States, for which he had a valid visa. However, the Spanish authorities refused him entry. On the night of 26–27 September 1940, before he could be deported back to France where he faced the danger of being arrested and interned, he took an overdose of morphine. There are several memorials to Benjamin in and around Portbou.

Where to stay and eat Most of the accommodation in Portbou is in apartments and holiday villas, available via online booking sites. **Voramar** (Passeig de la Sardana 6; w voramarportbou.com; ⏲ lunchtime only Mon–Thu; €€€€) is right on the seafront and serves gourmet tasting menus.

What to see Walter Benjamin committed suicide at the Hotel Francia de Portbou, now a private building, on Carrer Mar 5. He is buried in an unmarked grave in the **town cemetery** (⏲ 24hrs daily), which is located on the hill on the south side of the town and has stunning sea views. There is a memorial to Benjamin in the cemetery.

Next to the cemetery, the **Memorial Walter Benjamin a Portbou** (Passeig de la Sardana 11; ⏲ 24hrs daily) was designed by the Israeli sculptor Dani Karavan. The monument is in the form of a tunnel leading down to the sea but which is blocked by a pane of glass. Named *Passages*, it honours not only Benjamin but all the other refugees who made the journey to Portbou. The inscription is taken from Benjamin's essay *On the Concept of History* (Verso, 2016). Every September a memorial ceremony is held here.

Portbou is surrounded by hiking trails. It is possible to walk along the route Benjamin took across Coll de Rumpissar to the French town of Banyuls-sur-Mer. For details, see w historia-viva.net.

Further afield

Miranda de Ebro In Franco's Spain, there was a network of concentration camps where political opponents were imprisoned. The main camp for male foreign internees was at Miranda de Ebro, a small city in the north of the country. Conditions in the camp were appalling and British consular officials made regular visits to negotiate for the release of escaped servicemen and members of the French resistance. Parts of the camp buildings are still visible. Free guided tours of the camp are offered at the **visitors' centre** (Raimundo Porres Civic Centre, Avenida República Argentina 93; w mirandamemoria.es; ⏲ 09.00–15.00 & 17.00–21.00 Mon–Sat; tours bookable online).

MADRID Spain's first Holocaust memorial was dedicated in 2007, in Madrid's **Park of the Three Cultures** (Jardin de Las Tres Culturas), which symbolises the coexistence of Christians, Jews and Muslims. Muslims were also persecuted during the Inquisition, as were Protestant Christians. The memorial, made of railway tracks in the form of a Star of David, was designed by artist Samuel Nahon and architect Alberto Stisin.

PORTUGAL

Portugal had a tiny Jewish community of just 1,000 on the eve of World War II, although in the rural villages in the north of the country many Marrano Jewish families were still practising in secret, notably in Belmonte.

HISTORY From 1932 to 1968, Portugal was ruled by an authoritarian regime under the leadership of António de Oliveira Salazar, though, significantly, Salazar's nationalist politics did not have a racial element. Like Spain, Portugal remained technically neutral during World War II, and between 1939 and 1945 as many as 60,000–80,000 Jews passed through the country on their way to the Americas. A number of foreign Jewish relief organisations existed in Lisbon to assist them. Attempts were also made to intercede by Salazar's administration on behalf of the 4,300 Portuguese Sephardic Jews living in the German-occupied Netherlands, though these failed.

While Portugal was more sympathetic to the Allies than to Franco's Spain, it did, however, continue to trade with Nazi Germany until mid-1944.

PORTO Porto is Portugal's second largest city. After the end of the Inquisition, Jews started to settle again in Porto in the late 19th century and the community saw a modest cultural revival in the 1920s and 30s during a drive to bring back to Judaism those who had been forced to convert. The Spanish and Portuguese congregations of London with other members of the Sephardic diaspora funded the construction of a synagogue in Porto. Thanks to a law granting Portuguese citizenship to anyone who can prove their Portuguese Jewish origins, the Jewish community in Porto now numbers more than 500.

Where to stay and eat The **Hotel da Música** (Mercado do Bom Sucesso, Largo Ferreira Lapa 21 a 183; w hoteldamusica.com; K; €€) is a modern hotel near the Kadoorie Mekor Haim Synagogue. Porto is dotted with bakeries and pastry shops, and sandwiches are a lunchtime favourite. **Le J** (Rua de Vale Formoso 314; K; €€) serves Jewish deli-style sandwiches and salads, and also sells challah.

What to see The **Holocaust Museum of Porto** (Museu do Holocausto do Porto; Rua do Campo Alegre 790; w mhporto.com; ☉ 14.30–17.30 Mon–Thu, 14.30–16.00 Fri; free) was set up by the Jewish community of Porto and opened in 2021. A small, modern museum, it houses an exhibition on the Holocaust and the Jewish refugees who came to Portugal, and also remembers those Portuguese citizens who helped save Jews during the Holocaust. Many of the artefacts on display relate to the more than 60,000 Jewish refugees who passed through Portugal on their way to the Americas. There is also a reproduction of a barracks from the Auschwitz-Birkenau extermination camp.

The **Jewish Museum of Porto** (Museu Judaico do Porto; Rua Guerra Junqueiro 325; w mjporto.com; ☉ 10.00–noon Mon–Fri; €5) tells the story of the return of the Jews to the city. The museum is opposite the Kadoorie Mekor Haim Synagogue, which played a key role in sheltering refugees during World War II.

LISBON At the time of writing, the construction of a new Jewish museum, the **Tikvá Museu Judaico Lisboa** (Rua das Hortas, Belém; w mjlisboa.com) was in the

17

planning stages. The modern building was designed by Polish-American architect Daniel Libeskind, who also chose the museum's name *tikva*, which in Hebrew means 'hope'.

In 2006, a small travertine **memorial** on Praça Dom Pedro IV sponsored by the Portuguese Jewish community was erected in front of Lisbon's National Theatre to remember the victims of the Jewish massacre that took place in the city at Easter 1506.

18

Ukraine

One in every four Jewish victims of the Holocaust was murdered within the present-day borders of Ukraine. Most died in a hail of bullets in or near their homes in a massacre that was dramatically different from the organised and industrial mass murder carried out in Auschwitz. Long before the extermination camps in occupied Poland began operation, the Nazis, Romanians and Ukrianian collaborators were murdering Jews in what is now known as the Shoah by Bullets. The earth that covered many of the death pits moved for days after, as many of the victims were buried alive. By the end of the war 1.5 million to 1.6 million of the Jews in Ukraine had been murdered.

Across the country hundreds of mass graves remain unmarked and unprotected. False rumours persist even to this day that the Jews managed to conceal valuable items, which are buried alongside them, and there are frequent stories of looting and vandalism. In reality, victims were forced to undress and were stripped of their possessions. Men were usually shot first, then the women and children. According to the Central Database of Shoah Victims' Names kept by the Holocaust Remembrance Centre at Yad Vashem, around 50% of the Jewish victims have yet to be identified.

GETTING THERE

Ukrainian airspace was closed at time of writing because of the ongoing invasion by Russia. Road and train routes remain open with numerous crossings along the Hungarian, Moldovan, Polish, Romanian and Slovakian borders, but the main entry point for Ukraine is the Polish border town of Przemyśl, from which there are bus and train connections to Lviv, on the other side of the border. However, current UK government advice is against all or all but essential travel to parts of Ukraine. Check **w** gov.uk/foreign-travel-advice/ukraine or your embassy for updates.

ONLINE RESOURCES

Centropa **w** centropa.org. The Vienna-based institute (page 340) is an invaluable resource on Jewish life in Ukraine past and present.
History of Jewish Communities in Ukraine **w** jewua.org. Provides a lot of detailed information & individual shtetl stories.
Jewish Galicia & Bukovina **w** jgaliciabukovina. net. A useful website for visitors to western Ukraine.
Lviv Center for Urban History **w** lvivcenter. org/en/en. Many resources including an interactive

map showing current & vanished buildings of interest.
Protecting Memory Project **w** protecting-memory.org. This project, managed by the Memorial to the Murdered Jews of Europe Foundation (page 169), has transformed many mass Jewish & Roma graves in present-day Ukraine into dignified sites of remembrance.
Rohatyn Jewish Heritage
w rohatynjewishheritage.org. The murdered Jews of Rohatyn, 72km south of Lviv, are remembered

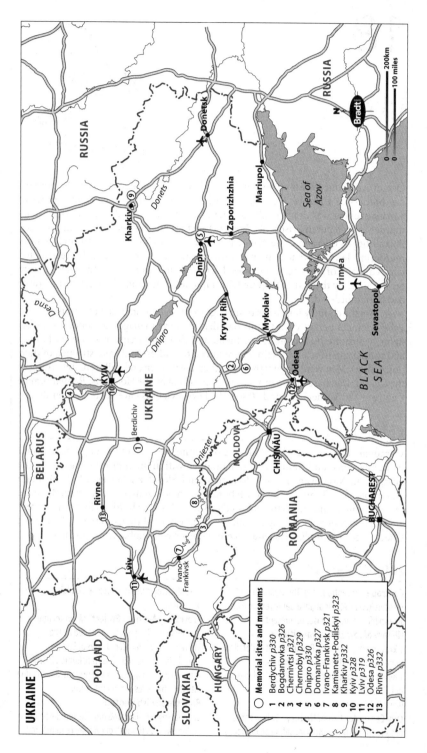

UKRAINE

Memorial sites and museums

1 Berdychiv p330
2 Bogdanovka p326
3 Chernivtsi p321
4 Chernobyl p329
5 Dnipro p330
6 Domanivka p327
7 Ivano-Frankivsk p321
8 Kamianets-Podilskyi p323
9 Kharkiv p332
10 Kyiv p328
11 Lviv p319
12 Odesa p326
13 Rivne p332

POLAND

SLOVAKIA

HUNGARY

BELARUS

ROMANIA

MOLDOVA

UKRAINE

RUSSIA

CHISINĂU

BUCHAREST

KYIV

Lviv

Ivano-Frankivsk

Rivne

Berdichiv

Kharkiv

Dnipro

Kryyyi Rih

Mykolaiv

Zaporizhzhia

Mariupol

Donetsk

Odesa

Sevastopol

Crimea

Sea of Azov

BLACK SEA

Dnipro

Donets

Dniester

Desna

Bradt

N

200km
100 miles

0
0

by this independent NGO project. A voluntary organisation based in both the Ukraine & the USA, it has placed memorials at the mass graves near the town & other Jewish sites.

Shoah Atrocities Map w shoahatlas.org. There are more than 1,500 Holocaust mass murder sites across Ukraine. As well as mapping those sites, this useful website also contains a historical overview of Jewish life in Ukraine & details about the Nazi occupation & statistics on the Holocaust in the country.

Trans History Audiowalks w audiowalks. centropa.org/chernivtsi. To find out more about Jewish life in Chernivtsi, follow Centropa's excellent audio walk.

Tsal Kaplun Foundation w tkfshtetl.org. Shtetl stories from the former Soviet Union.

Ukrainian Jewish Encounter w ukrainianjewishencounter.org. Another invaluable resource on Jewish life in Ukraine.

HISTORY

Before World War I, what is now Ukraine was part of Imperial Russia and the Austro-Hungarian Empire. In the wake of the Russian Revolution and the end of World War I, independent Ukrainian republics were declared in Kyiv and in the west. Civil war (and pogroms) wracked the country. The Bolsheviks eventually prevailed in most of the former Russian imperial territories while the Poles defeated the Ukrainians in the west.

INTERWAR YEARS In the interwar years, what is now western Ukraine was part of Poland; while most of the rest was the Ukrainian Soviet Socialist Republic, part of the Soviet Union from 1922. Transcarpathia (Carpathian Ruthenia/Subcarpathian Rus) was part of Czechoslovakia and northern Bukovina part of Romania as what is now Ukrainian Bessarabia. Much of what is now Transnistria (page 304) was an autonomous part of Ukraine until 1940. Crimea was a part of Soviet Russia until it was transferred to Soviet Ukraine in 1954.

One-and-a-half million Jews lived in Soviet Ukraine in the interwar years. It had the largest Jewish population in the Soviet Union, and one of the biggest Jewish populations in Europe, owing in part to the fact that before the Russian Revolution, most of it had been part of the Russian Empire's Pale of Settlement, to which Jews were confined between 1791 and 1917.

1939–41 In 1940, Stalin occupied most of eastern Galicia, western Volhynia, northern Bukovina, and southern Bessarabia, in accordance with the secret protocol of the 1939 Molotov–Ribbentrop Pact. The pact partitioned Poland and allowed the Soviet Union to annex the Baltic states. In the wake of this, the number of Jews in Ukraine rose to 2.75 million, not just because so many lived in the newly acquired territories but because many fled into them from German-occupied Poland.

In June 1941, the Germans invaded the Soviet Union, pushing the Soviets out of the territories they had taken in 1940 and going on to occupy most of the territories covered by present-day Ukraine. In the south, the Romanians reclaimed the territory they lost in 1940, in Bessarabia and northern Bukovina. Although never formally annexed by Romania, they also created a large area between the Dniester and Bug rivers including the historic port city of Odesa, called the Transnistria Governorate.

The utter chaos that followed the invasion is brilliantly captured in Vasily Grossman's novel *The People Immortal* (MacLehose Press, 2023). As depicted in the book, many Ukrainians supported the Germans, whom they regarded as their liberators. Areas under Soviet control had suffered a devastating famine in 1932–33, known as the Holodomor, which was caused by the Soviet collectivisation of farms and which killed millions. There was also a widespread belief that Jews were Bolsheviks. In the west, in the former Polish territories, where Ukrainian nationalist sentiment had traditionally been strong, many welcomed the arrival of the Germans believing that the invasion heralded the creation of an independent Ukrainian state and tens of thousands joined collaborationist units which participated in the Holocaust. But many Ukrainians also fought the Nazis as soldiers of the Red Army.

SHOAH BY BULLETS The months that followed the German invasion saw a radicalisation of Nazi policy towards Jews. Mobile killing units (Einsatzgruppen) were deployed by the Germans in their aim to murder the entire Jewish population who were considered a dangerous fifth column.

The Holocaust in Ukraine was a public affair. Local policemen and German officials requisitioned non-Jewish civilians to dig pits, fill in mass graves, collect Jewish clothing, sort through Jewish valuables, pull out teeth, or transport Jews to the pits in their carts. Research into the Shoah by Bullets, however, began only in the 1990s after the fall of communism. During the Cold War, Soviet officials sought to repress discussion of the unique fate of Jews under Nazi rule. The scale of the mass murder also meant there were few survivors to remember the killing sites and the names of the victims. Wendy Lower's *The Ravine: A Family, a Photograph, a Holocaust Massacre Revealed* (OUP, 2021) is a highly readable account of one mass shooting which is written much like a detective story.

LVIV

Like Vilnius in Lithuania and Thessaloniki in Greece, Lviv is a city where the people who live there today are completely different to those who lived there before 1945; the buildings are all that is left to tell their tales. In 2022, only 1,500 Jews were believed to be living in Lviv.

Although long neglected, the process of memorialisation has gathered pace in Lviv in recent years; but in the wider region it is still mostly neglected or forgotten.

As ever, memorialisation is complicated. Nationalist Ukrainians who fought the Soviets for example also often participated in the murder of Jews and Poles here.

GETTING AROUND It is easy to see all the sites in Lviv on foot or by tram or bus, but to explore the wider region it helps to have a car. Regional public transport is efficient but time consuming.

There are trains from Lviv to Chernivtsi, Ivano-Frankivsk, Kamianets-Podilskyi, Ternopil and Rohatyn. If you are already in Chernivtsi, the quickest way to get to Kamianets-Podilskyi is to take a bus.

Rakhiv is 200km from Chernivtsi. Public transport connections are poor, but it is possible to take a bus. To explore the Carpathians, it pays to have your own transport. Trains run from Košice in Slovakia to Uzhhorod (Uzgorod) and Mukachevo via Chop. If you are going to Uzhhorod this way, get out in Chop and take a taxi from in front of the station.

WHERE TO STAY AND EAT The **Ibis Styles** (Shukhevycha 3; w ibis.com; €) close to the city centre is a good budget option. The **Grand Café Leopolis** (Rynok Sq 1; w fest.lviv.ua/uk/restaurants/grandcafeleopolis; €) is famous for its desserts.

HISTORY When Lviv was part of the Austro-Hungarian Empire, it was known as Lemberg, the German name for the city. During this period, it was home to the Diet or regional assembly of the Kingdom of Galicia and Lodomeria, of which it was the capital. Galicia stretched from Auschwitz in the west to the Austrian province of Bukovina in the east. To the north it was bordered by the Russian Empire. Poles, Ukrainians (then more often known as Ruthenians), Jews and others lived here, co-existing for the most part, but not all of the time. Poles, Jews and Ukrainians competed politically, and Jews came under physical attack in times of crisis, for example during the Polish–Ukrainian war. Galicia's countryside was muddy and poor, and in the decades before World War I hundreds of thousands emigrated to the Americas or the bright lights of Vienna. It was a land where Zionism flourished but was also the home of great rabbis and yeshivas. It is a world that lives on the works of Jewish writer Yosef Shmuel Agnon (1888–1970).

After World War I, the Poles and Ukrainians fought for possession of the city, and in the wake of the Ukrainian collapse in 1919 it was secured for the new Polish state.

World War II When Hitler and Stalin invaded Poland in September 1939, according to a secret protocol of the Molotov–Ribbentrop Pact that Nazi Germany and the Soviet Union had signed the previous month, Poland was to be divided between them. The Soviet zone, which included Lviv, was annexed to the USSR – until it was lost to the Nazis when they attacked the Soviet Union in June 1941. At this point, half the city's population was Polish and Jews made up a third of the people who lived there. Ukrainians lived mostly in the surrounding countryside.

The Soviets arrested Poles, intellectuals and anyone connected with the Polish Army and police. Many Jews considered 'class enemies' were also arrested. They were held by the Soviet secret police, the NKVD, in prisons in the city. In total, 3,391 prisoners were murdered by the NKVD in Lviv.

When the Germans discovered thousands of bodies in the city's prisons, notably the Lonsky Prison (page 320), they blamed the Jews for the massacre of 22–23 June 1941, claiming they had worked for the secret police. Jews were made to clean up the mess and exhume bodies from mass graves, which fuelled the belief that all

Jews were Bolsheviks. A pogrom, known as the Prison Aktion, erupted, in which some 4,000 Jews were murdered by the Germans and Ukrainians. Another pogrom followed in July in which more than 2,000 Jews died.

After the massacres, in the early winter of 1941 the Germans created a labour camp at Janowska in the northwest of the city and resettled Lviv's 60,000 surviving Jews into a Jewish Quarter in the northern suburbs on the other side of the railway bridge on Chornovola. As they walked under the bridge, at least 3,000 men, women and children were stopped and taken to the forest next to the village of Lysynychi, 10km east of the city.

Mass deportations to Bełżec extermination camp began in March 1942 and Janowska began to be used as a site of mass murder, especially after Bełżec ceased operations in early 1943. The ghetto was liquidated in June 1943.

To escape the mass shootings and deportation of 1942, dozens of Jews hid in Lviv's sewers. Their story inspired the Polish film *W ciemności* (*In Darkness*; 2011).

Aftermath At the Allies' Tehran Conference in 1943, Stalin had demanded that, in the post-war settlement, Lviv and its surrounding territory which had been Polish before World War II should be recognised as part of the Soviet Union. The British and American leaders agreed to this, but not formally until the Potsdam Conference of 1945. This meant that, when the Red Army retook Lviv and the region in July 1944,

WEAPONISING HISTORY

The Russian leader Vladimir Putin has justified his full-scale invasion of Ukraine in 2022 as a war against 'neo-Nazis', even though the country has a Jewish president, who lost relatives in the Holocaust and heads a Western-backed democratically elected government. Ukrainian Jews have rallied to the flag and fought and died for the country just like others. However, history is complicated. For many Ukrainians the 16th Cossack Bohdan Khmelnytsky is a hero, but Jews remember him as being responsible for the deaths of thousands. Similarly, a significant number of Ukrainians today laud Stepan Bandera, whose followers fought the Nazis and the Soviets after 1944, but they know little about how those same followers murdered Poles and Jews. During the war tens of thousands of Ukrainians collaborated with the Nazis in the Holocaust but 7 million also fought against them as members of the Red Army.

When the Nazis invaded the Soviet Union in June 1941, Bandera's Organisation of Ukrainian Nationalists (OUN) declared an independent state in Lviv. Members of the OUN were also prominent in the Ukrainian Nachtigall Battalion which participated in the attack on the Soviet Union and Lviv, and OUN activists took part in the pogroms that rocked Lviv in June and July 1941. However, as the Germans did not support an independent Ukraine, Bandera was arrested and detained by them until 1944. After the war he was assassinated by a KGB agent in Munich in 1959. Followers of Bandera fought a guerrilla war against the Soviets for years after the end of World War II.

In Lviv there is a large statue of Bandera off Stepan Bandera Street; and the red-and-black flag – representing red Ukrainian blood spilled on the country's black earth – of the wartime and post-war Ukrainian nationalists of the Ukrainian Insurgent Army is ubiquitous now that Ukraine is at war again.

Also memorialised in the city in the famous Lychakiv cemetery is the Ukrainian SS Galicia Division, recruited by the Nazis in 1943.

it along with its people were still recognised as Polish. In August 1945, however, the USSR and Poland's provisional government signed a treaty whereby Poland ceded the territory to the Soviet Union – this came into force in February 1946. Poland was compensated with former German lands to the west; in East Prussia the Polish population was 'repatriated' to Poland and Ukrainians likewise were uprooted from their homes in Poland and sent to, now Soviet, western Ukraine. Records vary, but in the order of 1.1 million Poles including surviving Jews were sent to Poland and some half a million Ukrainians were sent the other way.

Lviv was repopulated at first by Ukrainians coming from the east of the country and Soviet administrators and or secret police personnel. Most of Lviv's Jews had been killed in the Holocaust so Jews in the post-war city came in the main from other parts of the Soviet Union.

WHAT TO SEE Lviv has a fabulous collection of Gothic, Renaissance, Baroque and Classical 19th-century buildings. Any visit to the city starts in its beautiful old town.

Old Jewish quarter
The old Jewish quarter centres on Ivana Fedorova and Staroevreiska streets south of Rynok Square and is marked by a series of information boards. The remains of the Turei Zahav or Golden Rose Synagogue destroyed by the Nazis and Ukrainian collaborators in 1942 were a wasteland for decades but are now marked by a memorial, the **Space of Synagogues** (Простір синагог; Staroievreiska 37; ⊕ 24hrs daily), which opened in September 2016. The synagogue, built in 1582, had been considered one of Europe's most beautiful. In front of the remains of the Golden Rose, the black stone slabs of the Perpetuation memorial include quotations from former Jewish residents of the area and are meant to symbolise voices from the past we cannot hear.

There is also a memorial to Lviv's Great Synagogue, destroyed by the Nazis in 1941, at Sianska 4 and to the Temple Synagogue which stood on Staryi Rynok Square 14.

An exhibition, 'Those Who Saved the World' created by the **Lviv Museum of the History of Religion** (Львівський музей історії релігії; Staroevreiska 36; w museum.lviv.ua; ⊕ 10.00–17.00 Tue–Sun; UAH30), tells the story of Lviv's Jews, but its main aim is to focus on Ukrainians of the Greek Catholic Church who rescued Jews, above all Archbishop Andrey Sheptytsky. A controversial figure, Sheptytsky welcomed the Nazis in the hope the invasion would lead to a Ukrainian state but, in a pastoral letter titled 'Thou Shalt Not Kill', protested to Himmler about Ukrainians being used to kill Jews. He then blessed the SS Galicia Division while he was hiding 150 Jews in church buildings, among them the former shoe factory in the Krochmalevychi townhouse on vulytsya Shevska.

The Krakivsky Market on Bazarna Street, 1.5km away in the northwest of the city, stands on the site of Lviv's **old Jewish cemetery**, whose destruction was begun by the Nazis and finished by the Soviets. Gravestones from the cemetery – where over a period of 500 years, up to 30,000 people had been buried – were used to pave roads and make walls. At time of writing there were plans to turn a small park, which was also part of the cemetery, into a memorial park. It is just north of the former Jewish hospital at Rappoporta 8, now the city's 3rd Clinical Hospital.

Lviv Ghetto area
Lviv's **Ghetto Memorial**, on busy Chornovola, is on the northern side of the railway bridge where the 'gates of death', or main gates, of the former ghetto stood. It was here that a deadly selection took place. Designed by Holocaust survivor Luisa Sternstein (1926–2015), who was born in the city, the sculpture represents a man who has one hand thrust heavenwards, a symbol of

pain and revenge, and another turned upwards in prayer. At its foot are gravestone fragments. A short alley with memorial plaques put up by families leads to a stark black menorah with an inscription calling on readers to remember.

Not far from the memorial, the **Territory of Terror Memorial Museum of Totalitarian Regimes** (Меморіальний музей тоталітарних режимів 'Територія Терору'; Chornovola 45; w museumterror.com; ⊕ 10.00–18.00 Wed–Thu, 11.00–19.00 Fri–Sun; UAH60; English audio guide) is located on the spot where Jews boarded trains to the Bełżec extermination camp in Poland. The largest action took place on 10–12 August 1942, when 38,000 Jews were deported. A further 2,000 were shot on sight. In June 1943, when the ghetto was liquidated, 3,000 people committed suicide and 5,000–6,000 Jews were deported to the Sobibór death camp. The Soviet Transfer Prison No. 25 was set up here after Lviv was reincorporated into the Soviet Union and closed only in 1955. It was used to hold prisoners of war and Ukrainian nationalists, many of whom were transferred to the Soviet Gulag. The museum, like other museums in Ukraine and parts of eastern Europe, equates the Nazi and Soviet occupation.

Janowska The site of the former **Janowska labour camp** is in the northwest corner of the city, opposite Klepariv railway station on Shevchenka (formerly Janowska) Street. On arrival at the camp, there was a selection: those considered unfit were deported to Bełżec or were shot in the Piaski ravine north of the camp. When Bełżec was closed in 1943, Janowska became an extermination camp, where as many as 50,000 Jews were murdered. Conditions were barbaric, and the commandant and his wife shot prisoners for entertainment. Prisoners in Janowska tried to organise a resistance and planned to use weapons smuggled into the camp in an uprising, but were caught by surprise when the camp was liquidated in November 1943.

After the war, the site was taken over by the NKVD and part of it still remains a prison. Part of the camp is accessible near the Tatarbunarska bus terminal located just before the prison. If coming from the centre, take tram 7 to the Tatarbunarska Street stop and walk the last 8 minutes. Apart from a central mowed area, monuments and signs are engulfed in undergrowth, though there are plans to create a memorial and small museum.

There is a memorial at the Piaski ravine on Omeliana Kovcha opposite the prison, and another at **Klepariv Station** (opposite the Shell petrol station), from where Jews were deported.

'Lonsky Prison' National Memorial Museum of Victims of Occupation Regimes (Національний музей-меморіал жертв окупаційних режимів 'Тюрма на Лонцького'; Stepana Bandery 1; w lonckoho.lviv.ua; ⊕ 10.00–13.00 & 14.00–19.00 Tue–Fri & Sun; free) The former Łackiego Prison was turned into a museum in 1996. The former Lonsky Habsburg barracks was used as an NKVD prison from 1939 to 1941. On 22–23 June 1941 during the German invasion of the Soviet Union, the NKVD murdered 1,681 people here. The Germans' discovery of the bodies prompted a pogrom in the city. Much of the building remains eerily as it was in 1941. Half the victims of the massacre were Ukrainian, a quarter Polish and the rest Jews although one can easily come away with the impression that its prisoners were all Ukrainian nationalists. Many of the prisoners held here by the NKVD were sent to the Gulag.

The Soviet secret police, the NKVD, and then the mobile killing units of the German Security Police, had their headquarters at **Vitovskoho 55** in a building constructed in 1935 originally for the electricity board.

FURTHER AFIELD

Ivano-Frankivsk Lying 140km southeast of Lviv, Ivano-Frankivsk (formerly known as Stanislav or Stanisławów in Polish) was home to around 40,000 Jews, among them many refugees, when it was occupied first by the Hungarians and then by the Nazis in July 1941. Up to 12,000 were killed in the Jewish cemetery on 12 October 1941, 'Bloody Sunday', during a selection prior to the creation of a ghetto in the town.

After the fall of communism, the striking 19th-century Moorish-style synagogue was given back to the Jewish community. Since 1989, Rabbi Moyshe Kolesnik has compiled an impressive collection of thousands of prayerbooks and scrolls, as well as various historical documents, maps and photographs of Jewish cultural and religious life from the region. The Torah scroll that he reads from every week was saved from the ghetto during the German occupation and hidden in the city. The synagogue is usually open in the morning, but if not, and you would like to see the collection, it is best to knock on the door and ask.

The current war has made Ivano-Frankivsk one of many towns in western Ukraine whose Jewish population has risen dramatically, from just 150 to more than 1,000 as refugees have fled the fighting further east. It looks increasingly as if they will stay for the foreseeable future and put down roots. Many of them have found that the refugee experience has drawn them closer to the Jewish community.

Chernivtsi The capital of Bukovina, 135km southeast of Ivano-Frankivsk, was once a bustling Austro-Hungarian city, known then as Czernowitz. Until the German invasion of the Soviet Union in 1941, Chernivtsi had a unique multi-cultural life and was home to some 45,000 Jews, but its cultural heart was ripped out by the Holocaust and then destroyed by communism. Those events have left it a sad and rather barren place, but it is nevertheless worth visiting to appreciate the desolation that the Holocaust left in its wake. Centropa has a useful audio walk of Chernivtsi (page 340).

Pack a copy of Gregor von Rezzori's novel *Memoirs of an Anti-Semite* (NYRB, 2007). A scion of Austro-Hungarian aristocrats in Chernivtsi, he describes the atmosphere of the interwar years. The novelist Aharon Appelfeld, who was born in a nearby village, was nine when the Romanians returned. His novels evocatively recall pre-war Jewish life, the horrors of the Holocaust and the struggles that faced the survivors. Appelfeld survived by living feral in the forest for three years. He then joined the thousands of Jewish refugees who made their way to Italy on a journey that would end in Israel (page 223).

History Chernivtsi's university was founded in 1875 and 50% of its lecturers were Jewish. While rural Bukovina was a Hasid stronghold, many of Chernivtsi's Jews were German speaking and highly assimilated. It was also home to many Yiddish writers.

In the interwar years, as Cernăuți, the city was part of Romania and the Jewish community faced discrimination. During the brief Soviet occupation of the region in 1940, Jewish institutions were closed down and 12,000 people from Bukovina were deported to Siberia and Kazakhstan, 30% of whom were Jewish. When Romania joined Germany in invading the Soviet Union in June 1941, Romania again took control. A ghetto was set up and deportations to Transnistria began. About 15,000 Jews from Chernivtsi survived the war.

What to see The **Chernivtsi Museum of Bukovinian Jewish History and Culture** (Музей історії євреїв Буковини; Teatralnaya 5; **w** muzejew.org.ua;

⏲ 10.00–15.00 Tue–Fri, 10.00–14.00 Sat, 10.00–13.00 Sun; UAH12) in the Central Palace of Culture, the former Jewish community building, is a good place to get a feel for what was lost in Chernivtsi.

Two vast cemeteries, both Jewish and Christian on vulytsya Zelena, are testament to the once multi-ethnic culture that was destroyed. In the **Jewish cemetery** there is a mass grave and memorial for those killed by the Romanians soon after they occupied the city. In recent years much work has been done to rehabilitate the cemetery, and there has long been a plan to convert the cemetery's ceremonial hall into a Holocaust museum.

Chernivtsi has several other memorials. At the end of vulytsya Pidhajetska, where the wood begins and 200m from the Prut River, a monument commemorates the lives of 400 Jews shot by the Germans in July 1941. In 2016, a major new memorial was built, at Sahaidachnoho 22a, to commemorate the **Chernivtsi Ghetto**, in which

THE CARPATHIANS

From 1920 to 1938, Carpathian Ruthenia (Transcarpathia, Zakarpattia, Sub Carpathian Rus) was part of Czechoslovakia. Unlike most parts of Europe where the Jews lived in cities and towns, in the Carpathians 80% were farmers and lived in rural areas or very small towns and were among the poorest Jews in Europe. As a result, traces of the world they lived in have all but disappeared. There were, however, significant Jewish populations in the bigger towns of Uzhhorod, Mukachevo, Khust and Berehove.

In 1938 after the Munich Conference, Czechoslovakia was divided and Hitler in effect gave the region to Hungary. On 15 March 1939 the independent state of Carpatho-Ukraine was declared. It lasted barely a few days before being snuffed out by the invading Hungarians, who annexed it along with southern Slovakia. Jewish life was supressed, and many Jewish men were gradually conscripted to forced labour within the ranks of the Hungarian Army. After the German invasion of Hungary in March 1944, though, Jews were forced into ghettos in **Berehove**, **Khust**, **Mukachevo**, **Uzhhorod** and **Vynohradiv**, and then deported to Auschwitz-Birkenau. Of some 100,000 Jews in the region, only 15,000–20,000 survived, if that. Reported numbers vary. Between 1945 and 1946, 270 teenage survivors from the Carpathians were brought to the UK by the Central British Fund, an organisation now called World Jewish Relief. They were among 732 child Holocaust survivors brought to the UK, and their stories are told on the '45 Aid Society website (w 45aid.org) named after the charitable organisation they set up in London in the 1960s.

The Red Army occupied the region in 1944, and in 1946 it was formally annexed from the restored Czechoslovakia by the USSR, becoming part of Soviet Ukraine. Before the Soviet borders were sealed, tens of thousands fled including Jews, leaving only some 4,000 by 1948.

The largest Jewish community in the region was in **Mukachevo**, then known by its Hungarian name of Munkács. In 1930 Jews accounted for 43% of the population. They were famous for their religious fervour but there was also an important Zionist movement. In 1920, the first Hebrew-speaking school in Czechoslovakia was established in Mukachevo, followed by the Hebrew Gymnasium in 1925, which soon became one of the most prestigious Hebrew high schools in eastern Europe. Mukachevo also had a large Hasidic community. On the eve of the Holocaust, there were nearly 30 synagogues in town, many of which were small some 50,000 people were initially forced to live. A plaque at Zankovetskoi Street 6 marks the house of **Traian Popovici**, the Romanian-appointed mayor in 1941–42. He compiled a list of some 20,000 Jews eligible for exemptions from deportation to Transnistria or to enable those who had already been sent to return. He was sacked in spring 1942. In 1969 he was recognised as a Righteous Among the Nations.

Kamianets-Podilskyi

Known as Komenets in Yiddish and Kamenets-Podolsk in Russian, this beautiful city with a fairy-tale castle is located 90km northeast of Chernivtsi. After the collapse of the Russian Empire and the civil war, the city became part of Soviet Ukraine. About 12,000 Jews lived here before World War II. That number swelled to 26,000 when Hungary began deporting Jews who were not Hungarian nationals, or who could not prove their citizenship, just as it joined Germany in attacking the Soviet Union. The majority were Jews from

Hasidic ones. The **Old Jewish Cemetery** on vulytsya Myra and Akademik Pavlova was razed in the communist-era and turned into a car park. Now it is full of lines of symbolic tombstones but has a Holocaust memorial topped with a menorah at its centre. There is also a newer memorial inscribed in Ukrainian. The new Jewish cemetery is 2km east at Tomas Masaryk Street 21.

In March 1944, a **ghetto** was established in Mukachevo. It was extremely overcrowded, with 10,000 people crammed into buildings which had previously housed just 3,000. A memorial, depicting a menorah growing from a map of the land of Israel, was put up in 1994 to mark the ghetto entrance, at the corner of Valenberha (Wallenberg) Street just where it meets Kosmonavta Belyaeva. Right next door to it is a 2013 plaque that commemorates the Swedish diplomat Raoul Wallenberg, who saved Jews in Budapest – though he had no tangible connection to Mukachevo.

In May 1944, the SS liquidated the ghetto, with the help of the Hungarian police. The Jews were then marched to brick factories on the edge of town. Forced to live in the factory's giant kilns, they were kept here for a week before being deported to Auschwitz – 28,587 Jews were despatched from Mukachevo and Carpathian Ruthenia on nine transports. Some of the striking photographs you may see of Jews sitting on the grass at Birkenau, waiting to be murdered in the gas chambers, are of the Jews of Mukachevo.

Between 1935 and 1938, the photographer Roman Vishniac (1897–1990) was sent by the American Jewish Joint Distribution Committee to photograph the Jewish communities in eastern Europe, including the Carpathians, as part of a fundraising campaign. Vishniac was a Russian-born Jew who was based in Berlin, where he also documented the Nazis' rise to power.

In 1983, some of his photographs were published in his book *A Vanished World* (Farrar Straus & Giroux, 1983). His daughter Mara Vishniac-Kohn has made the entire collection of his work available to the public to keep his legacy alive and also in the hope that some of the people in the pictures he took can be identified – see w vishniac.icp.org. Vishniac wanted to capture the very essence of these communities, not knowing that in a few years they would be wiped from the face of the earth. During the war Vishniac escaped to the US. Laura Bialis' documentary *Vishniac* (2023) tells the story of this man who was both an extraordinary photographer and controversial and complicated character.

Transcarpathia, which the Hungarians had seized from Czechoslovakia in March 1939 and which had a large Jewish population.

German and Hungarian troops occupied the city in the summer of 1941, and on 26 August, Jews were ordered to gather at the train station for resettlement. Instead, they were taken to pits and shot. The execution site is north of the fortress and is now a public park, Skver Vasylyeva, on Yevhena Konovaltsaya Street. There are memorials in the northwestern sector of the park. Between 26 and 28 August, 23,600 men, women and children were murdered by the German occupiers, assisted by Hungarian troops and Ukrainian police auxiliaries. This mass murder was a significant turning point in the Holocaust as it was one of the first to include children. There is a monument to the children murdered in the Jewish cemetery on vulytsya Mykola Hodiichuka in the eastern Bilanivka district.

ODESA

The great Black Sea port city of Odesa, immortalised in the 1925 film *Battleship Potemkin*, was founded in 1795 by the Russian Empress Catherine the Great. Its historic centre is much like St Petersburg's. Odesa was a cosmopolitan city made up of Russians, Armenians, Greeks and Ukrainians. Jews played an important part in the commercial life of the city during the Tsarist period.

The Jewish story in Odesa matters because it illustrates the extent to which regimes allied to the Third Reich took part in mass murder and that the Holocaust was a Europe-wide crime.

Odesa is an overwhelmingly Russian-speaking city but, as elsewhere since the beginning of the Russo-Ukrainian war in 2014 and especially since the full-scale invasion of 2022, Ukrainian is heard here more and more.

GETTING AROUND Odesa can be easily explored on foot. To see Bogdanovka (Bohdanivka), you need your own transport, to hire a driver or get there by minibus.

GOOD TO KNOW

Odesa was occupied by Romania in 1941–44. At his trial after the war, the Romanian leader Ion Antonescu claimed that he had protected the Jews in the pre-war territory of Romania that remained under Romanian control. While it is true that there were no deportations from these territories, in Bessarabia, northern Bukovina (Chernivtsi) and the Transnistria Governorate between the Dniester and Bug rivers it was quite another story.

The massacres carried out by the Romanians in Odesa and its surrounding area are little known in the English-speaking world. Historians estimate that about 240,000 Jews were murdered in the region, many of them burned alive. One reason these horrific events have slipped out of mind is that after the end of the war the Soviet narrative turned Odesa into a hero-city, in which the Red Army had won a great victory. There was little space for the story of what had befallen its civilian population, and Soviet politics allowed no place for the specifics of the Holocaust. Matters were further complicated by Romania for decades denying its involvement in the Holocaust. Many Odesans also reported their Jewish neighbours to the occupiers, which was a story that ran in contradiction to the official Soviet version of history, in which Odesans stood united against the common enemy.

WHERE TO STAY AND EAT Brik (Mayakovs'koho Ln 7; w brikhotel.com.ua; €) is a stylish modern hotel within walking distance of the centre and has a restaurant. One of many Jewish dishes that has been given a distinctly Odesan touch is *forshmak*, a herring pâté spread over rye bread – the fish is often soaked in milk and blended with sour apples and walnuts. Try it at **Tyulka** (46 Koblevskaya St; w tulka.od.ua; €).

HISTORY From 1880 to 1920, Odesa had the second largest Jewish population in the Russian Empire, and at the end of the 19th century 70% of Odesa's trading companies and 90% of its grain-trading firms belonged to Jews. Jews lived all over the city, though many, especially poorer and Orthodox Jews, lived in the Moldovanka area.

Odesa was also an important centre for Jewish culture. It was home to the writer Isaac Babel (1894–1940), who wrote about Jewish life in his *Odessa Stories* (Pushkin, 2016), and Ze'ev Jabotinsky (1880–1940), the Zionist journalist and founder of the right-wing self-defence group Betar.

Jabotinsky was influenced by Odesa's tendency to tip over the precipice into violence. Contrary to the traditional Yiddish phrase 'Lebn vi Got in Odes' ('To live like a God in Odesa'), in the 19th and early 20th centuries Jews were murdered on the city's streets in a serious of pogroms. In 1821 and 1859, Greeks in Odesa blamed Jews for a series of imagined crimes: from aiding the Turks in their battles with Greek revolutionaries to conspiring against Greek grain merchants. In 1871, the first large-scale pogrom in Russian history broke out. It was followed by two more in 1881 and 1905. To find out more read Charles King's *Odessa: Genius and Death in a City of Dreams* (Norton, 2012).

World War II Before World War II, there were some 180,000 Jews living in Odesa but by the time the city was occupied by Romania on 16 October 1941 after two months of fierce fighting, that number had dropped to 80,000–100,000. Odesa then became the capital of the Romanian-controlled area of Transnistria.

At 17.35 on 22 October 1941 a huge explosion destroyed the former NKVD headquarters on Marazliivska Street, which had been taken over by the occupying Romanian forces just a week before, killing 67 including Romanian and German officers. The explosives had been planted by the Red Army. Just as a similar explosion in Kyiv weeks before had prompted the massacre of more than 33,000 Jews at Babyn Yar, the one in Odesa also triggered a spate of killings. One of the most horrific spectacles was on Aleksandrovsky Prospekt (Oleksandrivs'kyi Av), where about 400 people were hanged on the tramlines. Over the following days, the Romanian and German forces hunted down Jews. Some 23,000 were shot in the city's port. Others – Jewish men, women and children – were taken to a local prison, from where the Romanian Army transferred them to Dal'nyk (Dalnik), west of Odesa. On arrival a group of 40–50 people were tied together with rope, thrown into a pit and shot dead. Some 5,000 more people were imprisoned in four barracks – the men in three and the women and children into the fourth. On 24 October the men in the first barracks were shot with machine guns through premade holes in the walls; but this method proved so time-consuming that the remaining three barracks were doused with petrol and set on fire. On the evening of 25 October, the last barracks was blown up with dynamite.

Even beginning before the explosion, Jews were taken to empty Red Army artillery depots on Lyustdorfs'ka Street near Tolbukhina Square. In the course of a few days up to 25,000 Jewish people were murdered here. In the 1990s a small memorial was erected by Jewish organisations.

After the massacres a ghetto was set up in Slobodka on the outskirts of the city.

WHAT TO SEE **Prokhorovs'ka Square**, the assembly point for deportations, is easy to reach as there are stops for several trams and buses here. It is the site of the city's main Holocaust memorial, a sculpture of a group of naked and emaciated victims. The monument sits in an alley planted with trees, each marked with the name of one of scores of Odesans who saved Jews. At the beginning of the alley there is a stark black cube marked with a Star of David and a menorah. The memorial square was founded in 1994 and refurbished in 2023, and has become the focal point of official commemoration.

The nearby **Odesa Holocaust Museum** (Музей Голокосту та пам'яті жертв нацизму; vul. Malaya Arnautska 111; ⓕ; ⏲ 11.00–18.00 Tue–Fri, 10.00–14.00 Sun; UAH15) near Privoz market is a small, privately funded initiative which opened in 2009. It has a permanent exhibition on the fate of Transnistria's Jews and a memorial room. Fifteen minutes' walk away, the **Jewish Museum 'Migdal-Shorashim'** (vul. Nizhyns'ka 66; w jewishmuseum.org.ua; ⏲ 12.30–18.00 Mon–Thu, closed Jewish holidays) has a Holocaust section. At time of writing, plans for the construction of a new Holocaust museum and memorial were on hold because of the ongoing war with Russia.

In the meantime, discovering the story of what happened here requires some imagination.

The former NKVD headquarters on Marazliivska Street, the site of the explosion that prompted the killing of thousands of Jews in the city (page 325), is across from the entrance to **Taras Shevchenko Park**.

On the hillside west of the village of **Velyky Dal'nyk**, 15km from Odesa city centre (not to be confused with the village of Dal'nyk 38km south of Odesa), is a marked mass grave of the 5,000 victims of the reprisals who were murdered in the barracks there.

In the 1990s a small **memorial** was erected by Jewish organisations to the 25,000 Jews murdered in the Red Army artillery depots on Lyustdorfs'ka Street near Tolbukhina Square. There are two memorials here but they are hard to find because the streets do not have names. To get to the first, travel northeast up Lyustdorfs'ka in the direction of Tolbukhina Square. At a monument of a flame with leaves, by the tram tracks, turn right on a small street between the Lyustdorfs'ka blocks numbered 49 and 50. Two hundred metres down this street is a black memorial to 'the shot and burned Jews', unveiled in 1975. There is a another memorial next to it with an Orthodox Christian cross commemorating soldiers who died. To get to the second Holocaust memorial, walk up the lane to the left of these two. It is 200m away behind Lyustdorfs'ka 47 and next to a children's playground. This granite memorial is the original Soviet one but it has been restored several times.

After the massacres a ghetto was set up in **Slobodka**, now a sprawling residential area but then on the outskirts of the city. There is a small plaque commemorating it by the gate of the Odesa Maritime Academy at Malov'skoho 10. It is just up from the tram stop after the railway bridge.

FURTHER AFIELD

Bogdanovka Over the course of the winter of 1941–42, Odesa's remaining 35,000 Jews were forced to walk in freezing weather from Prokhorovs'ka Square to Bogdanovka (Bohdanivka in Mykolaiv region), a collective farm on the southern Bug River, 190km northeast of Odesa. They were forced to live in pigsties. Between December 1941 and April 1942, 54,000 Jews were murdered here by the Romanians, helped by Ukrainian auxiliaries and civilians and local ethnic Germans. Although it was one of the largest atrocities of the Holocaust, it is largely forgotten. Roma and

CRIMEA

NOTE: Crimea was occupied and annexed by Russian forces in 2014 and at time of writing it is not possible to reach it from unoccupied parts of Ukraine.

Crimea had an unusual Jewish community which included Krymchaks, who followed rabbinical Judaism, and Karaites, who rejected what is called the Oral Torah. Both groups had lived on the peninsula for over 2,000 years. After Russia took control of the region from the Ottoman Empire in 1783, Ashkenazi Jews began to settle in Crimea which was made part of the Pale of Settlement.

In the interwar period, Crimea was a Zionist centre, where pioneers intending to settle in Palestine were trained on farms financed by foreign Jews. According to the 1939 Soviet census, 65,452 Jews (5.8% of the population) lived in Crimea.

German and Romanian forces arrived in Crimea in September 1941 but fighting continued for months. Sevastopol fell eventually in July 1942.

Many Jews had fled with the retreating Red Army, but of those who remained some 30,000–40,000 people were murdered. After some initial hesitation, Krymchaks were included in the mass murder. Krymchaks themselves estimate that more than 5,500 members of their community were killed by the Germans. Since Crimea was home to most of the world's Krymchaks, this means that more than 70% of their pre-war population was exterminated in 1941–44. The Nazis did not consider the Karaites as Jewish and the community was largely untouched by the Holocaust, though some were victims of mass shootings and forced into labour battalions.

There are several memorials at the mass graves in the city of Kerch on the east of the Crimean Peninsula which commemorate the approximately 7,000 Jews from Kerch and surrounding areas who were murdered by SS mobile killing units in 1941–42. For a full list of mass graves, consult the website Atlas of Holocaust Killing Sites in Ukraine (w shoahatlas.org).

Crimea was an autonomous republic of Soviet Russia until 1954, when it was transferred to Soviet Ukraine. In the 1990s, many Jews from Crimea, among them 500 Karaites, emigrated to Israel where the Israeli Chief Rabbinate has ruled that Karaites are Jews under Jewish law.

Sinti were also murdered here and are also mentioned on the memorial which has been vandalised several times in recent years. Centropa's interview with survivor Ivan Barbul (w centropa.org/en/biography/ivan-barbul) brings the horrors of the site to life.

In **Domanivka**, 35km away, where 20,000 Jews perished in a similar camp, a mass grave is marked by a memorial.

KYIV

There has been a significant Jewish community in Kyiv for more than 1,000 years. Israeli leaders Golda Meir and Ephraim Katzir, as well as the Soviet poet Ilya Ehrenburg, were born in the city. Sholem Aleichem, the Yiddish writer, Isaac Babel and Vasily Grossman, two of the most important Soviet writers, also lived some of their lives in Kyiv. The construction of the Bessarabskyi Market in 1910–12 was financed by Jewish patrons.

Before World War II some 160,000 Jews (20% of the population) lived in the Ukrainian capital, Kyiv. By the time the Germans entered the city on 19 September 1941, that number had dropped to perhaps 60,000 as many had fled, been evacuated or joined the Red Army.

GETTING AROUND Much of central Kyiv is accessible on foot. The city also has an impressive Soviet-era metro system. Take the metro to see the memorial site at Babyn Yar. To visit Chernobyl (Chornobyl), you must take an organised tour or hire a guide with a car – all hotel receptions will be able to help you arrange this. The best way to get to Berdychiv and Rivne is to take the train. They are on the main Kyiv–Lviv line. All big cities are easily accessible by train and night trains are a good way to travel. Seats and beds can be booked online.

WHERE TO STAY AND EAT The best budget accommodation option in Kyiv is the **Ibis Kyiv City Centre** (Shevchenko Bd 25; w ibis.com; €) located not far from the station. Kyiv has a lively café and restaurant scene. **Musafir** (Bohdana Khmel'nyts'koho St 3b; w musafir.com.ua; ⊕ 10.00–22.00 daily; €€) is a very popular Crimean Tatar restaurant serving small platters meant for sharing.

HISTORY On 24 September 1941 a series of bombs planted by the Soviet NKVD destroyed a large part of the city centre. The Germans used this as an excuse to carry out the mass murder of the city's Jewish population.

On 29–30 September 1941, Kyiv was the site of the most infamous of the massacres of the Shoah by Bullets at Babyn Yar, known in Russian as Babi Yar. Some 33,771 Jews (a German statistic), mainly older adults, women and children, were taken and shot in a ravine by the Germans, aided by Ukrainian auxiliaries and other collaborators. In all, 100,000 Jews, Roma, communists, Soviet prisoners of war, Ukrainian nationalists and others were eventually murdered at the site.

The mass killing at Babyn Yar has come to symbolise the Shoah by Bullets. The site has long been the focus of the country's collective memory of the Holocaust. Initially, the Soviet Union banned any kind of memorialisation at Babyn Yar, but after an earth dam built here for waste from a brickworks unleashed a mudslide in March 1961 causing some 1,500 deaths, discussion of what had happened there grew. Jewish dissidents began to gather at the site on the anniversary, many of whom were arrested. In the 1960s cultural thaw, the Soviet poet Yevgeny Yevtushenko demanded recognition of the massacre in his poem 'Babi Yar', which reverberated around the USSR. Eventually, in 1976 a massive bronze memorial was erected in the middle of what is now a large park to commemorate Soviet citizens, prisoners of war and soldiers executed here – there was no mention of the murder of the Jews. In October 1991, weeks before the final collapse of the Soviet Union, a large bronze menorah commemorating Jewish victims was inaugurated in a ceremony by Leonid Kravchuk, who had been vested with presidential powers after the Act of Declaration of Independence and was at that point the de facto president.

WHAT TO SEE The former Jewish area was in Podil, but the main draw for visitors interested in the Holocaust is at Babyn Yar, where the most infamous of the massacres of the Shoah by Bullets took place. Before leaving Kyiv, it is worth visiting the **National Museum of the Holodomor-Genocide** (Національний музей Голодомору-геноциду; Lavrska St 3; w holodomormuseum.org.ua; ⊕ 10.00–18.00 Thu–Sun; UAH30), which remembers Stalin's manmade famine of

1932–33 in which some 3.9 million died in Ukraine. It is important to understand the Holodomor's central place in contemporary Ukrainian historical memory and how that feeds into equalising the Soviet and Nazi regimes. Holodomor means 'death by hunger'.

Babyn Yar (Dorohozhychi; w babynyar.org; ⊕ 24hrs daily; free) In 2021, 80 years after the mass shootings at Babyn Yar, plans were unveiled for a new memorial complex at the site, which was due for completion in 2026. The project has been stalled by the ongoing war with Russia. However, much has been done here in the past few years, and there are now 20 memorials and things to see on both sides of the park here. The memorials include one to Roma, one to Ukrainian nationalists and one to those who died in the 1961 disaster.

Unlike most Holocaust memorials it was not state funded. Much of the money behind the recent project was donated by two Ukrainian-born Russian Jewish oligarchs, Mikhail Fridman and German Khan, who had benefited from the Putin regime. Before the 2022 Russian invasion, critics of the memorial claimed that the long arm of the Kremlin was interfering in historical memory in Ukraine and that was the reason for the enormous size of the project. In the wake of the full-scale invasion, both men were targets of Western sanctions; they resigned from the supervisory board and discontinued their funding. Another donor, the Ukrainian Jewish oligarch Viktor Pinchuk, diverted his funds to humanitarian projects. With the economic foundations of the project destroyed, the memorial institution turned to documenting war crimes in the current conflict and helping Holocaust survivors leave war-torn Ukraine. Despite claims to the contrary, the site was not damaged by a Russian missile in March 2022, and the target of that attack was the nearby TV tower.

Some critics say the new memorials are a Disneyfication of the Holocaust. It is an overly harsh criticism. They are modern and imaginative and make a change from some of the more predictable, arguably rather dull, memorials that are scattered across the continent. At the entrance to the park by the main exit from Dorohozhychi Metro, there is a map explaining what is where.

Be sure to see the imposing original **Soviet memorial** (see opposite). There are also several large rocks with spy holes – peer into them and you will see pictures of the exact same location during the massacres. Read the alley of highly informative panels. A bronze wagon remembers the **Roma** killed at Babyn Yar. The artistic **Mirror Field** and the **Crystal Wall of Crying**, designed by Marina Abramovic, the celebrated Serbian performance artist, are an extraordinary new approach to remembering the Holocaust.

FURTHER AFIELD
Chernobyl The 1986 nuclear disaster is what brings most tourists to Chernobyl (Chornobyl), 135km north of Kyiv. The power plant is 19km further north, but Chernobyl itself was an important Jewish settlement and the home of a Hasidic dynasty founded here in the 18th century.

No strangers to violence, Chernobyl's Jews were attacked repeatedly over the centuries. At the end of the 19th century, Jews made up half of the town's population of just over 5,000 people. In the interwar period, Jews left Chernobyl to find work in Kyiv and in 1939 only 1,783 remained. In August 1941, 450 were murdered in the Jewish cemetery on the edge of town with the help of local police. A small monument was erected by relatives after the war. Once a year, followers of the Chernobyl dynasty come to pray at the tombs of their rabbis.

Berdychiv One of the heartlands of Jewish culture in the Russian Empire and a large centre of Hasidic Judaism, Berdychiv is 190km southwest of Kyiv. In the late 19th century, 80% of its population was Jewish. The **Jewish Museum** (Музей Єврейства; Yevropeyska 15; ▓; ⊕ 09.00–17.00 Sun–Fri; UAH15), in the same building as the library, offers an introduction to pre-war Jewish life. Although in the early 20th century many Jews emigrated, in 1939 Jews still accounted for some 37.5% of the city's inhabitants. On the eve of war there were about 30,000 Jews in Berdychiv, the number having swelled with refugees coming from German-occupied Poland.

The German army occupied Berdychiv on 7 July 1941, and in August they forced Jewish citizens into a ghetto in a poor area known as Yatki. The Germans began shooting Jews in different actions from the end of August. In one, German soldiers amused themselves by forcing dozens of Jewish women to swim across the city's Hnylopiat River, knowing they would all drown. A memorial to some 1,300 young people who were taken from the ghetto on 4 September 1941, ordered to dig potatoes and then shot, was erected in 2019, close to the village of **Khazyn**, 6km south of the city.

A series of memorials that form the **Monument to the Victims of Nazism** (Пам'ятник жертвам нацизму) are by the road at Molodohvardiis'ka Street 3. There is information and maps for all the Holocaust sites in and around the city here, including all the mass graves. There is an especially moving **Jewish cemetery** on Zhytomyska Street which features unique shoe-shaped tombs and a memorial to those shot at the airfield. In all, some 30,000 Jews from Berdychiv and the surrounding area were shot.

UKRAINE WITHOUT JEWS

Berdychiv was the birthplace of the Soviet journalist Vasily Grossman, author of the epic novel *Life and Fate* (Vintage, 2006), published in the West long after his death in 1964. The book's accounts of the Holocaust are unforgettable. They include a letter written by the leading character's mother from the Berdychiv Ghetto which remains an extraordinary description of what it was like and how people in the town reacted.

Grossman made his name following the Red Army on their assault westwards towards Berlin and spent years reporting from frontlines. The offensive westwards from Kyiv reached Berdychiv in January 1944. Advancing westwards in the months before, Grossman had come to realise the enormity of what had happened and wrote his searing piece 'Ukraine without Jews', which was published in November 1943. He interviewed eyewitnesses, both the few Jewish survivors and Ukrainians, and was shocked to discover the major role that his former neighbours had played in the murder and pillage of the thousands who had lost their lives here. He wrote:

How is this murder different from the hundreds and thousands of people that the Germans executed elsewhere in fascist-occupied Europe? There is a difference, and it lies in the fact that the fascists execute French, Dutch, Serbian, Ukrainian, Russian and Czech people for violating fascist rules and laws—hiding a switchblade or an old revolver, accidentally uttering an angry word, a young man refusing to abandon his elderly parents for a German labour camp, or offering a sip of water to a partisan. But the Germans execute the Jews only because of the fact that they are Jews. In their view, Jews have no right to be alive.

Yitzhak Kaplan's home in Haifa in Israel has a stunning view south across the coast towards Atlit, the former British detention centre, where he was held when he arrived in Palestine in 1946. There are pictures of Kaplan's children and grandchildren by the television.

He was born in 1930, 15km east of Rivne in the small village of Babyn, where his parents had a shop. The Kaplans were one of two Jewish families who lived there. The young Yitzhak was sent to the Hebrew school in Rivne. He had two brothers and four sisters. His older brother was conscripted into the Red Army when the war broke out and was never heard of again. Although he says the family were '50–50' about Zionism, one of his sisters, Chaya, left for Palestine in 1936. When the Germans invaded in 1941, Kaplan, his parents, two sisters and a brother fled deep into the Soviet Union as the Nazis advanced.

His sister Fani, however, chose to stay in Rivne to wait for her husband who was in the Polish Army. She was one of those murdered in Sosenki Forest along with her two small children, who were taken from her and shot at the separate death pit (page 332). What Kaplan's sister went through before she died, let alone her children, is unimaginable; but it was not the reason that the family left for Palestine.

The warm winter sun streams in through the window as Kaplan describes how his surviving family was torn apart. His father fell sick and died and his other brother became a pilot in the Red Army. He would not see him again until the 1980s. Kaplan had wanted to enlist too, but a broken wrist changed the course of his life.

'In the summer of 1944, the war was finally over in Rovno and my sister Pola, who was 25, decided that she would go back to find out if it was safe to return.' He speaks slowly and matter-of-factly. 'There she met and married a partisan, Iser Glazer, who had lost his family. He was one of the partisans who had liberated the city. It was dangerous to travel, so she sent her new husband to collect us.'

The remaining members of the family returned with Glazer. They intended to go home and carry on with their lives, but it was too dangerous to go back to their house in Babyn, lest they be lynched by their former neighbours. 'The village was full of Banderists and someone else was living in our house,' Kaplan says. Decades later Kaplan was to return to the village again, only to discover that the house had been destroyed and, where it had once stood, there was just an empty lot.

The family decided to start a new life in Rivne. Yet Kaplan makes it clear that, as the months passed, his brother-in-law decided that they had no choice but to leave because everyday life was simply too dangerous. In the early spring of 1945, a few months before Rivne reverted to formal Soviet rule and it was still possible to leave, they decided to try to go to Palestine. Their story reflects the larger one in Rivne. It was a place where it was not safe to be Jewish in the years after the war.

Kaplan and his surviving family first made their way to Italy, where he endured the hunger strike in La Spezia (page 225), on the Liguria coast, before sailing illegally for Palestine in June 1946.

Rivne Before World War II, Rivne (Rovno), which lies 220km northwest of Berdychiv, was in eastern Poland and then called Równe. It was a thriving commercial centre; half of its population was Jewish and about a third was Polish.

In the early hours of 7 November 1941, Rivne's Jews were gathered and marched out of the city to the nearby Sosenki pine forest. In an orgy of killing that lasted for two days, 17,500 adults were shot or thrown alive into a large pit that had been specially prepared; 6,000 children suffered the same fate in an adjacent pit. The massacre was timed to be carried out before the ground froze and probably to coincide with the anniversary of the Bolshevik Revolution. The **Sosenki Forest**, a short drive out of town, is a depressing, bleak place. Rivne is still on the frontline where history is a weapon. On my last visit a dead dog covered in blood lay in the snow at the entrance.

On the western side of the city, across the Ustya River past the former ghetto area, **Dubens'ka Street** was the home of the wealthy Mussman family. Hertz Mussman was a mill owner who had the foresight to move to Palestine in 1934. Fania, one of the family's three daughters, was the mother of Israeli novelist Amos Oz. The large red-brick building and its courtyard and outhouses is at number 29, but oddly a plaque commemorating the family has been placed on a small grey stone house at number 31. It seems fitting that the surreal haunting memories of life in Rivne that tormented his mother and that Oz described in his memoir *A Tale of Love and Darkness* (Vintage, 2005) are clouded in a blur.

Rivne is important as it was the first city in Poland to be liberated by the Red Army. Among the soldiers were a significant group of Jewish partisans who made the Great Synagogue on **Shkil'na Street** (vul. Shkolnaya) their headquarters. (Today, the dumpy yellow building, behind a shopping centre, is a sports centre. The present-day **synagogue** is now in the former yeshiva further along at No. 39.) The Jewish partisans cleaned up the mass grave in the Sosenki Forest and set out to help survivors among the children who had been hidden in the countryside.

The tale of Jews helping Jews hit the headlines but, on a fundraising trip to Moscow, they were tipped off that Jews identifying as distinct from other victims was not compatible with the Soviet way of thinking and they could be arrested and sent to the Gulag. It was also simply too dangerous for Jews to remain in Rivne. Poles, Ukrainians and Russians were all keen to claim ownership here and of the surrounding countryside. Followers of the Ukrainian nationalist Stepan Bandera murdered Jews along with Poles.

Unlike the surviving Jews in Soviet Ukraine to the east, the Jews of Rivne were at this point regarded as Polish citizens, so survivors were free to leave. Although war was still raging across eastern Europe the partisans decided to lead their people out towards the Mediterranean. That exodus is known by its Hebrew name, Ha Bricha (The Flight).

KHARKIV

Kharkiv, an industrial powerhouse in the Soviet Union, was badly destroyed in World War II as the Red Army advanced eastwards. Since the Russian attack on Ukraine in 2022 the city has been once again on the frontline and has been badly shelled. Most locals speak Russian and use its Russian name of Kharkov.

GETTING AROUND Kharkiv is connected by good night and day trains to Kyiv. Sites in central Kharkiv are accessible by foot. To see the Drobytsky Yar memorial take a taxi. At the time of writing travelling east and southeast led to an active frontline. If you want to visit Dnipro, the best way is by minibus.

WHERE TO STAY AND EAT **Four Rooms Hotel** (vul. Mayakovs'koho 5, **w** 4-rooms. com.ua; **€**) is a designer hotel in the downtown area of Kharkiv. The nearby upscale **Sumsky market** has lots of restaurants. The Georgian restaurant **Toy Samyy Baranets'** (vul. Sumska; ⏰ noon–22.00 daily; **€**) just off the city's huge and imposing Freedom Square is popular.

HISTORY Kharkiv, which was outside the restricted area of Jewish settlement known as the Pale, acquired a significant Jewish population in the early 20th century as it industrialised. Although antisemitism was rife in the city under Tsarism, unusually there were no pogroms here. By the late 1930s, there were around 130,000 Jews living in the city; when Germany invaded the Soviet Union in June 1941, 100,000 of them fled the city. Anywhere between 16,000 and 30,000 Jews died in Kharkiv during World War II.

In 1959, although the synagogue and the Jewish theatre were closed under communism, 84,000 Jews lived in Kharkiv. The Choral Synagogue reopened in 1990 and is today the hub of Jewish life. Although many Jews left for Israel, 50,000 remained in the city in 2000. Since the Russian invasion many of the city's Jews, especially those with small children, have left.

WHAT TO SEE The main Holocaust site in Kharkiv is the **Drobytsky Yar Holocaust Memorial Park and Museum** (Дробицький Яр; **w** drobytskyyar.org; ⏰ 24hrs) on the eastern outskirts of the city. An obelisk to the 'victims of fascist terror' was put up in 1955, but the first proper commemoration only took place in 1989. The present large memorial complex, which opened in 2012, commemorates some 15,000 Jews who were massacred by the Nazis at a ravine here between December 1941 and January 1942. It consists of a 20m-tall menorah, an imposing white arched memorial and a memorial hall and museum underneath, where the names of the victims are engraved on the Chalice of Grief. In 2021, a new interactive exhibition at the memorial museum was installed. Roma were also killed at the site. And to save bullets, children were thrown into the death pits alive. The mass graves are clearly marked. The remains of 150 people found in a mass grave during building work in the area of the former ghetto in 2007 have been reburied at the site. There are plans to further landscape the site, creating a memorial walk. The menorah was badly damaged by Russian shelling in March 2022 and the arch peppered with shrapnel but the area is now open to the public again.

The former **ghetto** was located in the southwest of the city and is commemorated by memorials on Prospekt Heroi Kharkiva by the underpass close to the corner of 12-ho Kvitnya vulytsya. The closest metro is Industrialna. There is a small **Kharkiv Holocaust Museum** (Харківський музей Голокосту; Yaroslava Mydrogo 28; **w** holocaustmuseum.kharkov.ua; ⏰ 11.00–17.00 Mon–Fri; UAH10) in the city centre.

At the former **synagogue** at vulytsya Hromadyanska 9, the Germans gathered over 400 sick and elderly and sealed the entrance. Those inside died of cold and hunger. A memorial plaque has been mounted on the wall.

FURTHER AFIELD

Dnipro Formerly known as Dnipropetrovsk and before that Yekaterinoslav, Dnipro is 220km south of Kharkiv and was home to 80,000 Jews before 1941. Since the 2012 opening of the Menorah Centre, one of the largest Jewish civic centres in the world, the city has undergone a Jewish renaissance. The civic centre is built around the old synagogue and has a conference centre and two kosher hotels.

It is also home to the **Museum of Jewish Memory and Holocaust in Ukraine** (Музей Пам'ять єврейського народу і Голокост в Україні; Sholom Aleichem 4; w jmhum.org; ⏰ 10.00–19.00 Wed & Sun; UAH50), one of Ukraine's most important Jewish museums. The exhibition covers the history of Jews in Ukraine with a part dedicated to the Holocaust; there is also a Memory Hall dedicated to the memory of the 6 million.

On 13 October 1941, the Jewish population of Dnipro were assembled on the square behind the Lüx department store, now Dmytra Yavornytskoho 52. A plaque marks the spot. Their valuables were confiscated before they were grouped in columns and escorted under convoy to a ravine near the Botanical Garden. Two stelae commemorate the victims in Gagarin Park on either side of the running track. One dates from the Soviet period and the other is more modern. Over two days approximately 10,000 people were shot dead.

Appendix 1

GLOSSARY

Aktion	a Nazi military or police operation to forcibly assemble Jews prior to shooting or deportation.
Allies	group of 26 nations led by Great Britain, the United States and the Soviet Union, which opposed the Axis powers in World War II.
Anschluss	the annexation of Austria by Germany on 13 March 1938.
Appellplatz	the square where prisoners were forced to assemble for roll calls.
Aryan	term used in Nazi Germany to refer to non-Jewish and non-Roma white Europeans, especially northern Europeans with blonde hair and blue eyes, who were considered by the Nazis to be the most superior of Aryans and members of a 'master race'.
Aryanisation	the Nazi term for the seizure of Jewish property and Jewish-owned businesses and its transfer to non-Jews.
Ashkenazi	a Jewish diaspora that emerged in the Holy Roman Empire in the 8th and 9th centuries. Ashkenazim traditionally spoke Yiddish and largely migrated towards northern and eastern Europe during the late Middle Ages to escape persecution.
Axis	a political, military and ideological alliance created by Nazi Germany, Italy and Japan in Berlin on 27 September 1940. Bulgaria, Croatia, Serbia, Hungary, Romania and Slovakia eventually also joined the Axis.
bimah	platform in a synagogue from which the Torah is read.
blood libel	a false antisemitic accusation levelled at Jews, who from the medieval period onwards were wrongly accused of killing Christian children to use their blood during the Passover festival.
concentration camp	a prison camp used to detain enemies of the state, including Jews, Roma, political and religious opponents, members of national resistance movements, homosexuals, and others. Imprisonment was of unlimited duration, not linked to a specific act, and not subject to any judicial review. Inmates were often forced to undertake hard labour.
death march	a forced march of prisoners, especially Jews, from the concentration and labour camps in eastern Europe to

camps further west, which began in autumn 1944 as the Red Army advanced. Many prisoners who could not keep up were shot and many died of starvation and exhaustion.

deportation   forced removal from their homes of Jews in the Third Reich and German-occupied countries to ghettos, concentration, labour and extermination camps.

displaced persons camp   camps established by the Allies after World War II to house survivors of Nazi persecution and refugees from eastern Europe, known as displaced persons, or DPs, while they awaited repatriation to their home countries or resettlement elsewhere.

Einsatzgruppen   the German word for an Operational Task Force. Einsatzgruppen were mobile SS and SD (see opposite) killing units that were supported by personnel and auxiliary units of Ukrainian, Latvian, Lithuanian and Estonian volunteers. The units followed the German Army as it invaded the nations of central and eastern Europe. Their duties included the arrest or murder of political opponents and potential resistance.

extermination camp   a camp set up by the Nazis for the mass murder of Jews, primarily by poison gas.

Final Solution   translation of the German word *Endlösung*, a Nazi euphemism for the plan to murder all European Jews.

gas van   vehicle whose exhaust was redirected to its rear compartment to poison those people trapped inside.

General Government   part of German-occupied Poland which was not directly annexed to Germany, attached to German East Prussia, or incorporated into the German-occupied Soviet Union. It was administered by a German civilian governor-general and included Poland's major Jewish communities of Warsaw, Kraków and Lublin.

Gestapo   the SS-controlled German Secret State Police responsible for investigating political crimes and opposition activities. Gestapo is a contraction of Geheime Staatspolizei.

ghetto   the word was first used in Venice in 1516 to describe an area of a town or city where Jews were required to live. Under the Nazis a ghetto was a very clearly defined district, often walled or fenced in and surrounded by armed guards, in which Jews were forced to live in the worst possible conditions. All, except the Theresienstadt Ghetto, were eventually dissolved and the Jews murdered.

Haganah   underground paramilitary organisation in British Mandate Palestine from 1920 to 1948.

Judenrat   Jewish councils set up to maintain order and carry out the orders of the German Army.

Kapo   a concentration camp prisoner selected to oversee other prisoners.

Kindertransport   literally 'children's transport' in German; a programme whereby the British government allowed the admission of almost 10,000 mostly Jewish child refugees from central Europe after Kristallnacht, until the outbreak of war curtailed the operation.

Kommando	the German word for 'detachment', such as a group of concentration camp prisoners at forced labour.
Kristallnacht	the 'Night of Broken Glass' in German; a widespread pogrom that occurred throughout Germany, Austria and the Sudetenland region of Czechoslovakia, organised by the Nazis, on the night of 9–10 November 1938.
labour camp	a camp where Jews and other prisoners were subjected to forced labour for either military or government purposes.
Lebensraum	a basic principle of Nazi foreign policy, meaning 'living space' in German. Hitler believed that eastern Europe had to be conquered to create a vast German empire.
matzo	an unleavened bread traditionally eaten at Passover.
menorah	the candelabra lit on the Jewish festival of Hanukkah.
Muselmann	a term widely used by concentration camp prisoners to refer to inmates who were on the verge of death from starvation, exhaustion and despair.
Operation Barbarossa	code name for the German invasion of the Soviet Union, which began on 22 June 1941.
Pale of Settlement	the western part of the Russian Empire in which Russian Jews were allowed to live from 1835 to 1917.
pogrom	a Russian word meaning 'thunder' or 'storm' used to describe a violent attack on a Jewish community.
police battalion	armed unit of German regular policemen; along with the Einsatzgruppen (see opposite), the police battalions played a leading role in the mass executions of Jews in eastern Europe.
Red Army	the Workers' and Peasants' Red Army, usually referred to simply as the Red Army, was the army and air force of the Soviet Union from 1922 to 1946, when it was renamed the Soviet Army.
SD	abbreviation for *Sicherheitsdienst*; the SD was the political intelligence agency of the SS and played a central role in carrying out the Holocaust.
selection	the process of separating Jews deemed suitable for hard labour from the remainder, who were then sent to their deaths. This usually took place either in a ghetto round-up or on arrival at a concentration camp.
Sephardi	Sephardic Jews are a diaspora community, who in 1492 were forced to convert to Catholicism or face expulsion from Spain. Between 100,000 and 300,000 Spanish Jews left Spain and settled in different parts of Europe and the Middle East.
shtetl	a community with a large Jewish presence.
Sonderkommando	a term meaning 'special detachment' in German and used to describe an SS or Einsatzgruppe detachment. It also refers to the Jewish forced labour units in extermination camps who were forced to work in and around the gas chambers.
SS	abbreviation of *Schutzstaffel*, German for 'protection squad'. The SS was a paramilitary formation of the Nazi party created to serve as bodyguards to Hitler and other Nazi

leaders. The SS later took charge of political intelligence gathering, the German police and the central security apparatus, the concentration camps, and the systematic mass murder of Jews and other victims.

T4 Programme — a euthanasia programme, which was effectively the state-sponsored murder of the incurably ill, physically or mentally disabled, emotionally distraught, and elderly people considered 'not worthy of living' in the new German Reich.

Torah — the Hebrew word *torah* literally means direction or instruction but is also the name of the law given to Moses and written in the first five books of the Hebrew scriptures. Torah is also sometimes used to refer to the Talmud and other rabbinic writings (known as the Oral Torah).

transit camp — a camp in which Jews were held before deportation to extermination camps.

transport — the forced movement of prisoners from one place to another. The word was also used to refer to the movement of refugees both before and after the war.

Umschlagplatz — the German word for a transfer point.

Wehrmacht — the unified armed forces of Nazi Germany from 1935 to 1945.

yeshiva — a traditional Jewish school dedicated to the study of the Torah and rabbinic commentaries.

Yiddish — historically spoken by Ashkenazi Jews, a Germanic language with elements of Hebrew and Aramaic.

Zyklon B — a chemical developed as an insecticide, used in gas chambers during the Holocaust.

Appendix 2

There is a plethora of books on the Holocaust. What follows here is a selective list of texts and websites on the general history of the Holocaust. Books, memoirs and online resources related to specific events and places are cited in the destination chapters of this guide.

FURTHER INFORMATION

BOOKS

Browning, Christopher *The Origins of the Final Solution: The Evolution of Nazi Jewish Policy 1939–1942* Arrow, 2005. A detailed and comprehensive analysis of the descent of the Nazi persecution of the Jews into mass murder.

Bullock, Alan *Hitler: A Study in Tyranny* Penguin, 1990. Bullock's biography of Adolf Hitler remains a masterpiece.

Cesarani, David *Final Solution: The Fate of the Jews 1933–49* St Martins, 2016. A highly readable and sweeping reappraisal of the anti-Jewish politics of Nazi Germany and the inevitability of the 'Final Solution'.

Evans, Richard J *The Coming of the Third Reich: How the Nazis Destroyed Democracy and Seized Power in Germany* Penguin, 2004; *The Third Reich in Power, 1933–1939: How the Nazis Won Over the Hearts and Minds of a Nation* Penguin, 2006; *The Third Reich at War: How the Nazis Led Germany from Conquest to Disaster* Penguin, 2009. The trilogy by British historian Richard Evans is key to understanding the Third Reich.

Friedländer, Saul *The Years of Extermination: Nazi Germany and the Jews, 1939–1945* HarperCollins, 2007. A comprehensive study that also looks at international reactions to the Nazis' persecution of the Jews.

Gilbert, Martin *The Routledge Atlas of the Holocaust* Routledge, 2023. Gilbert is the author of many books on the Holocaust, but this volume is perhaps the best companion for the traveller.

Rees, Laurence *The Holocaust: A New History* Viking, 2017. An account of the roots and development of Nazi policy and how the Holocaust unfurled across Europe.

Snyder, Timothy *Bloodlands: Europe between Hitler and Stalin* Yale, 2010. Hitler's vision of racial superiority and Lebensraum came into both conflict and co-operation with Stalin's Soviet Union and caused millions of deaths.

Stone, Dan *The Holocaust: An Unfinished History* Pelican, 2023. Stone shines the spotlight on the mass murder in the east and argues that we need to stop seeing the Holocaust as an exclusively German project. Also useful is his *The Liberation of the Camps: The End of the Holocaust and Its Aftermath* Yale, 2015.

ONLINE RESOURCES

Arolsen Archives w arolsen-archives.org. The largest archives of Holocaust documentation, containing information on 17.5 million people.

Centropa w centropa.org. This Vienna-based organisation tells the story of Jewish communities in central and eastern Europe throughout the 20th century.

Gedenkstättenportal zu Orten der Erinnerung in Europa w memorialmuseums. org. A list of European sites of remembrance run by the Berlin-based Foundation Memorial for the Murdered Jews of Europe.

Ghetto Fighters' Museum w gfh.org.il. The Ghetto Fighters' Museum in Israel was founded in 1949 by Holocaust survivors to educate the public about Jewish resistance movements.

Remember.org w remember.org. Useful resource with art, photos, testimonies and educational programmes.

Simon Wiesenthal Center w wiesenthal.com. A Jewish global human rights organisation based in Los Angeles researching the Holocaust and hate in a historic and contemporary context. See also w museumoftolerance.com.

United States Holocaust Memorial Museum w ushmm.org. The United States' official Holocaust Memorial based in Washington DC. Highly informative, it has an extensive archive, much of which is accessible online and includes a victims database.

USC Shoah Foundation – The Institute for Visual History and Education w sfi.usc. edu. A non-profit organisation established by the film director Steven Spielberg, dedicated to making audio-visual interviews with genocide survivors.

World Holocaust Forum w worldholocaustforum.org. An international organisation dedicated to preserving the memory of the Holocaust and its important lessons for humanity.

Yad Vashem: The World Holocaust Remembrance Center w yadvashem.org. Israel's official memorial to the victims of the Holocaust has extensive archives, a database of victim's names and a wealth of educational material.

YIVO Institute for Jewish Research w yivo.org. Set up in Vilnius in 1925, but now based in New York, YIVO preserves, studies and teaches the cultural history of Jewish life throughout eastern Europe, Germany and Russia.

Index

Page numbers in **bold** refer to main entries; those in *italics* refer to maps

343

THE BRADT STORY

In the beginning
It all began in 1974 on an Amazon river barge. During an 18-month trip through South America, two adventurous young backpackers – Hilary Bradt and her then husband, George – decided to write about the hiking trails they had discovered through the Andes. *Backpacking Along Ancient Ways in Peru and Bolivia* included the very first descriptions of the Inca Trail. It was the start of a colourful journey to becoming one of the best-loved travel publishers in the world; you can read the full story on our website (**bradtguides. com/ourstory**).

Getting there first
Hilary quickly gained a reputation for being a true travel pioneer, and in the 1980s she started to focus on guides to places overlooked by other publishers. The Bradt Guides list became a roll call of guidebook 'firsts'. We published the first guide to Madagascar, followed by Mauritius, Czechoslovakia and Vietnam. The 1990s saw the beginning of our extensive coverage of Africa: Tanzania, Uganda, South Africa, and Eritrea. Later, post-conflict guides became a feature: Rwanda, Mozambique, Angola, and Sierra Leone, as well as the first standalone guides to the Baltic States following the fall of the Iron Curtain, and the first post-war guides to Bosnia, Kosovo and Albania.

Comprehensive – and with a conscience
Today, we are the world's largest independently owned travel publisher, with more than 200 titles. However, our ethos remains unchanged. Hilary is still keenly involved, and **we still get there first**: two-thirds of Bradt guides have no direct competition.

But we don't just get there first. Our guides are also known for being **more comprehensive** than any other series. We avoid templates and tick-lists. Each guide is a one-of-a-kind expression of an expert author's interests, knowledge and enthusiasm for telling it how it really is.

And a commitment to wildlife, conservation and respect for local communities has always been at the heart of our books. Bradt Guides was **championing sustainable travel** before any other guidebook publisher. We even have a series dedicated to Slow Travel in the UK, award-winning books that explore the country with a passion and depth you'll find nowhere else.

Thank you!
We can only do what we do because of the support of readers like you – people who value less-obvious experiences, less-visited places and a more thoughtful approach to travel. Those who, like us, take travel seriously.

Bradt GUIDES
TRAVEL TAKEN SERIOUSLY